P9-BJB-716

LEGAL INFORMATION ONLINE

www.nolo.com

24 HOURS A DAY

AT THE NOLO PRESS SELF-HELP LAW CENTER ON THE WEB, YOU'LL FIND:

○ **Nolo's comprehensive Legal Encyclopedia, with links to other online resources**

○ **Downloadable demos of Nolo software and sample chapters of many Nolo books**

○ **An online law store with a secure online ordering system**

○ **Our ever-popular lawyer jokes**

○ **Discounts and other good deals,**
our hilarious SHARK TALK **game**

THE NOLO NEWS

Stay on top of important legal changes with Nolo's quarterly magazine, *The Nolo News.* Start your free one-year subscription by filling out and mailing the response card in the back of this book. With each issue, you'll get legal news about topics that affect you every day, reviews of legal books by other publishers, the latest Nolo catalog, scintillating advice from Auntie Nolo and a fresh batch of our famous lawyer jokes.

WITHDRAWN

6TH EDITION

PATENT IT
YOURSELF

by Patent Attorney David Pressman

Edited by Attorneys Stephen Elias & Patricia Gima

Illustrations by Linda Allison

NOLO PRESS ⚖ BERKELEY

Your Responsibility When Using a Self-Help Law Book

We've done our best to give you useful and accurate information in this book. But laws and procedures change frequently and are subject to differing interpretations. If you want legal advice backed by a guarantee, see a lawyer. If you use this book, it's your responsibility to make sure that the facts and general advice contained in it are applicable to your situation.

Keeping Up to Date

To keep its books up to date, Nolo Press issues new printings and new editions periodically. New printings reflect minor legal changes and technical corrections. New editions contain major legal changes, major text additions or major reorganizations. To find out if a later printing or edition of any Nolo book is available, call Nolo Press at 510-549-1976 or check the catalog in the *Nolo News*, our quarterly publication. You can also contact us on the Internet at www.nolo.com.

To stay current, follow the "Update" service in the *Nolo News*. You can get a free one-year subscription by sending us the registration card in the back of the book. In another effort to help you use Nolo's latest materials, we offer a 25% discount off the purchase of the new edition of your Nolo book if you turn in the cover of an earlier edition. (See the "Special Upgrade Offer" in the back of this book.) This book was last revised in **October 1997**.

SIXTH EDITION	
Second Printing	OCTOBER 1997
Editor	STEPHEN ELIAS
Illustrations	LINDA ALLISON
Production	STEPHANIE HAROLDE
Book Design	TERRI HEARSH
Cover Design	TONI IHARA
Index	SAYRE VAN YOUNG
Proofreading	ROBERT WELLS
Printing	CONSOLIDATED PRINTING, INC.

Pressman, David, 1937–
    Patent it yourself / by David Pressman ; edited by Stephen Elias ;
illustrations by Linda Allison. -- 6th ed.
      p.   cm.
    Includes index.
    ISBN 0-87337-395-2
    1. Patent laws and legislation--United States--Popular works.
I. Elias, Stephen.   II. Title.
KF3114.6.P74 1997
346.7304'86--dc21

                96-31498
                CIP

For information on bulk purchases or corporate premium sales, please contact the Special Sales Department. For academic sales or textbook adoptions, ask for Academic Sales. Call 800-955-4775 or write to Nolo Press, Inc., 950 Parker Street, Berkeley, CA 94710.

Acknowledgments

My deep thanks go to my clients, and other inventors whose creativity and genius I so greatly admire and envy. My readers have given me much valuable feedback and suggestions, and I am grateful to them as well.

Thanks also to librarians par excellence, Mrs. Margreta J. Nisbett and Dr. Mary-Jo Di Muccio of the Patent Information Clearinghouse in Sunnyvale, California, and Primary Patent Examiner John S. Heyman, for their generous help.

I also wish to thank the staff at Nolo Press, including Steve Elias, Patti Gima, Stephanie Harolde and Ralph Warner for their ideas, contributions and support, Linda Allison for her clever drawings, Toni Ihara for her wonderful cover, and, especially, Terri Hearsh for substantially improving the look and feel of the Sixth Edition.

Finally, I wish to thank my wife Roberta for her unflagging support and contributions.

About the Author

David Pressman is a member of the Pennsylvania (inactive), California, and Patent And Trademark Office bars. He's had over 35 years' experience in the patent profession, as a patent examiner for the U.S. Patent Office, a patent attorney for Philco-Ford Corp., Elco Corp., and Varian Associates, as a columnist for EDN Magazine, and as an instructor at San Francisco State University. He contributed the Patent, Trademark and Copyright entries to the World Book Encyclopedia. He's also an inventor, with two patents issued. When not writing, dabbling in electronics, programming, inventing, or playing his trumpet, he practices as a patent lawyer in San Francisco. Originally from Philadelphia, he has a BS in Electrical Engineering from Pennsylvania State University. He spent his first year in law school at the University of Pennsylvania and completed his second and third years at George Washington University, where he served on the Law Review and received a Juris Doctor degree. He is also active in the general semantics and vegetarian movements.

Table of Contents

3 Documentation Can Be Vital

4 Will Your Invention Sell?

5 What Is Patentable?

6 Search and You May Find

7 Consider Your Options

8 How to Draft the Specification and Initial Drawings

9 Now for the Legalese—The Claims

10 Finaling and Mailing Your Application

11 How to Market Your Invention

12 Going Abroad

13 Getting the PTO to Deliver

14 Your Application Can Have Children

15 After Your Patent Issues: Use, Maintenance and Infringement

16 Ownership, Assignment, and Licensing of Inventions

A Appendices

Index

Introduction

What *Patent It Yourself* Does

Here's a book that allows you, the inventor, to patent and commercially exploit your invention by yourself. It provides:

- Step-by-step guidance for obtaining a U.S. patent, together with tear-out forms that are necessary for each step of the process;
- An overview of the procedures and requirements for getting patent protection abroad and concrete suggestions for finding the necessary resources to help you do this;
- An overview of the alternative and supplementary forms of protection available for inventions, such as trade secreting, copyrighting, trademarks, and using unfair competition law; and
- Detailed information and advice on how to commercially evaluate and market your invention.

By following the instructions set out here, you'll not only save healthy attorney fees, but you'll be personally involved with every step of the patenting process. This is a wise way to proceed, since you know your invention better than anyone else, and assuming you're willing to wade through a fair number of patent technicalities, you're the best person to patent it.

I think of the book as a great equalizer, since it provides the know-how to enable the garage-shop or basement do-it-yourselfer to get as good a patent as a large corporation. It provides the legal tools necessary for inventors (whether large or small) to provide first class legal protection for their work. And it especially gives the small inventor the tools to competently and efficiently protect an invention, whether or not he or she can afford a patent attorney.

You Don't Have to Use a Patent Attorney

In this view, it's almost a universal misconception that one must use a patent attorney to get a valid patent. This isn't true. First, the laws contain absolutely no requirement that one must have a patent attorney to file a patent application, deal with the Patent and Trademark Office (PTO) concerning the application, or to obtain the patent. In fact, PTO regulations [MPEP, Section 707.07(j)] specifically require patent examiners to help inventors in *pro se* (no lawyer) cases. Second, and perhaps more persuasive, it's a simple fact that many hundreds of patent applications are filed and successfully prosecuted each year by *pro se* inventors.

A Layperson Can Do a Quality Job

The quality of a patent is mainly dependent upon three basic factors:

1. whether the patent application contains a full, clear, and accurate description that tells how to make and use the invention,
2. whether the reach of the patent is as broad as possible, given the state of prior developments in the field, and
3. whether the application "sells" the advantages of the invention.

Fortunately, it takes no special legal expertise to do an excellent job for these factors.

Using an Attorney

Even if you do choose to work with an attorney, or have one available to you through the process, you'll find that this book allows you to take an active role in the process, do a better job of monitoring your attorney (no trivial consideration), and greatly adds to your understanding of the ways in which the law is willing to protect your invention. No matter how competent an attorney is, the client who understands what's going on will always obtain better service. Indeed, many corporate legal departments use this book to educate their inventors and support personnel to deal with patent attorneys and to protect their inventions more effectively.

Should You Do It Yourself?

The big question is, of course, even though it's possible to prosecute your own patent application, should you do so on your own or hire an expert? After all you probably hire people to do all sorts of things for you, from fixing your car to cleaning the chimney, that you could in theory do yourself. The most powerful incentive for patenting it yourself is the amount of money expert help costs. Or put another way, even though most car mechanics make a pretty good living, most of them can't afford to belong to the same country club as patent attorneys. The cost factor alone may dictate your decision for you if you can't afford the $3,000 to $5,000 most attorneys now charge to prepare a patent application on a simple invention.

On the other hand, if you're fortunate enough to be able to afford an attorney and you either don't have enough time to do it yourself, you don't think you'll be able to write a detailed description of your invention in conjunction with drawings (it's easier than you think), you aren't diligent and committed enough to complete projects in a reasonable time, or you don't think you can complete a detailed writing job in a fairly high quality manner, then perhaps you should use an attorney in conjunction with *Patent It Yourself*, to monitor and enhance the attorney's work, as stated above.

The above can be expressed by the following proportion:

$$\text{DIY } \alpha \ \frac{AT \cdot WA \cdot D \cdot DC}{AF}$$

which means you should be inclined to *Do It Yourself* in direct proportion to your *Available Time*, your *Writing Ability*, your *Diligence*, and your *Desire to Control* things, and in inverse proportion to your *Available Funds*. While this proportion isn't even an approach at precision, it provides the appropriate criteria and how to use them when making the do-it-yourself v. hire-an-attorney decision.

The best answer for some inventors may be to do some of both. Using this approach, diligent inventors will do much of the patent work themselves, only consulting with an attorney at an hourly rate if snags develop, or to check the patent application before submission.

The Sixth Edition Contains New Material On:

- rules governing the dimensions of drawing sheets,
- the new fee transmittal form that must accompany each application
- the techniques that can be used to prepare your own patent drawings
- the IBM patent search site on the World Wide Web
- the doctrine of equivalents, and
- international treaty membership.

How to Use *Patent It Yourself*

The book is organized primarily for chronological use, starting with an overview of the entire intellectual property field (which includes patents, trademarks, copyright and trade secret law) and then sequentially covering the steps most inventors will take to protect and profit from their inventions. I strongly recommend that you first read the book all the way through, skimming lightly over the many chapters that actually tell you how to do things.

In this way you'll first get an overview of the patent forest before you return and deal with the individual steps (trees) necessary to fully protect your invention.

Throughout the book I refer to a number of forms and in many instances reproduce them in the text. A tear-out version of each is also located in Appendix 7 for your use. I recommend that you make photocopies so you'll have ample spares for drafts and extra copies for your records.

Also throughout the book I refer to various statutes and governmental administrative rules, mostly in the patent area. I use standard forms of legal citation; these are interpreted as follows:

35 USC 102 = Title 35 of the U.S. Code, Section 102

37 CFR 1.111 = Title 37 of the [U.S.] Code of Federal Regulations, Section 1.111

Title 35 of the U.S. Code (USC) comprises all of the federal statutes patents and Title 37 of the U.S. Code of Federal Regulations (CFR) comprises all of the federal administrative rules issued by the Patent and Trademark Office and Copyright Office that deal with patents, trademarks, and copyright matters. Part 1 of 37 CFR is concerned with patents. Thus

Patent Rule 111 = 37 CFR 1.111.

Both the U.S. Code and the CFR are available in any law library and as indicated in Appendix 2, Books of Use and Interest.

I've used many abbreviations throughout *Patent It Yourself* to save space and spare you the tedium of repeatedly reading long phrases. I've tried to define each abbreviation the first time I've used it and again if there is a long break before it is used again. If at any time you need to refresh your memory about a particular abbreviation, please refer to Appendix 1, Abbreviations Used in *Patent It Yourself*.

The law is constantly changing. We try to update the important changes in each printing, and the *Nolo News*, but in the meantime you can get updates from the following Website on the Internet:

www.PatentItYourself.com/update.html.

ICONS USED IN THIS BOOK

Look for these icons, which alert you to certain kinds of information.

 The caution icon warns you of potential problems.

 The "fast track" arrow alerts you that you can skip some material that isn't relevant to your case.

 This icon indicates that the information is a useful tip.

 The note icon highlights information which pertains only to a specific patent field.

 This icon refers you to helpful books or other resources.

Good luck and successful inventing! ■

CHAPTER

1

Introduction to Patents and Other Intellectual Property

INVENTOR'S COMMANDMENT #1

Prior to deciding how to proceed with any creation, you should learn and be familiar with the various forms of intellectual property, including utility patents, design patents, trademarks, copyright, trade secrets, and unfair competition, so that you will be able to select and employ the proper form(s) of coverage for your creation.

IMPORTANT DEFINITIONS

While these definitions may seem elementary, I provide them here so that you will know exactly what I mean when I use these terms later.

An **invention** is any new article, machine, composition, or process or new use developed by a human.

A **patent application** is a set of papers that describe an invention and that are suitable for filing in a patent office in order to obtain a patent on the invention.

A **patent** is a grant from a government that confers upon an inventor the right to exclude others from making, using, or selling an invention for a fixed period of time.

In this chapter I'll first introduce you to the world of patent law. Each of the patent-related items discussed here I'll amplify in subsequent chapters, as they relate to the actual process of obtaining and profiting from a patent. I also present an overview of the other forms of "intellectual property" (including trademarks, copyright, and trade secrets), which are potentially available to you. Although you may think that a patent is the only form of protection for your creation, you should be familiar with and consider the alternatives, some of which you can use in addition to or in lieu of a patent.

Who can apply for a patent? Anyone, regardless of age, nationality, mental competency, incarceration, or any other characteristic, so long as he or she is a true inventor of the invention. Even dead or insane persons may apply through their personal representative. (See Chapter 16 for more on patent ownership.)

A patent is a form of personal property and can be sold outright for a lump sum, or its owner can give anyone permission to use the invention covered ("license it") in return for royalty payments. More on this in Chapter 16.

A. What Is a Patent and Who Can Apply for It?

What is a patent? It's a right granted by the government to a person or to a legal entity (partnership or corporation).

What is the nature of the patent right? A patent gives its holder the right to exclude others from making, using, or selling the invention "claimed" in the patent deed for approximately 17 to 18 years, provided certain fees are paid. (See Chapter 9 for more on patent claims, and Chapter 15 for more on maintenance fees.) You can use this right to exclude others by filing a patent infringement lawsuit in federal court.

B. The Three Types of Patents

There are three types of patents—utility patents, design patents, and plant patents. Let's briefly look at each.

- **Utility Patents**: As we'll see in Chapters 7 to 9, a utility patent, the main type of patent, covers inventions that function in a unique manner to produce a utilitarian result. Examples of utility inventions are Velcro hook-and-loop fasteners, new drugs, electronic circuits, software, semiconductor manufacturing processes, new bacteria, new animals, plants, automatic transmissions, and virtually anything else under the sun that can be made by humans. To get a utility patent, one must file a patent application that consists of a detailed description telling how to make and use the invention, together with claims (formally written sentence fragments) that define the invention, drawings of the invention, formal paperwork, and a filing fee. Again, only the actual inventor can apply for a utility (or any other) patent. The front or abstract page of a typical utility patent is illustrated in Fig. 1A.
- **Design Patents**: As discussed in more detail in Chapter 10, a design patent (as opposed to a utility patent)

Bovine Fly Guard.
No. 3,104,508

United States Patent [19]

Holmes

[11]	Patent Number: **4,949,887**
[45]	Date of Patent: **Aug. 21, 1990**

[54] **INSULATED MULTI-USE SEAT CUSHION WITH CLOSABLE HAND AND FOOT OPENINGS**

[76] Inventor: **William A. Holmes,** 209 Highland Ave., Piedmont, Calif. 94611-3709

[21] Appl. No.: **132,982**

[22] Filed: **Dec. 15, 1987**

Related U.S. Application Data

[63] Continuation-in-part of Ser. No. 867,453, May 28, 1986, abandoned.

[51] Int. Cl.⁵ **A61G 1/00**

[52] U.S. Cl. **224/151**; 224/205; 224/236; 2/66; 2/202; 126/204; 297/188

[58] Field of Search 224/151, 153, 202, 205, 224/257, 206, 207, 236, 237; 2/66, 91, 93, 108, 202, 203; 383/61, 110, 98, 99, 8; 128/382; 190/107, 102; 5/417–421; 297/230, 188, 192, 219; 126/204, 207, 208

[56] **References Cited**

U.S. PATENT DOCUMENTS

273,523	3/1883	Havasy	190/102
1,137,049	4/1915	Bushwick	190/107
2,835,896	5/1958	Giese	2/66
3,460,740	8/1969	Hagen	383/110
3,793,643	2/1974	Kinoshita	2/66
4,423,834	1/1984	Rush	224/151
4,604,987	8/1986	Keltner	5/421

Primary Examiner—Linda J. Sholl
Attorney, Agent, or Firm—David Pressman

[57] **ABSTRACT**

An insulated hollow cushion has a neck strap (30), an interior portion (72) sufficiently large to accommodate a portable heating source and/or hot and cold foods (74, 76), two side slits through which hands can be inserted for warmth, sealable flaps (16, 20) for closing the side slits when insulation is desired, a slit (36) at the top of the cushion for insertion of items into the cushion's interior, a closeable top flap (28) to seal the top opening for insulation purposes, and a closeable top small flap (56) to insulate the gap between a user's ankles when such user's feet are inserted through the top slit. The side flaps can be insulated so that they can be tucked into the side openings to narrow these openings to provide a tight seal when small hands are inserted into these openings. The insulating layer within the front (10) or the back panel can have multiple perforations (92) over an area thereof and this area can be covered, uncovered, or partially covered by a releasably closable flap (84), thereby to provide a "heat window" which allows maximum transmission of heat (or cold) from an internal hot (or cold) source, or partial transmission, or no more transmission than would occur through an intact insulated wall.

20 Claims, 6 Drawing Sheets

Fig. 1A—Utility Patent Abstract Page

covers the unique, ornamental or visible shape or design of an object, even if only on a computer screen. Thus if a lamp, a building, a computer case, or a desk has a truly unique shape, its design can be design patented. Even computer screen icons can be patented. However, the uniqueness of the shape must be purely ornamental or aesthetic; if it is functional, then only a utility patent is proper, even if it is also aesthetic. A good example is a jet plane with a constricted waist for reducing turbulence at supersonic speeds: although the shape is attractive, its functionality makes it suitable only for a utility patent.

A useful way to distinguish between a design and a utility invention is to ask, "Will removing or smoothing out the novel features substantially impair the function of the device?" If so—as in the jet plane with the narrowed waist—this proves that the novel features have a significant functional purpose, so a utility patent is indicated. If not—as in a woodshop wall clock that is shaped like a circular saw blade, or a phone that is shaped like a shoe—a design patent is indicated. Another useful question to ask is, "Is the novel feature(s) there for structural or functional reasons, or only for the purpose of ornamentation?"

The design patent application must consist primarily of drawings, along with formal paperwork and a filing fee.

• **Plant Patents:** A plant patent covers asexually reproducible plants (that is, through the use of grafts and cuttings), such as flowers (35 USC § 161). Sexually reproducible plants (that is, those that use pollination), can be monopolized under the Plant Variety Protection Act (7 USC § 2321). Both sexually and asexually reproducible plants can now also be monopolized by utility patent (35 USC § 101).

C. The Novelty and Unobviousness Requirement

With all three types of patents, a patent examiner in the Patent and Trademark Office (PTO) must be convinced that your invention satisfies the "novelty" and "unobviousness" requirements of the patent laws.

The novelty requirement is easy to satisfy: your invention must be different from what is already known to the public. Any difference, however slight, will suffice.

Novelty, however, is only one small hurdle to overcome. In addition to being novel, the examiner must also be convinced that your invention is "unobvious." This means that at the time you came up with your invention, it would have

been considered unobvious to a person skilled in the technology (called "art") involved in your creation. As we'll see in Chapter 5, unobviousness is best shown by new and unexpected, surprising, or far superior results, when compared to previous inventions and knowledge ("prior art") in the particular area you're concerned with.

D. How Long Do Patent Rights Last?

How long can you, the patent owner, exclude others from infringing the exclusive rights granted by your patent? Until recently, in the U.S., utility patents were granted for a period of 17 years (assuming required maintenance fees were paid). However, under new legislation stemming from the GATT (General Agreement on Tariffs and Trade) treaty, utility, and plant patents issuing from applications filed after June 7, 1995, will expire 20 years from the date of filing. The terms of patents for certain products whose commercial marketing has been delayed due to regulatory review (such as for drugs or food additives) can be extended beyond the statutory period under the new statutes (35 USC 155-156). GATT does not affect the terms for design patents (14 years from the date of issue).

The patent's enforceable monopoly period starts when the patent issues, usually about one to two years after the application is filed. From the date of filing to issuance (termed "pendency period") the inventor has no rights. However, when and if the patent later issues, the inventor will obtain the right to prevent the continuation of any infringing activity that started during the pendency period. Patents aren't renewable, and once patented, an invention may not be repatented.

Since under GATT, the patent expires 20 years from date of filing, and since the enforcement period only begins when the patent issues, it behooves an inventor to get a utility or plant patent issued as soon as possible, in order to obtain the longest possible monopoly period.

I provide a time chart in Appendix 6 and a "Life of an Invention" sidebar at the end of Section J, below, to indicate these and other pertinent times.

E. Patent Filing Deadlines

As we'll see in more detail in Chapter 5, in the United States you must file your patent application within one year after you first commercialize or publish details of the invention. However most foreign countries don't have this one-year grace period, so there's some disadvantage if you sell or publish before filing. For this reason, your safest route is to file a complete U.S. patent application before you publish or commercialize your invention. Under new legislation, you are permitted to file a "provisional patent application" (PPA) describing your invention in detail, in accordance with the instructions in Chapters 3 and 8. (No claims, discussed in Chapter 9, are needed.) This PPA can be used, under most circumstances, to defeat or block a patent application or invention of someone else who may subsequently file a patent application on the same invention. However, a regular patent application must be filed within one year after the PPA's filing date—more on this in Chapters 7 and 8.

F. Patent Fees

How much will it cost to get a patent? Assuming you use this book and don't use any patent attorneys or agents, and not including costs of drawings, typing, photocopying, and postage, the only fees you'll have to pay are government fees.

The amounts of these fees are listed on the PTO Fee Schedule in Appendix 4. As indicated in the Schedule, most PTO fees are two-part: large entity and small entity. The large-entity fees are generally paid by large corporations, while the small-entity fees, which are half the large-entity fees, are generally paid by independent inventors. For more on this, see Chapter 10, Section H. The names of these fees and the circumstances when they're due are as follows:

- **Utility Patents:** To file a provisional patent application, you'll have to pay a PPA filing fee. To file a utility

patent application, you must pay a *Utility Patent Application Filing Fee*. To have the PTO issue your utility patent, you must pay a *Utility Patent Application Issue Fee*. To keep the patent in force for its full statutory term, you must pay the PTO three maintenance fees, as follows:
  - *Maintenance Fee I*, payable 3.0 to 3.5 years after issuance.
  - *Maintenance Fee II*, payable 7.0 to 7.5 years after issuance.
  - *Maintenance Fee III*, payable 11.0 to 11.5 years after issuance.
- **Design Patents:** To file a design patent application, you must pay a *Design Patent Application Filing Fee*. To have the PTO issue your design patent, you must pay a *Design Patent Application Issue Fee*. The law doesn't require maintenance fees for design patents, and there's no PPA for a design patent application.
- **Plant Patents:** To file a plant patent application, you must pay a *Plant Patent Application Filing Fee*. To have the PTO issue your plant patent, you must pay a *Plant Patent Application Issue Fee*. Again, the law doesn't require maintenance fees for plant patents, and there's no PPA for a plant patent application.

G. The Scope of the Patent

The patent right extends throughout the entire U.S., its territories, and possessions. It's transferable by sale or gift, by will, or by descent (under the state's intestate succession [no-will] laws). The patent rights can also be licensed, that is, you can own the patent and grant anyone else, including a company, the right to make, use, or sell your invention in exchange for the payment of fees, called "royalties" (more on licensing in Chapter 16). As mentioned, the patent right is granted by the federal government, acting through the Patent and Trademark Office (a division of the Department of Commerce), in Arlington, Virginia. The patent right is recognized and enforced by the U.S. (federal) courts.

H. How Patent Rights Can Be Lost

The patent right isn't an absolute monopoly for the period that it is in force (from date of issuance until the expiration date—20 years from date of filing). It can be lost if:
- maintenance fees aren't paid;
- it can be proved that the patent either (a) fails adequately to teach how to make and use the invention, (b) improperly describes the invention, or (c) contains claims that are legally inadequate;

- one or more prior-art references (earlier patents or other publications) are uncovered which show that the invention of the patent wasn't new or wasn't different enough when the invention was made;
- the patent owner engages in certain defined types of illegal conduct, that is, commits antitrust or other violations connected with the patent; or
- the patent applicant committed "fraud on the Patent and Trademark Office (PTO)" by failing to disclose material information, such as relevant prior-art references, to the PTO during the period when the patent application was pending.

In short, the patent monopoly, while powerful, may be defeated and is limited in scope and time.

I. What Rights a Patent Grants and the Prior-Art Reference Value of a Patent

The patent grant gives its owner the right to file, maintain, and recover in a lawsuit against any person or legal entity (infringer) who makes, uses, or sells the claimed invention, or an essential part of it. If the patent owner wins the lawsuit, the judge will issue an injunction (a signed order) against the infringer, ordering the infringer not to make, use, or sell the invention any more. Also, the judge will award the patent owner damages—money to compensate the patent owner for loss due to the infringement. The amount of the damages is often the equivalent to a reasonable royalty (say 5%), based on the infringer's sales. However, if the patent owner can convince the judge that the infringer acted in bad faith—for example, infringed intentionally with no reasonable excuse—the judge can triple the damages and make the infringer pay the patent owner's attorney fees.

In addition to bringing in licensing income and enabling a manufacturer to charge more for a unique product, patents also have other uses. Some inventors file for and obtain patents mainly for vanity, or the prestige a patent brings. Others use patents to impress and obtain financing from investors. And many organizations obtain large portfolios of patents simply to assert them as a defense against any company who charges the organization with patent infringement.

The value of patents cannot be overestimated. As Dr. Edwin Land, the investor and founder of Polaroid, stated, "The only thing that keeps us alive is our brilliance. The only way to protect our brilliance is patents."

Since the patent defines the invention monopoly very precisely, the patent owner can use the patent only against supposed infringers who make, use, or sell things or pro-

cesses that fall within the defined monopoly. This means that not everyone who makes something similar to your invention will be an infringer; you can validly sue only those whose products or processes fall within the scope of the claims in your patent. (See Chapters 9, 13, and 15 for more on claims.)

In addition to its above-described use as an offensive weapon, a patent also provides a prior-art reference that will block others from getting a patent on anything disclosed in the patent. In this respect, a patent is like a periodical (magazine) article or book. This dual nature of a patent is illustrated in Fig. 1B.

WHEN I'M USED AS AN OFFENSIVE WEAPON	WHEN I'M USED AS A PRIOR-ART REFERENCE
1. My claims can be used to stop infringers or obtain damages from them.	1. My specification and drawings constitute prior art, just like any magazine article or book. They can be used to prevent others from getting a patent on what I disclose.
2. My offensive rights start when I issue and expire 20 years from my filing date, provided my maintenance fees are paid.	2. I'm effective as of my filing date and am good forever.
3. My powers are based solely upon my claims.	3. My claims are irrelevant. Think of me simply as a book, a magazine article, or any other publication.

Fig. 1B—A Patent Can Be Used As an Offensive Weapon or As a Prior-Art Reference

J. What Can't Be Patented

You can't patent any process that can be performed mentally. The reason is that the law doesn't wish to limit what people can do essentially with just their brains. The same

THE LIFE OF AN INVENTION

Although most inventors will be concerned with the rights a patent grants during its monopoly or in-force period (from the date the patent issues until it expires (20 years after the filing date)), the law actually recognizes five "rights" periods in the life of an invention. These five periods are as follows:

1. **Invention Conceived but Not Yet Documented:** When an inventor conceives of an invention, but hasn't yet made any written, signed, dated, and witnessed record of it, the inventor has no rights whatsoever.

2. **Invention Documented but Patent Application Not Yet Filed:** After making a proper, signed, dated, and witnessed documentation of an invention, the inventor has valuable rights against any inventor who later conceives of the same invention and applies for a patent. The invention may also be treated as a "trade secret"—that is, kept confidential. This gives the inventor the legal right to sue and recover damages against anyone who immorally learns of the invention—for instance, through industrial spying.

3. **Patent Pending—Patent Application Filed but Not Yet Issued:** During the patent pending period, including the one-year period after a provisional patent application is filed, the inventor's rights are the same as in Period 2 above. A patent application gives an inventor no rights whatsoever—only the hope of a future monopoly, which doesn't commence until a patent issues. However, most companies that manufacture a product that is the subject of a pending patent application will mark the product "patent pending" in order to warn potential copiers that if they copy the product, they may have to stop later (and thus scrap all their molds and tooling) if and when a patent issues. The Patent and Trademark Office (PTO) by law must keep all patent applications preserved in secrecy. The patent pending period usually lasts from one to three years.

4. **In-Force Patent—Patent Issued but Hasn't Yet Expired:** After the patent issues, the patent owner can bring and maintain a lawsuit for patent infringement against anyone who makes, uses, or sells the invention without permission. The patent's in-force period lasts from the date it issues until 20 years from its filing date, provided maintenance fees are paid. Also, once the patent issues, it becomes a public record or publication that can block others who file later from getting patents on the same or similar inventions—that is, it becomes "prior art" to anyone who files after its filing date.

5. **Patent Expired:** After the patent expires (20 years after the filing date, or sooner if a maintenance fee isn't paid), the patent owner has no further rights, although infringement suits can be brought for any infringement that occurred during the patent's in-force period. An expired patent remains a valid "prior-art reference" (as of its filing date) forever.

---

rule applies to abstract ideas that aren't reduced to hardware form, naturally occurring articles, business forms and other printed matter per se (not associated with some hardware), scientific principles in the abstract (without hardware), inventions that won't work to produce the result claimed for them (such as perpetual motion machines), and atomic energy inventions. See Chapter 5.

COMPUTER PROGRAM NOTE

Computer programs, including algorithms, cannot be patented per se. However, if the program, software, or algorithm affects some hardware or process—for instance, if the algorithm controls a display, a memory, a keyboard, any other hardware or process, or if it processes or analyzes a signal—then it can be patented. If the algorithm merely manipulates numbers, such as calculating π, or merely solves an algorithm, then it can't be patented. Computer programs and algorithms per se (without hardware) can alternatively be protected by copyright, and sometimes by trade secret law. See *Software Development: A Legal Guide*, by Stephen Fishman (Nolo Press).

With respect to designs, as explained, the PTO won't grant design patents on:
- any design that has significant functional utility (use a utility patent) or
- ornamentation that is on the surface only, rather than forming an integral part of a device.

K. Some Common Patent Misconceptions

Over the years that I've practiced patent law, I've come across a number of misconceptions that laypersons have about patents. As part of my effort to impart what a patent is, I want to clear up a few of the most common here at the outset.

Common Misconception: *A patent gives its owner the right to practice an invention.*

Fact: *If you come up with an invention, you may practice (make, use, and sell) it freely, with or without a patent, provided that it's not covered by another's "in force" patent, that is, a patent that is within its 20-year term.*

Common Misconception: *Once you get a patent, you'll be rich and famous.*

Fact: *A patent is like a hunting license: it's useful just to go after infringers. If the invention isn't commercialized, the patent is usually worthless. You won't get rich or famous from your patent unless you also get the invention into widespread commercial use.*

Common Misconception: *If a product has been patented, it's bound to be superior.*

Fact: *Although Madison Ave. would like you to believe this, in reality a patent merely means the invention is significantly different, not necessarily superior.*

L. How Intellectual Property Law Works to "Protect" Inventors

Many people speak of a patent as a form of "protection." The fact is that, as stated, a patent is an offensive weapon, rather than "protection," which is a defensive shield. To properly benefit from a patent, as we'll see in Chapter 15, the patent owner must sue or threaten to sue anyone who trespasses on the right. The patent doesn't provide any "protection" in its own right. Although the word "protection" is in common usage for all types of intellectual property, it's more accurate to say that a patent—as well as a copyright, trade secret, and trademark—gives its owner "offensive rights" against infringers. In other words the patent, copyright, trade secret, or trademark provides a tool with which you can enforce a monopoly on your creation. The distinction between protection (a defense) and offensive rights is as important in intellectual property law as it is in football or basketball: while a good defense may be valuable, you'll need a powerful offense to win the game or stop the infringer.

To help you keep this distinction in mind, I try consistently to use the term "offensive rights" instead of "protection." However, if I slip up from time to time, please remember that by protection I only mean that inventors have the right to affirmatively come forward and invoke the court's help in preventing infringement by others.

Common Misconception: *If you make or sell a device on which you have a patent, your patent will protect you against the infringement claims of others.*

Fact: *A patent is for offensive use only and has no value in defending against infringement charges from other patents, except that your patent sometimes will have value in a counterattack if the other patent owner infringes your patent.*

Common Misconception: *If a product, such as a tooth whitener, says "patented," no one else can make a product with a similar function.*

Fact: *Most patents cover only one specific aspect or version of a product, rather than the basic function of the product. For instance, the patent on the tooth whitener may cover only a specific composition, and many other compositions that perform the same function (albeit in an inferior—or superior—way) may exist that don't infringe the patent.*

M. Alternative and Supplementary Offensive Rights

As you probably realize, there are several alternative and often overlapping ways to acquire offensive rights on intellectual property. Let's think of these as different roads to the same destination. While the immediate filing of your patent application is one of these roads, it is only one. The purpose of this chapter is to provide you with a map to the other roads and to help you decide which is the best way to travel, given your circumstances.

The value of your invention can sometimes be better monopolized by using one of the other forms of intellectual property and can almost always be enhanced by simultaneously using a patent with one or more of these other forms—such as unique trade dress, a good trademark, and copyright-covered labels and instructions—and by maintaining later improvements as a trade secret.

N. Intellectual Property—The Big Picture

"Intellectual property" (sometimes called "intangible property") refers to any product of the human mind or intellect, such as an idea, invention, expression, unique name, business method, industrial process, or chemical formula, which has some value in the marketplace, and that ultimately can be reduced to a tangible form, such as a computer, a chemical, a software-based invention, a gadget, a process, etc. Intellectual property law, accordingly, covers the various legal principles that determine:

- who owns any given intellectual property
- when such owners can exclude others from commercially exploiting the property, and
- the degree of recognition that the courts are willing to afford such property (that is, whether they will enforce the owner's offensive rights).

In short, intellectual property (IP) law determines when and how a person can capitalize on a creation.

Formerly, patents were the most overwhelmingly significant part of IP law, so most attorneys who handled trademarks, copyright, trade secrets, and unfair competition, as well as patents, called themselves "patent attorneys." Nowadays, the non-patent forms of IP law have become far more significant, so most patent attorneys now call themselves IP attorneys.

Over the years, intellectual property law has fallen into several distinct subcategories, according to the type of "property" involved:

- **Patent Law** deals with the protection of the mental concepts or creations known as inventions—an example is the flip-top can opener. As indicated earlier, we have three types of patents: utility, design and plant.
- **Trademark Law** deals with the degree to which the owner of a symbol (for example, a word, design, or sound) used in marketing goods or services will be afforded a monopoly over the use of the symbol (that is, offensive rights against others who try to use it). Examples of trademarks are *Ivory, Coke, Nolo,* the *Mercedes-Benz* star, and the *NBC* chimes. With regard to advertising slogans, while the courts generally do not regard them as trademarks, they will afford them trademark rights provided their owners have used them consistently as brand names on the goods and not just in the media. Slogans are primarily covered by copyright law and unfair competition (see below).
- **Copyright Law** grants authors, composers, programmers, artists, and the like the right to prevent others from copying or using their original expression without permission and to recover damages from those who do so. Copyright law gives me offensive rights against anyone who copies this book without my permission.
- **Trade Secret Law** deals with the acquisition of offensive rights on private knowledge that gives the owner a

competitive business advantage—for example, manufacturing processes, magic techniques, and formulae. The method of producing the laser light shows and fireworks are trade secrets. Unless its owner makes substantial efforts to keep the knowledge secret, any trade secret rights will be lost.

- **Unfair Competition Law** affords offensive rights to owners of non-functional mental creations that don't fall within the rights offered by the four types of law just discussed, but which have nevertheless been unfairly copied by competitors. For example, "trade dress" (such as *Kodak*'s yellow film package), a business name (such as *Procter & Gamble Co.*), a unique advertising slogan (for example, "Roaches check in but they don't check out"), or a distinctive packaging label (such as *Duracell*'s copper-top energy cells) may all enjoy offensive rights under unfair competition principles.

Having covered patent law earlier in this chapter, let's now wade a little deeper into the other forms of intellectual property law, all of which are shown and briefly depicted in Fig. 1C, The Intellectual Property Mandala, below.

O. Trademarks

This is the most familiar branch of intellectual property law. On a daily basis, everyone sees, uses, and makes many decisions on the basis of trademarks. For instance, you probably decided to purchase your car, your appliances, much of the packaged food in your residence, your magazines, your computer, and your watch on the basis of their trademarks, at least to some extent.

1. Trademarks Defined

In its most literal meaning, a trademark is any word or other symbol that is consistently attached to, or forms part of, a product to identify and distinguish it from others in the marketplace. In other words, a trademark is a brand name.

An example of a word trademark is *Kodak,* a brand of camera. In addition to words, trademarks can be other symbols, such as designs or logos (the AT&T bell), sounds (the NBC chimes), shapes (the truncated, contrasting, conical top of Cross pens), smells, and even colors. For example, the PTO recently granted a trademark registration on a specific color used for a line of dry-cleaning ironing pads. (*Qualitex Co. v. Jacobson Products Co., Inc.,* 115 S.Ct 1300(1995).)

Many patented goods or processes are also covered by trademarks. For example, *Xerox* photocopiers have many patents on their internal parts, and also are sold under the

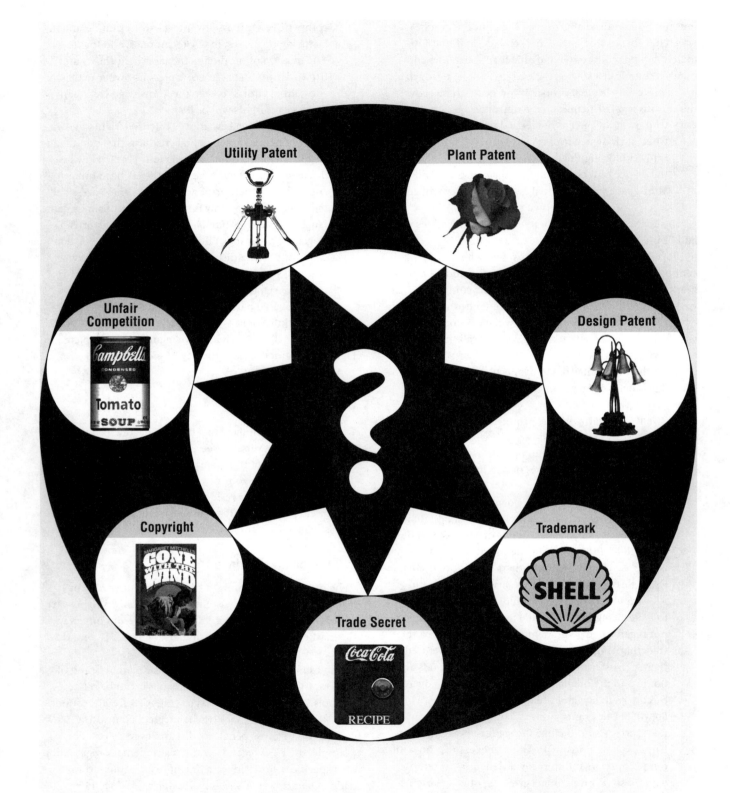

Fig. 1C—The Intellectual Property Mandala

well-known *Xerox* trademark. Without the patents, people could copy the internal parts, but *Xerox* would still have a monopoly on its valuable and widely recognized trademark.

The term "trademark" is also commonly used to mean "service marks." These are marks (words or other symbols) that are associated with services offered in the marketplace. The letters *NBC* in connection with the broadcast network are one example of a service mark. Another is the emblem used by *Blue Cross–Blue Shield* for its medical/insurance services. Other forms of marks commonly included within the term "trademark" are "certification marks" (the identifying symbol or name of an independent group, board, or commission that judges the quality of goods or services—such as the Good Housekeeping seal of approval), and "collective marks" (an identifying symbol or name showing membership in a organization—for example, the FDIC's symbol to show that deposits in a bank are insured).

An important third category of business identifier that is often confused with trademarks is called a "trade name." In the law, trade name is the word or words under which a company does business, while a trademark is the word or other symbol under which a company sells its products or services. To understand this better, let's use *Procter & Gamble* as an example. The words *Procter & Gamble* are a trade name, while *Ivory* is a trademark, that is, a brand name for *Procter & Gamble's* white soap. However, the media often refer to trademarks as trade names. Also, many companies such as Ford, use the same words as a trade name and a trademark, so the difference sometimes becomes academic.

Trademarks, such as *Ivory*, enjoy offensive rights under both federal and state trademark laws. The trade name *Procter & Gamble*, however, enjoys offensive rights primarily under state law (corporation registrations, fictitious name registrations, and unfair competition law). However, a federal law can also be used to slap down a trade name infringement as a "false designation of origin" (17 USC 1125).

2. Monopoly Rights of a Trademark Owner

Briefly, the owner of a trademark may or may not be entitled to legal offensive rights depending on how distinctive (or strong) the law considers the trademark. Trademarks that are arbitrary (*Elephant* floppy disks), fanciful (*Double Rainbow* ice cream), or coined terms (*Kodak*) are considered strong, and thus entitled to a relatively broad scope of offensive rights. On the other hand, marks that describe some function or characteristic of the product (such as "*RapidCompute* computers" or "*RelieveIt*" for an analgesic) are considered weaker and won't enjoy as broad a scope of offensive rights. Although the above differences may seem somewhat arbitrary, they really aren't. The courts give

fanciful, coined, or other arbitrary marks a stronger and broader monopoly than descriptive marks because descriptive marks come close to words in common usage and the law protects everyone's right to use these.

In addition to the strong/weak mark dichotomy, trademark owners may be denied offensive rights if the trademark becomes commonly used to describe an entire class of products, that is, it becomes "generic." For example, "aspirin," once a trademark that enjoyed strong offensive rights, became a generic word (no offensive rights) for any type of over-the-counter painkiller using a certain chemical. Why? Because its owner used it improperly as a noun (such as "Buy *Aspirin*") rather than as a proper adjective (such as "Buy *Aspirin* [brand] analgesic"), and the public therefore came to view it as synonymous with the product it described.

3. Relationship of Trademark Law to Patent Law

As indicated above, trademarks are very useful in conjunction with inventions, whether patentable or not. A clever trademark can be used with an invention—whether patentable or not—to provide it with a unique aspect in the marketplace so that purchasers will tend to buy the trademarked product over a generic one. For example, consider the *Crock Pot* slow cooker and the *Hula Hoop* exercise device. These trademarks helped make both of these unpatentable products successful. In short, a trademark provides brand name recognition to the product and a patent provides a tool to enforce a monopoly on its utilitarian function. Since trademark rights can be kept forever (as long as the trademark continues to be used), a trademark can be a powerful means of effectively extending a patent monopoly.

4. Overview of How Offensive Rights to Trademarks Are Acquired

Here's a list of steps you should take if you come up with a trademark and you want to acquire offensive rights to it and use it properly. Because this is a patent book, I haven't covered this topic in detail. Probably the best available source for learning how to search for, understand, and acquire offensive rights in your trademarks is *Trademark: How to Name Your Business & Product*, by McGrath & Elias (Nolo Press).

a. Preserve Your Mark as a Trade Secret Until You Use It

As I explain in Subsection d, below, you must take certain actions before you can acquire offensive rights in a mark. This means that during the developmental stage you must treat your trademark as a trade secret so that others won't adopt your proposed mark and use it first. (See Section Q, below, for an overview of acquiring offensive rights to trade secrets.)

b.   Make Sure the Mark Isn't Generic or Descriptive

Ask yourself if the mark is generic or descriptive. A generic mark is a word or other symbol that the public already uses to designate the goods or service on which you want to use the mark. Thus you can't acquire offensive rights on "The Pill" for a birth-control pill since it's already a generic term. A descriptive mark is similar to a generic mark in that it describes the goods, but hasn't yet gotten into widespread public use. For instance, if you came up with a new electric fork, you cannot acquire offensive rights in the mark *Electric Fork*, since it merely describes the product.

c.   Make Sure Your Mark Isn't Already in Use

It's essential not to select a mark that is in use by someone else. The good will you develop around the mark may go up in smoke in the event of a trademark infringement contest and you may be liable for damages as well. Even if your proposed mark isn't identical to the already-used mark, if it is similar, you're likely to be prevented from using it by the other mark's owner if, in the eyes of the law, there is a likelihood of customer confusion, mistake, or deception. To determine if your mark is already in use, you'll have to make a trademark search or hire someone to do it for you.

A complete trademark search should cover registered and unregistered (common law) marks, of which there are about one million. A trademark search firm, such as Trademark Service Corporation (800-872-6275) or Thomson and Thomson (800-692-8833), will make a complete search for you for about $350. However, you can do it yourself by searching registered marks in "The Trademark Register of the U.S." or *CompuMark Directory of U.S. Trademarks* (available in most libraries) or in a computer database called "TrademarkScan," available through Dialog or CompuServe. (See Chapter 6, Section L.) Then search unregistered marks in various trade directories, such as *McRae's Blue Book*, the *Gale Trade Names Register* and *Thomas Register*. Unregistered marks are also searchable through Dialog.

d.   Use or Apply to Register Your Trademark

The first to actually use or file an intent-to-use (ITU) application to register the trademark owns it—that is, acquires offensive rights against infringers. Actual use means shipping goods or advertising services that bear the trademark. If an ITU application is filed, the trademark owner must actually use the mark within the required period of time. As a trademark owner, you can validly sue a person who later

uses a similar mark for similar goods in a context that is likely to mislead the public. Contrary to popular belief, trademarks do not have to be registered for offensive rights to be acquired. However, as explained in Subsection e, just below, registration can substantially add to these offensive rights.

TRADE GROUP REGISTRATION OF TRADEMARKS

Instead of (or in addition to) registering your trademark with one or more state trademark offices and the U.S. Patent and Trademark Office (PTO), you can register it with an appropriate specific trade organization. For example, suppose you're an automobile manufacturer and you intend to come out with a new car, the *Zenith*, in a few years. Instead of applying to register it with the PTO, whose requirements are relatively complex, whose procedures are slow, and that will keep an intent-to-use application alive for only three years (at a relatively great expense), you can register your mark with the Automobile Manufacturer's Association under a relatively simple, economical procedure. The AMA-registered mark will be published for all other members of the AMA to see, so that they will know not to use the *Zenith* mark while your registration is alive. Similarly, movie titles can be registered with a movie industry association. So if you intend to use a trademark in a given industry, check with the industry's main association to see if you can register your mark with them as an alternative or in addition to a PTO or state registration.

---

e.   Use and Register Your Trademark

If you apply to register your mark federally on the basis of your intent to use it, you will, as stated, eventually have to actually use it on your goods to get it registered. You must thus follow through by actually using it and proving such use as part of your registration application.

If you do adopt and use a trademark on your goods before applying for registration, you should register it in your state trademark office if it's used exclusively in your state, and/or the PTO if it's used across a territorial or international border. Once your mark is federally registered, it will be much easier to sue infringers. The federal registration will cause the court to presume that you have exclusive ownership of the mark and the exclusive right to use it. If you don't register your trademark and it's infringed, you'll have much more difficulty when you go to court.

To register a trademark in your state, call or write to your Secretary of State in your state's capital for a trademark application form and instructions; the cost will be from about $50 to $120.

f.   Use Your Trademark Properly

The law considers it very important to use a trademark properly once you've adopted it as a brand name for your goods. Before it's registered, you should indicate it's a trademark by providing the superscript "™" after the mark. If it's a service mark, such as a restaurant name or a name for a service business, use the "SM" superscript—for example, "Alice's SM Restaurant." Once the mark is federally registered, provide the superscript "®" or indicate that the mark is registered in the PTO—such as "Reg. U.S. Pat. & TM. Off."

Word trademarks should always be used as brand names. That is, they should be used as adjective modifiers in association with the general name of the goods to which they apply, and shouldn't be used as a substitute for the name of the goods. For example, if you're making and selling can openers and have adopted the trademark *Ajax*, always use the words "can opener" after *Ajax* and never refer to an *Ajax* alone. Otherwise, the name can become generic and be lost, as happened to "cellophane" and "aspirin," and as could soon happen to *Xerox*. (Doesn't it somehow feel more natural to use the word "Xerox" than "photocopy" or "Kleenex" rather than "tissue"?)

5.   What Doesn't Qualify as a Trademark (for the Purpose of Developing Offensive Rights)

The courts won't enforce trademark offensive rights, nor will the PTO or state trademark offices grant trademark registrations, on the following:
- lengthy written matter (copyright is the proper form of coverage here);
- slogans that are merely informational or laudatory, such as "Proudly made in the U.S.A.";
- trade names not being used as a trademark or service mark ;
- immoral, deceptive, scandalous or disparaging matter;
- governmental emblems, personal names, or likenesses without consent;
- marks that they consider close enough to existing marks as to be likely to cause confusion;
- pure surnames or purely geographical designations; or
- generic or descriptive words.

P.   Copyright

A copyright is another offensive right given by law, this time to an author, artist, composer, or programmer, to exclude others from publishing or copying literary, dramatic, musical, artistic, or software works. While a patent can effectively provide offensive rights on an idea per se, assuming it's reduced to hardware form, a copyright covers only the author's or artist's particular way of expressing an idea. Thus, while a copyright can provide offensive rights on the particular arrangement of words that constitute a book or play, it can't cover the book's subject matter, message, or teachings. Put otherwise, you are free to publish any of the ideas, concepts, and information in this (or any) book, provided that you write it in your own words. But if you copy the specific wording, then you'll infringe the copyright on this book.

Some specific types of works that are covered by copyright are books, poetry, plays, songs, catalogs, photographs, computer programs, advertisements, labels, movies, maps, drawings, sculpture, prints and art reproductions, game boards and rules, and recordings. Certain materials, such as titles, slogans, lettering, ideas, plans, forms, useful things, non-original material, and non-creative material (such as a list of names and telephone numbers) can't be covered through copyright. U.S. government publications, by law, aren't covered by copyright and may almost always be freely copied and sold by anyone, if desired.

While I provide a brief overview of copyright principles in the rest of this section, more complete discussions of this subject are available in *The Copyright Handbook,* by Steven Fishman (for written works), *Copyright Your Software,* by Steven Fishman (for software and computer-related expressions), and *Software Development: A Legal Guide,* also by Stephen Fishman. All three books are published by Nolo Press.

1. What Is Copyright?

Now that we've seen what a copyright covers, what exactly is a copyright? As stated, a copyright is the offensive right that the government gives an author of any original work of expression (such as those mentioned above) to exclude others from copying or commercially using the work of expression without proper authorization.

To obtain copyright rights, the work must be "original," not merely the result of extended effort. Thus, in 1991, the Supreme Court held that a telephone company that compiled, through much work, an alphabetical directory of names and addresses could not prevent another publisher from copying the directory, since it had no originality. (*Feist Publications Inc. v. Rural Telephone Service Co.,* 111 S. Ct. 1282 (1991).) Also, a copyright cannot cover any system, method, process, concept, principle or device, although it can cover a specific explanation or description of anything.

The copyright springs into existence the instant the work of expression first assumes some tangible form, and lasts until it expires by law (the life of the author plus 50 years, or for works made for hire, 75 years from publication or 100 years from creation, whichever is shorter). A work made for hire is one made by an employee in the course of the employment or by an independent contractor under a written work-made-for-hire contract.

2. Copyright Compared With Utility Patent

The process involved in obtaining a patent differs significantly from that of registering a copyright. A copyright is deemed to exist automatically upon creation of the work, with no registration being necessary. On the other hand, to obtain patent rights, an application must be filed with the PTO, and that office must review, approve, and issue a patent.

If a copyright is registered with the Copyright Office (which technically is part of the Library of Congress) on any copyrightable material, a certificate of registration will be granted without examination as to the work's novelty. The PTO (part of the U.S. Department of Commerce), on the other hand, makes a strict and thorough novelty and unobviousness examination on all patent applications and won't grant a patent unless it considers the invention novel and unobvious.

Finally, with some exceptions, the two forms of offensive rights cover types of creation that are mutually exclusive. Simply put, things that are entitled to a patent are generally not entitled to a copyright, and vice versa. However, it's important to understand that there is a small gray area where this generalization isn't necessarily true. A few creations may be eligible for both types of coverage.

HOW TO SECURE OFFENSIVE COPYRIGHT RIGHTS IN A WORK

While no longer necessary for works published after March 1,1989, it's still advisable first to place the familiar copyright notice (for example, Copyright © 1995 David Pressman) on each published copy of the work. This tells anyone who sees the work that the copyright is being claimed, who is claiming it, and when the work was first published. (The year isn't used on pictures, sculptures, or graphic works.) This notice prevents an infringer from later claiming that the infringement was accidental.

Next you should register the work with the U.S. Copyright Office. If done in a timely manner, registration makes your case better if and when you prosecute a court action (for example, you can get minimum statutory damages and attorney fees). It's useful to distinguish between steps (a) and (b), placing the copyright notice on the work and actually getting a copyright registration. Thus I suggest that you don't say, "I copyrighted my program," but rather say, "I put a copyright notice on my program," or "I applied for a copyright registration on my program."

3. Areas Where Patent and Copyright Law Overlap

Let's look at these principal areas where you may be able to obtain offensive rights on intellectual property under either patent or copyright coverage, or both.

a. Computer Software

Computer programs are the best example of a type of creative work that may qualify for both a patent and copyright protection.

Viewed one way, computer programs are in fact nothing more than a series of numerical relationships (termed "routines") and as such cannot qualify for a patent (although they can, of course, be covered under the copyright laws because they have been held to constitute a creative work of expression). However, viewed from another perspective, computer programs are a set of instructions that make a machine (the computer) operate in a certain way. And, in recent years, many patents have been issued on computer programs where the program was claimed (described in the patent application) to affect some hardware or process. Simply put, a programmed machine, programmed system, or process using an algorithm to affect some hardware or process may qualify for a patent, whereas the algorithm per se couldn't. More on this in Chapter 5, Section C, and Chapter 9, Section G13.

Why patent a program as opposed to simply registering a copyright on it? Because the patent affords up to 20 years of broad, hard-to-design-around offensive rights for the program, even if an infringing program is created independently. What is the drawback? It takes about two years, a considerable amount of work, and a fair amount of money, even if you do it all yourself, to obtain a patent. Because much software becomes obsolete in a much shorter time, your software may not be worth protecting by the time the patent issues. Thus, you often don't need the full term of coverage a patent offers, and money spent on obtaining one may well be wasted.

While copyrighting of programs is relatively inexpensive as well as easy to accomplish, the coverage gained isn't as broad as is offered by a patent. This is so because copyright covers only the particular way the program is written, not what it does. For instance, all major word processing programs accomplish pretty much the same tasks (such as cursor movement, screen and print formatting, search and find functions, and moving text from one location to another) but each does so through a differently expressed program, and thus each is entitled to separate copyright status. Also, a copyright isn't available against independent creators—that is, those who write a similar or even identical program without copying it from the copyrighted program.

So when choosing whether to rely on copyright or a patent for software (assuming the software can be "claimed" as part of a physical structure or process) the software author must weigh the broader offensive rights that a patent brings against the expense and time in obtaining one. Likewise, the ease with which copyright is obtained must be counterbalanced by the narrow nature of its coverage.

There is one further drawback to copyright for programs: if you do choose to rely on copyright rather than a patent to cover your program, and you don't bring the program, or a device embodying it in a PROM (Programmable Read-Only Memory), out for a while, you take the risk that someone else may patent it in the meantime.

SIX SHOOTER DIAPER
No. 231,879

b.   Shapes and Designs

The inventor may also have a choice of utility patent or copyright in areas where an object's shape or design is both functional and aesthetic. Consider, for example, a new alphabet with letters that are attractive, yet which also provide more efficient, unambiguous spelling (such as the efficient alphabet that Shaw used to write *Androcles and the Lion*), or which are easier to read in subdued light. Patent or copyright can be used. The former will afford broader coverage to whatever principles can be identified and the latter will be cheaper, quicker, and easier to obtain, but limited to the specific shapes of the letters. Note that unlike design patents, copyright can be used to cover some aesthetic shapes even if they also have a significant function.

In many areas both forms of coverage can be used together for different aspects of the creation. Thus in parlor games, the game apparatus, if sufficiently unique, can be patented, while the gameboard, rules, box, and design of the game pieces can be covered by copyright. The artwork on the box or package for almost any invention can be covered by copyright, as can the instructions accompanying the product. Also the name of the game (for example, *Dungeons and Dragons*) is a trademark and can be covered as such.

If the invention can also be considered a sculptural work, or if it's embodied or encased in a sculptural work, copyright is available for the sculpture. However, copyright can't be used for a utilitarian article, unless it has an aesthetic feature that can be separated from and can exist independently of the article. This rule, known as the "separability requirement," is very important in copyright law.

Of course, to emphasize my earlier point, both copyrights and patents generally have their exclusive domains. Assuming they don't have any aesthetic components, patents are exclusive for machines, compositions, articles, processes, and new uses per se. On the other hand, copyrights are exclusive for works of expression, such as writings, sculpture, movies, plays, recordings, and artwork, assuming they don't have any functional aspects.

c.   Copyright Compared to Design Patents

There's considerable overlap here since aesthetics are the basis of both forms of coverage. Design patents are used mainly to cover industrial designs where the shape of the object has ornamental features and the shape is inseparable from, or meaningless if separated from, the object. For example, a tire tread design, a computer case, and the workshop sawblade clock (see Section B, above) are perfect for a design patent, but a surface decal, which could be used elsewhere, is not. Copyright, on the other hand, can be used for almost any artistic or written creation, whether or not it's inseparable from an underlying object, so long as the aspect of the work for which copyright is being sought is ornamental and not functional. This means copyright can be used for pure surface ornamentation, such as the artwork on a can of beans, as well as sculptural works where the "art" and the object are integrated, such as a statue. For instance, the shape of a toy was held to be properly covered by copyright since the shape played no role in how the toy functioned and since a toy wasn't considered to perform a useful function (although many parents who use toys to divert their children would disagree). The same principle should apply to "adult toys," provided they are strictly for amusement and don't have a utilitarian function.

What are the differences in the coverage afforded by design patents and copyright? Design patents are relatively expensive to obtain (the filing fee is higher, an issue fee is required—see Fee Schedule in Appendix 4), a formal drawing is required, a novelty examination is required, and the rights last only 14 years. However, a design patent offers broader rights than a copyright in that it covers the aesthetic principles underlying the design. This means that someone else coming up with a similar, but somewhat changed design would probably be liable for patent infringement.

Copyright, on the other hand, provides relatively narrow offensive rights (minor changes in all of the artwork's features will usually avoid infringement), the government fee for registration is very small (see Fee Schedule), the term is long (the life of the creator plus 50 years, or a flat 75 or 100 years for works classified as made-for-hire). And as no novelty examination is performed, you're virtually assured of obtaining a copyright registration certificate if you file.

Because the distinctions between design patents and copyrights are especially confusing, I've provided a comparison chart to summarize the distinctions between these two forms in Fig. 1D.

4.   When and How to Obtain Copyright Coverage

If you desire to obtain copyright coverage for an invention, program, creation, or for instructions, packaging or artwork that goes with your invention, you don't need to do anything until the item is distributed or published. This is because, as mentioned, your copyright rights arise when your work is first put into tangible form. And, although there is no requirement for a copyright notice on your work before it's generally distributed to the public, I strongly advise you to put the proper copyright notice on any copyrightable material right away, since this will give anyone who receives the material notice that you claim copyright in it and they shouldn't reproduce it without permission.

When your material is distributed to the public, it's even more desirable (though no longer mandatory for works published after March 1, 1989) that you place a copyright notice on it to notify others that you claim copyright and to prevent infringers from claiming they were "innocent" and thus entitled to reduced damages. This notice should consist of the word "Copyright," followed by a "c" in a circle © (or a "p" in a circle ℗ for recordings and records), followed by the year the work is first published (widely distributed without restriction), followed by the name of the invention's owner. Thus the copyright notice on this book appears as "Copyright © 1995 David Pressman. All Rights Reserved."

If anyone infringes your copyright (that is, without your permission someone copies, markets, displays, or produces a derivative work based on your original work) and you want to go to court to prevent this from happening and collect damages, you first have to register your work with the U.S. Copyright Office. Moreover, if you register within three months of the time your item is distributed or published, or before the infringement occurs, you may be entitled to attorney fees, costs, and damages that don't have to be proved by you (called "statutory damages"). All things considered, I strongly advise you to register your work as soon as it's published if you think you're entitled to copyright coverage.

Again, for detailed step-by-step guidance regarding copyright, I recommend *The Copyright Handbook*, by Steven Fishman (for written works), *Copyright Your Software*, by Steven Fishman (for software and computer-

DESIGN PATENT	**COPYRIGHT**
Permissible for All of the Following: The aesthetic aspects of articles of manufacture, such as jewelry, furniture, musical and other instruments and fabrics.	**Permissible for All of the Following:** Literary and artistic content of written materials, lectures, periodicals, plays, musical compositions, maps, artworks, software, reproductions, photographs, prints, labels, translations, movies, sculpture.
Disadvantages: Must prepare a formal application with ink drawings, must prosecute before the PTO with legal briefs, large filing fee and issue fees, lasts only 14 years, takes a long time (one to three years) to secure rights.	**Disadvantages:** Gives a narrow scope of offensive rights, no doctrine of equivalents, no protection of concepts (only particular form of expression thereof), only good against proven actual copiers (not independent creators).
Advantages: Broader scope of offensive rights, including doctrine of equivalents (see Chapter 15), can cover concepts, good against independent creators.	**Advantages:** Only need fill out a simple form with samples of the actual work, no formal drawings needed, no need for legal briefs, only small filing fee, no issue fee, lasts a very long time (life + 50 years or 75–100 years), instant offensive rights.
Can't Be Used For: Articles where the novel features have a utilitarian function (use utility patent); writings, flat artwork, photos, maps, drawings, programs, prints, labels, movies (use copyright), or surface ornamentation.	**Can't Be Used For:** Utilitarian articles, unless the aesthetic features are separable from and can exist independently of the article (toys aren't considered utilitarian), machines, processes, systems, concepts, principles or discoveries.
Recommended For: The aesthetic shape or layout of utilitarian articles.	**Recommended For:** Articles of manufacture that aren't utilitarian, or if utilitarian, have aesthetic aspects that can be separated and exist independently, jewelry, furniture, fabrics, literary content of written materials, lectures, periodicals, plays, maps, musical compositions, artworks, software, reproductions, photographs, prints, labels with artwork, translations, movies, sculpture.

Fig. 1D—Design Patents Compared to Copyrights

related expressions), and *Software Development: A Legal Guide,* also by Stephen Fishman. All three books are published by Nolo Press. Also, the Copyright Office, Washington, DC 20559, provides free information and forms on copyright. Tel. Nos.: 202-707-9100 for forms (24 hours) and 202-479-0700 for information.

Q. Trade Secrets

Here we provide a basic definition of trade secrets, distinguish trade secret protection from patents, list the advantages and disadvantages of trade secret vs. patenting, and tell you and how to acquire and maintain trade secret rights.

1. Definition

Thanks to the intensive coverage of the high-tech industry by the media, the term "trade secret" has become virtually a household word. You've probably heard of the recent case where an employee of a biotech (gene splicing) company tried to sell his employer's secrets to some FBI undercover agents.

What are these trade secrets and why are they valuable enough to warrant corporations paying millions of dollars to high-priced attorneys to protect them? In a sentence, a trade secret is any information, design, device, process, composition, technique, or formula that is not known generally and that affords its owner a competitive business advantage.

Among the items considered as trade secrets are:
- chemical formulas, such as the formula for the paper used to make U.S. currency
- manufacturing processes, such as the process used to form the eyes in sewing needles
- "magic-type" trade secrets, such as the techniques used to produce laser light shows and fireworks, and
- chemical recipes, such as the recipes for certain soft drinks, cosmetics, and chemicals.

Even if the ingredients of a chemical are publicly known, the method of combining the ingredients and their sources of supply can still be a trade secret.

Obviously, since these types of information and know-how can go to the very heart of a business and its competitive position, businesses will often expend a great deal of time, energy, and money to guard their trade secrets.

When I refer to trade secrets in this book, I mean those that consist of technical information, such as in the examples given above. However, virtually every business also owns "business-information" type trade secrets, such as customer lists, names of suppliers, and pricing data. The law will enforce rights to both types of trade secrets, provided the information concerned was kept confidential and can be shown to be non-public knowledge and truly valuable.

More so than in any of the other intellectual property categories, the primary idea underlying trade secrets is plain common sense. If a business knows or has some information that gives it an edge over competitors, the degree of offensive rights that the law will afford to the owner of a trade secret is proportional to the business value of the trade secret and how well the owner actually kept the secret. If a company is sloppy about its secrets, the courts will reject its request for relief. Conversely, a company that takes reasonable measures to maintain the secret will be afforded relief against those who wrongfully obtain the information. These central factors underlying trade secrets have profound implications for those who are seeking patents, as I discuss below.

2. Relationship of Patents to Trade Secrets

When a patent issues, the public has complete access to the ideas, techniques, approaches, and methods underlying the invention. This is because, as we'll see in Chapter 8, a patent application must clearly explain how to make and use the invention. Since the application is printed verbatim when the patent issues, all of this "know-how" will become public. This public disclosure doesn't usually hurt the inventor, however, since the patent can be used to prevent anyone else from commercially exploiting the underlying information.

What happens, however, if the patent isn't granted? Because patent applications are treated as confidential by the PTO, it is possible to apply for a patent and still maintain the underlying information as a trade secret during the patent application process. Then, if the patent is later denied, the competition will still not know about the invention and any competitive advantage inherent in that fact can be maintained and the trade secret will remain intact.

Even if a decision is made by the PTO to grant a patent, you'll have an opportunity to reject it and continue relying on trade secret principles to enforce offensive rights on your invention. This means, in essence, that provided the invention has been kept secret, every patent applicant can both apply for a patent and maintain the invention as a trade secret for the full pendency of the patent application process, which usually takes about two years. Only later, in the event the PTO decides to award a patent, need a decision be made as to which path to follow.

LOSS OF TRADE SECRET RIGHTS IF 18-MONTH PUBLICATION RULE TAKES EFFECT

Recently there have been proposals to publish every patent application 18 months after filing—for inspection by the public—as is done in almost all foreign countries. The PTO has already held public hearings on this issue based on its belief that such a law would be enacted prior to January 1, 1996. As of May 1997, no law has been enacted, although legislation has been introduced and one version has been passed by the House of Representatives. If such a rule is enacted into law, and you file a patent application on an invention that you might wish to keep as a trade secret if the patent isn't granted, you will have to take affirmative steps to withdraw your application before publication to prevent loss of your trade secret rights.

If you maintain an invention as a trade secret and put it into commercial use, you *must* file a patent application within one year of the date you first used it commercially. If you wait over a year, any patent that you do ultimately obtain will be held invalid if this fact is discovered. More on the "one-year rule" in Chapter 5, Section E.

The following material discusses the pros and cons of each form of offensive rights.

3. Advantages of Trade Secret Protection

Often I advise people to choose trade secret rights over those afforded by a patent, assuming it's possible to protect the creation by either. Let's look at some of the reasons why:

- The main advantage of a trade secret is the possibility of perpetual protection. While a patent is limited by statute to 20 years from filing and isn't renewable, a trade secret will last indefinitely if not discovered. For example, some fireworks and sewing needle trade secrets have been maintained for decades.
- A trade secret can be maintained without the cost or effort involved in patenting.
- There is no need to disclose details of your invention to the public for trade secret rights (as you have to do with a patented invention).
- With a trade secret, you have definite, already existing rights and don't have to worry about whether your patent application will be allowed.
- Since a trade secret isn't distributed to the public as a patent is, no one can look at your trade secret and try to design around it, as they can with the claims of your patent.
- A trade secret can be established without naming any inventors, as must be done with a patent application. Thus no effort need be made to determine the proper inventor and a company needn't request its inventor-employee to assign (legally transfer) ownership of the trade secret to it, as is required with a patent application.
- A trade secret doesn't have to be a significant, important advance, as does a patented invention.
- A trade secret can cover more information, including many relatively minor details, whereas a patent generally covers but one broad principle and its ramifications. For example, a complicated manufacturing machine with many new designs and that incorporates several new techniques can be covered as a trade secret merely by keeping the whole machine secret. To cover it by patent, on the other hand, many expensive and time-consuming patent applications would be required, and even then the patent wouldn't cover many minor ideas in the machine.
- Trade secret rights are obtained immediately, whereas a patent takes a couple of years to obtain, in which time rapidly evolving technology can bypass the patented invention.

4. Disadvantages of Trade Secret Versus Patenting

Before you stop reading this book, please understand that I spent three years writing it for a good reason. Or put more clearly, there are many circumstances in which the trade secret rights have important disadvantages. In these contexts, using the rights provided by a patent is essential.

The main reason that trade secrets are often a poor way to cover your work is that they can't be maintained when the public is able to discover the information by inspecting, dissecting, or analyzing the product (called "reverse engineering"). Thus mechanical and electronic devices that are sold to the public can't be kept as trade secrets. However, the essential information contained in certain chemical compositions sold to the public (cosmetics, for example), and in computer programs (assuming they're distributed to the public in object code form), often can't be readily reverse engineered, and thus can be maintained as trade secrets. However, because very sophisticated analytic tools are now available, such as chromatographs, Auger analyzers, spectroscopes, spectrophotometers, scanning electron microscopes, and software decompilers, most things can be analyzed and copied, no matter how sophisticated or small they are. And remember, the law generally allows anyone to copy and make anything freely, unless it is patented or subject to copyright coverage, or unless its shape is its trademark, such as the shape of the Photomat huts, or unless its shape has become so well-known or distinctive as to be entitled to trade dress rights. (See Section R, below.)

Strict precautions must always be taken and continually enforced to maintain the confidentiality of a trade secret. If your trade secret is discovered legitimately, or by any other method, it's generally lost forever, although you do have rights against anyone who purloins your trade secret by illegal means. You can sue the thief and any conspirators for the economic loss you suffered as a result of the thief's actions. In practice this amount can be considerable, since it will include the economic value of the trade secret.

Regardless of these offensive rights, individuals rarely will be able to respond adequately in damages; hence the individual's new employer or the purchaser of the trade secret (who usually has a deeper pocket) is usually sued. For example, when some Hitachi employee purloined some IBM trade secrets, IBM sued Hitachi as well as the individuals concerned and actually obtained millions of dollars in compensation from Hitachi. In addition, a trade secret is more difficult to sue on and enforce than a patent. A patent must be initially presumed valid by the court, but a trade secret must be proven to exist before the suit may proceed.

A trade secret can be patented by someone else who discovers it by legitimate means. For instance, suppose you invent a new formula, say for a hair treatment lotion, and keep it secret. Jane M., who is totally unconnected with you and who has never even heard of your lotion, comes up with the same formula and decides to patent it, which she does successfully. She can legitimately sue and hold you liable for infringing her patent with your own invention!

What conclusion should you draw from this discussion? Because offensive rights connected with trade secrets continue as long as the trade secret itself is maintained, and because infringement of patents on "trade-secretable" inventions is difficult to discover, if you have an invention that can be kept as a trade secret for approximately 20 years, you may be better off doing so than obtaining a patent on it.

5. Acquiring and Maintaining Trade Secret Rights

After I explain the differences between trade secret and patents, inventors will often say to me, "I've decided trade secret is the way to go; how do I get one?" The inventor is pleased to learn that acquiring and maintaining trade secret rights involves only simple, commonsense procedures and doesn't require any governmental or bureaucratic paperwork. All that is necessary is that the inventor take reasonable precautions to keep the information confidential. Also, an employer should have all employees who have access to company trade secrets sign an agreement to keep the information confidential; see Fig. 16A (in Chapter 16) for a typical employment agreement regarding trade secrets and other employer rights. Over the years the courts have devised a number of tests for determining what these reasonable precautions should be and whether a trade secret owner has taken them.

Most states now have a statute that makes the theft of a trade secret a criminal offense as well as a civil action (for instance, the Uniform Trade Secrets Act, California Civil Code § 3246 et seq.). Moreover, there is now a federal statute for the same purpose (Economic Espionage Act, 18 USC §1831 et seq.).

If you're interested in further reading on the subject, I recommend *Software Development: A Legal Guide,* by Stephen Fishman (Nolo Press), and *Trade Secrets,* by Pooley (Osborne-McGraw Hill). Also, see the heading "Law Books Relating to Patents" in Appendix 2, Books of Use and Interest.

R. Unfair Competition

The area of "unfair competition" is the most difficult to explain. Although anyone who is creative, or is in a competitive business, will encounter unfair competition problems or questions from time to time, any attempts to define this area are necessarily fraught with confusion. And no wonder! The scope of unfair competition law is nebulous in the first place and is regularly being changed by judges who make new and often contradictory rulings.

1. When Unfair Competition Principles Create Offensive Rights

Fortunately, this is a patent book rather than a law school course. And, for the purpose of this book, all you really need to understand about unfair competition law can be summarized in several sentences.

- An unfair competition situation exists when one business represents its goods or services in such a way as to potentially cause the class of buyers who purchase the particular type of goods or services to confuse them with goods or services offered by another business.
- Unfair competition law is usually available only as a source of offensive rights under the Federal "false designation of origin" statute (15 USC 1125(a)), or when no offensive rights are available under the trademark, copyright, or patent laws.
- Unfair competition can be used to cover such items as advertising symbols, methods of packaging, slogans, business names, "trade dress" (that is, anything distinctive used by a merchant to package or house its goods, such as the yellow container that has come to be identified with *Kodak* film), and titles. Also, Bette Midler successfully sued an advertising agency for using a singer whose voice sounded like Ms. Midler's. And Mother Fuddrucker's restaurants sued a competitor that copied Mother's distinctive restaurant layout. In other words, when the characteristics of a product or service aren't distinctive or defined enough to be considered a trademark, then unfair competition may be the appropriate way to cover it.
- If an injured party can prove that a business has engaged in unfair competition, a judge will issue an injunction (legal order) prohibiting the business from any further such activity or defining what the business can and can't do. Further, the court may award compensation (monetary damages) to the injured business (that is, the business that lost profits because of the public's confusion).

2. How Does the Law of Unfair Competition Affect You?

There are several ways in which the law of unfair competition can affect you.

- If you already have a product or service you find has been copied or pirated, and the traditional methods (patents, copyrights, trademarks, and trade secrets) are no help (perhaps because it's not patentable or it's too late to patent it, it doesn't qualify under the copyright or trademark laws, or it doesn't qualify as a trade secret), you still may be able to get relief under the doctrine of unfair competition.

- If you're contemplating coming out with a product or service, try to make it as distinctive as reasonably possible in as many ways as reasonably possible so that you'll easily be able to establish a distinctive, recognizable appearance (termed in the law as "secondary meaning"). For example, you would be wise to use unique and distinctive packaging ("trade dress"), unique advertising slogans and symbols, a unique title, a distinctive business name, and a clever advertising campaign. And the more you advertise and expose your product, and the more distinctive (different) it is, the stronger your unfair competition rights will be.

3. Comparison of Unfair Competition With Design Patents

Some inventors confuse the trade dress area of unfair competition law with design patents. Trade dress refers to the distinctive appearance of a business, a product, or product packaging, where the appearance distinguishes the product or business from other similar products or businesses but isn't significant or specific enough to be considered a trademark. The coloring of a package or label, or the layout of a business, are good examples of distinctive trade dress.

Patentable designs, on the other hand, relate to the appearance of an article that enhances its aesthetic appeal, which is more than mere surface ornamentation and which is novel and unobvious. Examples are a modernistic lamp design and the pattern of a fabric. While trade dress can be mere coloring, surface ornamentation, or a general appearance, a design patentable invention has to be a shape or appearance of a specific article which is more than a surface appearance, which relates to the overall appearance of the article, and which is different enough to be considered unobvious.

S. Acquisition of Offensive Rights in Intellectual Property—Summary Chart

The following chart summarizes intellectual property law as it applies to various types of mental creations.

UNDERLYING MENTAL CREATION	HOW TO ACQUIRE OFFENSIVE RIGHTS	LEGAL REMEDY FOR MISAPPROPRIATION
Invention (machine, article, process, composition, new use).	File a utility patent application as soon as possible, but within one year of offer of sale or publication, and get a patent.	Patent infringement litigation.
Industrial or aesthetic design.	File design patent application as soon as possible, but within one year of offer of sale or publication, and get a design patent.	Patent infringement litigation.
Brand name for a good or service; certification or collective mark or seal.	Use the trademark as a proper adjective with the "™" or "℠" superscript; register the trademark as soon as possible, with the state and/or the PTO, and get a trademark registration.	Trademark infringement litigation, either before or after registration.
Writings, music, recordings, art, software, sculpture, photos, etc.	Put a copyright notice on the work; also advisable to register copyright within three months of publication. Get a copyright registration.	Copyright infringement litigation, after registration.
Confidential technical or business information.	Keep it secret; keep good records so you can prove you kept it secret. Have employees sign "keep-confidential" agreements. The protected information is a trade secret.	Trade secret litigation.
Distinctive trade dress, informative slogans, novel business layout, etc.	Advertising and frequent use. The distinctive appearance is protectible trade dress.	Unfair competition litigation.

T. Selection Guide to Which Type of Intellectual Property Is Best for Your Creation

Now that you're familiar with all of the types of intangible property, let's summarize how to select the appropriate form for any type of mental creation.

IF YOUR CREATION RELATES TO:	ACQUIRE OFFENSIVE RIGHTS BY:
The functional aspect of any machine, article, composition, or process or new use of any of the foregoing—such as circuits, algorithms that affect some process or hardware, gadgets, apparatus, machinery, tools, devices, implements, chemical compositions and industrial or other processes or techniques that one could discover from final product, toys, game apparatus, semiconductor devices, buildings, receptacles, and vehicles, cloth and apparel, furniture (functional structure), personal care devices, scientific apparatus, abrasives, hardware, plumbing, parts, alloys, laminates, protective coatings, drugs[1], sporting goods, kitchen implements, locks and safes, timekeeping apparatus, cleaning implements, filters, refrigeration apparatus, environmental control apparatus, medical apparatus, new non-human animals, new bacteria, plant (sexually or asexually reproducible), or anything else made by humans where the novel aspects have a functional purpose.	Utility patent (use the rest of this book).
Any new design for any tangible thing where the design is nonfunctional and is part of and not removable from the thing, such as a bottle, a computer case, jewelry, a type of material weave, a tire tread design, a building or other structure, any article, item of apparel, furniture, tool, computer screen icon, etc.	Design patent (use Chapter 9).
Any asexually reproduced plant.[2]	Plant patent (see PTO Rules 61-167).
Any symbol, sign, word, sound, design, device, shape, smell, mark, etc., used as a brand name (trademark), service mark, certification mark or collective mark, such as "Ajax™ tools." (The symbol cannot be generic or descriptive—e.g., "electric fork.")	Using it as a trademark with "™" or "SM" superscript and then registering it in state and/or federal trademark offices. Also, you can apply to register federally before using, based upon your intent to use the mark.
Any book, poem, speech, recording, computer program, work of art (statue, painting, cartoon, label), musical work, dramatic work, pantomime and choreographic work, photograph, graphic work, motion picture, videotape, map, architectural drawing, artistic jewelry, gameboard, gameboard box and game instructions, etc.	Placing a correct copyright notice on the work, e.g., "© 1991 M. Smith"; apply for copyright registration, preferably within three months of publication. (See Section P, above.)

[1] Orphan drugs (those useful in treating rare diseases) can be covered under the Orphan Drug Act, 21 USC 360; write to the Food and Drug Administration for details.

[2] Sexually reproduced plants can be monopolized under the Plant Variety Protection Act, 7 USC 2321; write to Plant Variety Protection Office, National Agriculture Library, Room 500, 10301 Baltimore Blvd., Beltsville, MD 20705. Also, both types of plants (sexually and asexually reproducible) can be covered by utility patent.

IF YOUR CREATION RELATES TO:	ACQUIRE OFFENSIVE RIGHTS BY:
Any information whatever that isn't generally known that will give a business advantage or is commercially useful, such as formulae, ideas, techniques, know-how, designs, materials, processes, etc.	Identifying it as proprietary information or a trade secret, such as "This document contains Ajax Co. confidential information:"; or put it on an invention disclosure-type form (see Chapter 3) and limit its dissemination using appropriate means. (See Section Q, above.)
Any distinctive design, slogan, title, shape, color, trade dress, package, business layout, etc.	Using it publicly as much as possible, in advertising, etc., so as to establish a "secondary meaning" to enable you to win an unfair competition lawsuit. (See above.)

NOTE ON GAMES
You can theoretically acquire offensive rights on games by four different intangible property enforcement tools. Initially, the game idea and design is a trade secret. Then you can patent the game apparatus (assuming it's sufficiently different from the prior art) by a utility patent, treat the name of the game as a trademark, and cover the gameboard, rules, and box design by copyright.

NOTE ON COMPUTER PROGRAMS
These can also be covered by patents, copyright, trademark, or trade secret. If the program is to be narrowly disseminated under a license agreement so that you have some control over its purchasers or users, keep it as a trade secret, having your purchasers or users sign non-disclosure agreements. If the program is to be widely disseminated, so that trade secret protection wouldn't be practicable, apply for a patent if the program involves one or more valuable or highly novel algorithms that affect hardware or a process and that you expect to be useful for more than a few years. Use copyright if the algorithms aren't that valuable or novel. Also, the name of the program is a trademark and should be treated accordingly. The instructions should be covered by copyright.

U. Invention Exploitation Flowchart

To get you oriented and make it easier to use this book, here's a chart that shows the overall steps to use to exploit your invention and where the details of these steps are found.

Fig. 1E—Patent Exploitation Flowchart

CHAPTER

2

The Science and Magic of Inventing

INVENTOR'S COMMANDMENT #2

To invent successfully, be aware of problems you encounter. Also, take the time to study and investigate the practicality of new phenomena that occur by accident or flash of insight. Persevere with any development you believe has commercial potential.

Before we get to patents, the primary subject of this book, I want briefly to talk about inventions and inventing. Why do this? To begin, you may be a first-time inventor and thus have no experience in the real world of protecting and patenting inventions. I believe that too many first-timers get discouraged without trying hard enough. To inspire you to hang in there, I include here some past success stories. Hopefully, when you see that many other small, independent inventors have found their pot of gold, you'll be stimulated to press on.

Inventing provides things that enhance our lives, making them more interesting, pleasurable, exciting, rewarding, and educational. As the noted Swiss psychologist, Piaget, once said, "We learn most when we have to invent." Remember that everything of significance, even the chair you're probably seated in now, started with an idea in someone's brain. If you come up with something, don't dismiss it; it could turn out to be something great!

Common Misconception: The day of the small inventor is over; an independent inventor no longer has any chance to make a killing with his or her invention.

Fact: As you'll see by the examples given later in this chapter, many small, independent inventors have done extremely well with their inventions. Billions of dollars in royalties and other compensation are paid each year to independent inventors for their creations. In fact 73% of all inventions that have started new industries have come from individual inventors. So, don't be a victim of the "no-use-going-on-with-it-because-surely-someone-has-invented-it-already" syndrome. While I recommend that you don't rush blindly ahead to patent your work without making a sensible investigation of prior inventions and your creation's commercial potential (in the ways I discuss later), I urge you not to quit without giving your invention a fair chance.

Another reason for this chapter is that many inventors come up with valuable inventions, but they haven't developed them enough so that they can be readily sold. If their creations could be improved with further work, they'd have a far greater chance of success. So here I'll also give some

hints about such things as improving your inventions, solving problems about workability, and drawbacks.

If you've already made an invention, or are even in the business of inventing, I believe the techniques in this chapter that increase your creativity and provide additional stimulation will help you to make more and better inventions. On the other hand, I also recognize that the information in this chapter may not be particularly helpful to the experienced inventor or the corporate inventor—after all, you're already firmly in the inventing business. If you would rather skip this information for now, go to Chapter 3, where my discussion of recordkeeping should prove of value to even the most seasoned of inventors.

A. What I Mean by "Invention"

For the purpose of this book, an invention is any thing, process, or idea that isn't generally and currently known; which, without too much skill or ingenuity, can exist in or be reduced to tangible form or used in a tangible thing; which has some use or value to society; and which you or someone else has thought up or discovered.

Note that under this definition, an invention can be a process or even an idea, so long as it can be made tangible in some way, "without too much skill or ingenuity." On the other hand, the definition eliminates fantasies and wishes, such as time-travel or perpetual motion machines, since these obviously (at least to me) can't be made tangible.

An invention must have some use or value to society; otherwise what good is it, and how will you sell it? It must be generally unknown anywhere in the world (at the time you invent it), and it must have been thought up or discovered by you or someone else—otherwise it doesn't really have inventive value.

Why do I bother to define the term invention in such detail? So you'll begin to understand it and have a better feel for it, as well as to define the limits of its usage in this book. As you'll see, my primary concern is with inventions that qualify for a patent (that is, patentable inventions). However, nonpatentable inventions can also be valuable as long as society finds them at least somewhat special and useful.

B. Inventing by Problem Recognition and Solution

Now that you know what an invention is, how do you make one? Most inventions are conceived by the following two-step procedure: 1) recognizing a problem, and 2) fashioning a solution.

Although it may seem like duck soup, recognizing a problem often amounts to about 90% of the act of conceiving the invention. "To be an inventor is to perceive need." In these situations, once the problem is recognized, conceiving the solution is easy. Consider some of the Salton products—the home peanut butter maker, for instance, or the plug-in ice cream maker for use in the freezer. In both cases, once the problem was defined (the need for an easy homemade version of a product normally purchased at the store) implementing the solution merely involved electrification and/or size reduction of an existing appliance. Once the problem was defined, any competent appliance designer could accomplish its solution. True, during the implementation of the idea, that is, the design of the actual hardware, designers and engineers often contribute the very aspects of the invention that make it ingenious and patentable. Still, the main ingredient leading to a successful outcome for most inventions consists of recognizing and defining the problem that needs to be solved. Although Edison seemed to contradict this when he said that inventing is 10% inspiration and 90% perspiration, he was referring to the whole experience of inventing, including conception, making a practicable model, and licensing or selling the invention. Here, I'm referring just to the conception part of inventing—what Edison called "inspiration."

Of course, in some contexts, the recognition of a problem plays no part in the invention. Most improvement inventions fall into this category, such as, for example, the improvement of the mechanism of a ball-point pen to make it cheaper, more reliable, stronger, etc. But in general, you will find it most effective to go about inventing via the two-step process of identifying a problem and solving it. Or, as famed inventor Jacob Rabinow said, "You invent because something bothers you."

Let's look at some simple inventions that were made using this two-step process and which have been commercially implemented. I delineate the problem **P** and solution **S** in each instance. Where I know an Independent Inventor was responsible, I add an "**II**".

1. **Grasscrete.** **P** Wide expanses of concrete or asphalt in a parking lot or driveway are ugly. **S** Make many cross-shaped holes in the paving and plant grass in the earth below so that the grass grows to the surface and makes the lot or driveway appear mostly green; grass is protected from the car's tires because of its subsurface position.

2. **Intermittent Windshield Wipers.** **P** In drizzles, the slowest speed of windshield wipers was unnecessarily fast, and merely slowing the wipers was unsatisfactory, since a slow sweep was annoying. **S** Provide a "drizzle" setting where the windshield wipers made normally fast sweeps but paused after each sweep. (Robert Kearns, **II**. Mr. Kearns's brilliantly ingenious yet utterly ingenuous solution, has earned him at least $20 million in royalties thus far.)

3. **Buried Plastic Cable-Locator Strip.** **P** Construction excavators often damage buried cables (or pipes) because surface warning signs often are removed or can't be placed over the entire buried cable. **S** Bury a brightly colored plastic strip parallel to and above the cable; it serves as a warning to excavators that a cable is buried below the spot where they're digging. (This is a "new-use" invention since the plastic strip per se was obviously already in existence.)

4. **Magnetic Safety Lock for Police Pistols.** **P** Police pistols are often fired by unauthorized persons. **S** A special safety lock inside the pistol releases only when the pistol is held by someone wearing a finger ring containing a high-coercive-force samarium-cobalt magnet.

5. **Wiz-z-er™ Gyroscopic Top.** **P** Gyroscopes are difficult to get running: they require the user to wind a string around a shaft surrounded by gimbals and then pull it steadily but forcefully to set the rotor in motion. **S** Provide an enclosed gyro in the shape of a top with an extending friction tip that can be easily spun at high speed by moving it across any surface. (Paul Brown, **II**. Mr. Brown came up with this great invention because, while at a party, he had repeated difficulty operating a friend's son's gyro. His first royalty check from Mattel was five times his annual salary!)

6. **Dolby® Audio Tape Hiss Elimination.** **P** Audio tapes played at low volume levels usually have an audible hiss. **S** Frequency-selective compounding of the audio during recording and expanding of the audio during playback to eliminate hiss. (Ray Dolby, perhaps the most successful **II** of modern times.)

7. **Xerography.** **P** Copying documents required messy, slow, complicated photographic apparatus. **S** Xerography—the charging of a photosensitive surface in a pattern employing light reflected from the document to be copied and then using this charged surface to pick up and deposit black powder onto a blank sheet. (Chester Carlson, **II**. When Mr. Carlson, a patent attorney, brought his invention to Kodak, they said it could never be commercially implemented and rejected it. Undaunted, he brought it to The Haloid Co., which accepted it and changed its name to Xerox Corporation; the rest is history.)

8. **Flip-Top Can.** **P** Cans of beverage were difficult to open, requiring a church key or can opener. **S** Provide the familiar flip-top can. (Ermal Frase, **II**.)

EYE PROTECTOR FOR FOWL
NO. 620,832

Fig 2.

9. **FM, CW, and AGC. P** Information wasn't conveyable by radio due to noisy, limited frequency response and fade-out of AM reception. **S** Provide CW, FM, and AGC circuitry, familiar to all electronic engineers. (Edwin Howard Armstrong, **II**, the genius of high fidelity.)

10. **Thermostatic Shower Head. P** Shower takers sometimes get burned because they inadvertently turn on the hot water while standing under the shower. **S** Provide a thermostatic cut-off valve in the supply pipe. (**II**)

11. **VCR Plus. P** Most people are too lazy or too put off by technical matters to learn how to enter a date, time, and channel into their VCR. **S** With VCR Plus, each program is assigned a special code number in the newspaper and the VCR owner need merely enter the number and transmit it to the VCR.

12. **Organic Production of Acetone. P** During WWI, the U.K. desperately needed acetone to make explosives. since its normal source was cut off. **S** Use an anaerobic bacterium to produce acetone from locally available corn mash. (Dr. Chaim Weizmann. This invention helped save one nation and start a new one: It was instrumental in helping the U.K. and the Allies survive WWI and defeat the Germans. The U.K. rewarded Weizmann with the Balfour Declaration, which helped lead to the eventual formation of the State of Israel.)

13. **Grocery Shopping Cart. P** Shoppers in grocery stores used their own small, hand-carried wicker baskets and bought only the small amounts which they could carry in the baskets, thereby necessitating several trips to the grocery and causing sales to be relatively low per customer visit. **S** Provide a "grocery cart," that is, a large wire basket in a frame on wheels so that it can be rolled about and carry a large amount of groceries. (Sylvan Goldman, **II**. When Mr. Goldman first introduced his carts (about 1925), shoppers wouldn't use them and stores wouldn't buy them despite his extensive efforts. He eventually found a way to get his carts accepted: he hired crews of men and women to wheel the carts about his store, pretending they were shoppers, and also hired a woman at the entrance to the store to offer the carts to entering shoppers. Goldman then made millions from patents on his cart and its improvements (nesting carts and airport carts). This illustrates the crucial value of perseverance and marketing genius.)

The inventors of these inventions necessarily went through the problem-solution process (though not necessarily in that order) to make their invention. Even if an inventor believes the invention came spontaneously, you'll usually find that problem-solution steps were somehow involved, even if they appear to coalesce.

So, if you either don't have an invention or want to make some new ones, you should begin by ferreting out problem or "need" areas. This can often be done by paying close attention to your daily activities. How do you or others perform tasks? What problems do you encounter and how do you solve them? What needs do you perceive, even if they're as simple as wanting a full month's calendar on your calendar watch? Ask yourself if something can't be done more easily, cheaply, simply, or reliably, if it can't be made lighter, quicker, stronger, etc. Write the problems down and keep a list. Make sure you take the time to cogitate on the problems or needs you've discovered.

Sometimes the solution to the problem you identify will be a simple expedient, such as electrification or reduction in size. Generally, however, it will be more involved, as in some of the examples listed above. But you don't have to be a genius to come up with a solution. Draw on solutions from analogous or even nonanalogous fields. Experiment, meditate, look around. When a possible solution strikes you, write it down, even if it's in the middle of the night. History records a great number of important scientific and conceptual breakthroughs occurring during sleep or borderline-sleep states.

Also, remember that sometimes the "problem" may be the ordinary way something has been done for years, and which no one has ever recognized as a problem. Consider shower heads. Although essentially the same device operated satisfactorily for about 50 years, the inventor of water-massaging shower heads recognized the deficiency of an ordinary constant spray that didn't create any massage effect. He thus developed the water-massaging head that causes the water to come out in spurts from various head orifices, thereby creating the massaging effect.

Don't hesitate to go against the grain of custom or accepted practice if that's where your invention takes you. Many widespread erroneous beliefs have abounded in the past which were just waiting to be shattered. The medical field, in particular, had numerous nonsensical practices and beliefs, such as the use of "poudrage" (pouring talcum powder onto the heart to stimulate it to heal itself), blood-letting, and blistering, and the belief that insanity could be cured by drilling holes in the head to let the demons out.

You'll probably find the going easier if you invent in fields with which you're familiar. In this way you won't tend to "reinvent the wheel." Also, think about uncrowded fields or newly emerging ones where you will find ample room for innovation. But even if you work in an established area, you will find plenty of opportunity for new inventions. For example, more patents issue on bicycles than anything else. Still, you would make millions if you could invent an automatic, continuous bicycle transmission to replace the awkward derailleur. Or how about a truly compactable bicycle (or wheelchair) which could easily be carried onto a train or into the office but worked as well as the standard variety?

The U.S. Government publishes a quarterly list of needed products requiring inventive effort. Write to the U.S. Small Business Administration, Office of Innovation, Research and Technology, SBIR, 1441 L Street, NW, Washington, DC 20416; ask to be put on the list to receive its Quarterly Solicitation Announcements.

One important principle to successful inventing is to remember the acronym KISS (Keep It Simple, Stupid!). If you can successfully eliminate just one part from any machine, its manufacturer (or a competing manufacturer!) will be overjoyed: the cost of the machine will be reduced, it will be lighter, and, of course, it will be more reliable. Another way to look at this is Sandra Bekele's (an inventor-friend) admonition to (figuratively) "eliminate the corners." Or, to quote jazz great Charlie Mingus, "Anybody can make the simple complicated. Creativity is making the complicated simple."

Lastly, says highly successful toy inventor Richard Levy, don't go into inventing for money alone; you've got to enjoy the game and the hunt to make it all truly worth-while.

C. Inventing by Magic (Accident and Flash of Genius)

When I don't understand how something is done, I some-times call it "magic." Inventions made by "magic" don't involve the problem-solution technique which I just described; rather, they usually occur by "accident" or by "flash of genius." The PTO and the courts really don't care how you come up with an invention, so long as they can see that it wasn't already accomplished and it looks substan-tially different from what's been done before. In the hope-lessly stilted language of the law, "Patentability shall not be negatived by the manner in which the invention was made" (35 USC 103).

Many famous inventions have resulted from accident or coincidence. For example, Goodyear invented rubber vulca-nization when he accidentally added some sulphur to a rubber melt. A chemist accidentally left a crutcher (soap-making machine) on too long, causing air to be dispersed into the soap mixture. He found that the soap floated when it hardened, thus giving birth to floatable soap bars, such as Ivory® brand. Another chemist accidentally mixed some chemicals together and spilled them, finding they hardened to a flexible, transparent sheet (later known as "cellophane"). When Alexander Fleming accidentally contaminated one of his bacterial cultures with a mold, he was sufficiently alert and scientifically minded to notice that the mold killed the bacteria, so he carried this discovery forward and isolated the active ingredient in the mold, which later was named penicillin. (Unfortunately he didn't patent it, so he got the fame, but not the fortune.)

The law considers the fact that these inventions came about by total accident, without the exercise of any creativ-ity by their "inventors," legally irrelevant. All other things being equal, a patent on cellophane would be just as strong as one on nylon (another former trademark), the result of 12 years' intensive and brilliant work by duPont's now-deceased genius, Dr. Wallace Carothers of Wilmington, Delaware.

Since I don't understand how the "magic" occurs, I can't tell you or even suggest how to invent by accident. Please remember, however, that in case you ever come up with an accidental development, take the time and apply the effort to study, analyze and try to "practicalize" it. If it has poten-tial value, treat it like any other invention; the law will.

The other type of "magical" invention I'll refer to as the product of a "flash of genius." While "flash of genius" inventions inherently solve a need, the inventive act usually occurred spontaneously and not as a result of an attack on any problem. Some examples of this type are the electric knife and the previously discussed Salton inventions which actually created their own need, the Pet Rock (not a real invention by traditional definitions, but rather a clever trademark and marketing ploy, but highly profitable just the same), Bushnell's "Pong" game, the Cabbage Patch dolls, Ruth Handler's Barbie Dolls, and a client's Audochron® clock, which announces the time by a series of countable chimes for the hours, tens of minutes, and minutes. With these inventions, the inventor didn't solve any real problem or need, but rather came up with a very novel invention which provided a new type of amusement or a means for conspicuous consumption (showing off).

Although I don't understand how the creativity in these types of cases occurs, I suggest in Section E of this chapter several techniques for stimulating and unlocking such creativity. Using these techniques, many inventors have come up with valuable inventions and profitable ideas and marketing ploys.

D. Making Ramifications of Your Invention

Once you've made an invention, write down the problem and solution involved. Then, try to ramify it—that is, to do it or make it in other ways so it will be cheaper, faster, better, bigger (or smaller), stronger, lighter (or heavier), longer- (or shorter-) lasting, or even just different. Why ramify?

1. Most inventors usually find that their initial solution can be improved or made more workable.
2. By conceiving of such improvements first, you can foreclose future competitors from obtaining patents on them.
3. Even if you believe your first solution is the best and most workable, your potential producers or manufacturers may not see it that way. So, it's best to have as many alternatives handy as possible.
4. When you apply for a patent, the more ramifications you have, the easier it will be to make your patent stronger. (See Chapter 8.)
5. Conversely, if the broad concept or initial embodiment of your invention is "knocked out" by a search of the "prior art" (see Chapter 5, Section B3) made by you, your searcher, or the examiner in the Patent and Trademark Office, you'll have something to fall back on, so you'll still be able to get a patent.
6. Ramifications often help you understand your basic invention better, see it in a new light, see new uses or new ways to do it, etc.
7. Ramifications can be held back and introduced later, after the basic invention has been "milked" commercially, thereby prolonging the profits, as duPont did

with its Teflon®II. Be sure to try to patent the ramifications as soon as possible, however, to foreclose someone else from doing so.

In some situations, you'll find that you won't be able to ramify beyond your basic conception. But give it a try anyway, and make sure you record in writing any ramifications you do come up with as soon as possible. (See Chapter 3.)

One way to make ramifications is to pretend that a part of your device can't be made due to a law or crucial material shortage and then try to come up with a replacement.

E. Solving Creativity Problems

Unfortunately, hardly any invention ever works right or "flies" the first time it's built. You need to build and test it to be aware of the working problems. If you don't, the first builder, whoever it is, will inevitably face them. If this is a corporation to which you've sold or licensed your invention, it's sure to create problems. If your first construction doesn't work, don't be discouraged; expect problems and expect to solve them through perseverance. If you don't believe me, consider Edison's views on this subject:

Genius? Nothing! Sticking to it is the genius! Any other bright-minded fellow can accomplish just as much if he will stick like hell and remember nothing that's any good works by itself. You've got to make the damn thing work!... I failed my way to success.

If you show your invention to someone and you get static in return, don't necessarily get discouraged; the history of invention abounds with quotes from naysayers who were proved to be disastrously wrong. The enlightening book *303 of The World's Worst Predictions*, by W. Coffey (see Appendix 2, Books of Use and Interest), is full of amusing and insightful erroneous quotes. Here are a few teasers:

Everything that can be invented has been invented.
—U.S. Patent Office Director,
urging President McKinley to abolish the Office (1899).

What, sir? You would make a ship sail against the wind and currents by lighting a bonfire under her decks? I pray you excuse me. I have no time to listen to such nonsense.
—Napoleon Bonaparte to Robert Fulton, after hearing
Fulton's plans for a steam engine driven boat.

I think there is a world market for about five computers
—Thomas J. Watson, IBM President (1958).

Man won't fly for a thousand years.
—Wilbur Wright to Orville after a disappointing experiment
in 1901.

Many have analyzed the creative process, but so far no one has come up with a foolproof recipe or technique for innovating. However, almost all writers recommend that, unless you already have a "flash of genius," you first thoroughly prepare and familiarize yourself with the field, always keeping an open mind. Thereafter, some writers recommend you wait a while (allot an incubation period) to let your mind digest and work on the problem. Following incubation, insight usually comes, sometimes in bits and pieces. Alternatively, some experts recommend that, after preparation, one make a concentrated effort, which may lead to frustration and withdrawal. But be patient, since the insight, which may be an image or a fantasy, will usually come thereafter. Of course follow-through is necessary to implement and profit from the insight or fantasy.

If you have creativity problems, such as how to make that great idea work, here are some specific techniques you can use to enhance your creativity, and hopefully solve that problem.

Frame It Differently: One of the most effective ways to solve a problem is to "frame" the problem properly. Framing is another way of describing the way in which one looks at a situation. A common example of framing a problem occurs when you try to move a bulky sofa through a small doorway. If the first way doesn't work, frame the problem differently by turning the sofa upside down and trying again. Or take another example: If you have an apparatus which includes a lever, and you can't find a design shape for the lever which the machine will accommodate, look at the situation another way; perhaps you can redesign the apparatus to eliminate the lever altogether!

Use Your Right Brain: In the course of trying to solve a problem with an invention, you may encounter a brick wall of resistance when you try to think your way logically through the problem. Such logical thinking is a linear type of process (that is, one step follows another), which utilizes our rational faculties, located in the left side of our brains. This works fine when we're operating in the realm of what we know or have experienced. However, when we need to deal with new information, ideas, and perspectives, linear thinking will often come up short. On the other hand, creativity by definition involves the application of new information to old problems and the conception of new perspectives and ideas. For this you will be most effective if you learn to operate in a nonlinear manner, that is, use your right brain or creative faculties. Stated differently, if you think in a linear manner, you'll tend to be conservative and keep coming up with techniques which are already known. This, of course, is just what you don't want.

One way to engage your right-brain faculties in a search for a creative solution to your quandary is to pose the problem in clear terms and then forget about it and think of something completely different. For example, if you can't fit that lever in your apparatus, think of a different activity, or just take a break (how about a nice boating trip or a hike in the woods). Your subconscious will work on the problem while you're "away." Then come back to the problem and force your different activity onto your problem. In other words, try to think of the apparatus and your boating trip or hike simultaneously. You may find that a solution appears by magic (for example, you may realize a way to design the machine without the lever!).

Let Go of Assumptions: If you adhere to assumptions, you'll never innovate, since innovation, by definition, is the adoption of something new, the embarkation on an untrodden path. As Erich Fromm said, "Creativity requires the courage to let go of [assumed] certainties." So if you've got a problem, try to see what assumptions you're making (they're usually hidden) and then let them go or try to cancel them and see what you come up with.

Meditation: Another way to bring out your creativity is to meditate on the problem or meditate merely to get away from the problem. Either will help. As strange as it seems, some experts say that creativity can be enhanced during reverie by listening to a largo movement from a baroque symphony. At least you'll enjoy it! Also, the use of biofeedback machines can induce or teach deep relaxation with enhanced alpha, or even theta brain waves, a very effective stimulus to creativity.

Dreams: Most creative people find dreams the most effective way of all to solve problems. Or as Edison said: "I never invented anything; my dreams did."

Elias Howe solved the basic problem of his sewing machine in a dream. He saw some tribal warriors who ordered him to come up with a solution or they would kill him. He couldn't make a solution, so the warriors then threw their spears at him. When the spears came close, he saw that each had a hole near its tip. He awoke from the nightmare in terror, but soon realized the symbology: he put a hole near the tip of his bobbin needle and passed the thread through. Again, the rest is history.

Similarly, Mendeleev came up with the periodic table of the elements in a dream.

To stimulate creative dreaming, first immerse yourself in the problem near bedtime. Then forget about it—do something completely different and go to sleep. Your subconscious will be able to work on the problem. You'll most likely have a dream with an inspiration or insight. Then remember the dream and evaluate the insight to find out if it's correct (sometimes it won't be!).

Note that you'll forget most dreams, so keep a dream diary or notebook handy, by your bedside. Also, you'll find a pen with a built-in flashlight is also helpful. Before you go to bed, repeat fifteen times, "I'll remember my dreams." Whenever you do dream, wake up (you'll find it possible to do this if you intend to do so beforehand) and write your dreams down promptly. Once they are written down, forget about them, go back to sleep, and try to figure them out in the morning. Sometimes a week or more will pass before the meanings become clear. Or talk your dreams over with an equally inventive friend and see if he or she can get the meaning—sometimes talking about it helps.

Good luck. And pleasant dreams!

Computerized Creating: As strange as it may seem, computers can be used to enhance creativity, solve problems, bust through conceptual roadblocks and get into the recesses of your memory. Several "mindware" or "CAT" (computer-aided thinking software) programs for this purpose exist, and I believe they can be of significant help in this area. The programs work by first asking you to enter lots of details of your problem or area and then they rearrange the details and suggest lots of modifications and permutations for you to consider. One good program is called "The Idea Generator" from Experience In Software, Inc., Berkeley, California.

The Hot Tub Method: This has been used by many creative geniuses, starting with Archimedes who discovered the principle of volumetric measurement while in his tub. It works like this: When you relax in a hot tub for a long period, the heat on your body mellows you out and dilates your blood vessels so as to draw blood from your analytical brain, allowing your creative subconscious to come to the fore.

Unstructured Fanaticism: As "excellence guru" Tom Peters states, structured planners rarely come up with the really great innovations; monomaniacs who pursue a goal with unstructured fanaticism often do. So let yourself go and become an unreasonable madman—it may do the trick!

Group Brainstorming: If all else fails, get a group of friends or trusted associates together (or on a computer network) and throw the problem to the group. For some unknown reason, a group of people working together often come up with more good ideas than the same individuals working separately. This synergistic method is often used in corporations with great success. The use of others to help innovate has been called "leveraging knowledge," since one's knowledge and abilities are multiplied by others in a group.

Increase Self-Confidence: Those with more self-confidence and self-esteem tend to be more venturesome, and hence more creative. If you suffer from low self-confidence or low self-esteem, you may wish to explore local courses or read some of the self-improvement books in Appendix 2, Books of Use and Interest.

F. Contact Other Inventors

In recent years, many inventors' organizations have developed or sprung up in order to provide inventors with information and ideas, model makers, lists of searchers, speakers, patent attorneys, etc., as well as to sponsor various seminars and trade fairs where inventions can be exhibited. One or more of these organizations may provide you with invaluable assistance in your inventing efforts. As far as I'm aware, all of these organizations are legitimate and honest, and provide reasonable value for the membership or other fees charged, but check for yourself before investing a significant amount of your time or money. Some of these organizations are:

American Society of Inventors
Box 58426
Philadelphia, PA 19102

Central Valley Inventors' Association
P.O. Box 1551
Manteca, CA 95336

Ideas to Market Network
Box 12248
Santa Rosa, CA 95406
800-ITM-3210

BEARD GRINDER
No. 521,786,329

Inventors Alliance
Hayward, CA
510 -321-3172

Inventors' Assistance League
345 West Cypress
Glendale, CA 91204

Inventors' Workshop International
3201 Corte Malpaso, Suite 304
Camarillo, CA 93010
(has local branches)

Minnesota Inventors' Congress
Box 71
Redwood Falls, MN 56283

Mississippi Society of Scientists & Inventors
Box 2244
Jackson, MS 39225

Nevada Inventors Association
P.O. Box 9905
Reno. NV 89507-0905
702-322-9636

Ohio Inventors' Association
146 South High Street, Suite 206
Akron, OH 44308

Oklahoma Inventors' Congress
Box 53043
Oklahoma City, OK 73152

You can find other inventors' groups by asking at the Patent and Trademark Depository Library close to you. (See Chapter 6.) Also, a complete list of all inventors' organizations is available in *Inventor Assistance Source Directory*, published by Pacific Northwest Laboratory, P.O. Box 999, Mail Stop K8-11, Richland, WA 99352, Tel. 509-372-4274, Fax 509-372-4369.

G. Beware of the Novice Inventor's "PGL Syndrome"

As highly successful inventor (Whiz-z-er top) Paul Brown has discovered, many novice inventors have a very different attitude from experienced inventors. This attitude can be summarized as the "PGL (Paranoia, Greed, Laziness) syndrome." Let's discuss the components of this syndrome in more detail since each usually is a significant hindrance for inexperienced inventors.

Paranoia: Extremely common with inexperienced inventors, paranoia (excessive suspicion of other people's motives) makes them afraid to discuss or show their invention to others—some even go as far as refusing to disclose it

to a patent attorney. I do advise some measure of caution with unpatented inventions. However, once you record your invention properly (as discussed in Chapter 3), you can and should disclose it to selected persons, provided you take adequate measures to document whom you've disclosed it to and when. Don't be as paranoid as my friend Tom who invented a very valuable stereo movie invention but kept it totally to himself out of fear of theft, only to see it patented and commercialized by someone else.

Greed/Overestimation: Most people have heard fabulous stories of successful inventors who've collected millions in royalties. As a result, some novice inventors think that their invention is worth millions and demand an unreasonably large royalty or lump-sum payment for their creation. This is seldom wise. It is much better to set your sights at a reasonable level (see Chapter 16) so you won't miss out on commercial opportunities.

Laziness: Some novice inventors believe that all they need to do is show their invention to a company, sign a lucrative contract, and let the money roll in. Unfortunately it hardly ever happens so easily. To be successful, you usually have to record your invention properly (Chapter 3), build and test a working model (desirable but not always necessary), file a patent application, seek out suitable companies to produce and market the invention, and work like hell to sell the invention to one of these companies.

H. Don't Bury Your Invention

If you believe that you have what will turn out to be a successful idea, but you have doubts because it's very different, or you get negative opinions from your friends, consider that Alexander Graham Bell was asked by an irate banker to remove "that toy" from his office. The "toy" was the telephone. Or if that doesn't convince you, ponder these words of Mark Twain and Albert Einstein:

The man with a new idea is a crank—until the idea succeeds.
—Mark Twain

For an idea that does not at first seem insane, there is no hope.

—Albert Einstein

And as a recent successful inventor, Nolan Bushnell, (Pong) said, "Everyone who's ever taken a shower has an idea. It's the person who does something about it who makes a difference."

Don't forget that, in addition to making money if you're successful, an invention can create jobs, make our lives easier and more interesting and eliminate drudgery. Consider the Linotype® machine, where each machine eliminated 90 manual typesetters and their arduous task and spawned a new industry and profession. Then came the computer; where each modern computer replaced nine Linotype machines, spawned another new industry and gave almost anyone the ability to create typeset documents.

I hope you've received my message in this chapter loud and clear. If you have a worthwhile invention, and you scrupulously follow all the advice and instructions given in this and the succeeding chapters, and persevere, I believe you'll have a very good chance of success. ∎

CHAPTER

3

Documentation Can Be Vital

INVENTOR'S COMMANDMENT #3

After conceiving of an invention, you shouldn't proceed to develop, build or test it, or reveal it to outsiders, until you (1) make a clear description of your conception (using ink), (2) sign and date the same, and (3) have this document signed and dated by two trustworthy people who have "witnessed and understood" your creation. (As an alternative to documentary conception in this manner, you can use the PTO's Disclosure Document program, but be aware of the disadvantages and limitations of the DDP.)

INVENTOR'S COMMANDMENT #4

(1) Try to build and test your invention (if at all possible) as soon as you can, (2) keep full and true written, signed, and dated records of all the efforts, correspondence and receipts concerning your invention, especially if you build and test it, and (3) have two others sign and date that they have "witnessed and understood" your building and testing. (As an alternative—or in addition—to documenting, building and testing in this manner, you can use the PTO's Provisional Patent Application program, but be aware of the disadvantages and limitations of the PPA.)

A. Introduction

It's true in life generally that the better the documentation you keep, the easier it will be for you to retrieve important ideas, information, and, when necessary, proof that something happened. When it comes to inventing, good documentation is even more vital than in most other aspects of our lives. There are two distinct and important reasons why all inventors should document all of their work. The first has to do with the inventing process itself. The second involves the possibility that you will need to prove (1) that you are the inventor, and (2) that you came up with the invention first. Let's examine these reasons in order.

To help you properly document your invention, Nolo Press publishes *The Inventor's Notebook*. See the back of this book for more information.

B. Documents Are Vital to the Invention Process

It takes more than a good idea to sustain the invention process. It is absolutely essential to keep good, sound records, for the following reasons:

1. Good Engineering Practice

It's good engineering practice to keep a "technical diary," containing accurate, detailed documents of your ideas, work done and accomplishments. Good engineers and technicians record their developments in chronological order so that they can refer back to their engineering diary days, weeks, months, or even years later. First, this enables them to avoid running up the same blind alley twice. Second, good records will shed light on subsequent developments, will allow the inventor to find needed data and details of past developments, and will provide a base for new paths of exploration and ramifications, especially if failures have occurred.

2. Psychological Stimulus

Many of us come up with great ideas, especially when we're engaged in some other activity (including dreaming), and we forget to write them down. Later, we may recall that we had a brilliant idea the night before, or during the office party, but because we went back to sleep or were too busy, we forgot it. If we could get into the habit of writing down our thoughts on a piece of paper, later on we'd find that piece of paper there to bug us, almost forcing us to do something about it. So, keep a small pencil or pen and some paper with you at all times, even by your bedside, and in your wallet, and write down your thoughts as soon as they occur. Later on, you'll be glad you did.

3. Analyzation Stimulus

WWII Admiral Raborn once said: "If you can't write it down, you don't really know what you are doing."

Have you ever had an idea, plan, or concept that you really didn't fully understand yourself? I'll bet you discovered that when you tried to write a description of it, you were forced to figure it out, and only then finally realized fully or exactly what you had. Putting a description of your idea in writing forces you to think about it and crystallize it into communicable form. Note that no matter how great your idea, and no matter how much of the work you do yourself, you'll never be able to make a nickel from it until you can communicate it to others, for example, to get a patent, to license it, or to sell the product.

C. Documentation Is Vital to Prove Invention

If you keep clear, signed, dated, and witnessed documents of your creations, this will prove to others that you made the invention yourself, when you did so, and that you are a methodical, diligent, and reliable person. Who cares about the last point? While you may not be particularly interested in establishing such a reputation, you'll find it invaluable in case you ever get into any dispute over your invention. Also, when you go to license the invention, or undertake any other activity with it, as well as taking any tax deductions for your expenditures (see below), you'll find that having such documents will greatly enhance your standing with anyone who sees, evaluates, or considers your invention, or any aspect of your inventive activity.

There are six reasons why it's legally important promptly and properly to record your conception of your invention:

1. In Case of an Interference

The primary legal reason to record your inventive activities is to counter the claims of others that they invented your invention first. Many valuable inventions are independently and simultaneously conceived and brought to fruition, while others are misappropriated from the true inventor. In either case, for the first and true inventor to prevail, it's important to use the very specific recordkeeping techniques suggested later in this chapter.

Unfortunately, justice isn't automatic. A signed, dated, and witnessed description of your invention will be an invaluable item of proof to show that you came up with the invention on the date given and that you (and your co-inventor(s), if any) are the actual and true inventor(s) of the creation. As you'll see throughout the rest of the book, dates are crucial in patent law; thus you should date everything you receive or send; you can never tell when you'll need to rely on (prove) any date.

2. Proof in Case of Theft

Similarly, if someone sees or hears about your invention and attempts to "steal" it by claiming it as his or her own invention (in actuality, a rare occurrence), there will probably be a lawsuit or other proceeding in which the true and first inventor must be ascertained. In such a proceeding, the side with the earliest, best and most convincing evidence will win. 'Nuff said!

3. Proof in Case of Confusion of Inventorship

There's also, commonly, confusion as to who is the actual, true, and first inventor of a particular invention. Often several engineers or friends will be working on the same problem, and if conception isn't promptly recorded, memories fade and there will be confusion as to who is (are) the actual inventor(s). Also, bosses and other supervisors have been known to claim inventorship, or joint inventorship, in an employee's invention. If all inventors would promptly record their inventions and get them witnessed, preferably by coworkers (including bosses), there would be very few cases of such confusion of inventorship.

4. Antedate References

As we'll see later in Chapter 13, if the PTO examiner cites a "prior-art reference" against your application (that is, finds a prior publication that casts doubt on the originality of your invention), you can eliminate that reference as prior art (that is, prevent the examiner from using it) if you're able to show:

- you filed your application within the year after the reference's publication date and you built and tested the invention prior to the reference's effective date, or
- you conceived of the invention prior to the reference's effective date and you were then diligent in "reducing it to practice" (building and testing it, or filing a provisional or regular patent application).

As I'll explain in Chapter 5, Section E, a reference's effective date is its filing date if it's a U.S. patent, or its publication date if it's any other publication. This process of antedating a cited reference is called "swearing behind" the reference. Naturally, to be effective and acceptable when swearing behind a reference, your records should be detailed, clear, signed, dated, and witnessed.

5. Supporting Tax Deductions

Once you make an invention and spend any money on your creation, the IRS considers that you are "in business," thus enabling you to file a "Schedule C" or "Schedule E" (Form 1040) with your tax return to deduct all expenditures you made on your invention, from even ordinary income that you received. The IRS will be far more inclined to allow these deductions (assuming you're audited) if you can support them with full, clear and accurate records of all of your invention activities, including, but not limited to, conception, building and testing (Form 3-2 in Appendix 7), and expenditures for tools, plastics, etc.

6. Avoidance of Ownership Disputes

Suppose you make an invention in a specific area—say bicycles—and later you go to work for a company engaged in this area—say a bicycle manufacturer. If you haven't already filed a patent application on your bike, you'll have a very hard time proving you already made the invention before your employment with this company if you haven't kept a proper record. In this situation and in many others, the company (or an individual or other organization with whom you deal) will likely claim ownership of your prior invention under your employment (or other) agreement (see Chapter 16, Section D) unless you have the "paper" to prove prior invention.

D. Trade Secret Considerations

In Chapter 1, Section Q, you learned that an invention can qualify as a trade secret right up until the time a patent issues on it. Keeping an invention secret can provide its owner with certain obvious commercial advantages, and the owner may have recourse in the courts against any person who improperly discloses the secret to others.

Making a witnessed record of your invention doesn't conflict in any way with this trade secret protection. Even if you show your invention to witnesses, this won't compromise the trade-secret status of your invention because of the implied understanding that witnesses to an invention should keep it confidential. However, I recommend that you don't merely rely on this implied understanding, but actually have your witnesses agree to keep your invention confidential. A verbal agreement is good, but a written agreement is far better and will really tie down the confidentiality of your invention. I've incorporated a keep-confidential agreement in the disclosure form (Form 3-2, discussed below), but you can also have your witnesses sign the "Proprietary Materials Agreement" (Form 3-1, discussed below) when you give them your lab notebook or disclosure to sign.

Whether your invention is to be patented or kept as a trade secret (you can decide later—see Chapter 7), you should first record it properly so that you can prove that you invented it and that you did so as of a certain date. Since you can keep your notebook confidential, at least for the time being, no loss of any potential trade secret protection will result from your making a proper record of your conception.

Remember that while recording your invention can be vital in the situations outlined above, it provides only limited rights, since it won't give you any weapon to use if anyone independently comes up with your creation, or if anyone copies your invention once it's out on the market. To acquire full offensive rights in these situations, you need to obtain a patent on your invention. As discussed in Chapter 1, only a patent will give you rights against independent creators of your invention and those who copy it once it's out on the market.

E. Record the Building and Testing of Your Invention

After you conceive of your invention and prepare the proper record, you should follow my Inventor's Commandment #4 at the beginning of this chapter—that is, try to build and test your invention as soon as you can and keep detailed and adequate records of your efforts.

1. Keep Good Records of Building and Testing Activity

You may now well ask, if I've conceived of my invention and have properly recorded conception, why should I also build and test it? A good question. The main legal reason is in the U.S. patent statutes, specifically part of § 102 (35 USC. § 102), which states:

"In determining priority of invention there shall be considered not only the respective dates of conception and reduction to practice of the invention, but also the reasonable diligence of one who was first to conceive and last to reduce to practice, from a time prior to conception by the other."

The arcane phrase "reduction to practice" (RTP) means building and testing the hardware of the invention (called an "actual RTP") or the filing of a patent application on the invention (called a "constructive RTP," since the law construes this as an RTP). This part of § 102 (the "first to invent" law) means that if two inventors file patent applications on the same invention, the PTO will award the patent to the one who first "reduced the invention to practice," unless the other inventor conceived of it first and was diligent in reducing it to practice. It also means that if the PTO cites a "prior art" publication having an earlier date than your filing date, you can often "swear behind" the publication if you can prove that you invented before the date of the publication. (More on this in Chapter 13.) So in order to win any possible interference, or swear behind any earlier reference, you should build and test your invention as soon as possible if you aren't going to file on it right away. (But see Section I, below, for a discussion of the new Provisional Patent Application process—a legal alternative to building and testing your invention.)

There are other, non-legal reasons for building and testing. These are stated in Sections B and C, above. Specifically, it's good engineering practice, it provides psychological stimulus, it helps you analyze the invention, and it is of inestimable aid in case of theft, or confusion of inventorship or ownership. Even more importantly, as we'll learn in Chapter 4, building and testing is vital in evaluating the invention for commercial value, including operability, suitability, usability, etc. In addition, as I'll explain in Chapter 11, if you can build and test a working model of your invention, you can use this to great advantage in selling or licensing it to a manufacturer. So try to build and test it ASAP, if at all possible

Why should you painstakingly record the activities involved in the building and testing of your invention? This is an easy question to answer. All of the reasons discussed for recording the facts of your invention in the first place are applicable here, in spades. This is because the building and testing of an invention can be as (or even more) important than its conception, especially as proof of your invention in case of theft, confusion of inventors, interferences, the need to swear behind references, and the need to establish tax deductions. However, recordation of your efforts to build and test your invention isn't necessary to obtain a patent, unless an interference or other special situation occurs that requires you to prove your development efforts.

To illustrate the value of recordation, I recently prepared a patent application for a client. As she was reviewing it, I got a flyer in the mail from a store listing for sale an item almost identical to that which my client wished to patent! Since the item was being sold and was published before she had filed the application, the flyer constituted "prior art," which, on its face, would preclude my client's invention from being considered as novel and thus lead to the rejection of her application. But fortunately, my client had built and tested the invention, had made records of her conception and of her building and testing, and had signed and dated these and had gotten them witnessed months before. She could thus go ahead and file without fear, even though the flier was published before her filing date. This is because she could use her records to "swear behind" the flyer. Simply put, by documenting her invention and her efforts to build and test it, my client was still able to obtain a patent. On the other hand, had she failed to properly record her conception and building and testing, her application would have been barred and she would have lost all rights to her invention!

2. Keep Your Building and Testing Activity Confidential

If, as part of the testing of your invention, you have to order any special part or material, or if you have to reveal to or discuss your invention with anyone to get it built, be cautious about how and whom you contact. And when you do make any specific revelation, have the recipient of the information about your invention sign a Proprietary Materials (or "keep-confidential") Agreement (Form 3-1 in Appendix 7).

GETTING THE AGREEMENT SIGNED

Model makers and machine shops are used to signing these agreements. When you make an appointment to show your invention and you wish to have the recipient sign the agreement before viewing, it's only courteous and proper business practice to advise the recipient that you are bringing along a keep-confidential agreement before signing. Don't spring the agreement in a surprise manner.

The agreement is completed merely by specifically identifying the materials (documents or hardware) in the first section, your name in the second section (you're the Lender), and the name of your recipient in the third section (he, she, or it is the Borrower). Have your Borrower initial (1)(a) if you've already loaned the materials or (1)(b) if you'll be sending the materials after you receive the signed agreement back from the Borrower. Then have the Borrower fill in, sign and date the bottom of the agreement. I recommend that you give a copy of the signed agreement to your Borrower, as well as any extra copies that may be needed if any other persons in your Borrower's organization are to sign also.

Note that the agreement calls the delivery of your proprietary materials to the recipient a "loan." This will give you maximum rights if the recipient makes unauthorized use of or refuses to return the materials.

This agreement will cover almost all situations where you need to deliver proprietary materials under a keep-confidential arrangement. However, it isn't cast in stone: If, for example, you are making more than a loan of the materials, feel free to redraft the agreement, for example, by changing "loaned" to "delivered" and "Lender" to "Owner."

The agreement will also cover oral disclosures, but for reasons of difficulty of later proof (if needed) you should make disclosures only by actually delivering written materials.

F. How to Record Your Invention

Hopefully, I've managed to sell you on the need to carefully and accurately record your thoughts and activities that normally occur in the course of inventing. There are several ways to do the recording. These are discussed below, together with examples.

1. The Lab Notebook

The best, most reliable and most useful way to record an invention project (conception, building and testing, marketing, etc.) is to use a lab notebook, such as *The Inventor's Notebook,* by Grissom and Pressman (Nolo Press). Specifically designed for use with this book, *The Inventor's Notebook* provides organized guidance for properly documenting your invention. More information about *The Inventor's Notebook* and how to order it can be found at the end of this book.

   If you're a prolific inventor, or are employed as an engineer or the like, you will want to record a number of inventions as you make and develop them. The best way to do this is by using a blank or lab notebook. Preferably, it should have a closed spiral binding or a stiff cover, with the pages bound in permanently, such as by sewing or gluing. Also, the pages should be consecutively numbered. Lab notebooks of this type are available at engineering and laboratory supply stores, and generally have crosshatched, prenumbered pages with special lines at the bottom of each page for signatures (and signature dates) of the inventor

and the witnesses. As should be apparent, the use of a bound, paginated notebook that's faithfully kept up provides a formidable piece of evidence if your inventorship or date of invention is ever called into question, for instance, in an interference proceeding or lawsuit. A bound notebook with consecutively dated, signed and witnessed entries on sequential pages establishes almost irrefutably that you are the inventor—that is, the first to conceive the invention—on the date indicated in the notebook.

   If you don't have or can't get a formal lab notebook like this, a standard bound letter-paper-size crackle-finish school copybook will serve. Just number all of the pages consecutively yourself, and don't forget the frequent dating, signing, and witnessing, even though there won't be special spaces for this. Date each entry in the notebook as of the date you and your co-inventor(s), if any, make the entries and sign your name(s). If you made the entries over a day or two before you sign and date them, add a brief candid comment to this effect, such as, "I wrote the above on July 17, but forgot to sign and date it until now." Similarly, if you made and/or built the invention some time ago, but haven't made any records until now, again state the full, specific and truthful facts and date the entry as of the date you write the entry and sign it. For example, "I thought of the above invention while trying to open a can of truffles at my sister's wedding reception last July 23 (1995), but didn't write any description of it until now when I read *Patent It Yourself.*"

2. How to Enter Technical Information in the Notebook

Fig. 3A is an example of a properly completed notebook page showing the recordation of conception, and Fig. 3B shows recordation of building and testing.

   The sketches and diagrams should be clearly written (preferably double-spaced) in ink to preclude erasure and later-substituted entries. Your writing doesn't have to be beautiful and shouldn't be in legalese. Just make it clear enough for someone else to understand without having to read your mind. Use sketches where possible. Many inventors have told me they put off writing up their invention in a notebook or invention disclosure because they didn't know the proper "legal" terms to use, or had writer's block. However, as indicated, legalese isn't necessary or desirable. There are two very good ways to bypass writer's block:

   • Rely mostly on sketches, with brief labels explaining the parts and their functions, or
   • Make sketches, describing them orally to a friend, and record your oral description with a tape recorder. Then go back and transcribe your description.

TITLE: Self-Adjusting Can Opener   23

PURPOSE: To provide a can opener that self-adjusts to any size can.

DESCRIPTION: The can opener has a sliding clamp with a locking groove at its edge
[etc.] ... I conceived of this while I was at my friend Roberta's wedding last Sunday and
saw the caterer having trouble opening small and large cans with several openers...

Locking groove — SKETCH — Sliding clamp

RAMIFICATIONS: Instead of the locking groove, a special notch could be used as follows:

Notch — SKETCH

POSSIBLE NOVEL FEATURES: The sliding clamp with a raised frammis arm is believed entirely
new. Also, [etc.]...

ADVANTAGES: This can opener would eliminate the need for separate can openers for
different sized cans, thereby providing economy, ease of use, [etc.]...

INVENTOR: DATED:

Irma Inventor   *9X/8/25*

THE ABOVE CONFIDENTIAL INFORMATION IS WITNESSED AND UNDERSTOOD:

Wilfred Witness   *9X/9/25*

Alberta Attestor   *9X/9/25*

Fig. 3A—Properly Completed Notebook Page Showing Conception

27

TITLE: Self-Adjusting Can Opener — Building & Testing

REFERENCE: Conception recorded on page 23.

DESCRIPTION: A working model of this opener was made for me by Fred Smith of
Model Makers, Inc. starting Sept. 1. It was finished Sept. 13. It was made of cold-
rolled steel, 13 mm. thick, with brass bearings [etc.]…

Here is the photo we took on Sept. 15:

Locking groove

Sliding clamp

PHOTO

RAMIFICATIONS: We also tried a nylon hinge, but it did not work because…

TEST DESCRIPTION: We tried the opener on fifty different cans, from size __ to
size __ …

TEST RESULTS: For the size __ cans, the opener worked as well as the Ajax brand,
opening each can in an average time of 8.3 seconds, the same as we obtained with
the Ajax brand. [etc.]…

INVENTOR: DATED:

Irma Inventor   *9X/8/27*

THE ABOVE CONFIDENTIAL INFORMATION IS WITNESSED AND UNDERSTOOD:

Steve Elias   *9X/9/27*

Fred Friendly   *9X/9/27*

Fig. 3B—Properly Completed Notebook Page Showing Building and Testing

Do not leave any large blank spaces on a page—fill the page up from top to bottom. If you do need to leave space to separate entries, or at the bottom on a page where you have insufficient space to start a new entry, draw a large cross over the blank space to preclude any subsequent entries, or, more accurately, to make it clear that no subsequent entries could have been made in your notebook.

If you make a mistake in an entry, don't attempt to erase it; merely line it out neatly and make a dated note why it was incorrect. The notation of error can be made in the margin adjacent to the correct entry, or it can be made several pages later, provided the error is referred to by page and date. Don't make cumulative changes to a single entry. If more than one change is required, enter them later with all necessary cross-references to the earlier material they supplement. Refer back to earlier material by page and date.

If possible, make all entries directly in the notebook, or transfer them there from rough notes on the day the notes were made. If this isn't possible, make them as soon as practicable with a notation explaining when the actual work was done, when the entries were made and why the delay occurred.

If you've made an invention several months ago, and are now going to record it because you've just read this book, you should date the entries in the notebook when you actually write them, but you should also write when you actually made the invention and explain the delay with honesty and candor! Since the notebook is bound, you will have to handwrite the entries in it. Again, don't worry about the quality of your prose—your goal is only to make it clear enough for someone else to understand; use labeled sketches or the tape recorder/transcription techniques given above if writer's block occurs.

3.   What Should Be Entered in the Notebook

Your notebook should be used as a "technical diary"—that is, you should record in it anything you work on of technical significance, not just inventions. The front of the notebook should have your name and address and the date you started the notebook. When you record the conception of your invention, you and anyone who later sees the notebook will find it most meaningful if you use the following headings:

- Title (what your invention is called)
- Purpose (what purpose the invention is intended to serve)
- Description (a functional and structural description of the invention)
- Sketch (an informal sketch of the invention)
- Ramifications (all ramifications of the invention that you have conceptualized)

- Novel features (all possible novel features of the invention)
- Closest known prior art (the closest known existing approach of which you're aware)
- Advantages (of the invention over previous developments and/or knowledge—see the example in Fig. 3A).

Don't forget to sign and date your conception and have two witnesses also sign and date the record of conception. See Section 5, below.

To record the subsequent building and testing of your invention at a later page of the notebook, you will find it most useful to record the following items:

1. Title and Back Reference
2. Technical Description
3. Photos and/or Sketches
4. Ramifications
5. Test Description
6. Test Results
7. Conclusion

Fig. 3B (above) shows a properly done lab notebook record of the building and testing of an invention. Don't forget to sign and date, and have your witnesses also sign and date, the building and testing record, as well as the conception record. (See Section 5, below.)

If you're skilled enough to conceive, build and test your invention all at once, just combine all of the items of Figs. 3A and 3B as one entry in your notebook.

I strongly recommend that you record as much factual data as possible; keep conclusions to a minimum and provide them only if they are supported by factual data. Thus, if a mousetrap operated successfully, describe its operation in enough detail to convince the reader that it works. Only then should you put in a conclusion, and it should be kept brief and nonopinionated. For example, "Thus this mousetrap works faster and more reliably than the Ajax brand." Sweeping, opinionated, laudatory statements tend to give an impartial reader a negative opinion of you or your invention. However, it's useful to include the circumstances of conception, such as how you thought it up and where you were. This makes your account believable and helps refresh your memory later.

Word all entries so that they're complete and clear in themselves—that is, so that anyone can duplicate your work without further explanation. While you shouldn't use the lab notebook as a scratch pad to record every calculation and stray concept or note you make or think about, you also shouldn't make your entries so brief as to be of no value should the need for using the notebook as proof later arise. If you're in doubt as to whether to make an entry, make it; it's better to have too much than too little.

Also, you'll find it very helpful to save all of your "other paperwork" involved with the conception, building, and testing of an invention. Such paperwork includes correspondence and purchase receipts. These papers are highly trustworthy and useful as evidence, since they are very difficult to falsify. For example, if you buy a thermometer or have a machine shop make a part for you in January 1995, you should save receipts and canceled checks from these expenditures since they'll tie in directly with your notebook work.

4. How to Handle Large or Formal Sketches, Photos, Charts, or Graphs Drawn on Special Paper

If you have any items that by their nature can't be entered directly in the notebook by hand, you should make or enter them on separate sheets. These, too, should be signed, dated, and witnessed and then pasted or affixed in the notebook in proper chronological order. The inserted sheet should be referred to by entries made directly in the notebook, thus tying them in to the other material. Photos or other entries that can't be signed or written should be pasted in the notebook and referenced by legends (descriptive words, such as "photo taken of machine in operation") made directly in the notebook, preferably with lead lines that extend from the notebook page over onto the photo, so as to preclude a charge of substituting subsequently made photos (see Fig. 3B). The page the photo is pasted on should be signed, dated, and witnessed in the usual manner.

If an item covers an entire page, it can be referred to on an adjacent page. It's important to affix the items to the notebook page with a permanent adhesive, such as white glue or nonyellowing transparent tape.

If you have to draw a sketch in pencil and want to make a permanent record of it (to put in your notebook) without redrawing the sketch in ink, simply make a photocopy of the penciled sketch: voilà—a permanent copy!

5. Witnessing the Notebook

As I've repeatedly stressed earlier in this chapter, it's important that the notebook entries be witnessed. This is because an inventor's own testimony, even if supported by a properly completed notebook, will often not be adequate for proving an entry date. The witnesses chosen should be as impartial and competent as possible, which means they shouldn't be close relatives or people who have been working so closely with you as to be possible co-inventors. A knowledgeable friend, business associate, or professional will make an excellent witness, provided he or she has the necessary

technical ability or background to understand the invention. The witness should also be someone who's likely to be available later. Obviously, a person who's seriously ill, or of very advanced age, wouldn't be a good choice. Don't ask your patent attorney (if you are using one) to perform this function since the courts and the PTO won't allow an attorney to represent someone and also be that person's witness.

If the invention is a very simple mechanical device, practically anyone will have the technical qualifications to be a witness. But if it involves advanced chemical or electronic concepts, obviously a person with an adequate background in the field will have to be used. If called upon later, the witnesses should be able to testify to their own knowledge that the physical and/or chemical facts of the entry are correct. Thus they shouldn't just be witnesses to your signature, so you should not use a notary or a layperson who just witnesses your signature, as do witnesses to a will. Rather the witnesses should actually read or view and understand the actual technical subject material in the notebook, including the actual tests if they are witnessing the building and testing (Fig. 3B). Obviously, then, you should call in your witnesses to observe your final tests and measurements so that they can later testify that they did witness them.

While one witness may be sufficient, two are preferred, since this will enhance the likelihood of at least one of them being available to testify at a later date. If both are available, your case will be very strong. Also, if a dispute occurs between two inventors, the one with the greater number of witnesses will prevail, assuming all other considerations are substantially a wash.

Some notebooks already contain, on each page, a line for the inventor's signature and date, together with the words "Witnessed and Understood" with lines for two signatures and dates. If your notebook doesn't already contain these words and signature lines, merely write them in as indicated in Figs. 3A to 3C. To really tie down the trade secret status of your invention, you should add the words "The above confidential information is" just before the words "Witnessed and Understood," as has been done on Form 3-2 and on Figs. 3A, 3B, and 3C. You and the witnesses should sign and enter the date on the appropriate lines at the end of your description of the conception of your invention and at the end of your description of your building and testing.

6.   What to Do With the Notebook

Now that you've made those nice notebook records of conception and hopefully building and testing, what should you do with the notebook? Basically nothing, except to keep it in a safe place in case it's ever needed (hopefully not!) for one of the six "legal" reasons under Section C, above, and to use it liberally as needed for one of the "invention process" reasons under Section B, above.

G.   Another Way to Record Conception or Building and Testing— The Invention Disclosure

Suppose you conclude that for some good reason it's too difficult or inconvenient for you to keep a notebook or technical diary. There's a second, albeit somewhat inferior, way for you to record the conception or building and testing of your invention. This is by using a document called an "Invention Disclosure."

Despite its formidable name, an Invention Disclosure is hardly different from a properly completed notebook entry of an invention. It should be a complete record of your invention, including a title, its purpose(s), advantages, a detailed description of it, possible novel features, ramifications, details of its construction if you built it, and results obtained, if any. While it might better be called an "Invention Record," in the arcane world of patents it's called a

"disclosure," since an inventor often uses it to disclose an invention to others to get their opinion, have them develop it, and show what progress is being made. These entries should be made on a separate sheet of paper that has no other information on it except details of your invention and your name and address. For your convenience, Form 3-2 in Appendix 7 provides an Invention Disclosure form, and Fig. 3C illustrates how the form should be completed to record conception.

Since an Invention Disclosure isn't bound, the writing on it can, and preferably should, be printed or typed. But if you do write rather than type, just make sure your handwriting is legible. A sheet of professional or personal letterhead (if you have it) is suitable for an Invention Disclosure. Otherwise print your name, address, and telephone number at the top (or bottom, after your signature). Business letterhead is okay if the invention is to be owned by your business. If the disclosure runs to more than one page, you should write the title of your invention on the second and each succeeding page, followed by the word "continued," numbering each page and indicating the total number of pages of the entire disclosure—for example, "Page 1 of 3."

As before, the description of your invention should be signed and dated by you, marked "The above confidential information is Witnessed and Understood," and signed and dated, preferably by two witnesses, who, as before, are technically competent to understand your invention and who actually do understand and have witnessed the subject matter you have entered on your Invention Disclosure. (See Section F5, above.) If you use more than one page, each should be signed and dated by both the inventor and the witnesses.

As with the notebook, if you conceive of an invention on one date, and build and test the invention later, you should make two separate invention disclosures, one to record conception and the second to record the building and testing. The second should refer to the first, and both should be signed and dated by you and the witnesses. I haven't provided an example of an invention disclosure completed to show building and testing, but, as stated, it would be similar to the notebook entry to record building and testing (Fig. 3B set out in Section F, above).

Also, as with the notebook, keep the disclosure in a safe place and use it as discussed in Section F6, above.

If you've conceived of or have effectively built and tested your invention on a computer, you must print out a hard copy on paper so that you and your witness can sign it properly. Computer records are too impermanent to be given legal credibility.

EXAMPLE: Nellie Nerdle, while mousing around with a drawing program on her XYZ-98000, puts some triangles, ovals, and bars together and comes up with a new brassiere design. She not only saves it on her hard disk and makes a backup copy, but also makes a paper printout, signs and dates it, writes "Witnessed and Understood:" below her signature, and has her friends, Paul Pocketprotector and Gretchen Guru, sign and date as witnesses so that she'll have a permanent, signed and dated hard copy of her invention.

H. The Disclosure Document Program (DDP)— Or How to Make the PTO Your Witness to Conception

Several years ago the Patent and Trademark Office (PTO) started a program under which it accepts Invention Disclosures and preserves them for two years, or longer if a patent application is filed which refers to the Invention Disclosure. The purpose of this service, for which the PTO charges a small fee (see Appendix 4, Fee Schedule), is to provide credible evidence of the conception date and inventorship for inventors who, for some reason, cannot or don't wish to rely on witnesses. There's no doubt that, in case of an interference or other proceeding where the date of invention or inventorship itself is at issue, the PTO will regard a copy of a PTO-filed Disclosure Document as excellent evidence of conception.

Despite these advantages, I generally recommend that most inventors *not* use the DDP. Although the PTO's small fee per invention may not seem like much, the methods I've described earlier for recording your invention are free and, in fact, will give you (a) equally good or better evidence of conception and, more importantly, (b) evidence of building and testing. This is because live witnesses can testify to additional facts surrounding conception, and can also testify that they actually saw the building, testing, and operation of your invention. Also, a DDP record isn't as usable in court as a notebook or invention disclosure, since you won't have witnesses to validate the DDP record. Simply put, I hate to see you unnecessarily spend money for an inferior "product."

⚠️ In the event you do choose to utilize the PTO's DDP, remember several things that I've put into Form 3-3 to remind you: the DDP is not a substitute for filing a patent application or for building and testing the invention. Also, it won't provide you with any "grace period" or any other justification for delaying the filing of a patent application. It's merely an alternative way to get your conception disclosure witnessed. Moreover, even if you use the DDP to record your conception, you should still use a lab notebook or separate sheets with proper witnessing to record all the pertinent facts if you build and test your invention. Finally, filing a Disclosure Document with the PTO doesn't allow you to refer to the invention as "Patent Pending" or "Patent Applied For." (It's actually a criminal offense, punishable by a $500 fine, to refer to an invention as "Patent Pending" where no provisional or regional patent application has been filed.)

If you still wish to file a disclosure with the PTO under its Disclosure Document Program, simply send the following four items to Box DD, Assistant Commissioner for Patents, Washington, DC 20231:

1. A letter requesting that the attached disclosure be accepted under the Disclosure Document Program (complete Form 3-3 in Appendix 7)
2. A check for the specified fee, payable to the Commissioner of Patents and Trademarks. (Regrettably, I can't provide a form for this; you'll have to use your own check!)
3. One copy of your notebook entry (see Section F, above) or Invention Disclosure (completed Form 3-2—see Section G, above)
4. A stamped receipt postcard. The postcard should have your name and address on the front side and a description of your disclosure on the reverse side.

Disclosure Documents may also be filed (by hand delivery only) with the Sunnyvale (CA) Center for Innovation. See Fig. 6K.

The disclosure sheets must be numbered and letter size (8.5" x 11") or A4 size (210 mm x 297 mm). You should submit a photocopy of your original signed and witnessed disclosure and keep your original. (You don't have to have an original ink signature, or any signature at all, on the copy of the disclosure that you send to the PTO, but I recommend that you do sign and date your notebook or disclosure to make them more believable in case you ever have to go to court.)

The PTO will stamp all of the papers with the date of receipt and an identifying number and will return the postcard. The date and number on the returned postcard is important and should be carefully preserved.

If you file a Disclosure Document with the PTO and then do nothing else, the PTO will keep the original of your request letter and your disclosure for two years and then

Invention Disclosure

Sheet __1__ of __1__

Inventor(s): _____Irma Inventor_____

Address(es): _____1919 Chestnut St., Philadelphia, PA 19103_____

Title of Invention: __Self-Adjusting Can Opener_____

To record **Conception**, describe: 1. Circumstances of conception, 2. Purposes and advantages of invention, 3. Description, 4. Sketches, 5. Ramifications, 6. Possible novel features, and 7. Closest known prior art. To record **Building and Testing**, describe: 1. Any previous disclosure of conception, 2. Construction, 3. Ramifications, 4. Tests, and 5. Test results. Include sketches and photos, where possible. Continue on additional identical copies of this sheet if necessary; inventors and witnesses should sign all sheets.

1. I thought of this can opener while at my friend Roberta's wedding last Sunday. I saw the caterer having trouble opening small and large cans with several openers. Thinking there was a better way, I recalled my Majestic KY3 sewing machine clamp and how it was adjustable and thought to modify the left arm to accommodate a can opener head.

2. My can opener will work with all sizes of cans and is actually cheaper than the most common existing one, the UR4 made by Ideal Co. of Racine, WI.

3. My can opener comprises a sliding clamp 10, a pincer groove 12, (etc.) as shown in the following sketch:

4. Sketch:

10 → SKETCH ← 12

5. Instead of sliding clamp 10, I can use a special notch as follows:

Notch → SKETCH

6. I believe that the combination of sliding clamp 10 and pincer groove 12 is a new one for can openers. Also I believe that it may be novel to provide a frammis head with my whatsit.

7. The Acme KZ122 can opener, mfgd. by Acme Kitchenwares of Berkeley, CA and p. 417 of "Kitchen Tools & Their Uses" (Ready Publishers, Phila. 1981) show the closest can openers to my invention, in addition to the devices already mentioned.

Inventor(s): *Irma Inventor* _____ Date: *199X Jul 6*

_____ Date:____ / ___ / ___

The above confidential information is Witnessed and Understood:
_____*Griselda Hammelfarb*_____ Date: *199X Jul 7*
_____*Neonore Zimla*_____ Date: *199X Jul 10*

Fig. 3C—Invention Disclosure (Form 3-2 in Appendix 7)

destroy them. However, if you later file a patent application on the invention described in your disclosure, you should do so within two years of filing the disclosure. You should also file a separate reference letter in the application, referring to the disclosure (use Form 3-4 in Appendix 7). The PTO will then retain the disclosure indefinitely in case you ever need to rely on it in connection with your patent application. Be sure to file the reference letter within two years of filing the disclosure document; otherwise the disclosure will have already been destroyed by the PTO, even if you have filed a patent application. (This is another serious disadvantage of the DDP.)

As I'll discuss in more depth later, in Chapters 11 and 16, many disreputable organizations exist to prey on and exploit inventors. They've even gotten to the DDP. Here are three scams I recently encountered involving the DDP. In one, an inventor was charged $200 by an "invention developer" to file his DDP. In another, a company advertised as follows:

In a third, an organization advertised that there's no need to search inventions or file patent applications—they're a waste of time and money. An inventor, the ad said, can secure adequate protection for an invention by using a "special government program" whereby the Patent Office will record and preserve any invention for a nominal fee. All the inventor had to do was to sign up and pay the organization about $400 to enter this "special" program.

All three scams indicated that the inventor could "secure priority," "reserve rights" or take advantage of a "grace period" for two years. However, as stated, the DDP is merely a substitute for witnesses to your *conception*— nothing more! If you want to secure proper and full offensive rights on your creation against independent creators and copiers, you *must* patent it. If you want to record conception and/or building and testing to take advantage of the benefits enumerated in Sections B and C, just fill out Form 3-2; you needn't pay anybody anything!

I. The Provisional Patent Application— A Substitute for Building and Testing, With Some Disadvantages

⚠ For reasons explained in Section E, above, it's very important to build and test your invention as soon as possible. If you haven't read that section yet, do so now.

Suppose you don't have the facilities, skill, or time to build and test your invention, and you are not in a position to file a complete utility patent application right away. Inventors may file a Provisional Patent Application (PPA) which will serve as a legal alternative to building and testing their utility invention. (The PPA is not available for designs.) Let's explore the PPA and the advantages and disadvantages of using it.

1. What a Provisional Patent Application (PPA) Is

A PPA is a short version of a regular patent application. It is used to establish an early filing date for a later-filed Regular Patent Application (RPA). A PPA must contain:
  a. a detailed description of the invention telling how to make and use it,
  b. drawing(s), if necessary to understand how to make and use the invention,
  c. a cover sheet,
  d. a fee (small entity (SE) or large entity—see Appendix 4, Fee Schedule), and
  e. an SE declaration if you're an SE and want to file the PPA with an SE fee.

2. What a PPA Is Not

A PPA is not a regular patent application (RPA) and therefore cannot by itself result in a patent. For those readers already familiar with the regular patent application process described in Chapter 8, the PPA, unlike an RPA, does not require:
  • a Patent Application Declaration (PAD)
  • an Information Disclosure Statement (IDS)
  • patent claims
  • an abstract and summary
  • a description of the invention's background, or
  • a statement of the invention's objects and advantages.
  If you don't file an RPA within a year of your PPA's filing date, your PPA will go abandoned and will be forever useless. Also, your PPA cannot provide a filing date for subject matter that is not disclosed in it.

3. What a PPA Accomplishes

You can use a PPA in several ways, but only one use—the substitute for building and testing—is relevant here, so I'll detail only this use now, but will mention the other uses briefly.

If you choose to not build and test your invention right away, or are unable to do so, the next best step would normally be to file an RPA as soon as possible. But this approach can be very costly, especially if you are not sure that your invention will bring in very much money, assuming a patent issues on it. So, assuming you decide that an RPA is not appropriate, your next best step is to file a PPA. Not only are the filing fees associated with a PPA much less than an RPA ($75 as opposed to $385 as of Fall 1996), but the cost of preparing a PPA can also be a small fraction of what's involved with an RPA.

Once you file a PPA, you will be considered to have reduced your invention to practice, even if you've done nothing to build and test it, assuming that:

- an RPA (and optionally one or more foreign patent applications) are filed on the invention within one year, and
- the PPA fully describes the invention claimed in the RPA.

Being able to claim the PPA's filing date as a reduction to practice means you can use that date to:

- overcome the date of any prior art reference that is cited in opposition to your application, and
- establish your invention's priority in an interference (a procedure conducted by the PTO to decide which of two or more pending patent applications which claim the same invention should receive the patent).

PROVISIONAL PATENT APPLICATION COMPARED TO THE DOCUMENT DISCLOSURE PROGRAM

In a way, the PPA program is analogous to the Document Disclosure Program (DDP—Section H, above). The DDP provides a record of conception for those who don't have any witnesses, while the PPA provides the equivalent of an RTP for any inventors who can't get witnesses to their building and testing, or who aren't able to build and test. In both cases, the filed documents only establish priority over other inventions or prior art references, and don't themselves lead to a patent or affect its term—for that, a regular patent application is required.

4. Advantages of a PPA Over Building and Testing

In addition to the benefits of an early filing date, the PPA gives you the right to claim that your invention has "patent pending" status. In common parlance this means that you can publish, sell, or show your invention to others without fear of theft or loss of any domestic rights. (See Chapter 11, Section G.) This is because anyone who sees and steals your invention after you file your PPA would have a later filing date than yours, so you would almost certainly be able to win any interference with the thief. To win, the thief would have to prove that he/she conceived of the invention before you did, and was diligently attempting to reduce it to practice (by filing a PPA, RPA or building and testing it) at the very time that you filed your PPA. This would be very hard to prove unless it were true.

There are other advantages to using a PPA in place of actually building and testing the invention. These are:

- You need not incur the expense and time usually involved in building and testing an invention in order to reduce it to practice.
- You need not keep meticulous records of whatever building and testing you do accomplish.
- You need not obtain witnesses.
- You will be certain that your PPA's early filing date can be relied upon, provided your description of the invention in the PPA is legally sufficient as described below. (To rely on an actual reduction to practice by building and testing your invention, you have to keep adequate records of your building and testing activities and be prepared to prove the validity of these records in a court or in an interference.)
- You can file a technical article (which you might have written anyway) as a PPA. (But remember, the PPA article must fully disclose the invention claimed in the RPA, which must be filed within one year.)
- You can file a PPA, then within one year, file an RPA, which has the practical effect of delaying examination of the RPA and extending—up to one year—your patent's expiration date.
- You can file an RPA, convert it to a PPA one year later, and then file a second RPA based upon the PPA to extend your patent's expiration date for two years.

5. Disadvantages of the PPA

Alas, every silver box seems to contain a cloud: The disadvantages of filing a PPA may be as follows:

1. You may tend to forego building and testing and lose the concomitant advantages such as determining whether the invention is operable, practical, or useful, and having a working prototype to demonstrate to prospective manufacturers. (See Section E above.)
2. Your PPA may fail to contain a full a description of the actual nuts and bolts and use of the invention that you want to claim in your RPA, which means

you won't be able to rely on the PPA for any purpose related to that invention.

3. You may unintentionally forego foreign protection. This is because you cannot wait one year after filing the RPA, as is usually done, to foreign file. Instead you must make your foreign filing decision, as well as your regular U.S. filing decision, within one year after your PPA is filed.

6. Should You File a PPA?

For the reasons stated above, I recommend that you file a PPA only if:

a. you are not in a position to build and test your invention, properly document your activities and have your documentation witnessed, and

b. you are not currently in a position to file an RPA on the invention, and

c. you wish to establish an early filing date since you feel the invention is potentially valuable and might be independently developed by others or stolen from you.

7. How to Prepare and File a PPA

Ideally, the more your PPA resembles the RPA you file within the following year, the more you can be assured that you will be able to claim the PPA filing date. Conversely, the less the PPA resembles the RPA, the more work the patent examiner will have to do to determine whether your PPA fully discloses the invention being claimed in the RPA—which means the greater the chance you will be denied the PPA filing date. And so, my general recommendation is that you follow the basic rules for writing an RPA set out in Chapter 10 (double- or 1.5-spacing and with 1" margins, ample headings, short sentences, and a clear description). But, since your PPA will not be examined by the PTO unless and until you file an RPA—and then only to see whether it adequately describes the invention being claimed in the RPA—your description need not:

• be well written,
• use any legal terms, or
• be typed in any particular format.

To prepare and file a PPA, you should complete six steps:

1. prepare drawings, if necessary,
2. prepare a complete description of the structure and operation of your invention,
3. prepare a cover letter and fee transmittal,
4. prepare any needed small-entity declarations,
5. attach a check for the filing fee and a postcard, and
6. mail all papers to the PTO.

In keeping with my recommendation that you make your PPA look as much like your RPA as is feasible, I recommend that you prepare your drawings and description as I describe in Chapter 8. Although you legally don't need to include the Background, Objects and Advantages, Description of Drawing Figures, List of Reference Numerals, Summary, Conclusion or Abstract parts of the specification, it won't hurt if you do, and including these parts will make your PPA that much more effective if it is later examined. Your drawings can be informal drawings; they need not be inked or done carefully with a CAD program, but they (and the description) must be in permanent form (no pencil).

You also don't need to include any claims (Chapter 9). However, if possible, it is a good idea to draft some claims before filing the PPA, since this exercise will help you determine whether your detailed description includes everything necessary about your invention.

⚠ PROVIDE A FULL DESCRIPTION OF YOUR INVENTION. While it need not be well written or use any legalese, your "description" MUST comply with the full disclosure requirements—that is, it MUST clearly teach how to make and use the invention and it MUST disclose the best mode or version you currently prefer, if it has several modes or versions. To this end, I suggest you carefully review and follow Chapter 8, Section F, which discusses these requirements in detail.

After you feel that you've prepared an adequate and full description of your invention—and any necessary drawings—you're ready to prepare the cover letter and fee transmittal. You'll be relieved to learn that this is a simple matter. A cover letter form is provided in Appendix 7 as Form 3-5, and the fee transmittal is Form 10-1A; completion is straightforward (the fee is in Appendix 4). First read the cover letter to note all of the disadvantages of the PPA. I put these in the cover letter to warn you of these as they are significant. If you understand and accept these disadvantages, then simply fill in the name(s) of the inventor(s), a title, the number of sheets of specification, and the number of sheets of drawing. The title and name(s) of the inventor(s) are tentative and can be changed later, so long as one inventor named in the PPA is also named in the RPA and that inventor's invention is claimed in the RPA and fully disclosed in the PPA. However, if your RPA contains any essential information that isn't in your PPA, you may not be able to rely on your PPA. So again, be sure your description is adequate and complete.

See Chapter 10, Section H, to determine if you're entitled to file as a small entity (SE). If you are, you can file with half the fees of a large entity. Fill out a Small Entity Declaration (Form 10-3) and have any assignees or licensees fill out Forms 10-4A, 10-4B, or 10-4C as appropriate. Indicate on Form 3-5 the number of SE declarations you're sending. Complete the "Check" line as appropriate—the fee schedule is in Appendix 4. Then each inventor should sign and write his or her address. If you have more than two inventors, retype the form or photocopy the name and signature lines, splice them in, and recopy the form on legal-size paper.

If you want to get an instant filing date, obtain an Express Mail envelope and label from your post office and complete the Express Mail Declaration. (See Chapter 10, Section L.)

Make a complete copy of all papers of your PPA and mount them in a separate "legal" file.

Attach a check for the appropriate filing fee and a stamped receipt postcard. Address the front of the postcard to yourself and list on the back all of the papers you're sending for the PPA. Fig 3D provides an example of a completed postcard. If you don't have any postcards, just use a blank 4" x 6" card (preferably colored, so it can be spotted more readily if mixed with other mail) and a postcard-rate stamp.

> Provisional Patent Application of Ignatz Inventor and Imogene Inventress consisting of ten sheets of specification, three sheets of drawing, cover letter and fee transmittal, two small-entity declarations (inventor and assignee), $75 check for filing fee, and receipt postcard filed today.

Fig 3D—Back Side of Exemplary Receipt Postcard for PPA

Mail all papers to the address on the cover letter—that is, Box Provisional Patent Application, Assistant Commissioner for Patents, Washington, DC 20231. If you use Express Mail (advisable), you can consider your PPA filed as soon as you receive the express mail receipt from the postal clerk. About two weeks after you mail the PPA, you'll receive your postcard back, stamped with its date of receipt in the PTO and a serial number that the PTO has assigned to your PPA. If you use regular mail, the date stamped on your postcard will be the filing date of your PPA. Staple your postcard to the back of your PPA cover letter.

About a month later, you'll receive an official filing receipt from the PTO for your PPA. Mount this in the file with your PPA. Now determine the date that is ten months after your PPA's filing date and mark this date on your calendar to remind you to consider following through with an RPA and possible foreign patent applications. A suitable reminder is "Consider filing regular and foreign patent applications on PPA filed [filing date of your PPA]." You won't receive any further communication from the PTO about your PPA. Also, as stated, if you don't file an RPA referring to your PPA (see Chapter 10) within a year of your PPA's filing date, the PTO will forever disregard your PPA.

Even though you've filed a PPA as a substitute for building and testing, you should still try to build and test it if at all possible, for reasons explained in Section E, above.

8. PPAs and Foreign Filing

The effect of PPAs on foreign filing is a bit complicated, but not difficult to understand. As we'll learn in Chapter 12, there are two types of foreign jurisdictions in the patent world—those that are members of the Paris Convention and those that are not. If you file a PPA and then file in any Convention jurisdiction (for example, the European Patent Office, Patent Cooperation Treaty (PCT), the U.K., or Japan) within a year, your application in the Convention jurisdiction will be entitled to the priority of your PPA's filing date. Thus, after you file a PPA, you can then freely publish and sell your invention without loss of any rights in any foreign Convention jurisdiction, provided you file in the foreign

Convention jurisdiction within a year. Unfortunately, non-Convention countries, for example, China-Taiwan and India, do not provide any priority, so you must file in these countries before you publish or offer your invention for sale publicly, as fully explained in Chapter 12.

J. Don't Use the So-Called "Post Office Patent" to Document Your Invention

There's a myth that you can document the date you conceived of your invention (or even protect your invention) by mailing a description of your invention to yourself by certified (or registered) mail and keeping the sealed envelope. In fact, law regards the use of these "Post Office Patents" as tantamount to worthless and no substitute for the signatures of live witnesses on a description of your invention, or even for the PTO's Disclosure Document Program. The PTO's Board of Appeals and Patent Interferences, which has great power in these matters, has specifically said that it gives a sealed envelope little evidentiary value. ■

CHAPTER

4

Will Your Invention Sell?

INVENTOR'S COMMANDMENT #5

Don't spend significant time or money on your creation until you have thoroughly evaluated it for commercial potential, including considering all of its advantages and disadvantages.

A. Why Evaluate Your Invention for Salability?

Now that you've made an invention (Chapter 2) and properly recorded your conception (and building and testing, if done—Chapter 3), it's time to do two things before proceeding further: evaluate it for commercial potential and make a patentability search. While you can do these in any order, I recommend that you do the easiest and/or cheapest one first. Since, for most people, it's the commercial evaluation, I put this chapter first. However, if you live across the street from the PTO, then go to Chapters 5 and 6 first. Also, if you're a corporate inventor, the decision as to whether a particular invention is sufficiently marketable to justify applying for a patent may not be yours. In any event I recommend that you at least skim through this material for new ideas that might help you assess your work in a different light before proceeding to Chapters 5 and 6, where I discuss patentability and searching.

The commercial evaluation is so important that I've made it an Inventor's Commandment. Why is a commercial evaluation so important? Because the next steps you take will involve the expenditure of significant money and effort. Specifically, your next step, in addition to searching the invention, is to build and test it for feasibility and cost (if possible), and then to file a patent application on the invention. Naturally, you won't want to take these substantial labor and financial risks unless you feel you have some reasonable chance that your efforts and expenditures will be justified.

Many people believe that if they get a patent, they'll be assured of fame and fortune. However, the fact that you can get a patent doesn't mean that you'll make any money from the invention. In fact, less than one out of ten patented inventions make any money for their owners, mainly because the commercial prospects of the inventions were not adequately assessed at the outset.

The purpose of this chapter, then, is to help you reduce the risk of a "patented failure" by assisting you in checking your invention out for salability. In fact, before you proceed with a search, or the actual filing of a patent application, I recommend that you be reasonably confident that your invention is likely to make you at least $50,000, or at least twenty times the cost of what you plan to spend for searching, building a model, and patenting. Of course if you can do the search easily, or if you're into inventing for the sheer fun of it, or you want to get a patent to stroke your ego, you can disregard these financial requirements.

Also, if you come up with a technical breakthrough in a high-tech field, or a highly novel invention, you should consider patenting it even though you don't think it has immediate commercial value: it may become very profitable some years later, and your early patent will block later inventors from patenting it.

If after reading this chapter, you're still not sure about the commercial prospects of your invention, you may want to test market it. This can legally be done for up to one year since you can file a patent application up to one year after the invention is first sold or offered for sale. A test marketing is feasible if you're able to make (or have made) reasonable quantities of your invention cheaply. However, you must be willing to sacrifice your foreign rights. See Chapter 12, where I explain that you'll lose most of your foreign rights if you sell or otherwise release your invention to public scrutiny before you file for a patent in the U.S. Obviously, a field or use test of a working model of an invention will tell you much more than a theoretical "paper" evaluation discussed in this chapter.

If you do decide to test market the invention before filing, you must keep in mind the "one-year rule," which I'll also discuss in the next chapter. This rule, contained in Section 102 of the patent statutes (35 USC 102), requires that in order to be valid, a U.S. patent application *must* be filed within one year after you first sell your invention (this includes test marketing), offer it for sale or publish it. (See Chapter 5, Section E.)

B. Start Small but Ultimately Do It Completely

When you evaluate your invention for commercial potential, try to do it on a small scale at first in order to avoid a large, wasted expenditure. For example, if you make metal parts as part of building a prototype to test operability, try to have them made by the economical electric discharge machining (EDM) technique rather than with molds. Similarly, prior to conducting extensive interviews, try to consult with a single expert to be sure you're not way out in left field. If your initial, small-scale investigation looks favorable and you don't run into any serious impediments, I advise that you then do it carefully, completely, and objectively, using the techniques of this chapter.

If after you do the full evaluation your idea looks like it has great commercial potential, but some other factor such as patentability or operability doesn't look too promising, don't make any hasty decision to drop it. Continue to explore the negative areas. On the other hand, if after a careful evaluation you are truly convinced that your invention won't be successful, don't waste any further time on it. Move on.

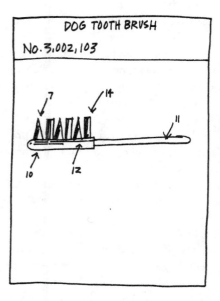

C. You Can't Be 100% Sure of Any Invention's Commercial Prospects

There's only one question you need to answer in commercially evaluating your invention: If my invention is manufactured and sold, or otherwise commercially implemented (for example, as a process that is put into commercial use), will it be profitable? Unfortunately, no one can ever answer this question with complete certainty. The answer will always depend on how the invention is promoted, how well it's designed, how well it's packaged, the mood of the market, the timing of its commercial debut, and dozens of other intangible factors. Most marketing experts say that five "P" factors must all be "right" for a new product to make it: Production, Price, Position (its place in the market), Promotion, and Perseverance.

In addition to the "Five Ps," the packaging (outer box as well as the shape of the device itself) can be crucial to its success. Consider a relatively recent invention, the Audochron® clock which indicates the time by a series of countable chimes. Given this technical feature only, the clock probably wouldn't have sold too well. But a talented designer put the works in a futuristic case shaped like a flattened gold sphere on a pedestal in which a plastic band at the center of the sphere lit with each chime. As a result, it became a status symbol and sold relatively large quantities at a high price; it even appeared in *Architectural Digest*, shown in a photo of a U.S. President's desk!

The trademark you select for your invention can also make a big difference as to whether it's a commercial success. If you doubt this, consider Vaseline's hand lotion. The lotion would very likely have been just another member of the bunch, consigned to mediocre sales, had not some clever marketing person come up with the trademark *Intensive Care*. This helped make it a sales leader. Ditto for the *Hula-Hoop* exercise device and the *Crock Pot* slow cooker, both of which certainly weren't hurt by evocative names. Even something as dull as roach traps were blasted into marketing stardom by the trademark *Roach Motel* and its brilliant ad campaign ("Roaches check in, but they don't check out"). Even something as prosaic as raisins were given a mighty boost recently with the "dancing raisins" TV campaign thought up by a marketing genius.

D. Take Time to Do a Commercial Feasibility Evaluation

Despite the marketing uncertainties, most experts believe that you can make a useful evaluation of the commercial possibilities of an untested invention if you take the time to do some scientific and objective work in three areas:

- the positive and negative marketing factors attached to your invention;
- consultation with experts, potential users of the invention, marketing people, and others; and
- research into prior developments in the same area as your invention.

Let's take a look at each.

The Positive and Negative Factors Test

Every invention, no matter how many positive factors it seems to have at first glance, inevitably has one or more significant negative ones. To evaluate the positive and negative factors objectively, carefully consider each on the list below. Using Form 4-1, the Positive and Negative Factors Evaluation Sheet (a copy is in Appendix 7), assign a commercial value or disadvantage weight to each factor on a scale of −100 to +100, according to your best, carefully considered estimate. If the factor is irrelevant to your invention, assign a weight of 0.

For example, if an invention provides overwhelming cost savings in relation to its existing counterparts, assign a +80 or higher to the "Cost" factor (#1) in the positive column. But if it requires a high capital expenditure (tooling) to build, a –50 would be appropriate for this factor (#43), and so on.

The following balance scale analogy will help you to understand the positive and negative factors evaluation: Pretend the positive factors are stacked on one side of a balance scale and the negative factors are stacked on the other side, as indicated in Fig. 4A.

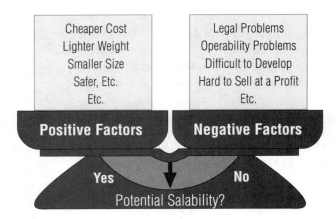

Fig. 4A—Conceptual Weighing of Positive v. Negative Factors

If the positive factors (those given a weight from +1 to +100) strongly outweigh the negative (those from –1 to –100), you can regard this as a "go" indication, that is, the invention is commercially viable. Obviously this balance scale is just an analogy. It can't be used quantitatively because no one has yet come up with a way to assign accurate and valid weights to the factors. Nevertheless, you'll find it of great help in evaluating the commercial prospects of your invention.

Before you actually take pen (or word processor) in hand and begin your evaluation, read through the following summary of positive and negative factors.

You should consider each factor carefully, especially if you assign a negative value, even if the negative value is merely due to the need to change or design and produce new production equipment. I've seen inventions and developments that were better in every way than what already existed, but which weren't used solely because the improvement didn't justify the cost of replacing existing production equipment, or the cost associated with manufacturing and promoting the device.

The factors of your invention with negative values are generally more important and require more consideration than do those with positive values, since if your invention fails, it will obviously be one or more of the negatives that causes it.

Factors Affecting the Marketability of Your Invention

1. **Cost.** Is your invention cheaper or more expensive to build or use than current counterparts? An example where making something more expensive to build would be an advantage is a credit or eligibility card; a more expensive card would be more difficult to counterfeit.

2. **Weight.** Is your invention lighter (or heavier) in weight than what is already known, and is such change in weight a benefit? For example, if you've invented a new automobile or airplane engine, a reduction in weight is a great benefit. But if you've invented a new ballast material, obviously an increase in weight (provided it doesn't come at too great a cost in money or bulk) is a benefit.

3. **Size.** Is your invention smaller or larger in size or capacity than what is already known, and is such change in size a benefit?

4. **Safety/Health Factors.** Is your invention safer or healthier to use than what is already known? Clearly there's a strong trend in government and industry to improve the safety and reduce the possible chances for injury, harm, and product liability suits in most products and processes, and this trend has given birth to many new inventions. Often a greater increase in cost and weight can be tolerated if certain safety and health benefits accrue.

5. **Speed.** Is your invention able to do a job faster (or slower) than its previous counterpart, and is such change in speed a benefit? This advantage, like #6, is important in software inventions.

6. **Ease of Use.** Is your invention easier (or harder) to use (the current buzzword is "ergonomic") or learn to use than its previously known counterpart? An example of a product where an increase in difficulty of use would be a benefit is the child-proof drug container cap. This advantage is especially important if you have a software innovation: if it enables you to use the computer or any other machine more facilely, this counts a great deal.

7. **Ease of Production.** Is your invention easier or cheaper (or harder or more expensive) to manufacture than previously known counterparts? Or can it be mass-produced, whereas previously known counterparts had to be made by hand? An example of something that is

more difficult to manufacture yet that is highly desirable is the new credit cards with holographic images: they're far more difficult to forge.

8. **Durability.** Does your invention last longer (or wear out sooner) than previously known counterparts? While built-in obsolescence is nothing to be admired, the stark economic reality is that many products, such as disposable razors, have earned their manufacturers millions by lasting for a shorter time than previously known counterparts.

9. **Repairability.** Is it easier to repair than previously known counterparts?

10. **Novelty.** Is your invention at all different from all previously known counterparts? Merely making an invention different may not appear to be an advantage per se, but it's usually a great advantage: It provides an alternative method or device for doing the job in case the first method or device ever encounters difficulties (such as from government regulation), and in case the first device or method infringes a patent that you want to avoid infringing. It also provides something for ad people to crow about.

11. **Convenience/Social Benefit/Mechanization.** Does your invention make living easier or more convenient? Many inventions with a new function provide this advantage. Although you may question the ultimate wisdom and value of such gadgets as the electric knife, the remote-control TV, and the digital-readout clock, the reality remains that, in our relatively affluent society, millions of dollars have been and are being made from devices that save labor and time (even though the time required to earn the after-tax money to buy the gadget is often greater than the time saved by using it). Even if the invention has one or more serious drawbacks, if it mechanizes a manual operation, it may still fly. Consider the Epilady® leg-hair remover: Even though its rotating spring ripped out m'lady's leg hairs in an extremely painful manner, it became a great success because it eliminated shaving and depilatories.

Then too, many new industries have been started by making an existing invention easier and convenient to use. Henry Ford didn't invent the automobile; he just produced it in volume and made it convenient for the masses to use. Ditto for George Eastman with his camera. And in modern times, the two Steves (Jobs and Wozniak) did much the same for the computer.

In the software field, especially nowadays, people seem willing to buy almost any program that will computerize a manual task, even if the time required to earn the money to buy the program, learn the program, and use it is much greater than the manual route.

12. **Reliability.** Is your invention apt to fail less or need repair less often than previously known devices?

13. **Ecology.** Does your invention make use of what previously were thought to be waste products? Does it reduce the use of limited natural resources? Does it produce less waste products, such as smoke and waste water? If so, you have an advantage that is very important nowadays and that should be emphasized strongly.

14. **Salability.** Is your invention easier to sell or market than existing counterparts?

15. **Appearance.** Does your invention provide a better-appearing design than existing counterparts?

16. **Viewability.** If your invention relates to eye use, does it present a brighter, clearer, or more viewable image? For example, a color TV with a brighter picture, or photochromic eyeglasses that automatically darken in sunlight were valuable inventions.

17. **Precision.** Does your invention operate or provide greater precision or more accuracy than existing counterparts?

18. **Noise.** Does your invention operate more quietly? Does it turn unpleasant noise into a more acceptable sound? Or does it make noise in a desirable situation—for example, a device that produced a warning noise when a VCR cartridge was inserted in the wrong manner would be desirable.

19. **Odor.** Does your invention emanate less or more unpleasant fumes or odors?

20. **Taste.** If your invention is edible or comes into contact with the taste buds (for example, a pill or a pipe stem), does it taste better? A foul taste (or smell) can also be an

advantage, such as for poisons to prevent ingestion by children, and for telephone cables to deter chewing by rodents.

21. **Market Size.** Is there a larger market for your invention than for previously known devices? Because of climatic or legal restrictions, for example, certain inventions are only usable in small geographical areas. And because of economic factors, certain inventions may be limited to the relatively affluent. If your invention can obviate these restrictions, your potential market may be greatly increased, and this can be a significant advantage.

22. **Trend of Demand.** Is the trend of demand for your device increasing? Of course you should distinguish, if possible, between a trend and a fad. The first will provide a market for your invention while the second is likely to leave you high and dry unless you catch it in the beginning stages.

23. **Seasonal Demand.** Is your invention useful no matter what the season of the year? If so, it will usually have greater demand than a seasonal invention, such as a sailboat. But sometimes this will be a negative rather than a positive, if the invention is something like skis or a holiday decoration, which does have a seasonal demand, rather than an all-year-around one.

24. **Difficulty of Market Penetration.** Is your device an improvement of a previously accepted device? If so, it will have an easier time penetrating the market than a device that provides a completely new function.

25. **Potential Competition.** Is your invention so simple, popular, or easy to manufacture that many imitators and copiers are likely to attempt to design around it, or break your patent as soon as it's brought out? Or is it a relatively complex, less popular, hard-to-manufacture device, which others wouldn't be likely to produce in competition with you because of such factors as the large capital outlay required for tooling and production?

26. **Quality.** Does your invention produce or provide a higher quality output or result than existing counterparts? For example, compact disks provide a much better audio quality than do phonorecords or magnetic tape.

27. **Excitement.** (The Neophile and the Conspicuous Consumer/Status Seeker). Almost all humans need some form of excitement in their lives: some obtain it by watching or participating in sports, others by the purchase of a new car or travel, and still others by the purchase of new products, such as a 50-inch TV, a laser disk player, or a friendly household robot. Such purchasers can be called "neophiles" (lovers of the new); their excitement comes from having and showing off

their new "toy." Purchasers of expensive products, like the Mercedes-Benz or a Rolex watch, are commonly motivated by what Thorsten Veblen has called "conspicuous consumption," and what we now call "status seeking." They enjoy showing off an expensive or unique item which they've acquired. Thus, if your invention can provide consumer excitement, either through sheer newness or through evidence of a costly purchase, it has a decided advantage.

28. **Markup.** If your invention is in an excitement category (that is, if it's very different, novel, innovative, or luxurious), it can command a very high markup, a distinct selling advantage.

29. **Inferior Performance.** Yes, I'm serious! If your invention performs worse than comparable things that are already available, this can be a great advantage, if put to the proper use. Consider the 3M Company's fabulously successful Scotch® Post-It® note pads: Their novelty is simply that they have a strip of stickum that is *inferior* to known adhesives, thus providing removable self-stick notes. Here the invention may not be so much the discovery of an inferior adhesive as the discovery of a new use for it.

30. **"Sexy" Packaging.** If your invention is or comes in a "sexy" package, or is adaptable to being sold in such a package, this can be a great advantage. Consider the Hanes l'Eggs® stockings where the package (shaped like an egg) made the product!

31. **Miscellaneous/Obviation of Specific Disadvantages of Existing Devices.** This is a catchall to cover anything I may have missed in the previous categories. Often the specific disadvantages that your invention overcomes will be quite obvious; they should be included here, nonetheless.

32. **Long Life Cycle.** If your invention has a potentially long life cycle, that is, it can be made and sold for many years before it becomes obsolete, this is an obvious strong advantage that will justify capital expenditures for tooling and conducting a big ad campaign.

33. **Related Product Addability.** If your invention will usher in a new product line, as did the computer, where many related products, such as disk drives, printers, and software can be added, this will be an important advantage with potentially enhanced profits.

34. **Satisfies Existing Need.** If your invention will satisfy an existing, recognized need, such as preventing drug abuse, or avoiding auto collisions, your marketing difficulties will be greatly reduced.

35. **Legality.** Does your invention comply with, or will its use fail to comply with, existing laws, regulations, and product and manufacturing requirements? Or, are

administrative approvals required? If your invention carries legal difficulties with it, its acceptance will be problematic no matter how great its positive advantages are. And if ecological or safety approvals are required (for example, for drugs and automobiles), this will be viewed as a distinct disadvantage by prospective buyers.

36. **Operability.** Is it likely to work readily, or will significant additional design or technical development be required to make it practicable and workable? Usually problems of operability will become abundantly clear when you try to build a working model, which you should try to do as soon as possible, even if you've filed a PPA (Chapter 3, Section I). (Don't forget to fill out another copy of Form 3-2 after you build and test it.)

37. **Development.** Is the product already designed for the market, or will such things as additional engineering, material selection, and appearance work be required?

38. **Profitability.** Because of possible requirements for exotic materials, difficult machining steps, great size, and so on, is your invention likely to be difficult to sell at a profit, or at an acceptable price level?

39. **Obsolescence.** Is the field in which your invention is used likely to be around for a long time or die out soon? If the latter, most manufacturers won't be willing to invest money in production facilities.

40. **Incompatibility.** Is your invention likely to be compatible or incompatible with existing patterns of use, customs, and so on?

41. **Product Liability Risk.** Is your invention in a "safe" area, such as a ruler, or in a problem area, such as safety devices, drugs, firearms, contact sports, and automobiles? In the latter area, the risks of lawsuits against the manufacturer, due to product malfunction or injury from use, are likely to be greater than average. For example, a client of mine invented an ingenious, economical, and highly useful device for preventing a revolver from being accidentally fired. But, alas, though he tried everywhere, he couldn't get any company to take it on because they were afraid of product liability lawsuits if the device ever failed.

42. **Market Dependence.** Is the sale of your invention dependent on a market for other goods, or is it useful in its own right? For example, an improved television tuner depends on the sale of televisions for its success, so that if the television market goes into a slump, the sales of your tuner certainly will fall also.

43. **Difficulty of Distribution.** Is your invention easy to distribute, or is it so large, fragile, or perishable that it will be difficult or costly to distribute?

44. **Service Requirements.** Is your invention free from service requirements or will it require frequent servicing

and adjustment? If the latter, this is a distinct disadvantage. But consider the first commercial color TVs which, by any reasonable standard, were a service nightmare, but made millions for their manufacturers.

45. **Production Facilities.** Almost all inventions require new production facilities, a distinct disadvantage. This is because the manufacture of anything new requires new tooling and production techniques. But some inventions require only a modest change or no change, a tremendous advantage.

46. **Inertia Need Not/Must Be Overcome.** An example of a great invention that so far has failed because of user inertia is the Dvorak typewriter keyboard, which, although much faster and easier to use, was unable to overcome the awkward but entrenched Qwerty keyboard. The same goes for the easier-to-use, less confusing, military-European time, or a decimal time system. There's a risk in introducing *any* new product, and when any invention is radically different, potential manufacturers, users and sellers will manifest tremendous inertia, regardless of the invention's value.

47. **Minor/Great Technical Advance.** In the 60s, I got a client a very broad patent on a laser pumped by a chemical reaction explosion; we were very pleased with this patent. However, it was so advanced at the time that the technology behind it is just now being implemented in connection with the "Star Wars" defense effort. Unfortunately, the patent expired in the meantime. The same goes for the computer mouse patent, which expired in 1980, just before "mice" became popular. The moral? Even if you have a great invention, make sure it can be commercially implemented within about 17 years.

48. **Learning Required.** If consumers will have to undergo substantial learning in order to use your invention, this is an obvious negative. An example: the early personal computers. On the other hand, some inventions, such as the automatically talking clock, make a task even easier to do and thus have an obvious strong advantage.

49. **Difficult/Easy to Promote.** If it will be difficult to promote your invention, e.g., because it's technically complex, has subtle advantages, or is very expensive, large, or awkward, you've got an obvious disadvantage. But if it solves an omnipresent problem and is cheap and easy to use, this is a clear advantage.

50. **Lack/Presence of Market.** If no market already exists for your invention, you'll have to convince the public that they need it—that is, that you have a "product in search of a market." While not a fatal flaw, and while this type of invention can be most profitable, you (or your licensee) will have to be prepared to expend substantial sums on promotion.

51. **Crowded/Wide Open Field.** If the field is already crowded, you'll have an uphill battle.

52. **Commodities.** If you've invented a new commodity—such as a better plastic, solvent, or grain—you'll face stiff price competition from the established, already streamlined standards.

53. **Combination Products.** If you've invented a "combination product"—that is, a product with two inventions that don't really groove together, like a stapler with a built-in beverage cup holder, people won't be beating a path to your door. On the other hand, the clock-radio was just the ticket.

54. **Entrenched Competition.** Despite its overwhelming advantages, Edison had a terrible time promoting his light bulb because the gas companies fought him bitterly.

55. **Instant Anachronism.** A clever inventor in Oakland, California, invented a wonderful dictionary indexing device which made it much faster to look up any word. However, he was unable to sell it to any dictionary publisher because the dictionary is being replaced by computerized devices. His clever invention was an "instant anachronism."

Now that you have a grasp of the factors that can influence the commercial viability of an invention, complete Form 4-1 by assigning a weight to each listed factor, either positive or negative. Also list and assign weights to any other factors you can think of which I've omitted. Then compute the sum of your factors and determine the difference to come up with a rough idea of a net value for your invention. I suggest that you continue to pursue inventions with net values of 50 and up, that you direct your efforts elsewhere if your invention has a net value of less than 0, and that you make further critical evaluation of inventions with net values between 0 and 50.

The list has many other valuable uses:

- Using the list may cause you to focus on one or more drawbacks that are serious enough to kill your invention outright.
- The list can be used to provide a way of comparing two different inventions for relative value so that you'll know which to concentrate more effort on.

You now should extract all factors on the list of Form 4-1 that have any value other than 0 and write these factors and their weights on Form 4-2, the Positive and Negative Factors Summary Sheet. (A copy is in Appendix 7.) This sheet, when completed, will provide you with a concise summary of the advantages and disadvantages of your invention. You can use it in at least four valuable ways:

1. To provide you with a capsule summary of your invention for commercial evaluation purposes (this chapter);

2. To help you prepare the "selling" parts of your patent application (see Chapter 8);

3. To help you to sell or license your invention to a manufacturer (see Chapter 11); and

4. To help you to get the PTO to grant you a patent (see Chapter 13).

Don't hesitate to update or redo Forms 4-1 and 4-2 if more information comes to mind.

E. Check Your Marketability Conclusions Using the Techniques of Consultation and Research

Once you reach some tentative conclusions about the commercial viability of your invention, it's time to get a reality check.

1. How to Go About It

If your evaluation of the above positive and negative factors affecting the marketability of your invention gives the positive side the edge, I recommend that you extend your investigation by doing some consultation and research. If you continue to get positive signs, extend your search still further until you've learned all you can about the field of your invention. This knowledge will also be of great benefit when you make your patentability search, prepare your application, market your invention, and deal with the PTO.

In Section 2, below, I suggest a number of procedures to use when you're disclosing your ideas to others so that they won't be stolen and so their trade secret (TS) status will be maintained. Here, I simply warn you at the outset that you shouldn't disclose ideas and information without utilizing appropriate safeguards; otherwise you may lose them to others.

The areas of consultation and research which you should investigate include asking both nonprofessionals and experts in the particular field for an opinion, and researching the relevant literature. As you do this, keep in mind and ask about all of the positive and negative factors listed above. Your consultation efforts and research will almost surely give you more information useful in assessing many of them. If so, again don't hesitate to redo your Forms 4-1 and 4-2.

As indicated, nonprofessionals can often be an excellent source of information and advice, especially if your invention is a consumer item that they are likely to have an opportunity to purchase if it's ever mass-produced. Consult your lay friends and associates, that is, those who have no special expertise in the field in which you are interested, but whose opinion you trust and feel will be objective. Often you may find it valuable *not* to tell them that you are the inventor so you'll get a more objective evaluation. You may also want to inquire as to what price they'd be willing to pay. It's especially helpful if you've built a working model (see Section F, below) so you can show it to them and ask if they'd buy it and for what price.

Experts to be consulted in the particular field of your invention include any and all of the following who can supply you with relevant feedback:

- salespeople and buyers in stores that sell devices similar to yours;
- engineers, managers, or technicians in companies in the field of your invention;
- scholars, educators, or professors who do research in the area of your invention; and
- friends who are "in the business."

Naturally you may not know all of these experts. Getting to them will require the creative use of the contacts you do have so as to arrange the proper introductions. Once you do, however, most people will be flattered that you've asked for their advice and pleased to help you.

After you show your invention—preferably a working model—note the person's initial reaction. If you hear a "Well, I'll be damned!" or "Why didn't I think of that!," you know you're on the right track.

For your literature search, I suggest that you start by locating a research librarian who's familiar with the area of your concern. Large technical and business libraries and those associated with major universities are obvious places to start. The library literature that you should investigate includes product directories, how-to-do-it books, catalogs, general reference books, and patents if they are available. (See Chapter 6.)

Remember that the purpose of the literature search isn't to determine whether your invention is new or patentable, but rather to give you additional background in the field so you can evaluate the positive and negative factors listed above. However, while you're doing your literature search, you may find that your invention was publicly known before you invented it. This is especially likely to occur if you search the patent literature. If so, you'll either have to drop the invention, since you'll know you aren't the first inventor, or try to make a new invention by improving your first effort. You'll be surprised how much better a feel you'll have for your invention once you've done some research and become familiar with the field.

If you work for or have access to a large company, visit its purchasing department and ask for permission to look through its product catalogs. Most companies have an extensive library of such catalogs and you'll often find much relevant and valuable information there that you won't find in even the biggest and best public libraries.

This search isn't the equivalent of the "patent search" that occurs before you apply for your patent. Covered in the next chapter is the more formal patent search, which obviously will provide you with considerably more background in the area of your invention.

2. Precautions to Take During Consultation

If you do show your invention to others or discuss it with them to any extent, a degree of care is mandatory to preserve the trade secret status of your invention and to prevent theft of your ideas, or to prove it in case it occurs. (See Chapter 1, Section Q.) Remember that any of the agreements discussed below are only as good as the parties who have signed them. Thus you shouldn't disclose your invention to anyone you don't trust. Suing someone for breaching a non-disclosure agreement is no substitute for picking a trustworthy person in the first place.

Here are some good alternatives that can be used to protect your invention from being misappropriated by others:

- Have disclosees sign a receipt or log book entry indicating that they have seen your invention. The log book entry can be simply a page in your inventor's notebook that says at the top, "The undersigned have seen and understood Tom Brown's confidential [name of invention] as described on pages ___ of this book, on the dates indicated." You may also want to add a "Comments" column to your book to indicate that you value their opinion. Doing this also makes it easier to ask your consultants to sign your receipt page or log notebook.

• Ask those to whom you show your invention to sign and date your disclosure as witnesses. Witnesses can hardly ever claim that they invented independently of you if they're on record as having witnessed your invention. If there are more than two or three witnesses, however, this method won't work as there won't be room in your book for more.

• Get your consultants to sign the Proprietary Materials Agreement (Form 3-1). However, it may be difficult for you to ask someone who's doing you a favor to sign this agreement.

• Although inferior to the other devices listed above, send a confirming or thank-you letter before and/or after your consultation so you'll have written, uncontradicted records that you showed your invention to the person on a specific date and that you asked it to be kept confidential. A confirmatory after-the-fact letter can simply say, "Thanks very much for looking at my [name of invention] at your office last Wednesday, July 3. This letter is to confirm that you agreed that the details of my [name of invention] should be maintained in strictest confidence. Thanks for your cooperation. Sincerely, [your name]." Photocopy any such letter and keep a copy for your records.

While care in disclosing your invention is necessary to prevent loss of its trade secret status and theft, don't go overboard with precautions. Many new inventors get such a severe case of "inventor's paranoia" that they're afraid to disclose their brainchild to anyone, or they're willing to disclose it only with such stringent safeguards that no one will want to look at it! In practice, most stolen inventions are taken only after they're out on the market and proven successful. This is because thieves are most interested in sure things. While I don't totally approve, highly successful inventor Paul Brown usually shows his inventions freely: he says, "Let them steal it—they don't know how much work they're in for!"

F.   Now's the Time to Build and Test It (If Possible)

Now that you have completed the conceptual process of your invention, it's time to build and test a working model or engage someone who will do it for you for a fee.

1.   Why Do It?

As stated under #36 in Section D, above, if you haven't already done so, it's very desirable to build and test a working model (prototype) of your invention, if at all possible. The reasons: a working model will give you something real to show your marketing consultants, plus valuable information about operability, cost, technical problems, and most of the other factors on the positive and negative factors list. If it's impractical to build a working model, often a non-working model, or scale model, will give you almost as much valuable data. As stated, don't forget to fill out another copy of Form 3-2 (Invention Disclosure) after you build and test it, in order to have a legal record of your building and testing.

2.   If You Use a Model Maker, Use a Consultant's Agreement

If you can't build and test it yourself, many model makers, engineers, technicians, and teachers are available who will be delighted to do the job for you for a fee, or for a percentage of the action. If you do use a model maker (consultant), you should take precautions to protect the confidentiality and proprietary status of your invention. There's no substitute for checking out your consultant carefully by asking for references (assuming you don't already know the consultant by reputation or referral).

In addition, have your consultant sign a copy of the Consultant's Work Agreement (Form 4-3 in Appendix 7). Note that this Agreement includes fill-in blanks to describe the names and addresses of the inventor and consultant, the name of the project or invention (such as "New Sweater-Drying Form"), detailed description of the work to be done (such as "build a wire-frame, plastic-covered, sweater-drying collapsible form in accordance with plans in attached Exhibit A—finished form to operate smoothly and collapse to 14" x 23" x 2" (or less) size"), and manner of payment (usually ⅓ at start, ⅓ upon construction, and ⅓ on acceptance by you, the Contractor) and which state's law should govern (pick the state where you reside if the Consultant is out-of-state).

Note that I've provided (see paragraph 7) that any changes in the work to be performed or payment to be made shall be in writing. I've done this because I've been involved in many disputes where the consultant does additional or more difficult work and wants more money, but the parties' memories differ as to what changes were agreed to, if any.

The Agreement also requires the Consultant to perform in a timely manner or you can void the Agreement and pay only 50%, or have the Consultant pay an agreed-upon penalty for every day he or she is delinquent.

3. What If the Consultant Invents?

Since many consultants are quite clever, they often come up with patentable improvements, ramifications, or even better versions of the basic invention which they're hired to build, test, or develop. This naturally brings up the issue of who will own and be able to use the consultant's inventions. Having been involved in many disputes in this area, I know that an ounce of prevention—that is, a prior stipulation as to who will own any inventions the Consultant makes—can prevent many misunderstandings, arguments, and even lawsuits later on.

With this end in mind, I've written the agreement to require the Consultant to disclose all innovations made to you, to sign any patent applications which you choose to file on the Consultant's inventions, and also to assign such inventions to you. Note also that the inventions that belong to you (the Contractor) are those that arise out of the Consultant's work under the agreement, even if conceived on the Consultant's own time. This is a customary clause in employment agreements (see Chapter 16) and is provided so that the Consultant won't be able to claim that a valuable invention made under the agreement isn't yours because it was made on the Consultant's time. Generally the Consultant will be a sole inventor (who should be the only one named in the patent application if the Consultant's invention can exist independently of yours), and a joint inventor with you if the invention is closely related to or improves on yours. (More on inventorship in Chapter 10, Section F.) This is because all of the true inventor(s) must be named as inventor(s) in all patent applications. I provide an assign-ment form and a Joint Owners' Agreement in Appendix 7. (See Chapter 16.)

G. Summary

Once you've commercially evaluated your invention—that is, garnered all your input and filled out your evaluation and summary sheets with the positive and negative factors—you're in a better position to decide whether or not to go ahead. If you decide to, your next step is to decide whether the invention will qualify for a patent under the patent laws. To do this, you should first learn the basic four legal requirements for getting a patent. (See Chapter 5.) Then, if it meets the first two of these requirements, make a formal patent search (see Chapter 6) to determine if it's sufficiently novel to satisfy the other two requirements.

If, on the other hand, your commercial evaluation leaves you uncertain, though you feel there's good potential, wait a while before proceeding. The passage of time may give you a new perspective that can make your decision easier. If after a couple of weeks you still can't make up your mind, it's probably best to proceed to the next step (the determination of patentability, including a search). If this determination discloses that your invention is already known or otherwise unpatentable, that's the end of the road. But if it shows that you have a patentable invention, you should probably attempt to patent and market it rather than let a potentially valuable and profitable idea die without being given its day in the sun. ■

CHAPTER

5

What Is Patentable?

INVENTOR'S COMMANDMENT #6

One-Year Rule: Treat the "one-year rule" as holy. You must file your regular patent application or Provisional Patent Application within one year of the date on which you first publish, commercially use, sell, or offer your invention, or any product that embodies it, for sale. If you wish to preserve your foreign rights and prevent theft of your creation, file your patent application before you publish details of or sell your creation.

INVENTOR'S COMMANDMENT #7

To evaluate or argue the patentability of any invention, use a two-step process: a) First determine what novelty the invention has over the closest prior-art reference(s). Novelty can be a new physical (hardware) feature, a new combination of two separate old features, or a new use of an old feature; and b) Then determine if the novelty produces any new and unexpected results or otherwise indicates unobviousness.

Here we deal with the specific subject of what's legally patentable and what's not. Over many decades, both Congress and the courts have hammered out a series of laws and accompanying rules of interpretation that the PTO and the courts (and hence you) must use to separate the patentable wheat from the unpatentable chaff. All of these laws and rules are introduced in this chapter and then referred to repeatedly in later chapters where I take you through the ins and outs of obtaining a patent.

Because an understanding of the material in this chapter is crucial to the rest of the book and to an understanding of patents in general, I urge you to relax and read it carefully. If later you become confused by terminology or about the criteria for determining the patentability of an invention, return for a refresher.

A. Patentability Compared to Commercial Viability

If you assessed the commercial potential of your invention, as suggested in Chapter 4, and your invention received a passing grade, your next question probably is, "Can I get a patent on it?" The answer to this question can be crucial, since you're likely to have a difficult time commercially exploiting an invention that isn't patentable, despite its commercial feasibility. Although you may be able to realize value from an invention by selling it to a manufacturer as a trade secret (a difficult sale to make!), or by selling it yourself and using a clever trademark, or (in some cases) by relying on copyright protection and unfair competition laws (as explained in Chapter 1), such approaches are usually inferior to the broad offensive rights that a patent offers. Concisely put, if your invention fails to pass the tests of this chapter, reconsider its commercial prospects and whether other areas of intellectual property will provide adequate offensive rights in the absence of a patent.

B. Legal Requirements for Getting a Utility Patent

As you can see from Fig. 5A, the legal requirements for getting a utility patent can be represented by a mountain having four upward sections, each of which represents a separate test that every invention must pass to be awarded the patent. The PTO is required by statute to examine every utility patent application to be sure it passes each of these tests. If it does, the PTO must award the inventor(s) a patent.

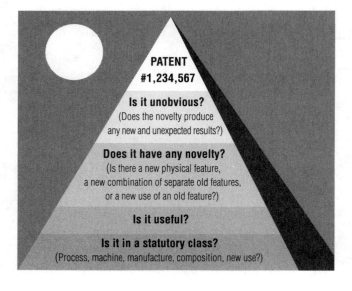

**Fig. 5A—Patentability Mountain:
The Four Legal Requirements for Getting a Utility Patent**

DESIGN AND PLANT PATENTS

Design patent applications must cover a new, original, and ornamental design for an article of manufacture and are examined in the same way and must pass the same unobviousness test as utility patent applications, except that the "better functioning" tests that are used to evaluate unobviousness (see Section F, below) are not used, since only the aesthetics of a design invention are relevant.

Plant patent applications are subject to the same legal requirements as utility patent applications, except that the statutory class requirement (first test) is obviously not relevant: plants provide their own statutory class. Since plant patents are relatively rare and are of very specialized interest, I won't go into detail except to set forth the additional legal requirements for getting one. They are: (1) the plant must be asexually reproduced; and (2) the plant must be a new variety. These may include cultivated sports, mutants, hybrids, and newly found seedlings, but should not be a tuber, propagated plant, bacterium, or a plant found in an uncultivated state.

The four requirements and the pertinent respective statutes are:

1. **Statutory Class:** Does the invention fit into one of five classes established by Congress? (35 USC 101.) Or put concretely, can it reasonably be called a:
   • process (method)
   • machine
   • notice of manufacture
   • composition, or
   • a "new use" of one of the first four.
2. **Utility:** Can the invention properly be regarded as a useful one (or ornamental in the case of designs)? (35 USC 101.)
3. **Novelty:** Can the invention properly be regarded as novel—that is, does it have an aspect that is different in any way from all previous inventions and knowledge (that is, the relevant prior art)? (35 USC 102.)
4. **Unobviousness:** Can the invention be properly regarded as unobvious from the standpoint of someone who has ordinary skill in the specific technology involved in the invention—that is, does it provide one or more new and unexpected results? (When dealing with designs, the question becomes: Are the novel features of the design unobvious in an ornamental or aesthetic sense?) (35 USC 103.)

As Fig. 5A shows, the first three tests are represented by relatively short steps. The last one, unobviousness, is relatively high. This is a real-life reflection of what commonly happens to patent applications before the PTO (or to patents when they're challenged in court). In other words, most inventions are found to (1) fit within at least one statutory class, (2) have utility (or ornamentality for designs), and (3) possess novelty. However, most of the patent applications that fail to reach the patent summit (almost half of all patent applications that are filed) are rejected because the PTO believes the invention is obvious.

THE PATENT LAWS

Congress derives its power to make the patent statutes from the U.S. Constitution (Art. 1, Sec. 8). The patent statutes passed by Congress can be found in Title 35 of the United States Code (35 USC). Patent statutes are typically referred to by the section of the USC they are put into. So, the statute that creates the five statutory patent clauses is referred to as 35 USC 101. The statutes, in turn, authorize the PTO to issue its Rules of Practice (which are relatively broad, and are termed in the law 37 CFR [Code of Federal Regulations] 1.1, etc.), and its Manual of Patent Examining Procedure (MPEP is relatively specific)—see Appendix 2, Books of Use and Interest. Fig. 5B illustrates the relationship between these authorities. The size of each authority varies from one sentence in the Constitution to about 600,000 words in the MPEP.

Fig. 5B—Patent Authorities

Let's now look at each of these requirements in more detail.

C. Requirement #1: The Statutory Classes

To be patentable, your invention must fall into one of the five statutory classes. If it does, it's "within a statutory class or category." That is, it's one of the five types of subject matter on which the law authorizes the PTO to grant a patent, assuming the other requirements for a patent are met.

Fortunately, the statutory categories established by the patent laws, although only five, are very comprehensive. Accordingly, you'll usually be able to squeeze most inventions into at least one of them. In many instances an invention will fit into more than one category, since they overlap to some extent. This isn't a problem, since you don't have to specify the one to which your invention belongs when you file your patent application. But you should be fairly sure it fits into at least one category. Otherwise, the PTO may reject it under Section 101 as "nonstatutory subject matter."

Let's discuss the five statutory classes in more detail:

1. Processes, Including Software

Sometimes termed "methods," processes are ways of doing or making things that involve more than purely mental manipulations. Processes always have one or more steps, each of which expresses some activity and manipulates or treats some physical thing.

a. Conventional Processes

Examples of conventional processes are heat treatments, chemical reactions for making or changing something, and ways of making products or chemicals. To give you an example of an extreme process patent, I represented one side in a patent lawsuit that involved a patent on a process of attaching a hairpiece to a bald person's scalp by putting suture anchors in the scalp and sewing the piece to the suture anchors. However, although surgical operations can still be patented, it no longer makes sense to do so since new legislation exempts medical practitioners from infringing any patent on a medical procedure per se.

b. Software Processes

Since most software-related inventions are claimed as processes, I'll discuss them here. However, be aware that software inventions can also be claimed as machines. As indicated in Chapter 1, computer software and algorithms can't be patented per se. (Software is a set of instructions that includes an algorithm and that controls a computer. An algorithm is a step-by-step problem-solving procedure.) However if the software or algorithm affects some hardware or process, it falls within a statutory class as a machine or a process. If it merely manipulates numbers or solves an algorithm, then the PTO will not consider it within a statutory class. For example, if the process analyzes EKG, spectrographic, seismic, or data bit signals, controls a milling machine, creates images on a computer screen, formats the printing of mathematical formulae, or recognizes patterns or voices, then it is considered to control hardware or a process and is statutory subject matter. However, if the process merely crunches numbers, generates a curve or calculates distances, then it is considered to be non-statutory. Some writers have stated that the issue is human control: if humans have the power to control the process or operation or make it stop, then it is statutory subject matter. However if the process or operation will occur or be valid no matter what humans can do, then it will be considered non-statutory.

If you have a software-related invention, here are some questions you can ask to help decide whether it is statutory or not (affirmative answers indicate your process is in a statutory class):

- Do the steps do something, independent of how they are implemented?
- Does the process apply a law of nature to a known structure or process?
- If the algorithm is removed, is there a viable (statutory) process left?
- Does the process do more than perform a numerical calculation or solve a mathematical algorithm?
- Are other uses of the algorithm possible?
- Is the process more than a post-solution display of an algorithm?
- Did you actually invent more than just an algorithm?
- Is a hardware (a machine or apparatus) involved?
- Does the process do more than manipulate abstract ideas?

For a more detailed discussion of patents on software-related inventions, see *Software Development: A Legal Guide*, by Stephen Fishman, Nolo Press.

If all of this seems unclear, one writer, Gregory A. Stobbs, Esq., of Harness, Dickey & Pierce, Birmingham, Michigan, has postulated that a common thread—the matter of human control—exists in all software inventions that the court or the PTO determines to be statutory subject matter (SSM). If humans have the ability to control the relationship of the algorithmic steps, then the software will be held to be SSM, but if humans have no ability to control the relationship, then it will not be held to be SSM. For example, an algorithm for determining π to 50 decimal places would be held to be non-SSM, since humans have no ability to control the relationships involved—they exist no matter what humans do. However, the main patent court—the CAFC—determined that an algorithm for making a diagonal line on a monitor smoother is SSM, probably because a human could make the line appear or disappear. *(In re Alappat.)* Also, the CAFC has held *(In re Lowry)* that a general purpose computer data structure that organizes information into different categories (selected from an infinite number of categories) is SSM, no doubt because humans can control the selection. On the other hand, the court held *(In re Trovato)* that a determination of the least costly route from geographical point A to point B by assigning a cost to each leg of every possible route and trying all possible combinations is not SSM because the least costly route is always the sum of the cheapest segments—humans have no power to change this relationship. Similarly, in *In re Warmerdam*, the court held that the use of circles aligned along an axis of an object to model the space taken by the object is non-SSM because Warmerdam made no more than an abstract observation—that an object always fits within a series of boundaries aligned along its axis—which all humans are powerless to change. So if you have an invention involving an algorithm, ask if humans can control the relationship involved. If so, you're probably in a statutory class, provided you claim it properly. The PTO has set forth the test for determining whether software is Statutory Subject Matter, see Fig. 5C below, and for claims, see Chapter 9.

The PTO has published guidelines (*Official Gazette* of 1996 Mar 26) for examiners to use in determining whether a claim to a software-related invention is SSM or not. These guidelines are summarized in the flowchart of Fig 5C. The chart is largely self-explanatory; however, it uses a different conceptual scheme to analyze the patentability of software than that employed by Gregory Stobbs. Also, the meanings of certain terms may not be apparent and therefore are defined as follows:

"**functional descriptive material (a data structure per se)**" is a compilation of data that performs a function, such as a set of instructions for a milling machine;

"**a computer program per se**" is the listing of a software program not inherently associated with any hardware, such as a tax return preparation program;

"**non-functional descriptive material per se**" is pure data, such as a telephone directory or the score of an opera;

"**a natural phenomenon**" is a fact or occurrence in nature, such as the force experienced by a current-carrying electrical conductor placed in a magnetic field;

"**independent physical acts, i.e., post-computer activity**" are acts performed under computer control, such as machining metal or playing music by a speaker;

"**the collection of data representing physical objects or activities (pre-computer activity) followed by the analysis and manipulation of such data to achieve a practical application**" can be exemplified by an electrocardiograph which receives and analyzes electrical signals from a human heart to indicate any heart damage;

"**merely manipulate an abstract idea or solve a purely mathematical problem without any limitation to a practical application**" can be exemplified by a program which analyzes statements using fuzzy logic to provide a conclusion, or which calculates the value of π. But a program which analyzes conflicting witness statements to determine guilt or innocence or calculates the required tire size of a truck given its weight, size, and other parameters would qualify for a patent because each has a practical application.

2. Machines

Machines are devices or things used for accomplishing a task. Like processes, they usually involve some activity or motion that's performed by working parts, but in machines the emphasis is on the parts or hardware, rather than the activity per se. Put differently, while a process involves the actual steps of manipulation of an item or workpiece (the machine that does the manipulation is of secondary import), a machine is the thing that does the manipulating and the steps or manner of its operation, and the process itself, or material worked upon, are of lesser import.

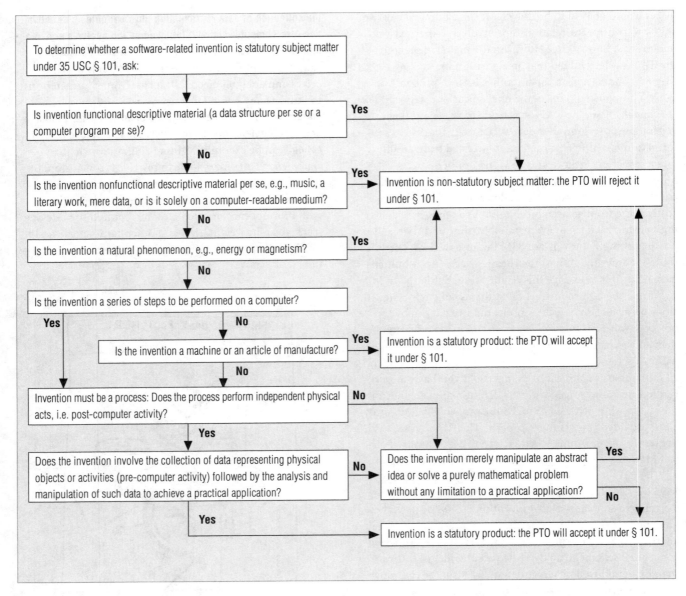

Fig. 5C—Flowchart to Determine Whether a Software-Based Invention Is Statutory Subject Matter

a. Conventional Machines

Examples of machines are cigarette lighters, robots, sewage treatment plants, clocks, all electronic circuits, automobiles, boats, rockets, telephones, TVs, computers, VCRs, disk drives, printers, lasers, and photocopiers. Many inventions can be claimed as a process and/or as a machine. For instance, an electric circuit or a weaving machine can be claimed in terms of its actual hardware and/or as a process for manipulating an electrical signal or weaving fabrics.

b. Software Machines

As stated in the previous section ("1. Processes, Including Software"), while most software inventions are claimed and regarded as processes, they can usually also be claimed and regarded as machines. For example, a system for controlling a milling machine according to certain measured parameters of an object can be claimed and regarded either as a process or a machine. As a process the system would be regarded and claimed as follows: (a) measuring an object to obtain a set of measurements, and (b) controlling a milling machine according to the set of measurements. As a machine the system would be regarded and claimed as follows: (a) means [or an apparatus] for measuring an object to obtain a set of measurements, and (b) means [or an apparatus] for adjusting a milling machine according to the set of measurements.

Note that the first step or "means" (the mensuration or the means for measuring) can be regarded as either an action or as the hardware for performing the action. This applies equally to the second step. Sometimes a software invention can't be regarded as a machine; for example, consider the software inventions defined by the two sample claims in Ch. 9, Sec. G13. The two inventions relate exclusively to process-type inventions and are actually so close to being all mental steps as to be non-SSM.

On the other hand, virtually every machine-type software invention can also be regarded as a process since each part of a "software" machine always performs some action or step. Insofar as possible, both types of claims can and should usually be provided in a single patent application. As stated in the previous paragraph, it's not important which category (process or machine) you subsume your software invention under, so long as you can subsume it under at least one of them.

As I've said, there are no clear lines between the five statutory classes. The important thing to realize is that it doesn't matter as long as your invention fits into at least one of them. Put differently, you needn't be able to tell a machine from a process to qualify for a patent.

3. Manufactures

Manufactures, sometimes termed "articles of manufacture," are items that have been made by human hands or by machines. This excludes naturally occurring things, like rocks, gold, shrimp, and wood, or slightly modified naturally occurring things, like a shrimp with its head and vein removed. But if you discover a new and unobvious use for a naturally occurring thing, such as a way to use the molecules in a piece of gold as part of a computer memory, you can patent the invention as a new use (see below), or as a machine (the gold with the necessary hardware to make it function as a memory).

Manufactures are relatively simple things that don't have working or moving parts as prime features. Clearly, you will see some overlap between the machine and the manufacture categories. Many devices, such as mechanical pencils, cigarette lighters, and electronic circuits can be classified as either. Examples of manufactures are erasers, desks, houses, wires, tires, books, cloth, chairs, containers, transistors, dolls, hairpieces, ladders, envelopes, buildings, floppy disks, knives, hand tools, and boxes. I was recently involved with a patent on a most unusual article—a musical dildo.

4. Compositions of Matter

Compositions of matter are items such as chemical compositions, conglomerates, aggregates, or other chemically significant substances that are usually supplied in bulk (solid or particulate), liquid, or gaseous form. Examples are road-building compositions, all chemicals, gasoline, fuel gas, glue, paper, soap, drugs, microbes, animals (nonhuman), food additives, and plastics.

Although, as stated, naturally occurring things such as wood and rocks can't be patented, purified forms of naturally occurring things, such as medicinals extracted from herbs, can be. One inventor even obtained a composition of matter patent on a new element he discovered. And recently, genetically altered plants, microbes, and nonhuman animals have been allowed under this category. Compositions are usually homogeneous chemical compositions or aggregates whose chemical natures are of primary importance and whose shapes are of secondary import, while manufactures are items whose physical shapes are significant, but whose chemical compositions are of lesser import.

5. New Uses of Any of the Above

A new-use invention is actually a new and unobvious process or method for using an old and known invention, whether it be an old and known process, composition, machine, or article. The inventive act here isn't the creation of a new thing or process per se, but the discovery of a new use for something that in itself is old.

If you discover a new and unobvious (unrelated) use of any old invention or thing, you can get a patent on your discovery. For example, suppose you discover that your venetian-blind cleaner can also be used as a seed planter. You obviously can't get a patent on the physical hardware that constitutes the venetian-blind cleaner, since you didn't invent it—someone already patented, invented, and/or designed it first—but you can get a patent on the specific new use (seed planting) of the hardware you've invented. In another example, one inventor obtained a patent on a new use for aspirin: feeding it to swine to increase their rate of growth.

New-use inventions are relatively rare and technically are a form of, and must be claimed as, a process. (35 USC 100(b).) However, most patent experts treat them as a distinct category. See Chapter 9 for a discussion of patent claims.

EXAMPLES OF INVENTIONS THAT DON'T FIT WITHIN A STATUTORY CLASS

- Processes performed solely with one's mind (such as a method of meditation or a method of speed-reading).
- Naturally occurring phenomena and articles, even if modified somewhat.
- Laws of nature, including abstract scientific or mathematical principles. (John Napier's invention of logarithms in 1614 was immensely innovative and valuable, but it would never get past the bottom level of the patentability mountain.)
- An arrangement of printed matter without some accompanying instrumentality. Printed matter per se isn't patentable, but a printed label on a mattress telling how to turn it to ensure even wear, or dictionary index tabs that guide you to the desired word more rapidly, have been patented as articles of manufacture.
- Methods of doing business that do not manipulate hardware in some unique way. Examples are sales plans, ad schemes, ideas for a quiz show, and a method of teaching firewalking. However, securities trading systems, credit accounting systems, etc., involving account and file postings, have been held patentable.
- Computer programs per se, naked computer instructions, or algorithms. See the flowchart of Fig. 5C showing the tests which help determine whether a computer program fits within a statutory class. Also see Chapter 9, Section G13, where I describe how any software or algorithm can be claimed to fit in a statutory class by relating it to physical elements or process steps.
- Ideas per se. Thoughts or goals not expressed in concrete form or usage are obviously not assignable to any of the five categories above. If you have an idea, you must show how it can be made and used in tangible form so as to be useful in the real world, even if only on paper, before the PTO will accept it.

D. Requirement #2: Utility

To be patentable your invention must be useful. Problems are seldom encountered with the literal utility requirement; *any* usefulness will suffice, provided the usefulness is functional, and not aesthetic. But remember, in Chapter 4, I recommend that the usefulness of your invention be rela-

tively great in order to pass the "commercial viability" test. It's hard for me to think of an invention that couldn't be used for some purpose. However, utility is occasionally an issue in the chemical area when an inventor tries to patent a new chemical for which a use hasn't yet been found but for which its inventor will likely find a use later. If the inventor can't state (and prove, if challenged) a realistic use, the PTO won't grant a patent on the chemical. A chemical intermediate that can be used to produce another useful chemical is itself regarded as useful. Software-based inventions almost always inherently satisfy the utility requirement since virtually all software has a utilitarian function, even if used to create aesthetic designs on an idle monitor, compute the decimal value of π, or evaluate golf scores. Why would a programmer spend tens or hundreds of hours writing code if not for a useful purpose? The main problem with software-based inventions is that they may not fall (or may not be claimed in a way so that they fall) into a statutory class, as noted in the previous section. (Also see Chapter 9.) Nonetheless, a software invention should be tested for utility just like any other invention just in case it falls into one of the "legally not useful" categories listed below.

Notwithstanding the fact that virtually all inventions are useful in the literal sense of the word, some types of inventions are deemed "not useful" as a matter of law, and patents on them are accordingly denied by the PTO. Let's look at this more closely.

1. Unsafe New Drugs

The PTO won't grant a patent on any new drug unless the applicant can show that not only is it useful in treating some condition, but also that it's relatively safe for its intended purpose. Put another way, the PTO considers an unsafe drug useless. Most drug patent applications won't be allowed unless the Food and Drug Administration (FDA) has approved tests of the drug for efficacy and safety, but drugs that are generally recognized as safe, or are in a "safe" chemical category with known safe drugs, don't need prior FDA approval to be patentable.

2. Whimsical Inventions

Occasionally, the PTO will reject an application for a patent when it finds the invention to be totally whimsical, even though "useful" in some bizarre sense. Nevertheless, in 1937 the PTO issued a patent on a rear windshield (with tail-operated wiper) for a horse (patent 2,079,053). They regarded this as having utility as an amusement or gag.

Most patent attorneys have collections of humorous patents. I could easily fill the rest of this book with my collection, but I'll restrain myself and briefly describe just a few.

- a male chastity device (patent 587,994—1897);
- a figure-eight-shaped device to hold your big toes together to prevent sunburned inner thighs (patent 3,712,271—1973);
- dentures with individual teeth shaped like the wearer's head (patent 3,049,804—1962); and
- a dress hanger with breasts (design patent D226,943—1973).

Also, even though the PTO issued patent 2,632,266 in 1953 for a fur-encircled keyhole, the censor wouldn't let me show this on a TV show.

3. Inventions Useful Only for Illegal Purposes

An important requirement for obtaining a patent, which Congress hasn't mentioned, but which the PTO and courts have brought in on their own initiative (by stretching the definition of "useful"), is legality. For example, inventions useful solely for illegal purposes, such as disabling burglar alarms, safecracking, copying currency, and defrauding the public, might be incredibly useful to some elements in our society, but the PTO won't issue patents on them. However, most inventions in this category can be described or claimed in a "legal" way. For example, a police radar detector would qualify for a patent if it's described as a tester to see if a radar is working or as a device for reminding drivers to watch their speed.

4. Immoral Inventions

In the past, the PTO has—again on its own initiative—included morality in its requirements. But, in recent years, with increased sexual liberality, the requirement is now virtually nonexistent. Thus the PTO now regularly issues patents on sexual aids, gags, and stimulants.

5. Non-Operable Inventions, Including Perpetual Motion Machines

Another facet of the useful requirement is operability. The invention must appear to the PTO to be workable before they will allow it. Thus, if your invention is a perpetual-motion machine, or a metaphysical-energy converter, or, more realistically, a very esoteric invention that looks technically questionable (it looks like it just plain won't work or violates some well-accepted physical law), your examiner will reject it as lacking utility because of inoperability. In this case you would either have to produce a logical, technical argument refuting the examiner's reasons (you can include affidavits or declarations of witnesses and experts and test results), or bring the invention in for a demonstration to prove its operability.

Operability is rarely questioned, since most patent applications cover inventions that employ known principles or hardware and will obviously work as described. If the examiner questions operability, however, you have the burden of proof. And note that all patent examiners have technical degrees (some even have Ph.D.'s), so expect a very stringent test if the operability of your invention is ever questioned.

Despite the foregoing, the PTO occasionally issues a patent on what appears to be a perpetual-motion-like machine, as they did in 1979 (patent 4,151,431). This raises an important point. The fact that a patent is granted doesn't mean that the underlying invention will work. It only means that the invention appears to work on paper (or that the PTO can't figure out why it won't work).

The PTO, however, has recently become more careful about perpetual-energy or perpetual-motion machines, as you may have noted from a recently publicized case where it denied an inventor a patent on an energy machine. The inventor took the case to the courts, but lost after the National Bureau of Standards, acting as a court expert, found the machine didn't have an efficiency of over 100%.

It's a common misconception that the PTO won't "accept" patent applications on perpetual-motion machines: the PTO will accept the application for filing (see Chapter 13), since filing and docketing are clerical functions. However, the examiner (a degreed professional) will almost certainly reject it later as inoperative (giving reasons) after a formal examination.

6. Nuclear Weapons

The invention must not be a nuclear weapon; such inventions aren't patentable because of a special statute. However, if you've invented a doomsday machine, don't be discouraged: you can be rewarded directly by making an application with the DOE (Department of Energy), formerly the Atomic Energy Commission.

7. Theoretical Phenomena

Theoretical phenomena per se, such as the phenomenon of superconductivity or the transistor effect, aren't patentable. You must describe and claim (see Chapter 9) a practical, realistic, hardware-based version of your invention for the PTO to consider it useful.

8. Aesthetic Purpose

If the invention's sole purpose or "function" is aesthetic, the PTO will reject it as lacking utility; such inventions should usually be the subject of a design patent application. A beautiful vase of unique design, a computer case whose unique shape does not make the computer operate better, and a computer program for producing a low-brightness design on an idle computer monitor, where the only novelty is the aesthetic uniqueness of the design, are examples of inventions which the law considers to lack statutory utility. However, if the design of the vase made it easier and safer to lift, if the shape of the computer case made it cheaper to manufacture, or if the computer program produced, on an idle computer monitor, a unique design showing a low-brightness aesthetic conversion of the last file worked on in order to remind the user of that file, then statutory utility would be present.

E. Requirement #3: Novelty

Now let's look at the novelty requirement of a patent. Like "unobviousness" (discussed in Section F), this requirement is often misunderstood.

1. Prior Art

Your invention must be novel in order to qualify for a patent. In order for your invention to meet this novelty test it must differ physically in some way from all prior developments that are available to the public anywhere in the world. In the realm of patent law, these prior developments and concepts are collectively referred to as "prior art." Accordingly, before I tell you how to determine whether your invention is novel, it's vital to understand what your invention must differ from—that is, what "prior art" is.

a. What Is Prior Art?

According to Section 102 of the patent laws, the term "prior art" means generally the state of knowledge existing or publicly available either before the date of your invention or more than one year prior to your earliest patent application date.

b. Date of Your Invention

Clearly, in order to decide what prior art is with respect to any given invention, it's first necessary to determine the "date of your invention." Most inventors think it's the date on which one files a patent application. While this date is important, and you can always use it if you have nothing better, you can usually go back earlier than your filing date if you can prove the date you conceived of the invention or the date you built and tested it. (See Chapter 3.) That is, your date of invention is the earliest of:

- the date you filed your patent application (provisional or regular);

- the date you can prove you built and tested your invention in the U.S. or a country that is a member of NAFTA or the WTO (World Trade Organization). Most industrial countries are members. (35 USC § 104); or
- the date you can prove you conceived of your invention in a NAFTA or WTO country, provided you can also prove you were diligent thereafter in building and testing it or filing a patent application on it.

So, from now on, when I refer to "your earliest provable date of invention," this will mean the earliest of the above three dates (filing, building and testing, or conception accompanied by diligence) that you can prove.

REDUCTION TO PRACTICE

In the law, the building and testing of an invention is called a "reduction to practice." The filing of a patent application, while not an actual reduction to practice, is termed a "constructive" reduction to practice because the law will construe it in the same way it does an actual reduction to practice. As discussed in Chapter 3, Section I, the filing of a valid Provisional Patent Application (PPA) also qualifies as a constructive reduction to practice.

The kinds of proof that the PTO and the courts typically rely on are the witnessed records of the type I described in Chapter 3. If you follow my recommendations in Chapter 3 about making proper records, you'll be able to go back to your date of conception, which usually will be at least several months before your filing date. More on this in Chapters 13 and 16.

Now that you know what your earliest date of invention is, you also know that the relevant "prior art" is the knowledge that existed prior to that date. More precisely, prior art comprises all of the items in the categories discussed below in Subsection d. Any item in any of these categories can be used against your invention at any time, either by the PTO to reject your patent application, or later on (if the PTO didn't find it or didn't give it adequate weight) to invalidate your patent in court.

c. Your Invention Must Not Be Publicly Known More Than One Year Prior to Your Filing Date— The One-Year Rule

In addition to the six categories under subsection d, below, prior art is also knowledge about your invention that has become publicly known more than one year prior to the date you file your patent application (either a regular patent application or a valid Provisional Patent Application, as described in Chapter 3, Section I). Known as the "one-year rule," the patent laws state that you must file a patent application within one year after you sell, offer for sale, or commercially or publicly use or describe your invention. If you fail to file within one year of such sale, offer for sale, public or commercial disclosure or use, the law bars you from obtaining a valid patent on the invention. Another way to put this, since we're talking about novelty, is that after a year following a sale, offer of sale, public or commercial use, or knowledge about your invention, it will no longer be considered novel by the PTO. While I've listed this "one-year rule" under the "prior art" heading for the sake of logical placement, it's so important that I've made it Inventor's Commandment #6 at the beginning of this chapter.

FOREIGN FILING AND THE ONE-YEAR RULE

While you have a year after publication or use to file in the U.S., I advise you not to do so, since most foreign countries aren't so lenient. If you think you may want to foreign file, you shouldn't offer for sale, sell, publicly use, or publish before you file in the U.S. For instance, suppose it's 1998 November 16, and you've just invented a new type of paint. If you have no intention of filing in another country, you can use, publish, or sell your invention now and still file your U.S. patent application (PPA or regular) any time up to 1999 November 16. However, if you think you may eventually want to foreign file on your invention, you should file in the U.S. (PPA or regular) before publicizing your invention. Then you can publish or sell the invention freely without the loss of any foreign rights in the major industrial or "Convention" countries, provided you file there within one year after your U.S. filing date. This is because, under an international convention (agreement or treaty), you'll be entitled to your U.S. filing date in such countries. In "non-Convention" countries (such as India and the Republic of China-Taiwan) you must file before you publicize the invention. (See Chapter 12.)

(The above year-month-day date format is from the International Standards Organization (ISO). It is also commonly used in computerese and trademark applications. I use it because it provides a logical descending order that facilitates calculating the one-year rule and other periods.)

d. Specifics of Prior Art

Now that we've broadly defined prior art, let's take a closer look at what it typically consists of, per 35 USC 102.

i. Prior Printed Publications Anywhere

Any printed publication, written by anyone, and from anywhere in the world, in any language, is considered valid prior art if it was published either (a) before your earliest provable date of invention (see above), or (b) over one year before you file your patent application. The term "printed publication" thus includes patents (U.S. and foreign), books, magazines (including trade and professional journals), Russian (or former U.S.S.R.) Inventor's Certificates, and publicly available technical papers and abstracts. Even photocopied theses, provided they were made publicly available by putting them in a college library, will constitute prior art. The PTO has even used old Dick Tracy comic strips showing a wristwatch radio as prior art!

COMPUTER TIP
While the statute speaks of "printed" publications, I'm sure that information on computer-information utilities or networks would be considered a printed publication, provided it was publicly available.

The "prior printed publications" category is the most important category of prior art and will generally constitute most of the prior art that you'll encounter. And most of the prior printed publications that the PTO refers to (cites) when it's processing your application, and that you will encounter in your search, will be patents, mainly U.S. patents.

ii. U.S. Patents Filed by Others Prior to Your Invention's Conception

Any U.S. patent that has a filing date earlier than your earliest provable date of invention is considered valid prior art. This is so even if the patent issues after you file your application. For example, suppose you conceive of your invention on 1995 June 9, and you file your patent application on 1995 August 9, two months later. Then, six months after your filing date, on 1996 February 9, a patent to Goldberger issues that shows all or part of your invention. If Goldberger's patent was any other type of publication, it wouldn't be prior art to your application since it was published after your filing date. However assume that Goldberger's patent application was filed on 1995 June 8, one day earlier than your date of conception. Under Section 102(e) of the patent laws, the PTO must consider the Goldberger patent as prior art to your application since Goldberger's application was filed prior to your invention's date of conception.

A common misconception is that only in-force patents (that is, patents that haven't yet expired) count as prior art. This isn't true. Any earlier patent, even if it was issued 150 years ago, will constitute prior art against an invention.

iii. Prior Publicly Available Knowledge or Use of the Invention in the U.S

Even if there's no written record of it, any public knowledge of the invention, or use of it by you or others in the U.S., which existed or occurred either (a) before your earliest provable date of invention, or (b) over one year before you file your patent application, is valid prior art. For example, an earlier heat-treating process used openly by a blacksmith in a small town, although never published or widely known, can defeat your right to a patent on a similar process. Similarly, a talk at a publicly accessible technical society will constitute prior public knowledge. Recently, even a showing of a kaleidoscope without restriction at a party with 30 attendees was held to be prior public knowledge.

For another example, suppose that you invented a new type of paint and you use it to paint your building in downtown Philadelphia. You forget to file a patent application and leave the paint on for 13 months: it's now too late to file a valid patent application since you've used your invention publicly for over a year. Put another way, your own invention would now be prior art against any patent application you file.

This public-use category of prior art is almost never used by the PTO, since they have no way of uncovering it; they search only patents and other publications. Occasionally, however, defendants (infringers) in patent lawsuits happen to uncover a prior public use that they then rely on to invalidate the patent.

EXPERIMENTAL EXCEPTION

If the prior public use was for bona fide (good faith) experimental purposes, it doesn't count as prior art. Thus suppose, in the "painted Philadelphia building" example above, that you painted your building to test the durability of your new paint: each month you photographed it, kept records on its reflectivity, wear resistance, and adhesion. In this case your one-year period wouldn't be initiated (begin to run) until your bona fide experimentation stopped and you left the paint out for nonexperimental purposes.

iv. Your Prior Foreign Patents

Any foreign patent (this includes Russian (or former U.S.S.R.) Inventor's Certificates) of yours or your legal representatives that issued before your U.S. filing date and that was filed over a year before your U.S. filing date is valid prior art. This category is generally pertinent to non-U.S. residents who start the patenting process in a foreign country. If you're in this class, you must file your U.S. application either within one year after you file in the foreign country or before your foreign patent issues. However, if you want to get the benefit of a foreign filing date for your U.S. application, you should file in the U.S. within the one year after your foreign filing date. (See Chapter 12.)

v. Prior U.S. Inventor

If anyone else in the U.S. invented substantially the same invention as yours before your invention's date of conception, and he or she didn't abandon, suppress, or conceal it, then this other person's invention (even though no written record was made) can be used to defeat your right to a patent. However, under a new statute, if your invention clears Section 102 (that is, it is novel) and the prior inventor worked in the same organization as you, then the prior inventor's work won't be considered prior art under Section 103. This prior art problem usually occurs when two (or more) inventors each file a patent application on the same invention. The PTO will declare an "interference" between the two competing applications. (See Chapter 16.)

vi. Prior Sale or On-Sale Status in the U.S

Under Section 102, the law also considers certain actions by humans to be "prior art," even when no paper records exist. These actions involve the "sale" or "on-sale" category.

Suppose you (or anyone else) offer to sell, actually sell, or commercially use your invention, or any product embodying your invention, in the U.S. You must file your U.S. patent application (regular or PPA) within one year after this offer, sale, or commercial use. This is another part of the "one-year rule." This means that you can make sales to test the commercial feasibility of your invention for up to a year before filing in the U.S. Again, however, I advise you not to do so, since this will defeat your right to a patent in most foreign countries, as mentioned above, and as explained in more detail in Chapter 12.

The type of sale or offer of sale that would bar your patent application must be an offer to sell or a sale of actual hardware or a process embodying the invention; an offer to sell or a sale of the inventive *concept* to a manufacturer will not start the one-year period running.

ABANDONMENT

If you "abandon" your invention by finally giving up on it in some way, and this comes to the attention of the PTO or any court charged with ruling on your patent, your application or patent will be rejected or ruled invalid. I've never personally had a case where this happened, but it has occurred.

EXAMPLE: You make a model of your invention, test it, fail to get it to work, or fail to sell it, and then consciously drop all efforts on it. Later you change your mind and try to patent it. If your abandonment becomes known, you would lose your right to a patent. But if you merely stop work on it for a number of years because of such reasons as health, finances, or lack of a crucial part, but intend to pursue it again when possible, the law would excuse your inaction and hold that you didn't abandon.

---

e.   Summary of Prior Art

If these prior-art rules seem complicated and difficult to understand, you're not alone. Very few patent attorneys understand them fully either! Perhaps Congress will simplify Section 102 someday and enact a "first to file" law, like the rest of the world uses. (Write to your Congressperson!) In the meantime, don't worry about it if you can't understand all of the rules. All you really need to remember is that relevant prior art usually consists of:

• any published writing (including any patent) that was made publicly available either (1) before your earliest provable date of invention (see above), or (2) over one year before you can get your patent application on file;
• any U.S. patent whose issue date isn't early enough to stop you but that has a filing date earlier than your earliest provable date of invention;
• any relevant invention or development (whether described in writing or not) existing prior to when your invention was conceived; or
• any public or commercial use, sale, or knowledge of the invention more than one year prior your application filing date.

2.   Any Physical Difference Whatever Will Satisfy the Novelty Requirement

Any novel feature, no matter how trivial, will satisfy the novelty requirement. For example, suppose you've "invented" a bicycle that is painted yellow with green polka dots, each of which has a blue triangle in the center. Assume (this is easy to do) that no bicycle has been painted this way before. Your bicycle would thus clearly satisfy the requirement of novelty.

Rarely will an investigation into your invention's patentability (called a "patentability search") reveal any single prior invention or reference that could be considered a dead ringer. Of course, if your search does produce a dead-ringer reference for your invention—that is, an actual device or published description showing all the features of your invention and operating in the same way for the same purpose—obviously your patentability decision can be made immediately. Your invention lacks novelty over the "prior art." Another way of saying this is that your invention has been "anticipated" by a prior invention or conception and is thus definitely unpatentable. The concepts of anticipation and prior art are discussed in more detail in Requirement #4—unobviousness.

The law generally recognizes three types of novelty, any one of which will satisfy the novelty requirement of Section 102: (1) physical (hardware or method) difference, (2) new combination, and (3) new use.

a.   Physical Differences

This is the most common way to satisfy the novelty requirement. Here your invention has some physical or structural (hardware or method) difference over the prior art. If the invention is a machine, composition, or article, it must be or have one or more parts that have a different shape, value, size, color, or composition than what's already known.

It's often difficult for inventors to distinguish between a physical difference and a new result. When I ask clients, "What's physically different about your invention?" they usually reply that theirs is lighter, faster, safer, cheaper to make or use, portable, and so on. However, these factors are new *results* or *advantages*, not physical differences, and are primarily relevant to unobviousness (see Section F), not to novelty. That is, they won't help your invention satisfy the novelty requirement. Again, a new physical feature must be a hardware (including operational) difference.

Even omitting an element can be considered novel. For example, if a machine has always had four gears, and you find that it will work with three, you've satisfied the novelty requirement.

Also, the discovery of a critical area of a given prior-art range will be considered novel. That is, if a prior-art magazine article on dyeing states that a mordant will work at a temperature range of 100-150 degrees centigrade and you discover that it works five times better at 127-130 degrees centigrade, the law stills consider this range novel, even though it's technically embraced by the prior art.

A physical difference can also be subtle or less apparent in the hardware sense so that it's manifested primarily by a different mode of operation. For example, an electronic amplifying circuit that looks the same, but that operates in a different mode—say Class A rather than Class B—or is under the control of different software, or a pump that looks the same, but that operates at a higher pressure and hence in a different mode, will be considered novel.

✏ PROCESSES NOTE

If your invention is a new process, you don't need any novel hardware; your physical novelty is basically your new way of manipulating old hardware. Any novel step or steps whatever in this regard will satisfy the physical novelty requirement.

b. New Combinations

Many laypersons believe that if an invention consists entirely of old components, it can't be patented. A moment's reflection will show that this couldn't be true, since most inventions are made of old components. Thus, the PTO will consider your invention novel if two or more prior-art references (actual devices or published descriptions) together account for all of your invention's physical characteristics. That is, if your invention is a new combination of two old features, the law will consider it novel. For your invention to be considered as lacking novelty and thus subject to rejection under Section 102 of the patent laws, all of its physical characteristics must exist in a single prior-art reference. For example, getting back to your bicycle, suppose you now "invent" a bicycle made of one of the recently discovered, superstrength, carbon-fiber alloys. The bicycle per se is old, as is the alloy, but you're the first to "combine" the two old concepts. Your bicycle would clearly be considered novel since it has a new physical feature: a frame that is made, for the first time, of a carbon-fiber alloy. But, remember, just because it's novel, useful, and fits within a statutory class, doesn't mean the bicycle is patentable. It still must surpass the tough test of non-obviousness (covered in the following section).

c. New Use

As stated in Section C5, above, if you've invented a new use for an old item of hardware, or an old process, the new use will satisfy the novelty requirement, no matter how trivial the newness is. For example, Dorie invents a new vegetable cooker which, after a search, she discovers is exactly like a copper smelter invented by one Jaschik in 1830. Dorie's cooker, even though identical to Jaschik's smelter, will be considered novel, since it's for a different use. (If your invention involves novel physical hardware, technically it can't be a new-use invention.)

If you're the type of person who thinks ahead, you're probably asking yourself, "Why is he bothering with novelty—isn't this requirement inherent in unobviousness—that is, if the invention is found to be unobvious won't it also be found to be novel?" Well, you're 100% correct. If an invention is unobvious, *a fortiori* (by better reason) it must be novel. However, the law makes the determination in two steps (Sections 102 and 103) and most patent professionals have also found it far easier to first determine whether and how an invention satisfies the novelty requirement and then determine if it can be considered unobvious. This two-step process is so important that I've made it Inventor's Commandment #7. See the first page of this chapter.

F. Requirement #4: Unobviousness

We're now entering what's probably the most misunderstood and difficult-to-understand—yet most important—aspect of patent law—that is, whether your invention is unobvious. Let's start with a "common misconception."

Common Misconception: If your invention is different from the prior art, you're entitled to get a patent on it.

Fact: Under Section 103 of the patent laws, no matter how different your invention is, you're not entitled to a patent on it unless its difference(s) over the prior art can be considered "unobvious" by the PTO or the courts.

Most of the time a patentability search will produce one or more prior-art references that show devices similar to your invention, or that show several, but not all, of the physical features of your invention. That is, you will find that your invention has one or more features or differences that aren't shown in any one prior-art reference. However, even though your invention is physically different from such prior art, this isn't enough to qualify for a patent. To obtain a patent, the physical (or use) differences must be substantial and significant. The legal term for such a difference is "unobvious" or, commonly, "nonobvious." That is, the differences between your invention and the prior art must not be obvious to one with ordinary skill in the field. Because this concept is so important, let's examine it in detail.

1. Unobvious to Whom?

It doesn't tell anyone much to say an invention must be unobvious. The big question is, unobvious to whom? Under Section 103, you can't get a patent if a person having ordinary skill in the field of your invention would consider the idea of the invention "obvious" at the time you came up with it.

The law considers "a person having ordinary skill in the art to which said subject matter pertains" to be a mythical worker in the field of the invention who has (1) ordinary skill, but who (2) is totally omniscient about all the prior art in his or her field. This is a pure fantasy since no such person ever lived, or ever will, but realistically there's no other way to come even close to any objective standard for determining nonobviousness.

Let's take some examples. Assume that your invention has to do with electronics—say an improved flip-flop circuit. A person having ordinary skill in the art would be an ordinary, average logic-circuit engineer who's intimately familiar with all prior-art logic circuits. If your invention has to do with chemistry, say a new photochemical process, a typical photochemical engineer with total knowledge of all photochemical processes would be your imaginary skilled artisan. If your invention is mechanical, such as an improved cigarette lighter or belt buckle, the PTO would try to postulate a hypothetical cigarette-lighter engineer or belt-buckle designer with ordinary skill and comprehensive knowledge. If your invention is a design, say for a computer case, the PTO would invent a hypothetical computer-case designer of ordinary skill and full knowledge of all existing designs.

2. What Does "Obvious" Mean?

Most people have trouble interpreting Section 103 because of the word "obvious." If after reading my explanation you still don't understand it, don't be dismayed. Most patent attorneys, patent examiners, and judges can't agree on the meaning of the term. Many tests for unobviousness have been used and rejected by the courts over the years. The courts have often referred to "a flash of genius," "a synergistic effect (the whole is greater than the sum of its parts)," or some other colorful term. One influential court said that unobviousness is manifested if the invention produces "unusual and surprising results."

Technically (for reasons mentioned below, I stress the term "technically"), none of these tests is used any longer. This is because the U.S. Supreme Court, which has final say in such matters, decreed in the famous 1966 case of *Graham v. John Deere* that Section 103 is to be interpreted by taking the following steps:

1. Determine the scope and content of the prior art.
2. Determine the novelty of the invention.
3. Determine the level of skill of artisans in the pertinent art.
4. Against this background, determine the obviousness or unobviousness of the inventive subject matter.
5. Also consider secondary and objective factors such as commercial success, long-felt but unsolved need, and failure of others.

Unfortunately, while in theory the Supreme Court has the last word, in practice it added nothing to our understanding of the terms "obviousness" and "unobviousness"— in the crucial step (#4), the court merely repeated the very terms (obvious and unobvious) it was seeking to define. Therefore, most attorneys and patent examiners continue to look for new and unexpected results that flow from the novel features when seeking to determine if an invention is obvious.

Despite its failure to define the term "obvious," the Supreme Court did add an important step to the process by which "obviousness" is to be determined. In Step #5, the court made clear that objective circumstances must be taken into account by the PTO or courts when deciding whether an invention is or isn't obvious. The court specifically mentioned three such circumstances: commercial success, long-felt but unsolved need, and failure of others to come up with the invention.

So, although your invention might not, strictly speaking, produce "new and unexpected results" from the standpoint of one with "ordinary skill in the art," it still may be considered unobvious if, for instance, you can show that the invention has enjoyed commercial success.

Normally, before you file a patent application you won't be able to consider commercial success as a factor in determining patentability, since I recommend (Chapter 7, Section H) that you don't sell the invention before you file. However, you can argue commercial success later to the examiner during the prosecution phase (Chapter 13, Section F) if your invention is commercially successful by then. Also, you can even consider commercial success before filing if you disregard my advice and take advantage of the "one-year rule" (Section E, above, and Chapter 7, Section H) by test-marketing your invention before filing.

Under the reasoning of the *John Deere* case, then, to decide whether or not your invention is obvious, you first should ask whether it produces "new and unexpected results" from the standpoint of one skilled in the relevant art. If it does, you've met the test for patentability. However, if there's still some doubt on this question, external circumstances may be used to bolster your position.

 If you feel your head spinning, don't worry. It's natural. Because these concepts are so abstract, there's no real way to get a complete and comfortable grasp on them. However, if you take it slow (and take a few breaks from your reading), you should have a pretty good idea of when an invention is and isn't considered "unobvious." In Section 3, directly below, I discuss examples of "unobviousness" and "obviousness." Then, in Section 4, I cover the types of arguments based on external circumstances (called "secondary factors") that can be made to bolster your contention that your invention is unobvious. I also provide a flowchart (Fig. 5D) that puts it all together in concise form.

3. Examples of Obviousness and Unobviousness

First, for some examples of unobvious inventions, consider all of the inventions listed in Chapter 2: the magnetic pistol guard, the buried plastic cable, the watch calendar sticker, "Grasscrete," the Wiz-z-er top, the shopping cart, etc. These all had physically novel features that produced new, unexpected results—that is, results that weren't suggested or shown in the prior art.

Although generally you must make a significant physical change for your invention to be considered unobvious, often a very slight change in the shape, slope, size, or material can produce a patentable invention that operates entirely differently and produces totally unexpected results.

EXAMPLE: Consider the original centrifugal vegetable juicer composed of a spinning perforated basket with a vertical side-wall and a nonperforated grater bottom.

When vegetables, such as carrots, were pushed into the grater bottom, they were grated into fine pieces and juice that was thrown against the cylindrical, vertical sidewall of the basket. The juice passed through the perforations and was recovered in a container but the pieces clung to the sidewalls, adding weight to the basket and closing the perforations, making the machine impossible to run and operate after a relatively small amount of vegetables were juiced. Someone conceived of making the side of the basket slope outwardly so that while the juice was still centrifugally extracted through the perforated side of the basket, the pulp, instead of adhering to the old vertical side of the basket, was centrifugally forced up the new sloped side of the basket where it would go over the top and be diverted to a separate receptacle. Thus the juicer could be operated continuously without the pulp having to be cleaned out. Obviously, despite the fact that the physical novelty was slight—that is, it involved merely changing the slope of a basket's sidewall—the result was entirely new and unexpected, and therefore was considered unobvious.

In general such a relatively small physical difference (changing the slope of the wall of a basket in a juicer) will require a relatively great new result (ability to run the juicer continuously) to satisfy the unobviousness requirement. On the other hand, a relatively large physical difference will need only minor new results for the PTO to consider it unobvious. That is, in Fig. 5A (The Patentability Mountain) the height of the fourth box can be shortened if the height of the third box is increased.

As indicated, new-use inventions don't involve any physical change at all in the old hardware. However, the new use must be (1) a different use of some known hardware or process, and (2) the different use must produce new, unexpected results.

EXAMPLE: Again consider the venetian blind cleaner used as a seed planter, and aspirin used as a growth stimulant, discussed in Section C5, above. In both instances, the new use was very different and provided a totally unexpected result: thus both inventions would be patentable. Also, in another interesting new-use case, the patent court in Washington held that removing the core of an ear of corn to speed freezing and thawing was unobvious over core drilling to speed drying. The court reasoned that one skilled in the art of corn processing could know that core removal speeds drying without realizing that core removal could also be used to speed freezing and thawing. Accordingly, the court held that the new result (faster freezing and thawing) was unexpected since it wasn't described or suggested in the prior art.

The courts have held that the substitution of a different, but similarly functioning, element for one of the elements in a known combination, although creating a "novel" invention, won't produce a patentable one. For example, consider the substitution, in the 1950s, after transistors had appeared, of a transistor for a vacuum tube in an old amplifier circuit. At first blush this new combination of old elements would seem to the uninitiated to be a patentable substitution since it provided tremendous new results (decreased power consumption, size, heat, weight, and far greater longevity). However, you'll soon realize that the result, although new, would have been entirely foreseeable since, just as in the carbon-fiber/bicycle case, the power reduction and reduced-weight advantages of transistors would have been already known as soon as a transistor made its appearance. Thus, substituting them for tubes wouldn't provide the old amplifier circuit with any *unexpected* new results. Accordingly, the PTO's Board of Appeals held the new combination to be obvious to an artisan of ordinary skill at the time.

If you're still a bit misty about all this, put yourself in the shoes of an electronic engineer who, at the time of the replacement of the vacuum tube with the transistor, was skilled in designing vacuum tube circuits and was currently designing a flip-flop circuit. Along comes this newfangled "transistor" that uses no heater and weighs 1/10th as much as a comparable tube, but which provides the same degree of amplification and control as the tube did. Do you think that it wouldn't be obvious to the engineer to try substituting a transistor for the tube in that flip-flop circuit? Similarly, the PTO would consider obvious the substitution of an integrated circuit for a group of transistors in a known logic circuit, or the use of a known radio mounting bracket to hold a loudspeaker enclosure instead of a radio.

The PTO will also consider as obvious the mere carrying forward of an old concept, or a change in form and degree, without a new result. For instance, when one inventor provided notches on the inner rim of a steering wheel to provide a better grip, the idea was held to be obvious because of medieval sword handles that had similar notches for the same purpose. And the use of a large pulley for a logging rig was held nonpatentable over the use of a small pulley for clotheslines. These cases are known as "obviousness by analogy."

On the other hand, one inventor merely changed the slope of a part in a papermaking (Fourdriner) machine; as a result the machine's output increased by 25%—a dramatic, new, and unexpected result that was held patentable.

In sum, the PTO will usually hold that substitution of a different material, shape, or size is obvious. But if the substitution provides *unexpected* new results, the law will hold it unobvious.

The courts and the PTO will also usually consider the duplication of a part obvious unless it can see new results. For instance, in an automobile, the substitution of two banks of three cylinders with two carburetors was held obvious over a six-cylinder, single-carburetor engine, since the new arrangement had no unexpected advantages. However, the use of two water turbines to provide cross flow to eliminate axial thrust on bearings was held unobvious over a single turbine; again, an *unexpected*, new result.

Similarly, making devices portable, making parts smaller or larger, faster or slower, effecting a substitution of equivalents (a roller bearing for a ball bearing), making elements adjustable, making parts integral, separable (modular), or in kit form, and other known techniques with their known advantages, will be held obvious unless new, unexpected results can be shown.

⚠️ If you create what you believe to be a valuable invention, but it seems simple and obvious to you, don't assume automatically that it's legally obvious. Some very simple inventions, like the vegetable juicer and the Fourdriner machine, have been granted very valuable patents!

📝 **DESIGN PATENT TIP**
In design cases, the design must have novel features, and the PTO must be able to regard these as unobvious to a designer of ordinary skill. If the design involves the use of known techniques that together don't produce any new and unexpected visual effect, then the PTO will consider it obvious. But if they produce a startling or unique new appearance, then the PTO will hold it to be unobvious.

HELPING HANDS HAT
No. 3,169,192.

Since only the ornamental appearance and not the function of a design is relevant, the degree of novelty of the design will be the main determinant of unobviousness: a high degree of novelty will always be patentable, while a low degree of novelty will encounter rough sledding unless you can set forth reasons why it has a very different appearance or visual effect.

4. Secondary Factors in Determining Unobviousness

As mentioned, if the new and unexpected results of your invention are marginal, you *may* still be able to get a patent if you can show that your invention possesses one or more secondary factors that establish unobviousness. While the Supreme Court listed only three in the *John Deere* case, I've compiled a list of twelve basic and nine combinatory secondary factors that the PTO and the courts actually consider. In the real world, these secondary factors must generally only be dealt with if the PTO makes a preliminary finding of obviousness or if your invention is attacked as being obvious. However, when deciding whether your invention is legally entitled to a patent, you'll have a much better idea of how easy or difficult it will be to obtain if you apply these secondary factors to your invention.

➡️ If you're sure that your invention is unobvious, feel free to skip this section, and Section 6, and proceed directly to Section 7.

Although some of these secondary factors may appear similar, try to consider each independently, since the courts have recognized subtle differences between them. As part of doing this, remember that lawyers like to chop large arguments into little ones so that it will appear that there are a multitude of reasons for their position rather than just one or two. While this approach may seem silly, it's nevertheless a fact (however sad) that the PTO and courts are used to hearing almost exclusively from lawyers (and, in the case of the PTO, from highly specialized patent agents). Accordingly, the general rule is, the more arguments you can use to claim unobviousness, the better your chances will be of getting a patent.

Now let's look at the secondary factors in detail.

Factor 1. Previous failure of others

If the invention is successful where previous workers in the field were unable to make it work, this will be of great help to your application. For instance, many previous attempts were made to use electrostatic methods for making photocopies, but all failed. Chester Carlson (a patent attorney himself) came along and successfully used an electrostatic process to make copies. This greatly enhanced his case for the patentability of his dry (xerographic) photocopying process.

Factor 2. Solves an unrecognized problem

Here the essence of your invention is probably the recognition of the problem, rather than its solution. Consider the showerhead that automatically shuts off in case of excess water temperature discussed in Chapter 2. As the problem was probably never recognized in the prior art, the solution would therefore probably be patentable.

Factor 3. Solves an insoluble problem

Suppose that for years those skilled in the art had tried and failed to solve a problem and the art and literature were full of unsuccessful "solutions." Along you come and finally find a workable solution, such as a cure for the common cold: you'd probably get a patent.

EXAMPLE: Consider an invention made by a client of mine—a circuit that, when connected across a light switch, holds the light on for about twenty seconds after the light is switched off, and can be used repeatedly and always operates in the same manner. The prior art showed "delayed-off" circuits, but all of these could only be used once every several minutes. By incorporating special discharging and reset circuits that had never before been used or suggested, my client's invention successfully solved a problem (lack of instant resettability) that was either not recognized before, or if recognized, wasn't soluble before. Thus the circuit was patentable over the prior art.

Factor 4. Commercial success

If your invention has attained commercial success by the time the crucial patentability decision is made, this militates strongly in favor of patentability. Nothing succeeds like success, right?

Factor 5. Crowded art

If your invention is in a crowded field (art)—that is, a field that is mature and that contains many patents, such as electrical connectors or bicycles—a small advance will go further towards qualifying the invention for a patent than it will in a new, blossoming art, such as monoclonal antibodies.

Factor 6. Omission of element

If you can omit an element in a prior invention without loss of capability, this will count a lot, since parts are expensive, unreliable, heavy, and labor-intensive (an example would be eliminating an inductor in an oscillator circuit).

Factor 7. Unsuggested modification

If you can modify a prior invention in a manner not suggested before, such as by increasing the slope in a paper-making machine, or by making the basket slope in a centrifugal juice extractor, this act in itself counts for patentability.

Factor 8. Unappreciated advantage

If your invention provides an advantage that was never before appreciated, it can make a difference. In a recent case, a gas cap that was impossible to insert in a skewed manner was held to be patentable since it provided an advantage that was never appreciated previously.

Factor 9. Solves prior inoperability

If your invention provides an operative result where before only inoperability existed, then it has a good chance for a patent. For instance, suppose you come up with a gasoline additive that prevents huge fires in case of a plane crash; you've got it made since all previous fire suppressant additives have been largely unsuccessful.

Factor 10. Successful implementation of ancient idea where others failed

The best example I can think of is the Wright Brothers' airplane. For millennia humans had wanted to fly and had tried many schemes unsuccessfully. The successful implementation of such an ancient desire carries great weight when it comes to getting a patent.

Factor 11. Solution of long-felt need

Suppose you find a way to prevent tailgate-type automobile crashes. Obviously you've solved a powerful need and your solution will be a heavy weight in your favor on the scales of patentability.

Factor 12. Contrary to prior art's teaching

If the prior art expressly teaches that something can't be done or is impractical—for example, humans can't fly without artificial propulsion motors—and you prove this teaching wrong, you've got it made.

5. Secondary Factors in Determining Unobviousness or Combination Inventions

Inventions that combine two or more elements known in the prior art can still be held patentable, provided that the combination can be considered unobvious—that is, it's a new combination and it produces new and unexpected results. In fact, most patents are granted on such combina-

tions since very few truly new things are ever discovered. So let's examine some of the factors used especially to determine the patentability of "combination inventions" (that is, inventions that have two or more features that are shown in two or more prior-art references).

 The following material is conceptually quite abstract and difficult to understand, even for patent attorneys. I'm presenting it in the interest of completeness. However, if you wish, you can safely skip it for now and proceed directly to Section 7. If the PTO or anyone else suggests that two or more prior-art references, taken together, teach that your invention is obvious, come back and read it then.

Factor 13. Synergism (2 + 2 = 5)

If the results achieved by your combination are greater than the sum of the separate results of its parts, this can indicate unobviousness. Consider the pistol trigger release (Chapter 2) where a magnetic ring must be worn to fire the pistol. The results (increased police safety) are far in excess of what magnets, rings, and pistols could provide separately.

EXAMPLE: For another example, suppose that a chemist combines, through experimentation, several metals that cooperate in a new way to provide added strength without added density. If this synergistic result wasn't reasonably foreseeable by a metallurgist, the new alloy would almost certainly be patentable.

Generally, if your invention is a chemical mixture, the mixture must do more than the sum of its components. For this reason, food recipes are difficult to patent unless an ingredient does more than its usual function or produces a new and unexpected result. Or, if you come up with a new technique of cooking that produces a new and unexpected result—for example, a cookie that is chewy inside and crisp outside—you've got a good chance of prevailing. Similarly, if you combine various mechanical or electrical components, the courts and the PTO will usually consider the combination patentable if it provides more than the functions of its individual components.

As an example of an unpatentable combination without synergism, consider the combination of a radio, waffle iron, and blender in one housing. While novel and useful, this combination would be considered an aggregation and obvious, since there's no synergism or new cooperation: the combination merely provides the sum of the results of its components and each component works individually and doesn't enhance the working of any other component. On the other hand, the combination of an eraser and a pencil would be patentable (had it not already been invented) because the two elements cooperate to increase overall writing speed, a synergistic effect. The same would hold true for mounting loudspeakers in a plastic insulating picnic box, where new cooperation results: the box holds the food and provides a baffle for the speakers.

Factor 14. Combination unsuggested

If the prior art contains no suggestion, either expressed or implied, that the references should be combined, this militates in favor of patentability. Examiners in the PTO frequently are assigned to pass on patent applications for combination inventions. To find the elements of the combination claimed, they'll make a search, often using a computer, to gather enough references to show the respective elements of the combination. While the examiners frequently use such references in combination to reject the claims of the patent application on unobvious grounds, the law says clearly that it's not proper to do so unless the references themselves, rather than an applicant's patent application, suggest the combination.

> **EXAMPLE:** Arthur B. files a patent application on a pastry-molding machine. The examiner cites (or your search reveals) one patent on a foot mold and another on a pastry mold to show the two elements of the invention. It wouldn't be proper to "combine" these disparate references since they're from unconnected fields and thus it wouldn't be obvious to use them together against your invention.

An example of where the law would consider it obvious to combine several references is the case where, as discussed, you make a bicycle out of the lightweight carbon-fiber alloy and, as a result, your bicycle is lighter than ever before. Is your invention "unobvious"? The answer is "No," because the prior art implicitly suggests the combination by mentioning the problem of the need for lighter bikes and the lightness of the new alloy. Moreover, the result achieved by the combination would be expected from a review of existing bicycles and the new lightweight alloy. In other words, if a skilled bicycle engineer were to be shown the new, lightweight alloy, it would obviously occur to the engineer to make a bicycle out of it since bicycle engineers are always seeking to make lighter bicycles.

Factor 15. Impossible to combine

This is the situation where prior-art references show the separate elements of the inventive combination, but in a way that makes it seem they would be physically impossible to combine. Stated differently, if you can find a way to do what appears to be physically impossible, then you can get a patent. For example, suppose you've invented the magnetic

pistol release. The prior art shows a huge magnetic cannon firing release attached to a personnel shield. Since the step from a cannon to a small handgun is a large one, physical incompatibility might get you a patent—that is, it would be physically impossible to use a huge cannon shield magnet on a small and very differently shaped trigger finger. Note, however, that sometimes by analogy the large can properly be used on the small if a mere change in size is all that's required.

Factor 16. Different combination

Here your combination is A, B, and C, and the prior-art references show a different, albeit possibly confusingly similar combination, say A', B, and C. Since your combination hadn't been previously created, you've got a good case for patentability even though your creation is similar to an existing one. Again the last analogy holds: a personnel shield for a cannon, even though it has a magnetic firing release, is so far different from a finger ring that the prior-art combination must be regarded as different from that of the invention.

Factor 17. Prior-art references would not operate in combination

Here the prior-art references, even if combined, wouldn't operate properly, such as due to some incompatibility. Suppose you've invented a radio receiver comprising a combined tuner-amplifier and a speaker, and the prior art consists of one patent showing a crystal tuner and an advertisement showing a large loudspeaker. The prior-art elements wouldn't operate if combined because the weak crystal tuner wouldn't be able to drive the speaker adequately; thus a combination of the prior-art elements would be inoperative. This would militate strongly in favor of patentability.

Factor 18. Over three prior-art references necessary to show your invention

While not a very strong argument, if it takes more than three references to meet your inventive combination, this militates in your favor.

Factor 19. References teach away from combining

If the references themselves show or teach that they shouldn't be combined, and you're able to combine them, this militates in favor of patentability. For example, suppose a reference says that the new carbon-fiber alloy should only be used in structural members that aren't subject to sudden shocks, but you were able to make a bike out of the carbon-fiber alloy. If you're able to use it successfully to make a bike frame, which is subject to sudden shocks, you should be able to get a patent.

Factor 20. Awkward, involved combination

Suppose that to make your inventive combination, it takes the structures of three prior-art patents, one of which must be made smaller, another of which must be modified in shape, and the third of which must be made of a different material. These factors can only help you.

Factor 21. References from a different field

If the references show structures that are similar to your invention, but are in a different technical field, this militates in favor of unobviousness and hence of patentability. I used this argument successfully to get a food mold patented over a similarly shaped device for molding a horse's foot.

6. How Does a Patent Examiner Determine "Unobviousness"

Because it's usually helpful to understand how a bureaucracy operates when you're dealing with it over significant issues, let's take a minute to examine how a patent examiner proceeds when deciding whether or not your invention is obvious. When patent examiners turn to the question of whether an invention is unobvious, they first make a search and gather all of the patents that they feel are relevant or close to your invention. Then they sit down with these patents (and any prior-art references you've provided with your patent application) and see whether your invention, as described in your claims (see Chapter 9), contains any novelty (novel physical features, new combination, or new use) that isn't shown in any reference. If so, your invention satisfies Section 102—that is, it is novel.

Next they see whether your novelty produces any unexpected or surprising results. If so, they'll find that the invention is unobvious and grant you a patent. If not (this usually occurs the first time they act on your case), they'll reject your application (sometimes termed a "shotgun" or "shoot-from-the-hip" rejection) and leave it to you to show that your new features do indeed produce new, unexpected results. To do this, you can use as many of the reasons listed above that you feel are relevant. If you can convince the examiner, you'll get your patent.

If a dispute over unobviousness actually finds its way into court (a common occurrence), however, both sides will present the testimony of patent lawyers or technical experts who fit, or most closely fit, the hypothetical job descriptions called for by the particular case. These experts will testify for or against obviousness by arguing that the invention is (or isn't) new and/or that it does (or doesn't) produce unexpected results.

Again, because the question of whether an invention is unobvious is obviously crucial to whether a patent will issue and because Sections 102 and 103 are widely confused, I have made the two-step evaluation Inventor's Commandment #7 at the beginning of this chapter.

7. Weak Versus Strong Patents

Although in this section I've covered the basic legal requirements for obtaining a patent on an invention, there is, in reality, an additional practical requirement. If the claims in your patent are easy to design around or are so narrow as to virtually preclude you from realizing commercial gain, it's virtually the same as if a patent had been denied you in the first place. I'll come back to this point when I cover how to conduct a patent search (Chapter 6) and how to draft your claims (Chapter 9).

8. The Inventor's Status Is Irrelevant

You may have noticed that in discussing the requirements for obtaining a patent, I didn't mention the inventor's status or personal qualifications (such as, the applicant should be an engineer, over 21, and so on). That is because status and personal qualifications are totally irrelevant. An invention need merely meet the four legal criteria (Section B, above). The applicant must qualify as a true inventor of the invention (discussed in Chapter 10), but his, her, or their age, sex, citizenship, country of residence, mental competence, health, physical disabilities, nationality, race, creed, religion, state of incarceration, and so on, are irrelevant. Even a dead or insane person can apply (through a legal representative, of course).

The manner of making the invention is also irrelevant, as we'll see by the next Common Misconception.

Common Misconception: *If a complete moron discovers something by accident, the law won't consider it to be as good an invention as if a genius had come up with it through years of hard, brilliant work.*

Fact: *The manner of making an invention is totally irrelevant to patentability. The invention is looked at in its own right as to whether or not it would be obvious to one skilled in the art; the way it was made or the qualifications or competence of the applicant are never considered by the PTO.*

G. The Patentability Flowchart

To get a better grasp of the admittedly slippery concept of unobviousness and the role it plays in the patent application process, consider Fig. 5D—The Patentability Flowchart. This flowchart is like a computer programmer's flowchart, except that all blocks have been made rectangular to use space more efficiently. In addition to presenting all of the criteria used by the PTO and the courts for determining whether an invention is unobvious, the chart also incorporates the first three tests (statutory class, usefulness, and novelty) of Fig. 5A. I strongly advise that you study this chart and the following description of it well, since it sums up the essence of this crucial chapter. Also, you'll want to use this chart when making your search (next chapter) and when prosecuting your patent application (Chapter 13). This chart has been designed to cover and apply to anything you might come up with, so you can and should use it to determine the patentability of any utility invention whatever.

Box A: Assuming that you've made an invention, first determine, using the criteria discussed above, whether you can reasonably classify your invention in one of the five statutory classes indicated. If not, take the "N" (No) output of Box A to the Box X on the left bottom of the chart.

As indicated in Box X, the PTO will probably refuse to grant you a patent, so see if you can gainfully use another form of coverage (such as trade secret, copyright, design patent, trademark, or unfair competition, as discussed in Chapter 1). If this possibility also fails, you'll have to give up on the creation and invent something else. If the invention can be classified within a statutory class ("Y" or Yes output of Box A), move on to Box B.

Box B: Now determine, again using the criteria above, whether the invention has utility, including amusement. If not, move to Box X. If so, move on to Box C.

Box C: Here's the important novelty determination. If an invention has any physical features that aren't present in any single prior-art reference, or if it is a new combination of old features, or a new use of an old feature or old hardware, no matter how trivial, it will clear Section 102—that is, it has novelty: take the Yes output to Box D. If not, it lacks novelty, so take the No output and go to Box X again.

Box D: This is the heart of the chart. You should now determine whether the novelty of your invention produces any new and unexpected result ("N&UR"). Use the criteria and examples presented in Sections F1 through F4. If you definitely feel that your invention does not provide N&UR, take the No output from Box D to Box X. On the other hand, if your answer is a clear "Yes" (you're sure you have N&UR), it's likely you'll be able to get a patent. While not mandatory, I recommend that you obtain additional reasons for patentability to boost your confidence by taking the Yes output to Box E to consider the "secondary" factors.

If, however, at this point you can't come up with a clear "Yes" or "No" as to N&UR—that is, your invention falls somewhere between these two extremes—it can still qualify for a patent if it has one or more secondary factors. In this case, follow the broken-lined "Possibly" output of Box D to Box E to determine whether your invention qualifies for a patent, even though it doesn't produce any N&UR. From here on, if you took the Yes output of Box D, you'll follow a solid-line route, but if you took the Possibility output, you'll follow the broken-line route.

Boxes E, F and G: No matter which route you take from Box D ("Yes" = solid line or "Possibly" = broken line), you should next answer all of the questions in Box E. Then move to Box F, which tells you to answer all of the questions in Box G if you have a combination invention, or to go directly to the end of Box G if it's not a combination invention. The more questions in Boxes E and G to which you can answer "Yes," the better your chances will be. No matter how you go through Boxes E to G, there are four possibilities, identified below as 1 (A&B) and 2 (A&B).

1. N&URs exist ("Yes" from Box D—solid-line route):
   A. If you answered "Yes" to Box D and to one or more questions in Boxes E and G (there are N&URs and one or more secondary unobviousness factors), take the Yes/solid-line output from Box G to Box H, where you'll see that the PTO is very likely to grant you a patent.
   B. If you were not able to answer "Yes" to any question in Boxes E and F (there are N&URs, but no secondary unobviousness factors), take the No/solid-line output from Box G to Box I, where you'll see that you'll still be likely to get a patent, based on your N&URs (Box D).

2. Possible N&URs ("Possibly" from Box D—broken-line route):
   A. If you answered "Possibly" to Box D and "Yes" to one or more questions in Boxes E and G (you're unsure about N&URs but you have one or more secondary unobviousness factors), take the Yes/broken-line output from Box G to Box J, where you'll see that the PTO will still probably grant you a patent.
   B. If you answered "Possibly" to Box D, but were not able to answer "Yes" to any question in Boxes E and G (you're unsure about N&URs and there are no secondary unobviousness factors), take the No/broken-line output from Box G to Box X, where you'll see that you probably won't be able to get a patent. Don't give up though, if you still think you might be able to prove some secondary factors later, such as commercial success after it hits the market.

Fig. 5D—The Patentability Flowchart

Search and You May Find

INVENTOR'S COMMANDMENT #8

You should make (or have made) a thorough patentability search of your invention before you decide whether to file a patent application.

Since you've learned how to determine patentability from Chapter 5, you can now make a patentability search. The Patent and Trademark Office (PTO) doesn't require a search, but I strongly believe that all inventors should make (or have made) a search prior to deciding whether to file a patent application. Thus I've made the "pre-ex" (pre-examination) patentability search the Inventor's Commandment #8.

A. Why Make a Patentability Search?

I've come up with fourteen reasons for making a patentability search. Let's look at each of them in detail.

1. To Determine Whether You Can Get a Patent

The main reason for making a patentability search of your invention is to discover if the PTO will be likely to grant you a patent on your invention. You may wonder why this should make any difference. After all, why worry about what the PTO will do before it does it? Simply because, if your search indicates that your invention is likely to qualify for a patent, you can go ahead with your development, marketing, and other work on the invention with far more assurance that your efforts will eventually produce positive results. Obviously, if a patent is ultimately granted, you will have a monopoly in the field of the invention for a number of years. Assuming, of course, that your invention has economic value, this will allow you to sell or license it for a reasonable amount, since you'll have at least some assurance that a right to exclude copiers will go with the invention.

If, on the other hand, your patentability search indicates that a patent isn't likely to be granted on your invention, you'll have to think long and hard about whether to proceed. The hard truth is that most manufacturers won't want to invest the money in tooling, producing, and marketing something that their competition can freely copy, and perhaps even sell, at a lower cost. As we'll see in Chapter 7, however, this isn't always true. While it's somewhat unusual, fortunes have sometimes been made manufacturing and selling unpatentable inventions.

2. To Avoid Needless Expenditures and Work

Another reason to make a patentability search has to do with time and money. It's a lot easier (and cheaper) to make a patentability search than to prepare a patent application that must contain a specification, drawings, claims, a filing fee, forms, etc. It makes sense to do a relatively small amount of work entailing a modest expenditure in order to gain useful information that may well allow you to avoid wasting considerable time and/or spending a relatively large amount of money.

3. To Provide Background to Facilitate Preparation of Your Patent Application

You'll find it far easier to prepare a patent application on your invention if you make a patentability search first. This is because a search will bring out prior-art references (prior publications including patents and literature) in the field of your invention. After reading these, you're almost sure to learn much valuable background information that will make the task of writing your patent application far easier. Even patent attorneys routinely review some sample patents from the field of an invention before they begin preparation of a patent application in order to give them a "feel for the art" involved.

4. To Know Whether to Describe and Draw Components

This reason is closely allied with Reason #3. As we'll see in Chapter 8, a patent application must contain a detailed description of your invention, in sufficient detail to enable a person with ordinary skill in the "art" involved to make and use it. If your invention has certain components with which you aren't familiar, you won't have to take the trouble to draw and describe these in detail if you find them already described in prior-art publications, including patents.

5. To Provide More Information About Operability and Design

When you make a search, you will almost always find patents in the field of your invention, possibly on inventions similar to yours. A reading of these patents will give you valuable technical information about your invention, possibly suggesting ways to make it work better and improve its design, or possibly indicating technical approaches that you should avoid.

6. To Learn Commercial Information

The patents and other references that you uncover in your search will give you valuable commercial information about your invention, including possible additional advantages and disadvantages, possible new uses, past commercial failures, etc. For instance, suppose you see many patents on inventions that produce the same result as yours, and you know from your familiarity with the field (as a result of your commercial evaluation in Chapter 4 and your preliminary look—see Section D, below) that none of these has attained commercial success. In this event, you might want to reconsider the wisdom of pushing ahead with your own invention. Or you might conclude that you can do better, because the prior inventions were not commercially exploited properly or because they did not operate properly due to lack of proper components, proper materials, etc.

7. To Obtain Possible Express Proof of Unobviousness

Sometimes a search will uncover references that actually "teach away" from your invention—for example, by suggesting that your approach won't work. You can cite such a reference to the PTO to help convince the examiner to regard your invention as unobvious. (See secondary reason #3 in Chapter 5, Section F4.)

For instance, suppose you've invented a bicycle frame made of a new carbon-fiber alloy that makes your bike far lighter and stronger than any previously made. Ordinarily, as discussed in Chapter 5, Section F, the substitution of a new material (here a carbon-fiber alloy for steel) would not be patentable, since the substitution would not provide any *unexpected* results. But suppose during your search you find a prior-art reference (such as an article in *Metallurgic Times*) that expressly states that the author has tried to use carbon-fiber alloys for bicycle frames without success. If you've found a way to use such alloys successfully, you can cite this reference to the PTO to show that you've turned a past failure into success. Thus you'll have express, positive proof that your invention provides unexpected results and is unobvious.

8. To Define Around the Prior Art to Facilitate Prosecution

By familiarizing yourself with the prior art, you'll be able to tailor and define the general thrust and advantages of your patent application around such art and its deficiencies, thus saving work and arming yourself with the proper terminology that you may need later in the "prosecution" stage (that is, the stage where you actually try to obtain a patent from the PTO). More about this in Chapter 13. Also, an international application, discussed in detail in Chapter 12, requires that an invention be defined in a way that distinguishes it from the prior art. Your search will be of great help here.

9. To Learn Your Invention's Novel Features So As to Expedite Prosecution

After making a thorough search of the prior art, you'll be able to make an informed determination of all your invention's novel features (Box C of Patentability Flowchart—Fig. 5D). By listing its novel features and their attendant advantages, you'll be able to stress and recite all of those features and advantages in your application, its claims and, if necessary, your arguments during prosecution, so as to expedite the ultimate allowance of your case and avoid an early "final action." (See Chapter 13, Section J.)

10. To Facilitate Licensing or Sale of Your Invention

When you attempt to sell or license your invention rights, your potential licensees will want to know if your patent application will be likely to get through the PTO. You can answer their concern, at least partially, by showing them your search results. This will give them confidence in your invention and will save them from having to do their own search, thereby speeding up and facilitating negotiations.

11. To Find Out What You've Really Invented

Yes, I'm serious! From over 30 years' experience I've found that many inventors don't realize or understand exactly what they've invented until they see a search report. Indeed, many inventors get a severe case of "search shock" when their "major advance" turns out to be relatively minor. If this happens, don't give up on your brainchild, since your minor advance may be extremely valuable and vital. On the other hand, occasionally an inventor, believing that the invention is a relatively small advance and that its basic broad idea must have already been invented, is very pleased to learn from the search results that the invention's a gold mine instead of a nugget!

12. To Get a Stronger Patent

The PTO itself will usually make a better search than you or a professional searcher will be able to do. Nevertheless, some examiners, at certain times, may miss a highly relevant reference. If anyone uncovers such a reference later, after you get your patent, and brings this reference to the attention of the PTO or any court, it may cast a cloud over, or even invalidate, your patent. However, if you find such a reference in your search, you can (and must) make a record of it in the PTO's file of your patent application, tailor your claims around it (see Chapter 9), and avoid any potential harm it may cause you later, thus making your patent stronger and less vulnerable.

13. To Get Your Patent Application Examined Ahead of Turn

For reasons explained in Chapter 10, Section P, I don't always recommend that you get your patent application issued sooner, but if you really need to speed things up, you'll be entitled to get it examined ahead of its turn if you've made a pre-examination search. More on how to make a patent application "special" in order to speed up examination in Chapter 10, Section P.

14. To Determine If Your Invention Will Infringe Any In-Force Patents

While the PTO doesn't care one bit about infringement, and will allow your patent application even if your claimed invention would infringe ten in-force patents, you may wish to know if your invention, if made, used, or sold will infringe any existing patents. A search will reveal this.

B. When Not to Search

Despite my inventor's commandment about doing a patent search prior to filing, there are at least two situations where you can "skip the search."

If you are dealing in a very new or arcane field with which you're very familiar, obviously a search is highly unlikely to be profitable. For example, if you're a biotech engineer who's familiar with the state of the art, the newness of your field makes it highly unlikely that you will find any early "prior art." Or, if you make semiconductors and have up-to-the-minute knowledge of all known transistor-diffusion processes, and you come up with a breakthrough transistor-diffusion process, a search will probably not produce any reference showing your idea. Before deciding not to search, however, you should be reasonably certain that you or someone else with whom you are in contact knows all there is to know about the field in question, and that you are fairly confident there is no obscure reference that shows your invention.

In addition, if you've made an improvement to an earlier invention that you've already searched, and you feel the search also covered your improvement, there's obviously no need to make a second search.

DESIGNS

Generally I recommend not searching design inventions, since the cost and time required to make the search is greater than the time and cost to prepare a design patent application. However, if you believe that reasons 6, 7, 9, 10, 11 and/or 12 of Section A, above, may be particularly relevant to your situation, you should make a search of your design.

Common Misconception: *It's not necessary to make a patentability search prior to considering whether to file a patent application, since the PTO will make one anyway.*

Fact: *While it's not necessary to make a search, it's highly desirable, for the 14 reasons given above.*

C. The Two Ways to Make a Patentability Search

Basically, there are only two ways in which you can get your search done: have someone do it for you or do it yourself. If you're a conscientious worker and you have the time, and access to a search facility, or you have computer search capability (see below), I recommend that you do the search yourself in order to make sure that it is done thoroughly and in your desired time frame. In addition, this will save you money and enable you personally to accumulate valuable information, as suggested above.

However, you may have very good reasons for having a professional searcher—for example, you live far from any search facility or you don't have a computer or enough time. Also, there's the procrastination factor: half the time the only way some of us will ever get a job done, even though we're capable of doing it, is to turn it over to a pro. If for geographical or other reasons you choose to hire a searcher, you'll find advice on choosing one in Section F, below. Even if you do use a searcher, read through the instructions on do-it-yourself searching (Sections I-L, below) in order to understand what you're paying for and to be able to recognize whether the searcher has done a thorough job.

Some inventors, because of the importance of the reasons for searching listed above, prefer to do the search themselves and also have a professional search done, just to double-check their work. I don't recommend this, since I've found that an inventor's diligent search is usually adequate. Still, if you feel insecure about your search, you might want to use a computer search as a rough double check (Section M, below). Don't rely on the computer completely, however, unless your invention is in a new field, such as biotechnology or computers. This is because computer searches go back only about 20 years. From my experience, most manual searches produce many relevant prior-art references that were published in much earlier periods, some even as far back as the 1800s.

If you do the patentability search yourself, there are three sub-possibilities:

1. You can search in the PTO in Arlington, Virginia (definitely the best place), or
2. You can search in a local Patent and Trademark Depository Library, or even a regular library that has the *Official Gazettes*, or
3. You can do a computer search if your invention is in a new field.

Read through Sections I and K, below, to compare these alternatives.

D. How to Make a Preliminary Search

If you don't live near the PTO in Arlington, Virginia, I recommend that you conduct a brief preliminary search before spending the money or time for a formal search. Sometimes you will quickly "knock out" your invention and save yourself cost and effort. If you haven't made the preliminary search already as part of your commercial evaluation (see Chapter 4), do so now. Look for your invention in one of two ways:

a. In stores, catalogs, reference books, product directories, etc.: an hour or two in your local library, and perhaps a visit or two to likely stores or suppliers, should be sufficient.

b. Make a quick, free, Internet search of recent patents. The Internet now has several excellent services (all listed on the PTO's World Wide Web site (http://www.uspto.gov/other.html) which enable one to make a *free* search of all patents issued since 1971 using key words. These services and their addresses (on the World Wide Web) are as follows:

IBM's Patent Server:

   http://patent.womplex.ibm.com

Internet Multicasting Service:

   http://town.hall.org/cgi-bin/srch-patent

EDS Shadow Patent Office:

   http://www/spo.eds.com/patent.html

STO's Internet Patent Search System:

   http://sunsite.unc.edu/patents/intropat.html

I provide instructions on making a computer search in Section M of this chapter. You can also use any references you uncover with a computer search to work backward to make a reference "tree" to get more patents, as explained in Section M5. Note, however, that all computer searches, while alluring, are incomplete, since they don't go back far enough and most don't provide patent drawings.

If you don't find anything in your preliminary search, and if your invention doesn't fall into the category discussed under "When Not to Search" (Section B, above), you're ready to make a full search.

E. The Quality of a Patent Search Can Vary

Like anything else, the quality of your patentability search can vary from very bad to near perfect. It can never be perfect since, because of their confidential status, there is no way to search pending patent applications. (As stated in the last chapter, a patent application that was filed before your date of invention is valid prior art against your application, even if the application issues after you file.)

Other reasons why your search may not be perfect are:

• some prior-art references can be missing (stolen or borrowed) from the area you're searching ("class and subclass"—see Section I, below);

• the area in which you're searching may not contain foreign, non-patent, or exotic references (such as theses);

• very recently issued patents may not have been placed in the search files yet;

- a relevant reference (patent or non-patent) may not have been classified in the proper class or in a way that conforms to your view of reality—that is, because of human variability, it may be classified where you wouldn't expect it to be; or
- your invention may have either been used publicly (without being published) before your invention, or it may have been previously invented by someone else who did not abandon, suppress, or conceal it.

F. How to Hire a Patent Professional

Suppose you decide to "let the pros handle it." Here are some suggestions for how to find a patent professional and what your role in the process should be.

1. Lay Patent Searchers

Many patent searchers can be located in the Yellow Pages of local telephone directories under "Patent Searchers." Others advertise in periodicals, such as the *Journal of the Patent and Trademark Office Society,* a publication for patent professionals edited and published by a private association of patent examiners, or *The Dream Merchant* (see Appendix 2, Books of Use and Interest). I have had far better results with patent attorneys and agents than with lay searchers. Attorneys and agents understand the concept of unobviousness (see previous chapter) better and thus dig in more places than might at first appear necessary. However, lay searchers have one big advantage: they charge about half of what most attorneys and agents charge. Nevertheless, before hiring a lay searcher, I would find out about the searcher's charges, technical background, on-the-job experience, usual amount of time spent on a search and where the searcher searches (in the PTO's main search room or in the examining division). Most importantly, I would also ask for the names of some clients, preferably in your city, so that you can check with them. Lay searchers do not have to be licensed by any governmental agency, so you should exercise more care in selecting one and you should be aware that they're not allowed to express opinions on patentability.

2. Patent Agents

A "patent agent" is an individual with some technical training (generally an undergraduate degree in engineering) who is licensed by the PTO to prepare and prosecute patent applications. A patent agent can conduct a patent search and is authorized to express an opinion on patentability, but cannot appear in court, cannot handle trademarks, and cannot handle licensing or infringement suits. All other

things being equal, I recommend using an attorney rather than an agent for searching (and patent application work), since attorneys' experience in licensing and litigation will usually lead them to make wider and stronger searches for possible use in adversarial situations.

3. Patent Attorneys

A "patent attorney" or "patent lawyer" is licensed to practice both by the PTO and the attorney licensing authority (such as the state bar, state supreme court, etc.) of at least one state. Thus patent attorneys must be licensed by two authorities. A "general" lawyer licensed to practice in one or more states, but not before the PTO, is not authorized to prepare patent applications or use the title "patent attorney."

4. Finding Patent Agents and Attorneys

All patent agents and attorneys are listed in the PTO's publication *Attorneys and Agents Registered to Practice Before the U.S. Patent and Trademark Office* (A&ARTP). This is available in all medium- to large-sized public libraries as well as Patent and Trademark Depository Libraries (see Section K, below), government bookstores, and on the PTO's electronic Bulletin Board System (see Appendix 5, Mail, Telephone and Computer Communications With the PTO).

For patent search purposes, you will want to find an attorney or agent in the Washington, D.C., area. Most patent attorneys and agents who do searching in the PTO can be found in the District of Columbia section, or the Virginia section of A&ARTP under zip code 22202. Pick one or more of these and then call or write to say you want a search made in a particular field. (Generally, hiring an attorney in your locality to do the search is a very inefficient and costly way to do the job, since the attorney or agent will have to hire an associate in or travel to Arlington to make the search for you. This means you'll have to pay two patent professionals or travel expenses for the search.)

HOW TO FIND "DISCOUNT" PATENT ATTORNEYS AND AGENTS

Active patent professionals (attorneys and agents) are either in private practice (a law firm or solo practice) or employed by a corporation or the government. Most patent professionals in private practice charge about $100 to $300 an hour. But many corporate-employed or semiretired patent professionals also have private clients and charge considerably less. If you want or ever need to consult a local patent professional, you'll save money by using one of these "discount" patent professionals; their services are usually just as good or better than those of the full-priced law firm attorneys. Also, since they have much less overhead (rent, books, secretaries), they'll be more generous with their time (except that patent professionals employed by the federal government are not allowed to represent private clients). Look in the geographical section of A&ARTP for corporate-employed or retired (but still licensed) patent professionals in your area; the latter can usually be identified by their corporate addresses or addresses in a residential, rather than a downtown, neighborhood. You can expect to pay substantially more for attorneys in downtown high-rise office buildings.

Of course, finding a good patent professional often involves more than checking a list. The best way is by personal referral. Ask another inventor, your employer, your local inventors' organization, a general attorney whom you like, a friend, etc. If you do find someone who seems good, make a short appointment to discuss the broad outlines of your problem. This will give you a feel for the attorney, whether the chemistry's good between the two of you, whether the fees are acceptable, etc. Ask what undergraduate degree the attorney has (almost all have undergraduate degrees in engineering or a science); you don't want to use a mechanical engineer to handle a complex computer circuit.

Your next question should be, Will the professional help you help yourself or demand a traditional attorney-client relationship (attorney does it all and you pay for it)? Many corporate-employed and retired patent professionals will be delighted to help you with your search, preparation, and/or prosecution of your patent application. Using this approach, you can do much of the work yourself and have the professional provide help where needed at a reasonable cost.

When it comes to fees, you should always work these out in advance. Some patent professionals charge a flat fee for searches (and also for patent applications and amendments); others charge by the hour. If you plan to do much of the work yourself, you'll want hourly billing. Also, be sure it's clear who will pay for other costs associated with prosecuting a patent, such as copies, postage, drafting, filing fees, etc.

G. How to Prepare Your Searcher

You'll want to use your patent searcher to maximum efficiency. Do this by sending your searcher a clear and complete description of your invention, together with easily understandable drawings. You won't compromise any trade-secret status of your invention by such a letter since by law it's considered a confidential communication. If you wish any type of particular emphasis applied to any aspect of your search, be sure to inform the searcher of this fact. If your notebook record of your invention or your invention disclosure is clear enough, you can merely send the searcher a copy. Whether you send a copy of your notebook entries or a separate disclosure (Form 3-2), I recommend that you blank out all dates on any document you send to anyone: this will make it more difficult for any potential invention thief (extremely rare) who might gain access to your disclosure to antedate you. Fig. 6A is an example of a proper search request letter from an inventor and Figs. 6B (a, b, c) are copies of the attachments to the search request letter of Fig. 6A.

You don't need to have a patent agent or a patent attorney sign a Keep-Confidential Agreement (Chapter 3), since registered patent professionals are strictly bound to keep all client communications confidential. However, if you feel insecure, or you are using a layperson to search, you certainly can ask your searcher to sign Form 3-1. In any case, you should always keep a "paper trail" of all disclosures you make to anyone.

Millie Inventress
1901 JFK Blvd.
Philadelphia, PA 19103

1995 Jan 22, Tue
Samuel Searcher, Esq.
2001 Jefferson Davis Highway
Arlington, VA 22202

Patentability Search: Inventress: Napkin-Shaping Ring

Dear Mr. Searcher:

As we discussed on the phone yesterday, you were highly recommended to me as an excellent searcher by Jacob Potofsky, Esq., who is a general attorney here and a cousin of my friend, Shirley Jaschik. You said that you would be able to make a full patentability search on my above invention, including an examiner consultation and a search in the examiner's files to cover foreign and non-patent references, for $500, including patent copies and postage. I have enclosed this amount as full payment in advance, per your request. You said that you would mail the search report (without an opinion on patentability) and references to me within three weeks from the date you receive this letter.

Enclosed are three sheets of drawings from my notebook (I have properly signed, witnessed, and dated records elsewhere); these sheets clearly illustrate my napkin-shaping ring invention. As you can see from the prior-art Figs 1 (A and B), previous napkin rings were simple affairs, designed merely to hold a previously rolled or folded napkin in a simple shape. In contrast, the napkin ring of my invention, shown in Fig 2, and made of metal or plastic, has a heart-shaped outer member 12, an inner leg 14, and two curved-back arms 16. As shown in Fig 3, it is used by introducing a corner 8 of a cloth napkin 10 between an end 4 of leg 4 and the adjacent portion of outer member 12. When napkin 10 is pulled partially through the ring, as indicated in Fig 4, it will be forced to assume the shape of the space between arms 16 and outer portion 12, as indicated.

Thus my napkin-shaping-and-holding ring can be used to make a napkin have an attractive, graceful shape when it is laid flat and placed adjacent to a place setting, as indicated in Fig 5. The extending portion of the napkin can also be folded up and around, as indicated in Fig 6-A, so that the napkin and its ring can be stood upright.

In addition to the specific shape shown, you should of course search the broader concept of my invention, namely a ring-shaped outer member with an inwardly extending tongue or leg that can be used to shape napkins pulled partially through the structure. I believe that I have provided you with sufficient information to fully understand the structure and workings of my invention so that you can make a search, but if any further information is needed, please don't hesitate to call me.

I understand that you will, in accordance with the ethics of your profession, keep all details of my invention strictly confidential, except to consult an examiner.

Most sincerely,

Millie Inventress

Millie Inventress (215-776-3960)
Encs.: $500 check, 3 sheets of drawings
(My file: 60:Search.ltr)

Fig. 6A—Inventor's Search Request Letter to Patent Searcher

FIG 1
PRIOR ART
NAPKIN RINGS

FIG 2
CIRCULAR SHAPING
RING

Fig. 6B(a)—Drawing of Invention, Part a

FIG 3
NAPKIN INTRODUCED

FIG 4
NAPKIN PARTIALLY
INSERTED

Fig. 6B(b)—Drawing of Invention, Part b

FIG 5
NAPKIN FULLY INSERTED

FIG 6A
TIP FOLDED UP AROUND
RING-SIDE VIEW

Fig. 6B(c)—Drawing of Invention, Part c

H. Analyzing the Search Report

After you send out your search request, the searcher will generally take several weeks to perform the patentability search, obtain copies of the patents and other references that the searcher feels are relevant, and report back. Most search reports have four parts:

1. A description of your invention provided by the searcher to assure you that the searcher has understood your invention and to indicate exactly what has been searched.
2. A list of the patents and other references discovered during the search.
3. A brief discussion of the cited patents and other references, pointing out the relevant parts of each.
4. A list of the classes and subclasses searched and the examiners consulted, if any.

The searcher will enclose copies of the references (usually U.S. patents, but possibly also foreign patents, magazine articles, etc.) cited in the search report and enclose a bill. Most searchers charge separately for the search, the reference copies, and the postage. If you've paid the searcher a retainer, you should be sent a refund unless your retainer was insufficient. In this case, you'll receive a bill for the balance you owe.

EXAMPLES:

- Fig. 6C is an example of a typical, competently done search report sent by Samuel Searcher, Esq., in response to Millie Inventress' letter of Fig. 6A.
- Fig. 6D(a) is a copy of page 1 (the drawing) of the Gabel patent cited in the search report.
- Fig. 6D(b) is a copy of page 2 of Gabel (the first page of Gabel's specification).
- Fig. 6D(c) is a copy of page 1 of the Le Sueur patent cited in the search report.

I haven't shown the other cited patents and the rest of the Gabel and Le Sueur patents, as these aren't necessary for our patentability determination.

You should now read the searcher's report and the references carefully. Then, determine whether your invention is patentable over the references cited in the search report. Let's use Millie's search report as an example of how to do this.

First, note from Fig. 6B that the napkin-shaping ring of the invention has an annular (ring-shaped) outer member with an inwardly projecting leg. The leg has flared-back arms at its free end. When a folded napkin is drawn through the ring, tip first, the arms and annular member will shape the napkin between them in an attractive manner, as indicated in Fig. 6B(c).

Of the four previous patents cited, let's assume that only Gabel and Le Sueur are of real relevance. Gabel, a patent from 1930, shows a curtain folder comprising a bent sheet metal member. A curtain is folded slightly and is drawn through the folder that completes the folding so that the curtain can be ironed when it is drawn out of the folder. Le Sueur, a patent from 1976, shows a napkin ring with a magnetized area for holding the letters of the name of a user.

Now, as part of analyzing this sample search report, we'll use the master flowchart of Fig. 5D. To save you from having to turn the pages repeatedly, I've reproduced it below, as Fig. 6E. If any part of this chart confuses you, reread the part of Chapter 5 that explains each box in detail.

Okay, now let's work our way through the chart:

Box A: Millie's napkin-shaping ring can be classified within a statutory class as an article (or even a machine since it shapes napkins).

Box B: It clearly has usefulness, since it provides a way for unskilled hostesses or hosts to give their napkins an attractive, uniform shape.

Box C: We must now ask whether the invention is novel—that is, physically different from any single reference. Clearly it's different from Le Sueur because of its inwardly extending leg 14. Also, it's different from Gabel because, comparing it with Gabel's Fig. 6, it's rounder and it has a complete outer ring with an inwardly extending leg, rather than a folded piece of sheet metal. It's important to compile a list of the differences that the invention has over the prior-art references, not the differences of the references over your invention.

Box D: The question we must now ask is, Do the novel features (the roundness of the ring, the inwardly extending leg, and the flared-back arms) provide any new and unexpected results? After carefully comparing Gabel with Millie's invention, we can answer with a resounding "Yes!" Note that Gabel states, in her column 2, lines 62 to 66, that the strip of cloth is first partially folded along its side edge and then it is placed in the folder. In contrast, Millie's shaping ring, because of its roundness and leg, can shape a totally unfolded napkin—see Millie's Figs. 3 and 4. This is a distinct advantage, since Millie's shaper does all of the work automatically—the user does not have to specially fold the napkin. While not an earthshaking development or advance, clearly Millie's ring does provide a new result and one that is unexpected, since neither Gabel, Le Sueur, nor any other reference teaches that a napkin ring can be used to shape an unfolded napkin. Thus we take the solid-line "Yes" output of Box D to Box E.

Box E: Although not mandatory, we next check the secondary factors (1 to 21) listed in Boxes E, F, and G.

SAMUEL SEARCHER
Patent Attorney
2001 Jefferson Davis Highway
Arlington, VA 22202
703-521-3210
1995 Feb 21, Thu

Ms. Millie Inventress
1901 JFK Blvd.
Philadelphia, PA 19103

Search Report: Inventress: Napkin-Shaping Ring

Dear Ms. Inventress:

In response to your letter of Jan. 22, I have made a patentability search of your above invention, a napkin-shaping ring comprising an outer portion with an inwardly extending leg and flared-back arms at the end of the leg. I have also searched the broader concept of an annular member with an inward cantilevered leg for shaping a napkin that is drawn therethrough. My bill for $400, the total cost of this search, including the references and postage, is enclosed and is marked "Paid"; I thank you for your check.

I searched your invention in the following classes and subclasses in the actual examining divisions: 40/21, 40/142, D44/20, and 24/8. In addition, I consulted Examiner John Hayness in Group Art Unit 353 regarding this invention. Otherwise, I kept your invention strictly confidential. In my search, I thought the following references (all U.S. Patents) were most relevant, and I enclose a copy of each: **Bergmann,** 705,196 (1902); **Gabel,** 1,771,328 (1930); **Hypps,** 3,235,880 (1966); and **Le Sueur,** 3,965,591 (1976).

Bergmann shows a handkerchief holder that comprises a simple coiled ring with wavy portions.

Gabel is most relevant; she shows a curtain folder comprising a folded metal device through which a curtain (already partially folded) is inserted and then pulled through and ironed at the exit end.

Hypps shows a necktie and holding device.

Le Sueur shows a napkin ring with magnetically attachable names.

I could not find any napkin-shaping devices as such and Examiner Hayness was not aware of any either. However, be sure to consider the Gabel patent carefully, as it appears to perform a somewhat similar function, albeit for curtains.

It was my pleasure to serve you. I wish you the best of success with your invention. Please don't hesitate to call if you have any questions.

Most sincerely,

Samuel Searcher

Samuel Searcher
Encs: $100 Check, Bill and References

Fig. 6C—Patent Searcher's Search Report

July 22, 1930   L. GABEL   1,771,328

FOLDER

Filed March 16, 1923

Louise Gabel
INVENTOR

BY *Victor J. Evans*
ATTORNEY

WITNESS:

Fig. 6D(a)—Drawing of Prior-Art Gabel Patent

1,771,328

UNITED STATES PATENT OFFICE

LOUISE GABEL, OF COLUMBUS, NEBRASKA

FOLDER

Application filed March 16, 1928. Serial No. 262.243.

This invention relates to cloth holding devices and more particularly to a device adapted for holding cloth in the form of plaits while ironing and sewing.

An other object of the invention comprehends an enlarged entrance opening in one end of the device within which the cloth may be introduced.

A further object of the invention contemplates tongue members adapted to form creases in the cloth.

An additional object of the invention consists of a portion removed from the discharge end of the device whereby binding action of a sad iron therewith is obviated while pressing the cloth.

With the above and other objects in view, the invention further consists of the following novel features and details of construction, to be hereinafter more fully described, illustrated in the accompanying drawing and pointed out in the appended claim.

In the drawing:—

Figure 1 is a side elevation of the invention while in use and followed by a sad iron.

Figure 2 is a top plan view of Figure 1.

Figure 3 is a top plan view of the invention per se.

Figure 4 is a sectional view taken on line 4—4 of Figure 3.

Figure 5 is a bottom plan view of the invention.

Figure 6 is a front elevation of the invention per se.

Referring to the drawing in detail, wherein like characters of reference denote corresponding parts, the reference character 10 indicates a plate member having a curved outwardly projecting forward end 11 and a concaved inner end 12.

The sides of the plate are bent upon themselves upwardly and inwardly upon the plate to provide horizontally disposed guide members 13.

As illustrated in Figures 1, 3, 4 and 6, the outermost end, namely 11, is flared to provide an enlarged entrance and to accomplish such construction the outermost ends of the guide members 13 are upwardly flared, as indicated at 14 and concaved, as indicated at 15 upon the foremost edges thereof.

Tongues 16, carried by 13, are extended reversely, posed in spaced relation the plate member 10. tongues being also spaced members. The foremost 16 are rounded, as indicated, jected forwardly for guide the adjacent ends of the

In the use and operation of the invention, lengths of cloth, such as indicated at 18, of a desired width, are partially folded along the side edges thereof and the strip per se laid upon the upper side of the plate member 10. The folded portions of the strip being adapted to repose upon the upper sides of the tongues 16 and to be projected within the spaces as defined between the tongues and the guide members. Due to the fact that the outermost end of the device is flared, an enlarged entrance is provided by means of which the cloth may be readily introduced and fed. The rounded portions 17 for the tongues also permit ease in the drawing of the cloth through the device or the sliding of the device upon the cloth. As illustrated in Figures 1 and 2 of the drawing, a sad iron, such as indicated at 19, may travel upon the cloth 18 immediately behind the device to press the folded side edges or plaits of the cloth. By the same token, the invention could be used in the formation of different kinds of braids and etc., and to effectively feed the cloth or strip to a sewing machine, in the event the plaits are to be held against displacement from the strip per se.

The concaved portion 12, upon the innermost end of the strip 10, is adapted to prevent binding action of the sad iron 19 therewith when the latter closely pursues the plate member. Such construction will also prevent injury to the strip and plaits.

Although I have shown, described and illustrated my invention as being primarily adapted for use in the manufacture of plaits, it is to be obviously understood that the invention could be effectively employed for

Fig. 6D(b)—Specification of Prior-Art Gabel Patent

United States Patent [19]

Le Sueur

[11]   **3,965,591**

[45]   **June 29, 1976**

[54]   NAPKIN RING

[75]   Inventor: **Alice E. J. Le Sueur, Cobble Hill, Canada**

[73]   Assignee: **The Raymond Lee Organization, New York, N.Y. ; a part interest**

[22]   Filed: **Nov. 26, 1974**

[21]   Appl. No.: **527,216**

[52]   U.S. Cl.. **40/21 R**
[51]   Int. Cl.² **G09F 3/14**
[58]   Field of Search.................. 40/142 A, 63, 21 A, 40/21 B, 10; 63/2; 24/8

[56]   **References Cited**
UNITED STATES PATENTS

198,065   12/1877   Annin .... 63/1 X

2.600.505   6/1952   Jones .... 40/142 A
2.653.402   9/1953   Bonagura .... 40/21 A

FOREIGN PATENTS OR APPLICATIONS

1.308.888   10/1962   France 40/142

Primary Examiner—Louis G. Mancene
Assistant Examiner—Wenceslao J. Contreras
Attorney, Agent, or Firm—Howard I. Podell

[57]   ABSTRACT

An open cylindrical napkin ring fitted with magnetic means for attaching an identifying name or set of initials in a recess on the outside of the ring.

3 Claims, 4 Drawing Figures

Fig. 6D(c)—Abstract Page of Prior-Art Le Sueur Patent

Fig. 6E—Patentability Flowchart

Reading through these factors, we find first that #2 in Box E applies—that is, the invention solves a problem (the inability of most persons to quickly and neatly fold napkins so that they have an attractive shape) that was never before even recognized. Also, we can provide affirmative answers to factors #8 and #11, since the invention provides an advantage that was never before appreciated and it solves a long-felt, but unsolved need—the need of unskilled persons to shape napkins quickly and gracefully (long felt by the more fastidious of those who hate paper napkins, at least).

Boxes F and G: Since two references are present, and each shows some part of Millie's invention, we have to answer "Yes" to Box F and proceed to Box G to consider the possible effect that a combination of these would have on the question of obviousness ("combinatory unobviousness"). In Box G we see that factors 13, 15, 18, 19 and 21 can reasonably be argued as relevant to Millie's invention. The invention has synergism (#21), since the results (automatic napkin folding) are greater than the sum of the references, the combination of the two references is not suggested (#13) by the references themselves; and even if the two references were combined, Millie's inward leg would not be shown (#15). The references are complete and fully functional in themselves, and hence teach by implication that they should not be combined (#18). And it would be awkward, requiring redesign and tooling, to combine the references (#19). Thus we can with conviction state that several secondary factors are present, so we take the solid-line "Yes" output of Box G. Here (Box H) we see that the PTO is very likely to grant a patent, and our determination on patentability is accordingly positive.

In fact, this exercise is a real case: An examiner initially rejected an application for the napkin-shaping ring as unpatentable over Gabel and Le Sueur. However, he agreed to grant a patent (#4,420,102) after I filed an argument forcefully stating the above considerations.

Although I've analyzed the search report to determine whether Millie's invention was patentable, it's important to remember that a weak patent isn't much better than no patent. Put differently, a very weak patent and $3.00 will get you a cable car ride in San Francisco. So in addition to reaching a decision on patentability, you should also walk the extra mile to determine whether your patent is likely to be of broad enough scope to make it economically worthwhile. I tell you how to do this in Section J of this chapter.

Note that we have done our own patentability evaluation—the four-part list, above—and that the search report of Fig. 6C didn't include an opinion on patentability. There are several reasons for this.

First, if your searcher is a layperson (not a patent attorney or agent), the searcher is not licensed to give opinions on patentability since this constitutes the practice of law.

Second, even if your searcher is an attorney or agent, the searcher usually won't provide an opinion on patentability because most searchers are used to working for other patent attorneys who like to form their own opinions on patentability for their clients.

Third, if the searcher's opinion on patentability is negative, a negative written opinion might be damaging to your case if you do get a patent, sue to enforce it, and the opinion is used as evidence that your patent is invalid. This would occur, for example, if your court adversary (the defendant-infringer) obtains a copy of the opinion by pretrial discovery (depositions and interrogatories), shows it to the judge, and argues that since your own search came up with a negative result, this militates against the validity of your patent. However, a negative written opinion can be "worked" in court—that is, distinguished, explained, rebutted, etc.—so if you want the searcher's opinion on patentability in addition to the search, most patent attorney/agent searchers will be glad to give it to you without extra charge, or for an slight additional cost of probably not more than $100 to $200.

Fourth, armed with the knowledge you've gained from Chapter 5, you should be able to form your own opinion on patentability by now; the exercise will be fun, educational, and insightful to your invention.

In any case, don't hesitate to ask any questions about the searcher's practices in advance, and be sure to specify exactly what you want in your search. It's your money and you're entitled to buy or contract for whatever services you desire.

I.   Do-It-Yourself Searching in the PTO

Almost all pre-examination searches should be made primarily in patent files (paper or computer). This is because patents are classified according to a detailed scheme (discussed later in this chapter). Also, there are about ten times as many devices and processes shown in the patent files as in textbooks, magazines, etc., primarily because commercial practicability is not a requirement for patentability. All PTO examiners make their searches in the patent files for these reasons, so you should also. However, if you have access to a good non-patent data bank—such as a good technical library in the field of your invention, you can use this as a supplement or alternative to your search of the patent files.

Searching is a strange business—it's one of the few times you'll look for something with the hope that you won't find it! Nevertheless, you should do it carefully and thoroughly, because searching is one of the main areas where an ounce of early work can save you pounds of later work and disappointment.

1.   Getting Situated at the PTO

As we have said, the best place to make a search of the patent files is in the PTO in Arlington (unless you have access to the files of a large company that specializes in your field). This is because the PTO's search facilities have all U.S. patents arranged by subject matter. For example, all patents that show bicycle derailleurs are physically grouped together, all patents that show transistor flip-flop circuits are together, all patents to diuretic drug compositions are together, etc. Also, the PTO has foreign patents and literature classified along with U.S. patents according to subject matter (but only in the examiner search areas). Remember (Chapter 5, Section E1) that foreign patents are valid prior art in the U.S.

The PTO is located in a complex of modern medium-rise buildings in Arlington, Virginia, informally called "Crystal City." Although all mail must be addressed to the Assistant Commissioner for Patents, Washington, DC 20231, the PTO is physically located at South 23rd Street and U.S. 1 (Jefferson Davis Highway) in Arlington, about half-a-mile due west of the Washington National Airport. It

receives over three million pieces of mail a year, more than any other governmental agency except the IRS.

The PTO is technically part of the Department of Commerce (headquartered in Washington) but operates in an almost autonomous fashion. The first floor of the main PTO building (Crystal Plaza 4) contains the main search room. The various examining divisions and administration departments are upstairs in this and adjacent buildings.

The PTO employs about 1,200 examiners, all of whom have technical undergraduate degrees in such fields as electrical engineering, chemistry, or physics. Many examiners are also attorneys. The PTO also has about an equal number of clerical, supervisory, and support personnel. The Commissioner of Patents and Trademarks is appointed by the President, and most of the higher officials of the PTO have to be approved by Congress. Most patent examiners are well paid; a journeyman examiner (ten years' experience) usually makes $50,000 to $100,000 a year.

Assuming you do go to the PTO in Arlington, here's what you'll find. There are two places you can make the search:

• the public search room, and
• the examiners' search files in the actual examining division.

Most searchers make their search in the public search room because it's more convenient—it's on the first floor, there are search tables, and it's large and well lighted. However, I recommend putting up with a little inconvenience and going upstairs to the examiners' search files. There are several reasons to do this: the examiners are there to assist you; literature and foreign patents are available; it's much quieter; the patent files are likely to be more intact; and finally, of at least minor importance, the chairs are more comfortable. To get into the search room or upstairs, you must apply for a user pass, which will take only a few minutes. You must also ask permission from an examiner or clerk before commencing your particular search.

If you need help with your search, you can ask any of the search assistants in the search room or (even better) an examiner in the actual examining division. You won't be endangering the security of your invention if you ask any of these people about your search and give them all the details of your invention. They see dozens of new inventions every week and they are quite used to helping searchers and others. I've never heard of an examiner or search assistant stealing an invention. They could not do so personally, anyway, because employees of the PTO are not allowed to file patent applications. True, in theory a PTO employee could reveal an invention to a friend or relative who could file, but it's absurdly unlikely to occur.

2. How to Do the Search

Okay, now that you know something about the PTO and where to search, what do you do next? There are four basic steps to take when conducting a patent search; these are depicted in Fig. 6F and listed below:

Step 1: Articulate the nature and essence of your invention, using as many different terms as you can think of to describe it.

Step 2: Find the relevant classification(s) for your invention.

Step 3: Note relevant prior art (patents and other publications) under your classification.

Step 4: Carefully review the prior art to see whether it anticipates your invention or renders it obvious.

Let's take these one at a time.

Step 1: Write Out the Nature and Essence of Your Invention

As with any other classification or indexing system, your success will depend on the degree to which the words and phrases you use to define your invention coincide with the terms used by the classifier or indexer. For this reason, you should first figure out several ways to describe your invention. Start by writing down all the physical features of your invention in a brief, concise format so that you'll know exactly what to look for when searching.

For example, if you're searching a bicycle with a new type of sprocket wheel, write down "bicycle, sprocket wheel," and add briefly the details. If you're searching an electronic circuit, write down in a series of phrases like the foregoing or, in a very brief sentence, the quintessence of your invention, such as "flip-flop circuit with unijunction transistors" or some other very brief and concise description. Do the same for chemical inventions.

Form 6-1 is a Searcher's Worksheet that you can use to facilitate your searching, and Fig. 6G is a completed version of Form 6-1 that you might produce if you had searched Millie Inventress's invention. Note that the invention description part of the worksheet contains a concise description of the invention for easy reference.

Once you've written a concise description of your invention, think of some alternative key words or phrases to add to your description. Don't hesitate to define your invention in still additional ways that may come to you during your search. Then, take your worksheet with this brief description and the drawing(s) of your invention to the public search room. Even if you're not going to do your search there, use that room to find out how your invention is classified.

Step 2: Find the Proper Classification for Your Invention

To find the place to search your invention, you'll need its most relevant search classification (called class and subclass). To obtain this, first look at the searcher's "tools" or reference publications, all of which are available in book or CD-ROM form. (See sidebar, CD-ROM Products at PTDLs, in Section K, below.) These consist of:

- the *Index to the U.S. Patent Classification*
- the *Manual of Classification*, and
- the *Classification Definitions*.

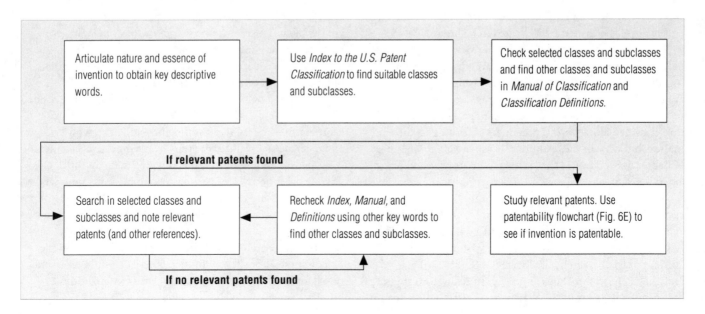

Fig. 6F—Searching Process

Searcher's Worksheet

Sheet ___1___ of ___1___

Inventor(s): __Millie Inventress__

Invention Description (use key words and variations): __Napkin folder—Annular member with inner leg__
__and flared-back arms__

Selected Search Classifications

Class/Sub	Description	Checked	Comments
40-21	Napkin holders	✓	very relevant—the right place
40-142	Misc. tableware	✓	mostly utensils—not too good
D44-20	Napkin holders	✓	somewhat relevant
24-8	Shaping devices	✓	N.G.

Patents (and Other References) Thought Relevant

Patent #	Name or Country	Date	Class/Sub	Comment
705,196	Bergmann	1902	40-142	Plain ring
1,771,328	Gabel	1930	40-21	Curtain folder
3,235,880	Hypps	1966	40-21	Necktie and holder
3,965,591	LeSueur	1976	40-21	Ring with magnetic letters

Consulted Examiner
Hayness, John   Ext. 353

Searcher: __S. Searcher__   Date: __9X-1-12__

Fig. 6G—Completed Searcher's Worksheet (Form 6-1 in Appendix 7)

Again, let's slow down and look at each of these in detail.

The Index to the U.S. Patent Classification

While bearing an awkward title, this will be your main reference tool. It's a paperbound 8.5" x 11" book that alphabetically lists all possible subject areas of invention, from "abacus" to "zwieback," together with the appropriate class and subclass for each. The *Index* also lists the classes alphabetically. Let's assume that you've invented a gymnastic exercising apparatus. The first thing to do is to look in the *Index* under "Gymnastic Devices." We come to page 96 (Fig. 6H), a typical page from the *Index*. It shows, among other things, that "Gymnastic Devices" are classified in class 272, subclass 109.

Manual of Classification

Now that we've found the class and subclass numbers, it's time to turn to the *Manual of Classification*, which lists the classes of invention numerically. (As stated, there are about 430 classes.) Each class is on its own page(s), together with about 300 to 400 subclasses under each class heading, for a total of about 140,000 subclasses. The *Manual* lists design as well as utility classes; the classes are not in any logical order. To see where class-subclass 272-109 fits, let's look at the first page that covers class 272. Fig. 6I is a copy of this page. It shows the first part of "Class 272—Amusement and Exercising Devices." Note that subclass 93 in this class covers "Exercising Equipment," and that subclass 109, which is indented under subclass 93, states "Gymnastic"; thus, class-subclass 272-109 covers gymnastic exercising equipment. Note that under 272-109 are further subclasses that may be of interest; these cover trapezes and rings, horizontal bars, etc.

As I'll explain below, this manual is used as an adjunct to the *Index*, to check your selected classes, and to find other, closely related ones.

Classification Definitions

To check our selected class and subclass still further, we next consult a third source, known as the *Classification Definitions*. This is a series of loose-leaf books or CD-ROM disks that contain a definition for every class and subclass in the *Manual*. At the end of each subclass definition is a cross-reference of additional places to look that correspond to such subclass. Fig. 6J shows the classification definition for 272-109. This definition is actually a composite that I've assembled from several pages of the *Definitions*—that is, it includes definitions for class 272 per se and the superior class/subclass 272-93. Note that the class definition (272 per se), as well as many of the subclass definitions (see, for example, 272-110) contain cross-references to other classes

and subclasses. You should consider these when selecting your search areas.

Be sure to spend enough time to become confidently familiar with the classification system for your invention. Check all of your subclasses in the *Manual of Classification* and the *Class Definitions* manual to be sure that you've obtained all of the right ones. Usually, two or more subclasses will be appropriate. For example, suppose your gymnastic device uses a gear with an irregular shape. Naturally, you should search in the gear classes as well as in the exercising device classes. Note that the cross-references in the exercising device classes won't refer you to "gears," since this is too specific—the cross-references in the PTO's manuals are necessarily general in nature. It's up to you to consider all aspects of your particular invention when selecting search categories.

Another excellent example of using your imagination in class and subclass selection for searching is given in the paper, "The Patent System—A Source of Information for the Engineer," by Joseph K. Campbell, Assistant Professor, Agricultural Engineering Department, Cornell University, Ithaca, New York, which was presented at the 1969 Annual Meeting of the American Society of Agricultural Engineers, North Atlantic Region. The ASAE's address is P.O. Box 229, St. Joseph, MI 49085. The publication number is NA-64-206. The article costs $7.00. Call 616-429-0300 for more information.

GETTING CLASSIFICATION FROM THE PTO OR A PTDL

You can get a free, informal mail-order classification of your invention for search purposes by sending a copy of your invention disclosure, with a request for suggestions of one or more search subclasses, to Search Room, Patent and Trademark Office, Washington DC 20231. However, unless you're really stuck in obtaining subclasses, I don't recommend using this method, since you have the interest and familiarity with your invention to do a far better job if only you put a little effort into it.

Also, to save time if you intend to go to the PTO in Arlington, you can get the search classifications locally at a PTDL (Patent Trademark Depository Library) by using its CD-ROM CASSIS (Classification and Search Support Information System). Instructions will be provided at the computer or by the librarian.

Professor Campbell postulates a hypothetical search of a machine that encapsulates or pelletizes small seeds (such as

Gun   **INDEX TO CLASSIFICATION**   **Hammer**

	Class	Subclass
Water pistol	222	79
Well tubing perforator	175	2
Y gun	89	1R
Gussets		
Garment	2	275
Pocketbook body construction	150	30
Gut or Gut Treatment	8	94.11
Splitter	83	926A*
Guttapercha	260	709
Gutter	405	119
Eaves trough	52	11
Electric conductor underground structure	174	39
Road and pavement	404	2
Support design	D 8	363
Guy	52	146
Bed spring and frame	52	272
Gymnastic Devices	272	109
Coin controlled apparatus	194	
Gypsum	423	554
Calcining	106	100
Coating or plastic compositions containing	106	109
Alkali metal silicate	106	77
Gyrating		
Reciprocating sifter		
Actuating means	209	366
Horizontal and vertical shake	209	326
Horizontal shake	209	332
Gyratory Crusher		
Jaw crushers rotary component	241	207
Parallel flow through plural zones	241	140
Series flow through plural zones	241	156
Gyro Stabilized		
Article support	248	183
Furniture for ships	114	119
Gyroplane (See Aircraft)	244	17.11
Gyroscope	74	5R
Aerial camera combined	354	70
Aircraft control	244	79
Ammunition digest	102	DIG 3
Direction indicator	33	318
Gimbals	248	182
Gun sight combined	33	236
Gyroscopic compass	33	324
Telemetric system combined	340	870.7
Monorail rolling stock	105	141
Suspended	105	150
Rotors	74	572
Rotors and flywheels	74	
Ship antiroll	114	112
Ship stabilizer	114	122
Ship steering	114	144R
Speed responsive devices	73	504
Torpedo	114	24
Torpedo steering	114	24
Toy	46	50
Transmission	74	64

H

	Class	Subclass
H Acid	260	509
Haberdashery Item	D 2	378
Habitat, Submarine	114	314
Hack Saw	145	31R
Combined	7	149
Design	D 8	96
Hanging	83	783
Hackling		
Combing	19	115R
Decorticating	19	5R
Hacks Tree	30	121
Haemocytometer	356	39
Testing lenses	356	124
Hair		
Artificial furs	428	85
Artificial structure	132	5
Beauty parlor equipment	D28	10
Brush	15	160
Carried hat fasteners	132	60
Clippers	D28	52
Coating compositions	106	155
Curlers		
Curling iron	D28	38
Electrically heated	219	222
Fluid fuel heated	126	408
Cutters	30	
Design	D 8	57
Design clippers	D28	52

	Class	Subclass
For inside ear or nose	30	29.5
Hair planers	30	30
Drying on head		
Apparatus	34	96
Processes	34	3
Supports for	34	101
Dye applicator	D28	7
Dyeing and dyes	8	405
Fasteners	132	46R
Design	D28	39
Fertilizer from	71	18
Hairpiece	D28	92
Inserters	128	330
Jeweled fastener	63	2
Net	132	49
Pins (See hairpins)	132	50R
Planers	30	30
Removing (See notes)	30	32
Burial preparation	27	21
Butchering	17	1D
Coarse or water hair from fur	69	24
Cutters for inside ear or nose	30	29.5
Depilating untanned skins	8	94.16
Depilatories	8	94.16
Electric needle	128	303.18
Electric needle supports	128	303.19
Fiber liberating	19	2
Fur treatment	69	24
Process	17	47
Razors	30	32
Surgical instruments	128	355
Tweezers	128	354
Shampooing apparatus	4	515
Shearing, fur finishing	26	15R
Thinning shears	30	195
Springs	368	175
Strand making		
Covering by spinning etc	57	4
Spinning etc	57	28
Textile spinning etc	57	29
Thinners	30	195
Design	D28	52
Toilet preparations	424	70
Treating process	132	7
Vulcanizable natural hydrocarbon gums with	260	748
Waving	132	7
Hairpin	132	50R
Design	D28	39
Dispenser	132	1A
Hat fastener cord or loop and	132	61
Making	140	87
Packaging	227	25
Half Belts	2	309
Half Wave		
Gas rectifier	313	216
With hot cathode	313	211
High voltage rectifier	313	317
With emissive cathode	313	310
With thermionic cathode	313	310
Rectifier system	363	13
Circuit interrupter for	200	
Dynamoelectric machine	310	10
Electronic tube for	313	317
Gas tube type	363	114
Power packs	307	150
Unidirectional impedance for	357	
Vacuum tube type	363	114
With filter	363	39
With voltage regulator	363	84
Halftone		
Blanks and processes printing	101	401.1
Etching	156	654
X-art	156	905*
Photographic process	430	396
Photographic screens	350	322
Chemically defined	430	6
Printing plates	101	395
Halides (See Material Halogenated)		
Hydrocarbon	570	101
As azeotropes	203	67
Electromagnetic wave synthesis	204	163R
Electrostatic field or electrical discharge synthesis	204	169
Metal	423	462
Electrolytic synthesis	204	94
Nitroaromatic	568	927
Nonmetal inorganic	423	462
Organic acid	260	543
Rubber	260	772

	Class	Subclass
Hydrohalide	260	771
Mixtures containing	260	735
Hall Effect Means in an Amplifier	330	6
Haloamines	564	114
Acyclic	564	118
Hydroxy or ether containing	564	119
Plural difluoramine groups	564	121
Unsaturated	564	120
Alicyclic	564	117
Amidines	564	116
Halogen Compounds (See Material Halogenated)		
Halogenated Carboxylic Acid Esters	560	1
Acyclic acid esters	560	226
Of phenols	560	145
Acyclic amino acid esters	560	172
Acyclic carbamic acid esters	560	161
Acyclic oxy acid esters	560	184
Acyclic polycarboxylic acid esters	560	192
Acyclic unsaturated acid esters	560	219
Alicyclic	560	125
Aromatic amino acid esters	560	47
Aromatic carbamic acid esters	560	30
Aromatic polycarboxylic acid esters	560	23
Oxybenzoic acid esters	560	65
Phenoxyacetic acid esters	560	62
Halogenation (See Halides)	260	694
Halohydrin	568	841
Halowax	570	181
Halter		
Brassiere type garment	128	425
Feed bags supported on	119	66
Harness	54	24
Design	D30	19
Poke with bar and	119	141
Snap releasers	119	114
Hamburger		
Cookers	99	422
Grinders	241	
Molding and shaping (See briquetting meat)		
Hames	54	25
Collar combined	54	18R
Design	D30	23
Traces and connectors	54	30
Tugs	54	32
Hammer	145	29R
Automobile fender straightening	72	705
Burglar alarm	116	88
Claw	254	26
Combined with additional tools	7	143
Design	D 8	75
Drop forging	72	435
Earth boring tool combined	175	135
Firearm	42	
Forging	72	476
Heads for piano actions	84	254
Impact clutch type	173	93.5
Implement combined	81	463
Awl or prick punch	30	358
Internal combustion charge igniter rocking electrode	123	157
Leather compacting	69	1
Magazine	227	133
Making		
Forging dies for	72	470
Processes of	76	103
Metal bending	72	462
Mills	241	185R
Parallel material flow	241	138
Perforated discharge	241	86
Process	241	27
Series material flow	241	154
Musical instruments		
Piano	84	236
Stringed instrument	84	323
Tuning	84	459
Nut cracker	30	120.1
Pile driver	173	90
Punching machine	83	
Riveting	72	476
Road rammer	404	133
Rock drilling	175	135
Rod encircling type	145	30.5
Saw stretching machine	76	26
Scale removing	29	81D
Shoe lasting stretcher and	12	109
Stoneworking combined	125	6
Impact tools	125	40
Tool driving	173	90

Fig. 6H—Sample Page of *Index to Classification*

272-1

CLASS 272   AMUSEMENT AND EXERCISING DEVICES

DECEMBER 1983

1 R	AMUSEMENT	
1 A	..Sand boxes	
1 B	..Water sports	
1 C	..Aircraft simulation	
1 D	..Stick horses and body supported devices	
1 E	..Birling devices	
2	.Houses	
3	.Arenas	
4	..Racing	
5	...Horse	
6	.Elevating devices	
7	..Combined roundabouts	
8 R	.Illusions	
8 M	...Mirrors	
8 N	...Novelties	
8 F	...Fire	
8 D	...Display	
8 P	...Projected light	
8.5	..By transparent reflector	
9	..Stage	
10	...Special projected picture or light effects	
11	...Settings	
12	....Rapid movement	
13	...Mirror	
14	...Sound imitation	
15	...Rain, snow and fire	
16	..Trip simulation	
17	...In passenger-carrying devices	
18	....With projected picture scenery	
19	..Maze or labyrinth	
20	..Pyrotechnic display	
21	.Stage appliances	
22	..Shifting scenery	
23	...Guides, braces and clips	
24	..Aerial suspension devices	
25	..Properties	
26	...Stage tanks	
27 R	.Initiating devices	
27 B	...Blowing and cards	
27 W	...Pins and water jets	
27 N	...Novelties	
28 R	.Roundabouts	
28 S	...Vertical shaft mounting	
29	..Combined with transporting vehicle	
30	..Combined seesaw	
31 R	..Toy	
31 A	....Aircraft	
31 B	....Helicopter	
31 P	....Phonograph driven	
32	..Marine	
33 R	..Occupant propelled	
33 A	....Bowl shape	
33 B	....Bicycle type	
34	..Auto-propelled carriages	
35	..Free carriage	
36	..Vertical and horizontal axes	
37	..Plural vertical axes	
38	..Plural horizontal axes	
39	..Vertical axis only	
40	...Suspended vehicle or rider support	
41	....Circular swings	
42	....With rotating platform	
43	...Rotating vehicle or rider support and stationary track or platform	
44	....Vertically undulating track or platform	
45	....Horizontally undulating track or platform	
46	...Rotating disk, ring or bowl	
47	....Concentric rings or disks	
48	....With vehicle or rider supports	
49	...Horizontal axis only	
50	..Gyrating axis	
51	..Inclined axis	
52	.Hobby horses	
52.5	..Combined or convertible	

53.1	..With actuating means	
53.2	..With movable elements	
54	.Seesaws	
55	..One person	
56	..Rocking support	
56.5 R	.Slides	
56.5 SS	...Ski slopes	
85	.Swings	
86	..Motor operated	
87	..Hand and foot operator	
88	..Hand operator	
89	...Horizontally reciprocating	
90	...Cable grasp	
91	....Pulley mounted	
92	..Foot operator with separate suspender	
93	EXERCISING EQUIPMENT	
94	.For head (e.g., jaws, neck, etc.) or foot	
95	..Face (e.g., jaws, lips, etc.)	
96	..Foot	
97	.For simulating skiing	
98	.For thrusting a simulated weapon (e.g., fencing foil, etc.)	
99	.For improving user's respiratory function	
100	.For track or field sports	
101	..For jumping, vaulting or hurdling	
102	...Cross-bar or support therefor (e.g., hurdle, etc.)	
103	....Means to facilitate adjustment of cross-bar height	
104	...Vaulting pole or stop therefor	
105	..Starting block for track runner	
106	.For throwing (e.g., javelin, hammer, etc.)	
107	...Discus	
108	...Shot put	
109	.Gymnastic	
61	..Trapezes and rings	
62	..Horizontal bars	
63	...Parallel bars	
64	..Vaulting horses	
65	..Projectors	
66	...Spring boards	
110	.Swinging tower or pole	
111	..Balancing bar or rope	
112	..For hanging or climbing by the arms	
113	.Playground climber (e.g., for use by children)	
67	.Hand and wrist	
68	..Grips	
69	.Tread mill	
70	.Walking or skating	
70.1	..Stilts	
70.2	...Steps	
70.3	..Occupant propelled frame	
70.4	...Armpit engaging	
71	.Swimming	
72	.Rowing	
73	.Bicycle	
74	.Skipping	
75	..Ropes	
76	.Striking	
77	..Striking bags	
78	...Supports	
114	.For user locomotion (e.g., pogo stick, etc.)	
115	..Translatable with user inside	
116	.User-manipulated force-resisting mechanism or element	
117	..User-manipulated weight	
118	...Including guide for vertical array of weights	
119	...Worn on user's body	
120	...Utilizing user's body weight	
121	..Part of user's body	
122	...Dumbbell or barbell	
123	....Barbell	

Fig. 6I—Sample Page of *Manual of Classification*

petunia or lettuce seeds) so they may be accurately planted by a mechanical planter. To find the appropriate subclasses, he first looks in the *Index of Classification* under the "seed" categories. He finds a good prospect, "Seed-Containing Compositions," and sees that the classification is Class 47 (Plant Husbandry), sub 1.

After checking this class/subclass in the *Manual of Classification* to see where it fits in the scheme of things and in the *Class Definitions* to make sure that it looks OK (it does), he would start his first search with Class 27, Sub 1. Then, using his imagination, Professor Campbell also realizes that some candies, such as chocolate-covered peanuts, are actually encapsulated seeds. Thus, he also looks under the candy classifications and finds several likely prospects in Class 107: "Bread, Pastry and Confection-Making." Specifically, sub 1.25, "Composite Pills (with core)"; sub 1.7, "Feeding Solid Centers into Confectionery"; and sub 11, "Pills" look quite promising. Thus he adds class 107, subs 1.25, 1.7, and 11 to his search field. The moral is this: When you search, look not only in the obvious places, but also use your imagination to find analogous areas, as Professor Campbell does.

For another example of searching in analogous areas, consider an automobile steering wheel that you've improved by adding finger ridges to improve the driver's grip. In addition to searching in the obvious area (automobile steering wheels), consider searching in any other areas where hand grips are found, such as swords, tools, and bike handlebars.

Fortunately, the cross-references in the Class Definitions manual will be of great help here—note (Fig. 6J) the copious cross-references at the top of Class 272. Also, as stated, the PTO and all PTDLs have the CASSIS system, which will be of great assistance.

Note how Sam Searcher, Esq., has completed the "Selected Search Classifications" section of the search worksheet with appropriate classes to search for prior art relevant to Millie Inventress's invention.

Step 3: Note Relevant Prior Art (Patents and Other Publications) Under Your Classification

After obtaining a list of classes and subclasses to search, find the actual examining division (or location in the search room if you choose to stay downstairs) where these classes and subclasses are actually located. Then go to your search area and look through all the patents in your selected subclasses. The PTO recently implemented several automated search systems; ask the search assistants in the main search room if they have one in your field. If so, you're lucky.

In the public search room, you'll have to remove bundles of patents from slot-like shelves in its huge stack area. Bring them to a table in the main search area, and search them by placing the patents in a bundle holder and flipping through them. In the examiners' search room, the patents are found in small drawers, called "shoes" by the examiners. You should remove the drawer of patents, hold it in your lap, and flip through the patents while you're seated in a chair; generally, no table will be available.

As you flip through the patents, you may at first find it very difficult to understand them and to make your search. I did when as an examiner I made my first search in the PTO. Don't be discouraged! After just a few minutes the technique will become clear and you may even get to like it! You'll find it easier to understand newer patents (see Le

Date: March 1973   CLASSIFICATION DEFINITIONS   Page 272-1

Class 272, AMUSEMENT AND EXERCISING DEVICES

CLASS DEFINITIONS.

This class is generic for amusement and exercising, and includes devices whose purpose is amusement, recreation, exercising, gymnastics, or athletics, unless by analogy of structure or by other functions they are classified in other classes. It includes apparatus used at amusement parks and in theaters, unless otherwise classified, also houses, arenas, and elevators where the sole function is amusement.

SEARCH CLASS:

9, Boats, Buoys and Aquatic Devices, appropriate subclasses for buoyant structure disclosed, but not claimed with features simulating birds, fish, fowl, etc. See (3) Note in Class Definitions of Class 9 for statement of the line.

46, Amusement Devices, Toys, for species of amusement devices commonly called toys which are principally for the amusement of children.

104, Railways, subclass 53+, for amusement railways.

182, Fire Escapes, Ladders, Scaffolds, subclass 137+, for a body catcher or life net.

187, Elevators, appropriate subclasses, for elevators of general utility.

273, Amusement Devices, Games, for species of amusement devices commonly called games which involve skill or competition.

280, Land Vehicles, appropriate subclasses for various types of land vehicles, particularly subclass 1.1+ for simulations, especially progressive hobby horses; subclass 11.1 for skates; subclass 12+ for sleds; and subclass 47.1 for person supporting bodies connected to wheels so as to effect body rocking as the wheels rotate.

404, Road Structure, Process and Apparatus, subclasses 17+ and 71 for pavement and road structure.

Subclasses.

■ ■ ■

93. Apparatus under the class definition intended to be operated by a user of such apparatus for the purpose of developing the muscles of the user's body by repetitive or continuous activity of the user, such activity being facilitated by such apparatus.

(1) Note. Patents placed into this and indented subclasses clearly show that the disclosed purpose is to condition or develop the user's own body. Apparatus that is used by one person to move another person's body will be found in Class 128, Surgery (see the Search Class Note below). Apparatus that is used for moving a user's body for a purpose other than exercising (e.g., transport) will be found in classes that are exemplified in the Search Class notes found under the definition of this class.

(2) Note. The following terms, used in subsequent definitions of the subclasses hereunder, are defined and explained herein: CONTRACTION (i. e., of a muscle) is the physiological effort of the muscle which produces a force that tends to result in shortening of the muscle tissue. It does not necessarily result in an actual me-

chanical change in the length of the muscle, but rather in a tendency to change. The effort may result in shortening of the muscle ("concentric" contraction), or may occur during lengthening of the muscle ("eccentric" contraction), or may occur while the muscle is constrained to remain at substantially the same length ("isometric" contraction), but the tendency to shorten the muscle tissue is generally termed "contraction". Force is the result or effect of the effort exerted by a generator of such effort upon an object. As used in this schedule and in the definition of these subclasses, the term "force" replaces the previously-used terms "push" and "pull", because push and pull are easily confused. As commonly used in this context, "push" refers to a force exerted by a person away from the person's body and "pull" refers to a force exerted by a person towards the person's body; however, in a physiological context, all muscles pull when exercised in the sense that they tend to shorten the muscle tissues when contracted. The term "force" also includes a twisting or turning effort, i.e., a torque as well as a push or pull effort.

■ ■ ■

109. Apparatus under subclass 93, wherein significance is attributed to the use of said apparatus for acrobatic purposes.

(1) Note. The terms "gymnastic" and "acrobatic" have come to denote and describe various pieces of equipment such as trapezes, bars, vaulting horses, etc., that are used in the physical activities known by such names. These activities are characterized by extreme movements of the user, who used the equipment as a fulcrum or starting area to launch his/her body through space, or swing therefrom, or perform other such physical activities thereon. As in previously-described athletic activities, the significance of the apparatus is more in the activity for which the apparatus is used than in the structural differences between the apparatus.

110. Apparatus under subclass 109, including an elongated slender rod, of which one end is secured to the ground and the other end serves as a support for the user as his/her body is exercised thereon.

SEARCH THIS CLASS, SUBCLASS:
104, for a structurally similar flexible pole that is used to help launch a pole vaulter over a high bar.

111. Apparatus under subclass 109, including a relatively slender, horizontally-positioned member, on which member a user supports his/her body with the center of gravity of said body above the member while attempting to maintain the body in a state of equilibrium.

112. Apparatus under subclass 109, including equipment that is grasped by a hand or the hands of the user, and from which equipment the user suspends his/her body or ascends the equipment using only his/her arm(s).

Fig. 6J—Sample Page of *Classification Definitions*

Sueur—Fig. 6D(c)), since they have an abstract page up front that contains a brief summary of the patent and the most relevant figure or drawing.

You'll find that the older patents (see Gabel—Fig. 6D(a)) have several sheets of unlabeled drawings and a closely printed description, termed a "specification," after the drawings. However, even with older patents, you can get a brief summary of the patent by referring to the summary of the invention, which is usually found in the first or second column of the specification. Near the end of each patent, you'll find the claims (Chapter 9). See any utility patent, or Fig. 6M, below, for some examples of claims. These are formally worded, legalistic sentence fragments that usually come after and are the object of the heading words "I [or "We"] claim." As mentioned in the last chapter (and as you'll learn in detail in Chapter 9), the claims define the legal scope of offensive rights held by the owner of the patent. I have seen more confusion about claims than perhaps any other area of patent law. If you'll read and heed well the next common misconception, you'll avoid falling into what I call the "claims trap," which technically is known as a confusion of infringement with anticipation. (See sidebar.)

Common Misconception: *If the claims of a prior patent don't cover your invention, you're free to claim it in your patent application.*

Fact: *The claims of a patent are there solely to define the monopoly or scope of offensive rights held by the owner of the patent. Patent owners use claims mainly in licensing or in court to determine whether the patent is infringed—that is, whether the hardware that an alleged infringer makes, uses, or sells violates the patent. Thus, when you encounter a relevant patent during a search, you should not read its claims. You should treat the patent like any other publication (book, magazine article, etc.) to see if the patent's specification ("spec.") or drawings disclose (anticipate) your invention, or any part of it. Since the patent's claims merely repeat what's already in the spec. and drawings, they won't contain anything new, so you need not even read the patent's claims to understand the full technical disclosure of any patent. The spec. and drawings will almost always contain more than what is in the claims anyway. So even if a patent's claims don't cover your invention, its spec. and drawings may still disclose your invention. Since the patent is a prior publication as of its filing date, it can thus anticipate your invention, even if it doesn't claim your invention. (If you were free to claim an invention that a prior patent disclosed but did not claim, that would make patents worth less as prior art than other publications, such as magazine articles!)*

ANTICIPATION VS. INFRINGEMENT

Many inventors have actually asked me, "How can an expired patent block me from patenting my invention?"— that is, how can an expired patent be a valid prior-art reference? However, a moment's thought will show that if a patent ceased to be a valid prior-art reference when it expired, then inventors could (a) re-patent the same invention approximately every 17 years, (b) patents would have a lower status than other prior-art publications, such as periodicals, which remain valid prior art forever, and (c) inventors could patent things that were not new. The misconception that a patent ceases to be a prior-art reference when it expires represents a confusion of *anticipation* with *infringement.* They are entirely separate areas in patent law and should be considered independently.

Anticipation is a situation that occurs when a proposed or new invention is discovered or found anywhere in the "prior art" (prior public use or prior publications, including the specification of any in-force or expired U.S. or foreign patent, any prior book, periodical article, etc.). Since the existence of the prior art proves the invention isn't new, the putative invention is said to be *anticipated* by the prior art and thus can't be patented. (35 USC 102.)

Infringement is a situation that occurs only when the claims of an in-force patent "read on" a product or process. If so, then the product or process *infringes* (violates) the patent and the patent owner may be able to negotiate licensing royalties from the infringer, or successfully sue the infringer for money damages and/or an injunction ordering the infringer to cease infringing. (35 USC 271.) (Note that a patent application can't infringe anything.)

If an invention is anticipated by a prior-art reference, that does not necessarily mean that it would infringe the reference, since the reference may be (a) a periodical article or book, which can't be infringed, (b) a foreign patent, which can't be infringed by activity in the U.S., or (c) an expired U.S. patent, which can no longer be infringed. Even if an invention is anticipated by an in-force U.S. patent, the invention usually will not infringe the patent. Why? Because the patent's claims usually will not read on the invention, most likely because the patentee was not able to get broad enough claims allowed due to even earlier prior art. The PTO is never concerned with and never takes any action with regard to any infringement; their main concern is to find anticipations to prevent the issuance of patents on old inventions.

If an invention infringes an in-force U.S. patent, that patent will necessarily anticipate such invention.

Another reason for not reading the claims of searched patents is that they're written in such stilted legalese that they're difficult to understand. Nevertheless, some searchers do like to read claims of patents to get a quick "handle" on the patent's technical content. Also, if you make an *Official Gazette* search in a Patent and Trademark Depository or regular library (see Section K, below), you'll have to rely on claims for the most part, since most of the OGs contain only a single claim of each patent.

If you do read the claims, keep in mind three important considerations:

1. If a prior-art patent shows (that is, describes) but doesn't formally claim your invention, this doesn't mean you're free to claim it.

2. A patent contains much more technical information than what's in its claims; all of this technical information can be used as prior art, just as if the patent were an article in a technical magazine. Thus, you should use the claims only to get a "handle" on the patent; you should not regard them as a summary or synopsis of the patent's disclosure.

3. The scope of coverage you will likely be able to obtain for your invention (see Section J, below) will usually be narrower than the scope of the claims of the closely relevant prior-art patents you uncover. (See Chapter 9 to see how to determine the breadth of claims.)

Common Misconception: *If your invention is covered by the claims of a prior patent, you will be liable as an infringer if you file a patent application on the invention.*

Fact: *Neither a patent application nor its claims can infringe a prior patent. Only the manufacture, use, or sale of an invention in physical form can infringe.*

Don't think about obviousness as you search since this may overwhelm you and detract from the quality of your investigation. Rather, at this stage, try to fish with a large net by merely looking for the physical features of your invention.

As you search, keep a careful record of all patent classes and subclasses you've searched, as indicated in Fig. 6G, above. Probably 95% of the references you encounter when you search will not be relevant. If you find relevant patents or other art, write their numbers, dates, names, or other identification, and order copies later; again see Fig. 6G. Although you need only the number to order a patent, I recommend that you write the issue date, first inventor's name, and classification as well to double-check later in case you write down a wrong number.

If you do find an important relevant reference, don't stop; simply asterisk it (to remind you of its importance) and continue your search to the end. When you note a relevant reference, also write down its most relevant features to refresh your memory and save time later.

If you still don't find any relevant patents, double-check your search classes using *Classification Definitions*, the *Manual of Classification*, and some help from a patent examiner or assistant in the search room. If you're reasonably sure you're in the right class and still can't find any relevant references, write down the closest ones you can possibly find, even if they're not relevant. This will establish that you made the search, what the closest art is, and how novel your invention is, and you'll have references to cite on your Information Disclosure Statement (see Chapter 13, Section A) to make the PTO's file of your patent look good; you should never finish any search without coming up with at least several references. If you do consult examiners, write their names in the comments section of the worksheet.

In each subclass, you'll find patents that are directly classified there, and "cross-references" (XRs), patents primarily classified in another subclass, but also classified in your subclass because they have a feature that makes the cross-reference appropriate. Be sure to review the cross-references as well as the regular patents in each subclass.

The public search room has copiers for making instant copies of patents for a per-page fee, but if you don't need instant copies, you can buy a complete copy of any patent for one patent copy coupon, or use two coupons per patent for rush service. To do this, purchase an adequate supply of coupons from the PTO's cashier (see Appendix 4, Fee Schedule); then write down the number of each patent you select on a coupon, add your name and address, and deposit them in the appropriate box in the search room. The patents you request will be mailed to you, generally in several weeks if you use one coupon per patent, or in several days if you staple two coupons together per patent. Also, there are various services that can supply patent copies immediately by fax, or in a few days by mail, at about the same price that the PTO charges. Several of these are Faxpat (800-666-1233), Optipat (800-445-9760), and ReedFax (800-422-1337). Also, the PTO itself now furnishes patent copies by rapid mail return, fax, and FedEx at competitive prices and by charge card or check: You can order by telephone (703-305-8716), fax (703-305-8759), and Internet message (http://www.uspto.gov/web/uspto/patsales.patsales.html). Representative patent copy prices as of Fall 1996 were as follows: three-day mail or fax return: $3.00, one-day fax return: $6.00.

Step 4: Carefully Review the Prior Art to See Whether It Anticipates Your Invention or Renders It Obvious

After you've made your search and obtained copies of all the references you thought were pertinent, study them carefully at your leisure. I recommend you write a brief summary of each relevant patent, even if it has an abstract, to force you to really understand it. Then, determine if your invention is patentable over the patents you've found. Follow the steps described earlier in this chapter (Section H) for analyzing the search report when your search is done by someone else.

J. The Scope of Patent Coverage

Although you'd probably like things to be simpler, the determination of whether your invention is patentable will rarely be a "yes" or "no" one, unless your invention is a very simple device, process, or composition. Many inventions are complex enough to have some features, or some combination of features, that will be different enough to be patentable. However, your object is not merely to get a patent, but to get *meaningful* patent coverage—that is, offensive rights that are broad enough that competitors can't "design around" your patent easily. As I've said elsewhere, designing around a patent is the act of making a competitive device or process that is equivalent in function to the patented device but that doesn't infringe the patent.

Many "modern" inventions are actually old hat—that is, the basic ideas were known many years before and the real inventions are actually just improvements on old ones. For example, the first computer was a mechanical device invented in the 1800s by Charles Babbage. The ancient Chinese used a soybean mold to treat infections. One J. H. Loud received a patent on a ballpoint pen in 1888, and the first 3D film was shown in 1922!

Simply put, you'll often find that your invention, while valuable, may be less of an innovation than you thought it was. You'll thus have to determine whether or not your invention is sufficiently innovative to get meaningful patent protection. In other words, your scope of coverage will depend upon how close the references that your search uncovers are to your invention—that is, how many features of your invention are shown by the references, and how they are shown. In the end, your scope of coverage will actually depend upon the breadth of the claims that you can get the PTO to allow, but this is jumping the gun at this stage; I cover claims in Chapter 9.

For an example, let's take a simple invention. As stated, in a simple invention patentability will usually be a black or white determination, and you won't have much of a prob-lem about your scope of coverage. Suppose you've just invented a magnetically operated cat door—that is, you provide a cat with a neck-worn magnet that can operate a release on a cat door. Your search references fail to show any magnetically operated pet release door. Thus, the neck magnet and the magnetic door release are the novel features of your invention. To get a patent, your invention would have to be limited to these specific features, since neither could be changed or eliminated while producing the same result. However, there is no harm in limiting the invention to these features, since it would be difficult for anyone to "design around" them—that is, it would be difficult or impossible for anyone to provide the same result (a cat-operated door release) without using a neck magnet and a magnetic release.

With other inventions, however, your scope of coverage won't be so broad—that is, it won't be as difficult for someone to design around it. For example, suppose you invented the centrifugal vegetable juicer mentioned previously in Chapter 5—that is, a juicer with a sloping side basket permitting the solid pulp to ride up and out so that juicing could continue without having to empty the pulp from the basket.

If the prior art were not "kind" to you—that is, your search uncovered a patent or other publication that showed a juicer with a basket with sloping sides and with a well at the top to catch and hold the pulp—your application would not be allowed if you claimed just the sloping sides (even though it would be superior to the prior art due to the complete elimination of the pulp). To get the patent, you would have to also claim another feature (say, the trough shape). Thus, by having access to the prior art you would know enough to claim your invention less broadly.

Also, suppose you've invented the napkin-shaping ring of Fig. 6B. Suppose further that Gabel did not exist and that your search uncovers only the Le Sueur patent (see Fig. 6D(c)), which shows a plain, circular napkin ring. You'd be entitled to relatively broad coverage, since your novel features are themselves broad: namely, a ring with inner parts that can shape a napkin when it is pulled through the ring.

However, assuming the Gabel patent does exist and your search uncovers it as well as Le Sueur, what are your novel features now? First, your device has a circular ring with a leg extending inwardly from the ring; neither Gabel nor Le Sueur, nor any possible combination of these references, has this combination. Second, your invention has the flaring arms that shape the napkin; these are attached to the end of the inner leg; the references also lack this feature. Thus to distinguish over Le Sueur and Gabel, you'll have to rely on far more specific features than you'd have to do if only Le Sueur existed. Hence your actual invention would be far narrower, since you'll have to limit it to the novel features that distinguish it from Gabel as well as Le Sueur. Unfortunately, this will narrow your scope of coverage, because competitors can design around you more easily than they could do if only Le Sueur existed.

As you've probably gathered by now, your scope of coverage will be determined by what novel features you need to use to distinguish your invention over the prior art and still provide new results that are different or unexpected enough to be considered unobvious. The fewer the novel features you need, the broader your invention or scope of coverage will be. Stated differently, if you need many new features, or very specific features, to define over the prior art and provide new results, it will usually be relatively easy for a competitor to use fewer or alternative features to provide the same results without infringing your patent.

You should make your scope of coverage determination by determining the fewest number or the broadest feature(s) you'll need to distinguish patentability over the prior art. Do this by a repetitive narrowing trial-and-error process: First, see what minimum feature(s) you'll need to have some novelty over the prior art—that is, enough to distinguish under Section 102 (Box C of Figs. 5D and 6E)—and then see if these would satisfy Section 103 (Boxes D, E, and G)—that is, would they provide any unexpected new results?

If you feel that your minimum number of features are enough to ascend the novelty box (pictured in Fig. 5A in Chapter 5), but would not be sufficient to climb the big unobviousness box—that is, you don't have enough features to provide new and unexpected results—then try narrowing your features or adding more until you feel that you'll have enough to make it to the patentability summit.

This is another one of those aspects of patent law that may have your head spinning. Fortunately, the material covered here under determining the scope of your protection is also discussed in the different context of drafting your claims. (See Chapter 9.) By the time you read this book thoroughly, you will understand all of this a lot better.

After you evaluate your search results, you'll have a pretty good idea of the minimum number of novel features that are necessary to sufficiently distinguish your invention over the prior art. If you're in doubt that you have enough such features, or if you feel that you'd have to limit your invention to specific features to define structure that would be considered unobvious over the prior art, it probably isn't patentable, or even if patentable, it isn't worth filing on, since it would be easy to design around. One possibility, if

you can't make a decision, is to pay for a professional's opinion.

On the other hand, if you've found nothing like your invention in your search, congratulations. You probably have a very broad invention, since, of the 5+ million patents that have issued thus far, one or more features of almost all inventions are likely to be shown in the prior art.

K. Searching It Yourself in a Patent and Trademark Depository Library

If you can't search in the PTO, the next possibility, although somewhat inferior, is to search your invention in one of the Patent and Trademark Depository Libraries listed below in Fig. 6K, all of which currently receive all patents issued by the PTO. Before going to any PTDL, call to find out their hours of operation and what search facilities they have.

Why is searching at a PTDL less useful than searching at the PTO? Simply because not all PTDLs have all patents issued from No. 1 to the present, none have them physically separated by subject matter into searchable classifications as does the PTO in Arlington, and none have foreign patents or non-patent literature (books, magazines, etc.). Using a PTDL is therefore more difficult and time-consuming than if you use the PTO. You should carefully balance the large expenditure of your time and the inferiority of the search materials against the $200 to $500 or so you would spend for a professional searcher to do the job at the PTO. Of course, as I suggested, the optimum solution is to visit Arlington yourself.

I like to assign percentage values to the various types of searches: I roughly estimate a good examiner's search at 90% (that is—it has about a 90% chance of standing up in court), a good search by a non-examiner in the PTO at 80%, and a good search in a PTDL at 70%. (Unfortunately, as in business, there's no certainty in the law.) If your invention is in an active, contemporary field, such as a computer mouse, you should reduce the value of the two non-examiner types of searches somewhat, due to the fact that patent applications in this field are more likely to be pending.

If you do make a search at a PTDL, you should go through the same four steps given above. First, articulate your invention (in the same manner as before), and second, use the reference tools to find the relevant classes and subclasses. The third step is a review of the patents in the selected classes and subclasses. And finally, you should analyze all relevant prior-art references for their effect on your invention's patentability.

REFERENCE COLLECTION OF U.S. PATENTS AVAILABLE FOR PUBLIC USE IN PATENT AND TRADEMARK DEPOSITORY LIBRARIES

The following are designated as Patent and Trademark Depository Libraries (PTDLs) and receive current issues of U.S. patents and maintain collections of earlier-issued patents. The scope of these collections varies from library to library, ranging from patents of only recent years to all or most of the patents issued since 1790.

These patent collections, which are organized in patent number sequence, are available for use by the public free of charge. Each of the PTDLs, in addition, offers supplemental reference publications of the U.S. Patent Classification System, including the *Manual of Classification, Index to the U.S. Patent Classification, Classification Definitions*, and provides technical staff assistance in their use to aid the public in gaining effective access to information contained in patents. CASSIS (Classification And Search Support Information System—see the sidebar below), which

provides direct access to Patent and Trademark Office data, is available at all PTDLs. Facilities for making paper copies of patents from either microfilm or paper collections are generally provided for a fee.

Since there are variations in the scope of patent collections among the PTDLs and in their hours of service to the public, anyone contemplating use of the patents at a particular library is urged to contact that library, in advance, about its collection and hours in order to avert possible inconvenience. Additional libraries are added from time to time, so check a recent edition of the *Official Gazette* to see if a library closer to you has opened. (This list is printed in every issue of the OG.)

Currently, 12 of these libraries have APS (Automated Patent System) search terminals which can search text of patents back to 1971. (See Section M1.)

State	Name of Library	Telephone
Alabama	Auburn University Libraries	205-844-1747
	Birmingham Public Library	205-226-3620
Alaska	Anchorage: Z.J. Loussac Public Library	907-562-7323
Arizona	Tempe: Noble Library, Arizona State Univ.	602-965-7010
Arkansas	Little Rock: Arkansas State Library	501-682-2053
California	Los Angeles Public Library	213-228-7220
	Sacramento: California State Library	916-654-0069
	San Diego Public Library	619-236-5813
	San Francisco Public Library	415-557-4500
	Santa Rosa: Bruce Sawyer Center (not a PTDL, but useful)	707-524-1773
	Sunnyvale Center for Innovation (has APS Image terminals—see Section M1)	408-730-7290
Colorado	Denver Public Library	303-640-6220
Delaware	Newark: University of Delaware Library	302-831-2965
D.C.	Washington: Howard University Libraries	202-806-7252
Florida	Fort Lauderdale: Broward County Main Library	305-357-7444
	Miami: Dade Public Library	305-375-2665
	Orlando: Univ.of Central Florida Libraries	407-823-2562
	Tampa: Campus Library, University of South Florida	813-974-2726

State	Name of Library	Telephone
Georgia	Atlanta: Price Gilbert Memorial Library, Georgia Institute of Technology	404-894-4508
Hawaii	Honolulu: Hawaii State Public Library System	808-586-3477
Idaho	Moscow: University of Idaho Library	208-885-6235
Illinois	Chicago Public Library	312-747-4450
	Springfield: Illinois State Library	217-782-5659
Indiana	Indianapolis: Marion County Public Library	317-269-1741
	West Lafayette: Purdue University Libraries	317-494-2872
Iowa	Des Moines: State Library of Iowa	515-281-4118
Kansas	Wichita: Ablah Library, Wichita State Univ.	316-689-3155
Kentucky	Louisville Free Public Library	502-574-1611
Louisiana	Baton Rouge: Troy H. Middleton Library, Louisiana State University	504-388-8875
Maine	Orono: Raymond H. Fogler Library, University of Maine	207-581-1678
Maryland	College Park: Engineering and Physical Sciences Library, University of Maryland	301-405-9157
Massachusetts	Amherst: Physical Sciences Library, University of Massachusetts	413-545-1370
	Boston Public Library	617-536-5400 Ext. 265

Fig. 6K—List of Patent and Trademark Depository Libraries

REFERENCE COLLECTION OF U.S. PATENTS AVAILABLE FOR PUBLIC USE IN PATENT AND TRADEMARK DEPOSITORY LIBRARIES (CONTINUED)

State	Name of Library	Telephone	State	Name of Library	Telephone
Michigan	Ann Arbor: Engineering Transportation Library, University of Michigan	313-647-5735	Oregon	Portland: Paul L. Boley Law Library Lewis & Clark College	503-768-6786
	Big Rapids: Abigail S. Timme Library, Ferris State University	616-592-3602	Pennsylvania	Philadelphia, The Free Library of	215-686-5331
				Pittsburgh, Carnegie Library of	412-622-3138
	Detroit Public Library (has APS Image Terminals—see Section M1)	313-833-3379		University Park: Pattee Library, Pennsylvania State University	814-865 4861
Minnesota	Minneapolis Public Library and Information Center	612-372-6570	Puerto Rico	Mayaguez General Library, University of Puerto Rico	787-832-4040 Ext. 3459
Mississippi	Jackson: Mississippi Library Commission	601-359-1036	Rhode Island	Providence Public Library	401-455-8027
Missouri	Kansas City: Linda Hall Library	816-363-4600	South Carolina	Clemson University Libraries	803-656-3024
	St. Louis Public Library	314-241-2288 Ext. 390	South Dakota	Rapid City: Devereaux Library, S.D. School of Mines and Technology	605-394-1275
Montana	Butte: Montana College of Mineral Science & Technology Library	406-496-4281	Tennessee	Memphis & Shelby County Public Library and Information Center	901-725-8877
Nebraska	Lincoln: Engineering Library, University of Nebraska	402-472-3411		Nashville: Stevenson Science Library, Vanderbilt University	615-322-2717
Nevada	Reno: University of Nevada-Reno Library	702-784-6500	Texas	Austin: McKinney Engineering Library, University of Texas at Austin	512-495-4500
New Hampshire	Concord: New Hampshire State Library	603-271-2239			
New Jersey	Newark Public Library	201-733-7782		College Station: Sterling C. Evans Library, Texas A & M University	409-845-3826
	Piscataway: Library of Science & Medicine, Rutgers University	908-445-2895		Dallas Public Library	214-670-1468
New Mexico	Albuquerque: University of New Mexico General Library	505-277-4412		Houston: The Fondren Library, Rice University	713-527-8101 Ext. 2587
New York	Albany: New York State Library	518-474-5355		Lubbock; Texas Tech University	806-742-2602
	Buffalo and Erie County Public Library	716-858-7101	Utah	Salt Lake City: Marriott Library, University of Utah	801-581-8394
	New York Public Library (The Research Libraries)	212-592-7000	Vermont	Burlington: Bailey/Howe Library, University of Vermont	Not yet operational
North Carolina	Raleigh: D.H. Hill Library, N.C. State U.	919-515-3280	Virginia	Richmond: James Branch Cabell Library, Virginia Commonwealth University	804-828-1104
North Dakota	Grand Forks: Chester Fritz Library, University of North Dakota	701-777-4888	Washington	Seattle: Engineering Library, University of Washington	206-543-0740
Ohio	Akron: Summit County Public Library	330-643-9075	West Virginia	Morgantown: Evansdale Library, West Virginia University	304-293-2510
	Cincinnati and Hamilton County, Public Library of	513-369-6936			
	Cleveland Public Library	216-623-2870	Wisconsin	Madison: Kurt F. Wendt Library, University of Wisconsin	608-262-6845
	Columbus: Ohio State University Libraries	614-292-6175			
	Toledo/Lucas County Public Library	419-259-5212		Milwaukee Public Library	414-286-3051
Oklahoma	Stillwater: Oklahoma State Univ. Library	405-744-7086	Wyoming	Casper: National County Public Library	307-237-4935

Fig. 6K (cont'd)—List of Patent and Trademark Depository Libraries

In a PTDL these steps are more difficult than in the PTO. First, you must get a list of the patents in your selected classes and subclasses. Most of the PTDLs have lists of patents in each class and subclass on microfilm or CD-ROM. (See the sidebar, CD-ROM Products at PTDLs, below) But if your PTDL doesn't have such a list, you'll have to order one from the PTO in Arlington; this may take several weeks to arrive. The staff will show you how to do this.

Fig. 6L is a typical sample of a microfilm printout—a list of patents that are classified in our old friend, class 272-109, gymnastic devices.

Once you've obtained a list such as this for the first of your selected classes and subclasses, you'll have to locate each patent (or an abstract of it) individually and examine it. There are two ways to access each patent:

1. Look at an abstract of the patent in its *Official Gazette* (OG) volume, or
2. Look at the entire patent in a numerically arranged stack or on microfilm or microfiche.

THE *OFFICIAL GAZETTE*

The *Official Gazette* (Patents) is a thick periodical published weekly, listing the main facts (patentee, assignee, filing date, classification) plus the broadest claim and main drawing figure of every patent issued that week. It also contains pertinent notices, fees, and a list of all PTDLs (Fig. 6K). Its price is outrageously high (about $600/year). Ralph Nader and Jacob Rabinow (a famous inventor) have railed against this high price as a disincentive to U.S. innovation.

If you make an OG search (this will be much easier), each patent entry you find will contain only a single claim (or abstract) and a single figure or drawing of the patent, as indicated in Fig. 6M (a typical page from an OG).

Note that for each patent, the OG entry gives the patent number, inventor's name(s) and address(es), assignee (usually a company that the inventor has transferred ownership of the patent to), filing date, application serial number, international classification, U.S. classification, number of claims, and a sample claim or abstract. If the drawing and claim look relevant, go to the actual patent, order a copy of it, and study it at your leisure.

Remember that the claim found in the *Official Gazette* is not a descriptive summary of the technical information in the patent. Rather, it is the essence of the claimed invention. The full text of the patent will contain far more technical information than the claim. So, even if a patent's *Official Gazette* claim doesn't precisely describe your invention, the rest of the patent may still be relevant.

EXAMPLE: When recently performing a PTDL search, a client of mine passed over a patent listed in the OG because the single drawing figure appeared to render the patent irrelevant. In fact, another drawing figure in the passed-over patent (but not found in the OG) anticipated my client's invention and was used by the PTO to reject his application (after he had spent considerable time, money, and energy preparing and filing it). The moral? Take an OG search with a grain of salt. Note well that a figure of the patent that isn't shown in the OG may be highly relevant; thus it's best to search full patents.

To make an OG search of the patents in Class 272, subclass 109 (Fig. 6L), start with the first patent in this list, D-262,394X. The "D" means that the patent is a design patent and the X means that this patent is a cross-reference. To locate patent D-262,394, look in the back of any OG for the section with the design patents, and see what range their numbers cover. If the patent numbers are too low, go to a later OG. If those are too high, go to an earlier OG. You'll be able to locate the right OG in a few minutes. You'll find that the present patent, D-262,394, was issued in 1980. Look at the figure from the patent printed in the OG and, if you find it relevant, write its identifying data down on your Searcher's Worksheet, Form 6-1.

Currently, 18 of these libraries have APS (Automator Patent System) search terminals that can search text of patents back to 1971. (See Section M1.)

LISTING | CLASS 272 | REEL NO. 7   PAGE   19

CLASS 272

105	★ 107	★ 109	★ 109	★ 110
80 1,701,026	1,134,008	1,747,352X	3,659,844X	3,754,758
53 1,709,832	1,492,976	1,779,903	3,735,979X	3,834,695
01 1,785,968	1,570,185	1,914,555	3,764,446X	3,837,641X
98X 1,793,898	1,947,025X	1,918,559X	3,778,054X	3,880,422
13X 1,990,497	1,958,807X	1,928,089X	3,785,642X	3,896,858X
28X 2,004,172	2,223,091	2,048,587X	3,825,252X	3,923,302
86 2,144,962	2,640,699X	2,107,377	3,857,561X	4,084,814
22X 2,165,749X	2,864,201X	2,167,696X	3,857,563X	
44 2,323,510	3,312,472X	2,169,710X	3,874,657X	111
31 2,341,473	4,121,826X	2,262,761X	3,891,207X	
97 2,505,784		2,324,970X	3,895,795X	D 175,729X
92 2,534,159	108	2,496,748	3,912,262	159,301
62 2,890,048		2,572,149X	3,915,451	971,003
16X 2,900,187	450,759	2,595,111X	3,937,461	1,001,300X
18 2,937,871	807,770	2,652,966X	3,947,023X	1,407,642
10X 2,978,692X	1,036,138	2,671,229X	3,966,200	1,419,191X
09 3,010,321X	1,805,121X	2,706,632X	3,969,871X	1,537,686X
22 3,244,421X	1,996,687	2,722,360X	3,971,561X	1,747,721
06 3,400,928	1,997,958X	2,738,189X	3,981,500X	2,000,250
82 3,401,931	2,117,938	2,771,615X	4,014,057X	2,197,600X
91 3,494,615	3,548,420X	2,795,423	4,026,547	2,343,204X
88X 3,608,897	3,759,513	2,829,892X	4,037,834X	2,646,280X
64 3,665,452X	3,884,465X	2,858,132X	4,125,257	2,855,201
64 3,724,843	4,121,826X	2,859,967X	4,137,583X	2,939,704
00X 3,731,298X		2,885,233X	4,147,129X	3,062,542
81 3,746,335	(109)	2,897,013X	4,147,828X	3,083,964
67 3,799,542		2,944,815	4,204,719X	3,173,415X
32 3,809,392X	D 262,394X	2,953,376X	4,210,322	3,339,920
17 4,089,519	RE 25,843	3,006,645	4,216,958	3,404,884
12 4,134,583X	9,695	3,044,773X	4,225,131	3,416,792X
48	174,499	3,085,357	4,274,626	3,485,493X
04 106	233,273	3,105,982X	4,275,880X	3,545,747X
24	233,274	3,106,395X	4,325,546X	3,547,435
94X 610,131X	233,540	3,204,259X	4,340,215	3,570,847
16X 649,885	233,541	3,205,888X	4,340,216	3,570,848
80 1,122,157	451,411	3,207,511X	4,344,617	3,580,568
88 1,552,442	649,914	3,211,452X	4,350,721X	3,582,068
68X 1,569,395	664,414	3,242,509X	4,410,175X	3,589,716
34X 1,731,686	802,338	3,251,076X		3,616,126X
1,994,089	811,417	3,262,134X	110	3,658,325
2,036,524X	907,075	3,284,819X		3,722,881
2,044,092	932,413	3,319,273X	D 198,923X	3,754,757
66 2,122,023	932,902	3,372,920	D 199,984X	3,781,931X
01 2,180,384	998,634	3,379,439X	1,085,505X	3,806,118X
54 2,196,610	1,003,797	3,391,414X	1,100,180X	3,837,644X
26 2,214,464	1,013,687	3,399,407	1,141,292X	3,850,428X
22X 3,163,421X	1,015,208	3,405,939X	1,482,910X	3,944,654
00 3,181,864X	1,126,082	3,409,294X	1,865,095X	3,990,697
78 3,746,334	1,128,201	3,419,270X	1,907,451	4,105,201
65 3,942,793X	1,130,813	3,432,163	1,916,809X	4,133,524
20X 4,084,813	1,142,137X	3,433,477X	2,198,537	4,183,521X
99 4,333,643	1,177,473X	3,459,611X	2,723,855X	4,197,839X
37X 4,337,940	1,204,329X	3,526,911X	2,906,531X	4,204,719X
14X 4,404,053X	1,256,734	3,580,569	2,949,298X	4,258,915
07	1,479,830	3,598,406X	3,246,893X	4,272,073
70 107	1,501,823X	3,628,790X	3,250,532	4,278,250X

112	★ 113
D 155,940X	D 173,173
D 208,924X	D 176,999
D 212,021X	D 187,138
D 214,572X	D 187,380
239,970X	D 187,381
450,187	D 187,656
775,309	D 198,532
786,672	D 218,455
950,100	D 218,460
1,485,135	D 218,765
1,585,748	D 224,029
1,670,390	D 224,796
1,676,061	D 227,381
2,240,407	D 227,792
2,303,223X	D 231,550
2,365,117	D 232,4
2,429,939	D 238,694
2,706,632X	D 250,723
2,800,105X	D 250,783
2,838,307	D 250,784
2,929,627	170,495
2,977,118	209,511
3,032,344	77,550
3,090,617X	796,159
3,156,465	821,391
3,342,484X	1,126,082
3,445,108	1,185,176
3,483,999X	1,351,053
3,501,140X	1,471,465
3,506,261	1,488,244
3,526,399	1,488,245
3,547,435X	1,488,246
3,563,539X	1,707,854
3,598,406X	1,765,361
3,606,315	1,822,786
3,638,602X	1,877,833
3,642,277	1,901,964
3,771,784X	1,917,018
3,782,718	1,929,822
3,794,316	2,126,636
3,837,642X	2,151,403
3,982,754X	2,206,581
4,018,437X	2,222,119
4,077,403X	2,500,425
4,116,433X	2,584,742
4,149,712	2,620,185
4,159,113	2,648,538
4,161,998X	2,648,539
4,272,073X	2,704,667
4,278,250X	2,720,430
4,335,538X	2,723,853
4,355,633X	2,768,823
4,372,552	2,795,423
	2,843,379
113	2,883,192
	2,886,317

Fig. 6L—List of Patents in Class 272-109 from Microfilm Printout

AUGUST 24, 1976   GENERAL AND MECHANICAL   1395

a plurality of bristles slidingly extending through said sleeve about said head for locking said electrode into heart tissue,

a slide assembly disposed within said sleeve and about said hose for movement toward and away from said head, said

assembly mounting said bristles for movement in and out of said sleeve as said assembly is moved by a catheter inserted in the rear of said sleeve to engage said slide assembly, and

means adjacent the rear of said sleeve for preventing withdrawal of said assembly from said sleeve.

3,976,083
BRASSIERE HAVING SIMULATED NIPPLES
Jakob E. Schmidt, 934 Monroe St., Charlestown, Ind. 47111
Filed Feb. 27, 1975, Ser. No. 553,779
Int. Cl.² A41C 3/00
U.S. Cl. 128—425   8 Claims

1. An improved brassiere comprising a pair of breast receiving cups, said cups comprising an outer layer of flexible fabric material; and a simulated nipple attached to said outer layer of each cup, said nipple comprising a stud element having distal and proximal ends and an exterior profile simulating the profile of the nipple of a human female breast, said stud element being positioned interiorly of said cup with a portion of said outer layer deformed over said distal end, and means cooperating with said proximal end and said outer layer for attaching said stud element to said breast receiving cup, whereby the exterior profile of said stud element is noticeable exteriorly of said brassiere to enhance the appearance of bralessness when said brassiere is worn beneath outer garments.

3,976,084
RETHRESHER BLOWER FOR A COMBINE
Wilbert D. Weber, Mississauga, Canada, assignor to Massey-Ferguson Industries Limited, Toronto, Canada
Filed Apr. 23, 1975, Ser. No. 570,901
Int. Cl.² A01F 12/18
U.S. Cl. 130—27 F   4 Claims
1. An agricultural combine harvester including a frame; a thresher housing; grain threshing, separating and cleaning apparatus including sieves mounted on the frame in the thresher housing; a conveyor mounted below said sieves for receiving tailings that overflow the sieves and conveying the tailings to one side of the combine; and a tailings rethreshing and blower assembly mounted on the frame for receiving tailings from the conveyor mounted below the sieves, for rethreshing the tailings and for blowing the rethreshed tailings

back into the thresher housing for cleaning, the rethresher and blower assembly including a chamber defined by two end walls and arcuate wall sections joining the two end walls, a blower rotatably mounted between the two end walls, said blower including vanes extending outwardly from the axis of rotation of the blower, rasp bar sections detachably mounted on the outer ends of the blower vanes, stationary threshing elements mounted on at least a portion of the arcuate wall of the chamber to cooperate with the rasp bar sections on the blower vanes to rethresh tailings, a tailings inlet aperture in

said arcuate wall sections, conveyor means connecting the conveyor mounted below the sieves and the tailings inlet aperture to direct tailings from conveyor mounted below said sieves through the tailings inlet aperture and into said chamber, a threshed tailings outlet in said arcuate wall sections, conveyor means connecting the threshed tailings outlet to the thresher housing to direct rethreshed tailings from the tailings outlet in said arcuate wall sections up and into the thresher housing, at least one air intake in one of the two end walls which define the chamber, and drive means to rotate the blower.

3,976,085
AUTOMATIC CIGARETTE FEED MACHINE
Floyd Vameda Hall, Durham, N.C., assignor to Liggett & Myers, Incorporated, Durham, N.C.
Continuation of Ser. No. 353,372, April 23, 1973, abandoned. This application Sept. 26, 1974, Ser. No. 509,702
Int. Cl.² A24C 5/35
U.S. Cl. 131—25   11 Claims

1. In combination in a one-to-one relationship,
a cigarette making machine for producing cigarettes at a high rate of speed, wherein said making machine includes a means for dispensing cigarettes individually in a spaced relationship,
a cigarette packaging machine for packaging cigarettes at approximately said high speed rate, and
a cigarette feed machine connected between said making machine and said packaging machine to convey the cigarettes made in said making machine directly to said ciga-

---

Fig. 6M—Page of _Official Gazette_ Showing Various Patent Abstracts

The second patent in the list, RE-25,843, is a reissue patent. Reissues are discussed in Chapter 14. For now, all you have to know is that reissues are listed in the front of each OG. Find the right OG, and in the same manner as you did with the design patent, locate the patent and list it on your worksheet if you feel it's relevant.

All of the rest of the patents in subclass 109 are regular utility patents in numerical and date order. Start with patent 9,695, which issued in the middle 1800s. You'll be able to locate it easily, since the outside of the binder of each OG volume usually lists the numbers of the utility patents which that volume contains. (If your PTDL doesn't carry OGs this far back, they'll probably have it on microfilm; ask your librarian for assistance.) Once you locate the OG (or microfilm reel), look at the patent in the usual manner to see if it's relevant. If so, write its data on your worksheet.

If your PTDL has full copies of patents readily accessible (each patent usually consists of several pages), you can look at the full text of each patent, one by one, in a similar manner as you looked at their abstracts in the OGs. If you find that the patent is relevant, usually you'll have access to a photocopy machine where you'll be able to make a copy of the whole patent, or just its relevant parts, on the spot.

CD-ROM Products at PTDLs

The PTO periodically publishes various CD-ROM disks that contain classification and bibliographic information about patents. All PTDLs subscribe to these disks and have one or more computers with CD-ROM drives for reading the disks. While the disks can't be used to make a true patentability search, they can be used as a searching aid and to provide other information about patents that you may find useful. The two most helpful disks are:

- CASSIS/CLASS disks (go back to 1790) can be used to find the classification of any patent, or the list of patents in any class.
- CASSIS/BIB disks (go back only about 20 years) can be used to find the classification of any recently issued patent, to find all patents assigned to any company or individual, to find a list of patents by year of issue, status (expired, reexamined, etc.), all patents by inventor's residence, all recently issued patents with a certain word or words in their title or abstract (this feature can be used to perform a crude search), and to find the field of search (class and subclass) for any type of invention.

Alternatively, if you don't want to interrupt the flow of your searching, you can save your patent numbers and order copies later. The PTDL may have PTO patent copy order coupons. If not, you can order patent copies from the PTO by writing a letter listing the numbers of the patents you want (be sure they're accurate!) to "Commissioner of Patents and Trademarks, Washington, DC 20231" with a check for the price per patent (Appendix 4, Fee Schedule) times the total number of patents you've ordered, or you can order copies from a private patent copy sales company. (See Section I, Step 3, above.)

If you can't get to a PTDL, note that most large public or university libraries at least subscribe to the *Official Gazette*. If, in addition to this resource, a local library also has an *Index of Classification,* you can make a cursory search there.

After you've completed Step 3, the review of patents, then perform Step 4, the analysis and decision, in exactly the same manner as outlined above for the PTO search.

L. Using the Shadow Patent Office to Search Via Internet

One of my favorite and easiest computer search services is available to anyone who can send e-mail through the Internet. This includes subscribers to America Online, Prodigy, and CompuServe, as well as a large number of other bulletin boards and online services. Operated by the Shadow Patent Office (SPO), a division of EDS, this service uses statistical algorithms to analyze your search request, and a powerful parallel-processing computer to search for conceptually related patents and send the results of the search back to you by e-mail through the Internet.

Most searches will produce the patent's face-sheet information, including the abstract, although it is also possible to obtain the full text of specific patents for an additional fee (drawings not included).

You may search by subject and by specific patent (called an infringement or validity search). To search by subject, you send an e-mail message consisting of a brief description of your invention and any key words that you think will help narrow the search. This type of search produces information on either 25 or 50 conceptually related patents (depending upon how much you wish to pay).

You can also make a validity search using SPO. (See Chapter 15, Section K, for more about this.) This works pretty much the same way. All you have to do is identify the patent you want searched, plus any key words. You will then receive information about 25 or 50 patents that are similar to the initial patent.

The SPO search service is as reasonable in cost as it is powerful. For about $80, you can discover as much relevant prior art in the U.S. patent database as you can for double or even triple that sum when using the other computer searching services (see Section M, below).

For complete information about how to sign up for this excellent service, call 800-258-6739, fax 800-533-3122 or send an e-mail message to spo_patent@spo.eds.com.

If you do use the SPO, remember that, like any other computer search service, it goes back only about 25 years, and thus will not provide a complete search for low-tech inventions. To complete an SPO search, you must go to the PTO or to a PTDL and do the job manually to cover patents before 1971.

M. Computer Searching

Although computer searching is beginning to come of age, you should not use it in place of a full manual search for low-tech inventions. The main reason for this is that the patents in most computer search data banks usually go back to only 1971 (some to 1950). Nevertheless, I cover it here because for most high-tech inventions there is no need to search prior art prior to 1971. Also, computer searching does have some advantages that make it useful as a supplement to a manual search. Since I believe that computer searching will eventually virtually replace manual searching, you may be able to avoid a bad case of "future shock" by becoming familiar with computer searching now.

Most basic computer search systems don't show the drawings of any prior patents. However, some services are now offering drawings from the patents being searched. Nor do most computer search systems use the PTO classification system. Instead, they search solely for Boolean combinations of key words in the texts—specification claims, abstract, or title—of prior patents. For example, suppose you've invented the bike with a frame made of a certain carbon-fiber alloy. To make a manual search, you would look through the patents in the bike and metallurgical (carbon-fiber alloy) classifications, hoping that if a relevant patent exists, someone would have classified it in either or both of these places. However, to make a computer search, you would select a combination of key words to describe your invention. Here you should use "bicycle" and "carbon fiber alloy." You then send these words to the computer and tell it to look through its data bank for any patent that contains all of these words. When it finds any patents that contain your key words in the combination you specify in your search request, it will identify these patents, regardless of their classifications.

If the computer reports too much data for you to conveniently examine—say it's found 200 patents with your words in combination—you should first look at one or two of the patents (the computer will show you the relevant text) to see if your invention is shown in an earlier patent (that is—your invention has been "knocked out"). If so, your search is over. If not, you'll need to narrow your search. This is easy. Simply add one or more additional key words, say "frame," or some details of the alloy, and redo the search with these increased key words until you've few enough patents to manually review conveniently. Also, you can narrow the search by using narrower (more specific) key words.

If you get extremely specific, the computer is likely to report no patents, or just one or two. If this occurs, you'll need to broaden your search. This is just as easy. Merely remove one or more key words, or broaden your present key words, and redo the search until you get back what you want. For example, you could eliminate "bicycle" or substitute "frame" for "bicycle" to broaden the search. Note that to broaden your search (pull out more prior art), you should use fewer key words, and to narrow your search (pull out less prior art), you should use more key words.

SIMILARITY OF CLAIMS TO COMPUTER SEARCHES

If you can understand this Boolean-logic concept now (you narrow your search by using more key words and/or making your key words more specific; you broaden your search by using fewer key words and/or making your key words more general), you'll have an easy time understanding patent claims (Chapters 9 and 13), since in claims, the more elements that are recited, the narrower the coverage.

The data that you search by computer (that is—the texts or claims of patents) is made available to anyone (for a fee) by several computer search service firms. These are private companies that in turn get this data in the form of machine-readable tapes as a by-product of the patent printing process from the Government Printing Office, which prints all patents. However, to produce a truly effective patent search report, these companies will have to find some way, such as using optical character recognition technology, to incorporate the data from earlier patents into their data banks. It doesn't take much imagination to realize what will happen when all patents and possibly other literature are added to the data banks, when the computers can also display and print out the drawings of patents, and when more terminals become available in libraries, service centers, etc. When this occurs, computer searching will be paperless, faster, and more thorough, as well as being independent of the PTO's classification system, which is subject to human error and troubled by missing patents.

Computer searching is presently used by the PTO's examiners to supplement their searches. As a result, we're getting better examinations and stronger patents. When computer searching is perfected and completed, I believe that patent application pendency time will be reduced from its present level of about 1.5 to three years to about six months or less, and that, more importantly, hardly any patent will ever be questioned for validity—that is, almost all patents will be virtually incontestable. (See Chapter 15 for more on patent validity.)

1. Available Computer Search Resources

Now that you get the general idea, how do you go about supplementing your manual search with a computer search? There are two ways to gain access to a computer search service's data bank:

- Via a personal computer (or terminal) with a modem—in this case you'll have to make a suitable agreement with a service or have access to the Internet
- Via an existing terminal that is dedicated to patent searching, such as at a PTDL, large company, law firm, or in the PTO.

In either case there are now two types of computer search services available: those which are free on the Internet and those which charge. The first free service is the PTO itself. It provides free key-word combination searches, but

only of abstracts of patents since about 1975. To use this service, visit http://patents.cnidr.org and search the bibliographic database. International Business Machines Corporation (IBM) offers free searching of the full text of patents back to 1971 and provides the drawings of patents since 1987. The IBM site is at http://patent.womplex.ibm.com.

While all of the seven fee based computer search services listed below provide the capability of searching the prior art to determine whether an invention is novel, they also provide other "patent search" capabilities, such as searching for all of the patents issued to a specific inventor, searching for all of the patents assigned to (legally owned by) a specific company, searching for a list of all of the patents in a specific search class, etc. Hence, it's important to be sure, when you sign up for a "patent search," that you make it clear that you need the capability of making a novelty search, the process I describe in this chapter.

Here are the six search services (six commercial and one at the PTO) that provide patent searching, together with their telephone numbers:

Dialog (Claims): 800-334-2564
Bibliographic Research Service (BRS/SEARCH):
  800-289-4277
Mead Data Central (Lexpat): 800-543-6862
Permagon: 800-336-7575
Orbit/Questel: 800-424-9600
Corporate Intelligence Corp. (CIC): 206-925-1000
APS Search Terminals at the PTO or certain PTDLs (see below).

Call any of the first six (commercial) services and they will be delighted to send you information about their patent search services, or advise you where you can access a terminal near you. If you only need to make a one-time search, clearly it won't pay to make an ongoing agreement with a company for their services. If you want to use your personal computer, or a company computer, as a patent search terminal, you'll have to sign a contract with one of the services. The good news is that all of the services except one have no sign-up or monthly minimum charge, although some services levy a one-time charge of about $50 for their instruction manual. The bad news is that the one with the sign-up and monthly minimum charge, Mead Data Central, along with CIC and the APS terminals at the PTO and certain PTDLs, are the two best services, since they can search and send back the full text and drawings of any patent in their data bases (back to 1974 or 1971); all of the others search only the abstract or claims of the patents.

The APS search terminals in the PTO's search room and in certain PTDLs can be used by anyone who has taken their course. Inquire at the PTO's search room or PTDL for details.

All services charge for the amount of time that you use to search their database; the fee runs from about $20 per hour for off-time (night/weekend) searching to $200 per hour for weekday use. These fees include telephone toll costs. A typical search will cost around $10–$150.

While I'm reluctant to recommend any vendors in this book, because of changing conditions, at present there is no question that CIC, Mead, and APS are the unqualified "best." If you can gain access to CIC or a terminal with a Lexpat search capability near you, or you can go to the PTO's search room or a PTDL, go no further. If not, most of the other databases are in my opinion about even in their capabilities, except for Orbit/Questel, which can provide an image of one figure for each patent.

The Sunnyvale, California, and the Detroit Public Library PTDLs have two image search workstations, which, in addition to providing text-searching back to 1971, also can display the full text and drawings of all U.S. patents back to 1790.

2. Vocabulary Associated With Computer Searches

How do you use a database? Assuming you're going to do the search yourself, first thoroughly study the service's instruction manual so that you'll be able to conduct your search in as little time as possible, thereby minimizing user time charges. While every system is different, and while space constraints preclude coverage of them all, the following usage terms are common to all systems. If you're going to do any patent searching, you should learn these terms now.

- A **File** is the actual name of the patent search database provided by the service; for example LEXPAT is the name and trademark for Mead Data General's patent search database; CLAIMS is Dialog's patent search file.
- A **Record** is a portion of a file; the term is used to designate a single reference, usually a patent within a database.
- A **Field** is a portion of a record, such as a patent's title, the names of the inventors, its filing date, its patent number, its claims, etc.
- A **Term** is a group or, in computerese, a "string," of characters within a field—for example, the inventor's surname, one word of the title of a patent, etc., are terms.
- A **Command** is an instruction or directive to the search system that tells it to perform a function. For example, "Search" might be a command to tell a system to look for some key search words in its database.

- A **Key Word** or a **Search Term** are the words that are actually searched. "Bicycle" and "carbon fiber alloy" are the key words for our example above.
- A **Qualifier** is a symbol that is used to limit a search or the information that the search displays for your use. Normally no qualifier would be used in novelty searches, but if you're looking for a patent to a certain inventor, you could add a qualifier that limits the search to the field of the patentee's name.
- A **Wild Card Symbol** is an ending (familiar to users of sophisticated word processing programs) that is used in lieu of a word's normal ending in order to broaden a *key word*. The wild card cuts off immaterial endings so that only word roots are searched. For example, if we were searching Millie's annular napkin-shaping ring, we would want our search to include the words "annular" and "annulus." Thus, instead of using both key words and the *Connector Symbol* "or" (see below), we might search for "annul*" where "*" was a wild card symbol that tells the computer to look for any word with the root "annul" and any ending.
- **Connector Words** are those (such as "or," "and," and "not") that tell the computer to look for certain defined logical combinations of *key words*. For instance, if you issued a *command* telling the computer to search for "annulus or ring and napkin," the computer would recognize that "or" and "and" were connector words and would search for patents with the words "annulus" and "napkin," or "ring" and "napkin," in combination.

  Obviously, the use of more *key words* joined by the Boolean "and" connector will narrow your search, since it will add more *key words* to the search; this will cause the computer to pull out fewer patents, because only patents with all of the *key words* connected by "ands" will satisfy your search request. However, the use of more *key words* joined by the "or" connector will broaden your search, since any patent with any one of the *key words* joined by an "or" will be selected. The "not" connector is seldom employed, but it can be used to narrow a search when you want to eliminate a certain class of patents that contain an unwanted *key word*. (Note that when you get to writing your claims (Chapter 9), "ors" and "nots" are generally verboten.)
- **Proximity Symbols** are those that tell the computer to look for specified *key words*, provided they are not more than a certain number of terms apart. Thus, if you told the computer to search for "napkin w/5 shaping" it would look for any patent that contained the words "napkin" and "shaping" within five words

of each other, the symbol "w/5" meaning "within five words of." If no proximity symbol is used and the words are placed adjacent to each other—such as "napkin shaping"—the computer will pull out only those patents that contain these two words adjacent to each other in the order given. However, if a *connector word* is used—such as "napkin and shaping"—the computer will pull out any patent with both of these words, no matter where they are in the patent and no matter in what order they appear.

3. Think of Alternative Search Terms

Before you even approach the computer, no matter what search system you use, be well prepared with a well-thought-out group of key words and all possible synonyms or equivalents. Thus, to search for Millie's napkin-shaping ring, in addition to the obvious key words "ring," "annular," "napkin," and "shaping," think of other terms from the same and analogous fields. In addition to napkin, you could use "cloth." Or, in addition to shaping, you could use "folding" or "bending." In addition to "annulus" or "ring," you could try "device," etc.

4. Using the Computer

From here on, simply follow the instructions in the service manual for operating the computer and gaining access to the database. As with the manual search, pull out all relevant patents without any consideration of obviousness. Then later, at your leisure, analyze them as instructed earlier in this chapter. Good luck and smooth searching!

5. Using Computer-Generated References to Work Backward

After making a computer search and obtaining a group of relevant references generated by the computer, it's possible (and very easy) to use these references to work back and obtain additional, earlier relevant references that antedate the computer's database. How? Simply look at and/or order each of the "References Cited," which are listed on the abstract page (see Fig. 6D(c)) of each computer-generated patent. These references (usually patents) were cited by the PTO during prosecution of the patent and are usually very relevant. You can even look up the "References Cited" in the additional references to go back even earlier, thereby making a "tree" of references. However, the PTO didn't list the "References Cited" before the '50s, and in earlier patents "References Cited" are listed at the end of the patent.

N. Searching Software Inventions in the Software Patent Institute's Database

Many software experts have recently complained that the PTO has been issuing patents on software inventions that aren't novel and unobvious over the prior art. I believe that there is much validity to this charge—that is, many software patents really don't claim a novel and unobvious invention and could be invalidated by a proper search. As a result, some people even want to do away with software patents. I strongly disagree with this proposal, since this would be throwing out the baby with the bathwater.

I believe that much, if not most, future technological progress will occur in software, but without the incentive of a patent monopoly, software developers will not have an adequate incentive to innovate. There are many other arguments in favor of software patents, but they're beyond the scope of this book. Suffice it to note that I prefer strengthening the PTO's software search capability.

If you agree and want to support the continued existence of software patents, keep your eyes peeled for any legislative developments and do whatever you can to support the continued existence of software patents. Also, one organization that has been in the forefront of preserving software patents deserves your support: It is The Abraham Lincoln Patent Holders Association (ALPHA), 146 Main Street, Suite 404, Los Altos, CA 94022, tel. 415-965-0327, Fax 415-968-7319, founded by programmer Paul Heckel. ALPHA took its name from Lincoln's famous and still-pertinent aphorism, emblazoned over a door of the former Patent Office in the Commerce Department building in Washington, through which I passed every day when I worked there: "The patent system added the fuel of interest to the fire of genius."

But I digress. As a result of the PTO's problems with searching and maintaining an adequate software patent database, the Software Patent Institute, 2901 Hubbard Street, Ann Arbor, MI 48105-2467, tel. 313-769-4606, Fax 313-769-4054, Internet: spi@spi.org, URL: http://www.spi.org/, was born. The SPI maintains, catalogs, and has the best software prior art database in the world. The SPI doesn't do searching, but they now make their database open to the public. They allow QuickLook users to explore their databases without viewing records for free and Guest users to look at synopses of records for free for up to one hour. I strongly recommend that you take advantage of these generous services of the SPI before you make your actual search, in order to familiarize yourself with their search systems. To make a useful search, one must be a subscriber or an SPI member, but their fees are reasonable. Most casual searchers will want to become a subscriber; as of Summer 1996 subscribers had to pay a one-time administrative sign-up fee of $100 and a searching fee of $1.00 per 1,000 characters displayed from the SPI's databases. Making a search in the SPI's databases is similar to making any other computer search: you simply enter a search string in a Text Box in a Search Query section of the interface and the SPI's computer will execute the search. The search can be narrowed or broadened in the same way that it's done for other computer searches; see Section M or the SPI's instructions for guidance. You can also access the SPI's database via the BRI/SEARCH service; their telephone number is 800-289-4277.

The SPI also likes to receive prior art on software inventions, such as old instruction books and manuals, and will also receive and provide a defensive publication service for software inventions. (See Chapter 14, Section F, for more on defensive publications.)

0. The IBM Patent Searching System on the Internet

The patent searching system described here is best thought of as a useful tool for conducting a preliminary patent search for inventions using recent technologies. The older the field of inventing, the less useful this system will be. In any event, if you become serious about applying for a patent on your invention, you will be well advised to conduct a more thorough patent search using the techniques and/or resources described elsewhere in this chapter.

If the computer age is newly upon us, the Internet is its cutting edge. And as you might expect, there are now ways to do at least cursory patent searches on the World Wide Web. The best of these is the IBM Patent Server on the Internet (http://patent.womplex.ibm.com), a searching system and database (generously provided by IBM) that contains over two million patents that date back 26 years to January 5, 1971.

1. No Specfication or Drawings for Patents Issued Between 1971 and 1973

For all patents issued between 1971 and 1973, the site provides only the following information, which can be searched, viewed, downloaded, and printed:

Patent Number
Title
Inventor

Relevant Prior Art
Assignees
Agent or Attorney
Abstract
Claims.

The specifications and drawings of these patents cannot be searched. To see the specification and drawings, it is necessary to obtain a copy of the full patent, which you can do directly from this site.

2. Text and Images for Patents Issued Between 1974 and the Present

For patents issued after 1973, you can search, view, download and print the same parts of the patent as described in Section 1 above. In addition, although the drawings and specifications can't be searched as text, they may be viewed as scanned images, which are akin to photographs. But be prepared for possible frustration. The images are slow to download, and appear to be browser dependent (the system works better on some browsers than on others).

3. Limitations of the IBM System

The fact that you can only search patents issued since 1971 can itself be an extremely important limitation. As I stress in Chapter 5, Section E, all previous inventions (prior art) can be used to determine whether a new invention qualifies for a patent. Therefore, to be effective, a patent search must reach back to the earliest prior art that might relate to (teach) the new invention. Since the IBM system reaches back only to 1971, you can only have confidence in your search results if your invention technology wasn't around prior to 1971. For an invention that requires searching back considerably beyond the 1971 date (for instance, an invention related to bicycles) the IBM system will only provide a fraction of the total prior art for that invention.

A secondary limitation of the IBM system is that you are unable to search the entire patent. If you are searching for patents whose subject matter is similar to yours, your search is limited to the patent's title, abstract, and the claims. The patent specification (covered in Chapter 8 of this book), which includes detailed descriptions of the underlying invention and its background, is not included in the search. Since the IBM search system depends upon the use of key words (see Section 4 below), the inability to search the specification means that your key words may produce a more limited list of relevant patents than would otherwise be the case. By contrast, the computerized search system available in the PTO and some Patent and Trademark Depository Libraries (PTDLs) do in fact allow you to search the entire patent, including the specification.

A third limitation is the fact that you must depend on key words. Traditional patent searching involves an analytical system that uses a classification scheme to find relevant prior art (see Section I above). This analytical system is the result of a human being grouping like inventions together and does not depend on the whimsy of which search terms you select. The key-word system, on the other hand, depends on you coming up with the right words in your search request. However, patents are often written with legal-sounding terms or technical jargon in place of otherwise ordinary terms. For example, a patent for a telephone may be titled Full Duplex Voice Telecommunication Device. Such a patent may never be found with telephone as the search term. This limitation is inherent in any computerized searching system based on search terms. The disadvantages of the key-word search system can to some extent be overcome by following the tips described in Section 6 below as well as by using the logic implicit in the Boolean search technique (Section 4).

Additional limitations are the inability to search by year or date, and the inability to display more than the first 200 patents found in each search. Of course, if your search produces more than 200 patents, you can take this as a sign that your search is too broad and consider ways to narrow it. See Section J above.

A final limitation is that for patents prior to 1974 you can't see the full patent. Unless you are able to read the detailed description of the invention and its background, and view at least some of the drawings, it may be hard for you to judge its full effect as prior art on your ability to get a patent. That means that you will have to order the patent, a service provided by this site at a reasonable cost. (See Section 7 below)

4. Four Ways to Search

There are four ways to search the IBM system: Simple Text Search, Patent Number Search, Boolean Text Search, and Advanced Text Search. Again, only the information contained in the list in Section 1 above will be searched; the background of the invention and the complete description of the invention (the heart of the specification) are not available for searching.

Simple Text Search

Fig. 6N shows the Simple Text Search page, which is the first page of the IBM Web site. It is simply titled Search, although elsewhere on the Web site it is referred to as Simple Text Search. To use, enter one or more words in the text entry box, select the time period, and click Search. The system will search for an exact match of the words anywhere in the searchable parts of the patents (listed in Section 1). Examples of search words include "keyboard," "Smith John," "computer mouse," "Sony," etc.

Patent Number Search

Fig. 6O shows the Patent Number Search page. You must enter an exact patent number of seven alphanumeric characters, without any commas. For example:

4256879 — Searches for utility patent number 4256879.

D352640 — Searches for design patent number D352640.

RE30298 — Searches for reissued patent number RE30298.

PP03987 — Searches for plant patent number PP03987.

T962311 — Searches for defensive publication number T962311.

Boolean Text Search

Fig. 6P shows the Boolean Text Search page. It is for searching patents that contain—in their searchable portions—the precise combination of words that you designate as search terms. There are two boxes for entering search terms, and there is a pull-down menu to the right of each box. Each menu can be displayed or pulled down by clicking on the button with the down arrow, as shown in Fig. 6Q. Each menu for a box contains a selection of the following fields:

Any Field
Inventor
Assignee
Title
Abstract
Claims
Agent.

Selecting Any Field causes the system to search for the word or term in all fields. Selecting any other field limits the search to the selected field. Most inventors will be searching for a type of invention, so the most useful fields are Title, Abstract, and Claims, since these contain a description of the invention.

The menu between the field menus contains a selection for the Boolean connector, which includes And, Or, and And Not, as shown in Fig. 6R. The And connector causes the system to search for patents with both words or terms; the Or connector causes the system to search for patents with either term; and the And Not connector causes the system to search for patents with the first word or term, but

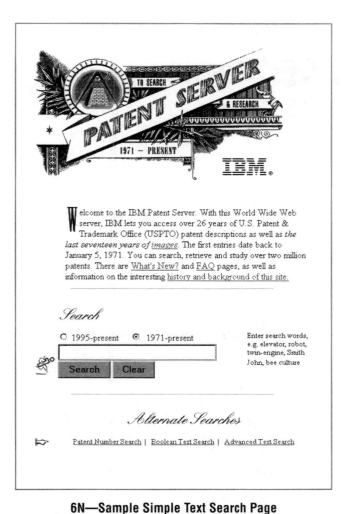

6N—Sample Simple Text Search Page

6P—Sample Boolean Text Search Page

6O—Sample Patent Number Search Page

**6Q—Choosing a Search Field in a Boolean
Text Search Page**

without the second word or term. For example, a search with Sony limited to the Assignee field, the And connector, and television limited to the Claims field, will find patents assigned to (owned by) Sony, and that include the word television in the claims. Words linked by Boolean connectors can occur separately in a document. For example, a search with computer limited to Any Field, the And connector, and mouse limited to Any Field, will find patents with computer anywhere within a searchable portion and mouse anywhere within a searchable portion; a patent that has an abstract or claim describing "a mouse connected to a computer" will still be found.

The "Maximum results" pull-down menu may be used for determining the maximum number of patents displayed in the results for each search. The maximum is 200.

6R—Choosing a Connector in a Boolean Text Search Page

Advanced Text Search

Fig. 6S shows the Advanced Text Search page. Different words or terms can be entered in up to seven different fields for producing more accurate search results. In most situations, only the Title, Abstract, and Claims fields are used, since these are the only ones that contain a description of the invention. Therefore, there is little practical difference between the Advanced Text Search and the Boolean Text Search, since the latter already enables you to search the same fields.

6S—Sample Advanced Text Search Page

Again, the Maximum results pull-down menu may be used for determining the maximum number of patents displayed in the results for each search. The maximum is 200.

5. Searching, Viewing, Saving, and Printing

As an example, a Simple Text Search was conducted with the words ergonomic computer mouse. Two patents that contain such words in their searchable parts were found, as shown in Fig. 6T. Clicking on a patent number displays all the information typically found on the first page of the actual patent, except for the drawing, as shown in Fig. 6U. The entire patent is available as a series of scanned images because the patent is dated after January 1, 1980. Clicking on the View Images link (underlined text; typically blue) at the top of the page displays the first page of the patent, as shown in Fig. 6V. The image is displayed in another window separate from the one displaying the information in Fig. 6U, so that you may switch back and forth between the windows.

You can scroll forward or backward through the images by clicking on the pointing hands at the top or bottom of the page. The pointing hand pointing at three bars is for advancing to the beginning or end of the patent. The magnifying glass with the wide slit is for zooming in to show the patent in greater detail, and the magnifying glass with the narrow slit is for zooming out to show the patent in lesser detail.

A text page, such as in Fig. 6U, can be saved to disk by clicking the File menu in your browser (a program used for surfing the Internet), and selecting Save As…. An image can be saved by clicking on it with the right mouse button (for PC users), and selecting Save Image As…. The text pages and images can thus be viewed later at any time, even when you are not connected to the Internet.

A text page can also be printed by clicking on the Print button in your browser. However, the images are printed at screen resolution, which is about 75 dpi, so that the output is almost unreadable. Here is a way to print at a higher resolution:

1. Zoom in at least twice to enlarge the image and increase the detail. Zooming in more than twice produces slightly better image quality, but the download time and file size are substantially increased.

2. Save the image to disk. On the PC, this is done by clicking on the image with the right mouse button, and selecting Save Image As….

3. Use a paint or image editing program to open and print the image, which is .gif type file. A full-featured word processor, such as Microsoft Word, can also be used to open the image with the Insert Picture command. Use the program's controls to make the image fill the whole page. As shown in Fig. 6W, the apparent printed quality is about 200 dpi, which is perfectly readable.

6. Important Searching Tips

Your searching can be more productive and accurate if you follow these important tips:

1. *Less is more.* The fewer words used to define a search, the broader the results, and vice versa. For example, a search done with the term ergonomic computer mouse found two patents; a search done with the term computer mouse found 157 patents; and a search done with the term mouse found 3,147 patents (only a maximum of the first 200 can be displayed).

2. *Use alternative terms.* A variety of different terms are often used in patents to describe similar inventions, so search with as many alternative terms as you can think of. For example, a computer mouse is also referred to as a computer input device or a pointing device. Incidentally, a search done with computer input device found 91 patents, and a search done with pointing device found 475 patents (only a maximum of the first 200 can be displayed).

3. *Make good use of Boolean connectors.* And, Or, And Not can be used to connect words or terms in a box

6T—Sample Search Results Page

Order Patent | Vote | View Images

5576733 : Ergonomic computer mouse

INVENTORS: Lo; Jack, Daly City, CA 94014
ASSIGNEES: **none**
ISSUED: **Nov. 19, 1996**   FILED: **May 25, 1994**
SERIAL NUMBER: **248737**   FEE STATUS:
INTL. CLASS (Ed. 6): G09G 3/02;
U.S. CLASS: 345-163, D14-114;
FIELD OF SEARCH: 345-163,164,165,166,168,160,179,157 ; 074-471 XY ; 341-20,22 ; 400-489,715 ; 248-918 ; 361-680 ; 401-6-8,48 ; 015-436,435,438,443,444 ; D14-114,107 ;
AGENTS: Lo; Jack;

ABSTRACT: An ergonomic computer mouse includes an upright, primary finger-supporting surface for supporting all of the fingers of an upright hand in straight positions and in an upright stack. It also includes an opposite thumb-supporting surface for supporting the thumb. A hand holding the ergonomic computer mouse will be in a naturally upright and relaxed position, without requiring twisting of the hand, wrist, or forearm. As a result, fatigue, discomfort, and pain are minimized or eliminated even after a long period of continuous use.

U.S. REFERENCES:

Patent No.	Patentee	Issue Date	No patents reference this one
5355147	Lear	Oct. 1, 1994	
5157381	Cheng	Oct. 1, 1992	
4780707	Selker	Oct. 1, 1988	
5160919	Mohler et al.	Nov. 1, 1992	
5296871	Paley	Mar. 1, 1994	
D302426	Bradley et al.	July 1, 1989	
5287090	Grant	Feb. 1, 1994	
2498105 *	Dolan	Feb. 1, 1950	
D328597	Clouss	Aug. 1, 1992	
5137384	Spencer et al.	Aug. 1, 1992	
4862165	Gart	Aug. 1, 1989	
3972628	Stevers	Aug. 1, 1976	
4917517	Ertz	Apr. 1, 1990	

* some details unavailable

17 CLAIMS First Claim Shown (Show all claims)

I claim:

- 1. An ergonomic computer mouse for translation over a horizontal stationary surface, comprising:
  - a generally horizontal bottom surface for stably and translatably positioning said mouse over said stationary surface;
  - a housing attached on top of said bottom surface, said housing having a forward end, a rear end, and opposite sides extending continuously between said forward end and said rear end;
  - one of said sides being a generally vertical finger-supporting surface for supporting the fingers of a generally upright hand in a generally vertical stack, so that the little finger is at the bottom thereof and the index finger is at the top thereof, said finger-supporting surface being generally elongated in a horizontal direction for supporting the fingers in generally straight positions, and
  - another one of said sides being a thumb-supporting surface for supporting the thumb of said hand, so that said mouse is securely gripped between the thumb and the fingers, and is easily maneuvered by flexing the straight fingers and the thumb, and the hand is in a relaxed, untwisted, and naturally upright position.

RELATED U.S. APPLICATIONS: **none**

FOREIGN REFERENCES:

Document No.	Country	Date	Intl. Class
41435	Switzerland	May 1, 1908	
413606	EPO	Feb. 1, 1991	
2244546	United Kingdom	Dec. 1, 1991	
2237160	United Kingdom	Apr. 1, 1991	

OTHER REFERENCES:

- Appoint Flashpoint, Guide to Operations, p. 2; Computer Shopper Magazine, May 1994, p. 548, describing operation and showing photo of mouse pen, respectively.
- Cadence Magazine, May 1994, p. 74, showing photo of mouse pen.
- Microsoft Mouse User's Guide, pp. 2, 22, and 23, showing drawings of the mouse being held by a hand.

PRIMARY/ASSISTANT EXAMINERS: **Hjerpe; Richard, Lao; Lun-Yi**
ADDED TO DATABASE: **Nov. 5, 1996**

☞ Patent Number Search | Boolean Text Search | Advanced Text Search

Home | Help | Search | Order Form | Guestbook | Legal | IBM

6U—Sample First Page Text of Patent

6V—Sample First Page Image With Drawing

6X—Patent Order Form

in any of the search methods, except for Patent Number Search. For example, ergonomic And mouse can be entered in the Simple Text Search box. When Boolean connectors are used, each multiple-word term must be enclosed in quotes. For example, "ergonomic" And "pointing device." Boolean connectors can also be used to search for inventions with alternative terms simultaneously. For example, "computer mouse" Or "pointing device" finds all patents with either set of words.

4. *Use Wild cards.* Use the asterisk * as a wild card to represent any character or characters. For example, John* finds patents by all inventors with the first or last name starting with John, and ending with any character or characters, including John, Johnny, Johnson, and Johnston. Use the question mark ? as a wild card to represent any single character. For example, ?am finds ram, cam, jam, etc.

5. *Inventor Names.* Always enter inventor names last-name first, for example, Edison Thomas.

6. *Class and References.* If you find a relevant patent, click on the Intl. Class and U.S. Class links (Fig. 6U) to display patents for potentially similar inventions, and the U.S. References link to view the patents specifically cited as being similar.

Information on using more advanced search techniques can be found by clicking the search language link in the Advanced Text Search page.

7. Ordering Patent Copies

Although the portions of the patents that are available (see Sections 1 and 2 above) can be printed directly from the Web site free of charge, they must be downloaded and printed one page at a time. If you wish to get numerous patents, this will be a very time consuming process. Instead, you may order copies of the patents and have them delivered to you, but at a cost. To order patents from the list shown in Fig. 6T, check the boxes next to ones you want, and click Order Checked Documents. You can also order a patent you are viewing, such as in Figs. 6U or 6V, by clicking on the Order Patent link on the top of the page to display the Patent Order Form page, shown in Fig. 6X. The patents are available in a variety of formats at different costs, starting from $2.50 per patent of up to 100 pages. Click on the price list link on the Patent Order Form page for details.

US005576733A

United States Patent [19]

Lo

[11] **Patent Number:** 5,576,733

[45] **Date of Patent:** Nov. 19, 1996

[54] **ERGONOMIC COMPUTER MOUSE**

[76] Inventor: **Jack Lo**, 1415 Eddington La., Daly City, Calif. 94014

[21] Appl. No.: **248,737**

[22] Filed: **May 25, 1994**

[51] **Int. Cl.⁶** G09G 3/02

[52] **U.S. Cl.** 345/163; D14/114

[58] **Field of Search** .... 345/163, 164, 345/165, 166, 168, 160, 179, 157; 74/471 XY; 341/20, 22; 400/489, 715; 248/918; 361/680; 401/6–8, 48; 15/436, 435, 438, 443, 444; D14/114, 107

[56] **References Cited**

U.S. PATENT DOCUMENTS

D. 302,426	7/1989	Bradley et al.	D14/114
D. 328,597	8/1992	Clouss	D14/114
2,498,105	2/1950	Dolan	401/48
3,972,628	8/1976	Stevers	401/48
4,780,707	10/1988	Selker	345/163
4,862,165	8/1989	Gart	341/20
4,917,517	4/1990	Ertz	401/6
5,137,384	8/1992	Spencer et al.	400/489
5,157,381	10/1992	Cheng	345/163
5,160,919	11/1992	Mohler et al.	340/711
5,287,090	2/1994	Grant	345/163
5,296,871	3/1994	Paley	345/163
5,355,147	10/1994	Lear	345/163

FOREIGN PATENT DOCUMENTS

413606	2/1991	European Pat. Off.	345/179
41435	5/1908	Switzerland	15/437
2237160	4/1991	United Kingdom	273/148 B
2244546	12/1991	United Kingdom .	

OTHER PUBLICATIONS

Appoint Flashpoint, Guide to Operations, p. 2; Computer Shopper Magazine, May 1994, p. 548; describing operation and showing photo of mouse pen, respectively.

Cadence Magazine, May 1994, p. 74, showing photo of mouse pen.

Microsoft Mouse User's Guide, pp. 2, 22, and 23, showing drawings of the mouse being held by a hand.

Primary Examiner—Richard Hjerpe
Assistant Examiner—Lun-Yi Lao
Attorney, Agent, or Firm—Jack Lo

[57]   **ABSTRACT**

An ergonomic computer mouse includes an upright, primary finger-supporting surface for supporting all of the fingers of an upright hand in straight positions and in an upright stack. It also includes an opposite thumb-supporting surface for supporting the thumb. A hand holding the ergonomic computer mouse will be in a naturally upright and relaxed position, without requiring twisting of the hand, wrist, or forearm. As a result, fatigue, discomfort, and pain are minimized or eliminated even after a long period of continuous use.

17 Claims, 2 Drawing Sheets

6W—Sample Enlarged Image

Consider Your Options

INVENTOR'S COMMANDMENT #9

After making your commercial evaluation and search, carefully consider the alternatives before proceeding or dropping it: file a utility patent application now, test the market for up to a year and then consider filing, keep it a trade secret, file a design application, use a clever trademark, use copyright coverage, and/or use distinctive "trade dress" for unfair competition coverage.

Now that you have a pretty good idea of the patentability and commercial status of your invention, it is time to make a plan for acquiring the maximum possible offensive rights under the law. While you might think that your next step would be to prepare and file a patent application, you would be wrong in doing so without first considering the information in this chapter. I suggest that your main goal should be to profit from your invention, not to get a patent.

I've provided a Decision Chart (Fig. 7A) to simplify and organize your alternatives. It consists of 23 boxes with interconnecting lead lines. The numbered, light-lined boxes (even numbers from 10 to 40) represent various tasks and decisions on your route to making decisions on available options. The lettered, heavy-lined boxes (A to F and X) represent your actual options.

The numbers in parentheses in the following discussion refer to the boxes on the chart. While there are seven options, several of these can be reached by several routes. Accordingly, the following discussion is divided into more than seven sections.

A. Drop It If You Don't See Commercial Potential (Chart Route 10-12-14-X)

This route has already been covered in Chapter 4, but in order to acquaint you with the use of the chart, I'll review it again.

Referring to the chart, assuming that you've invented something (Box 10—Chapter 2) and recorded the conception properly (Box 12—Chapter 3), you should then proceed to build and test your invention as soon as practicable, or consider filing a Provisional Patent Application (Chapter 3), provided you're aware of all of the disadvantages of the PPA (Box 12). If building and testing would present appreciable difficulty, you should wait until after you evaluate

your invention's commercial potential (Box 14—Chapter 4), or patentability (Box 16—Chapter 5). But always keep the building and testing as a goal; it will help you to evaluate commercial potential and may be vital in the event an "interference" occurs (different persons seek patents for the same invention). What's more, as you'll see in Chapter 11, you'll find a working model extremely valuable when you show the invention to a manufacturer.

Your next step is stated in Box 14—investigate your invention's commercial potential using the criteria of Chapter 4. Assuming you decide that your invention has no commercial potential, your answer to the commercial question is "No," and you would thus follow the "No" line from Box 14 to the ultimate decision, Box X, which says "Invent something else," as already covered in Chapter 4. See how easy it is?

B. Try to Sell Invention to Manufacturer Without "Regular" Patent Application (Chart Route 12-14-16-18-B)

This route is especially useful if you've filed a Provisional Patent Application (PPA) on the invention (Box 12), but can also be used if you've built and tested the invention and properly recorded your building and testing activities. After filing a PPA or building and testing and recording your efforts (Box 12), see if the invention has commercial potential (Chapter 4—Box 14) and if it's patentable (Chapters 5 and 6—Box 16). If so, whether or not you're able to prepare—or have prepared—a regular patent application, try to sell your invention to a manufacturer (Box B) in the hope that the manufacturer will have the application prepared for you, either on the basis of your PPA or without the PPA. If you take this route, you should be sure either that your PPA is properly prepared (see Chapters 3 and 8) or that you've properly documented conception, building and testing (Chapter 3). I recommend this route only if you can't prepare or can't afford to have prepared a regular patent application because:

- if you've only built and tested the invention without properly recording your activities, you run a risk of an unscrupulous manufacturer stealing your invention by filing a patent application on your invention before you do so, and
- if you've filed a PPA, you'll have all of the disadvantages of the PPA. (See Chapter 3, Section I, for a discussion of the advantages and disadvantages of filing a PPA.)

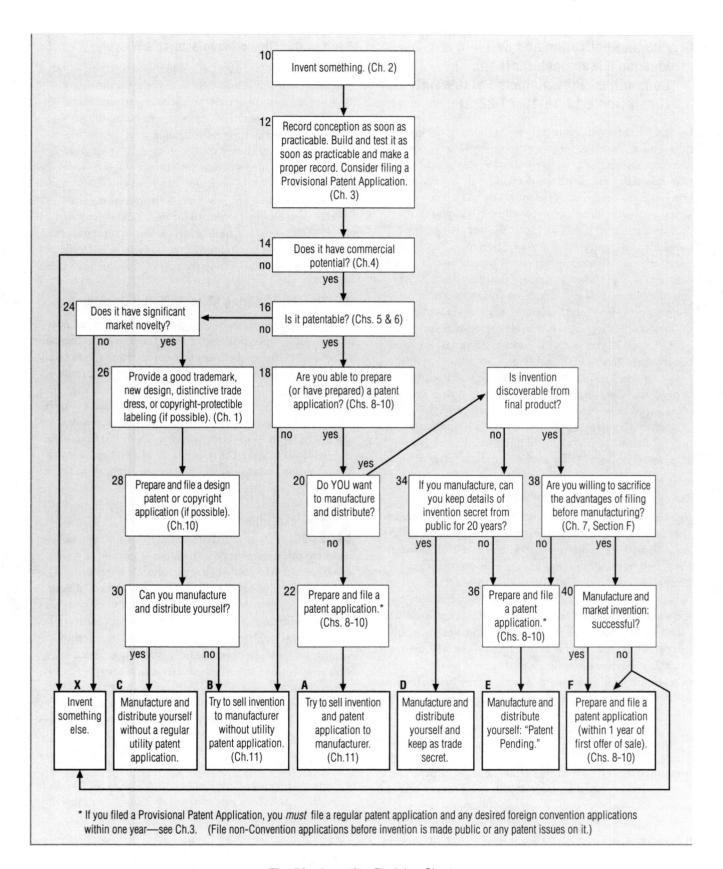

Fig. 7A—Invention Decision Chart

C. File an Application and Sell It to or License a Manufacturer If You See Commercial Potential and Patentability (Chart Route 14-16-18-20-22-A)

Filing a patent application and selling rights to the invention is the usual route for most inventors. This is because inventors seldom have the capability to establish their own manufacturing and distribution facilities. If a) your invention has good commercial potential (Box 14), b) your decision on patentability is favorable (Box 16), c) you're able to prepare a patent application (Box 18) (or have one prepared for you), and d) you don't wish to manufacture and distribute your product or process yourself (Box 20), your next step is to prepare a patent application (Box 22). After you prepare the patent application, you should then try to sell your invention (and accompanying patent application) to the manufacturer, as stated in Box A. Note that if you file a PPA (Box 12), you must file your "regular" patent application, and also any desired foreign convention applications (see Chapter 12) within one year. You should file any desired non-Convention applications before your invention is made public or before any patent issues on it.

Why file a patent application before offering the invention to a manufacturer? A good question, which has four good answers. Let's look at each one individually.

1. Offensive Rights for Your Invention

By preparing and filing a patent application, you've defined your invention and its ramifications in very precise terms, made formal drawings of it, and formally established your claim to it in the PTO. Thus anyone who later sees the invention and wants to steal or adopt it would have to engage in elaborate and (usually) illegal preparations. And, the would-be thief will have filed after you, a serious disadvantage. Thus once you file the application, you may publish details of your invention freely and show it to anyone you think may have an interest in it (unless you've chosen to maintain your invention as a trade secret during the pendency of the patent application process—see Section F, below).

2. Respect for Your Invention

A manufacturer to whom you show the invention, seeing that you have thought enough of your invention to take the trouble to prepare and file a patent application on it, will treat it, and you, with far more respect and give it much more serious consideration than if you offer an unfiled invention.

3. You Can Sign a Manufacturer's Waiver

As you'll see in Chapter 11, most manufacturers to whom you offer an invention will not deal with you unless you first waive (give up) certain potential claims that might arise from the transaction (such as your being able to charge the manufacturer with stealing your idea in the event this occurs). Simply put, signing a waiver if you haven't already filed a patent application will put you at the complete mercy of the company to whom you show your invention. Fortunately, however, such waivers do not involve your giving up your rights under the patent laws. Thus, having a patent application on file, in this context, affords you powerful rights against underhanded dealing by the manufacturer (assuming the patent subsequently issues).

4. You'll Be Offering More So You'll Get More

Most manufacturers want a proprietary or privileged position—that is, a position that entitles them to a commercial advantage in the marketplace that competitors can't readily copy and obtain. A patent provides a very highly privileged position: a 17- to 18-year (approximately) monopoly. Thus if you have a patent application that already covers your invention, manufacturers may be far more likely to buy your invention (with its covering patent application) than if you offered them a "naked" invention on which they have to take the time and trouble to file a patent application for you themselves.

AN EXCEPTION
Although, as stated, it's usually best to file your patent application as soon as possible, it may be to your advantage to delay and keep the invention secret or take your chances approaching manufacturers "naked" if your invention is so innovative that it's not likely to be commercialized for many years. Gordon Gould, the inventor of the laser, did this unintentionally when he filed his patent application years late because he mistakenly believed he needed a working model to file. His mistake worked to his great advantage, however, since his delay postponed his monopoly period so that it coincided with the laser's commercial period, thereby turning an otherwise worthless patent into pure gold.

Common Misconception: You shouldn't patent your invention, since someone will see your patent, copy your invention, and make it more cheaply.

Facts: Copiers rarely use patents as a basis for their activities. Usually they copy successful products in the marketplace by reverse engineering. They'll be less likely to do this if it is patented, and a patent will enable you to stop their production or get royalties from them.

Filing before marketing is so important that I've made it part of the Inventor's Commandment at the beginning of this chapter.

D. If You Have Commercial Potential Without Patentability, License or Sell Your Invention to a Manufacturer Without Filing (Chart Route 16-24-26-28-30-B)

If your invention isn't patentable (that is—the decision in Box 16 is negative), don't give up; there's still hope. Many fortunes have been made on products that weren't patentable. For instance, the Apple computer made its designer-promoters, Jobs and Wozniak, multimillionaires, yet lacked any significant inventive concepts and never was awarded a major patent. Ditto for Henry Ford's automobile and George Eastman's Kodak camera.

Thus you should now decide, on the basis of your commercial potential and patentability evaluations, whether your invention nevertheless possesses "significant market novelty" (Box 24). If so, it may in fact be quite profitable if introduced to the market. Put differently, if your patentability search produces close prior art, but not a dead ringer, this indicates that probably no one has tried your specific, particular idea before, although someone has come close enough to preclude you from getting a patent. However, if you feel, looking back on your commercial-potential

and patentability evaluations, that it doesn't have significant market novelty—that is, there's little chance of commercial success—then there isn't much hope and you'll have to try again (Box X).

Assuming that your invention does have significant market novelty (Box 24) but does not qualify for a utility patent, there are several ways that you can use to obtain proprietary rights on your invention and make it more attractive to potential manufacturers. Let's take a closer look at these.

1. Record Conception and Building and Testing (If Applicable) Properly

While recording won't provide you with any rights against independent creators, or "reverse engineers," it will establish you as the inventor, as well as the date of your invention, so you'll be able stop invention thieves who copy it illegally before it's out. (Chapter 3, Section C.)

Recently I came across several layperson "invention gurus" who advocated (for a fee) that inventors "protect" their inventions without a patent application by—and here's the secret—using the PTO's DDP (Chapter 3, Section H). For reasons stated in that section, I recommend not using the DDP. Since it's no better than a witnessed invention disclosure (Form 3-2), it can't document building and testing, and most inventors erroneously think it gives them a two-year grace period.

2. Provide a Clever Trademark

One good way to make your invention more attractive is to provide a clever trademark for it (Box 26). As stated in Chapter 1, Section O, a trademark is a brand name for a product. An excellent type of brand name is one that suggests the function of the product in a very clever way. A clever trademark can be a very powerful marketing tool—that is, a tool that will greatly enhance the value and salability of your invention and give you added proprietary rights to sell to a manufacturer. Examples of clever, suggestive trademarks are *Water Pic* for an oral irrigation device and *Hushpuppy* for shoes. Also consider *Sunkist* citrus fruit, *Shasta* soft drinks, *Roach Motel* roach traps, *Heavyhands* exercise weights, *Sun Tea* beverage containers, and *Walkman* portable tape players.

3. File a Design Patent Application

If the invention that fails to qualify for a utility patent is a tangible product, the second trick to obtaining proprietary rights is to give it a distinctive design (Box 26). Then, perhaps, a design patent can be obtained. By distinctive design,

I mean a shape or layout that is unique and different from anything you've seen so far. The design, in this case, doesn't mean the function or internal structure of the product, but only its outward, non-functional, ornamental, aesthetic shape or layout that makes it distinct visually.

For example, the D-shaped *Heavyhands* weights and Dizzy Gillespie's trumpet with its upwardly bent bell section are excellent examples of valuable design inventions. If you've invented a computer, a new case shape can be a design invention. For a bicycle, a new frame shape design would be a design invention. From abacuses to zithers, from airplanes to zippers, almost every humanly made object under the sun can be redesigned or reshaped in a new way so that it can be covered by a design patent.

However, remember from Chapter 1 that for a design patent to be applicable, the new features must be for aesthetic or ornamental purposes and should not have any significant functional purpose—otherwise the PTO will reject it as non-ornamental—that is, only a utility patent will be appropriate. Also, the design must be inseparable from the object and not merely surface ornamentation. In the latter case, copyright is the proper form of coverage. (See Chapter 1, Section P.) For example, the label design on a jar of juice cannot be protected by a design patent, but a new shape for the jar would qualify for one. If you do come up with a distinctive design, you should, of course, record it in the same manner as you recorded your invention. (See Chapter 3.) And as with your invention, you should build a prototype or model as soon as practicable. You should also prepare and file a design-patent application (Box 28) on the ornamental appearance (not workings) of your invention.

As stated in Chapter 6, unless you live near the PTO or a Patent and Trademark Depository Library, it doesn't pay to search a new design beyond the most cursory look in product catalogs. This is because the cost of the search will greatly exceed the cost and effort to prepare and file a design-patent application. As you'll see in Chapter 10, a design-patent application consists simply of a drawing and a few forms that you fill out; it's very easy and economical to prepare.

4. Provide Distinctive "Trade Dress"

If you can't come up with a new design (or even if you can), you can still enhance the proprietary value of your invention by providing it with a distinctive "trade dress," such as a special, uniform color (as Kodak does with its yellow film packages), a special "certificate of authenticity" (if appropriate) as some manufacturers do with their replicas of antique objects, and/or a unique advertising slogan. This type of enhanced uniqueness is not different or special

enough to qualify for a utility patent, design patent, copyright, or trademark. However, you can acquire offensive rights, at least before it is made public, under trade secret law. (See Chapter 1, Section Q.) And the law of unfair competition may provide some rights once it is commercially unveiled (Chapter 1, Section R). Be sure to record the trade dress properly (see Chapter 3) before showing it to anyone and be sure to use it (or have it used) consistently and as much as possible after marketing.

5. Provide Copyrightable Labeling

Look closely at some of the packaged products that you see in your home or on display in a store for a copyright notice, for example, "© 1980 S.C. Johnson & Son, Inc." This copyright is intended to cover either the wording on the label or container, the artwork thereon, or both. While relatively easy to design around (that is—come up with a close but non-infringing alternative), unique labeling with a copyright notice nevertheless provides a measure of offensive rights that is well worth the small effort it takes to invoke. Many market researchers have shown that an attractive label can make all the difference in the success of a product. Accordingly, it can pay, if you're marketing a packaged product, to spend some effort, either on your own or in hiring a designer, to come up with an attractive, unique label, affix a copyright notice, and apply for copyright registration. (See Chapter 1, Section P.)

6. Consider Trade Secret

Keep your invention secret, at least until you file. If you do offer it to any manufacturers, you should apprise them that it can be kept as a trade secret permanently, if it is trade-secretable. More on this in Section F, below.

E. Make and Sell Your Invention Yourself Without a Utility Patent Application (Chart Route 30-C)

Here we assume again that you have an unpatentable invention. If you can make and distribute it yourself (Box 30), it's better to do so (Box C) than to try to sell it to a manufacturer outright. Even if you have a trademark (even a good one), a design patent application, distinctive trade dress, and/or a unique label, the absence of a utility patent application means a manufacturer does not get a really good privileged position, and so will generally not be as inclined to buy your invention. However, if you decide to manufacture the invention yourself, and you reach the market first, you'll have a significant marketing advantage despite the lack of a utility patent. Also, since you're the manufacturer, you'll make a much larger profit per item than if you received royalties from a manufacturer.

F. Manufacture and Distribute Your Invention Yourself, Keeping It As a Trade Secret (Chart Route 20-32-34-D)

Even though your invention may be commercially valuable and patentable, it isn't always in your best interest to patent it. The alternative, when possible, is to keep an invention a trade secret and manufacture and sell the invention yourself, for example, by direct mail marketing, broadcast or periodical advertising, possibly eventually working your way up to conventional distributors and retailers. As explained in Chapter 1, Section Q, a trade secret has numerous advantages and disadvantages. While an invention can be maintained as a trade secret right up until the time a patent actually issues, once it does, the trade secret is lost through the mandatory public disclosure associated with the patent process. Conversely, if you either don't get a patent or choose to not pay the issue fee, your invention will remain a trade secret as long as you continue to treat it as one.

Remember that you can't maintain trade secret rights on an invention unless it's of the type that can't be discovered from the final product, even if sophisticated reverse engineering is used. One good example of an invention that was kept as a trade secret is the formula used in the *Toni* home permanent wave kit. Its inventor, Richard Harris, manufactured and sold the unpatented invention through his own company for many years, making large profits, and there-

after sold his business for $20 million when he decided to retire.

Although not specifically covered on the chart, there is another possibility in the trade secret category. That is, you may sell your invention to a manufacturer who may chose to keep it as a trade secret. This may occur with either unpatentable or patentable inventions (Chart routines 16-24-26-28-30-B or 16-18- 20-22-A), but you don't have to worry about this alternative since it's the manufacturer's choice, not yours.

If you've already filed a patent application and a manufacturer buys the patent application with a view to using your invention as a trade secret, the manufacturer can simply allow the patent application to go abandoned so it won't be published, thereby maintaining the trade secret. While you may lose the ego boost of a possible patent, your bulging wallet should provide adequate alternative compensation.

You shouldn't refer to your abandoned patent application in any other application that will issue as a patent, since anyone can gain access to an abandoned application that's referred to in a patent.

G. File Patent Application and Manufacture and Distribute Your Invention Yourself (Trade-Secretable Invention) (Chart Route 20-32-34-36-E)

Suppose your invention is not discoverable from your final product (Box 32) so that you can keep it secret for a while, but not for the life of a patent (Box 34). Or, suppose, after evaluating the advantages and disadvantages of a trade secret under the criteria above, you don't wish to choose the trade-secret route, preferring instead to patent your invention. You should then prepare and file a patent application (Box 36) (see Chapters 8 to 10) and then manufacture and distribute the invention yourself with the notice "patent pending" affixed to the invention (Box E).

KEEP IT SECRET
While the patent application is pending, you should not publish any details of your invention, since, if the patent application is finally rejected, you can allow it to go abandoned and still maintain your trade secret, as discussed above. Remember, by law, the PTO must preserve patent applications in secrecy, and, in practice, is very strict in this regard. Outsiders have no access to any pending patent

applications and PTO personnel must keep patent applications in strict confidence. (There are proposals for a new law (not yet introduced) that would require the PTO to publish every patent application 18 months after filing, if it doesn't issue by then, as is done in most foreign jurisdictions. If this legislation passes, and you decide to maintain your invention as a trade secret, be sure to formally withdraw your application before it's published.)

EFFECT OF "PATENT PENDING" NOTICE
The patent-pending notice on your product does not confer any legal rights, but it is used by most manufacturers who have a patent application on file in order to deter potential competitors from copying their inventions. The notice effectively warns competitors that the manufacturer may get a patent on the product, so that if they do invest the money and effort in tooling to copy the invention, they could be enjoined from further manufacturing, with a consequent waste of their investment. However, make sure you don't use a patent-pending notice with a product that is not actually covered by a pending application: to do so is a criminal offense.

H. File Patent Application and Manufacture and Distribute Invention Yourself (Non-Trade Secretable Invention) (Chart Route 20-32-38-36-E)

This will be the route followed by most inventors who wish to manufacture their own invention. Assume that the essence of your invention, like most, is discoverable from the final product (Box 32), and assume that it's cheaper to file a patent application than to manufacture and sell products embodying the invention yourself (Box 38). Alternatively, assume that you don't want to sacrifice the advantages of filing before manufacturing. In either case, you should prepare and file a patent application (Box 36) and then manufacture and distribute the invention yourself with the patent-pending notice (Box E).

I. Test Market Before Filing (Chart Route 20-32-38-40-F)

Although I know you'd like to manufacture and test market your invention before filing a patent application on it, I generally don't recommend this for patentable inventions because of the following:

1. You have less than one year to do the test marketing because of the "one-year rule" (Chapter 5, Section E).
2. You may get discouraged unjustifiably if you try to market your invention and you aren't successful; that is—you probably will be too discouraged to file a patent application and therefore you'll lose all rights on the invention forever.
3. You'll lose your foreign rights since most foreign countries or jurisdictions, including the European Patent Office (see Chapter 12), have an absolute novelty requirement, which means that if the invention was made public anywhere before its first filing date, such publication will prevent the issuance of a valid patent.
4. There is a possibility of theft since, anyone who sees it can (assuming it's not trade secretable) copy it and file a fraudulent patent application on it.
5. There are business disadvantages when:
   - the product has a short or seasonal selling period or limited market life;
   - test marketing would disclose an easily copyable product to competitors;
   - the cost of test marketing would be so high as to outweigh the risk of regular marketing;
   - the product is merely a response to competition; or
   - market conditions in the field are changing so fast that the results of a market test would soon be obsolete. (*Wall St. Journal*, 1984 Aug. 27, p. 12.)

So, assuming your invention is discoverable from the final product (Box 32), ask yourself whether it's easier and cheaper to manufacture and test market it than to file a patent application. If it is, and if you're also willing to sacrifice the above five advantages of filing before manufacturing (Box 38), and the above business disadvantages don't apply, you can manufacture and market your invention (Box 40) before filing. While you're test marketing, you can put a warning notice (no legal effect, but possibly a deterrent one) on your product, such as "Patent Rights Reserved," as Federal Express does on its envelopes.

If you discover, within about nine months of the date you first introduce your product, that it is a successful invention and likely to have good commercial success, begin immediately to prepare your patent application (Box F), so that you'll be able to get it on file within one year of the date you first offered it for sale or used it to make a commercial product.

If your manufacturing and market tests (Box 40) are not successful, you should generally drop the invention and concentrate on something else (Box X), although you still have the right to get a patent on your invention. Thus, if the market test is unsuccessful, but you feel that you don't want to give the invention up forever, by all means follow the line, and prepare and file the patent application within one year of the first offer of sale (Box F). If you do manufacture and market your invention, and then later file a patent application on it, be sure to retain all of your records and paperwork regarding the conception, building, testing, and manufacturing of your invention; these can be vital if you ever get into an interference. (See Chapter 13, Section K.)

Now that we've covered all possible routes on the chart, I hope you've found one that will meet your needs. If your choice is to file a patent application, move on to Chapters 8 to 10; if you want to try to market your invention first, skip over to Chapter 11. Chapter 10 also covers design patents.

PATENT IT YOURSELF SOFTWARE NOW AVAILABLE

To facilitate and partially automate the preparation of a patent application, a computer program version of *Patent It Yourself* is now available. This program will take you step-by-step through the entire process of preparing a patent application, in addition to facilitating the recording of the invention and evaluating its commercial potential. The program contains a complete text of this book online and also contains copious examples of every part of a patent application. Further, it automates many tasks associated with the preparation of an application, including the assignment of reference numerals. *The Patent It Yourself* program runs under the Windows™ operating system and is available from Nolo Press.

CHAPTER 8

How to Draft the Specification and Initial Drawings

INVENTOR'S COMMANDMENT #10

Your patent application must contain a description of your invention in such full, complete, clear, and exact terms that anyone having ordinary skill in the field will be readily able to make and use it.

INVENTOR'S COMMANDMENT #11

In your patent application, you should "sell" your invention to the examiner or anyone else who may read the application. List all the disadvantages of the prior art and all the advantages of your invention in the introduction, the operation sections, and a conclusion.

This and the next two chapters are the heart of this book: they cover the writing and transmittal of your patent application to the Patent and Trademark Office (PTO). This chapter provides an overview of the patent application drafting process and contains specific instructions on drafting a specification and preliminary drawings. Chapter 9 explains how to draft patent claims (sentence fragments that delineate the precise scope of the patent being sought). Chapter 10 explains how to "final" the application as well as the precise steps involved in transmitting it to the PTO. In addition, Chapter 10 covers design patent applications.

Because these subjects can be difficult to understand in the abstract, I use concrete examples throughout. And, at the end of this chapter, you'll find the specification (including the abstract) and formal drawings of a sample patent application. Similarly, at the end of Chapter 9, you'll find the patent claims of this same application. The completed formal papers for this application appear at the end of Chapter 10.

A. Lay Inventors *Can* Do It!

It's a common myth that a lay inventor won't be able to prepare a patent application, or prepare it properly. Having worked with many lay inventors I dispute this vigorously. I have found that lay inventors can and have done very good jobs, often better than patent attorneys, by following this book. To prepare a proper patent application, you should

be mainly concerned with three considerations:

1. The specification (description and operation of your invention and drawings) should be detailed enough so that there will be no doubt that one skilled in the art will be able to make and use the invention after reading it.
2. The main claims should be as broad as the prior art permits. (More about this in Chapter 9.)
3. You should "sell" your invention by stressing all of its advantages.

If you satisfy these three criteria, you'll be home free. All the other matters are of lesser import and can be fixed if necessary. I'll show you how to satisfy these three main criteria in this and the next chapter. Now let's get started by looking at what's contained in a patent application.

B. What's Contained in a Patent Application

A regular patent application consists of the following parts, which are all sent together to the PTO after assembly in the following order:

1. A self-addressed receipt postcard
2. A check for the filing fee (see Appendix 4, Fee Schedule)
3. A transmittal letter and fee transmittal
4. A drawing or drawings of the invention—either formal or informal
5. A "specification" (not "specifications") containing the following sections:
   a. Title of the Invention
   b. Background—Cross-Reference to Related Applications (if applicable)
   c. Background—Field of the Invention
   d. Background—Prior Art. This is a discussion and criticism of the relevant prior art (previous relevant developments in the same technological area)
   e. Objects and Advantages. These list all of the positive aspects of your invention
   f. Drawing Figures. These list the drawing figures, briefly.
   g. List of Reference Numerals (optional but desirable). Reference numerals are the numbers that you'll use on your drawings to designate the respective parts of your invention, such as 10 = motor and 12 = shaft
   h. Summary of the Invention
   i. Description—Main Embodiment. This is a narrative description of the structure of the invention's main embodiment.

j. Operation—Main Embodiment. This is an explanation of how the main embodiment of the invention works or operates.

k. Description and Operation—Alternative Embodiments. This is a narrative description of the structure and operation of any alternative embodiments of the invention.

l. Conclusion, Ramifications, and Scope. This part consists of one or more broadening paragraphs summarizing the invention's advantages, the alternative physical forms it can take, and an indication that it shouldn't be limited to the particular form(s) shown.

m. Program listing, if any.

6. Claims. These are precise sentence fragments that delineate the exact nature of your invention—see Chapter 9.

7. Abstract. This is a brief summary of what the invention is and how it works, technically considered part of the specification.

8. A completed patent application declaration form (statement under penalty of perjury that you're the true inventor and that you acknowledge a duty to keep the PTO informed of all material information and prior art related to your invention).

9. A small entity declaration if you're an individual and you haven't transferred (or agreed to transfer) ownership or license to a large entity (Form 10-3). If any owner of the patent application is an individual other than the applicant-inventor, a nonprofit organization, or one with 500 or fewer employees, an additional declaration for such owner is required. (See Chapter 16.)

10. A Disclosure Document Reference Letter to tie your application to any disclosure document you previously filed.

11. An Information Disclosure Statement, List of Prior Art Cited by Applicant, and copies of such prior art. Technically, these aren't part of the patent application, but since they're supposed to be sent to the PTO with or soon after the application, I've included them here. These inform the PTO of relevant prior art or any circumstances known to you that may potentially affect the novelty or obviousness of your invention.

Note that a printed patent contains additional data, such as references cited, field of search, and so on. You should not include this additional data in your patent application; the PTO will add this data when they print it.

A Provisional Patent Application (PPA) must include some, but not all, of the parts just listed for a regular patent application. These parts are:

- items 1-4 (postcard, check, transmittal letter, informal drawings)
- items 5a (Title), 5f (description of drawings), 5i (description-main embodiment), 5j (operation-main embodiment), 5k (description and operation—alternative embodiments), and
- item 9 (small entity declaration).

Note that the PPA uses a different transmittal letter (Form 3-5) and has a different fee. (See Fee Schedule).

C. What Happens When Your Application Is Received by the PTO?

When your application arrives at the PTO, their clerical personnel will deposit your check, put all of your papers in a folder (termed a "file wrapper"), assign a filing date and serial number to your application, stamp this information on your postcard, and return it. Then they'll send you an official filing receipt and forward your file to the drafting department, where your drawings will be reviewed for formal requirements. A drawing objection slip will be put in your file if your drawings have any formal errors, such as blurred lines. Next, the file is sent to an appropriate examining division.

When its turn is reached (within a few months to a year), your application will be reviewed by an examiner who will allow the application (rare) or, more commonly, send you an "Office Action." The Office Action will do one or more of the following:

- object to one or more aspects of your specification;
- reject some or all of your claims because of imprecise language;
- reject some or all of your claims because of unpatentability over the prior art.

To overcome these objections and/or rejections, you'll have to submit an "Amendment" (Chapter 13) in which you:

- make changes, additions, or deletions in the drawings, specification, and/or claims; and/or
- convince the examiner that the Office Action was in error.

If the examiner eventually decides to allow the application (either as originally presented or as amended), you'll be given three months to pay an issue fee and fix any drawing errors. Your specification and claims, along with certain other information (your name, address, and a list of all prior art cited by the examiner), will then be sent to the U.S. Government Printing Office. There they'll be printed verbatim as your patent. From filing to issuance, the process usually takes somewhere between six months to two years, but sometimes longer.

MODEL OF INVENTION
You never have to furnish or demonstrate a working model of your invention. However, in rare cases, if the examiner questions the operability of your invention, such as if you claim a perpetual motion or energy machine, one way for you to prove operability is by demonstrating a working model. Working models are also useful to enable the examiner to understand and appreciate the value of your invention.

D. Do Preliminary Work Before Preparing Your Patent Application

Before you begin the actual writing of your patent application or prepare any of the forms that go along with it, it's wise to make thorough preparations. Having worked on many patent applications, I can tell you that if adequate preparations are made beforehand, the actual writing of the application rarely takes more than several partial days. Here are the basic preparatory steps:

1. Review the Prior Art

Assemble all your prior-art references, including any references gleaned from textbooks, magazines, or journals you've searched or discovered that are relevant to your invention or to the field of your invention. Read each of these references carefully, noting the terms used for the parts or steps that are similar to those of your invention. Write down the terms of the more unusual parts and, if necessary, look them up in your prior-art patents, textbooks, magazine articles, Appendix 3, Glossary, or the *What's What* book (see Appendix 2, Books of Use and Interest), so that you'll be familiar with them and their precise meaning. Also, note the way the drawings in these prior-art references are arranged and laid out, paying particular attention to what parts are done in detail and what parts need be shown only very roughly or generally because they are well known or are not essential to the invention.

If you see any prior-art patent whose specification contains words, descriptions, and/or drawing figures that you can use in your application, feel free to plagiarize! Patents are not covered by copyright and it's considered perfectly legal and ethical to make use of them.

2. Review Your Disclosure

In Chapter 3, I strongly advised that you prepare a description (with sketches) of your invention and have this signed and witnessed, either in a laboratory notebook or on a separate piece of paper, called an invention disclosure. Review this now to be sure you have all of the details of your invention drawn or sketched in understandable form and that the description of your invention is complete. If you haven't done this yet, do it now, referring to Chapter 3 when necessary.

3. Ramifications

Write down all of the known ramifications (potential different uses and methods of operation) and embodiments (potential forms in which the invention can occur). That is, record all other materials that will work for each part of your invention, other possible uses your invention can be put to, other possible modifications of your invention, ways in which its size or shape can be altered, parts (or steps in its manufacture) that can be eliminated, and so on.

The more ramifications and embodiments you can think of, the broader your patent can be claimed, and the more you'll be able to block others from obtaining patents either on devices similar to your invention or on improvements to it. Also, you'll have something to fall back on if your main or basic embodiment is "knocked out" by prior art that your search didn't uncover or that surfaced after your search.

For instance, if your invention is a delaying device that you use to close the lid of a box automatically a few moments after the lid is opened, another embodiment that could make advantageous use of the delaying device might be in a "roly-poly man" toy to make the man stand up again automatically a few moments after he's tipped over.

SEVERAL RELATED INVENTIONS
If you have two or more related inventions, such as a car radio mount and a housing for the same radio, you may show, describe and claim both in the same application, since the examiner may allow both inventions at once and you'll save fees and effort. However, you're allowed only one invention per filing fee, so the examiner may require you to restrict your application to one invention (Chapter 13, Section M). If so, you can easily file a divisional application (Chapter 14, Section C) on the other inventions before the original application issues and still get the benefit of your original application's filing date. However, under the GATT law, passed Dec. 1994, your original application and any divisionals you file will expire 20 years from the filing date of your original application, so keep this in mind and

don't file your divisionals long after your original filing date. The advantage of filing a divisional later is that you postpone the second filing fee a year or two, and you'll avoid paying it altogether if you find the invention hasn't panned out and you decide to drop it. (In any case, don't include several inventions on one application if they're from different inventors.)

4. Sources of Supply

If your invention contemplates the use of any exotic or uncommon materials or components, or involves unusual manufacturing steps, obtain the names and addresses of potential suppliers and/or identify textbooks or other references outlining how one should obtain or make such unusual elements or procedures. Describe these unusual dimensions, materials, or components in detail.

For example, with an electrical circuit, you generally don't have to include the technical values or identifications of components. However, if the operation of the circuit is at all unusual, or if any component values are critical, write down their names or identifications. With a chemical invention, write down the source or full identification of how to make any unusual components or reactions. With a mechanical invention, if any unusual parts, assembly steps, or materials are required, be sure you provide a full reference as to where to obtain or how to perform them.

The reason why you will need the full details of any special aspects of your invention is simple. Section 112 of the patent laws (35 USC 112) mandates that the specification must be a "complete, clear, and concise" description of the invention such that anyone skilled in the art can make and use it without too much effort. More on this later.

5. Advantages/Disadvantages

List all disadvantages of the relevant prior art that your invention overcomes, referring to the checklist in Chapter 4 (Form 4-2) to make sure your listing is complete. Then list all the advantages of your invention over the prior art, and all of your invention's general disadvantages.

Now that we have reviewed these vital preliminary steps, let's turn to writing the specification.

E. Flowchart

To get you oriented, I've provided, in Fig. 8A below, a self-explanatory flowchart of the entire application preparation process. Steps A to O are covered in Chapter 8, Steps P to T in Chapter 9, and Steps U to W in Chapter 10.

F. Writing Your Patent Specification to Comply With the Full Disclosure Rules

In writing the specification of a patent application, including a PPA, your goal is to disclose clearly everything you can think of about your invention. In case of doubt as to whether or not to include an item of information, put it in. The statutory provision that mandates the inclusion of all this information in your patent application is Section 112 of the patent laws, paragraph 1, which reads as follows:

"The specification shall contain a written description of the invention, and of the manner and process of making and using it, in such full, clear, concise and exact terms as to enable any person skilled in the art to which it pertains, or with which it is most nearly connected, to make and use the same, and shall set forth the best mode contemplated by the inventor of carrying out the invention."

As part of doing this, it may help if you keep well in mind the "exchange theory" of patents. The government grants you a patent (that is, a monopoly on your invention) for a term of 17 to 18 years in exchange for your disclosing to the public the full details of your invention (how to make and use it) so that they'll get the full benefit of your creativity after your patent expires. Complete disclosure involves disclosing at least the "best mode" of the invention as contemplated by you, the inventor. So, if you have several different embodiments of your invention, make sure you identify the one you currently favor. If you can't decide which embodiment is the best, it's okay to list each embodiment and tell its relative advantages and disadvantages. For example, in the delay device referred to above, its use to close a box lid after a few minutes might be your preferred embodiment, and the delayed "roly-poly man" might be an alternative embodiment. In this case you need merely state that the box is your preferred practical application of the delay device.

Another reason for disclosing as much as you can about your invention is, as stated, to block others from getting a subsequent improvement patent on your invention. If you invent something and disclose only one embodiment of it, or only one way to do it, and get a patent that shows only that one embodiment, someone may later see your patent and think of another embodiment or another way to do it that may be better than yours. This person will then be able to file a new patent application on this "improvement invention" and thereby, assuming a patent is issued, obtain a monopoly on the improvement. If this occurs, you won't be able to make, use or sell the improvement without a license from the person who owns that patent. This is so even though you have a patent on the basic invention.

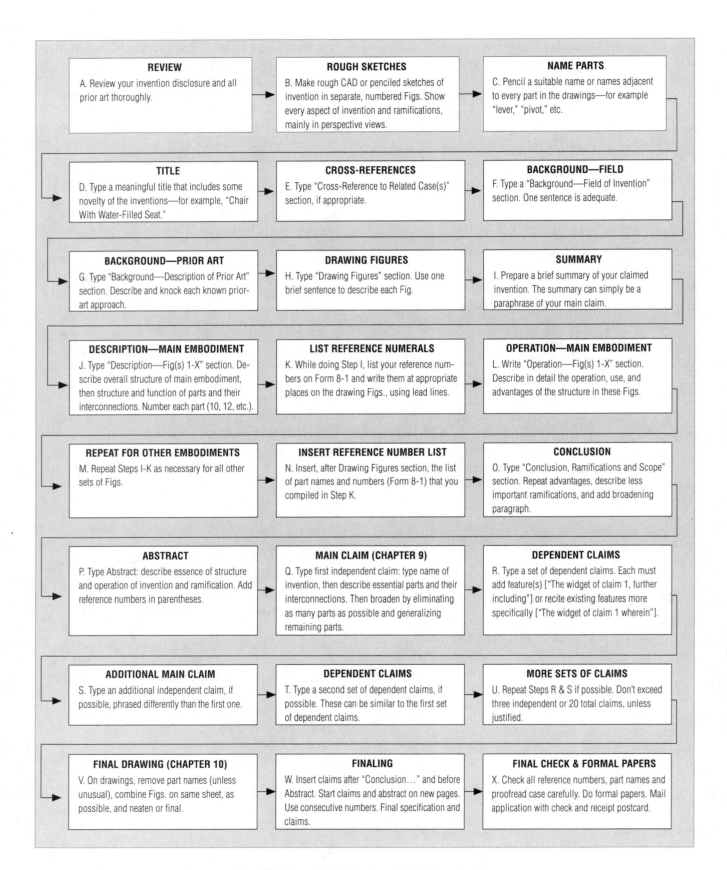

Fig. 8A—Steps in Preparing a Patent Application

NO NEW MATTER CAN BE ADDED

What happens if you don't put enough information in about your invention to enable "one skilled in the art" to make and use it without undue effort? Your entire application can either be rejected under Section 112 on the grounds of "incomplete disclosure," or it may be later invalidated if it is challenged by an infringer when you try to enforce it. Also, if your patent application is rejected because of incomplete disclosure, usually there is nothing you can do since you aren't allowed to add any "new matter" (additional technical information) to a pending application. (See Chapter 13.) In other words, "you must get it right the first time." While many inventors object to and rail against the "no-new-matter rule" ("Why can't I add improvements to my application?"), a moment's thought will convince you that the rule has a good purpose. Without the rule, an applicant could continuously add improvements and modifications, so that the filing date would be meaningless.

As mentioned earlier, you must provide enough information in your patent application to enable anyone working in the field of your invention to be able to build and use, without undue effort, a working version of your invention from the information contained in your patent application. However, to comply with this section, you ordinarily don't have to put in dimensions, materials, and values of components, since the skilled artisan is expected to have a working knowledge of these items. However, as described above, dimensions, materials, or components that are critical to the performance of your invention, or that are at all unusual, *must* be included. If in doubt, include this specific information.

Finally, having reviewed many patent applications prepared by laypersons, I find that the most common error in preparing the specification of a patent application is a failure to include enough detail about the invention, or enough ramifications. Thus, if you "sweat the details" like a good professional does, you'll seldom go wrong.

SOFTWARE NOTE

If your invention includes a microprocessor and an application program for it, either in software or in firmware, you should include a source or object code listing of the program with your patent application. If you don't have one, a detailed flowchart will do, so long as a programmer having no more than ordinary skill would be able to refer to your chart and then be able to write the program and debug it without undue effort or significant creativity, even if the task would take several months.

BIOTECHNOLOGY NOTE

If your invention requires a microorganism or a fusion gene that is not widely available, you must make a deposit of your "special" bug or plasmid in an approved depository; see MPEP *(Manual of Patent Examining Procedure)*, § 608.01(p)(c), and Chapter 2400, referred to in Appendix 2, Books of Use and Interest. If your application contains a nucleotide or amino acid sequence, you must describe your sequence according to the PTO's sequence rules (standard symbols and format). See MPEP § 2420 et seq. for the rules and availability of a program called "PatentIn" for submitting the sequence in electronic form.

TRADEMARKED CHEMICAL NOTE

If your invention uses a trademarked chemical—such as "Ajax developer"—and you don't know its composition, see if any other similar chemicals will work. If so, you can just refer to the chemical by its generic name, with a reference to a suitable manufacturer—for example, "developer, preferably Ajax brand, sold by Ajax Chemical Company, Inverness Park, California." If the trademarked chemical is critical, try your best to find its generic constituents—for example, by contacting the company or doing research. If you can't find the constituents, you'll have to refer to the chemical by its trademark and manufacturer, but this will limit your invention severely.

FORMULA NOTE

You can enter formulas in the text the same way you would do if you were writing a college paper or textbook. However, it's best to avoid formulas, Greek letters, and subscripts, if at all possible: the printer may get them wrong, and if your patent ever gets into court, they'll turn off a lay judge. Remember, the "KISS" rule (Keep It Simple, Stupid!)

G. Software and Other Computer-Related Inventions

Many inventors have asked me if I planned to write a separate book on how to patent software. I always answer in the negative because I believe there is no need for such a book: patent applications for software and other computer-related inventions (software) are prepared under the same rules and with the same general considerations as for any other invention. Inventors should be aware of one special consideration, but otherwise should follow the rules for any other invention, whether it's a mechanical device, an electrical circuit, a chemical composition, or a process (including a new use).

As indicated previously, the main patenting difficulty with software inventions has been whether they could be patented at all. However, numerous court decisions over the years and the PTO's specific guidelines and flowchart (See Chapter 5, Section C) have answered this question, so let's get to preparing the specification.

The special consideration applicable to software inventions is in meeting the full disclosure requirement. As stated in the preceding section, a patent application must contain a sufficiently detailed description of the invention so that one having skill in the art to which it pertains, or to which it is most nearly connected, will be able to make and use the invention without undue effort. In practice, the PTO and courts strictly enforce this requirement when software inventions are involved, since the newness of the field makes most people less comfortable with it. So if you're preparing a patent application on a software invention, be absolutely sure that no one will ever be able to challenge it for "incomplete disclosure." That is, make absolutely sure it contains a "full, clear, concise, and exact" description of the invention and how to make and use it.

How should you fulfill this requirement in practice with software inventions? Virtually every software invention uses a computer program of some sort, whether it's in a PROM (programmed read-only memory) or a separate program on a disk which is used with a general-purpose computer. To fulfill the complete disclosure requirement, it is essential that you disclose either a listing of the program or a detailed flowchart of the operations and steps involved with the invention that a programmer can use to create a working version.

If you've already written the program, the easiest way to provide the necessary disclosure is to supply the listing as part of the patent application. (See "Computer Programs Note" in Section I, below, for how to do this.) The listing can be in machine-readable form (object code) only; you *don't* have to supply the listing in humanly readable form (source code), since the requirement says you need merely disclose how to make and use it; you do not have to enable the public to modify it.

You should explain in the specification how to implement the listing and any special instructions which may be necessary to implement the invention without undue experimentation. The explanation should detail how to configure the computer to perform the required function and interrelate with any other elements to yield the claimed invention. For instance, you should state what program-

ming language the listing is in (for example, "C++"), how to use it to control the computer or microprocessor, what type of computer or microprocessor to use it with (for instance, "a Pentium chip"), and what hardware should be connected to the computer, both on the input and output sides as necessary (for instance, "a MIDI interface" and "a laser printer").

Of course you can also provide the source code and a flowchart, but to frustrate potential competition, I recommend you supply only the object code. The program should be free of any serious bugs and should not have too many minor bugs (virtually no program is 100% bug free). In other words, no one should be able to say your listing wouldn't function according to its specifications. (The PTO won't test your program, but if you get a patent and later seek to enforce it during license negotiations or in court, your adversary will!)

If you choose to provide only a flowchart, make sure it's complete and detailed enough to enable any reasonably skilled programmer to write a program, using only routine skills. The flowchart will be adequate even if it would take a programmer several months to write the program, so long as only routine skill and not extraordinary effort will be involved. In this connection, I like to think of a flowchart like the plans for a building: if the plans are adequate for an ordinary builder to construct the building, they will be adequate, even if it will take the builder several months, or even a year or more. However, if the plans are rough and sketchy, so that the builder has to hire an architect to complete them, or has to use a lot of imagination to fill in gaps, then they're inadequate. Fig. 8B shows adequately detailed flowcharts (from patent 5,170,279, 1992 Dec 8) in two parts: general and specific. The associated explanation in the specification (not provided) discusses each block in detail, lists the equations referred to in the blocks, and explains exactly how to implement the flowchart.

H. First Prepare Sketches

Before you even begin the actual nuts and bolts preparation of your specification, you should make (or have made for you) penciled sketches of your invention. These will form the basis of the drawings you'll eventually send to the PTO along with your patent application. (See Chapter 10, Part A). Your sketches will also be the foundation of your application. In other words, you'll build from these as you write your specification and claims.

The main reason I discuss sketches at this point is that you have to do your sketches prior to drafting the specification, as well as the other parts of the application. You don't have to worry about planning any layout of your figures on

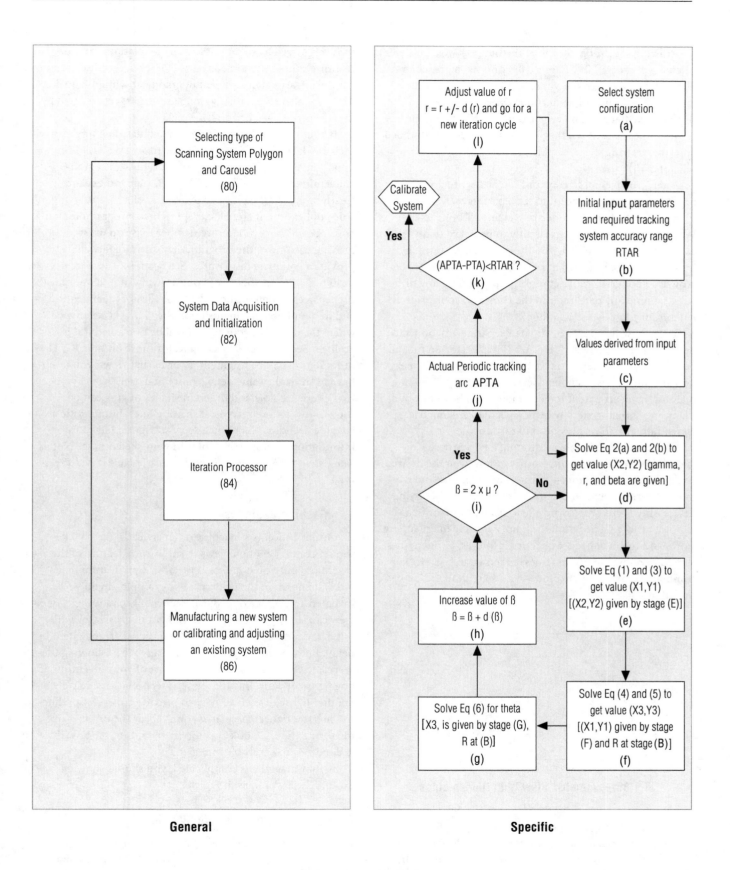

Fig. 8B—Software Flowcharts

the drawing sheets, or the size of the figures—yet. This will be covered in detail in Chapter 10. For now, merely complete a set of sketches showing all of the aspects of your invention without worrying about size or arrangement; these sketch-figures can even be done very large and on separate sheets. Later on they can be reduced and compiled onto the drawing sheets as part of the "finaling" process (Chapter 10).

After you've completed your sketches, write down a name for each part adjacent to such part in each sketch, such as "handlebar," "handgrip," "clamp," "bolt," etc. Write the names of the parts lightly in pencil so that you can change them readily if you think of a better term. Use lead lines to connect each name to its part if the parts are crowded enough to cause confusion. If you have any difficulty naming any part, refer to the Glossary, your prior-art patents, or the *What's What* book.

Your drawing should be done in separate, unconnected figures, each one labeled ("Fig. 1," "Fig. 2," etc.) so that all possible different views and embodiments of your invention are shown. Use as many views as necessary. Look at a relevant prior-art patent to get an idea as to how it's done. The views should generally be perspective or isometric views, rather than front, side, and top, engineering-type views. If you have trouble illustrating a perspective view, take a photo of a model of your invention from the desired angle and draw the photo—perhaps by enlarging and tracing it. Alternatively you can use a "see and draw" copying device of the type employing a half-silvered mirror in a viewing head on a pedestal; these are available in art supply stores and through gadget mail order houses. Hidden lines should be shown in broken lines, as shown in Fig. 8C. For complicated machines, exploded views are desirable as shown in Fig. 8D.

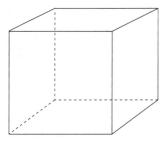

Fig. 8C—Isometric View With Hidden Lines

You can use any reasonable symbols for mechanical, electronic/electrical, and chemical parts; the PTO has no requirements in this area, except that the symbols not be outrageous. I suggest you use conventional symbols, such as those approved by the ANSI (American National Standards Institute), those used in conventional texts, or those used in your prior-art patents. In lieu of graphical symbols, labeled boxes are also acceptable, so long as the part represented by the box is standard or conventional.

If you have an electronic system, a block diagram with each block labeled (for example, "Schmitt Trigger," "flip-flop," "inverter") is fine. If any block represents a non-conventional circuit, however, be sure that you explain clearly what's in the block or provide a reference to a suitable publication. If any block represents a programmed microprocessor or computer, remember that you must provide a listing of the program or a software flowchart to provide a complete disclosure. (See Section F, above.)

If possible, one figure of your drawing should be comprehensive enough to show the basic idea of the invention and to be suitable for inclusion in the *Official Gazette*, where the details of your patent will be published if it is granted. See Chapter 6, Section K, for more on the OG. The other figures can be fragmentary or partial views; you don't have to show the same details more than once.

Different colors and different shades of gray can be shown with different types of shading lines, but provide a suitable decoding legend in a separate figure. For more information on imparting color in your sketches, see Nolo's *The Patent Drawing Handbook,* by Jack Lo and David Pressman.

1. Machine Sketches

If your invention is a machine or an article, your sketches should contain enough views to show every feature of the invention, but you don't have to show every feature that's old and known in the prior art. For example, if you've invented a new type of pedal arrangement for a bicycle, one view can show your pedal arrangement in gross view without detail. Other views can show your pedal arrangement in detail, but you don't have to include any views showing the bicycle itself in detail, since it isn't part of your invention. If one figure of your drawing shows a sectional or side view of another figure, it is customary to provide cross-section lines in the latter figure; these lines should bear the number of the former figure. Look at prior-art patents to see how this is done. See the example in Fig. 8E.

If your machine is complicated, you should show an exploded view of it, as in Fig. 8D.

2. Chemical Composition Sketches

If your invention is a chemical composition, the PTO won't generally require drawings unless your invention is a material that has a nonhomogeneous composition (internally

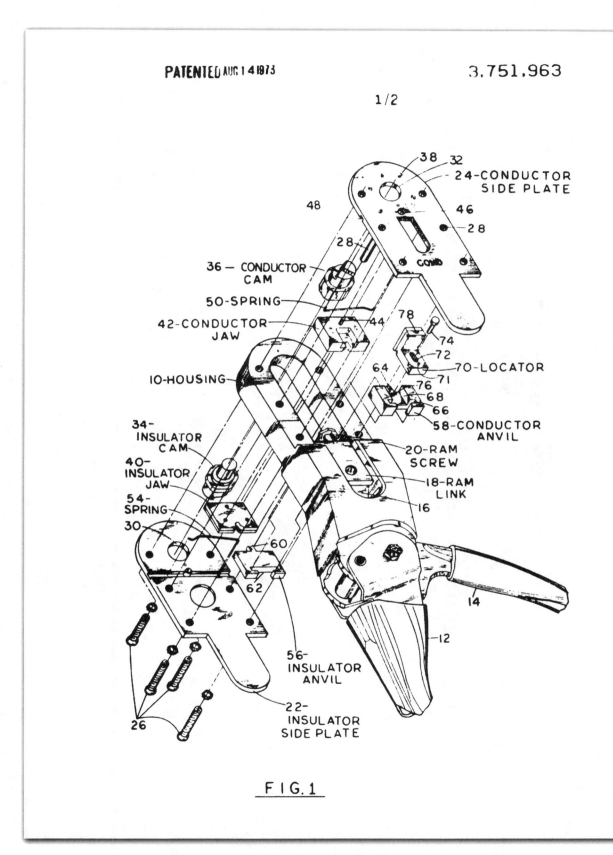

PATENTED AUG 1 4 1973   3.751.963

1/2

FIG.1

Fig. 8D—Isometric Exploded View

Fig. 8E—Views with Cross-Section Lines

differentiated through layering, for example), in which case you should show it in cross-section detail. Also, if a step-by-step process is involved, the PTO will require a flowchart, even though the process is fully described in your specification (see the next section). The reason: so future searchers will be able to understand your patent more rapidly. Benzene rings and other molecular diagrams can usually be presented in the specification.

3. Computer, Chemical, or Mechanical Process Sketches

If your invention includes a process of the electronic-computer, chemical, or mechanical type, you should, as stated, provide a flowchart (or a program listing for software inventions—see Section G above) showing the separate steps involved, each described succinctly in a different block. If your blocks are connected, they should all be labeled as one figure; if disconnected, they should be labeled as separate figures. As before, each figure should be labeled—for example, Fig. 1, Fig. 2, Fig. 3, etc. If several figures are related more closely to each other than they are to the rest of the figures, you can label the more closely related figures with the same number, but with different suffixes—for example, "Fig. 1-A, Fig. 1-B, Fig. 1-C."

If you desire, you can try providing a short title after each figure, giving a general description of the part of your invention shown in the figure, just as you would do if you were writing a scientific article for an engineering magazine or textbook. However, PTO drafting personnel often object to such titles for some unknown reason. If this occurs,

you'll have to delete the titles, which is easy to do by whitening out the titles on the originals of your drawing and sending in new photocopies.

If you believe it will help in understanding your invention, you may (and should) include a drawing of the prior art as one figure of your drawings. This figure must be labeled "prior art" to indicate that it isn't part of your invention.

I. Drafting the Specification

Once you've reduced your invention to sketches, it's time to begin drafting the specification portion of your patent application. Review the specifications of your prior-art patents—or the sample "spec." at the end of this chapter—to find out how they're written. Your specification should be written as one continuous document with separate sections, each with a heading, as in the following sections (except that "Title" should not be a heading).

1. Drafting Tips

Here are some general rules to keep in mind when drafting your specifications.

Avoid Legalese

As I'll discuss in more detail below, you should *not* try to write like a lawyer or use legalese. Such syntax is actually undesirable, since it only makes your writing stilted and less clear. Nothing reads as awkwardly as when a layperson tries to use legalese (except when a lawyer uses it). The only legal requirements for a patent specification are that it be a full, clear, concise, and complete description of how to make and use the invention. (The claims, however, should be written with extreme clarity and precision, and to do this you may have to use a few "saids" and "wherebys," but I'll explain this fully in Chapter 9.)

No Need for Legal Terms

I've been told countless times by inventors that they couldn't possibly prepare their own patent application because they don't know "the correct legal terms to use." However, the PTO specifically prohibits legal terms in a specification. Why? So that the specification will be easy to read and understand. Legal terminology was created by lawyers to make their writing less understandable and more obscure, so as to befuddle and confuse laypersons. This makes the law seem esoteric and impenetrable to all but the properly anointed. Happily, the law is moving away from these practices and is opening its doors to laypersons. So don't let any imaginary legal barriers deter you.

Two things are required from every specialized treatise: it should clarify its subject and, more importantly, it should tell us how and by what methods we can attain it and make it ours.

—Longinus

Use Short and Simple Sentences

It's best to write your description in short, simple sentences, with short paragraphs. Each paragraph should generally be shorter than 200–250 words, or one page (double-spaced), and should relate to one part or subpart of your invention. The Cybernetics Institute has found that short sentences communicate best. Also, they found that 50% of adults can't understand a sentence longer than 13 words anyway. Don't worry about the quality or style of your writing or the beauty of your language. Your main goal is to include all points of substance of your invention and make your description clear and understandable. If you get stuck and don't know how to phrase a description of a part or an operation, here's a helpful trick: simply pretend you're describing your invention aloud to a close friend. Remember what you said (or make an audio recording) and write it down. Then go back and polish the language. If you attack the job in small chunks or in piecemeal fashion, it usually will go much easier.

Use Copious Headings

Also, if you use copious subheadings (such as "Fig. 1—Description of Handlebar Attachment"; "Fig. 2—Front Fork Detail"; "Fig. 10—Operation of Derailleur"; etc.) throughout your specification (as I've done in this book), most people will find it far easier to read. This allows them to take in the information in separate, small, inviting chunks that are easy to digest one at a time. Refer to the specification at the end of this chapter (Fig. 8F) to see examples of headings in an application.

Getting started is the worst part.

—Roberta Pressman

If you have trouble getting started, don't worry; many writers have blocks from time to time, and lots of inventors initially (and erroneously) lament, "I could never write my own patent application." The words of Lao-Tse will encourage you:

A journey of a thousand miles begins with a single step.

An anecdote that will help is the story of a newly manufactured clock that couldn't bring itself to start when told it would have to tick 31,536,000 times per year; it was too daunting a job. However, when its maker cleverly pointed out to it that it would have to tick only once per second, it didn't seem so bad. So the clock started and has been going ever since.

If you still feel daunted, it will help you to know that virtually all inventors who have trouble getting started suffer from *lack of will,* not *ability*. I had a client who came to the U.S. from Hong Kong with little money or English, but with a great invention and tremendous drive. He wrote and filed his own application and got a valuable patent, after I fixed his English. If he could do it, surely you, with probably a much better command of English, can do so also.

If you feel that you can't write adequately, I suggest that you give it your best shot and then have a writer, college English major, high school English teacher, etc., edit your draft.

Now let's get to the nitty-gritty of preparing the specification portion of a patent application.

Make an Outline Before Starting

Prior to starting, in order to guide your path, you will find it helpful first to make an outline which should be the same as the headings set out below, except that you may want to make headings (Description and Operation) more specific and/or break them into several more specific headings each, in accordance with your figures and specific situation.

2. The Parts of the Specification

There are also some commonsense rules governing the best presentation of each of the separate parts of your specification. I'll briefly discuss each of these. Only the sections with an asterisk are needed to file a Provisional Patent Application. (See Chapter 3.)

a. Title*

Have your title reflect the essence of your invention without being too long (about seven words maximum) or so specific that it's narrower than your invention's full scope. On the other hand, don't pick a title so broad—such as "Electrical Apparatus" —as to be essentially meaningless. A look at some recently issued patents in your field should give you a good idea of how specific to make your title.

b. Background—Cross-References to Related Applications

If you have (or will file) any other patent applications on inventions that are related to the present invention, refer to them briefly here—for example, "This invention uses the transmission of my co-pending application, Ser. Nr. 07/

123,456, Filed 1991 Aug. 9." If you've filed a Provisional Patent Application (PPA, see Chapter 3) and you're filing the regular patent application within one year of your PPA's filing date, you should claim the benefit of your PPA's filing date here as follows: "This application claims the benefit of Provisional Patent Application Ser. #___/_____, filed 1999__ _____ _____." Otherwise, omit this section.

c. Background—Field of Invention

Your first sentence should be a brief, one-sentence paragraph stating the general and specific field in which your invention falls. For example, the sentence might read, "This invention relates to bicycles, specifically to an improved pedal mechanism for a bicycle." The field of your invention should be the technical, product, subject, or scientific area with which it's most nearly connected, such as bicycles, kitchenware, lasers, medical instruments, drugs or skiing. Don't mention any details of your invention here.

d. Background—Discussion of Prior Art

Here, discuss how the problem to which your invention is directed was approached previously (if it was approached at all), and then list all the disadvantages of the old ways of doing it. For example, you can start as follows: "Originally bicycles were made with a fixed transmission ratio. This made pedaling up hills difficult. This problem has been partially solved by the implementation of derailleur mechanisms, but these had and still have significant problems." Then list the derailleurs that were used in the past and their disadvantages. Again, look at prior-art patents to get an idea of what was done. If you can, tell why prior-art people failed to solve the problem and why a solution is needed.

While the PTO doesn't want needlessly derogatory remarks about the inventions of others, you should, as much as possible, try to "knock the prior art" here in order to make your invention look as good as possible. Keep your statements factual (for example, "The derailleur in patent 3,456,789 to Prewitt, 1982 May 3, had a limited number of discrete gear ratios") and not opinionated (don't say, "Prewitt's derailleur was an abject failure"). If applicable, tell why prior-art people didn't think of any solution before and why a solution is needed. Do not discuss any detailed structure or operation of any prior art in this section, since detailed mechanical discussions without the benefit of drawings will be incomprehensible to most people. Occasionally, you may have such a completely unique invention that there's really no prior art directly germane to your invention. If so, just state the general problem or disadvantage your invention solves.

e. Objects and Advantages

In the patent field, the term "objects" means "what the invention accomplishes." Thus, you should list here all the things your invention accomplishes and its advantages over the prior art. You can start this section as follows: "Accordingly, several objects and advantages of my invention are...." Then, include the objects or advantages of your invention that are the converse of the disadvantages of the prior art. For example, if in your prior-art section you stated that derailleurs were complex and unreliable, you should state now that your invention provides a simpler and more reliable derailleur. Then, in a separate section, starting with, for example, "Other objects and advantages are," add any additional objects and advantages of which you're aware. You already know these from your commercial evaluation. (See Chapter 4.)

Be sure to include all disadvantages of the prior art from your "Background" section and all of the positive factors of your invention from Form 4-2 (Chapter 4). (Remember, you're still selling your invention—to the examiner, to a potential licensee, and possibly to a judge!)

Avoid very narrow objects, such as "it is one object to provide a 14.5 mm carbon fiber lever," since these can be used to limit your invention. Similarly avoid objects that can't be accomplished, such as, "it is one object to provide a totally safe bike," since this can also be used against you.

At the end of this section, add a catch-all paragraph reading as follows: "Further objects and advantages of my invention will become apparent from a consideration of the drawings and ensuing description."

Your Objects and Advantages section should be like an ad or sales brochure for your invention: it should tell why someone should buy it, but without any technical details or operational descriptions that wouldn't be meaningful to a new prospective buyer.

It may seem needlessly repetitious to state the disadvantages of the prior art in the "Background" section and then repeat the converse of these in the "Objects" section. However, you'll soon find that this is but one instance of many where repetition is used in a patent application. For instance, the objects are effectively repeated again (a third time!) in the concluding paragraph of the specification. Moreover, the parts of the invention are actually repeated five times, under "Description," under "Operation," in the Claims, in the Abstract, and in your list of reference numerals.

Why is repetition used so much? Because it's one of the keys to effective communication. There's an apropos old saying:

To communicate effectively to someone, you should first tell your listener what you're going to say, then actually say it, and finally tell the listener what you said.

f. Description of Drawings

Here, provide a series of separate paragraphs, each *briefly* describing a respective figure of your drawing—for example, "Fig 1 is a perspective (or plan, side, exploded, or rear) view of my invention"; or, "Fig 2 is a view in detail of the portion indicated by the section lines 2-2 in Fig 1." Do not include any reference numerals, specific parts, or any other details in this section—just a brief overall description of each figure.

g. List of Reference Numerals

Although the PTO doesn't require or even recommend a separate list of the reference numerals and the names of their respective parts in an application, I strongly advise that you include such a list in a separately headed section, as I've done in the sample specification at the end of the chapter. Why? There are three very important reasons:

- To help you to keep your reference numerals straight—that is, to avoid using the same number for different parts.
- To help you to keep your nomenclature straight—that is, to avoid using different terms for the same part.
- To provide a very visible and easy-to-find place where examiners, searchers, and others who read your application or patent can go to instantly identify any numbered part on your drawings.

I find it helpful to compile this list on a separate sheet of lined paper as I write the patent application, and then incorporate the list in the text. I've provided a suitable worksheet as Form 8-1 in Appendix 7. Also, to keep confu-sion at a minimum, I advise that you don't use single-digit reference numerals, and that you begin your numbers with a number higher than your highest-numbered drawing figure—for example, if you have Figs 1 to 12 of drawings, begin your reference numerals with number 20.

Lastly, I advise that you use even-numbered reference numerals when you write the application; in this way, if you later have to add another reference number, you can use an odd number and put it between two logically related even numbers. (See the list in the sample specification at the end of the chapter.)

h. Summary

The PTO's Rule 73 requires that the specification contain a summary of the claimed invention, and Rule 72 requires an abstract of the entire specification. In practice, many patent attorneys omit any Rule 73 summary, since the abstract, as well as the claims, already provides one. Hardly any patent examiner will object if you omit a summary. However, I recommend that you include a summary in order to describe the forest before you describe the trees and to program your examiner to more readily understand what follows. Your summary can simply paraphrase your main claim (see Chapter 9) or can be a one- or two-sentence description of the essence of your invention.

i. Description of Invention*

Here you should describe in great detail the static physical structure of your invention (not how it operates or what its function is). If your invention is a process, describe the procedures or machinery involved in it. Begin by first stating what the figure under discussion shows generally—for example, "Fig 1 shows a perspective view of a basic version of my widget." Then get specific by describing the main parts and how they're connected. (These main parts can form the basis for your claims, as we'll see in Chapter 9.) Then get more specific: describe each main part in detail and all of the sub- or component parts in detail.

Start with the base, frame, bottom, input, or some other logical starting place of your invention. Then work up, out, or forward in a logical manner, numbering and naming the parts in your drawing as you proceed. Use the part names that you previously wrote on your sketches.

To number the parts, write a number near each part and extend a lead line from the reference number to the part to which it refers. Don't circle your reference numerals, since a PTO rule prohibits this. The lead lines should *not* have arrowheads—for example, a bicycle grip might be desig-nated "22————." However, to refer to a group of parts as a whole—for example, a bicycle, use an arrowhead on the lead line, thus, " 10———>." If you have several closely related or similar parts, you can give them the same reference number with different letter suffixes to differentiate, such as "arms 12a and 12b," or "arms 12L (left) and 12R (right)."

Although you may think that the patent examiner won't need to have parts that are clearly shown in the drawing separately described in detail, all patent attorneys provide such a description. This is part of the previously mentioned repetition technique that is used to familiarize the examiner with the invention and set the stage for the claims (Chapter 9) and operational description. When you mention each part twice, once in the description and again in the operation discussion, the first mention will initially program your reader to relate to the part so that the reader will really understand it the second time around, when it counts. This is the same technique as is used in the lyrics of blues songs, where the first two lines are always restated to enhance communication.

Another good technique is to use several different equivalent names for a part the first time you refer to it in order to provide one with which your reader will be familiar—for example, "connected to base 10 is a strut, pylon, or support 12." Then pick one name and use it consistently thereafter.

As stated, before you begin a description of any figure, refer to it by its figure number—for example, "Fig 1 shows an overall view of the can opener of the invention." Then as you come to each part or element, give it a separate reference number—for example, "The can opener comprises two handle arms 10 and 12 that are hinged together at a hinge 14."

Where several figures show different views of an embodiment of your invention, you can refer to several figures at once—such as "Figs 1 and 2 show plan and elevational (front) views of a scissors according to the invention. The scissors comprises first and second legs 12 and 14, the second leg being best shown in Fig 2." However, don't refer to too many figures at once, and always keep your reader advised as to which figure is under discussion.

Cover every part shown in your drawings and be sure to use consistent terminology and nomenclature for the parts in the drawing. For example, if gear 44 is shown in Fig 8 and also in Fig 11, label it with the reference numeral "44" in both figures. Fill out the Drawing Reference Numerals Worksheet (Form 8-1) as you write, to keep your numerals and nomenclature consistent. If you use a word processor, I suggest you refer to each part by a number only and then, when you're finished, use your "change" utility to add consistent part names—such as, you can write "44 is connected to 36" and later change "44" to "widget 44" and "36" to "base 36" throughout your specification.

Lastly, be sure to detail all the interconnections or mountings between parts—for example, "Arm 14 is joined to base 12 by a flange 16."

USE OF "A" AND "THE"

When you write the static description, use the indefinite article "a" (not "the") to introduce each part—for example, "<u>A</u> lever 14 is connected to <u>a</u> handle 12." Later on, when you refer to already-introduced parts, you can refer to them by their name and number, without any articles—for example, "Lever 14 preferably is made of wood and handle 12 is made of acrylic." Or, to vary the style of your writing, you can refer to familiar parts without any reference numeral, but with the definite article "the"—for example, "...is connected to the derailleur..."

DEM BONES

To understand the technique commonly used to describe the parts and their interconnections, think of the song, *Dem Bones.* The song details virtually every bone-to-bone connection in the body in logical order—for example, "The knee bone's connected to the thigh bone, the thigh bone's connected to the hip bone." In a similar manner, your description should also detail every part-to-part interconnection, even if you think the reader would find it obvious from your drawing.

DON'T BE COY

Suppose your invention uses some special or exotic parts, techniques, or relationships, but you don't want to describe these because such information is valuable and you want to keep it as a trade secret and not give it away to potential copiers and competitors. Unfortunately, you can't be coy. You must include complete detailed descriptions of these, including dimensions, relationships, materials, and sources of supply, as applicable, in this section in order to comply with the "full disclosure" statute (35 USC 112). Putting in such specifics will not limit your invention in any way since the claims (next chapter) will determine its scope. However, failing to include these specifics can render your patent application fatally flawed if they are necessary for one skilled in the art to make and use the invention.

Including details and dimensions at crucial places can also prove vital later if you have to rely on these in order to support and distinguish your claims over a close prior-art reference cited by the examiner. Thus, it's almost axiomatic in patent law that you should make your specification as long, specific, and detailed as possible, and your main claim as short, broad, and general as possible. If you're tempted to skip the details, remember that a few strokes on a keyboard now can save you from losing many thousands of dollars later. Be especially sure to expand your discussion in the areas where you feel that your invention is novel over the prior art.

TRADEMARKS

If any material, substance or component of your invention is a trademarked product, you should refer to it by its generic name, without using the mark—unless the mark is necessary for full identification. For example, if you have a hook-and-loop fastener, you can say, "'hook-and-loop fastener 20 holds tab to base 14." It is not necessary to use either of the marks *Velcro* or *Latchlok*, since H&L fasteners are well known. The same holds true for the trademark *Teflon*—use PTFE instead. However, if the product is not common, you can use its mark, provided you use it properly, which means capitalizing the mark, identifying it as a trademark, using the mark as an adjective with a generic descriptor, and identifying the owner of the mark—such as "Ajax™ developer, manufactured by Goldberger Graphics of San Francisco." If the trademarked product is crucial and you're going to recite it in your claims, and you don't know its composition, see "Trademarked Chemical Note" in Section F, above.

Avoid technical language, insofar as possible, but if you use any technical terms, be sure to define them for any lay judge or young examiner who may read your application. Try to make your description as simple as possible, without eliminating any crucial details. Avoid absolute terms, such as "always" and relative terms, such as "dense," "hot," or "hard"—use quantitative values that can be used in claims, such as "having a mass greater than 2.5 grams," "between 70° C and 100° C," or "having a hardness less than 10 durometer," or "having a thickness less than that of member 13."

COMPUTER PROGRAMS NOTE
As stated in Section G above, if your invention involves a computer program, include a program listing (or at least a detailed flowchart) with a detailed explanation as to how to configure the computer to perform the required function and interrelate with any other elements to yield the claimed invention. This can be submitted as part of the specification, or as part of the drawings, provided it's contained on ten printout pages or less. In either case, the listing should be a very black, camera-ready copy. If the printout is to be submitted on drawing sheets, these should be of the proper size (U.S. or international, see Chapter 10), with each sheet including a separate figure number (Fig 1, Fig 2, etc.; or Fig 1-A, Fig 1-B, etc.). If the printout is to be submitted as part of the specification, it must be on the same size sheets. The printout should be sent in a protective cover. If your program is longer than ten pages, it should be submitted on microfiche, as an appendix. It will not be printed with the patent, but will be referred to in the patent. The standards for the microfiche are contained in Rule 96 (37 C.F.R. 1.96—see Appendix 2, Books of Use and Interest), available at all Patent and Trademark Depository Libraries and over the PTO's bulletin service (see Appendix 5, Mail, Telephone and Computer Communications With the PTO).

j.   Operation of Invention*

After you complete the static description of your main or preferred embodiment, you should then describe in extensive detail the operation or function of the parts covered in your description. Refer to each part by its name and reference numeral, and be sure to include the working or function of every part. Your invention may be of such a nature that it may not be possible to include a physical description and an operational description in separate sections, but you'll find that this mode of description works generally for most inventions, and you should try to adhere to it since it will force you to be complete and comprehensive.

If your invention includes several embodiments and ramifications, you should fully describe the structure of the most preferred or most basic embodiment first, then describe its operation in a separate section immediately following the structural description. In this way, your reader or examiner will get a full understanding of the invention, including its operation. Then describe each additional embodiment in the same manner, but more briefly, since you only need detail the differences over the first embodiment. Thus, several sets of description/operation sections will result. For example, "Fig. 1—Description of Motor," "Operation of Motor," "Fig. 2—Description of Hand Version," "Operation of Hand Version." You must include a highly detailed description of each and every part of your invention, together with a highly detailed description of the operation of each part and its relation to the other parts.

I emphasize once again that you should include all reasonably important embodiments and ramifications so that you'll have more support for broader claims and so that if an infringer is making or selling a ramification, you'll be able to show the judge that you specifically showed that ramification in your application. Although infringement is supposed to be determined mainly by the wording of your claims, when you get to court, judges are psychologically influenced in your favor, as a practical matter, if your specification and drawings show and discuss the very embodiment that is being infringed.

THEORY OF OPERATION

If your invention operates by utilizing an interesting or unusual theory, you can include this also, either before or after describing the operation. If you're not sure about the correctness of your theory, you can state this—for example, "While I believe the reaction occurs because of a catalytic effect of the platinum, I don't wish to be bound by this." You are not required to give any theory of operation in your application, since this isn't necessary to enable one skilled in the art to make or use the invention. However if you can include any theory of operation, you should, since it will make your invention more interesting, believable, and likable to your readers (such as your patent examiner or a judge).

MEDICAL DEVICES AND DRUGS
If your invention is a medical device or drug, you don't need to supply proof of efficacy if it's obvious that it will work and be safe. For instance, if your invention is a drug that is close or analogous to an existing drug that is already recognized as safe and efficacious, you don't need further proof. But if your invention is a drug that is substantially different than anything on the market, and it's not apparent that the drug will be safe and efficacious, you must be prepared to prove those things. Applications for patents on drugs often are referred to the FDA, which has its own requirements, but in cases where the drug or device isn't radically different, declarations by experts regarding safety and efficacy will usually be accepted by the PTO.

k. Conclusion, Ramifications, and Scope of Invention

After you finish your detailed description of the invention's operation, add a "Conclusion, Ramifications, and Scope of Invention" section to sum things up and to remind the

judge who sees your patent that the claims control. Here's an example:

Thus the reader will see that the can opener of the invention provides a highly reliable, lightweight, yet economical device that can be used by persons of almost any age. [Keep selling it!]

While my above description contains many specificities, these should not be construed as limitations on the scope of the invention, but rather as an exemplification of one preferred embodiment thereof. Many other variations are possible. For example [then continue with brief description of possible variations that aren't important enough to show as ramifications in the drawing].

Accordingly, the scope of the invention should be determined not by the embodiment(s) illustrated, but by the appended claims and their legal equivalents.

In the first paragraph quoted above, the objects and advantages of the invention are restated and summarized to hammer home the greatness of your invention. In the "for example" portion of the second quoted paragraph, include a brief description of any alternative embodiments you can think of and that (as stated) you didn't consider important enough to show in the drawing and describe in detail in your description. I usually put exotic, untested embodiments, as well as minor variations in color, size, and materials in the broadening paragraph. It's desirable to include as many ramifications as possible in order to get any means clauses in your claims interpreted as broadly as possible. (See Chapter 9 on drafting claims for a discussion of "means clauses" and their relationship to the specification.)

Thus you should go through the entire application and, for each element of the inventive device or method, state in the ramifications paragraph whether that element can be:
- eliminated or duplicated,
- changed in size (made smaller or larger),
- made of a different material,
- made of a different shape,
- made of a different color,
- connected or associated with its adjacent elements in a different manner,
- given a different mode or function of operation—for example, suction rather than blowing, or
- made integrally or separately (modular or in sections).

It's very important to be as comprehensive as possible when describing ramifications because recent decisions of the Court of Appeals for the Federal Circuit (the sole patent appellate court) have tended to interpret claims narrowly, unless the infringed device is described or mentioned in the specification.

Look at the sample specification at the end of this chapter to see how this is done.

That's just about all there is to drafting the specification portion of your application. What's left, you ask? The small matter of "Claims," that's what. I'll tell you how to write these in the next chapter.

J.   Drafting the Abstract

Your abstract should come at the end of your patent application, on a separate sheet, after the claims. However, it will be printed on the first page of your patent and appears right after the sample specification of Fig. 8F, since the claims have been saved for the next chapter. The abstract is relatively easy to do once you've done the specification, and since it's very closely related to the specification, I'll cover it here.

The abstract should be put on a new page with the title and then the heading "Abstract." To do the actual abstract, write one paragraph providing a concise summary of the specification in about 250 words. Spend enough time writing the abstract to make it concise, complete, and clear. This is because the abstract is usually the part of an application that's read first and most frequently consulted. Look at the abstracts of several of your prior-art patents to get an idea of what's involved. To be concise, your abstract should not include throat-clearing phrases like "This invention relates to," but rather, should get right into it and state—for example, "An improved bicycle pedal mechanism having…, etc." If you think you may file the application in other countries, you should include reference and figure numbers in the abstract (with each one in parentheses) to comply with the international rules. International filing is covered in Chapter 12.

K.   Review Your Specification and Abstract Carefully

After you've completed your draft, be sure to review it carefully to be sure you've included everything about your invention you can think of, and that there is no possible ground for anyone to say that you haven't included enough to teach one skilled in the art how to make and use your invention. You may have to go through two, three, or more drafts to get it right. Be sure to compare your specification with those of other patents in the field so that yours is at least as complete as theirs. If you allow yourself plenty of time—for example, a few days to do the drawings, a few days to write the introductory parts of your specification,

and a few days to do the static description, you won't feel pressured and thus you'll be able to do a better, more readable, more legally adequate job.

Don't do your work in haste. The public won't ask whether it was completed in three days, but whether it's accurate and complete.

—Anon.

⚠️ Many prior-art patents are not properly described, especially under today's more demanding standards, so don't absolutely rely on them as a standard; rather, follow the guidelines of this chapter.

L.   Checklist for Your Patent Application Draft

After reviewing many patent applications prepared by laypersons, I've come up with three lists of the most common errors and areas generally needing improvement. The first list (in two parts) follows; it covers the preliminary drawings and draft specification. Before you go on to the claims (Chapter 9) or to the finaling process (Chapter 10), I suggest that you check this list carefully and make any needed corrections in your work. The specification checklist includes many grammar and punctuation rules that I see inventors violate frequently.

CHECKLIST FOR PRELIMINARY DRAWINGS

☐ D01. Every significant part in the drawings has its own reference numeral.

☐ D02. Every part has a different reference numeral—that is, the same reference numeral is never used to indicate different parts. (Suffixed numbers (10, 10'; 10A, 10B, etc.) can be used for different parts.)

☐ D03. The same reference numeral is always used to indicate the same part when such part is shown in different Figs; that is, two different numerals are never used to indicate the same part.

☐ D04. Arrowheads are not used on any lead line, unless it refers to an entire assembly of elements.

☐ D05. The drawings show enough details of your invention to enable it to be fully and readily understood by a lay judge.

☐ D06. The reference numerals start with a number higher than your highest Fig number.

☐ D07. Even reference numerals (10, 12, etc.) are used so you can add more numerals in sequence later, if needed.

☐ D08. The Fig details and reference numerals are large enough to be easily read.

☐ D09. A descriptive label is placed on or near each component whose function is not apparent.

☐ D10. The drawings show every part and modification that you intend to include in your claims. (See Chapter 9.)

☐ D11. No dimensions on drawings.

☐ D12. Each figure has a separate number. Suffixed figure numbers (Fig 1-A, Fig 1-B; Fig 1, Fig 1') are okay.

☐ D13. Separate figures are not connected by any line.

☐ D14. Separated parts of any figure are joined by projection lines (see Fig 8C) or a large bracket.

☐ D15. Exotic or special parts are labeled—for example, "saturated transistor"; "gray water"; "electric hose."

☐ D16. Perspective (isometric) views, rather than engineering (top, side, bottom) views, are used wherever possible.

CHECKLIST FOR DRAFT OF SPECIFICATION

Writing Generally

☐ W01. No sentence is over about 13 words (unless really necessary or unless two independent clauses are used).

☐ W02. A heading is supplied for approximately every two pages of discussion.

☐ W03. Each discussion relates to and explains only its heading.

☐ W04. Adjacent paragraphs are connected by transitions, and no paragraph is longer than about one page, double spaced.

☐ W05. Every sophisticated term is defined clearly.

☐ W06. The description is written in simple, nontechnical terms, insofar as possible, so that a lay judge can understand it.

☐ W07. All writing is clear, reads smoothly, and is logical.

☐ W08. Male personal pronouns (he, his, etc.) aren't used exclusively; your examiner may be a woman.

☐ W09. No sentence is started with a number.

☐ W10. Every reference numeral is preceded by a noun ("lever 21").

☐ W11. A comma isn't used between subject and verb. (Wrong: "Lever 24, is connected to brace 26.")

☐ W12. A comma is used at all natural pauses.

☐ W13. Don't omit "Oxford" comma: "He ate bread, ham, and eggs." (Comma indicates the ham and eggs aren't mixed.)

☐ W14. All possessives are apostrophized, except "its."

☐ W15. Loose, informal writing isn't used.

☐ W16. A descriptive noun ("lever") rather than a general term ("part") is used for every element.

☐ W17. A group of words serving as a single adjective is hyphenated—for example, "impact-resistant glass."

☐ W18. No sentence fragments are used. (Wrong: "Because the gear is made of nylon.")

☐ W19. Writing is proofread carefully.

☐ W20. The indefinite article "a" (rather than "the") is used to introduce parts in the specification.

☐ W21. The definite article "the" isn't used to refer to a part by its name and reference numeral.

☐ W22. Already-introduced parts are not referred to with the article "a."

☐ W23. Every part is referred to by the same word throughout.

☐ W24. Your writing does not contain "flab" phrases such as "It will be noted that." (Flab slows reader's pace and detracts from drama and strength of work.)

☐ W25. The writing doesn't change voices (active to passive, or vice versa) in a paragraph, and you use the active voice as much as possible.

☐ W26. The discussion discusses one Fig at a time, insofar as possible, and doesn't jump from figure to figure too much.

☐ W27. Your reader is always kept clearly advised which figure is under discussion.

☐ W28. "Fig" (rather than figure) is used throughout to speed reading.

Specification

☐ S01. The title indicates the essence of your invention without being too long.

☐ S02. The Background—Field of the Invention section is not longer than one sentence.

☐ S03. The Background—Prior Art section does not mention your invention.

☐ S04. All detailed technical discussions refer to a drawing Fig (many humans can't comprehend abstract technical discussions).

☐ S05. Each prior-art approach you discuss is knocked.

☐ S06. When any patent or prior-art reference is referred to, the inventor's or author's name(s), the patent #, or publication and page, and its issue date are included.

☐ S07. The Objects and Advantages section states all advantages of your invention. These include the converse of every disadvantage in the Prior-Art section. The Objects and Advantages section also concludes with a general reference to other objects and advantages that will become apparent from the specification and drawings.

☐ S08. The Drawing Description section has just one short sentence for each Fig.

☐ S09. A List of Reference Numerals section is included.

☐ S10. Every reference numeral on the drawings is used in the specification and every reference numeral in the specification is on the drawings.

☐ S11. The same reference numeral is not used for two different parts. (Suffixed numerals—10, 10A, 10' for different parts—are okay.)

☐ S12. The description and the operation of the invention are discussed in separate sections.

☐ S13. Overall or main parts and overall operation are described before describing details of parts and operation.

☐ S14. If any part mentioned in the specification isn't shown in the drawings (for example, because it's conventional), state this. (For example, "Output 24 of generator 22 is connected to a conventional storage battery (not shown).")

☐ S15. You don't refer to your device as an "invention"; you're specific. (Wrong: "My invention thus …" Right: "My can opener thus…")

☐ S16. Ramifications are discussed after the basic version is explained and a preferred embodiment is indicated.

☐ S17. A separate "Summary" section is provided after the List of Reference Numerals.

☐ S18. Wishy-washy descriptions ("a plastic brace might work here") are eliminated; all descriptions are firm, sure, and positive.

☐ S19. The dimensions, preferred materials, relationships and/or sources of supply are stated for all exotic or critical parts.

☐ S20. For ease of reading, a shorter term is used when you refer again to a part with a long name. For example, First time: "A liquid-overflow check valve 12." Second time: "Valve 12."

☐ S21. Generic terms, rather than trademarks, are used. Each trademark used is identified as such, typed in caps, used with a generic noun, and its owner is indicated.

☐ S22. No legal words, such as "said" or "means," are used in the specification or abstract.

☐ S23. Metric (or metric followed by British) dimensions are used.

☐ S24. The Description and Operation sections contain enough detail to enable your invention readily to be built and used. Every part of the invention is discussed, its purpose is stated, and the overall operation of the invention is explained.

☐ S25. The Operation section does not introduce any part.

☐ S26. A Conclusion, Ramifications, and Scope section is provided at the end of the specification to repeat the advantages, discuss all possible alternatives, less important embodiments and ramifications) and to indicate that the claims control.

☐ S27. The Abstract is technical and terse, without listing too many advantages.

☐ S28. The Abstract has a reference numeral in parentheses "(12)" ,after each named part, for possible foreign filing.

SPECIFICATION OF SAMPLE PATENT APPLICATION

Note: This application is reproduced in final form, ready for filing in the PTO. However, your application will be in draft form after completing Ch. 8.

A2-KoppeLam.SB   your disc and file # (optional)

Note: Dimensions and layout are indicated for typing or printing on letter-size paper (8.5" x 11") so that, if foreign filing is later desired (see Ch.12), photocopies made directly on A4 paper will have the proper format for foreign filing. If foreign filing is not likely to be desired, legal or letter-size paper with the usual margins (always provide at least a 1" top margin for hole punching), 1½ or double line spacing, and page numbers at bottom or top can be used as the US PTO has very loose formatting standards.

8-9 cm top margin on p. 1

Patent Application of

Lou W. Koppe

for

2.5 cm left margin

PAPER-LAMINATED PLIABLE CLOSURE FOR FLEXIBLE BAGS

Printout should have minimum 1.5 line spacing (4 lines/inch) but is shown with denser spacing since this example is shown on a reduced scale.

Background--Field of Invention

one sentence for field of invention

This invention relates to plastic tab closures, specifically to such closures which are used for closing the necks of plastic produce bags.

Background--Description of Prior Art

2.8–3.8 cm right margin on 8.5" x 11" paper

description of and knocking of prior art

Grocery stores and supermarkets commonly supply consumers with polyethylene bags for holding produce. Such bags are also used by suppliers to provide a resealable container for other items, both edible and inedible.

Originally these bags were sealed by the supplier with staples or by heat. However, consumers objected since these were of a rather permanent nature: the bags could be opened only by tearing, thereby damaging them and rendering them impossible to reseal.

Thereafter, inventors created several types of closures to seal plastic bags in such a way as to leave them undamaged after they were opened. U.S. patent 4,292,714 to Walker (1981) discloses a complex clamp which can close the necks of bags without causing damage upon opening; however, these clamps are prohibitively expensive to manufacture. U.S. patent 2,981,990 to Balderree (1961) shows a closure which is of expensive construction, being made of PTFE, and which is not effective unless the bag has a relatively long "neck".

type almost to bottom of page so A4 copies can be made with proper bottom margin

Thus if the bag has been filled almost completely and consequently has a short

Fig. 8F—Specification of Sample Patent Application

2

continue knocking the prior art

neck, this closure is useless. Also, being relatively narrow and clumsy, Balderree's closure cannot be easily bent by hand along its longitudinal axis. Finally, his closure does not hold well onto the bag, but has a tendency to snap off.

Although twist closures with a wire core are easy to use and inexpensive to manufacture, do not damage the bag upon being removed, and can be used repeatedly, nevertheless they simply do not possess the neat and uniform appearance of a tab closure, they become tattered and unsightly after repeated use, and they do not offer suitable surfaces for the reception of print or labeling. These ties also require much more manipulation to apply and remove.

Several types of thin, flat closures have been proposed—for example, in U.K. patent 883,771 to Britt et al. (1961) and U.S. patents 3,164,250 (1965), 3,417,912 (1968), 3,822,441 (1974), 4,361,935 (1982), and 4,509,231 (1985), all to Paxton. Although inexpensive to manufacture, capable of use with bags having a short neck, and producible in break-off strips, such closures can be used only once if they are made of frangible plastic since they must be bent or twisted when being removed and consequently will fracture upon removal. Thus, to reseal a bag originally sealed with a frangible closure, one must either close its neck with another closure or else close it in makeshift fashion by folding or tying it. My own patent 4,694,542 (1987) describes a closure which is made of flexible plastic and is therefore capable of repeated use without damage to the bag, but nevertheless all the plastic closures heretofore known suffer from a number of disadvantages:

(a) Their manufacture in color requires the use of a compounding facility for the production of the pigmented plastic. Such a facility, which is needed to compound the primary pigments and which generally constitutes a separate production site, requires the presence of very large storage bins for the pigmented raw granules. Also, it presents great difficulties with regard to the elimination of the airborne powder which results from the mixing of the primary granules.

(b) If one uses an extruder in the production of a pigmented plastic—especially if one uses only a single extruder—a change from one color to a second requires purging the extruder of the granules having the first color by introducing those of the second color. This process inevitably produces, in sizeable volume, an intermediate product of an undesired color which must be discarded as scrap, thereby resulting in waste of material and time.

Fig. 8F (cont'd)—Specification of Sample Patent Application

3

(c) The colors of the closures in present use are rather unsaturated. If greater concentrations of pigment were used in order to make the colors more intense, the plastic would become more brittle and the cost of the final product would increase.

(d) The use of pigmented plastic closures does not lend itself to the production of multicolored designs, and it would be very expensive to produce plastic closures in which the plastic is multicolored—for example, in which the plastic has stripes of several colors, or in which the plastic exhibits multicolored designs.

(e) Closures made solely of plastic generally offer poor surfaces for labeling or printing, and the label or print is often easily smudged.

(f) The printing on a plastic surface is often easily erased, thereby allowing the alteration of prices by dishonest consumers.

(g) The plastic closures in present use are slippery when handled with wet or greasy fingers.

(h) A closure of the type in present use can be very carefully pried off a bag by a dishonest consumer and then attached to another item without giving any evidence of such removal.

Objects and Advantages

reverse of disadvantages of prior art = praise of your invention

Accordingly, besides the objects and advantages of the flexible closures described in my above patent, several objects and advantages of the present invention are:

(a) to provide a closure which can be produced in a variety of colors without requiring the manufacturer to use a compounding facility for the production of pigments;

(b) to provide a closure whose production allows for a convenient and extremely rapid and economical change of color in the closures that are being produced;

(c) to provide a closure which both is flexible and can be brightly colored;

(d) to provide a closure which can be colored in several colors simultaneously;

(e) to provide a closure which will present a superior surface for the reception of labeling or print;

(f) to provide a closure whose labeling cannot be altered;

Fig. 8F (cont'd)—Specification of Sample Patent Application

4

(g) to provide a closure which will not be slippery when handled with wet or greasy fingers; and

(h) to provide a closure which will show evidence of having been switched from one item to another by a dishonest consumer—in other words, to provide a closure which makes items tamper-proof.

Further objects and advantages are to provide a closure which can be used easily and conveniently to open and reseal a plastic bag, without damage to the bag, which is simple to use and inexpensive to manufacture, which can be supplied in separate tabs en masse or in break-off links, which can be used with bags having short necks, which can be used repeatedly, and which obviates the need to tie a knot in the neck of the bag or fold the neck under the bag or use a twist closure. Still further objects and advantages will become apparent from a consideration of the ensuing description and drawings.

Drawing Figures

one short
sentence for
each figure

In the drawings, closely related figures have the same number but different alphabetic suffixes.

Figs 1A to 1D show various aspects of a closure supplied with a longitudinal groove and laminated on one side with paper.

Fig 2 shows a closure with no longitudinal groove and with a paper lamination on one side only.

Fig 3 shows a similar closure with one longitudinal groove.

Fig 4 shows a similar closure with a paper lamination on both sides.

Fig 5 shows a similar closure with a paper lamination on one side only, the groove having been formed into the paper as well as into the body of the closure.

Figs 6A to 6K show end views of closures having various combinations of paper laminations, longitudinal grooves, and through-holes.

Figs 7A to 7C show a laminated closure with groove after being bent and after being straightened again.

Figs 8A to 8C show a laminated closure without a groove after being bent and after being straightened again.

Fig. 8F (cont'd)—Specification of Sample Patent Application

5

Reference Numerals In Drawings

10	base of closure	12	lead-in notch
14	hole	16	gripping points
18	groove	20	paper lamination
22	tear of paper lamination	24	corner
26	longitudinal through-hole	28	neck-down
30	side of base opposite to bend	32	crease

Summary

summary paraphrases main claim

In accordance with the present invention a bag closure comprises a flat body having a notch, a gripping aperture adjacent the notch and a layer of paper laminated on its side.

Description—Figs. 1 to 6

static description of figures

A typical embodiment of the closure of the present invention is illustrated in Fig 1A (top view) and Fig 1B (end view). The closure has a thin base **10** of uniform cross section consisting of a flexible sheet of material which can be repeatedly bent and straightened out without fracturing. A layer of paper **20** (Fig 1B) is laminated on one side of base **10**. In the preferred embodiment, the base is a flexible plastic, such as poly-ethylene-tere-phthalate (PET—hyphens here supplied to facilitate pronunciation)—available from Eastman Chemical Co. of Kingsport, TN. However, the base can consist of any other material that can be repeatedly bent without fracturing, such as polyethylene, polypropylene, vinyl, nylon, rubber, leather, various impregnated or laminated fibrous materials, various plasticized materials, cardboard, paper, etc.

At one end of the closure is a lead-in notch **12** which terminates in gripping points **16** and leads to a hole **14**. Paper layer **20** adheres to base **10** by virtue either of the extrusion of liquid plastic (which will form the body of the closure) directly onto the paper or the application of heat or adhesive upon the entirety of one side of base **10**. The paper-laminated closure is then punched out. Thus the lamination will have the same shape as the side of the base **10** to which it adheres.

Fig. 8F (cont'd)—Specification of Sample Patent Application

6

The base of the closure is typically .8 mm to 1.2 mm in thickness, and has overall dimensions roughly from 20 mm x 20 mm (square shape) to 40 mm x 70 mm (oblong shape). The outer four corners **24** of the closure are typically beveled or rounded to avoid snagging and personal injury. Also, when closure tabs are connected side-to-side in a long roll, these bevels or roundings give the roll a series of notches which act as detents or indices for the positioning and conveying of the tabs in a dispensing machine.

A longitudinal groove **18** is formed on one side of base **10** in Fig 1. In other embodiments, there may be two longitudinal grooves—one each side of the base—or there may be no longitudinal groove at all. Grove **18** may be formed by machining, scoring, rolling, or extruding. In the absence of a groove, there may be a longitudinal through-hole **26** (Fig 6L). This through-hole may be formed by placing, in the extrusion path of the closure, a hollow pin for the outlet of air.

Additional embodiments are shown in Figs 2, 3, 4, and 5; in each case the paper lamination is shown partially peeled back. In Fig 2 the closure has only one lamination and no groove; in Fig 3 it has only one lamination and only one groove; in Fig 4 it has two laminations and only one groove; in Fig 5 it has two laminations and one groove, the latter having been rolled into one lamination as well as into the body of the closure.

There are various possibilities with regard to the relative disposition of the sides which are grooved and the sides which are laminated, as illustrated in Fig 6, which presents end views along the longitudinal axis. Fig 6A shows a closure with lamination on one side only and with no groove; Fig 6B shows a closure with laminations on both sides and with no groove; Fig 6C shows a closure with only one lamination and only one groove, both being on the same side; Fig 6D shows a closure with only one lamination and only one groove, both being on the same side and the groove having been rolled into the lamination as well as into the body of the closure; Fig 6E shows a closure with only one lamination and only one groove, the two being on opposite sides; Fig 6F shows a closure with two laminations and only one groove; Fig 6G shows a closure with two laminations and only one groove, the groove having been rolled into one lamination as well as into the body of the closure; Fig 6H shows a closure with only one lamination and with two grooves; Fig 6I shows a closure with only one lamination and with two grooves, one of the grooves having been rolled into the lamination as well as into the body of the closure; Fig 6J shows a closure with

Fig. 8F (cont'd)—Specification of Sample Patent Application

7

two laminations and with two grooves; Fig 6K shows a closure with two laminations and with two grooves, the grooves having been rolled into the laminations as well as into the body of the closure; and Fig 6L shows a closure with two laminations and a longitudinal through-hole.

From the description above, a number of advantages of my paper-laminated closures become evident:

(a) A few rolls of colored paper will contain thousands of square yards of a variety of colors, will obviate the need for liquid pigments or a pigment-compounding plant, and will permit the manufacturer to produce colored closures with transparent, off-color, or leftover plastic, all of which are cheaper than first quality pigmented plastic.

(b) With the use of rolls of colored paper to laminate the closures, one can change colors by simply changing rolls, thus avoiding the need to purge the extruder used to produce the closures.

(c) The use of paper laminate upon an unpigmented, flexible plastic base can provide a bright color without requiring the introduction of pigment into the base and the consequent sacrifice of pliability.

(d) The presence of a paper lamination will permit the display of multicolored designs.

(e) The paper lamination will provide a superior surface for labeling or printing, either by hand or by machine.

(f) Any erasure or alteration of prices by dishonest consumers on the paper-laminated closure will leave a highly visible and permanent mark.

(g) Although closures made solely of plastic are slippery when handled with wet or greasy fingers, the paper laminate on my closures will provide a nonslip surface.

Operation--Figs 1, 6, 7, 8

operational description of figures

The manner of using the paper-laminated closure to seal a plastic bag is identical to that for closures in present use. Namely, one first twists the neck of a bag (not shown here but shown in Fig 12 of my above patent) into a narrow, cylindrical configuration. Next, holding the closure so that the plane of its base is generally

Fig. 8F (cont'd)—Specification of Sample Patent Application

8

perpendicular to the axis of the neck and so that lead-in notch **12** is adjacent to the neck, one inserts the twisted neck into the lead-in notch until it is forced past gripping points **16** at the base of the notch and into hole **14**.

To remove the closure, one first bends it along its horizontal axis (Fig 1C—an end view—and Figs 7 and 8) so that the closure is still in contact with the neck of the bag and so that gripping points **16** roughly point in parallel directions. Then one pulls the closure up or down and away from the neck in a direction generally opposite to that in which the gripping points now point, thus freeing the closure from the bag without damaging the latter. The presence of one or two grooves **18** or a longitudinal through-hole **26** (Fig 6L), either of which acts as a hinge, facilitates this process of bending.

The closure can be used to reseal the original bag or to seal another bag many times; one simply bends it flat again prior to reuse.

As shown in Figs 1C, 7B, and 8B (all end views), when the closure is bent along its longitudinal axis, region **30** of the base will stretch somewhat along the direction perpendicular to the longitudinal axis. (Region 30 is the region which is parallel to this axis and is on the side of the base opposite to the bend.) Therefore, when the closure is flattened again, the base will have elongated in the direction perpendicular to the longitudinal axis. This will cause a necking down **28** (Figs 1D, 7C, and 8C) of the base, as well as either a tell-tale tear **22**, or at least a crease **32** (Figs 7A and 8A) along the axis of bending. Therefore, if the closure is attached to a sales item and has print upon its paper lamination, the fact that the closure has been transferred by a dishonest consumer from the first item to another will be made evident by the tear or crease.

Figs 7A and 8A show bent closures with and without grooves, respectively. Figs 7C and 8C show the same closures, respectively, after being flattened out, along their longitudinal axes, paper tear **22** being visible.

Conclustion, Ramifications, and Scope

Accordingly, the reader will see that the paper-laminated closure of this invention can be used to seal a plastic bag easily and conveniently, can be removed just as easily and without damage to the bag, and can be used to reseal the bag without requiring a new closure. In addition, when a closure has been used to seal a bag and is later bent and removed from the bag so as not to damage the latter, the paper

repeat advantages— keep selling it!

Fig. 8F (cont'd)—Specification of Sample Patent Application

9

lamination will tear or crease and thus give visible evidence of tampering, without impairing the ability of the closure to reseal the original bag or any other bag. Furthermore, the paper lamination has the additional advantages in that

• it permits the production of closures in a variety of colors without requiring the manufacturer to use a separate facility for the compounding of the powdered or liquid pigments needed in the production of colored closures;

• it permits an immediate change in the color of the closure being produced without the need for purging the extruder of old resin;

• it allows the closure to be brightly colored without the need to pigment the base itself and consequently sacrifice the flexibility of the closure; it allows the closure to be multicolored since the paper lamination offers a perfect surface upon which can be printed multicolored designs;

• it provides a closure with a superior surface upon which one can label or print;

• it provides a closure whose labeling cannot be altered or erased without resulting in tell-tale damage to the paper lamination; and

• it provides a closure which will not be slippery when handled with wet or greasy fingers, the paper itself providing a nonslip surface.

additional
ramifications

Although the description above contains many specificities, these should not be construed as limiting the scope of the invention but as merely providing illustrations of some of the presently preferred embodiments of this invention. For example, the closure can have other shapes, such as circular, oval, trapezoidal, triangular, etc.; the lead-in notch can have other shapes; the groove can be replaced by a hinge which connects two otherwise unconnected halves, etc.

broadening
paragraph

Thus the scope of the invention should be determined by the appended claims and their legal equivalents, rather than by the examples given.

**[CLAIMS FOLLOW, STARTING ON A NEW PAGE, BUT ARE
PRINTED IN THE NEXT CHAPTER]**

Fig. 8F (cont'd)—Specification of Sample Patent Application

start abstract on new page, after claims

12

reproduce title
from p. 1

PAPER-LAMINATED PLIABLE CLOSURE FOR FLEXIBLE BAGS

Abstract: A thin, flat closure for plastic bags and of the type having at one edge a V-shaped notch (12) which communicates at its base with a gripping aperture (14). The base (10) of the closure is made of a flexible material so that it can be repeatedly bent, without fracturing, along an axis aligned with said notch and aperture. In addition, a layer of paper (20) is laminated on one or both sides of the closure. The axis of the base may contain one or two grooves (18) or a through-hole (26), either of which acts as a hinge to facilitate bending.

inset reference numerals in parentheses
for possible foreign filing

Fig. 8F (cont'd)—Specification of Sample Patent Application

see Fig.10A for permitted drawing sizes

1/4

FIG.IA

FIG.IB

FIG.IC

FIG.ID

FIG.2

FIG.3

FIG.4

Fig. 8F (cont'd)—Specification of Sample Patent Application

2/4

FIG.5

FIG.6D   FIG.6G   FIG.6I   FIG.6K

3/4

FIG.6A   FIG.6B   FIG.6C   FIG.6E

FIG.6F   FIG.6H   FIG.6J   FIG.6L

Fig. 8F (cont'd)—Specification of Sample Patent Application

4/4

FIG.7A

FIG.7B

FIG.7C

FIG. 8A

FIG.8B

FIG.8C

Fig. 8F (cont'd)—Specification of Sample Patent Application

CHAPTER

9

Now for the Legalese—The Claims

INVENTOR'S COMMANDMENT #12

In your patent application, formulate at least one main (independent) claim. Make this claim as broad as the prior art permits by (1) reciting as few elements as you can, and (2) using the broadest possible terms for such elements, thereby to make it as difficult as possible for others to avoid infringing such claim.

INVENTOR'S COMMANDMENT #13

In your patent application, formulate (1) one or two alternative independent claims, making these as broad as possible, and (2) as many dependent claims as necessary to add all of the significant additional features of your invention, thereby to provide backup for your independent claim(s) and a range of coverage.

A. What Are Claims?

If you don't yet know what patent claims are, or have never read any, you're in for a surprise. The word "claim" in the patent context is definitely a term of art. A "claim" is not what the common dictionary definitions recite—it's not a demand for something due, a title to something in the possession of another, or that which one seeks or asks for. Rather, a "claim," in the arcane world of patents, is a very formally worded sentence fragment contained in a patent application or patent. Claims recite and define the structure, or acts, of an invention in very precise, logical, and exact terms. They serve as tools to determine whether an invention is patentable over the prior art, and whether a patent is infringed. Just as a deed recites the boundary of a real estate parcel, patent claims recite the "bounds" or scope of an invention for the purposes of dealing with the PTO and possible infringers. In other words, claims are the nitty-gritty of patents. While the specification must teach how to make and use the invention, the claims must define its scope.

While claims are literally sentence fragments, they are supposed to be the object of the words "I [or We] claim." They are actually interpreted, when in a patent application, as saying to the examiner, "Here is my definition of my invention. Please search to see whether my invention, as here defined, is patentable over the prior art." In a patent, claims are interpreted as little statutes that say to the public, "The following is a precise description of the elements of this invention; if you make, use, or sell anything that has all of these elements, or all of these elements plus additional elements, or that closely fits this description, you can be legally held liable for the consequences of patent infringement."

Since there are only five statutory classes of inventions (see Chapter 5), every claim must define something that is classifiable into one of these classes. Thus there are: (1) process or method claims; (2) machine claims; (3) article or article of manufacture claims; (4) composition of matter claims; and (5) claims reciting a new use of any of the previous four statutory classes. Again, the line between (2) and (3) is blurred. Fortunately, as mentioned in Chapter 5, you don't have to do the classifying unless the PTO decides that your invention doesn't fit within any class at all.

If all of this sounds a bit formidable, don't let it throw you; it will become quite clear as we progress, after you see some examples. What's more, when it comes to claims, every layperson who "prosecutes" (handles or controls) a patent application has a safety net: So long as you can convince the patent examiner that you have a patentable invention, the examiner is required by law to write at least one claim for you, for free. I discuss this, along with several aids to claim drafting, in Section G of this chapter.

But a word of caution. If you're tempted to skip this chapter and solely rely on the examiner, you can't. You must provide at least one claim in your application to obtain a filing date. In addition, familiarity with the information I provide here is essential to securing the strongest possible patent on your invention. So I urge you to approach this chapter as if there were no safety net. Take this chapter as I present it, in small, easy-to-digest chunks, and you'll have no trouble. If you don't understand something the first time, go back again so you'll be further down on the learning curve where you'll see things much more clearly.

B. The Law Regarding Claims

The law (statutes and PTO rules) concerning claims is written in only the most general and vague terms. Accordingly, I'll be turning to the real world of everyday practice to help you understand the actual requirements for drafting claims. Before I do, however, let's at least take a brief look at the law as it is written.

1.   Legal Requirements for Patent Claims

The only pertinent statute comprises the last five paragraphs of our old friend, Section 112 of the patent laws (35 USC 112), which states:

> *(2)   The specification shall conclude with one or more claims particularly pointing out and distinctly claiming the subject matter which the applicant regards as the applicant's invention.*
>
> *(3)   A claim may be written in independent or, if the nature of the case admits, dependent form.*
>
> *(4)   Subject to the following paragraph, a claim in dependent form shall contain a reference to a claim previously set forth and then specify a further limitation of the subject matter claimed. A claim in dependent form shall be construed to incorporate by reference all the limitations of the claim to which it refers....*
>
> *((5)   This paragraph refers to multiple dependent claims, but since examiners don't like them and since they require a stiff surcharge, I've omitted this paragraph and strongly recommend that you don't use them.)*
>
> *(6)   An element in a claim for a combination may be expressed as a means or step for performing a specified function without the recital of structure, material, or acts in support thereof, and such claim shall be construed to cover the corresponding structure, material, or acts described in the specification and equivalents thereof.*

Paragraph (2) is the one that mandates the use of claims in patents. It also means that the claims must be specific enough to define the invention over the prior art ("particularly pointing out") and also should be clear, logical, and precise ("distinctly claiming"). This sentence is the most important part of Section 112 and is referred to by patent examiners almost daily because of the frequency with which they reject claims for lack of clarity or for some other similar reason.

Paragraphs (3) and (4) define independent and dependent claims (more on this later) and make it clear that a dependent claim incorporates all the limitations of the claim to which it refers.

Paragraph (6) was enacted to overrule two famous Supreme Court decisions (*G.E. v. Wabash*, 304 U.S. 371 (1938) and *Halliburton v. Walker*, 329 U.S. 1 (1946)). These decisions held certain claims invalid on technical grounds, specifically for "functionality at the point of novelty" because they expressed the essence of an invention in terms of its novel function, rather than reciting the specific structure that performed the novel function. In other words, they contained a broad expression like "means for hardening latex" rather than a specific expression like " a sulfur

additive." Congress enacted this paragraph to enable patent applicants to continue to claim their inventions more broadly. Under paragraph (6), if a claim uses the word "means" for performing a function, it must be construed to cover the structure, material, or acts described in the specification, and their equivalents. That is, if a claim recites "means for conveying rotational energy from said pedals to said rear wheels" and the specification describes a link chain for performing this function, the "means" claim will be construed by the PTO and the courts to cover the link chain and any equivalents, such as a driveshaft, a gear train, etc. (*In re Donaldson Co., Inc.*, 29 U.S.P.Q. 2d 1845 (CAFC 1994)).

2.   Rules of Practice

In addition to Section 112, claims are governed by the PTO's "Rules of Practice." PTO Rule 75, parts (b), (d)(1), and (e) add these additional requirements:

> *(b)   More than one claim may be presented provided they differ substantially from each other and are not unduly multiplied....*
>
> *(d)(1)   The claim or claims must conform to the invention as set forth in the remainder of the specification and the terms and phrases used in the claims must find clear support or antecedent basis in the description so that the meaning of the terms in the claims may be ascertainable by reference to the description....*
>
> *(e)   Where the nature of the case admits, as in the case of an improvement, any independent claim should contain in the following order: (1) a preamble comprising a general description of all the elements or steps of the claimed combination that are conventional or known, (2) a phrase such as "wherein the improvement comprises," and (3) those elements, steps, and/or relationship that constitutes that portion of the claimed combination that the applicant considers as the new or improved portion.*
>
> *(f)   If there are several claims, they shall be numbered consecutively in Arabic numerals.*
>
> *(g)   All dependent claims should be grouped together with the claim or claims to which they refer to the extent possible.*

Part (b) requires that the claims differ substantially from each other and not be too numerous. In practice, minimal differences will suffice. The rule prohibiting numerous claims is more strictly enforced. If more than about twenty claims are presented, there should be some justification, such as a very complex invention or numerous embodiments. Also, there are substantial charges for each independent claim over three and each claim (independent or dependent) over 20—see Appendix 4, Fee Schedule.

Part (d)(1), enforced only sporadically, requires that the terms in the claims should correspond to those used in the specification. It has often been said that the specification should serve as a dictionary for the claims.

Part (e), a newcomer, was introduced to require that claims be drafted, insofar as practicable, in the German or "Jepson" style (from a famous decision of that name). The Jepson-type claim is very easy for examiners to read and understand. It puts the essence of the invention into sharp focus by providing in the first part of the claim an introduction that sets forth the environment of the invention—that is, what is already known, and in the second part, or body of the claim, the essence of the invention—that is, the improvement of the current invention. In practice, I've never seen this part of Rule 75 enforced.

Part (f) is self-explanatory and part (g) will be explained in Section J of this chapter.

C. Some Sample Claims

As mentioned, claims boil the invention down to its essence. In their broadest sense, they eliminate everything nonessential to the invention. In fact, many inventors first realize what their invention truly is when they write or see a claim to it, especially after the claim has been rejected in the patent prosecution process. Conversely, you won't be able to draft an adequate claim unless you have a clear understanding of your invention. Although not a patent attorney, the great theatrical producer David Belasco showed that he understood the principle behind claims well when he said,

"If you can't write your idea on the back of my calling card, you don't have a clear conception of your idea."

And claims are difficult to write just because they are so short. Blaise Pascal once concluded a letter to a friend as follows: "I have made this letter a little longer than usual because I lack the time to make it shorter." Nevertheless, don't get discouraged; if you follow the step-by-step, four-part procedure I give later, you'll find that writing claims is not too much more difficult than writing the specification.

Consider some hypothetical simple claims in the five respective statutory classes of invention. Patent applications containing the first four of these claims would now be rejected since the "inventions" they define are obviously old and in the public domain. The fifth—a "new use" claim—is from a patent.

1. Process or Method Claims— Conventional Process and Software Process

Here are examples of two method claims, one to a conventional process and one to a software-based process. Note that both claims recite a series of steps or individual operations, rather than a series of hardware elements as in an article claim. Note also that both claims are similar in construction, as discussed below, indicating that a software process is generally claimed the same way as any other process.

a. Conventional Process

For the conventional process, assume that you've just invented sewing and want to claim the process. Here's how you'd do it.

A method for joining two pieces of cloth together at their edges, comprising the steps of:
  a. positioning said two pieces of cloth together so that an edge portion of one piece overlaps an adjacent edge portion of the other piece, and
  b. passing a thread repeatedly through and along the length of the overlapping portions in sequentially opposite directions and through sequentially spaced holes in said overlapping adjacent portions,

  whereby said two pieces of cloth will be attached along said edge portions.

Note that the first part of this claim contains a title, preamble, or genus, which states the purpose of the method but doesn't use the term "sewing," because sewing is the invention and is assumed to be new at the time the claim is drafted. The claim contains two steps, (a) and (b), that state in sequence the acts one would perform in sewing two pieces of cloth. Note that each clause begins with an "—

ing" word. The claim also contains an optional "whereby" clause at the end to point out to the examiner or a judge the advantage of the process.

b. Software Process

For the software process, assume that you've just invented a word processor and want to claim the word insertion feature (which we now all take for granted) as a method. Here's how you'd do it.

A method of inserting additional characters within an existing series of characters on a display, comprising:

> *(a) providing a memory which is able to store a series of characters at an adjacent series of addresses in said memory,*
>
> *(b) providing a character input means which a human operator can use to store a series of characters in said memory at said respective adjacent series of addresses,*
>
> *(c) storing said series of characters in said memory at said adjacent series of addresses,*
>
> *(d) providing a display which is operatively connected to said memory for displaying said series of characters stored in said memory at said adjacent series of addresses,*
>
> *(e) providing a pointer means which said operator can manipulate to point to any location between any adjacent characters within said series of characters displayed on said display,*
>
> *(f) providing a memory controller which will:*
>
>> *(1) direct any additional character which said operator enters via said character input means to a location in said memory, beginning at an address corresponding to the location between said adjacent characters as displayed on said display, and*
>>
>> *(2) causing all characters in said series of characters which are stored in said memory at addresses subsequent said location in said memory to be transferred to subsequent addresses in said memory so that said additional character will be stored in said memory at said location and before all of said subsequent characters,*
>
> *whereby said display will display said additional character within said series of characters at said location between said adjacent characters, and*
>
> *whereby a writer can add words within existing body of text and the added words are displayed in an orderly and clean fashion without having to reenter said existing body of text.*

Note that the preamble of this claim states the purpose of the method. The series of steps in the body of the claim first state or lay out the hardware of the computer (the memory, the display, etc.) as a series of "providing" clauses since a method claim is not supposed to state hardware directly, that is, if this claim recited simply "a memory," rather than "providing a memory," the examiner in the PTO would object to it as an improper hybrid claim because it recited both hardware and method steps. More on this later. Finally, note that the end of this claim also contains a first optional "whereby" clause which states the internal function of the claimed method, and a second "whereby" clause which states an overall, external, and meaningful result or function of the method. The two whereby clauses help sell the method to the examiner, as well as any judge who has to decide on the validity or infringement of this claim.

2. Machine Claims—Conventional and Software Machines

Here are examples of two machine claims, one to a conventional machine and one to a software-based machine. Note that both claims recite a series of hardware elements, rather than a series of steps as in the process claims. Note also that both claims are similar in construction, indicating again that a software machine is generally claimed the same way as any other machine.

a. Conventional Machine

For the conventional machine, assume now that you've just invented the automobile. Here's how to claim it.

A self-propelled vehicle, comprising:

> *a. a body carriage having rotatable wheels mounted thereunder for enabling said body carriage to roll along a surface,*
>
> *b. an engine mounted in said carriage for producing rotational energy, and*
>
> *c. means for controllably coupling rotational energy from said engine to at least one of said wheels,*
>
> *whereby said carriage will be self-propelled along said surface.*

This claim again contains a title in the first part. The second part or body contains three elements, the carriage, the engine, and the transmission. These elements are defined as connected or interrelated by the statement that the engine is mounted in the carriage and the transmission (defined broadly as "means for controllably coupling …") couples the engine to at least one wheel of the carriage.

Again, the whereby clause recites the advantage of the hardware elements of the preamble and clauses a., b., and c.

b. Software Machine

For the software machine, let's make it easy and continue to assume that you've just invented a word processor and want to claim the word insertion feature as a machine. As I'll explain below, to obtain maximum coverage, it's best to provide both method and machine claims for an invention, if it's possible to do so. Here's the machine claim to the word processor:

A machine for inserting additional characters within an existing series of characters on a display, comprising:

    (a) a memory which is able to store a series of characters at an adjacent series of addresses in said memory,

    (b) a character input means which a human operator can use to store a series of characters in said memory at said adjacent series of addresses,

    (d) a display which is operatively connected to said memory for displaying said series of characters stored in said memory at said adjacent series of addresses,

    (d) a pointer means which said operator can manipulate to point to any location between any adjacent characters within said series of characters displayed on said display,

    (e) a memory controller which will:

        (1) direct any additional character which said operator enters via said character input means to a location in said memory, beginning at an address corresponding to the location between said adjacent characters as displayed on said display, and

        (2) cause all characters in said series of characters which are stored in said memory at addresses subsequent to said location in said memory to be transposed to subsequent addresses in said memory so that said additional characters will be stored in said memory at said location and before all of said subsequent characters,

whereby said display will display said additional characters within said series of characters at said location between said adjacent characters, and

whereby a writer can add words within the existing body of text and the added words are displayed in an orderly and clean fashion without having to reenter said existing body of text.

Note that this machine claim is essentially the same as the above method claim on word processing, but our machine claim contains only directly recited hardware elements and no method steps. It's simply an alternative

way of reciting the word processing invention. As I'll discuss below, it's desirable to provide as many different ways to claim an invention as possible, just as it would be desirable to go into battle with as many different weapons as possible (rifle, pistol, knife, grenade, etc.), since you never know which one will help you win the battle.

3. Article of Manufacture Claim

You've done it again! Here's a claim to the pencil you've just invented.

A hand-held writing instrument comprising:

    a. elongated core-element means that will leave a marking line if moved across paper or other similar surface, and

    b. an elongated holder surrounding and encasing said elongated core-element means, one portion of said holder being removable from an end thereof to expose an end of said core-element means so as to enable said core-element means to be exposed for writing, whereby said holder protects said core-element means from breakage and provides an enlarged means for holding said core-element means conveniently.

This claim, like the machine claim, contains a preamble and a body with two elements: (a) the "lead" and (b) the wood. As before, the elements of the body are associated; here the wood ("elongated holder") is said to surround and encase the lead ("elongated core"). The "whereby" clause at the end of the claim states the purpose and advantage of the lead and its holder.

4. Composition of Matter Claim

Now, great inventor that you are, you've come up with concrete. Here's your claim.

A rigid building and paving material comprising a mixture of sand and stones, and a hardened cement binder filling the interstices between and adhering to sand and stones, whereby a hardened, rigid, and strong matrix for building and paving will be provided.

This claim, although not in subparagraph form, still contains a preamble and a body containing a recitation of the elements of the composition (sand, stones, and cement binder), plus an association of the elements (sand and stones are mixed and binder fills volume between and adheres to sand and stones). Again, the whereby clause drives home the advantages of the components.

The height of brevity was reached (and will never be exceeded) in a composition of matter claim some years ago when the PTO issued a patent to Glenn T. Seaborg on a new element, Americium; the claim read simply, *Element 95.*

5. New Use Claim

Someone discovered that pigs put on weight faster if aspirin is added to their diet. Here's how to claim it.

A method of stimulating the growth of swine comprising feeding such swine aspirin in an amount effective to increase their rate of growth.

This claim recites the newly discovered use of aspirin and the purpose of the new use in a manner that defines over and avoids the known, old use of aspirin (analgesic). Note that it is a method claim (as all new-use claims must be). This is because aspirin per se is old and thus must be claimed more narrowly, as a new use.

Now that you've read a few claims, I suggest you try writing a practice claim or two of your own to become more familiar with the process. Try a simple article or machine with which you are very familiar, such as a table, chair, pen, etc. Write the preamble and then the body. To write the body, first list the elements or parts of the article or machine, and then associate or interconnect them. Don't worry too much about grammar or style, but try to make the claim clear and understandable.

D. Common Misconceptions Regarding Claims

In my experience, inventors' misconceptions about claims are more widespread than in any other area of the patent law, except possibly for the misconception regarding the "Post Office Patent" explained in Chapter 3. Consider some of the following:

Common Misconception: *The more claims that the PTO (Patent and Trademark Office) allows in your patent application, the broader your scope of coverage.*

Fact: *The scope of your monopoly is determined by the wording of your claims, not their number. One broad claim can be far more powerful than fifty narrow claims.*

Common Misconception: *If you want to get broad coverage on a specific feature of your invention, you should recite that specific feature in your claims.*

Fact: *If you recite a specific feature of your invention in a claim, that claim will be limited to that feature as recited, and variations may not be covered—for example, if you have a two-inch, nylon gear in your apparatus and you recite it as such in a claim, the claim may not cover an apparatus that*

uses a one-inch gear, or a steel gear. The best way to cover all possible variations of your gear is to recite it simply as a "gear," or better yet, "rotary transmission means."*

Common Misconception: *To cover a specific feature of your invention per se, you need merely recite it in a dependent claim.*

Fact: *As stated in the statute quoted in Section B, above (35 USC 112, ¶ 4), a dependent claim is construed (and reads) as if it incorporated all of the limitations of the claim to which it refers. Thus if your independent claim (#1) recites a telephone having a connecting cord and your dependent claim reads, "The telephone of Claim 1 wherein said connecting cord is coiled," the dependent claim doesn't claim the coiled cord per se, but rather the coiled cord in combination with the telephone. More on this later in Section J, Drafting Dependent Claims.*

Common Misconception: *If a claim doesn't recite a specific feature of your invention, then this feature is necessarily not covered. For example, if your invention includes a two-inch, nylon gear and you fail to recite it specifically in a claim, then anyone who makes your invention with this gear can't infringe your patent.*

Fact: *The fact that a feature isn't recited doesn't mean that it isn't covered. An absurd example will make this clear. Suppose your invention is a bicycle and you show and describe it with a front wheel having 60 spokes. You don't mention the spokes at all in a claim; you simply recite a "front wheel." Any bike that has all of the limitations of the claim will infringe it. Thus a bike that has any "front wheel" will infringe, whether it has zero or 600 spokes.*

As I'll explain from time to time, to infringe a claim, an accused apparatus must have at least all of the elements of the claim; if it has more elements than recited in the claim, it still infringes, but if it has less, then it doesn't infringe. Claim limitations are thus interpreted using Boolean logic, similar to computer search terms, as explained in Chapter 6, Section M.

Common Misconception: *The more features of your invention you recite in a claim, the broader that claim will be. (Stated differently, the longer a claim is, the broader it is.)*

Fact: *As will be apparent from the previous common misconception, the less you recite in a claim—that is, the fewer the elements you recite—the broader the claim will be. This seeming paradox exists because an accused infringing device must have all the elements of a claim to infringe. Thus, the fewer the elements specified in a claim, the fewer the elements an accused infringing device needs to have to infringe. Put* *differently, infringement is generally easier to prove if a claim is made shorter or has fewer elements. "To claim more, you should recite less" is a Boolean concept that is difficult for most inventors to absorb, but that you should learn well if you want to secure the broadest possible coverage. Again, see Computer Searching in Chapter 6, Section M, for further clarification of this point.*

E. One Claim Should Be As Broad As Possible

As stated in Inventor's Commandment #12, there are two ways to make a claim broader: (1) *minimize* the number of elements; and (2) *maximize* the scope of these elements. Let's see how this works.

1.   Minimize the Number of Elements

Take our automobile claim, above, which recites three elements, A, B, and C—that is, the wheeled carriage, the engine, and the transmission. If an accused machine contains just these three elements, it will, of course, infringe.

If it has these three plus a fourth, such as a radio, which we'll label D, it will still infringe.

But if our accused machine contains only elements A and B, the carriage and engine, it won't infringe, since it simply doesn't contain all of the claimed elements, A, B, and C.

If a claim contains many, many elements, say A to M, only devices with all thirteen elements, A to M, will infringe. If the maker of the device eliminates just one of the thirteen elements, say G, the device will *not* infringe. Thus, it's relatively easy to avoid infringing a claim with many elements.

If a claim contains only two elements, A and B, any device with these two elements will infringe, no matter how many other elements the device has. The only way to have the device avoid infringement is to eliminate either element A or element B, a relatively difficult task.

Thus, it should be very clear that the fewer the elements in a claim, the harder the claim will be to avoid, that is, the broader it will be and the more devices it will cover. Therefore, when drafting a main or independent claim to your invention, it will behoove you to put in as few elements of your invention as possible. (You do have to include sufficient elements so that the claim recites an operative, complete assemblage that is novel and unobvious over the prior art. More on this in Sections F and G, below.)

2.   Maximize the Scope of Elements

With regard to the second way of broadening a claim, that is, reciting existing elements more broadly, consider a few examples. Suppose an invention involves a chair. The chair can be drafted broadly as "a seat" or narrowly as a four-legged maple chair with a vinyl-covered padded seat and a curved plywood back. Obviously, a three-legged plastic stool would be "a seat," and it would infringe the broadly recited element, but would miss the narrowly recited maple chair by a country mile. In electronics, "controllable electron valve" is broader than "vacuum tube" or "transistor." In machinery, "rotational energy connecting element" is broader than "helically cut gear" or "V-belt."

One way of reciting elements broadly is to take advantage of paragraph 6 of Section 112 by reciting an element, wherever possible, as "means" plus a specific function. In this way, any device or means that performs the function and was the equivalent of the supporting structure in the specification would infringe. For example, "means for conveying rotational energy" is broader than a drive belt and covers gears, pulleys, and drive shafts if these are the equivalent of a belt, which they will be determined to be if you've mentioned them in the specification. "Amplifying means" is broader than and covers such items as transistor amplifiers, tube amplifiers and masers.

If you do use the word "means" in a claim, Section 112 requires that the claim recite a "combination"—that is, two or more elements or parts. Claims that recite a single element are not supposed to use the word "means" to describe the single element since this is considered too broad—for example, "17. Means for providing a continuously variable speed/power drive for a bicycle" would be an example of a prohibited "single means" claim. However, you can effectively obtain practically the same breadth of coverage by adding an immaterial second element to the claim to make it a combination claim. Thus, "17. In combination, a bicycle having a pedal mechanism and means for providing a continuously variable speed/power drive for coupling rotational energy from said pedal mechanism to a wheel of said bicycle" would satisfy Section 112.

Courts have recently been construing "means" clauses narrowly, so you should also include claims with "structural" (non-means) clauses; these clauses can be expanded under the "doctrine of equivalents" (Chapter 15, Section J).

To sum up, while you should write your specification as specifically and with as much detail as possible (Chapter 8), you should make the substance of your claims as general (broad) as possible by (1) eliminating as many elements as is feasible and (2) describing (reciting) the remaining elements as broadly as possible. In other words, make your specification specific and long and your main claims general and short.

F. The Effect of Prior Art on Your Claim

Now that you've learned how to make your claims as broad as possible, it's time for the bad news. What is "possible" has generally much less breadth than you'd like. This is because each claim must define an invention that is patentable over the prior art. Remember the issues of novelty and unobviousness? Well, they (especially unobviousness) are an ever-present factor always to be considered in claim drafting.

1. Novelty

Let's go back to Section 102, which deals with novelty (Chapter 5). A claim must define an invention that is novel in view of the prior art. It must recite something that no single reference in the prior art shows—that is, it must contain something new or novel. Your claim must recite novel hardware (or a novel process step) in a positive, structurally supported, unequivocal manner. For example, reciting "a wheel for providing lateral stabilization" won't adequately define over a prior-art wheel that doesn't provide lateral stabilization, since the function isn't supported by novel structure. The remedy: recite the novel structure

that does provide the stabilization—such as a guideway for the wheel, or a "means" for providing stabilization.

Just as a claim can be made broader by eliminating elements and reciting the existing elements more broadly, it can be made narrower in order to define novel structure (1) by adding elements, or (2) by reciting the existing elements more narrowly.

For an example of adding elements, suppose a prior-art reference shows a machine having three elements—A, B, and C, and your claim recites these three elements A, B, and C. Your claim would be said to lack novelty over the prior art and would be rejectable or invalid under Section 102. But if you added a fourth element, D, to the claim, it would clear the prior art and would recite a novel invention (but not necessarily a patentable one, because of the unobviousness requirement). (If the prior art were an in-force patent that *claimed* elements A, B, and C, and your *device* had elements A, B, C, and D, it *would* infringe for reasons given in Section E1, above. However, the PTO is never concerned with infringements, so you don't need to worry about this issue in a patent application.)

For an example of reciting existing elements more narrowly, suppose the prior art shows a machine having the same three elements—A, B, and C. You could also clear this prior art and claim a novel invention by reciting in your claim elements A, B, and C′, where C′ would be the prior-art element C with any change that isn't shown in the prior art. For example, if the prior art shows element C as a steam engine, and you recite a gasoline engine (C′), you've obviated any question of lack of novelty (though probably not obviousness).

In sum, although you'd like to be able to eliminate as many elements as possible and recite all of your elements as broadly as possible, you will usually have to settle for less because there will always be prior art there to make you toe the line of novelty.

2. Unobviousness

As I've stressed, novelty isn't enough. The claims must define an invention that would be unobvious to one having ordinary skill in the art. Or to use the paraphrase of the law from Chapter 5, the novel feature(s) of the invention defined by each claim must have one or more new features that are important, significant, and produce valuable, unexpected new results. Thus, when you have to narrow a claim to define over the prior art, you must do so by adding one or more elements or by reciting existing elements more narrowly, and you must be sure that the added or narrowed elements define a structure or step that is sufficiently different from the prior art to be considered unobvious. More on this in Chapter 13.

For the last bit of bad news, note that if the wording of a claim has several possible interpretations, the examiner is entitled to use any one, including the one least favorable to you, in determining whether the claim clears the prior art.

Now that I've given you the bad news, I suggest you ignore it at this stage. You should try to write your main claim(s) as broadly as possible while keeping in mind the prior art that you've uncovered. In case of doubt, you should err on the side of too much breadth, since you can always narrow your claims later if your examiner thinks they're too broad. Conversely, if your examiner allows your narrow claims on your first office action (rare), you'll find it very difficult to broaden them later.

G. Technical Requirements of Claims

As stated, in addition to defining adequately over the prior art, each claim must also be worded in a clear, concise, precise, and rational way. If the wording of a claim is poor, the examiner will make a "technical" (non-prior art) rejection under Section 112. It is this technical aspect of drafting claims that most often serves as a stumbling block to the layperson. Yet claim drafting really won't be that hard if you:

- Study the sample claims listed later in this chapter, plus those of a few patents, to get the basic idea;
- Use the four-step method (preamble-element-interconnections-broaden) set out in Section H, below; and
- Are conversant with the appropriate terminology associated with your invention's elements.

Remember also that you needn't write perfect claims when you file the application. Why? Because if you have a patentable invention, you can have the examiner write them for you. A provision of the *Manual of Patent Examining Procedure*, Section 707.07(j), states:

When, during the examination of a pro se [no attorney] case, it becomes apparent to the examiner that there is patentable subject matter disclosed in the application [the examiner] shall draft one or more claims for the applicant and indicate in office action that such claims would be allowed if incorporated in the application by amendment.

This practice will expedite prosecution and offer a service to individual inventors not represented by a registered patent attorney or agent.

Although this practice may be desirable and is permissible in any case where deemed appropriate by the examiner, it will be expected to be applied in all cases where it is apparent that the applicant is unfamiliar with the proper preparation and prosecution of patent applications.

You do have to at least give it a try, since you must file at least one claim with your application to get a filing date. But, as indicated, this claim need not be well written or narrow enough for patent coverage. Instead, during the ensuing prosecution stage, you can ask the examiner to write claims for you pursuant to this section if you feel yours aren't adequate. The examiner is bound to do so if your invention is patentable.

If you do choose this option, be sure the examiner's claims are broad enough, since it isn't in the examiner's own interest to write broad claims for you. As with any other claim, ask yourself if any elements of the examiner's claim can be eliminated or recited more broadly and still distinguish adequately over the prior art. If so, amend it as I suggest in Chapter 13, Section E.

Also remember that many patent attorneys and agents will be willing to review or draft your claims at their regular hourly rates. But use this as a last alternative, since most patent attorneys in private practice charge $100 to $300 per hour. If possible, you should choose a company-employed patent attorney or a retired patent attorney who works at home, since such attorneys' rates will usually be one-half to one-third of those charged by their downtown counterparts. See Chapter 6, Section F, for how to find patent attorneys and agents.

Now that you know there's help out here, let's look at some of the basic rules covering the drafting of claims.

1. Be Precise

Your claims must be precise, logical, and determinate. One of the most common reasons for claim rejections is the improper use of articles, such as "a," "the" and "said." Generally, the first time you recite an element, use the indefinite article "a," just as you would if you were speaking to someone who is not familiar with your device. If you refer to the same element again using exactly the same words to describe it, use the extremely definite article "said." "Said" actually means, in patent law, "the following part, which this claim (or its parent claim) previously recited in exactly the following words:" If you refer to the same element again by using different, but implicitly clear words to describe it, use the definite article "the" again, just as you would do in ordinary speech. Here's an example showing how "a," "said" and "the" are properly used in a claim to a table:

EXAMPLE:
An article of furniture for holding objects for a sitting human, comprising:

(a) a sheet of rigid material having sufficient size to accommodate use by a human being for writing and working,

(b) *a plurality of elongated support members of equal length,*

(c) *said support members being joined perpendicularly to the undersurface of said sheet of rigid material at spaced locations so as to be able to support said rigid member in a horizontal orientation.*

Note that the first time any element is mentioned, the article "a" is used, but when it's referred to again by its original designation, "said" is used. When it's referred to again with a different (but clear) designation—that is, the undersurface of the table—"the" is used.

In addition to being precise in the use of articles, you should avoid ambiguous references. For example, if "said elongated lever" is used in a claim and no "elongated lever" has previously been recited, a non-sequitur has occurred and a rejection for indefiniteness due to a "missing antecedent" will be made by the PTO. Or, if the same element is positively recited twice, such as "a lever" … "a lever," the claim is unclear. The solution is to change the second "a lever" to "said lever."

💡 COMPUTER HINT

To help provide proper antecedents, it's very helpful to use a computer and a word-processing program with a "windows" function so that you can display the first part of your claim (or your main claim if you're writing dependent claims) in one window and the latter part of your claim (or the dependent claim you're writing) in a second window. In this way, you'll be able to refer continuously to the previous writing to make sure your current writing corresponds.

Vagueness and indefiniteness can also occur if you use abbreviations—such as, "d.c." (say "direct current"); relative terms without any reference—such as, "large" (say "larger than…" or "large enough to support three adults"), or vague, casual language, such as "strong," "suitable," "standard," etc.

2. Use Only One Capital, One Period, and No Dashes, Quotes, Parentheses, Trademarks or Abbreviations

Amateurs violate this rule so often that a friend who has a foreign patent translation agency and who wants to show he's professional includes the following blurb in his ad flyer: "We promise never to include more than one period or capital letter in any translated claim, no matter how long it is." While it may be hard for you to accept, and while it may seem silly, the rules are that the only capital letter in a claim should be the first letter of the first word, the claim should contain a period only at its end, and there should be no dashes, quotes, or parentheses, trademarks or abbreviations. (You may use capitals, periods, and parentheses for the lettered subparagraphs of a claim, for instance, "A." or "(A)". Also, hyphens ("hand-held") are OK, but dashes ("—" or "--") are not.

3. Use Means Clause to Avoid Functionality of Claim

The technical error of "functionality" occurs when elements of the claim are recited in terms of their advantage, function, or result rather than in terms of their structure. The remedy is to recite the elements of the claim as "means" or a "device" for performing the function or achieving the result.

For example, here are some typical improper functional claims actually written by a layperson:

7. *An additive for paints that makes the paint dry faster.*

8. *A belt buckle that does not tend to snag as much.*

Both of these claims would be rejected under Section 112 because they don't particularly point out and distinctly claim the invention since they recite what the invention *does* rather than what it *is*.

The remedy: use "means" or "device" clauses and also recite the general composition or structure of the additive or buckle. But remember that the claim must be to a combination; a single "means" claim won't pass muster. Thus, even if Claim 7 were written as follows, it would violate Section 112:

7. *Additive means for paints for making them dry faster.*

Here's how the above two claims can be properly rewritten to pass muster under Section 112:

7A. *A paint composition comprising:*

(a) *a paint compound comprising an oil-based paint vehicle and a suspended pigment in said vehicle, and*

   (b) additive means admixed with said vehicle for decreasing the drying time of said paint compound and

   (b') a volatile solvent admixed [etc.].

8A. A belt buckle comprising:

   (a) a catch comprising two interlocking rigid parts that can be attached to opposite ends of a belt, and

   (b) anti-snag means for preventing said interlocking parts from snagging on cloth when placed adjacent said interlocking parts and

   (b') a shield for preventing [etc.].

Under the pertinent statute (35 U.S.C. §112, ¶7) and court decisions, a "means" clause is supposed to be interpreted according to the corresponding structure or material described in the specification and the equivalents of such structure or material. Thus, a means clause is not supposed to be interpreted literally to cover every possible means which fulfills the function of the means, but only according to the corresponding structure or material in the specification and its equivalents.

A moment's reflection will show you that claiming your invention in terms of its unique structure, rather than its results, effects, or functions, makes logical sense. This is because a monopoly, to be precise and to have reasonable limits, must be defined in terms of its structure, rather than the result such structure produces. In other words, if you recited "a belt buckle that doesn't snag" you would be claiming a result only, so that any belt buckle that fulfilled this result would infringe, regardless of its structure. This "functional" type of claim would accordingly be considered unreasonably broad and therefore would have to be narrowed and made more explicit by the addition of some additional structure or a means clause in order to make it more commensurate with the invention.

SOAP SHOOTER
NO. 756,329

USING MEANS CLAUSES IN SOFTWARE CLAIMS

If you use any means clauses in your claims, it is necessary to identify and describe in the specification what structure or material supports the means. If you have a software invention, this requirement is particularly important under the PTO's guidelines. While it's not necessary to use the term "means" in the specification, the specification should clearly describe an element or structure using the same words used in the claims to recite the function of the means. That is, if your claim recites a "means for displaying the three-dimensional structure of a compound," your specification should clearly describe specific software, for instance, a specific code segment or object, that you employ, and it should also state that this segment or object configures a general-purpose microprocessor to display the three-dimensional structure of the compound.

Of course, while both of the above claims (as I revised them) would pass Section 112, they would not be novel or patentable under Sections 102 or 103, since they recite nothing new according to our present state of knowledge.

4. Be Complete

Each claim must stand on its own—that is, it must recite enough elements to make a working, complete device in accordance with its recognized status in its art. For example, you can recite a light bulb per se (without reciting the entire lamp) since light bulbs are a well-known item of commerce. But a claim to just the glass envelope of a light bulb would probably be rejected as incomplete, since it won't do anything on its own and isn't a recognized item of commerce. The remedy for failing to include enough elements is simply to add the needed elements. Examiners and attorneys frequently disagree as to whether a claim is incomplete, the examiner wanting the claim narrowed by the addition of elements and the attorney wanting it to remain broad, that is, not to add any more elements.

5. Keep Language Straightforward and Simple

Properly drafted claims use a minimum number of words to delineate the essence of the invention. Excess wordiness of a claim, termed "prolixity" by the PTO, is a frequent error committed by beginners. The remedy is to reword the claim in more compact language.

6. All Elements of Invention Must Logically Interrelate

Each of the elements in a claim must be logically related and connected to the other elements. When the elements of an invention don't appear to cooperate and to be connected in a logical or functional sense, the PTO will reject the claim. This is a more substantive type of rejection, since it's often directed at the underlying invention rather than simply the way the claim is drafted. For example, if you claim the combination of a waffle iron and tape recorder, these elements don't cooperate and hence your claim would be rejected as drawn to an aggregation. But the elements don't have to work at the same time to cooperate; in a typewriter, for example, the parts work at different times but cooperate toward a unitary result.

7. Old Combination and Aggregation

Formerly, claims drafted in terms of an old or well-known combination, such as an automatic transmission and an automobile, where the invention was in the transmission, were rejectable on the ground of "old combination," but this rejection has been eliminated. However claims drafted to a combination of elements which don't cooperate toward a common end, such as a washing machine and a telephone, can be rejected on the ground of aggregation. But the elements do not have to function simultaneously to cooperate: a typewriter is a good example of elements (keys) which don't function simultaneously but do cooperate.

8. Use Only Positive Limitations

In the past, all negative limitations (for example, "noncircular") were verboten, but now only those that make the claim unclear or awkward are proscribed. However, because many examiners still wince when they see negative limitations in claims, it's best to avoid them by reciting what the invention is, rather than what it isn't. For instance, instead of saying, "said engine connected to said wheels without any transmission," say "said engine connected directly to said wheels." You are permitted to recite holes, recesses, etc.; see "Voids" in the Glossary for a list of "hole-y" words.

9. Use Proper Alternative Expressions

As with negative limitations, disjunctive expressions—that is, those using "or" or the like—are permissible so long as the two expressions are just different ways of reciting the same things. If two different things are meant, however, try to find a generic term to cover both, or use two separate claims. Thus, instead of saying, "said amplifying circuit containing a vacuum tube or transistor," say "said amplifying circuit employing an amplifying valve." You can also use two claims, one to recite the tube and the other to recite the transistor.

MARKUSH GROUP CLAIMS

A third, sophisticated way to write a claim for an invention with two or more elements is to recite the disjunctive elements by using a Markush group. A Markush (from a decision with that name) group is a series of related elements joined by "and" which follows these magic words: "selected from the group consisting of." Thus, a tube or a transistor could be recited in one claim as follows: "said amplifying circuit containing a device selected from the group consisting of tubes and transistors."

---

10. Avoid Too Many Claims

If you've put in too many similar claims, even though you've paid for them, you'll have to eliminate some to make the examiner's job easier. If you ever have more than 20 claims, the invention should be complex enough or have enough ramifications to justify them and the claims should differ substantially.

11. Make Sure Claims Correspond With Disclosure

First, the literal terms or words of the claim must be present somewhere in the specification. If they aren't, the remedy is to amend the specification by adding the exact terms used in your claims, or to amend the claims by eliminating those terms that aren't literally in the specification. Second, any operation, structure, or result recited in a claim must be clearly and completely described in the "spec."

12. Make Sure Claims Are Supported in Drawing

Nothing is really wrong with the claim here, but remember that the drawings must show every feature recited in the claims. If they don't, amend either the drawing or the claims. A broad recitation in a claim, such as "fuel atomizing means," can be supported by specific hardware, such as a carburetor, in the drawings. But remember that you can't add any new matter to an application once it's on file. So be sure to include all possibly relevant details of your invention in your drawings and spec. before you file. For example, if an examiner rejects a claim that recites "fuel atomizing means" for lack of support in the drawings, you can overcome this rejection by adding a box labeled "fuel atomizing means" to the drawings. You can't add a carbu-retor unless your spec. mentions a carburetor, since this would be verboten new matter.

13. Claim Computer Program as Manipulating Some Hardware or Process

If your invention involves (or actually is) a computer pro-gram or algorithm—that is, a set of instructions for a com-puter—you must claim it in relation to how it works to manipulate some physical structure (including a process), even though minimal. You can't simply claim the software as a process, since the PTO will reject it under 35 USC §101 as non-statutory subject matter (non-SSM). Why not? No one knows for sure why the PTO resisted the first pro-grams. My guess is because of neophobia (fear of the new), lack of understanding, and a wish to avoid work. Anyway, the courts have generally upheld the PTO on this point. See Chapter 5, Section C, for more on this point.

Here's an example of some "program" claims drafted to recite enough hardware to pass muster; these claims go about as far as one can go in claiming programs.

9. *A process of operating a general purpose data processor of known type to enable said data processor to execute formulas in an object program comprising a plurality of formulas, such that the same results will be produced when using the same given data, regardless of the sequence in which said formulas are presented in said object program comprising the steps of:*

  (a) *examining each of said formulas in a storage area of said data processor to determine which formulas can be designated as defined*

  (b) *storing, in the sequence in which each formula is designated as defined, said formulas that are desig-nated as defined, and*

  (c) *repeating steps (a) and (b) for at least undefined formulas as many times as required until all said formulas have been designated as defined and have been stored; thereby producing the same results upon sequential execution of said formulas stored by said process when using the same given data, regardless of the order in which said formulas were presented in the object program prior to said process.* (Pardo & Landau, patent 4,398,249; 1983.)

10. *A method for evaluating Boolean expressions in a computer system, comprising:*

  forming a first constant from the expression to specify rearrangement of the variables,

  setting said first constant into a work area,

  translating said first constant in said work area using the variables as a translate table,

  forming a second constant from the expressions where the second constant functions to change the values of the variables to position numbers having values one less and two less than the position number of the variable and where the second constant changes the zeros between variables into position numbers that point to previous positions in the result string containing values of previously evaluated subexpressions,

  logically combining said translated first constant with said second constant using an exclusive OR operation, and

  translating the result of said exclusive OR operation using the result as the translate table as the result is chang-ing during the translation, the result from last transla-tion in the result being the value of the Boolean expression being evaluated. (Berstis, patent 4,417, 305; 1983)

Note that in the Pardo & Landau patent, the claim recites an algorithm itself; it is limited by or applied to pro-cess steps beyond the algorithm per se. In the Berstis patent, "work area" and "exclusive OR" are part of the process, thereby making it more than an algorithm per se.

Here's an example of a program claim that was rejected as non-statutory because it was essentially just an algorithm:

"A method of diagnosing…comprising: performing lab tests …, producing from said test's parameter values…, compar-ing such values…, [etc.]"

However, here's a similar program claim that was held to be SSM:

"A method of using a computer processor to analyze electri-cal signals and data representative of human cardiac activ-ity by converting said signals to time segments, applying said time segments to a high-pass filter, using said computer processor to determine the amplitude of said filter's output, and comparing said amplitude to a predetermined value."

From a comparison of the last two claims it will be apparent that the claimed process or hardware must be more than a specified algorithmic function. This is because claiming an algorithmic function per se (as does the re-jected claim in the preceding paragraph) would cover the acts of a human using a pencil and paper or mental gym-nastics. If, however, the claim recites a "means" for performing an algorithmic function on or with some hard-ware or practical situation, it will be limited, under the *Donaldson* decision (see Section B, Part 1), to the hardware disclosed in the specification and its equivalents, and thus will pass muster, provided the specification clearly describes hardware which performs the function specified for the means. Also, the courts have held that the mere fact that a claim contains an algorithm will not make it objectionable, so long as it doesn't claim the algorithm per se—that is, it must be limited to hardware in some way. However, if the claim recites essentially an algorithm, and then adds some trivial or common hardware, such as a CRT, it may not pass muster.

14. Recite Each Element Affirmatively as Subject of Its Clause

For maximum clarity, the elements of your invention should be affirmatively and directly recited; don't bring them in by inference or incidentally—for example, say "A transmission comprising: (a) a gear, (b) a shaft, (c) said gear being mounted on said shaft" [etc.], and not "A transmission whose gear is mounted on its shaft " In other words, each significant element of the claim should be recited for the first time (introduced) in a positive manner, preferably with the word "a," so it's the subject of its clause, and not with wording that makes it part of the object or assumes that the reader already knows that it's there. This rule is especially important for do-it-yourselfers to follow in order to write clear and understandable claims.

15. Include Structural Support in Recitation of Operation

Assume a claim recites "a lever connected to move said pendulum to and fro at the same rate as said lights flash." The movement of the pendulum at this special rate is too much for the lever to do all by itself. In other words, there's not enough structural support for the operation recited. The remedy? Recite either (a) enough structure to do the job or (b) use a "means" clause. Here are examples of both methods:

(a) *a photoresponsive electromechanical circuit terminating in a lever that is connected to said pendulum and is arranged to move said pendulum at the same rate as said lights flash.*

(b) *means, including a lever connected to said pendulum, for moving said pendulum at the same rate as said lights flash.*

16. Format

If the claim has several elements or steps, each should be in a separate paragraph with the first line hanging out to the left (see the claims in Section 13 above) or indented.

H. Drafting Your Main (Independent) Claim

As indicated above, there are two basic types of claims: "independent" and "dependent." "Independent claims" are those that don't refer back to any preceding claim; they stand alone. Examples of independent claims are all of those given in the preceding sections of this chapter. Note that these claims don't refer back to any preceding claim and each defines a complete, operative invention by itself.

"Dependent claims," which will be covered in the next section, refer back to a preceding or "parent" claim (this preceding claim can either be independent or dependent). A dependent claim recites narrower subject matter than its preceding claim in either of the two standard ways—that is, either by adding an additional element(s) or defining one or more elements of the preceding claim more narrowly.

The reasons for providing dependent claims will be covered in the next section also; the main point to remember here is that your independent claims are the important ones since they're the basic and broadest definitions of your invention. If a dependent claim is infringed, its independent or parent claim(s) must also be infringed. If an independent claim is infringed, however, that's enough to win the case. You don't have to worry about your dependent claims.

To draft an independent claim, the easiest and most direct way to do it is to follow these four basic steps:

1. Write a preamble giving the name or title of the invention.
2. List the elements (or steps) of the claim.
3. Interconnect the elements or steps.
4. Broaden the claim.

The claim can be structured so that the elements of the claim appear together, followed by the interconnections. Or, each element can appear in conjunction with its interconnection(s) to adjacent element(s). Most patent attorneys use the latter method—see Claims (2), (3), and (4) in Section C, above, for examples—but you may find it easier to recite the interconnections separately. An exception is process claims, where you'll find it easier to directly associate each step with its predecessor.

Start by writing your first claim without regard to breadth—that is, just get a preamble written, set down the elements of the invention, and interconnect them, paying no attention to how broadly you can recite the invention. In other words, just define your invention as you believe necessary to "get it all down" in a complete manner.

Then, see how many elements (or steps) you can eliminate and how many remaining elements you can broaden so that the result maintains sufficient structure and yet does not tread on the prior art too much. Remember that the broadest way of defining any element is by using "means-plus-a-function" language. Don't forget to refer to your prior-art patents for examples.

To provide a real example that everyone can understand, let's assume you've just invented a table. Since you've already written your specification, you have a name for each part of your invention, so that chore is already behind you. (If you believe your part names leave something to be desired, you can get additional part names from your prior-art search patents, the Glossary at the end of this book, the *What's What* book (see Appendix 2, Books of Use and Interest), or in a thesaurus (in a book or computer). All that remains now is to provide a title or preamble. List the parts, interconnect them, and then broaden your claims.

1. The Preamble

To write the preamble, pick a name or title for the whole unit, remembering that you can't use the word "table" since it hasn't been invented until now. Try to put it in a class to which it belongs. Since a table is an "article of furniture," these words would be fine. You could also use any other suitable class, such as a "work station device," a "support for holding objects to be handled by a sitting human," etc. I've used "an article of furniture" and I've added the modifier "for holding objects for a sitting human, comprising" to narrow the field a bit and to make my title more meaningful.

2. The Elements

Next, to list the parts of the table, I'll start with the largest, most visible part, the top, and then add the smaller, less apparent parts, the legs. Since the table's just been invented, we'll assume that the words "top" and "legs" are still unknown, but even if they were, it's not wise to use "top" anyway, since it's a notoriously vague homonym (it can mean anything from a hat to a bottle cap to a toy). To define the top, then, we need a more meaningful term or phrase. Let's suppose we've made a model of our invention and have used a large sheet of chipboard for the top. All we need to do at this stage is to say so; thus our first and most basic element becomes "(a) a large sheet of chipboard."

Suppose our model table has four legs and we've made them of six-cm diameter circular oak dowels, each 65 cm long. Then our legs would be recited simply as "(b) four oak dowels, each having a circular cross section 6 cm in diameter and each 65 cm long." Our elements are now all recited—wasn't that easy!

3. Interconnections

Lastly, we have to interconnect the legs to the top, an easy task. Suppose our legs are joined at the underside of the top using four metal flanges, attached at the four corners of the top with each having a cylindrical portion with female threads, and with the top sections of the legs having mating male threads that are screwed into the respective flanges so that the legs extend at right angles to the top. Merely recite the flanges positively and add an interconnection clause as follows:

   (c) *four flanges, each having means for attachment to one side of said sheet of chipboard and each having a cylindrical portion with female threads, and*

   (d) *said four flanges being attached to one side of said sheet of chipboard at four respective corners thereof and said four oak dowels having male threads on a top section thereof and being screwed into the cylindrical portions of said respective flanges so that said dowels extend from said sheet of chipboard at right angles.*

Eureka! It's done. You've written a complete independent claim.

Here's how it looks:

11. *An article of furniture for holding objects for a sitting human, comprising:*
   (a) *a large sheet of chipboard,*
   (b) *four oak dowels, each having a circular cross section 6 cm in diameter and each 65 cm long, and*
   (c) *four flanges, each having means for attachment to one side of said sheet of chipboard and each having a cylindrical portion with female threads, and*
   (d) *said four flanges [etc.].*

Note that I always recite the elements and their inter-connections in lettered subparagraphs with a hanging indent style. The PTO and courts prefer (but do not require) this format, since it's easier to analyze than a continuous paragraph.

Is there anything wrong with this claim? Yes! As you probably will have realized by now, this claim is far too narrow—that is, it has many elements and each of these is recited too specifically. In fact it even recites specific dimensions, which you don't generally even need in the specification. Thus the claim as written would be easy to avoid infringing: all that an infringer would have to do is to use plywood instead of chipboard, use four pine dowels instead of oak, etc. Let's broaden it then.

Remember, you broaden a claim by (1) eliminating elements where possible, and (2) reciting the remaining elements as broadly as possible.

Going through the claim to eliminate elements, we see that the top can't be eliminated since it's an essential part. However, we don't need to recite four legs—we can eliminate one of these since three legs will support the top. But better yet, we can even use the word "plurality" since this covers two or more legs. (The term "plurality" means more than one. Used here, it is an example of how you'll sometimes need to search for a word or phrase that most broadly describes a particular element. Even though two may not be sufficient to support a top, the PTO will usually not object to this word in this context. We could even go further and eliminate the recitation of legs entirely by reciting "support means," but this would include solid supports, such as in a chest or bureau, which would not be suitable for table-type uses.) Lastly, we can eliminate the flanges, since these aren't essential to the invention and since there are many other possible ways of attaching legs to a table top.

Next, let's go through the claim to see which elements can be recited more broadly. First, the top. Obviously "a large sheet of chipboard" is a very narrow recitation since plywood, solid wood, metal, and plastic tops would avoid infringement. A broad recitation would be "a large sheet of rigid material," but, as stated above, the word "large" is frowned upon by the PTO as too vague to satisfy Section 112. So let's make the top's size more specific. Since we're interested in providing a working surface for humans, let's merely specify that the top is "a sheet of rigid material of sufficient size to accommodate use by a human being for writing and working."

Next the legs. Obviously, the recitation of four circular oak dowels with specific dimensions is very limiting. Let's eliminate the material, shape, and dimensions and recite the legs as merely "a plurality of elongated support members of substantially equal length." This covers square, round,

triangular, and oval legs, regardless of their length or material.

Lastly, instead of the flanges (that we've eliminated as unnecessary) to join the legs to the top, let's use "means" (to make it as broad as possible) as follows: "means for joining said elongated support members at right angles to the underside of said top at spaced locations so as to be able to support said top horizontally."

The result would look like this:

11. *An article of furniture for holding objects for a sitting human, comprising:*

    (a) *a sheet of rigid material of sufficient size to accommodate use by a human being for writing and working*

    (b) *a plurality of elongated support members of equal length*

    (c) *means for joining said elongated support members at right angles to the underside of said sheet at spaced locations so as to be able to support said top horizontally.*

Obviously, Claim 11 is now far broader than our first effort. Your first independent claims should be as broad as possible, but of course, you can't make it so broad that it lacks novelty or unobviousness. Thus, when you eliminate as many elements as possible, and when you broaden the remaining elements in the manner just described, keep in mind that you must leave enough structure or acts to define your invention over the prior art.

Put differently, writing claims is like walking on a fence: you can't sway too far on the side of specificity or you'll fall onto the side of worthlessness and you can't sway too far onto the side of breadth or you'll fall onto the prior art. To obtain the broadest possible coverage, you should not draft your main claim primarily to cover your invention; rather draft it as broadly as possible with at least some thought of clearing the prior art, then go back and make sure that it at least covers your invention.

Some patent attorneys compare the writing of their first claim to passing through a wall of fire. However, I have found that if I follow the above four steps—(1) write a preamble, (2) recite the elements, (3) interconnect them, and (4) broaden the claims—the going is relatively painless. In case of doubt, err on the side of breadth at this stage, since you can always narrow your claims later, but you may not be able to make them broader if the application's allowed on the first office action.

I. Other Techniques in Claim Writing

Now that you understand the basics, here are some other tricks you may want to use when writing your claims. Obviously, not all apply all of the time, but you will probably find that at least several can be used to improve your claim writing.

- Use "weasel" words like "substantially," "about," or "approximately" whenever possible—that is, whenever you specify a dimension or any other specific parameter to avoid limiting your claim to the specific dimension specified. The renowned judge, Learned Hand, who wrote many famous patent decisions, once opined that judges should read the modifier "substantially" into every claim, even if it's not already cited. However, I strongly recommend that you don't rely on a judge to broaden your claim for you, but rather, do it yourself when you first write the claim.

- Provide a proper antecedent in the beginning of your claim for every term you use in the latter part of the claim. For example, in Claim 11 in the preceding part, the clause "the underside of said top" near the end of the claim has no clear antecedent in the beginning of the claim and thus might be objected to by some examiners. The claim would be better if clause (a) were amended by adding, "said sheet having an undersurface" to provide unequivocal support for the underside phase later.

- At the end of your claim, I recommend adding a "whereby" clause to specify the advantage or use of the invention to hammer home to the examiner, or anyone else who reads your claim, the value of your invention. Thus in Claim 11, above, you should add at the end of this claim, "whereby a human can work, eat, and write in a convenient seated position." "Whereby" clauses don't help to define over the prior art, but they do force the examiner to consider the advantages (Section 103 features) of your invention and thus help to get the claims allowed.

- You may put the drawing's reference numerals in your claims after the appropriate elements, but this is seldom done unless the elements of the claim aren't clear.

- If your invention has an opening, hole, or recess in its structure, you may, as stated, recite the hole directly as such, even though it isn't tangible. For example, the recitation "said member having a hole near its upper end" is permissible.

- Sometimes, instead of using the preamble-elements-interconnections approach, it's desirable to omit the preamble, especially if you feel the preamble will be too restrictive, that is, if the elements of the body of the claims can be used for another function. For example, if we recited "A working surface comprising" as a preamble in the above claim and someone used

the actual structure claimed, but turned it upside down and used the legs for a quoit game, it would not infringe since it isn't being used as a working surface. In this case simply start the claim, "In combination:" or "A process comprising:" and then recite the elements or steps and their interconnections.

- With regard to the rarely enforced Rule 75(e) (quoted in Section B.2, above) requiring the use of Jepson (with a preamble containing old elements and body of claims containing improvements of your invention), most patent attorneys recommend that claims *not* be cast in this style unless the examiner requests it or unless the examiner is having trouble understanding exactly what your inventive contribution is. The reason for this is that a Jepson claim isolates and hence minimizes your improvement, making it easier to invalidate. If you do claim in the Jepson format, draft your preamble so that it includes all the elements or steps and their interconnections that are already known from the prior art; then add a "cleavage" clause such as "the improvement comprising" or "characterized in that"; and then recite the elements of your invention and their interconnections.

- Use the word "predetermined" to indicate that something has a size, thickness, length, quality, etc., without limiting the claim to any specific dimension or quality. For example, "said member having a predetermined cross-sectional shape" and "said valve arranged to open when a predetermined gas pressure is developed."

- A claim that recites a group of elements can be made "open" or "closed." An open claim (the normal case) will cover more elements than it recites, whereas a closed claim is limited to and will cover only the elements it specifically recites. To make a claim open, use "includes" or "comprising" —for example, "said machine *comprising* A, B, and C." In this case, a machine with four elements A, B, C, and D will infringe. To make a claim closed (rarely done), use "consist" or "having only"— for example, "Said machine *consisting* of A, B, and C." In this case, a machine with elements A, B, C, and D will not infringe, since, in patent law, the word "consist" is interpreted to mean "having only the following elements."

- Also, whenever you recite several units of anything, preface your recitation with "a plurality of"—such as, "a plurality of holes in said hose."

- Remember that, because of the Boolean "less is more" rule in interpreting claims, it's not necessary to recite a specific feature in your main claim in order to cover that feature in combination with the other elements of your invention. For example, once I drafted a claim for a client where one embodiment of her invention had a fingerlike support. Not seeing the finger in the main claim, she asked me, "Did you claim the finger?" I then explained to her that the main claim was broad enough to cover her invention with or without the finger.

- After drafting your claim, you or a friend should be able to make enough sense out of it to sketch your invention. If this isn't possible, the claim is unclear and needs to be reworked.
- You can use any technical or descriptive terms that you feel are reasonably necessary to define or describe your invention—the claim does not have to be limited to any special "legalese." One patent attorney I know had a devil of a time defining (to the satisfaction of the examiner) a convex transistor structure with a nubbin on top until he simply called it "mammary-shaped."
- If possible, provide a method claim to cover your invention; you usually can do this if there's any dynamic operation involved in the invention. Most machines and electrical circuits can be claimed in terms of a method. Method claims are usually broader than apparatus claims, since they're not limited to any specific hardware.
- Each substantive clause of a method claim must usually start with an "___ing" word, such as "attaching," "heating," "abraiding," etc. If you want to recite some hardware in a method claim, use "providing"—such as, "providing a central processor."
- If you do recite any "means," it's desirable to label the means with an adjective in order to provide a mnemonic aid in case you need to refer to the means later. For example, "distal means," "closing means," etc. Also, the "means" must be followed by or be modified by a function. For example, "plate means" isn't a means plus a function since "plate" isn't a function, but "printing means" is OK since "printing" is a function. (*Ex parte Klumb*, 159 U.S.P.Q. 694 (Pat. Off. Bd. App. 1967).)
- Lastly, many patent attorneys recommend that a claim not be too short. A claim that is short will be viewed adversely (as possibly overly broad) by many examiners, regardless of how much substance it contains. Thus, many patent attorneys like to "pad" short claims by adding whereby clauses, providing long preambles, adding long functional descriptions to their means clauses, etc. The trick here, of course, is to pad the claim while avoiding a charge of undue prolixity under Section 112.

PATENT ATTORNEY WORDS

If you get stuck and don't know how to phrase something, usually one of the "patent attorney words" below will help.

a (used to introduce a part)
about (used to fudge a specific quantity)
at least (used to hammer home that more elements can be used)
contiguous (used to indicate elements are touching)
device for (interpreted like "means for")
disposed (used to indicate a part is positioned in a particular place)
further including (used in dependent claims to add additional parts)
heretofore (used to refer back to something previously recited)
indicium (used to recite something that a human can recognize, such as a mark or a sound)
means for (used to claim something broadly, in terms of its function, rather than specific hardware)
member (used to recite a mechanical part when no other word is available)
multitude (used to recite a large, indefinite number)
pivotably (used to indicate that a part is rotatably mounted)
plurality (used to introduce more than one of an element)
predetermined (used to state that a part has a specific parameter)
providing (used to recite a part in a method claim)
respectively (used to relate several parts to several other parts in an individual manner)
said (used to refer to a previously recited part by exactly the same word)
sandwiching (used to indicate that one part is between two other parts)
selected from the group consisting of (used in a Markush claim to create an artificial group)
slidably (used to indicate that two parts slide with respect to each other)
so that (used to restrict a part to a defined function)
substantially (used to fudge a specific recitation)
such that (used to restrict a part to a defined function)
surrounding (used to indicate that a part is surrounded)
the (used to refer to a previously recited part by a slightly different word)
thereof (used as a pronoun to avoid repeating a part name)
urging (used to indicate that force is exacted upon a part)
whereby (used to introduce a function or result at the end of a claim)
wherein (used in a dependent claim to recite an element (part) more specifically)
(For names of components, see Appendix 3, Glossary.)

J.   Drafting Dependent Claims

In Section H, I pointed out that there are two basic types of claims—independent claims (these stand on their own) and dependent claims (these incorporate an entire other claim, which can be a previous independent or dependent claim). A dependent claim is simply a shorthand way of writing a narrower claim—that is, a claim that includes all the elements of the previous claim, and adds one or more additional elements or narrows one or more elements of the previous claim.

Reasons for Writing Dependent Claims:

1. **Backup.** Dependent claims are by definition always narrower than the claims on which they depend. You may accordingly be wondering, "If my broad independent claim covers my invention, why do I need any more claims of narrower scope?" True, if all goes well, your broad claim will be all you'll need. However, suppose you sue an infringer who finds an appropriate prior-art reference that neither you nor the PTO examiner found and that adversely affects the validity of ("knocks out") your broad claim. If you've written a narrower claim you can then disclaim the broad claim and fall back on the narrower claim. If the narrower claim is patentable over the prior art, your patent will still prevail. Each claim, whether independent or dependent, is interpreted independently for examination and infringement purposes. If the claim is dependent, it's interpreted as if it included all the wording of its parent (incorporated) claim or claims, even if the incorporated claim is held invalid.

2. **Reification of Broad Claims.** Dependent claims are useful to explain and reify (make real) some of the broad, abstract terms in your independent claims. For instance, if you recite in a claim "additive means," many judges may not be able to understand what the "additive means" actually covers, but if you add several dependent claims that state, respectively, that the additive means is benzine and toluene, they'll get a very good idea of what types of substances the additive means embraces. If your main claim recites a new parlor game, adding a dependent claim that recites that the game is simulated on a computer will make it clear that the main claim covers computer simulation as well as board versions. (Don't forget to show the computer version in your drawings and discuss it in your specification.)

3. **Provide Spectrum of Coverage.** Narrower claims can be used to provide a range, spectrum, or menu of proposed coverage from very broad to very narrow so that your examiner can, by allowing some narrower claims and rejecting the broader ones, indicate the scope of coverage the examiner's willing to allow.

4. **Prevent Premature Final Action.** Providing dependent claims of varying scope and approaches forces the examiner to make a wider search of your invention on the first examination. This will prevent the examiner from citing new prior art against your application on the second office action, which usually must be made "final." (See Chapter 13.) Thus, you should include every possibly novel feature (or novel combination of features) of your invention in your dependent claims.

5. **Provide Broader Base for Infringement Damages.** By providing dependent claims that add more elements, you define your invention (in these claims) as a more comprehensive structure, thereby providing a broader base upon which a judge can calculate infringement damages.

6. **Provide a Specific, Descriptive Recitation.** This reason is slightly different than ¶ 2 above. If the recitation in the independent claim is broad and abstract, such as, "urging means for …," I strongly recommend that you provide dependent claims with a descriptive, definite recitation (for example, "wherein said urging means is a coil spring") to hit the nail on the head, or provide a specific hardware recitation so a judge won't have to use his or her imagination.

For these reasons, when you're satisfied with your first, basic and broadest independent claim, you should write as many dependent claims as you can think of. Each dependent claim should begin by referring to your basic claim, or a previous dependent claim, using its exact title.

If the dependent claim is narrowing one or more elements of the independent claim, it should use the word "wherein"—for example, "The bicycle of Claim 1 wherein"—and then continue by narrowing the elements of the independent claim.

If the dependent claim is adding additional elements, it should use the words, "further including"—for example, "The bicycle of Claim 1, further including..."—then continue by reciting the additional feature(s) of your invention. The additional features can be those you eliminated in broadening your basic claims and all other subsidiary features, including all combinations and permutations of such features of your invention you can think of. The features added or narrowed by the dependent claims can be specific parameters (such as materials and temperatures) or other specifics of your invention (such as specific shapes, additional elements, or specific modes of operation). Refer to your prior art patents for guidance on how to draft these.

Note that a dependent claim must either recite the elements of its parent claim more specifically, or add additional elements. It may not change any element to a different type or kind. Thus, if your parent claim recites "1. A house made of red bricks," your dependent claim can't say "2. The house of Claim 1 wherein said bricks are yellow." It can say "2. The house of Claim 1 wherein said bricks are made of clay" (recites bricks more specifically) or "2. The house of Claim 1, further including a layer of paint over said bricks" (adds additional structure).

Here are some dependent claims for Claim 11 (set out in Section H, above). Note that each dependent claim either adds an element to the coverage of Claim 11 or narrows an already recited element.

11. *An article of furniture (etc.).*
  12. *The article of furniture of Claim 11 wherein said sheet of rigid material is made of wood.*
    13. *The article of furniture of Claim 12 wherein said sheet of rigid material of wood is made of chipboard.*
      14. *The article of furniture of Claim 13 wherein said sheet of chipboard has a rectangular shape.*
  15. *The article of furniture of Claim 11, wherein said means for joining comprises a set of flanges, each of which joins a respective one of said support members to the underside of said sheet of rigid material.*
    16. *The article of furniture of Claim 15 wherein each of said flanges is made of iron and includes a cylinder with female threads and wherein one end of each of said elongated members has male threads and is threadedly mated with the female threads of a respective one of said flanges.*

17. *The article of furniture of Claim 11, further including a layer of a rigid plastic laminate bonded to a top side of said sheet of rigid material.*

Note that a dependent claim may be dependent upon the parent claim or another dependent claim. A dependent claim should be numbered as closely as possible to the number of its parent claim. Note also how I've made a physical indication of claim dependency by indenting (nesting) each dependent claim under its parent claim(s) as shown above. This is optional, but makes things clearer for you and the examiner.

MULTIPLE DEPENDENT CLAIMS

A dependent claim may actually be made dependent upon several previous claims (called "multiple dependent claiming" and common in Europe), but I recommend that you do *not* include multiple dependent claims (e.g., "*3. The widget of claims 1 or 2 wherein…*) since the PTO's examiners dislike the practice, there's a stiff surcharge for the privilege, and for fee purposes each MDC counts as the number of claims to which it refers. (See Appendix 4, Fee Schedule.)

A dependent claim will be read and interpreted by examiners and judges as if it incorporated all the limitations of its parent claim(s). Thus suppose your independent and dependent claims read, respectively, as follows:

18. *A rifle having an upwardly curved barrel.*
  19. *The rifle of Claim 18 wherein said barrel is made of austenitic steel.*

The dependent claim (19) will be treated independently, but with Claim 18 incorporated, so that it effectively reads as follows:

19. *A rifle having an upwardly curved barrel, said barrel being made of austenitic steel.*

USE ONLY SIGNIFICANT LIMITATIONS

You can make your dependent claims as specific as you want, even to reciting the dimensions of the table top, its color, etc. However, extremely specific limitations like this, while possibly defining an invention that is novel over the prior art (Section 102), do not recite unobvious subject matter (Section 103), so they'll be of little use to fall back on if you lose your independent claim. Thus, you should mainly try to use *significant* limitations in your dependent claims—that is, limitations that an infringer might use if he or she made your invention.

You should try to draft at least one dependent claim with as many parts as possible so as to provide as broad a base as possible for maximizing infringement damages. Also try, insofar as possible, to draft at least one claim to cover parts of the invention whose infringement would be publicly verifiable, rather than a nonverifiable factory process or machine.

As with independent claims, you should not make your dependent claims purely "functional"—that is, each dependent claim should contain enough physical structure to support its operational or functional language. Here are some examples:

WRONG:

> 17. The bicycle of Claim 16 wherein said derailleur *operates with continuously variable speed-to-power ratios.* [This claim has no structure to support its operational limitation.]

RIGHT:

> 17. The bicycle of Claim 16 wherein said derailleur *contains means for causing it to operate with continuously variable speed-to-power ratios.* [The "means" limitation is a recitation of structure that supports the operational limitation.]

RIGHT:

> 17. The bicycle of Claim 16 wherein said derailleur *contains a cone-shaped pulley and a belt pusher for causing it to operate with continuously variable speed-to-power ratios.* [The pulley and pusher constitute structure that supports the operational limitation.]

If your independent claim recites a means plus a function, your dependent claim should modify the means and not the function. For example, assume an independent Claim 20 recites, "variable means for causing said transmission to have a continuously variable gear ratio." Here are the right and wrong ways to further limit this "means" in a dependent claim:

WRONG:

> 21. The transmission of Claim 20 wherein said continuously variable gear ratio ranges from 5 to 10.

RIGHT:

> 21. The transmission of Claim 20 wherein said variable means is arranged to provide ratios from 5 to 10.

Common Misconception: *If a dependent claim recites a specific feature of your invention, say a two-inch nylon gear, your invention will be limited to this gear so that if any copy of the invention uses a one-inch gear, or a steel gear, it won't infringe on your patent.*

Fact: *Although the copy won't infringe the dependent claim, it will infringe the independent claim so long as it isn't limited to this specific feature. And as long as even one claim of a patent is infringed, the patent is infringed and you can recover as much damages (money) as if 50 claims were infringed.*

Common Misconception: *The limitations in a dependent claim will narrow its independent claim.*

Fact: *The independent claim is interpreted independently of its dependent claims and the latter never narrow the former.*

If you still don't get the principle of broad and narrow claims, here are three simple claims that everyone can understand:

1. All eye-care professionals.
2. The persons of Claim 1 who are medical doctors.
3. The persons of Claim 2 who are strasbismologists living in the City of Belvedere.

Claim 1 is very broad: it will cover ophthalmologists, optometrists, and opticians all over the earth. Claim 2 is of intermediate scope: although it's longer than #1, it's narrower in scope since it eliminates everyone but MDs. Claim 3 is very narrow: it's still longer than Claim 2, but is far narrower since it eliminates all MDs except strasbismologists living in Belvedere.

As indicated above in Section G1, if you're working on a computer, use its "windows" function (if available) to keep your independent claim displayed while you write your dependent claims.

CLAIMS OF DIFFERENT SCOPE

The concept of claims of different scope (independent and dependent) is confusing to most inventors. Here's another way of explaining it, if you still don't understand.

An *independent claim* is one that *doesn't* refer back to any previous claim. For example, "*1. A telephone comprising (a) a base, (b) a handset, and (c) a rotary dial.*" is an example of an independent claim.

To write another independent claim like Claim 1 (C1), but which is narrower than C1 by reciting a base of black plastic, simply repeat all of Claim 1 and add that the base is black plastic. For example, "*2. A telephone comprising (a) a base of black plastic, (b) a handset, and (c) a rotary dial.*" is an example of a second independent claim which is narrower than C1.

However, there's an easier, shorter, and cheaper way to avoid repeating all of C1 each time: Simply write a claim that refers to the independent claim (#1) so as to incorporate all of it by reference, and then state how it should be narrowed. Such a shorthand claim is called a *dependent claim* (DC). A DC is thus one that refers back to and incorporates all of a preceding claim and adds or modifies one or more limitations to recite the invention more narrowly. For example, "*2´. The telephone of Claim 1 wherein said base is made of black plastic.*" is a claim of exactly the same scope as C2. C2´ will be interpreted as if it included *all* of the subject matter of C1, *together with the additional subject matter in C2´.*

It follows that to infringe a DC, a device must have all of the elements of the DC, *plus all of the elements of the preceding claim.*

Thus, adding a DC to recite a specific feature of your invention won't broaden or narrow your coverage; it will just provide another, yet more precise, missile. The six reasons for including DCs are in Part J.

Also note that a DC can refer back to a preceding claim, and the preceding claim can in turn refer back to a further preceding claim. To infringe such a *third-level DC*, the device must have *all* of the elements of *all three claims* in the chain.

K. Drafting Additional Sets of Claims

After you've written your first independent claim and all the dependent claims you can think of (all numbered sequentially), consider writing another set of claims (an independent claim and a set of dependent claims) if you can think of a substantially different way to claim your invention. See the prior-art patents and the sample set of claims at the end of this chapter (Fig. 9A) for examples of different independent claims on the same invention. Your second set of dependent claims can be similar to your first set; a word processor with a block copy function will be of great aid here. Writing more sets of claims will not give your invention broader coverage, but will provide alternative weapons to use against an infringer. That is, writing a second set of claims is like going into battle with a sword as well as a gun. Also, writing more sets of claims will give your examiner additional perspectives on your invention. That is, your chances of getting your examiner to bite will be increased if you present many flavors to choose from.

In the example above (Claim 11), I might start my second independent claim with the legs instead of the top and I might try to define the top and legs differently—for example, instead of "elongated members," I might call the legs "independent support means." Instead of calling the top a "sheet of rigid material," I might call it a "planar member having paralleled, opposed major faces."

Here are still other ways to write a different independent claim: (1) Rewrite one of the dependent claims from your first set in independent form; (2) wait a few days and write an independent claim again, with independent thought; and (3) write the second independent claim by reciting the elements of the first independent claim in reverse or inverse order.

Another valuable way to write a different independent claim is to provide a method (process) claim if your first independent claim is an apparatus claim, or vice versa; you're allowed to have both method and apparatus claims in the same case. You should always include an independent method claim if possible, since a method claim is usually not limited to specific hardware and thus affords broader coverage. Every step of each independent method claim must be an action step, for instance, "providing…" or "heating…."

Your filing fee entitles you to up to three independent claims and 20 total claims. I generally try to use up my allotment by writing three independent claims and three sets of five to seven dependent claims each. However, if I feel that I can write a fourth, substantially different independent claim and the cost can be borne by my client, I will add it, plus more dependent claims. The PTO charges for each independent claim over three, and for each claim (independent or dependent) over 20.

On the other hand, for relatively simple inventions, I may not be able to think of any substantially different ways to write an independent claim, so I may submit only one, plus a few dependent claims. I advise you generally not to submit more than the number of claims permitted for your basic filing fee—that is, three independent claims and 20 total claims—unless the complexity of your invention justifies it, or you have some other good reason.

As with the specification, be sure to review your claims very carefully after you've written them.

L. Checklist for Drafting Claims

Here's the second part of the application checklist that I started in Chapter 8. As before, I suggest you go through this list carefully and make any needed corrections in your claims before going on to Chapter 10.

CHECKLIST FOR DRAFT CLAIMS

☐ C01. Grammatical articles are used properly in the claims:

"a" or "an" to introduce any singular part,

"the" to refer to a part a second time when using a different (but clearly implied) term as before, and,

"said" only to refer to a part using the IDENTICAL term as before.

☐ C02. Two articles together, such as "the said," aren't used.

☐ C03. Every part and feature in every claim is shown in the drawings and discussed in the specification.

☐ C04. No claim uses any disjunctive ("or") expression (except to recite two equivalent parts or a disjunctive function of a machine).

☐ C05. No claim uses any naked functional clause; all claims contain a structural recitation or "means" to support every functional recitation.

☐ C06. A function is recited adjacent each "means"; also, each "means" has a label (such as "lever means") if the function itself doesn't provide a label.

☐ C07. For each unique "means" followed by a function in the claims, the specification describes some hardware or an element which implements or provides the function for such means, using the same words as used in the claim to describe the function.

☐ C08. "Consisting" isn't used in any claim (except to say "having only").

☐ C09. No claim uses any abbreviation, dash, parentheses, or quote.

☐ C10. No term is used for the first time in any claim.

☐ C11. The subparagraph form is used in long claims for ease of reading.

☐ C12. Each claim has just one capital letter and one period (except lettered paragraphs), and no parentheses (except lettered paragraphs, quotes, abbreviations, or trademarks.)

☐ C13. All significant parts are affirmatively recited in the claims as the subject and not the object of a clause.

☐ C14. The main (independent) claim is made as broad as possible by reciting minimum number of elements and by generalizing existing elements (without reading on prior art).

☐ C15. No vague, loose, or casual language is used in any claim.

☐ C16. Space between adjacent claims is greater than space between adjacent lines of a claim.

☐ C17. No dependent claim recites an additional function unless "means" or structure is specified to support such structure.

☐ C18. All parts recited in claims are connected together.

☐ C19. All claims recite enough parts to provide a complete assemblage.

☐ C20. You haven't submitted over 20 total or over three independent claims unless the case is very complex or extra claims are justified.

☐ C21. No independent claim refers to any other claim and all dependent claims refer to a previous claim in line 1 or line 2.

☐ C22. You've filed enough dependent claims to cover all features and permutations and you've filed second and third sets of claims (with differently phrased independent claims) if possible.

☐ C23. You've included an independent method claim and dependent method claims, if possible.

☐ C.24. You've included a structural (no "means" clauses) independent claim.

☐ C25. Every dependent claim starts with either:
"The _____of Claim x wherein..." to narrow existing element(s), or
"The _____of Claim x, further including..." to add new element(s).

☐ C26. No dependent claim is used to substitute a different part for any part recited in its parent claim; each dependent claim either narrows or adds to the existing parts of its parent claim.

☐ C27. No dependent claim recites a method limitation if its parent claim is an apparatus claim, and vice versa.

☐ C28. The same element isn't recited more than once in any claim unless the second and later recitations use "said" before the element.

start claims on new page

10

Printout should have minimum 1.5 line spacing (4 lines/inch) but is shown with denser spacing since this example is shown on a reduced scale.

first independent claim

Claims: I claim:

1. In a bag closure of the type comprising a flat body of material having a lead-in notch on one edge thereof and a gripping aperture adjacent to and communicating with said notch, the improvement wherein said closure has a layer of paper laminated on one of its sides.

2. The closure of claim 1 wherein said body of material is composed of polyethyleneterephthalate.

optional indent for dependent claims

3. The closure of claim 1 wherein said body is elongated and has a longitudinal groove which is on said one side of said body and extends the full length of said one side, from said gripping aperture to the opposite edge.

4. The closure of claim 3 wherein said groove is formed into and along the full length of said lamination.

5. The closure of claim 1 wherein said body is elongated and has a longitudinal groove which is on the side of said body opposite to said one side thereof and extends the full length of said one side, from said gripping aperture to the opposite edge.

6. The closure of claim 1 wherein said body is elongated and has two longitudinal grooves which are on opposite sides of said body and extend the full lengths of said sides, from said gripping aperture to the opposite edge.

7. The closure of claim 6 wherein the groove on said one side of said body is formed into and along the full length of said lamination.

8. The closure of claim 1 wherein said body has a paper lamination on both of said sides.

9. The closure of claim 8 wherein a groove is on one side of said body and extends the full length of said one side, from said gripping aperture to the opposite edge.

second independent claim, phrased differently than first

10. The closure of claim 8 wherein two grooves, on opposite sides of said body, extend the full lengths of said sides, from said gripping aperture to the opposite edge.

11. The closure of claim 10 wherein said grooves are rolled into and along the full lengths of said laminations, respectively.

Fig. 9A—Claims for Sample Patent Application

11

12. The closure of claim 1 wherein said paper lamination is colored.

13. The closure of claim 1 wherein said body is elongated and has a longitudinal through-hole.

14. A bag closure of the type comprising a flat body of material having a lead-in notch on one edge thereof, a gripping aperture adjacent to and communicating with said notch, characterized in that one of its sides has a layer of paper laminated thereon.

15. The closure of claim 14 wherein said body of material is composed of polyethyleneterephthalate.

16. The closure of claim 14 wherein said body is elongated and has a longitudinal groove on said one side of said body and which extends the full length of said one side, from said gripping aperture to the opposite edge.

17. The closure of claim 14 wherein said body is elongated and has a longitudinal groove which is on the side of said body opposite to said one side thereof and extends the full length of said one side, from said gripping aperture to the opposite edge.

18. The closure of claim 14 wherein said body is elongated and has two longitudinal grooves which are on opposite sides of said body and extend the full lengths of said sides, from said gripping aperture to the opposite edge.

19. The closure of claim 14 wherein said body has a paper lamination on both of said sides.

20. The closure of claim 19 wherein a groove is on one side of said body and extends the full length of said one side, from said gripping aperture to the opposite edge.

21. The closure of claim 19 wherein two grooves, on opposite sides of said body, extend the full lengths of said sides, from said griping aperture to the opposite edge.

22. The closure of claim 14 wherein said paper lamination is colored.

23. The closure of claim 14 wherein said body is elongated and has a longitudinal through-hole.

abstract follows on new page—
see Ch. 8

Fig. 9A (cont'd)—Claims for Sample Patent Application

CHAPTER

10

Finaling and Mailing Your Application

INVENTOR'S COMMANDMENT #14:

Before signing any document, whether in the patent field or elsewhere, read, understand, and agree to it fully. After signing, obtain and save an identical copy of what you signed.

INVENTOR'S COMMANDMENT #15:

Avoid Fraud: In addition to making a full disclosure, promptly tell the PTO, in Information Disclosure Statements, about any pertinent "prior art" or other material facts concerning your invention of which you are aware.

INVENTOR'S COMMANDMENT #16:

Every time you send any paper(s) to the PTO, include a receipt postcard addressed to you with all of the paper(s) listed on the back of the card. Also, be sure all blanks on all forms are completed, all forms are signed, a signed check is included, if needed, all pages are present, and the document is being timely mailed.

INVENTOR'S COMMANDMENT #17:

Orderly File: Prepare and maintain an "official papers" file jacket; in it, mount an identical copy of every paper you send to the PTO, together with every paper you receive from the PTO.

Now that you've drafted your patent application, it's time to put it in final form. Since the PTO places great emphasis on thoroughness, this chapter is, accordingly, filled with many picky details. In the event you want to rebel and simply pass over those requirements that are inconvenient, remember that the PTO has many rules you must comply with and that your patent examiner has enormous discretion over whether your application will be approved or rejected. An application that fully meets the requirements and standards of the PTO will have a better chance than one that doesn't.

Fortunately, while you must pay attention to detail, meeting the PTO's requirements and standards is relatively easy if you've followed my suggestions in the previous chapters. Because you've reviewed a number of patents in the same field as your own, you'll be familiar with the standards for writing the specification and claims (Chapters 8 and 9). Because you've prepared preliminary drawings (Chapter 8) in basic conformance with the rules for final drawings, putting them in final form will not involve great difficulty. Because you've analyzed all relevant prior art known to you and can distinguish it from your invention, you are in a good position to follow through with your application to a successful completion (Chapter 13).

Enough said. Let's get started.

A. The Drawing Choices

You have two basic choices for your drawings. You can file the application with:

- *Formal drawings* (generally CAD drawings or other computer-created drawings or xerographic copies of ink drawings done with instruments on Bristol board or Mylar film and in accordance with all the rules), or
- *Informal drawings* (generally xerographic copies of good pencil or ink sketches, which include all the details of the invention).

Further, in each case the drawings can be filed in either:

- The U.S. letter size (8.5" x 11"), or
- The A4 international size (210 mm x 297 mm).

Which type of drawing should you submit—formal or informal? I strongly recommend that, if at all possible, you do formal drawings. Formal drawings look much nicer and neater and thus will make a far better impression on the examiner, showing that you're serious about the invention. Remember, "Quality is remembered long after price is forgotten."—Stanley Marcus. However, if cost and time are important considerations, you should file informal drawings. If you do, the PTO will examine your application in the same way, but will require you to file formal drawings when and if any claims are allowed, or when the entire application is allowed. Also, you'll have to prepare formal drawings about 11 months after filing if you want to file abroad; see Chapter 12. Photographs (black and white or color) are now acceptable, provided a petition and a fee accompany the application; see below.

As far as the choice of the U.S. or international sizes is concerned, if you have any serious thoughts about filing abroad, it's better to use the international (A4) size, since you can make good photocopies, file these for your U.S. application, and later use the originals (or another good set of copies) for the international application. (I discuss foreign filing in Chapter 12.) If you do use the U.S. size and later decide to foreign file, you can still make A4 copies by using a photocopier or a patent drawing service in the Arlington, Virginia, area (about $17 a sheet).

Color photos or color drawings may also be used if necessary to illustrate the invention properly. File three sets of color photos or drawings in one of the four permitted sizes with:

1. a petition explaining why color is necessary
2. the petition fee (see Appendix 4, Fee Schedule), and
3. a statement in the specification just below the title reading as follows: "The file of this patent contains at least one color drawing. Copies of the patent with color drawings will be provided by the PTO upon payment of necessary fee."

Black and white photos may also be used for patent drawings, even if not necessary to illustrate the invention. File three sets of B&W photos in one of the four permitted sizes on double-weight photographic paper or mounted on Bristol board with:

1. a petition requesting that B&W photos be accepted (no explanation is necessary), and
2. the petition fee (see Appendix 4, Fee Schedule).

For the Petition (B&W or color), retype Form 10-7, changing the heading to "Petition to Submit B&W [Color] Drawings" and changing the body to "Applicant(s) request(s) that B&W [color] drawings be accepted in this application. Enclosed is a petition fee of $____. [Color drawings are necessary to illustrate the invention because ....]"

All photos must be of sufficient quality that all details can be reproduced in the printed patent and the photos must illustrate all features of the invention, just as ink or CAD drawings must do. It you can't draw too well, this may prove to be a viable alternative to hiring a patent drafter. However, weigh the petition and photo costs against the drafter's fee.

B. PTO Rules for Drawings

The PTO has a number of rules for preparing formal drawings. Even if you plan to submit informal drawings, the rules should be followed as much as possible so that much of the work will already be done in the event you later need to submit formal drawings (they are required if your patent application is allowed). For step-by-step instructions and examples on how to implement these rules, see *The Patent Drawing Book*, by Jack Lo and David Pressman (Nolo Press).

When your drawings arrive at the PTO, whether with your application or after allowance, your drawings are inspected by the PTO's drawing inspectors, who are themselves draftspersons. If they find that any of your drawings are informal or in violation of any of the above rules, they will fill out and insert a drawing objection sheet in your file. A copy of this (shown in Fig. 10A) will be sent to you with your first office action or after allowance. (See Chapter 13.) You must correct the drawings before a patent can issue by substituting new drawings. Because your drawings may no longer be borrowed from the PTO, you should keep the originals of your drawings and send in good photocopies. Then if you have to correct the drawings, you can correct your originals and then send in new photocopies.

The most common drawing defects are listed on the drawing inspector's sheet (Fig. 10A). These and other frequently encountered defects are as follows:

- Lines are pale
- Paper is poor
- Numerals are poor
- Lines are rough, blurred, or matrixy (zig-zag)
- Copier marks are on the drawing
- Shade lines are required
- Figures must be numbered
- Heading space is required
- Figures must not be connected
- Criss-cross or double line hatching is objectionable
- Arrowheads are used on lead lines for individual parts
- Parts in section must be hatched
- Solid black is objectionable
- Figure legends are placed incorrectly (for example, inside figure or vertically when drawing is horizontal)
- Drawing has mounted photographs
- Drawing contains extraneous matter
- Paper is undersized or oversized
- Margins are too small
- Lettering is too small
- Figures contain dimension lines
- The sheets contain wrinkles, tears, or folds
- Both sides of the sheet are used
- Margin lines have been used
- Sheets contain too many erasures

Rcd 950 28

Form PTO 948 (Rev. 10-93)   U.S. DEPARTMENT OF COMMERCE - Patent and Trademark Office   Application No. **07/883567**

NOTICE OF DRAFTSPERSON'S PATENT DRAWING REVIEW

PTO Draftspersons review all originally filed drawings regardless of whether they are designated as formal or informal. Additionally, patent Examiners will review the drawings for compliance with the regulations. Direct telephone inquiries concerning this review to the Drawing Review Branch, 703-305-8404.

The drawings filed (insert date) **9/27/95** , are
A. ___ not objected to by the Draftsperson under 37 CFR 1.84 or 1.152.
B. _✓_ objected to by the Draftsperson under 37 CFR 1.84 or 1.152 as indicated below. The Examiner will require submission of new, corrected drawings when necessary. Corrected drawings must be submitted according to the instructions on the back of this Notice.

1. DRAWINGS. 37 CFR 1.84(a): Acceptable categories of drawings:
Black ink. Color.
___ Not black solid lines. Fig(s)_____
___ Color drawings are not acceptable until petition is granted.

2. PHOTOGRAPHS. 37 CFR 1.84(b)
___ Photographs are not acceptable until petition is granted.

3. GRAPHIC FORMS. 37 CFR 1.84 (d)
___ Chemical or mathematical formula not labeled as separate figure.
Fig(s)_____
___ Group of waveforms not presented as a single figure, using common vertical axis with time extending along horizontal axis.
Fig(s)_____
___ Individuals waveform not identified with a separate letter designation adjacent to the vertical axis. Fig(s)_____

4. TYPE OF PAPER. 37 CFR 1.84(e)
___ Paper not flexible, strong, white, smooth, nonshiny, and durable.
Sheet(s)_____
___ Erasures, alterations, overwritings, interlineations, cracks, creases, and folds not allowed. Sheet(s)_____

Transparent objectionable Figs 1, 3

5. SIZE OF PAPER. 37 CFR 1.84(f): Acceptable paper sizes:
___ 21.6 cm. by 35.6 cm. (8 1/2 by 14 inches)
___ 21.6 cm. by 33.1 cm. (8 1/2 by 13 inches)
___ 21.6 cm. by 27.9 cm. (8 1/2 by 11 inches)
___ 21.0 cm. by 29.7 cm. (DIN size A4)
___ All drawing sheets not the same size. Sheet(s)_____
___ Drawing sheet not an acceptable size. Sheet(s)_____

_4 5 12_

6. MARGINS. 37 CFR 1.84(g): Acceptable margins:

Paper size			
21.6 cm. X 35.6 cm.	21.6 cm. X 33.1 cm.	21 cm. X 27.9 cm.	21 cm. X 29.7 cm.
(8 1/2 X 14 inches)	(8 1/2 X 13 inches)	(8 1/2 X 11 inches)	(DIN Size A4)
T 5.1 cm. (2")	2.5 cm. (1")	2.5 cm. (1")	2.5cm.
L .64 cm. (1/4")	.64 cm. (1/4")	.64 cm. (1/4")	2.5 cm.
R .64 cm. (1/4")	.64 cm. (1/4")	.64 cm. (1/4")	1.5 cm.
B .64 cm. (1/4")	.64 cm. (1/4")	.64 cm. (1/4")	1.0 cm.

___ Margins do not conform to chart above.
Sheet(s)_____
___Top (T) ___ Left (L) ___Right (R) ___Bottom (B)

7. VIEWS. 37 CFR 1.84(h)
REMINDER: Specification may require revision to correspond to drawing changes.
___ All views not grouped together. Fig(s)_____
___ Views connected by projection lines. Fig(s)_____
___ Views contain center lines. Fig(s)_____
Partial views. 37 CFR 1.84(h)(2)
___ Separate sheets not linked edge to edge.
Fig(s)_____
___ View and enlarged view not labeled separately.
Fig(s)_____
___ Long view relationship between different parts not clear and unambiguous. 37 CFR 1.84(h)(2)(ii)
Fig(s)_____
Sectional views. 37 CFR 1.84(h)(3)
___ Hatching not indicated for sectional portions of an object.
Fig(s)_____
_✓_ Hatching of regularly spaced oblique parallel lines not spaced sufficiently. Fig(s)_____
___ Hatching not at substantial angle to surrounding axes or principal lines. Fig(s)__ **3**
___ Cross section not drawn same as view with parts in cross section with regularly spaced parallel oblique strokes.
Fig(s)_____
___ Hatching of juxtaposed different elements not angled in a different way. Fig(s)_____
Alternate position. 37 CFR 1.84(h)(4)
___ A separate view required for a moved position.
Fig(s)_____

Modified forms. 37 CFR 1.84(h)(5)
___ Modified forms of construction must be shown in separate views.
Fig(s)_____

8. ARRANGEMENT OF VIEWS. 37 CFR 1.84(i)
___ View placed upon another view or within outline of another.
Fig(s)_____
___ Words do not appear in a horizontal, left-to-right fashion when page is either upright or turned so that the top becomes the right side, except for graphs. Fig(s)_____

9. SCALE. 37 CFR 1.84(k)
___ Scale not large enough to show mechanism without crowding when drawing is reduced in size to two-thirds in reproduction.
Fig(s)_____
___ Indication such as "actual size" or "scale 1/2" not permitted.
Fig(s)_____
___ Elements of same view not in proportion to each other.
Fig(s)_____

10. CHARACTER OF LINES, NUMBERS, & LETTERS. 37 CFR 1.84(l)
_✓_ Lines, numbers & letters not uniformly thick and well defined, clean, durable, and black (except for color drawings).
Fig(s)_____

11. SHADING. 37 CFR 1.84(m)
___ Shading used for other than shape of spherical, cylindrical, and conical elements of an object, or for flat parts.
Fig(s)_____
___ Solid black shading areas not permitted. Fig(s)_____

12. NUMBERS, LETTERS, & REFERENCE CHARACTERS. 37 CFR 1.84(p)
___ Numbers and reference characters not plain and legible. 37 CFR 1.84(p)(1) Fig(s)_____
___ Numbers and reference characters used in conjuction with brackets, inverted commas, or enclosed within outlines. 37 CFR 1.84(p)(1) Fig(s)_____
___ Numbers and reference characters not oriented in same direction as the view. 37 CFR 1.84(p)(1) Fig(s)_____
___ English alphabet not used. 37 CFR 1.84(p)(2)
Fig(s)_____
___ Numbers, letters, and reference characters do not measure at least .32 cm. (1/8 inch) in height. 37 CFR(p)(3)
Fig(s)_____

13. LEAD LINES. 37 CFR 1.84(q)
___ Lead lines cross each other. Fig(s)_____
___ Lead lines missing. Fig(s)_____
___ Lead lines not as short as possible. Fig(s)_____

14. NUMBERING OF SHEETS OF DRAWINGS. 37 CFR 1.84(t)
___ Number appears in top margin. Fig(s)_____
___ Number not larger than reference characters.
Fig(s)_____
___ Sheets not numbered consecutively, and in Arabic numerals, beginning with number 1. Sheet(s)_____

15. NUMBER OF VIEWS. 37 CFR 1.84(u)
___ Views not numbered consecutively, and in Arabic numerals, beginning with number 1. Fig(s)_____
___ View numbers not preceded by the abbreviation Fig.
Fig(s)_____
___ Single view contains a view number and the abbreviation Fig.
___ Numbers not larger than reference characters.
Fig(s)_____

16. CORRECTIONS. 37 CFR 1.84(w)
___ Corrections not durable and permanent. Fig(s)_____

17. DESIGN DRAWING. 37 CFR 1.152
___ Surface shading shown not appropriate. Fig(s)_____
___ Solid black shading not used for color contrast.
Fig(s)_____

ATTACHMENT TO PAPER NO. **9**   REVIEWER **CBR**   DATE **10/25/95**

Applicant's Copy

Fig. 10A—Draftman's Drawing Objection Sheet

Although the PTO form still refers to four sizes of paper, new rules only allow two sizes: 8 1/2 x 11" and A4.

- Sheets contain broken lines to illustrate regular parts of the invention
- Sheets contain alterations, interlineations, or overwritings
- Sheets contain unclear representations
- Sheets contain freehand lines
- Sheets contain figures on separate sheets that can't be assembled without concealing parts
- Sheets contain reference numerals that aren't mentioned in the specification
- Sheets contain the same reference numeral to designate different parts
- Figures aren't separately numbered
- Drawings contain dimensions.

SUMMARY OF PTO DRAWING RULES

1. **Need for Drawings:** Drawings (or only a single drawing) must be filed whenever necessary to understand the invention.
2. **Flowcharts:** Flowcharts should also be included whenever useful for an understanding of the invention.
3. **Must Show Features Claimed:** The drawings must show every feature recited in the claims.
4. **Conventional Features:** Conventional features that are not essential for an understanding of the invention, but are mentioned in the description and claims, can be shown by a graphical drawing symbol or a labeled rectangular box. For example, a motor can be shown by an encircled "M," and a CPU in a computer can be shown by a rectangle labeled "CPU."
5. **Improvements:** When your invention consists of an improvement in an old machine, the drawing should show the improved portion disconnected from the old structure with only so much of the old structure as is necessary to show how your improvement fits in. For example, if you've invented a new tail light for a bicycle, show the bicycle itself with the new tail light (without detail) in one figure. Then show just the portion of the bike where the tail light is mounted in detail in another figure, together with details of the mounting hardware.
6. **Paper:** The filed drawings (xerographic copies) should be on paper that is flexible, strong, white, smooth, non-shiny, and durable. Ordinary 20# bond is acceptable.

(You should do the originals on Mylar film, vellum, or hard, rather than soft, Bristol board; this is available in most good art supply stores. Strathmore Paper Co. makes excellent patent drawing boards in both U.S. and A4 sizes (about $1/sheet), but you can get your sheets more economically by buying larger sheets of hard Bristol board and cutting them to the proper size. If you're using CAD, do the originals on regular bond and, since additional originals are so easy to make, send the originals to the PTO. (Keep your disk copy and a backup of your drawing file!)

7. **Lines:** The main requirement for all drawings is that all lines must be crisp and perfectly black. A good photocopy on good quality bond paper is usually used, but the lines should be crisp and sharp. A good xerographic copy from a dark-penciled original will be accepted. Jagged slant lines from a dot matrix printer or bit-mapped drawing program are verboten for formal drawings.

Lines the PTO Recognizes on Drawings:

Normal Lines: Use a solid thin line (————) to show regular parts and a thick solid line (▬▬▬) to show a shadowed edge—see Rule #14—or hatching a cross-section.

Hidden Lines: This is a dashed line (– – – – – – –) to show a part behind another part—see Fig. 8C.

SUMMARY OF PTO DRAWING RULES (CONT'D)

Projection Lines: This is composed of alternating long dashes and dots (— • — • — •) and is used to connect exploded parts—see Fig. 8D.

Phantom Lines: Similar to a projection line, but which uses two dots instead of one (— • • — • • — • •); this is used to show an alternate position of a movable part.

8. **White Pigment:** The use of white pigment (for example, White Out™, Liquid Paper™) to cover lines is now acceptable, provided all lines are sharp and black.

9. **Uniform Size:** All drawing sheets in an application must be exactly sized in the same U.S. letter or A4 size. Fig. 10B shows these two sizes.

10. **Invisible Margins:** The margins must not contain any lines or writing; all writing and lines must be in the remaining "sight" (drawing area) on the sheet. Margin border lines are forbidden, but crosshairs (about 1cm long) should be drawn over two opposite (cater-corner) margin corners as shown in Fig. 10B.

11. **No Holes:** The drawing sheets should not contain any holes.

12. **Instrument Work:** All lines must be made with drafting instruments or a laser printer and must be very dense, sharp, uniformly thick, and black. Fine or crowded lines must be avoided. Solid black areas are not permitted. Freehand work must be avoided unless necessary.

13. **Hatching:** Parts in section must be filled with slanted parallel lines (hatching) that are spaced apart sufficiently so that they can be distinguished without difficulty. Crisscross and double-line hatching is forbidden.

14. **Shading:** Objects can be shaded with surface and edge shadings so that the light appears to come from the upper left at a 45-degree angle. Thus the shade sides of all objects (the right and bottom) should be done with heavier lines. Surface shading should be open. On perspective views, the closest edges should be made heavier. Edge and surface shading is mandatory in design patent applications.

15. **Scale:** The scale should be large enough to show the mechanism without crowding when the drawing is reduced to ⅔ of its original size for reproduction. Detailed parts should be shown on a larger scale, and spread out over two or more sheets if necessary, to accomplish this, but the number of sheets should not be more than necessary.

16. **Figures:** The different views should be consecutively numbered figures, for example, "Fig. 1-A," "Fig. 1-B," "Fig. 2," etc. Each figure should be separate and uncon-nected with any other figure. If possible, you should number the figures consecutively on consecutive sheets. However, if you want to arrange the figures in non-consecutive order to use space efficiently, that's okay, albeit less desirable.

17. **Reference Numerals and Lead Lines:** Numbers must be plain, legible, carefully formed, and not encircled. They should be at least 3.2 mm (⅛") high. When parts are complex, they should not be placed so close that comprehension suffers. They should not cross or mingle with other lines. When grouped around a part, they should be placed around the part and connected by lead lines to the elements to which they refer. They should not be placed on hatched or shaded surfaces unless absolutely necessary; if then, they should be placed in a blank space in the hatching or shading. (Numerals are preferred to letters.) Arrowheads should not be used on lead lines, but if a numeral refers to an entire assembly or group of connected elements, its lead line can have an arrowhead, or it can be underlined to distinguish it from the lead lines of numerals that refer to a single part.

18. **No Duplication of Reference Numerals:** The same part in different figures must always be designated by the same reference numeral. Conversely, the same reference numeral must never be used to designate different parts. Numbers with primes and letter suffixes are considered different numbers.

19. **Graphic Symbols:** These can be used for conventional parts, but must be defined in the specification. For instance, if you use an encircled "M" for a motor, the specification should say, for example, "A motor, represented in Fig. 2 by an encircled 'M.'" Conventional symbols, such as those approved by the IEEE, ASA, etc., or from any standards or symbols book, can be used. Arrows should be used to show direction of movement, where necessary.

20. **Descriptive Matter:** The rules state that descriptive matter on the drawings is not permitted. I vehemently oppose this rule, since the use of descriptive matter on drawings makes them far more meaningful, and since textbooks, magazine articles, etc., all use drawings with ample descriptive matter. Unfortunately, this rule is being enforced now, so just put the figure number and nothing else under each figure—for example, "Fig. 1."

The Rules do permit (and even require) legends to be used within rectangular boxes, on flowcharts, piping

SUMMARY OF PTO DRAWING RULES (CONT'D)

(plumbing) lines, or wherever else additional clarity is highly desirable. If used, the descriptive matter lettering should be as large, or larger, than the reference numerals.

21. **Views:** The drawings should have as many views (figures) as is necessary to show the invention. The views may be plan, sectional, exploded, elevational, or perspective; detailed larger-scale views of specific elements should be employed. Engineering views (such as front, side, bottom, or back) should not normally be used if perspective views can adequately illustrate the invention. If exploded views are used, the separated parts of the same figure must be joined by assembly lines or embraced by a bracket. (See Fig. 8D.)

    A large machine or schematic or flowchart can be extended over several sheets, but they should be arranged to be easily understandable and so that the sheets can be assembled adjacent each other to show the entire machine. Never place one figure within another.

22. **Sectional Views:** The plane upon which a sectional view is taken should be illustrated in the general view by a broken line, the ends of which should be designated by numerals corresponding to the figure number of the sectional view with arrows indicating the direction in which the sectional view is taken. For example, suppose your Fig. 1 shows a left side front view of your carburetor and Fig. 2 shows a cross-sectional front of the back half of the carburetor on a plane vertically bisecting the carburetor into front and back halves. In this case, Fig. 1 should contain a broken vertical line spaced halfway from left to right with arrows pointing to the right at the top and bottom of this line; the arrows should each be labeled "2" to indicate the section is shown in Fig. 2.

23. **Moving Parts:** To show two positions of a moveable part, show its main position in full lines and its secondary position in phantom lines, provided this can be done clearly. If not, use a separate view for the secondary position. (See this sidebar above for how to do a phantom line.)

24. **Modifications:** Show modifications in separate figures, not in broken lines.

25. **No Construction Lines:** Construction lines, center lines, and projection lines connecting separate figures are forbidden. However, projection lines to show the assembly of parts in an exploded view in one figure are permitted. (See Fig. 8D.)

26. **Position of Sheet:** All views (figures) on a sheet must have the same orientation, preferably so that they can be read with the sheet upright (that is, its short side at the top) so the examiner won't have to turn the sheets or the file to read the drawing. However, if views longer than the width of the sheet are necessary for the clearest illustration of the invention, the sheet can be turned on its side so that its short side and the appropriate top margin is on the right-hand side. The orientation of any lettering on a sheet must conform with the orientation of the sheet, except that the sheet number and number of sheets separated by a slash (1/2) must always be at the top. (See Fig. 10B.)

27. **OG Figure:** One figure should be a comprehensive view of the invention for inclusion in the *Official Gazette*, a weekly publication of the PTO that shows the main claim and drawing figure of every patent issued that week.

28. **No Extraneous Matter:** No extraneous matter—that is, matter that is not part of the claimed invention or its supporting or related structures—is permitted on the drawings. However, you can (and should) place additional matter, such as a hand on a special pistol grip, if necessary to show use or an advantage of the invention. Also, you should put the sheet number and total number of sheets ("1/4, 2/4," etc.) below the top margin, in centered numerals that are larger than the regular reference numerals. If the center space is occupied, the sheet number should be placed to the right.

29. **No Wrinkled Sheets:** The sheets should be sent to the PTO with adequate protection so that they will arrive without wrinkles or tears. You should send the sheets flat, between two pieces of corrugated cardboard within a large envelope, but they can also be rolled and sent in a mailing tube, provided they don't wrinkle. Never fold patent drawing sheets.

30. **Phantom Lines:** Parts that are hidden, but that you want to show, for example, the inside of a computer, should be shown in phantom lines—that is, broken lines. (See #7 above.) Reference numeral lead lines that refer to phantom parts should also be broken, in accordance with standard drafting practice. Broken lines must never be used to designate a part of the actual invention, unless to illustrate a phantom part or a moved position of a part.

31. **Identification on Back:** So that the PTO can identify and utilize the drawings in case they get separated from the file, you should include the title of the invention, and the first inventor's name and telephone number on the back of each sheet, at least 1 cm down from the top. Use a label or sticker if necessary to prevent this information from showing through to the front.

C. Doing Your Own Drawings

Many inventors sensibly choose to prepare their own patent applications instead of hiring a patent attorney or agent to do it for them. However, these same inventors frequently conclude that preparing the drawings is beyond their ability and turn the job over to a professional draftsperson. This can be costly. The typical draftsperson charges $75 to $150 per sheet of patent drawings (each sheet may contain several figures or separate drawings). Since most patent applications have between two to ten sheets of drawings, an inventor can easily shell out up to $1,500 per patent application.

Fortunately, patent drawings, like the application itself, are frequently susceptible to a self-help approach. To be sure, you'll need to learn some PTO rules and a certain learning curve is involved. However, the result will not only save you a ton of money over many patent applications, but also:

- You will be able to prepare promotional brochures for marketing your invention to prospective manufacturers or customers.
- You will be able to render your invention more accurately than a hired professional, because you know your invention best. By doing your own drawings, you do not have to take the time to make someone else understand your invention, or have to send the drawings back and forth for corrections.
- You will have the great satisfaction of properly completing the entire patent application by yourself—an impressive accomplishment for an inventor.

The Patent Drawing Book, also published by Nolo Press, provides detailed guidance on making the drawings yourself. Here is a brief overview of the three methods for making patent drawings: pen and ruler, computer-aided drafting, and photography.

1. Drawing With Pen and Ruler

The traditional or old way of making patent drawings is with pen and ruler. A set of basic tools for this method can be assembled relatively inexpensively, and making simple drawings is fairly easy. However, with pen and ruler, there is little room for mistakes, because except for very small marks, it is very difficult to correct misplaced ink lines. Nevertheless, with careful planning of drawing positioning (layout), and great care in laying down ink lines, drawing with pen and ruler is still a viable technique. In fact, according to one survey, most professional patent draftspersons still make drawings this way.

The necessary tools include pencils for preliminary sketches, ink drafting pens (also known as technical pens) for drawing ink lines, straight rules for drawing straight lines, triangles for drawing angled lines, templates for drawing certain standard shapes, curve rules for drawing curves, an optional drafting table, and good-quality ink drawing paper. Pen and ruler may be used to make patent drawings in the following ways:

a. Drawing From Scratch

You can draw an object by visualizing in detail what it should look like, carefully sketching that image on paper with a pencil, correcting it until it looks about right, and finally inking in the lines. The sketching of a telephone is illustrated in Fig. 10C. You must have some basic drawing skills to draw from scratch.

b. Tracing

Tracing is much easier than drawing from scratch. An obvious method is to trace a photograph of an object that you wish to draw, as shown in Fig. 10D. You can also trace an actual, three-dimensional object by positioning a transparent drawing sheet on a transparent sheet of glass or acrylic, as shown in Fig. 10E, looking at the object through the glass, tracing the lines of the object on the drawing sheet, and photocopying the tracing onto a sheet of paper. Tracing requires very little skill other than a steady hand.

c. Drawing to Scale

You can also draw by scaling—that is, reducing or enlarging—the dimensions of an actual object to fit on a sheet of paper, and drawing all the lines with exact scale dimensions. For example, if an object has a height of 20 inches and a width of 12 inches, you can reduce those dimensions by 50%, so that you would draw it with a height of ten inches and a width of 6 inches on paper, as shown in Fig. 10F. All other dimensions of the object are scaled accordingly for the drawing. Making a drawing that looks right is easier by drawing to scale than by drawing based on only a mental image.

2. Drawing With a Computer

CAD (computer-aided drafting or design) allows you to produce accurate drawings even if you consider yourself to have little or no artistic ability. In fact, no drawing skills in the traditional sense are needed at all. Furthermore, CAD enables you to correct mistakes as easily as a word processor enables you to edit words in a document. Even if you discover a mistake after you've printed a drawing, you can easily correct the mistake and print a new copy. To use CAD, you will need some computer skills, but if you know how to type letters on your computer, you can easily learn how to draw with it.

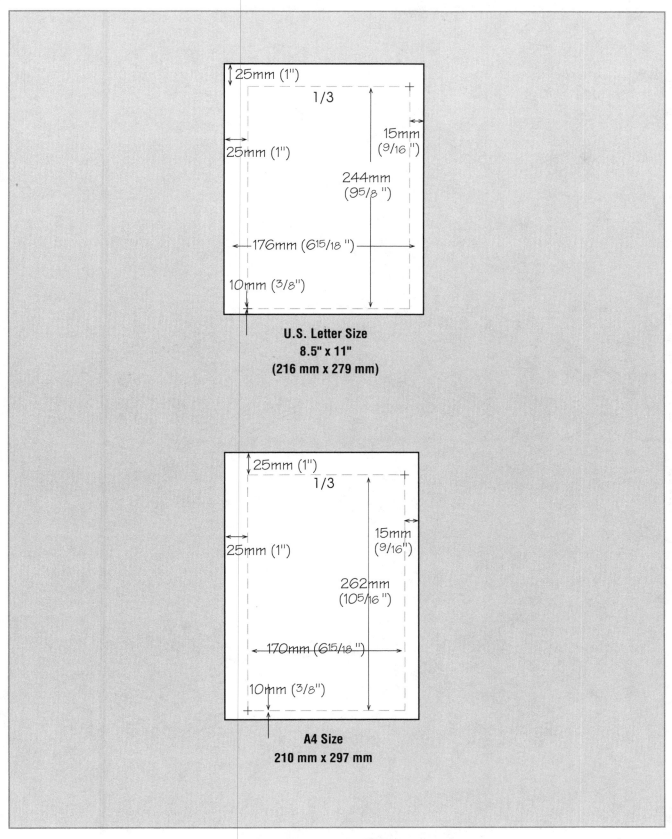

Fig. 10B—The Two Permitted Drawing Sizes

Fig. 10C—Sketching Techniques

Fig. 10D—Tracing a Photo

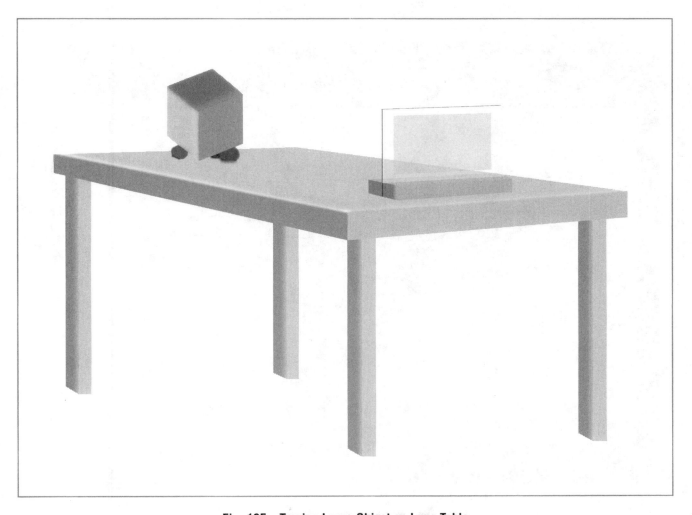

Fig. 10E—Tracing Large Object on Long Table

Fig. 10F—Drawing to Scale

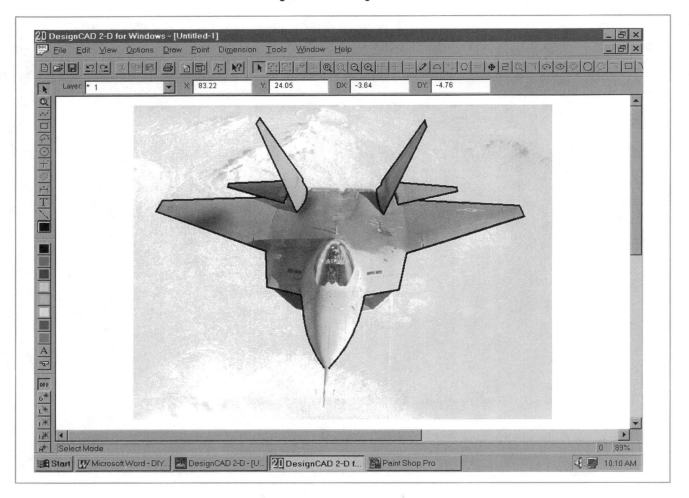

Fig. 10G—Tracing a Photo on a Computer

You will need either a PC (IBM compatible) or a Mac, an ink jet or laser printer, a CAD program, an optional scanner, and an optional digital camera. A computer may be used to make patent drawings in the following ways:

a. Tracing

If you have a scanner, you can scan a photograph of an object, import (load) the scanned image into a CAD program, and trace it easily, as shown in Fig. 10G, a photo of an aircraft (the black outlines are the tracing lines which are difficult to see in a black-and-white book). If you have a digital camera, you can take a photograph of the object and download (transfer) the image directly into your computer through a cable, without having to print and scan the photograph. Once it is in your computer, tracing the image is very easy. Since you use a mouse instead of an ink pen, you don't even need a steady hand.

b. Drawing From Scratch

A 3D (three-dimensional) CAD program enables you to construct an accurate, 3D representation of your invention within the computer, such as the pipe fitting shown in Fig. 10H. A 3D model is typically built by using and modifying basic geometric building blocks, such as boxes, cylinders, planes, and custom-defined shapes. You may create each part with specific dimensions, or you may simply draw a shape that looks about right. You can easily rotate the finished model to see it from any angle. You can also easily zoom in or out to adjust the viewing distance. Once you are satisfied with the view, you can print it as a line drawing (a drawing of dark lines on a light background). Therefore, you can make wonderful looking drawings with a computer, even if you consider yourself to be a terrible artist.

Fig. 10H. Building a 3D CAD Model

3. Photography

Almost everyone has some degree of familiarity with photography. Obviously, a camera can take an accurate photograph or "drawing" of an object. Photographs may be submitted as patent drawings, or they may be converted into line drawings by tracing them. Although photography spares you from having any drawing skills, you must have some photographic skills to take clear pictures, including a basic understanding of lighting and exposure. To take an accurate photograph, you will need a 35 mm camera with selectable aperture, zoom and macro (close up). You will also need a tripod.

D. Consider Using a Professional Patent Draftsperson

If you don't feel competent to do your own drawings, you'll want to hire someone to do them for you. You can locate people who specialize in preparing patent drawings by letting your fingers do the walking through the nearest metropolitan area Yellow Pages. Look under the heading "Drawing Services," which should list several patent drafters. While expensive (about $30 to $50 per hour, or $80 to $150 per sheet), these people should do the job correctly the first time with CAD or in India ink on Bristol board. Also, you can use a "starving artist" who's proficient in the medium to be used (such as India ink or CAD), and reads and understands the rules thoroughly.

E. Finaling Your Specification, Claims, and Abstract

Before putting them in final form, reread your specification, claims, and abstract, to make sure they're clear, complete, and understandable. Again, make sure that the main substantive requirements (Chapters 8 and 9) are satisfied.

As with your drawings, you may type your specification, claims, and abstract on either U.S. or A4-size paper. All sheets must be of the same size, free of holes, and have 2 cm top, bottom, and right margins, and a 2.5 cm left margin. Use 1.5 or double spacing and number the sheets at the top or bottom, inside the margin. (All correspondence that you send to the PTO at any time should always be 1.5 or double-spaced; never use single spacing and never type on both sides of a sheet.)

If you think you may later want to file corresponding foreign applications, it's easiest to type your application on U.S. letter-size paper with proper margins so that if photocopied onto A4 size paper, it will have the proper A4

margins. To do this print out or type the application on letter-size or computer paper (8.5" x 11" after removal of the selvage or carrier strip). Use a 1" left margin, 6.2" line width, 1" top margin (3" on p. 1), and a bottom margin of 0.3", so that the last line is almost at the bottom of the page. The sample specification in Chapter 8 (Fig. 8F) is typed this way, except that the 1" top margin has been omitted. Save the original for possible later use in making an A4 version for an international application. There is no typeface style requirement, and dot matrix printers are okay so long as the printout, or its photocopy, is clearly readable. You should never justify (line up the right margin of) your typing, since unjustified printing (as in this book) is easier to follow.

TYPING AND FILING APPLICATION ON A4 PAPER

Alternatively, you can type and file your U.S. application on A4 paper, following the proper requirements for such matters as margins and line spacing (the abstract page). However, I don't recommend this, since, although the rest of the world uses it everywhere, it's very hard to obtain A4 paper in the U.S., unless you cut it yourself or have it cut for you. If you do want to file on A4, the sheets should be 21 by 29.7 cm in size, with top margins of 8 to 9 cm on the first sheet and 2 to 4 cm thereafter, left margins of 2.5 to 4 cm, and bottom and right margins of 2 to 3 cm, with sheets numbered consecutively at the top and lines typed 1.5 spaces apart—that is, four lines per inch. Keep the originals and file an A4 xerographic copy. As stated, the PTO doesn't care much about format, but if you later file a PCT application (see Chapter 12) these measurements will be strictly enforced.

You should start your claims and abstract on new pages, with the abstract on the last sheet, *after* the claims. The titles should go on the first page. Don't submit an application on easily erasable paper, or on paper that has white pigment covering any typewritten lines, since these are not considered permanent, unaltered records. If you're not a good typist, and you don't have a word processor, one solution is to type your application on easily erasable paper or regular paper, cover the errors with white pigment, type in the corrections, and then make bond paper photocopies of your typewritten original for submission to the PTO.

If, after putting your specification in final form, you find you must make a few minor changes (one or two words in a few places), it's okay to do so, provided you make these changes neatly in ink—in handwriting—and date and initial the margin adjacent to each change *before* you sign the application.

You don't have to file your drawings and your type-written papers on the same size sheets; the drawings can be on A4 paper and the typewritten pages on U.S.-size paper, or vice versa. All drawing sheets must be the same size, as must all typed sheets. Never use both sides of a sheet, either for drawings or for the specification. A neatly typed specification will certainly make a very favorable impression on your examiner. If you can do your application with a laser printer with larger, bolder, and contrasting heading fonts, the result will be most impressive. As mentioned earlier, if you don't own a laser printer, consider using one at a copy center.

Some inventors have prepared their applications to look like patents, complete with narrow, single-spaced columns and cited references. Don't do this; your application should look like the sample in Chapter 8. The PTO will supply and print the list of references cited, your name, and all other data that normally goes on the abstract page. (See Fig. 1A.) You should not do this.

Minimize the potential for disaster by not placing cups of coffee or other beverages at your desk while completing your final papers.

F. Name All True Inventors and Only True Inventors

In several different parts of your application, you're required to name the applicants and inventors. For example, in Form 10-1, your transmittal letter, you must list the applicants. And Form 10-2 (your Patent Application Declaration) must be signed by the inventors (see Figs. 10I and 10J). These are discussed in the following sections.

As previously mentioned, while anyone can apply for a patent, the named applicant(s) must be the true inventor(s) of the invention. If you've conceived the invention (as defined by the claims) entirely on your own, of course there's no problem about who should be named co-inventor. On the other hand, if you've invented it with someone else, both of you should be named as "joint inventors." But be sure that both of you actually are joint inventors. If somebody other than you played a significant role in conceiving the invention, turn to Chapter 16, Section B, for a more detailed discussion on inventorship. Under no circumstances should you name your financier, your boss, or anyone else who was not an actual inventor.

G. Completing the Patent Application Declaration

Each patent application must be accompanied by a patent application declaration (PAD), which is a written statement under oath. The form for the PAD is provided as Form 10-2, and a completed version is provided below in Fig. 10I.

While completing the PAD is a straightforward process, you should not treat it lightly. Rather, you should read and review it very carefully before you sign. If anyone can prove that you signed the declaration knowing that any of its statements were false, your patent can be held invalid. In fact, I've seen so many inventors sign PADs without reading or keeping a copy that I've provided Inventor's Commandment #14 at the beginning of this chapter to remind you to read, agree with, and keep a copy of all documents you sign.

The title of the invention from p.1 of the specification goes in the space near the top; the name, residence, citizenship, and post-office address of each inventor (if there is more than one) go in the appropriate spaces. Your residence is the legal jurisdiction (city and state) where you reside. This will normally be the same as the city and state of your post-office address, unless you have a post office box or a postal address in a city other than the one in which you legally reside. If there are more than two inventors (see Chapter 16, Section B), photocopy or type the last few lines of the form on a second page as many times as necessary and label Form 10-2 "Page 1 of 2" and the second page "Page 2 of 2." Fig. 10I shows how the PAD is completed for two joint inventors.

Each inventor should then sign and date the appropriate spaces at the bottom of the form. Note that the PAD directs the PTO to send correspondence and calls to the first-named inventor. While every joint inventor must sign all papers that are sent to the PTO, the PTO will correspond with one inventor only. Therefore you should list the inventor who is most available (or who has best access to a photocopier) first.

Note the sentence of the PAD that states that you acknowledge a duty to disclose information of which you are aware and that is material to the examination of the application. This provision is designed to impress upon inventors their duty to disclose (to the PTO) any information that could affect the examination or validity of the application. This means you must disclose to the PTO all relevant prior art that you have uncovered, any disadvantages of your invention of which you are aware, or any other act you think the examiner would want to be aware of when examining the application. Normally, all of this information will be provided in your Information Disclosure Statement (see Section N, below).

This disclosure requirement is very important; so much so that courts have, as mentioned, held patents invalid for "fraud on the PTO" when inventors have neglected this duty. Thus I've made it Inventor's Commandment #15.

⚠ You must not sign the PAD until the entire application is completed; if the PTO finds out that you signed it before it was completed, or if you made any changes to the application after you signed the PAD, your application can be stricken or rejected entirely. If you need to make any changes to the application after it's finaled, you can do so neatly in ink, provided you date and initial each change and you do this *before* you sign the PAD. You can also make changes by amendment(s) after the application is filed (see Chapter 13), provided you don't add new matter to the application.

H. Fill Out the Small Entity Declaration If Appropriate

If you're a "small entity," that is, an independent inventor, or an independent inventor(s) who hasn't assigned or licensed, or isn't under an agreement to assign or license, the invention to a large, for-profit business (over 500 employees), you'll be entitled to pay small-entity filing, issue, and maintenance fees, which are half the large-entity filing fees. (See Appendix 4, Fee Schedule, for the amounts

of these fees.) To qualify, you must complete and send in a Small Entity Declaration (SED) with your application. You must send in an SED if you have an *obligation* to assign or license, even though you haven't yet filed an assignment. (The SED form is Form 10-3 in Appendix 7.)

HOW TO COMPLETE THE SED (FORM 10-3)

- Fill in the inventors' names adjacent the "Applicant" lines at the top of the form and add the title of the application where indicated.
- If you haven't sold or granted any interest in (assigned or licensed) your application to anyone (see Chapter 16), and aren't under any obligation to do so (this will be the normal case), check the box before the line reading, "there is no such person, concern, or organization."
- If you have sold or granted such an interest, or are obligated to do so, then check the line that ends in an asterisk, list the person or organization on the appropriate lines, and check the appropriate box to indicate whether this person or organization (your "assignee") is an individual, small business, or non-profit organization. (I cover assignments in Chapter 16, Section E.)
- Your assignee (or licensee) (if any) should complete and file a supplemental, non-inventor SED, if appropriate. Form 10-4A is for individual assignees, Form 10-4B is for small businesses, and Form 10-4C is for nonprofit institutions. (These forms are included in Appendix 7.)
- Print your name(s) and date, and sign the main SED at the bottom where indicated. If you have more than two joint inventors (see Chapter 16, Section B), add a line at the top of the SED reading "Joint/Third Applicant: _____" (squeeze it in or retype the form) and add another three-line signature section on a second page. Label these pages "Page 1 of 2" and "Page 2 of 2," as with the PAD.

If you're not fortunate enough to qualify as a small entity—that is, you (or any co-inventor) have assigned or licensed the invention, or are under an obligation to assign or license it, to a for-profit business with over 500 employees—omit the SED and pay the large entity filing (and other) fees. Also, if you initially qualify as a small entity and later you assign or license the invention to a large entity, you'll have to apprise the PTO of this fact and pay a large-entity issue fee.

Declaration for Utility or Design Patent Application

As a below-named inventor, I hereby declare that my residence, post office address, and citizenship are as stated below next to my name and that I believe that I am the original, first, and sole inventor [if only one name is listed below] or an original, first, and joint inventor [if plural names are listed below] of the subject matter which is claimed and for which a patent is sought on the invention, the specification of which is attached hereto and which has the following title:

" Food chopper with convolute blade   "

I have reviewed and understand the contents of the above-identified specification, including the claims, as amended by any amendment specifically referred to in the oath or declaration. I acknowledge a duty to disclose information which is material to the examination of this application in accordance with Title 37, Code of Federal Regulations, Section 1.56(a).

I hereby declare that all statements made herein of my own knowledge are true and that all statements made on information and belief are believed to be true; and further that these statements were made with the knowledge that willful false statements and the like so made are punishable by fine or imprisonment, or both, under Title 18, United States Code, Section 1001, and that such willful false statements may jeopardize the validity of the application or any patent issued thereon.

Please send correspondence and make telephone calls to the First Inventor below.

Signature: Sole/First Inventor: _Mildred Goldberger_

Print Name: ___Mildred Goldberger___   Date: _199X August 9_

Legal Residence*: _Philadelphia, PA_   Citizen of: ___Hungary___

Post Office Address: ___1901 Kennedy Blvd., Philadelphia, PA 19103___

Telephone: ___215-222-2972___

Signature: Joint/Second Inventor: _Nathaniel Briskin_

Print Name: ___Nathaniel Briskin___   Date: ___199X August 9___

Legal Residence*: ___Philadelphia, PA___   Citizen of: ___USA___

Post Office Address: ___1991 Chestnut St., Philadelphia, PA 19103___

Telephone: ___215-227-6639___

* City and state, county and state, city, state and country, if foreign.

Fig. 10I—Completed Patent Application Declaration (Form 10-2 in Appendix 7)

I. Complete the Transmittal Letter and Fee Transmittal, Check, and Postcard

Now it's time to prepare the routine paperwork necessary to actually send your patent application to the PTO. Here's how to do it.

1. Prepare a Transmittal Letter

The transmittal letter (Form 10-1) should be dated as of the date the entire patent application is mailed. Fig. 10J, below, shows how it's completed.

The names of the inventor(s), the title, the total number of pages of specification and claims, the number of sheets of drawing, and whether the drawings are formal or informal should all be indicated in the appropriate spaces on this form. If you attach any SEDs, check the SED box and indicate the number of SEDs attached; the number will be one if you're an independent inventor who hasn't assigned or licensed, or two (yours and your assignee/licensee) if you have assigned or licensed. The date the application was signed should also be indicated in the space provided. The application should be mailed to the PTO shortly after this date of signature.

If you filed a DDP or PPA (see Chapter 3, Sections H and I), check the DDP or PPA block and fill in the serial number and filing date if you filed a PPA. Your regular patent application must be filed within one year of your PPA's filing date if you want the benefit of such date. If the last day of the one-year period falls on a weekend or holiday, you must file your Regular Patent Application (RPA) on the next business day before the weekend or holiday. At least one inventor named in the RPA must have been named in the PPA.

If you're not sure your claims are entirely proper, you should check the "Request Under MPEP Section 707.07(j)" block to ask the examiner to write allowable claims for you, if necessary.

If there are two inventors, both should sign the letter, and their respective addresses should be provided. If there are more than two inventors, retype the form to have additional lines and spaces for the additional inventors, or splice these in and make a clean photocopy of the form. As stated, whenever there is more than one inventor, all inventors must sign every communication to the PTO.

2. Write a Check and Fill out Fee Transmittal

Fill out the Fee Transmittal (Form 10-1A) by completing the date, name of the first (or only) applicant and title.

Then enter the Basic Utility Application Filing Fee (from Fee Schedule in Appendix 4) in the blank on line 201 and in the blank on the line after "Subtotal (1)." This fee entitles you to file up to three independent claims and 20 total claims, assuming that each dependent claim refers back to only one preceding claim (independent or dependent).

Next enter the total number of claims (independent and dependent) in the blank after "203 Total claims:" If you're filing more than 20 total claims (not generally recommended), subtract 20 from this figure and enter the result in the next blank, enter the PTO's fee for each claim over 20 in the next blank and enter the product (if any) in the last blank, after the "=" sign.

Next enter the total number of independent claims in the blank after "202 Total indep. claims:" If you're filing more than three independent claims (not generally recommended):

- subtract 3 from the figure you entered after "202" and enter the result in the next blank,
- enter the PTO's fee for each independent claim over 20 in the next blank, and write the product (if any) in the last blank, after the "=" sign.

Next calculate and enter any applicable figure in Subtotal (2) and enter the sum of those subtotals in the blank after "Total Payment Enclosed" and in the blank just above "Sir:" Also indicate in the blank just above "Sir:" whether you're enclosing a check or money order.

Finally, sign and print your name and address at the end. (If you're obligated to pay large entity fees, change "small" to "large" in the form, double all fees, and change the fee codes as follows: 201 to 101, 202 to 102 and 203 to 103.)

You can obtain a somewhat speedier processing of your application than is usually the case by filing a Petition to Make Special along with your application (see Section P, below).

If you're enclosing an assignment (see Section O, below), check the "Assignment" box and the "Additional Fee" box and the assignment recording fee.

The check should be made out to Commissioner of Patents and Trademarks for the total amount, and should be attached to the transmittal letter. Be absolutely sure you have enough money in your checking account to cover the check; if the check bounces, you'll have to pay a stiff surcharge. Unfortunately, the PTO does not discount its fees for the needy, handicapped, or aged, or allow such individuals to postpone their fees.

In the United States Patent and Trademark Office

Mailed 199 <u>X</u> <u>Aug. 9</u>

Assistant Commissioner for Patents

Washington, District of Columbia 20231

Sir:

Please file the following enclosed patent application papers:

Applicant #1, Name: <u>Mildred Goldberger</u>

Applicant #2, Name: <u>Nathaniel Briskin</u>

Title: <u>Food Chopper with Convolute Blade</u>

☒ Specification, Claims, and Abstract: Nr. of Sheets <u>12</u>

☒ Declaration: Date Signed: <u>199x Aug. 9</u>

☒ Drawing(s): Nr. of Sheets Enc.: Formal: _____ Informal: <u>2</u>

☒ Small Entity Declaration Of Inventor(s)   ☐ SED of Non-Inventor / Assignee / Licensee

☒ Assignment; please record and return; recordal fee enclosed.

☒ Check for $ <u>425</u> for:

    ☒ $ <u>385</u> for filing fee (not more than three independent claims and twenty total claims are presented).

    ☒ $ <u>40</u> Additional if Assignment is enclosed for recordal.

☒ Disclosure Document Program reference letter.

☐ Pursuant to 35 U.S.C. §119(e)(i), applicant(s) claim priority of provisional patent application Ser. Nr. _____ ,

    filed _____ .

☐ Return Receipt Postcard Addressed to Applicant #1.

☒ **Request Under MPEP § 707.07(j):** The undersigned, a pro se applicant, respectfully requests that if the Examiner finds patentable subject matter disclosed in this application, but feels that Applicant's present claims are not entirely suitable, the Examiner draft one or more allowable claims for applicant.

Very respectfully,

Mildred Goldberger
Applicant #1 Signature

Nathaniel Briskin
Applicant #2 Signature

<u>1901 Kennedy Blvd.</u>
Address (Send Correspondence Here)

<u>1991 Chestnut Street</u>
Address

<u>Philadelphia, PA 19103</u>

<u>Philadelphia, PA 19103</u>

Express Mail Label # EH160200231US ; Date of Deposit 199 <u>X</u> <u>Aug. 10</u>

I hereby certify that this paper or fee is being deposited with the United States Postal Service using "Express Mail Post Office To Addressee" service under 37 CFR 1.10 on the date indicated above and is addressed to "Box Patent Application, Assistant Commissioner for Patents, Washington, DC 20231."

Signed: *Mildred Goldberger*
Inventor

Fig. 10J—Completed Patent Application Transmittal Letter (Form 10-1 in Appendix 7)
Use latest fees—See Appendix 4, Fee Schedule

3.   Postcard

As stated in Inventor's Commandment #16 at the beginning of this chapter, you should enclose a receipt postcard with every paper you send to the PTO. All attorneys use receipt postcards because the PTO receives many thousands of pieces of mail each day and occasionally loses some. It may be months before you receive any reply to a paper you've sent to the PTO, so you'll want to be assured it arrived safely.

Fig. 10K indicates how an application receipt postcard should be completed, front and back. Note that the back of the card contains the inventors' names, title of invention, number of pages of specifications, claims, and abstract, the date the Patent Application Declaration was signed, the number of sheets of drawing (and whether formal or informal), the Small Entity Declaration, and the check number and amount. Leave space at the bottom of the back of the card for the PTO's stamp. Occasionally, receipt postcards get lost because of their size and inconspicuous color. I have had better results by using colored (bright red) postcards.

The PTO will stamp your application postcard receipt with a date and serial number and mail it back to you as soon as they open your letter, which can take them two weeks.

J.   Maintain an Orderly File

I often consult with "pro-se" inventors (that is, those who have prepared and filed their own patent applications).

Usually they bring me their "application" in the form of a sloppy, loose stack of mixed-up—and occasionally missing—papers. You'll avoid this problem, and the serious trouble it can get you into, if you'll heed Inventor's Commandment #17, shown at the beginning of this chapter, which admonishes you to mount all official papers (those sent to and received from the PTO) in a separate folder.

A three-part folder for (a) your application, (b) correspondence from the PTO, and (c) correspondence to the PTO is useful. Keep your prior-art references in a large envelope loose inside the folder. To avoid confusion, I recommend that you keep other papers concerning your invention in a separate folder.

K.   Assembly and Mailing of Your Application—Final Checklist

Congratulations. You're now ready to mail your patent application to the PTO, unless you want to include an assignment (Section O), an Information Disclosure Statement (Section N), and/or a Petition to Make Special (Section P). If you do want to include any of these with your application (this is optional), consult the indicated sections, complete your paperwork, and then come back to this point.

Assemble in the following order—and carefully check—the following items, which are the third part of the checklist I started in Chapter 8; please do this carefully and methodically, as "haste makes waste," especially when applying for a patent.

The following received today:

Patent Application for Mildred Goldberger and Nathaniel Briskin for "Food Chopper With Convolute Blade," consisting of 12 sheets specification, claims, and abstract, declaration signed 199X Aug. 9, 2 sheets informal drawing, small entity declaration, and check nr. 334 for $ _____:

Back of Receipt Postcard

Mildred Goldberger
1901 Kennedy Blvd.
Philadelphia, PA 19103

Front of Receipt Postcard

Fig. 10K—Completed Postcard to Accompany Patent Application

FINAL CHECKLIST

☐ (a) **Return Receipt Postcard** addressed to you with all papers listed on back.

☐ (b) **Check or Money Order** for correct filing fee (basic fee and fee for any excess claims); adequate funds on deposit.

☐ (c) **Transmittal Letter and Fee Transmittal** properly completed and signed.

☐ (d) **Drawing sheets** all present; drawings clear, complete, and under–standable. The sheet number and total number of sheets (e.g. "1/3") is on the front (below top margin) and your name is on the top back. Originals of drawings (or disk file if CAD used) kept in safe place.

☐ (e) **Specification, Claims, and Abstract** included; description of invention clear and complete and claims drafted per Chapter 9.

    (i) Typing is clear and readable and 1.5 or double-spaced.

    (ii) Application is prepared in form for making proper A4 copies later if foreign filing contemplated (optional).

    (iii) Top margin (above page numbers) is at least 2.5 cm on all pages.

    (iv) No sentence is longer than about 13 words, paragraphs are not longer than about $1/2$ page, and a heading is supplied for about every two pages.

    (v) Claims are separated by an extra line.

    (vi) Claims and abstract start on new pages.

    (vii) No changes made after application signed.

☐ (f) **Patent Application Declaration** (PAD) completed, signed, and dated in ink. (The PTO will accept a PAD, or virtually any other document which has a photocopy of your signature, provided you can always produce the ink-signed original.)

☐ (g) **Small Entity Declaration** (SED) completed, signed, and dated in ink. Additional non-inventor SED(s) included if anyone else has any interest in the application.

☐ (h) Parts are assembled in above order and copies made for your file.

☐ (i) **Information Disclosure Statement and PTO-1449** with references attached if you're filing it with your application (see Section N, below).

☐ (j) **Petition to Make Special** (optional to speed application processing; see Section P, below).

☐ (k) **Assignment** if needed (see Section O, below).

☐ (l) **Disclosure Document Reference Letter** (Form 3-4) if you previously filed a Disclosure Document.

☐ (m) **Envelope** addressed to:
Box Patent Application
Assistant Commissioner for Patents
Washington, DC 20231

I suggest that you file a photocopy of your signed application and keep the original of your application so you can make copies later if you need to send them to manufacturers when you market your invention. (See Chapter 11.)

Staple the pages of the specification, claims, abstract and declarations together. Attach the drawings with a paper clip or other temporary device.

The papers can be transmitted in a large envelope, with one or two sheets of stiff cardboard to protect the drawing from bending, or, if they are thin enough, they can all be rolled and mailed in a mailing tube.

The application should be sent to the PTO by first-class mail. You may want to register the parcel to cover the expense of making new drawings in case it's lost. However, registering your mail will not cover you for loss of any legal rights in case your application is lost in the mail on the way to the PTO.

L. Using Express Mail to Get an Instant Filing Date

If you want to insure against loss of your application, secure full legal rights in case it is lost, get an "instant" filing date (the date you actually mail your application), or make absolutely sure your application is on file before the one-year period after a PPA was filed or the invention was put on sale, sold, or published expires, you should send it by Express Mail. You must use "Express Mail Post Office to Addressee" service and you must indicate that you're using this service by completing and signing an Express Mail Certification at the bottom of your transmittal letter (Form 10-1/Fig. 10J). Paste the Express Mail number strip right on Form 10-1 and then make a photocopy of Form 10-1. The PTO's Rule 10 (37 CFR 1.10) states, in effect, that mailing any paper to the PTO by Express Mail, with a properly completed Express Mail certification, is the same as physically delivering the paper directly to the PTO. Thus you can consider and call your application "patent pending" as soon as the postal clerk hands you the Express Mail receipt, and your filing date will be the date on this receipt, provided all papers of the application are present and are properly completed. That is, you've followed the final checklist.

⚠️ If you send your application by any other type of mail, with or without a "Certificate of Mailing" (Chapter 13), or by courier (Federal Express, etc.), your filing date will be the date the application is actually received at the PTO and you'll have no rights if it's lost.

M. Receipt That Application Was Received in PTO

About two to four weeks after you send your application to the PTO, you'll get your postcard back, stamped to indicate the filing date of your application, and also stamped with an eight-digit serial number (for example, "08/123,456") that has been assigned to your application. Within about a week to a month after that (sometimes longer), you should get a blue filing receipt back from the PTO indicating that your application has been officially filed.

If for any reason your application is incomplete or deficient, it will not be officially "filed" but will be regarded as "deposited." The Application Branch of the PTO will send you a letter stating the deficiency in your application and telling you to promptly remedy it. However, if you follow all the instructions in this chapter, including the checklist in Section K, carefully, you'll get your blue filing receipt in due course.

Once you get the filing receipt, your application is officially "patent pending," and unless you want to keep your invention a trade secret, as discussed in Chapter 7 (in case your patent application is eventually disallowed), you may publish details of your invention or market it to whomever you choose without loss of any legal rights in the U.S. or Convention or treaty countries (see Chapter 12). If you manufacture anything embodying your invention, you should mark it "patent pending" and keep your application, Ser. Nr., and filing date confidential to preserve rights in non-Convention countries and prevent access by potential copiers. If you mailed your application by Express Mail and it was properly completed, you may refer to your invention as "patent pending" as soon as you get the Express Mail receipt.

N. File the Information Disclosure Statement Within Three Months

The PTO's rules impose on each patent applicant a "duty of candor and good faith" toward the PTO. This means that all inventors (and attorneys) have a duty to disclose to the PTO information they are aware of which might influence the patent examiner in deciding on the patent application. (This duty is embodied in Inventor's Commandment #15, and discussed in Section G, above.) To comply with the "prior art" part of Inventor's Commandment #15, the PTO asks all applicants to submit an Information Disclosure Statement (IDS) at the time of filing the application or

within the following three months. Even if it weren't required, it is to your advantage to file an IDS and to list as many relevant prior-art references as possible in order to have them considered and noted by the examiner so that they will be listed as "References Cited" in the patent. This creates a presumption that your patent's claims are patentable over these references—that is, you'll have put these references behind you. I suggest that you use the option to file afterward; this will prevent overload while preparing your basic application.

The IDS actually consists of a transmittal letter and a "PTO-1449 Form," on which you list the prior art; these forms are provided as Forms 10-5 and 10-6. A filled-in sample is set out as Fig. 10L and 10M.

The IDS should list all prior-art references known to the inventors that are relevant to the patentability of the application. These should include all the references you discovered in the course of your patentability search (see Chapter 6), plus any other prior art of which you're aware, including even your own papers. In addition, the inventors must include with the IDS a copy of each cited reference and a discussion of the relevance of any non-English language references to the invention. You must cite them even if you discussed them in the prior-art section of your patent application. (If you aren't aware of any prior art, don't file an IDS.)

You may well ask why, if the prior art you discover consists of patents, you have to send patents to the PTO; isn't this like carrying coals to Newcastle? Well, yes, but the PTO claims that it's such a large and complex organization that it would cause too many administrative difficulties and require too much examiners' time to dig out all of the patents cited by applicants; thus, they want you to send them copies. If you found many relevant references, say so. Send in the 20 most relevant, but be sure not to omit any reference with a unique, relevant feature.

As mentioned, you can send the IDS with your application instead of taking advantage of the three-month grace period. In this event, the names of the inventors and title of your invention are the only information you need to put at the top of Forms 10-5 and 10-6. If you send it after your application is filed, you'll know the serial number, filing date, and group art unit, and can insert them. You normally won't know the examiner's name unless you've received a first "office action" from the PTO.

Complete Forms 10-5 and 10-6. Fill in all the blanks. The form blanks are self-explanatory, except that the U.S. class and subclass go in the "class" and "subclass" blanks. The Group or Group Art Unit (GAU) are on your filing receipt.

In the United States Patent and Trademark Office

Serial Number: <u>06 / 123 456</u>

Appn. Filed: <u>199X June 22</u>

Applicant(s): <u>Douglass, L. Clarkson</u>

Appn. Title: <u>Food Cutter</u>

Examiner/GAU: <u>   /3240</u>

Mailed: <u>199X Oct 24, Mon</u>

At: <u>San Francisco, CA</u>

Information Disclosure Statement

Assistant Commissioner for Patents

Washington, District of Columbia 20231

Sir:

Attached is a completed Form PTO-1449 and copies of the pertinent parts of the references cited thereon. Following are comments on any non-English-language references pursuant to Rule 98:

    Rasmussen shows a fruit peeler with a bent guide for controlling the thickness of fruit as it is being peeled. **Gillet** shows a knife mounted parallel to a space which knife can be tilted out or in to adjust the spacing of its edge.

    None of the references shows a knife for making a cut of controlled depth wherein a flat-bladed knife with an elongated sharpened edge with an outward protrusion attached to the blade that is spaced back from the edge for limiting the depth of cut that can be made by said edge when it is used to **cut** in a direction **perpendicular** to the plane of the blade, as it is recited in independent claims 1 and 17, and hence their dependent claims 2 to 11 and 18 to 20.

    To the contrary, all of the references show guides that are mounted generally parallel to the blade for limiting the thickness of the peel that can be cut by the blade when it used to **peel** in a direction **parallel** to its plane.

    Also, none of the references show any blade having a substantially right-angle bend parallel to its direction of elongation, as it is recited in independent claim 12 and its dependent claims 13 to 16.

Very respectfully,

Applicant(s): <u>*L. Clarkson Douglass*</u>

<u> </u>

Enc.: PTO-1449 & References

c/o: <u>L. Clarkson Douglass, Applicant Pro Se</u>

<u>   15 Chestnut Street</u>

<u>   San Francisco, CA 94109</u>

Telephone: <u>   415-227-4494</u>

Fig. 10L—Completed Information Disclosure Statement (Form 10-5 in Appendix 7)

Sheet ___1___ of ___1___

FORM PTO-1449 (Substitute)

| ATTY. DOCKET NO. Disc File 2403 | SERIAL NO. 07/123,744 |

LIST OF PRIOR ART CITED BY APPLICANT

(Use several sheets if necessary)

| APPLICANT Clarkson, L.D. | |
| FILING DATE 199X June 22 | GROUP 324 |

U.S. PATENT DOCUMENTS

*EXAMINER INITIAL		DOCUMENT NUMBER	DATE	NAME	CLASS	SUBCLASS	FILING DATE IF APPROPRIATE
	AA	21695	1858	Oot			
	AB	602758	1898	Lenders			
	AC	2083368	1937	Gambino	146	206	
	AD	2968867	1961	Wolff	30	284	
	AE						
	AF						
	AG						
	AH						
	AI						
	AJ						
	AK						

FOREIGN PATENT DOCUMENTS

	AL	69640	1949	DENMARK (Rasmussen)			
	AM	1029924	1953	FRANCE (Gillet)			
	AN						
	AO						
	AP						

OTHER PRIOR ART *(Including Author, Title, Date, Pertinent Pages, Etc.)*

	AR						
	AS						
	AT						

EXAMINER	DATE CONSIDERED

*EXAMINER: *Initial if reference considered, whether or not citation is in conformance with MPEP 609; Draw line through citation if not in conformance and not considered. Include copy of this form with next communication to applicant.*

Fig. 10M—Completed PTO Form 1449 (Attach to Information Disclosure Statement) (Form 10-6 in Appendix 7)

If you include any non-English-language reference on Form 10-6, Rule 98(a)(3) requires that you also provide a concise explanation of its relevance on a separate paper or in the specification. I recommend that you also state how your invention, as claimed, differs physically from this reference(s). State the relevance of any non-English references, and any discussion as to how your invention differs, on Form 10-5. Fig. 10L provides an example.

If you send in the IDS with the application, note this on the postcard and transmittal letter that you send with your application. If you send it in after the application is filed, send in a separate postcard. Again, the front of the card should be addressed to you; the back should read as in Fig. 10N.

If you haven't followed my instructions in Chapter 6—that is, you haven't made a search and are not aware of any prior art—as stated, you don't have to file an IDS: The PTO won't deny or delay your application if you don't file an IDS. However, if they (or an infringer whom you later sue for patent infringement) discover that you knew of relevant prior art and didn't file an IDS, your patent application or patent can be held invalid for "fraud on the PTO." This is so even if the examiner discovers the reference you withheld and cites it in a regular Office Action. (See Chapter 13, Fig. 13-A4.)

Information Disclosure Statement, Form PTO-1449, and (Number) References in patent application of (name(s) of inventor(s)), Serial No. _____, Filed _____ received for filing today:

Fig. 10N—Back of Postcard for Sending IDS

O. Assignments

As I mentioned, a patent application must be filed in the name or names of the true inventor or inventors of the invention claimed in the patent application. The inventors then become the applicants for the patent, and the law considers that they automatically own equal shares of the invention, the patent application, and any patents that may issue on the application (Chapter 16, Section B). However, inventorship can be different from ownership. Often all or part of the ownership of the invention and the patent application must be transferred to someone else, either an individual or a legal entity, such as a corporation, a partnership, or an individual. To make this transfer, the inventor(s) must "assign" (legally transfer) their interest. The assignment transfers ownership (or part of it) from the inventor(s) to another entity. However, inventorship remains the same after an assignment is made. (Directions and forms for making an assignment are in Chapter 16, Section E.)

If you have assigned the application to another and you want to send the assignment to the PTO for recording (highly advised), you can either send it in with the patent application or at any time afterward. I prefer to send in assignments later, after I get the postcard receipt back, when I know and can add the serial number and filing date of the application to the assignment, to make the two documents (the assignment and the application) correspond to each other more directly. In this case, you can add the serial number and filing date to the assignment in the spaces indicated. Then prepare an Assignment "Recordation Form Cover Sheet" (Form 16-2B). In space 1, the conveying parties are the inventor applicants. In space 2A, the receiving party is the assignee—the person or organization to whom you're assigning the application. The Internal Address is the mail stop or apartment number if any, in the assignee's building. In Space 3, the Conveyance is an assignment and the execution date is the date you signed the assignment. In Space 4, the Application Number is the Serial Number of your patent application. I recommend that you also type the filing date. If you don't know these numbers yet, just fill in the execution (signing) date of your PAD. If you're assigning a patent, fill in the patent number and issue date in Space 4B. "Additional numbers attached [ ] Yes [ ] No" should be checked to indicate whether or not you've listed additional cases on an attached sheet. The remaining blocks are self-explanatory. Make sure to include the recordation fee (see Appendix 2, Fee Schedule). If you wish to send the assignment in with your patent application, complete the Recordation Form Cover Sheet (Form 16-2B), check the "Assignment" and "$_____" additional boxes on Form 10-1, and increase your fee accordingly.

If an assignment of a patent application has been recorded and it is referred to in the issue fee transmittal form (see Chapter 13), the PTO will print the patent with the assignee's interest indicated. However, even if you fail to indicate the assignment on the issue fee transmittal, so that the patent doesn't indicate the assignment, the assignment will still be effective if it has been recorded.

If an assignment has been made, and as a result there are two or more owners of the patent application, then the owners should consider signing a Joint Owners' Agreement (Form 16-1) for the reasons indicated in Chapter 16, Section C.

P.   Petitions to Make Special

If you do need to have your patent issue sooner than in the normal course (one to three years) or want to have it examined sooner for any reason, you can have it examined ahead of its normal turn by filing a "Petition to Make Special" (PTMS—Form 10-7), together with a Supporting Declaration (SD). This can be filed with the application or at any time after. An example of a properly completed PTMS and an SD are shown below in Figs. 10O and 10P.

Before you get excited about filing a Petition to Make Special, however, please consider this. Unless you have a specific need for the early examination or issuance of a patent—for example, an infringement is occurring, you need a patent to get capital for manufacturing the invention, the technology is rapidly becoming obsolete, or you're contemplating foreign filing—most patent professionals agree that you will not gain much of an advantage in filing a PTMS. Why? From experience, I've found that filing a PTMS usually advances the examination only a few months. This is likely to be reduced under the new "20-year from filing" patent term, since more applicants will be likely to file a PTMS to extend the period of time their patent is in force.

Also, once a patent issues, the technology is made public (remember, the patent application must teach clearly how to make and use the invention), so that potential competitors can see the patent and start copying its technology and designing around it.

Lastly, most potential licensees (companies whom you'd like to license under your patent) would prefer to sign the license while the patent application is still pending and hence kept in secrecy in order to get an edge on the competition. As stated in the next chapter, you should try to license your invention as soon as your patent application is filed and not wait until the patent issues.

As you'll note on the PTMS, an application can be made special, and hence examined ahead of turn, for any of 11 reasons. Those reasons marked with an asterisk (*—numbers 1, 2, 7, 8, 10 and 11) will require a petition fee (for large or small entities). (See Appendix 4, Fee Schedule.) If you use any of the other reasons (numbers 3 to 6 and 9) you won't have to pay any fee, since these are "favorable public policy" (nonmercenary) reasons. Here are the 11 reasons:

1. **Manufacturer Available:** A manufacturer is available—that is, a person or company exists that will manufacture the invention provided the patent application is allowed or a patent issues.*
2. **Infringement Exists:** Someone is making, using, or selling the invention covered by the patent application and you need a patent to sue the infringer or get the infringer to pay you royalties.*
3. **Applicant's Health Is Poor:** You're in such poor health that your normal lifespan is likely to be shortened and you want to get the fruits of your invention before you depart this life.
4. **Applicant's Age Is 65 or Greater:** Self-explanatory.
5. **Environmental Quality Will Be Enhanced:** Your invention conserves natural resources and/or keeps the air, water, or landscape pristine. (See Fig. 10P.)
6. **Energy Savings Will Result:** The invention provides a way to use energy more efficiently, thereby also conserving natural resources.
7. **Recombinant DNA Is Involved:** Public policy favors the full and rapid exploitation of recombinant deoxyribonucleic acid.*
8. **Search Was Made:** If you've made a search and submitted an Information Disclosure Statement—as you're supposed to do anyway (see Section N above)—you can get the case made special, since the examiner's task is made easier by your search.*
9. **Superconductivity Is Advanced:** Public policy favors the exploitation of this phenomenon.
10. **Relates to HIV/AIDS or Cancer.** Self-explanatory.*
11. **Counters Terrorism.** You have a counter-terrorism invention, such as an explosive detector, an aircraft security system, or a vehicle barrier or disabler.

The supporting declaration that accompanies the PTMS should be in the format of Fig. 10P with the introductory paragraph, paragraph 1, and the last paragraph left intact. The remaining paragraphs must give detailed facts (MPEP 708.02) in support of the reason for the petition. Here are some suggestions:

- If reason 2 is applicable (infringement exists), you should state in your Supporting Declaration (SD) that you've made a rigorous comparison of the claims of your application with the infringer's device and find that the claims "read on" such device (that is, your claims apply to it). You should attach a two-column table, listing the elements of one of your claims as separate paragraphs in the left column and explaining how each element "reads on" the infringing device in corresponding paragraphs in the right column.
- If reason 4 (senior citizen) is applicable, you need merely state that you're over 65 and give your birthdate.

In the United States Patent and Trademark Office

Serial Number: _06/123,456_

Appn. Filed: _199X Aug 9_

Applicant(s): _Goldberger, David_

Appn. Title: _Wind Generator Using Stratus Rotor, Etc._

Examiner/GAU: _Hayness   /   654_

Mailed: _199X September 20_

At: _San Francisco_

Petition to Make Special

Assistant Commissioner for Patents
Washington, District of Columbia 20231

Sir:

Applicant hereby respectfully petitions that the above application be made special under MPEP Sec. 708.02 for the following reason; attached is a declaration in support thereof:

I. ☐ Manufacturer Available;*

II. ☐ Infringement Exists;*

III. ☐ Applicant's Health Is Poor;

IV. ☐ Applicant's Age Is 65 or Greater;

V. ☒ Environmental Quality Will Be Enhanced;

VI. ☐ Energy Savings Will Result;

VII. ☐ Recombinant DNA Is Involved;*

VIII. ☐ Special Procedure: Search Was Made;*

IX. ☐ Superconductivity Is Advanced;

X. ☐ Relates to HIV/AIDS or Cancer;*

XI. ☐ Counters Terrorism.*

*☐ Also attached, since reason I, II, VII, VIII, or X has been checked, is the $ _____ Petition Fee pursuant to Rules 102 and 17(i).

Very respectfully,

Applicant(s): _David Goldberger_

Attachment(s): Fee if indicated and supporting Declaration

c/o: _David Goldberger_

119 Walnut St.

San Francisco, CA 94123

Telephone: _415-722-0362_

Fig. 100—Completed Petition to Make Special (Form 10-7 in Appendix 7)

In the United States Patent and Trademark Office

Appn. Number: 06/123,456
Filing Date: 199X Aug. 9
Applicant(s): Goldberger, David
Examiner: Hayness / GAU 654

Mailed: 199X Dec 11 Wed
At: San Francisco

**Declaration In Support of Accompanying Petition to Make Special
Reason V—Enhancement of Environmental Quality**

In support of the accompanying Petition to Make Special, applicant declares as follows: *

1. I am the applicant in the above-identified patent application.

2. The invention of the above application will materially enhance the quality of the environment of human kind by contributing to the restoration or maintenance of the basic life-sustaining natural elements of air and water in the manner described below.

3. Specifically, the invention of the above application is an improved electrical power generator employing wind energy. It provides a more efficient wind power generator than heretofore available because it uses a highly efficient stratus rotor in combination with a Loopis vane, thereby intercepting an average of 25% more of the wind energy passing therethrough than prior-art conventional fan-blade wind turbines, as described in full detail on pages 3 to 5 of the specification.

4. By more efficiently using wind power, it enables the installed cost per average kilowatt of generated wind power on a yearly basis to be materially lowered. This will make wind power generators more economical, cost-effective, and attractive to investors, individual power consumers, and power companies. As a result, more utilization of wind power generation will occur, causing less dependence on and less utilization of conventional power plants using fossil-fuel sources such as coal and oil, or nuclear fission, thereby resulting in less air and water pollution due to reduced effluents in the air and waterways from such conventional power plants. Thus thermal and other pollution of such air and waterways will be reduce so that air and water quality will be maintained and will actually be restored due to national self-purification.

5. I further declare that all statements made herein of my own knowledge are true and that all statements made upon information and belief are believed to be true, and further that these statements were made with the knowledge that willful false statements and the like so made are punishable by fine or imprisonment, or both, under Section 1001 of Title 18 of the United States Code, and that such willful false statements may jeopardize the validity of the application and any patent issuing therefrom.

Very respectfully,

David Goldberger
David Goldberger

1919 Chestnut Street
Philadelphia, PA 19103
215-237-6639

Fig. 10P—Completed Declaration to Accompany PTMS
*This (and all other papers sent to the PTO) should always be typed with 1.5 or double spacing.

- If reason 7 or 9 (DNA or superconductivity) is involved, refer to your application and tell how it involves DNA or superconductivity.
- If reason 8 is applicable, state that an IDS has been filed or is enclosed, and state where (that is, class and subclass) and by whom the search was made.
- If any of the other reasons is involved, give detailed facts or reasoning in support of your main reason, as I have done in Fig. 10P. Don't hesitate to attach photocopies of such documents as letters and advertisements to your SD if they are relevant.

If you file your PTMS with the application, you should refer to it in your transmittal letter and your postcard receipt. In this case, you won't be able to include the PTO's filing data on the PTMS. If you file it later, add the application filing data to the PTMS, as I have done in Fig. 10P. As always, don't forget the postcard receipt.

If your PTMS is accepted, you'll receive a letter from the PTO stating that your petition has been granted and the examiner in charge of your application has been instructed to examine it ahead of turn.

You should then receive an official action (see Chapter 13) several months sooner than normal. If your PTMS isn't accepted, you'll also receive a letter telling you why. Usually the rejection will be because your facts and reasons in the Supporting Declaration aren't detailed enough. In this case, file a revised Declaration, beefing up your facts and reasons.

Q. Filing a Design Patent Application

As I've indicated in Chapter 1, Section B, a design patent covers the ornamental external appearance, rather than the internal structure, function, composition, or state of an invention. Fig. 10Q shows an example of a design patent. You may file both a design patent application and a separate utility patent application on the same device, but of course, they should not cover the same feature of the device. The utility patent application should cover only the structure (or a method) that makes the device or invention function or operate, while the design patent application should cover an entirely separate "invention," namely, the ornamental (aesthetic) external (nonfunctional) appearance of something. For example, you can file a utility patent application on a computer program (provided it's associated with some hardware), its circuitry, its keyboard mechanism, or its connector structure, and a design patent application on the shape of the computer's case.

You'll be relieved to know that design patent applications are very easy to prepare. A design patent application consists simply of the following:

- A preamble, specification, and claim (Form 10-8)
- A Fee Transmittal (Form 10-1A)
- The drawing(s)
- A PAD (Form 10-2)
- A SED (Form 10-3)
- The fee (see Appendix 4, Fee Schedule), and
- The receipt postcard.

A completed preamble, specification, and claim for a design application is shown in Fig. 10Q.

If you believe that your invention has a unique ornamental appearance that is significantly different from anything heretofore designed, you can file a design patent application on it.

Although not 100% kosher, some inventors file a design application on the external appearance of a utility invention that is unpatentable in the utility sense, and that has unfinalized or trivial novelty in the design sense. They do this mainly to be able to truthfully and legally state for a few years that the invention is "patent pending."

The first step in completing a design application is to prepare drawings in the same format as for a regular patent application. (See Section A, above.) However, the drawings for the design application should show only the exterior appearance of your invention; no interior parts or workings should be shown and no reference numerals are used. The drawings of a design patent application must, however, be done with good surface and edge shading; see Fig. 10R.

If your invention is a computer-generated symbol (such as an icon like a trash can or a type font), you can file a design patent application on it, but you must show more than just the symbol per se. This is because the pertinent statute (35 U.S.C. 171) requires that the design be "an article of manufacture" and the PTO does not consider a computer symbol, per se, as an article. The solution? Simply include a computer display (monitor or display panel) in your drawing and show the computer-generated symbol on the display. Both the symbol and the display should be drawn in solid lines.

Usually only one embodiment of a design is permitted. If you have several embodiments or versions of your design, you can include these all in one application. But if the examiner feels they don't all relate to the same inventive concept, you'll be required to restrict the application to one embodiment. In this case, you can file a divisional application(s) on the other embodiment(s), provided you do so before the original application issues. (See Chapter 14 for divisional applications.)

It's important to remember that drawings of your design application should have enough figures to show all of the details of the external surface of your design. A company I once worked for had an important design patent on a TV set held invalid because the design patent's drawings failed to show the rear side of the TV set.

Once you've made your drawings (in formal or informal form) fill out Form 10-8 from Appendix 7 as indicated in Fig. 10Q, below. The title of your design can be very simple and need not be specifically directed toward your invention. For example, "Bicycle" is sufficient. Each view of the drawing should be separately indicated. For example, "Fig. 1 is a front perspective view, Fig. 2 is a side view," etc.

Note that the design application has one claim only, and to write that claim you need merely fill in the blank on Form 10-8 with the title of your design. Fill out the fee transmittal (amount is in Appendix 4), the PAD (Form 10-2) and SED (Form 10-3) as instructed in Sections G and H above.

The design application with the declarations, drawings, and receipt postcard should be sent to the PTO in the same manner as your regular patent application. Be sure to keep an identical copy of your design application, including its drawings. (The filing fee is indicated in Appendix 4, Fee Schedule (large/small entity).) No transmittal letter is needed, since Form 10-8 inherently provides a transmittal letter.

DESIGN PATENT APPLICATIONS

Design patent applications, declarations, drawings and receipt postcards should be sent to the PTO using the following address:

Box Design
Assistant Commissioner for Patents
Washington, DC 20231

The same address should be used for subsequent communications with the PTO regarding your application.

You'll receive your receipt postcard back in a week or two, and you'll receive a blue filing receipt a month or so thereafter. If you're aware of any prior art, don't forget to file an Information Disclosure Statement (Part N, above) within three months of your filing date. The IDS should merely discuss how the appearance of your design differs from prior-art assigns.

PLANT PATENT APPLICATIONS

I haven't covered plant patent applications since they're extremely rare and specialized. If you do want to file a plant application, it will be easy to do if you familiarize yourself with this chapter and PTO Rules 161 to 167 (37 CFR 1.161-7).

Design Patent Application—Preamble, Specification, and Claim

Box Design
Assistant Commissioner for Patents
Washington, District of Columbia 20231

Sir:

Preamble:

The petitioner(s) whose signature(s) appear on the declaration attached respectfully request that Letters Patent be granted to such petitioner(s) for the new and original design set forth in the following specification. The filing fee of $ _(see Appendix 4)_, __4__ sheets of drawings (3 ccpies ea.), a patent application declaration, a small entity declaration, and a return receipt postcard are attached.

Specification:

The undersigned has (have) invented a new, original, and ornamental design entitled

"___Clothes Hanger_____"

of which the following is a specification. Reference is made to the accompanying drawings which form a part hereof, the figures of which are described as follows:

Fig. 1 is a ___front, elevational_____ view.

Fig. 2 is a ___left side_____ view.

Fig. 3 is a perspective view.

Fig. 4 is a rear view.

Claim: I (We) Claim:

The ornamental design for a ___Clothes Hanger_____

_____ , as shown.

Express Mail Label #   (**EH1602002311US**)   ; Date of Deposit 199 _X_ _Sept 8_____

I hereby certify that this paper or fee is being deposited with the United States Postal Service using "Express Mail Post Office To Addressee" service under 37 CFR 1.10 on the date indicated above and is addressed to "Assistant Commissioner for Patents, Washington, DC 20231."

Signed: ___Sandy Rand_____
Inventor

Fig. 10Q—Completed Design Patent Application (Form 10-8 in Appendix 7)
*Use latest fees—see Appendix 4, Fee Schedule.

United States Patent Office

Des. 226,943
Patented May 22, 1973

226,943

CLOTHES HANGER

Tom Erik Torbjorn Ahlström and Hans Otto Georg Ehrich, both of 13 Brannkyrkagatan, S–117 20 Stockholm, Sweden

Filed Aug. 11, 1971, Ser. No. 171,041

Claims priority, application Sweden May 6, 1971

Term of patent 14 years

Int. Cl. D6—08

U.S. Cl. D6—248

FIG. 1 is a front view of the clothes hanger of our design;
FIG. 2 is a right end view thereof;
FIG. 3 is a perspective view thereof;
FIG. 4 is a rear view thereof.
We claim:
The ornamental design of a clothes hanger, as shown.

References Cited

UNITED STATES PATENTS

D. 166,610   4/1952   Kerby -------------- D80—8
D. 205,256   7/1966   Poland -------------- D80—8
2,462,778   2/1949   Rosen.
2,446,832   8/1948   Insley.

JAMES R. LARGEN, Primary Examiner

Fig. 10R—Sample of Design Patent

How to Market Your Invention

INVENTOR'S COMMANDMENT #18

Try to market your invention as soon as you can after filing your patent application; don't wait until your patent issues. Favor companies who are close to you and small in size, and who already make and sell items close to yours.

INVENTOR'S COMMANDMENT #19

If you want your invention to be successful, pursue commercial exploitation with all the energy that you can devote to it.

INVENTOR'S COMMANDMENT #20

Never pay any money to any invention developer unless the developer can prove to you that it has a successful track record—that is, most of its clients have received more income in royalties than they have paid the developer in fees.

In this chapter I make an important detour from the central task covered by this book—obtaining a valid and effective patent on your invention. The reason for this sudden turn is simple. In the usual course of events, you'll have an interval (three months to one year) after you file your patent application before you need to either consider foreign filing or reply to an office action from the PTO. I strongly recommend that you use this interval to get your invention out on the market. This advice is so important that I've included it as Inventor's Commandment #18 at the beginning of this chapter.

THE PROJECT TEAM APPROACH

If you already know how your invention will be marketed, or you work for a corporation that plans to handle this task, you can skip this chapter and continue reading about obtaining patent coverage. Also, if you would rather spend all your time at your workbench and not have to deal with marketing, a good way to go is to put together a "project team," as suggested by Richard White in *The Entrepreneur's Manual.* Your project team should consist of several persons with diverse skills, such as an inventor, a marketer, a person to handle the legwork, a model maker, etc. Chapter 12 deals with obtaining patents in other countries and Chapter 13 with getting the U.S. PTO to grant your patent.

"Out on the market?" you ask. Shouldn't you keep your invention, and the fact that you've filed the application, secret? The answer is, "No." In fact, once you file a patent application (including a Provisional Patent Application; see Chapter 3, Section I) on your invention, you may show it to whomever you think might be interested in buying or licensing it without risk of having someone scoop you on your invention.

This is because it would be very difficult for someone to steal your invention when you're the first to file a patent application on it. A patent thief would have to:

- file another application (the filing date would necessarily be substantially later than yours due to the preparation time), and
- get into a patent contest with you (called an "interference"—see Chapter 13, Section K), and be able to win it. It's unlikely that this will happen because the later filing date would make the thief a "junior party" with a large burden of proof. You would also be able to prove that the thief "derived" the invention from you if you keep records of those to whom you reveal your invention. Moreover, the thief would have to commit perjury (a serious felony) by falsely signing the Patent Application Declaration (Chapter 10). Of course, if you plan to maintain the invention as a trade secret, you should take the proper precautions (Chapter 1, Section Q). At any rate, inventions are seldom stolen in their early stages, before they're proven in practice.

Your next question might be, why try to sell or license your invention before a patent has been issued? While there are advantages to selling an already-patented invention, generally it's best to try to sell or license your invention as soon as possible after filing your patent application. This is because prospective corporate purchasers of your invention will want time to get a head start on the competition and to have the time the patent is in force coincide with the time the product's actually on the market. Also, you'll be able to offer the manufacturer the right to apply for foreign patents; this right will be lost once your patent issues. The lack of prestige that a pending patent has as compared to an already issued patent can be compensated for by a favorable search report showing that there's no strong prior art—that is, that a patent is likely to issue on your invention.

A. Perseverance and Patience Are Essential

As Paul Sherman, N.Y. Asst. Attorney General, said in his excellent article, "Idea Promoter Control: The Time Has Come" (*Journ. Pat. Off. Soc.*, 1978 April, p. 261), "It is a failing of our system that there are no recognized avenues for amateur inventors to have their ideas evaluated and presented to manufacturers." Even if you get a patent, it will almost certainly be totally worthless unless it covers a commercially exploited invention. In fact, millions of patents have issued on inventions that were never successfully commercialized. None of these patents ever yielded a nickel to their owners.

To get your invention into commercial production, you'll have to persevere. There's no magic solution to the invention marketing process. As noted toy inventor Paul

Brown says, "You almost have to be obsessed with your invention to get it going." Or put another way, Emerson's famous adage about building a better mousetrap would have been better written, "If you build a better mousetrap, you'll still have to beat a path to many doors to get it sold." This brings us to Inventor's Commandment #19, regarding perseverance, which you should now reread.

Even though you believe you've got the greatest thing since sliced bread, the money won't start flowing in that quickly in most cases. It takes time to develop, market, and sell a product. Chester Carlson, a patent attorney and the inventor of xerography, may have exaggerated somewhat, but he wasn't too far off base when he said:

> *"The time scale of invention is a long one. Results do not come quickly. Inventive developments have to be measured in decades rather than years. It takes patience to stay with an idea through such a long period.*
> *"In my case, I am sure I would not have done so if it were not for the hope of the eventual reward through the incentives offered by the patent system."*

B. Overview of Alternative Ways to Profit From Your Invention

As you can see from the chart of Fig. 11A, there are seven main ways or routes for the independent inventor to get an invention into the marketplace and profit from it—Routes

Fig. 11A—Alternative Ways to Profit From Your Invention

1 to 7. These choices involve increasing difficulty and work for you. I recommend that most inventors use Route #3, and have accordingly highlighted this route.

1. Route 1: Using a Contingent-Fee Intermediary

Starting at the top, Route 1 involves getting a contingent-fee invention broker or intermediary to find a suitable manufacturer/ distributor for you and then using the broker to represent you in the sale or license of your invention.

Sometimes termed "invention developers," "invention marketers," "invention promoters," and the like, these contingent-fee brokers are firms that will represent you and try to market your invention by selling or licensing it for a percentage of your rights, the "contingent-fee basis." Most of the invention brokers are reputable and honest, and provide a legitimate service for a fair fee.

Obviously, Route 1 is the easiest possible path, since the broker will do all of the work for you. However, it's neither that difficult to find suitable manufacturer/distributors (Section D, below) if they exist, nor to present your invention to them once you locate them (Section G, below). Thus, I recommend that you consider handling this task yourself. No one can sell an invention as sincerely and with as much enthusiasm and conviction as you, the true inventor. Also, you'll get 100% of the benefits and won't have to share the fruit of your creativity with a salesperson.

If you do use an invention broker, you should be concerned about two main possibilities for harm:

1. Loss of your invention rights through theft or communication to a thief, and

2. Loss of time and hence other opportunities.

The first possibility isn't great because you've already got a patent application on file. However, the second possibility is very real, and you should accordingly verify the efficacy of any promoter beforehand. Unfortunately, about the only surefire way to do this is by word-of-mouth. Check with a patent attorney (Chapter 6, Section F), an inventors' organization (Chapter 2, Section F), or some of the intermediary's clients if your own associates are unable to provide you with a lead.

Once you're satisfied with the promoter's honesty and references, you should next investigate the contract you are offered by the promoter to be sure you don't lose time needlessly. Thus, the contract should specify that the promoter will perform substantial services, such as identifying the prospective manufacturers, preparing an invention presentation or demonstration, building and testing the invention, negotiating a license or sales agreement for you, etc. And most important, the agreement should set a time limit for the promoter to succeed—that is, get you a firm offer to

buy, license, or get your invention on the market in product form. I feel that a year is reasonable; 18 months, about the maximum you should ever consider. Make sure that if the promoter fails to succeed in the allotted time, all of your rights will be returned to you, together with all of the promoter's research, presentation documents, models, etc.

Here's a list of some invention brokers and developers who will work on a contingent-fee basis. If there are no results, there is no cost to you. I haven't made a detailed investigation of these or any other agencies; it's up to you to do this before you sign. Don't confine your efforts to this list, however; there are many other reliable, honest, contingent-fee promoters around the U.S. who are listed in local telephone and business directories or who are known to local patent attorneys and inventors' organizations.

Arthur D. Little, Inc.
Invention Management Group
Acorn Park
Cambridge, MA 02140
617-495-5000

Battelle Development Corporation
505 King Avenue
Columbus, OH 43201
614-424-6424

REFAC Technology Development Corporation
122 E. 42nd Street
New York, NY 10017
212-687-4741

In addition, many universities now have invention marketing departments that exist primarily to market the technology developed in the universities' research labs, but they also take ideas from outsiders on a contingent-fee basis. Check with your local colleges.

DON'T USE A FEE-BASED INVENTION INTERMEDIARY

There are other firms, which I call fee-based invention intermediaries, that you should generally avoid like the plague. Paul Turley of the FTC reported that of 30,000 people who paid such intermediaries a fee, not one ever received any payback. These companies or organizations run ads in newspapers, magazines, radio, and TV, stating something like "Inventions and Ideas Wanted!" They will commonly first send you an "inventor's kit" that includes a disclosure form similar to my Form 3-2 and that promises to "evaluate" your invention for free or for a relatively small fee (say $200 to $600). The evaluation almost always is glowingly positive. Then they'll ask for a relatively large fee— $1,000 to $5,000—using very high-pressure sales tactics. They'll promise to do "market research" and try to sell your invention or have it manufactured. They sometimes also take a percentage share (for example, 20%) of your invention.

Generally, they will do little more than write a brief blurb describing your invention and send it to prospective manufacturers in the appropriate fields. Their efforts are virtually 100% unsuccessful, as reported in the article "Patent Nonsense," in the *Wall Street Journal,* 1991 Sept 19, and on the TV program "20/20" on 1995 Jun 6. For this reason I recommend you not use an invention promoter unless you find one that can establish a successful track record—that is, a record of bringing its clients a significant percentage in royalties in relation to the fees it charged them. As Stephen Paul Gnass (Invention Convention) says, "Ask if the invention developer makes its money from inventions or inventors."

The fact is, no special expertise is needed to market an invention; a sincere approach directly to a suitable company from an independent inventor (using techniques of this chapter) will be far more effective than any "intermediary's" effort. I would look elsewhere.

2. Route 2: Partial Use of an Intermediary

Route 2 (a seldom-used path) is the same as Route 1, except that here you use a broker to find prospects and then you take over and do the selling. Contingent-fee brokers won't accept this type of arrangement, since they'll want to control the sales negotiations. However, there are many inventor assistance companies that will provide you with product evaluation, illustration, advertising, packaging design, market research, and product testing services for a fee; one such organization is Synergy Consultants, 2915 LBJ, Suite 254, Dallas, TX 75234. If you feel that your strong suit is in presenting and selling, and that sales research is for someone else, you can pay a broker or market researcher (either contingent-type or fee-based) to research possible purchasers. Then go out and present your invention yourself.

3. Route 3: Finding a Manufacturer and Distributor Yourself

Route 3 is the path I most favor and which most independent inventors use. Here you do your own research and selling. If you succeed, you'll get 100% of the rewards and you'll control the whole process, yet you won't be bothered with manufacturing or distributing.

4. Route 4: Having Your Invention Manufactured and Distributed for You

Route 4 is a viable alternative for some relatively uncomplicated products. Here you have your invention manufactured for you—a Far-Eastern manufacturer will usually be cheapest—and then use U.S. distributors to sell the product. Of course, you have the headaches of supervising a manufacturing operation, including such items as quality control and red tape associated with importing. But, if you succeed, you'll keep much of the manufacturing profit for yourself.

5. Route 5: You Distribute

In Route 5, you handle distribution as well as supervising manufacturing. More profit, but more headaches and work.

6. Route 6: You Manufacture

In Route 6, you really get into it; you have to do the manufacturing yourself, with all of its headaches (see Section J), but you'll get a lion's share of the profits, if there are any.

7. Route 7: You Manufacture and Distribute

Last, and most difficult, in Route 7 you do it all yourself— manufacturing and distributing. While you get all of the profits, you'll have all of the headaches, as explained in Section J.

Because, as I said, Route 3 makes the most sense for most independent inventors, I devote the bulk of this chapter to finding a manufacturer/distributor to build and market your patent. (If you want to pursue the possibility of manufacturing and distributing your invention, I've included an overview of potential resources in Section J, below, to help you do this.)

C. Be Ready to Demonstrate a Working Model of Your Invention to Potential Customers

Assuming that you choose Route 3, the best way to get a manufacturer or others to "buy" your invention is to demonstrate an actual working model. Pictures and diagrams may convey an idea and get a message across, but the working model is the thing that will make believers out of most people and show them that your invention is real and fulfillable, and not just chicken scratchings on paper. So, if you haven't made a model before, do your best to make one now, even if it has to be made of cardboard or wood. One essential is to make your model or prototype as simple as possible. Simplicity enhances reliability, decreases cost, decreases weight, and facilitates salability, both to a manufacturer and to the public.

If you're not handy, hopefully you can afford to have a professional model maker or artisan build the model, or you may have a handy friend or relative. Where can you find model makers? Ask your local inventors' organization. (See Chapter 2, Section F.) If that fails, the inventor's magazine, *Dream Merchant* (see Appendix 2, Books of Use and Interest), has ads in every issue from model makers. Another obvious place is in your nearest metropolitan area Yellow Pages under "Model Makers." Also try "Machine Shops" and "Plastics—Fabricating, Finishing, and Decorating."

In addition, your local college or community college may have a design and industry department that may be able to refer you to a model maker. If you live near an industrial plant that employs machinists or model makers, perhaps you can get one of these employees to moonlight and do the job for you—put a notice on the plant's bulletin board, call, or ask around.

If you do use a model maker and you disclose critical dimensions, materials, suppliers, or other information you consider to be proprietary (that is, maintained by you as a trade secret), it is best to have the model maker sign a Consultant's Work Agreement (Form 4-3) before you turn over your drawings or other papers. Follow the instructions in Chapter 4 to fill out this form. I also suggest that you add

a confidentiality legend to any drawings or descriptions you turn over to your model maker. Such a legend, which can be made in rubber-stamp form or can be typed on the drawings, can read as follows:

This drawing or description contains proprietary information of [your name] and is loaned for use only in evaluating or building an invention of [your name] and must be returned upon demand. By acceptance hereof, recipient agrees to all of the above conditions. © 199_ [your name].

After you've made a working model, you should take at least one good photograph of it. The photograph should be of professional quality—if you are not a good photographer, have a professional do it, and order several views if necessary. Have at least 50 glossy prints made of the photo, possibly with several views on one sheet. Then write a descriptive blurb about your invention, stating the title or the trademark, what it is, how it works, its main advantages and selling points, plus your name, address, telephone number, and the legend "Patent Pending." Don't get too bogged down in detail, however. In other words, make your write-up snappy and convincing. Then have it typed or printed and have at least 50 copies made to go with the photographs.

D. Finding Prospective Manufacturers/Distributors

The next step is to compile an initial listing of manufacturers who you believe could manufacture and distribute your invention profitably. You should keep your marketing notes, papers, and, correspondence in a separate file from your patent application (legal) file. Your initial list should comprise all the manufacturers who meet the following three criteria:
- They're geographically close to you
- They already manufacture the same or a closely related product, and
- They're not too large.

Nearby or local manufacturers who already work in your field are best. If they manufacture your invention, you can monitor their progress, consult with them frequently, and take any needed action more easily if anything goes wrong. Obviously, it's a big help to deal with a company that has experience with devices similar to yours. They already know how to sell in your field, are aware of competitive pricing policies, can make your invention part of their existing product line—which allows them to keep sales costs low—and presumably want new models related to their existing products in order to keep ahead of the competition. If the manufacturer is not in a closely allied line, both the seller and the product will be on trial, so why start with two strikes against you?

The reasons for avoiding giant manufacturers are these:

1. Smaller manufacturers are more dependent on outside designers. In other words, most don't have a strong inbred prejudice against inventions they did not invent themselves (see the "NIH" Syndrome in Section E, below).

2. You can contact the decision-makers or the owners of the company directly, or more easily.

3. Decisions are made more rapidly because the bureaucracies are smaller.

4. You are less likely to be required to sign a waiver form (see "The Waiver," in Section F, below).

5. Giant companies have a greater tendency to try to "get around" your invention by investigating and trying to invalidate your patent or trying to avoid infringing it. Medium and small companies, on the other hand, will be more interested in your invention's profit potential and its effect in the marketplace.

Obviously, you shouldn't use companies that are so small that they don't have enough money to finance the manufacture of your invention or the marketing of it adequately. Companies with sales of about $5 million to $50 million are best.

To find companies meeting the above criteria, start by first considering people you know. Which one of them is likely to have contacts in the field of your interest? Put them to work for you and you may be amazed that with a few phone calls you can get just the introduction you need.

If this doesn't work, try looking in your appropriate local stores for manufacturers of closely allied products that are already on the shelves. You'll know for sure that these companies have a successful distribution and sales system or operation.

Inventors' magazines, such as *Dream Merchant* (see Appendix 2, Books of Use and Interest), have ads from companies seeking new products from inventors; be on your guard for scams, however.

Also, check the library for books listing local manufacturers (such as the *California Manufacturers Register*) and check national resources such as the *Thomas Register* or *Dun's Million Dollar Directory*. In addition, check the ads in pertinent trade and hobby magazines. Lastly, stock advisory services, such as *Value Line Investment Survey, Standard & Poor's,* and *Moody's,* supply excellent information about companies. Get the names of the company presidents, vice presidents, directors of engineering, marketing, etc. Find out all you can about each company you select; know its products, sales and corporate history, profitability, and factory location(s).

If your invention is in the gadget category and you believe it would appeal to the affluent, your first choice might be Hammacher Schlemmer, a specialty store and mail-order house at 147 East 57th Street, New York, NY 10022. This outfit develops and sells a wide variety of gadget exotica, both through its catalogs and over the counter. The company receives about 3,000 ideas for inventions each year, accepts about 50 to 75 of these, and arranges to have them produced by manufacturers. Many items that Hammacher Schlemmer financed and had manufactured, or first sold as strictly luxury gadgets, have become commonplace in American homes. For example, the steam iron, the electric razor, the pressure cooker, the blender, the humidifier, the electric can opener, the high-intensity lamp, the microwave oven, and the automatic-drip coffee maker were first introduced by this unique and innovative firm. Many other "gadget exotica" mail order firms exist, such as The Sharper Image (which makes appointments with inventors to display their inventions) and JS&A, but these firms don't develop or manufacture any products. Also, trade fairs or shows—such as The Gift Show—are good places for you to wander about, looking for prospective manufacturers. Talk to the people who run the exhibits to get a feel for the companies, whom to contact, and what their attitude toward outside inventions is.

If your invention is a new automotive tool, Lisle Corp., 807 East Main St., Clarinda, IA 51632, actively seeks such inventions. Write them for their Invention Disclosure Agreement. If you have a sports or exercise machine, Nordic Track, tel. 800-967-2113, is hungry for new products. The Sharper Image, 415-445-6125, is hungry for new products in the "executive gadget" category, while Homax Products, 800-729-9029, wants home improvement inventions.

If you can't find any U.S. companies, try foreign ones. Sadly, there has been a recent trend in many U.S. firms to become complacent or tight. They've refused to undertake new ventures that foreign firms have jumped at, which can work to your advantage as an inventor.

E. The "NIH" Syndrome

Before presenting your invention to any manufacturer, two possible impediments should be kept in mind:

- the "NIH" (Not Invented Here) syndrome, and
- the common insistence that you give up many of your legal rights by signing a waiver (Section F, below).

Generally, the larger the manufacturer, the greater the chances of encountering one or both of these impediments.

The NIH syndrome is an unwritten attitude that handicaps inventors who submit their ideas to a company, no matter how meritorious such ideas may be. Put simply, many companies have a bias against any outsider ("the enemy") or any outside invention because it was "not invented here." This attitude prevails primarily because of jealousy. The job of the corporate engineering department is to create new and profitable products for their company. If an engineering department were to recommend an outside invention, it would almost be a tacit admission that the department had failed to do its job in solving a problem and coming up with the solution the outside inventor has found.

How can you overcome the NIH syndrome? First, realize that it's more likely to exist in larger companies, or companies with extensive engineering departments. Second, when forced to deal with engineering departments or any department in a company where the NIH syndrome may be present, always remember that the more your invention appears to be a logical extension of ideas already developed within the company, the better your chances of acceptance will be.

F. The Waiver and Precautions in Signing It

Most inventors affected with the paranoia part of the "Paranoia/Greed/Laziness Syndrome" (see Chapter 2, Section G) are afraid to show their invention to anyone, even after they've filed a patent application. The truth is, however, that most companies are far more afraid of you suing them for taking your invention than they are interested in stealing it. Most companies with access to legal advice will require you to sign their agreement (called a "waiver"), under which you give up a number of important rights that you would otherwise possess under the law. The reason for this waiver is that many companies have been sued by inventors claiming violation of an implied confidentiality agreement, or an implied agreement to pay if all or any part of the invention is used. Even though the company's own inventor may have come up with the invention independently of the outside inventor, many companies have lost these suits or were forced to compromise because of the uncertainties and expenses of litigation.

The waiver itself usually requires you to give up all your rights, except those which you may have under the patent laws. Specifically, the waiver typically asks you to agree that:

1. The company has no obligation to pay you if they use your idea.
2. The company isn't bound to keep your idea in confidence.
3. The company has no obligation to return any paper you submit.
4. The company has no obligation whatever to you, except under the patent laws.

Many companies add many other minor provisions, which are not significant enough to discuss here. The effect of the waiver is that you have no rights whatever against the company if they use your invention, except to sue them for patent infringement if and when you get a patent.

The usual procedure, if you send a letter mentioning your idea to the company, is for the company to route your letter to the patent or legal department, which will send you a form letter back stating their policy and asking you to sign the waiver before they agree to review your idea. Once you do so, the patent or legal department will approve your submission for review and send it to the appropriate engineering manager of the company.

Since you may not get a patent, since the company may use a variation of your idea that may not be covered by any patent you do get, and since you would like to have the company keep your submission in confidence, it's best to avoid signing any waiver if at all possible. For this reason, you should, at least initially, concentrate on smaller companies. The smaller the company, the less likely they are to make you sign a waiver. In fact, the best sort of relation you can have with a company to which you submit your ideas is to have them sign an agreement that you have drafted. Many small companies actually want to review outside inventions and are willing to sign a proprietary-submission agreement.

If the company is willing, or if you can swing it (say, by touting the commercial potential of your invention, being dramatic, establishing a rapport with the research people, etc.), have the company sign a Proprietary Submission Agreement such as the following:

Proprietary Submission Agreement

X Company agrees to review an invention from [your name] for a new and improved [describe invention], to keep in confidence such invention and all papers received, to return upon request all papers submitted, and to pay [your name] a reasonable sum and royalty to be settled by future negotiation or arbitration if X Company uses or adopts such invention.

If a company won't sign the above agreement, you can make it a bit more palatable by eliminating the last clause regarding the payment of a reasonable fee and royalty. Even with the last clause eliminated, you're in a very good position if you've gotten them to sign. If the company still refuses to sign your agreement, you can add the following clause:

The forgoing shall not obligate X Company with respect to any information which X Company can document (a) was known to it prior to receipt from me, either directly or indirectly, or (b) which is now or hereafter becomes part of the public domain from a source other than X Company.

If you can't get them to sign even this, you're still in a pretty good position legally if you can get them to review your invention without any agreement being signed by either side.

If all else fails and you do have to sign a waiver before the company will look at your invention (that's what will usually happen), it's not all that bad, since you do, at least, have a pending patent application. And most companies are far more afraid of you suing them (for taking your invention) than they are interested in stealing your invention. Now you can understand why I emphasized the need to file your patent application before submitting your invention to any company. If you sign the waiver, your position won't be seriously jeopardized if your patent issues. However, if you're submitting an invention to a company without having first filed a patent application (Block B of the Invention Decision Chart from Chapter 7), it's very important that you try to get the company to sign the above Proprietary Submission Agreement or, failing that, try to submit it without signing their waiver.

If you do have to sign a waiver, try to make sure the company is a reliable and fair one. Also, it's important to insist, by means of a separate letter, that the company make its decision within a given time, say six months, or else return all of your papers to you. This is because many companies, especially large ones, can take many months or years

to make a decision if you let them, which may interfere with your efforts to market the invention to others.

To the extent you are uncertain about whether signing a waiver is a good idea under the circumstances, a consultation with a patent attorney might be wise. On the other hand, don't let the waiver prevent you from showing your invention to a reputable manufacturer that promises to give you a decision in a reasonable time. As long as your patent is pending and eventually issues, you'll have reasonably strong rights.

G. The Best Way to Present Your Invention to a Manufacturer

The best and most effective way to sell your invention to a manufacturer is personally to visit the decision-maker in the company you elect and demonstrate a working model or prototype of your invention (or present drawings of it if you have no working model). To accomplish this, write a brief, personal, friendly, and sincere letter to the president of the company, saying that you have a very valuable invention you believe would be profitable for the company's business and that you would like to make an appointment when convenient to provide a brief demonstration. You can disclose the general area of your idea, but don't disclose its essence until you can present it properly. Keep the initiative by stating that you will call in a few days. Follow through accordingly. Here's an example:

Mr. Orville Billyer
President, Billyer Saw Co.
[etc.]

Dear Mr. Billyer:

I'm employed as an insurance agent, but in my spare time I like to tinker. While building a gun rack, I thought of and have perfected a new type of saw fence which I believe can be produced at 60% of the cost of your A-4 model, yet which can be adjusted in substantially less time with greater accuracy. For this reason, I believe that my fence, for which I've applied for a patent, can be a very profitable addition to your line. I'll call you in a few days to arrange a demonstration of my invention for you in your plant.

Most sincerely,

Marjorie Morgenstern
Marjorie Morgenstern

When you come to the demonstration, be prepared! Set up your presentation well in advance. Practice it on friends. Explain the advantages of your invention first: how it works, how it will be profitable for their business, and why it will sell. Make sure your model works. Also, prepare appropriate and attractive written materials and photos for later study by the decision-maker.

In your presentation and written material, it's wise to cover the "Three Fs"—Form, Fit, and Function.

Form is the appearance of your invention. Stress how it has (or can have) an attractive, enticing appearance.

Demonstrate how your invention fits with other products, or with the environment in which it is to be used. If your invention is a highly functional device, such as a saw fence, show and tell how it fits onto a sawing machine. If it's a clock, show (or present attractive pictures showing) how it looks attractive on a desk or coffee table.

Function is what your invention does, how it works, what results it attains. Demonstrate and discuss its function and its advantage here. Mention all of the advantages from your Positive and Negative Factors Evaluation (Form 4-1, Appendix 7). In addition, be prepared to discuss such items as cost of manufacture, profit, retail price, competition, possible product liability, and product life. Review all of the positive and negative factors from the list in Chapter 4 to be sure you've covered all possible considerations.

During the verbal part of your presentation, it's wise to use diagrams and charts, but keep your model, written materials, and photos hidden from view. Otherwise, the people you're trying to sell to will be looking at these instead of listening to you. Then, at a dramatic moment, bring out your model and demonstrate how it works. Don't apologize if your model is a crude or unattractive prototype, but radiate enough confidence in yourself and your invention that they will overlook any lack of "cosmetics." If you can't bring or show them your model for any reason, a videotape, filmstrip, drawing, diagram, or slide presentation that shows the three F's will be a viable, though less desirable way, to show the invention.

If possible, make them think that the invention is basically their idea. You can do this by praising their related product line and then showing how your idea compliments theirs, or by enthusiastically endorsing any reasonable suggestion they make for your idea.

At the end of your verbal presentation, produce your written materials and pictures for study (either then and there or at a later time). If they're interested in the invention, be prepared to state your terms and conditions. (See Chapter 16, Section G.) If they're really serious and ask for it, you can show them your patent application without your claims, but only with the understanding that it won't be copied and will be returned to you. You shouldn't offer the claims, prior art from your search, serial number, or filing date, unless you're asked. If you're relying on a Provisional Patent Application for your patent pending status, then you won't have drafted your claims yet, and you also may not have conducted a patentability search.

If you've done your best and still get a rejection, don't accept it blindly and walk away with your tail between your legs, but turn it into an asset for next time. Talk to the executives about it and learn exactly why they decided not to accept your idea so that in the future you'll be better prepared to answer and overcome the disadvantage that blocked your initial acceptance.

Assuming the company is interested, you shouldn't blindly or automatically accept it as your patron. Rather, you should evaluate the company to which you're demonstrating your invention just as they're evaluating you and your invention. For example, if the company seems to lack energy or vision, don't go with them. Also, you should check out the company with their local Better Business Bureau to see if they have a clean record. After all, you're risking a lot, too, when you sign up with a company. If the company doesn't promote your invention enthusiastically and correctly, it can fail in the market, even if it's the greatest thing to come down the pike in 20 years.

DON'T BE AFRAID OF SIMULTANEOUS SUBMISSIONS
If you're aware of several prospective companies that you feel might be interested, I recommend that you approach all of the companies simultaneously; otherwise, you'll waste too much time. If several companies "bite" concurrently, you'll be in the enviable position of being able to choose your licensee.

H. Presenting Your Invention by Correspondence

Another way to present your invention is by correspondence. Because letters are easy to file and forget, and because any salesman will tell you a personal presentation is a thousand times more likely to make a sale, I strongly advise against submitting an invention to a manufacturer by correspondence if you can avoid it. Try your utmost to arrange a personal demonstration with a working model as described in the previous section. Nevertheless, if you do have to resort to correspondence, don't let your efforts slacken.

Your letter should always be addressed to a specific individual. Find the president's name from the directories mentioned in Section D above. If you receive an expression of interest from the company, you will probably be faced with the waiver question. My comments in the previous discussion cover how to handle this problem. Before you send a model, get an advance written commitment from the company that they'll return it within a given time. You should send your model by certified, insured mail, return receipt requested, and make follow-up phone calls as appropriate.

I. Making an Agreement to Sell Your Invention

If you sell your invention to a manufacturer/distributor, the next step is to sign an agreement of some sort with the manufacturer. The question thus arises, what will be the terms of the agreement, exactly what will you sell them, and for how much? There are many possibilities. These are covered in Chapter 16, which deals with ownership and transfers of patents.

J. Manufacturing and/or Distributing the Invention Yourself

For reasons stated earlier, manufacturing and/or distributing a product embodying your invention—unless you already have manufacturing experience, a plant, and/or distribution facilities—is very difficult. Besides, you can spend your time more effectively selling your invention or patent application, rather than dealing with manufacturing and product-marketing problems.

If you do plan to manufacture and/or distribute your invention yourself (Routes 6 or 7), I strongly suggest that you learn about the subject thoroughly beforehand so you will know what is involved and which pitfalls to avoid. The best place to obtain literature and reading material is your local SBA (Small Business Administration) office, which has scads of literature and aids available to apprise you of the problems and pitfalls. They even have a service that allows you to obtain the advice of an experienced executive free; ask for a "Counseling Request from Small Business Firm" form. Nolo Press publishes an excellent book, *How to Write a Business Plan,* by Mike McKeever, which tells potential businesspeople how to assess the costs of a proposed business, how to draft a business plan, and how to obtain sufficient start-up money.

1. Financing the Manufacture of Your Invention

Financing any manufacturing venture of your own is a separate and formidable problem. If you have an untried and unsold product, most banks will not lend you the money to go ahead. However, if you can get orders from various local firms, the bank may lend you the money. Thus a local test-marketing effort on a limited scale may be desirable.

For obtaining money to finance untried products, a money lender who's willing to take more risk is needed. Such a person is usually termed a "venture capitalist" (VC). A VC will loan you money in exchange for shares or a portion of your enterprise. Pratt's *Guide to Venture Capital Sources* (listed in Appendix 2, Books of Use and Interest) is the most popular source of VCs, but most libraries have other VC resources. Also the Venture Capital Hotline, tel. 408-625-0700, will provide you with a list of suitable VCs for a fee (about $75). However, VCs won't lend you money on the same terms a bank would. Because of the higher risks they take, they demand a much larger return—namely a piece of the action. Also, they'll want to monitor your company and exercise some degree of control, usually by putting their people on your board of directors. A thorough discussion of the pros and cons of working with venture capitalists can be found in the Nolo Press book, *How to Write a Business Plan,* mentioned earlier. While most VCs are companies or partnerships, sometimes wealthy individuals finance inventions, so if you have a rich uncle or know of a suitable patron, include them on your list.

A recent development in the VC field is the "Incubator VC." This is a VC that provides several different inventors with offices, labs, and/or a manufacturing area in a special building, called an "innovation center." Also the VC may provide technical, financial, and marketing consultation, as well as other services, until each nurtured enterprise is ready to leave the "nest." The sources in the preceding paragraph, as well as inventors' organizations (Chapter 2, Section F), will give you the names of Incubator VCs; they are sponsored by academia, state and federal governments, and private organizations. One of the largest is Genexus International, Inc., 200 N. Main St., Suite 200, Salt Lake City, UT 84103, tel. 801-328-1504. They have several incubation centers around the U.S. Another is Inventure Place, Akron, OH.

2. Prepare a Business Plan

To obtain venture capital to start a business based on your invention, you'll have to prepare a business plan—a presentation that tells all about your invention, the market for it, and how you plan to use the money. You can get an excellent booklet from a national accounting firm gratis, which will tell you how to prepare your business plan. This is *Financing Business Growth* , available free from any office of Deloitte & Touche LLP. This practical guide tells how to write and present your business plan. Again, *How to Write a Business Plan* is also recommended for this purpose.

3. Distribution Through Mail Order

Mail order is often an easy way for an individual to distribute an invention, whether the inventor makes it or has it made. An excellent guide is *How I Made $1,000,000 in Mail Order,* by E. Joseph Cossman (Prentice-Hall). Once your mail order operation starts bringing in some cash, you can branch out and try to get some local, then regional, then state, and then (hopefully) national distributors who handle lines similar to yours.

There are two principal ways to contact your potential customers:
- magazine/media advertising, and
- direct mail advertising.

If you're interested in the latter, order the *Dunhill Marketing Guide to Mailing Lists* from Dunhill International List Company, Inc., 444 Park Avenue South, New York, NY 10016.

You can also try to use a mail order distributor. Many mail order houses will, if you send them a production sample and they like it and feel you can meet their demand, buy your production. They'll put in their own ads, manufacture, and distribute their own catalog, and thus are valuable intermediaries for many garage-shop manufacturers. Walter Drake & Sons, Colorado Springs, CO 80940, is one of the largest, but you can obtain the names of many others by looking for ads in *Redbook, House Beautiful, Better Homes and Gardens, Apartment Life, Sunset, Holiday,* etc. These mail-order firms are always looking for new gadgets, and most of their products come from small firms. While many of them will purchase quantities of your product outright, some will want to take them on consignment, which means they do not pay you until and unless they sell it themselves.

4. Utilize Government Services

If your invention is or can be used in a product that the federal government might purchase, write to the General Services Administration, Federal Supply Service, 1734 New York Avenue, NW, Washington, DC 20406, telling them that you're offering a product that you feel the government can use. They'll send you appropriate forms and instructions. Also, don't neglect your corresponding state and local purchasing agencies.

If you have an energy-related invention, the Department of Energy may give you a research grant if the National Bureau of Standards gives it a favorable evaluation. Write for an Energy-Related Inventions Program brochure from the U.S. Department of Energy, Office of Technical and Financial Assistance, Forrestal Building, CE-50, 1000 Independence Ave., SW, Washington, DC 20585.

5. Publicity

Publicity will sometimes be of great aid to you before you get your invention into production, and is invaluable once it's on the market. Assuming it's not yet on the market and you're either looking for a manufacturer, distributor, or thinking of manufacturing or distributing it yourself, publicity can cut both ways. As stated, many manufacturers like to get a secret head start on their competition and thus won't be too interested if your invention has already been disseminated to the public.

If you're going to make and sell it yourself, I believe you should wait until you've got the product out before you try to publicize it. Why? The public's memory span is short, so they'll be likely to forget about your product by the time you get it on sale. My advice is to not seek publicity until a product with your invention is almost or actually on the market, unless you've tried unsuccessfully, after substantial efforts, to get it on the market.

Assuming you're ready for publicity, one way to get it (at a price) is to hire a public-relations or marketing research firm to promote your invention for you. There are many reputable firms who can come up with many creative and valuable ideas for a fee. However, since the cost of public-relations services is very high, I don't recommend it unless you can bear the cost without difficulty.

Many magazines will feature new ideas free if you send them a clear, understandable, professional-quality photo or drawing of your invention, plus a brief, clear, and understandable description of it. They may even write a full-length feature about your invention if they think it's interesting enough. Suitable magazines are *Popular Science, Mechanics Illustrated, Popular Electronics, Better Homes and Gardens, Pageant, Parade, Playboy, This Week, True Story, Jet, Outdoor Life, House and Garden, House Beautiful, Outdoor Living, Changing Times, McCall's, Apartment Life, Argosy* and *Sunset.* You can obtain the addresses of those you think are relevant from *Ulrich's International Periodicals Directory* in your local library.

The magazine *Advertising Age* has a feature called "Idea Marketplace" in each issue in which they publicize new inventions gratis. Write to them at Crown Communications, Inc., 740 Rush Street, Chicago, IL 60611, sending a picture and brief description of your invention. Thomas Publications, 1 Pennsylvania Plaza, New York, NY 10119, has a bimonthly called *Technology Mart* that offers a similar service, as does *Dental Products Reporter,* 4849 Gulf Road, Skokie, IL 60077, and the "Form + Function" column of the *Wall Street Journal,* by John Pierson.

Review the trade magazines in the field of your invention for other ideas.

Nolo also publishes an excellent book, *Marketing Without Advertising*, by Phillips and Rasberry; its title is self-explanatory.

Other sources of publicity are exhibits, trade fairs, and business shows. I don't recommend that you use these, since I haven't heard many success stories from exhibitors. But if you feel that you may get a bite from this type of exposure, try one—the cost is usually a few hundred dollars. You'll be given a table or booth, or equivalent space to demonstrate your invention at the fair or show. Naturally, your exhibit should be attractive and interesting, and it is preferable to have a working model or very good literature available in connection with your invention. There are exhibition-service companies that will prepare a display exhibit for you for a fee. Also, several of the Contingent-Fee Invention Brokers listed above have exhibition areas.

Don't overlook the media (radio, TV, newspapers, and magazines) as an excellent source of free publicity, which most experts say is the best kind. Many local radio and TV stations feature talk shows whose hosts are always looking for interesting guests; some stations even have shows in which new inventors can demonstrate or discuss their inventions. To find the shows and get on them, call your local stations, ask what talk shows they have and which might be interested in interviewing an inventor with a hot new product, and who the appropriate producers are. Then send the producers a press kit or letter describing your invention and why it and you would be of interest to the show's listeners.

One of the best ways to get media publicity (and concomitant interviews) is to dream up or pull a stunt. For example, if you've invented a new bicycle drive mechanism, you might enter and win a local bike race, or sponsor some type of contest (which you can win!).

Lastly, don't overlook a new phenomenon—invention stores that sell newly invented products at retail. One is the New Products Showcase at the Irving Mall in Irving, TX. Also, there are a number of Sharper Image- and Nature Co.-like stores that sell dozens of new gadgets and are always looking for new ones to scoop their competition.

6. The Premium Marketing Route

If you can't get a manufacturer or distributor to take your invention, try offering it as a premium to accompany a related product that is already on the market. For example, one television magazine show featured a girl, Abbey Mae Fleck, 8, of St. Paul, Minnesota, who invented a great plastic hanger to suspend bacon in a microwave oven so that the grease dripped away while it cooked. However, none of the manufacturers of plastic microwave accessories would bite (their loss!). So ingenious Abbey approached a bacon company and got them to offer her MAKIN BACON® via a discount coupon on their bacon packages. The result: an instant success! The bacon company's investment was minimal, yet it profited handsomely by providing a way to cook its bacon dryly. And Abbey got her commercial distribution. Abbey's story also shows that creativity has no age limits. ■

INVENTOR'S COMMANDMENT #21

Foreign Filing: Don't file your invention in any foreign country unless you're highly confident it has extremely strong commercial potential there. File in Convention (major industrial) countries within one year of your earliest U.S. filing date (regular or Provision Patent Application) and in non-Convention countries before the invention becomes publicly known. Don't file abroad until you receive a foreign-filing license or until six months from your U.S. filing date.

A. Introduction

By now you've gotten your U.S. application on file and have taken steps to have your invention manufactured and distributed in anticipation of receiving a patent. Your next step will be either to file in one or more other countries (this chapter) or to deal with the first substantive response by the U.S. PTO (called an "Office Action") to your application (Chapter 13).

If you've already received your first Office Action from the U.S. PTO, you'll have a pretty good idea of the patentability of your invention and, consequently, your chance of getting foreign patents abroad. (If you want to help determine your chances of getting foreign patents, see Chapter 10, Section P, to see how to get your U.S. application examined earlier.)

Why file your patent application in other countries? Simply because a U.S. patent will give you a monopoly only in the U.S. If you think your invention is important enough to be manufactured or sold in large quantities in any other countries, so that you want to create a monopoly there, you'll have to go through the considerable effort and expense of foreign filing in order to eventually get a patent in each desired foreign country. Otherwise, anyone in the foreign country will be able to make, use, and sell your invention with impunity. However, they won't be able to bring it into the U.S. if you have a U.S. patent without infringing your U.S. patent.

This chapter doesn't give you the full, detailed instructions necessary to file abroad. That would take another book. Instead, my mission is to alert you to the basic procedures for foreign filing, so that you won't lose your opportunity to do so through lack of information. However, once you decide to foreign file, you'll probably need some professional guidance, notwithstanding the availability of other resources (discussed in Section K of this chapter) that will answer most of your questions.

The most important points you can learn from this chapter are presented in Inventor's Commandment #21 at the beginning of this chapter. It states (a) don't foreign file in any foreign country unless you're highly confident your invention has extremely strong commercial potential there, (b) don't foreign file until you get a foreign-filing license (see Section G, below) or until six months has elapsed from your U.S. filing date, (c) you must do any desired filing in non-Convention countries (see Section E, below) before you publish or sell the invention, and (d) in all other countries (Convention countries—see Section B, below) within one year of your earliest U.S. filing date (regular or Provisional Patent Application (PPA)).

Prior to discussing the ins and outs of foreign filing, it's important that you familiarize yourself with several important treaties and arrangements. As I'll explain in detail below, most industrialized countries are members of the "Paris Convention," which gives you the full benefit of your filing date in your home country, provided you file in a foreign Convention country within one year (Section B, below). Also, most of the countries of Europe have joined the European Patent Convention, which has created a single patent office—the European Patent Office (EPO—Section C, below)—to grant European patents that are good in all member countries. Lastly, most industrialized countries are also members of the PCT—Patent Cooperation Treaty—which enables applicants to file a relatively economical international application in their home country within one year of their home-country filing date. The PCT gives applicants up to a 30-month delay and enables them to have a search, and optimally an examination, performed before making an expensive filing abroad (Section D). Let's discuss these areas in detail.

B. The Paris Convention and the One-Year Foreign Filing Rule

The most important thing to know about foreign filing is the International Convention for the Protection of Industrial Property. Most people in the patent field call it the "Paris Convention" or simply "the Convention." The majority of industrialized nations of the world are parties to this international treaty, which was entered into in Paris in 1883 and has been revised many times since. Generally, the Paris Convention governs almost all reciprocal patent filing rights.

For the purpose of this chapter, there's only one thing you need to know about the all-important Paris Convention: If you file a patent application (regular or PPA) in any one member jurisdiction of the Paris Convention (such as the U.S.), you can file a corresponding application in any other member jurisdiction (such as the U.K., Japan, the EPO, the PCT, Australia, etc.), within one year of your earliest filing date—six months for designs. Your applications in the other jurisdiction will be entitled to the filing date of your U.S. application (regular or PPA) for purposes of overcoming prior art. ("Jurisdiction" refers to any country or group of countries that have joined under a treaty such as the EPO, PCT, or AIPO (the African Intellectual Property Organization).)

You do have to claim "priority" of your original application. If you fail to file any foreign applications under the Convention within the one-year period, you can still file after the one-year period in Convention jurisdictions, provided you haven't sold, published, or patented your invention yet. However, any such late application won't get the benefit of your original U.S. filing date, so any relevant prior art that has been published in the meantime can be applied against your applications. Put differently, once you miss the one-year deadline, your foreign application won't be entitled to the filing date of your original application. Rather, it becomes a non-Convention application, even in Convention countries. Also, once your U.S. application

issues, it's too late to foreign file anywhere (unless you file within the one-year period)—that is, you file a Convention application.

All jurisdictions that are members of the Paris Convention are indicated in Fig. 12A, where the most popular jurisdictions for foreign filing are indicated in boldface.

C. European Patent Office/Europäisches Patentamt/Office européen des brevets (EPO)

The European Patent Office (EPO) is a separate and vast trilingual patent office in Munich, across the Isar River from the famous Deutsches Museum. The EPO grew out of the earlier formation of the European Economic Community (EEC, also known as "the Common Market") and the economic integration that resulted. Member nations of the EEC are also members of a treaty known as the European Patent Convention (EPC). Under the EPC you can make one patent filing in the EPO, whose main branch is at Ehrhardstrasse 27, D-8000, München 2, Germany. If this filing matures into a European patent, it will, when registered in whatever individual member countries you select, cover your invention in these selected countries. And since the EPC is, in turn, considered the same as a single country (a jurisdiction) under the Paris Convention and the PCT, your effective EPO filing date will be the same as your original U.S. filing date, so long as you comply with the one-year foreign filing rule. In other words, filing in the EPO allows you to kill many birds with one stone.

Once your application is on file, the EPO will subject it to a rigorous examination, including an opposition publication 18 months after filing. (See Chapter 13.) Even though you'll have to work through a European agent, patent prosecution before the EPO is generally smoother than the PTO because the examiners are better trained (all speak and write three languages fluently) and because they actually take the initiative and suggest how to write your claims to get them allowed. If your application is allowed, you'll be granted a European patent that lasts for 20 years from your filing date (provided you pay maintenance fees in the member countries you've selected). Your patent will be valid automatically in each member country of the EPC that you've designated in your application, provided that you register it in and file translations in each country and appoint an agent there.

⚠ Filing in the EPO is extremely expensive for U.S. residents and you'll have to pay an annuity to the EPO each year your application is on file there until it issues. Thereafter, you'll have to pay annuities in each member country in which you've registered your Europatent. Therefore, as I suggest in Section H, below, you should not file for a Europatent unless you're extremely confident your invention will be commercially successful there, or unless someone else, such as a European licensee, is paying the freight.

All member countries of the EPO are indicated in Fig. 12A.

D. The Patent Cooperation Treaty (PCT)

The PCT is another important treaty to which most industrial countries are a party. Under the Patent Cooperation Treaty (PCT), which was entered into in 1978, you can file in the U.S. and then make a single international filing within the one-year period; this can cover all of the PCT jurisdictions, including the European Patent Office (EPO). Eventually, you must file separate or "national" applications in each PCT jurisdiction (including the EPO) where you desire coverage. These separate filings, which must be translated for non-English-speaking jurisdictions, must be made within 20 months after your U.S. filing date, or eight months after your PCT application is filed. However, if you elect a Chapter II of the PCT by 19 months after your U.S.

filing date, you can wait up to 30 months after your U.S. filing date to make these separate filings. Thus, except for the single international filing, the PCT affords you a 20- or 30-month extension in which to file in PCT countries or the EPO.

Also, you can file your first regular application under the PCT and then file in any PCT jurisdiction (including the U.S.) within 20 or 30 months from your PCT filing date. You should take this route if you've filed a PPA and you've decided to foreign file by one year after your PPA filing date.

Further, since the PCT is a member of the Paris Convention, if you file with the PCT first, you can file in any non-PCT Convention jurisdiction within one year from your PCT filing date. After you file your PCT application, you'll receive a "search report," but unless you continue with Chapter II, you'll have no opportunity to prosecute the application or get claims allowed. If you elect Chapter II of the PCT, you will receive an examination and can prosecute and amend your claims and receive a formal indication of allowability (or rejection!). A list of the PCT jurisdictions is indicated in Fig. 12A, including those that have accepted Chapter II. (Note that all PCT members are members of the Paris Convention, but not vice versa.)

The PCT is administered by the World Intellectual Property Organization in Geneva (address in Section K).

E. Non-Convention Countries

There are a significant number of countries (generally non-industrial, except for India) that aren't parties to the Paris Convention. These are indicated in Fig. 12A.

Filing isn't common in most of these countries, but if you do want to file in any of them, you may do so at any time, provided:

   a. Your invention hasn't yet become publicly known, either by your publication, by patenting, by public sale, or by normal publication, in the course of prosecution in a foreign jurisdiction (the PCT and the EPO publish 18 months after filing), and

   b. You've been given a foreign-filing license on your U.S. filing receipt (see Section G, below) or six months has elapsed from your U.S. filing date.

I won't discuss filing in non-Convention countries in detail, except to note that if you do wish to file in any, you should do so in exactly the same manner as you would for an individual filing in a Convention country (see Section J, below), except that you won't need a certified copy of your U.S. application.

Country or Jurisdiction	Paris Cnvn.	EPO	PCT	PCT Ch. II	Pan Am Cnvn.
Albania	■		■	■	
Algeria	■				
Argentina	■				
ARIPO *	■		■	■	
Armenia°	■		■	■	
Australia	■		■	■	
Austria	■	■	■	■	
Azerbaijan°	■		■	■	
Bangladesh	■				
Barbados	■		■	■	
Belarus°	■		■	■	
Belgium	■	■	■	■	
Bolivia	■				
Bosnia-Herzegovina	■		■	■	
Brazil	■		■	■	
Bulgaria	■		■	■	
Burundi	■				
Canada	■		■	■	
Chile	■				
China, Mainland	■		■	■	
China, Taiwan△					
Colombia					
Costa Rica	p				■
Croatia	■				
Cuba	■				
Cyprus	■				
Czech Republic	■		■	■	
Denmark	■	■	■	■	
Dominican Republic	■				
Ecuador	p				■
Egypt	■				
El Salvador	■				

Country or Jurisdiction	Paris Cnvn.	EPO	PCT	PCT Ch. II	Pan Am Cnvn.
Estonia	■		■	■	
Ethiopia					
European Pat. Off.	■	■	■	■	
Finland	■		■	■	
France	■	■	■	■	
Gambia	■				
Georgia	■		■	■	
Germany	■	■	■	■	
Ghana	■		■		
Greece	■	■	■	■	
Guatemala	p				■
Guinea-Bissau	■				
Guyana	■				
Haiti	■				
Holy See	■				
Honduras	■				
Hong Kong					
Hungary	■		■	■	
Iceland	■		■	■	
India△	■				
Indonesia	■				
Iran	■				
Iraq	■				
Ireland	■		■	■	
Israel	■		■	■	
Italy	■	■	■	■	
Jamaica					
Japan	■		■	■	
Jordan	■				
Kazakhstan°	■		■	■	
Korea, North	■		■	■	
Korea, South	■		■	■	

⚠ The PCT organization (WIPO) is a member of the Paris Convention.

* African Regional Industrial Property Organization: Ghana, Kenya, Malawi, Sudan, and Uganda.
° Also can be covered by Eurasian Patent from Eurasian Patent Office in Moscow.
△ Separate priority treaties between United States and Taiwan and India.

† Organisation Africain Proprété Intellectuel: Common patent system for French-speaking African countries: Benin, Burkina Faso, Cameroon, Central African Republic, Chad, Congo, Côte d'Ivoire, Gabon, Guinea, Mali, Mauritania, Niger, Senegal, and Togo.

p Pan-American Convention (similar to Paris Convention).

Fig. 12A—Memberships in Patent Conventions

Country or Jurisdiction	Paris Cnvn.	EPO	PCT	PCT Ch. II	Pan Am Cnvn.
Kuwait					
Kyrgyzstan°	■		■	■	
Latvia	■		■	■	
Lebanon	■				
Lesotho	■		■	■	
Liberia	■		■	■	
Libya	■				
Liechtenstein	■	■	■	■	
Lithuania	■		■	■	
Luxembourg	■	■	■	■	
Macedonia	■		■	■	
Madagascar	■		■	■	
Malaysia	■				
Malta	■				
Mauritania	■		■	■	
Mauritius	■				
Mexico	■		■	■	
Moldavia	■		■	■	
Moldoro, Republic of	■		■	■	
Monaco	■		■	■	
Mongolia	■		■	■	
Morocco	■				
Netherlands	■	■	■	■	
New Zealand	■		■	■	
Nicaragua	p				■
Niger	■		■		
Nigeria	■				
Norway	■		■	■	
OAPI †	■		■	■	
Pakistan					
Panama					
Paraguay	■				
Peru	■				
Philippines	■				
Poland	■		■	■	
Portugal	■		■	■	

Country or Jurisdiction	Paris Cnvn.	EPO	PCT	PCT Ch. II	Pan Am Cnvn.
Romania	■		■	■	
Russian Federation°	■		■	■	
Rwanda	■				
Saint Lucia	■		■	■	
St. Kitts & Nevis	■				
San Marino	■				
Sierra Leone					
Singapore	■		■	■	
Slovak Republic	■		■	■	
Slovenia	■		■	■	
South Africa	■				
Spain	■	■	■		
Sri Lanka	■		■	■	
Suriname	■				
Swaziland	■		■	■	
Sweden	■	■	■	■	
Switzerland	■	■	■	■	
Syria	■				
Tajikistan°	■		■	■	
Tanzania	■				
Thailand					
Togo	■		■		
Trinidad & Tobago	■		■	■	
Tunisia	■				
Turkey	■		■	■	
Turkmenistan°	■		■	■	
Ukraine	■		■	■	
United Kingdom	■	■	■	■	
United States	■		■	■	
Uzbekistan	■		■	■	
Venezuela					
Vietnam	■		■		
Yugoslavia	■		■		
Zaire	■				
Zambia	■				
Zimbabwe	■		■	■	

Fig. 12A—Memberships in Patent Conventions

F. Never Wait Until the End of Any Filing Period

As stated, you have one year after you file your U.S. application to file foreign Convention patent applications (and be entitled to your U.S. filing date) in the PCT, the EPO, or any other jurisdiction that's a member of the Paris Convention. You also have eight months (18 months under Chapter II) after you file a PCT application to file in the individual PCT countries, including the EPO. You have one year, if you file under the PCT first, to file in non-PCT Convention countries or 20 months (30 months under Chapter II) to file in the PCT countries, respectively. However, you should never wait until the end of any of these periods. You should normally make your decision and start to take action about two or three months before the end of the period. This is to give you and the foreign agents time to prepare (or have prepared) the necessary correspondence and translations and to order a certified copy, if needed, of your U.S. application. So mark your calendar in advance accordingly. (While you shouldn't wait until the very end of the one-year period, you shouldn't file until near the end since there's no advantage in filing early, unless you need an early patent—for example, because you have a foreign infringement.)

G. The Early Foreign Filing License or Mandatory Six-Month Delay

Normally, the blue official filing receipt that you get after filing your U.S. application (Chapter 13, Section A) gives you express permission from the PTO to file abroad. This permission usually will be printed on your filing receipt, as follows: "Foreign Filing License Granted 1995 Aug 9." However, if your filing receipt fails to include a foreign filing license (only inventions with possible military applications won't include the license), you aren't allowed to foreign file on your invention until six months following your U.S. filing date. What's the reason for this? To give the U.S. government a chance to review your application for possible classification on national security grounds. You probably won't be affected by any of this, as most applications get the foreign filing license immediately and, in any case, there is usually no good reason to file before six months after your U.S. filing. If your situation is different, however, and your filing receipt doesn't include a license, see a patent lawyer (Chapter 6, Section F). If your invention does have military applications, not only will you fail to get a foreign filing license on your filing receipt, but after you receive the receipt, you may receive a Secrecy Order from the PTO. This will order you to keep your invention secret until it's declassified, which often takes 12 years. Your patent can't issue till then, but the Government may compensate you if they use your invention in the meantime. You can foreign file an application that is under a secrecy order, but it's complicated; see a patent lawyer who has experience in this area.

H. Don't File Abroad Unless Your Invention Has Very Good Prospects in That Country

Because patent prosecution and practice in other countries is relatively complicated and extremely expensive, you should not file applications abroad unless:

- A significant market for products embodying the invention is *very* likely to exist, or
- *Significant* commercial production of your invention is *very* likely to occur, or
- You've got a foreign licensee (someone who's paying you money for your invention and know-how).

It's been my experience that far too many inventors file abroad because they're in love with their invention and feel it will capture the world. Unfortunately, this almost never happens. Almost all inventors who do file abroad never recoup their investment—that is, they usually waste tens of thousands of dollars in fees and hardly ever derive any royalties, let alone enough royalties to cover their costs. Thus, as a general rule, I suggest that you file in another country only if you feel that you're:

- very likely to sell at least $500,000 worth of your invention there, if you're selling it yourself, or

- very likely to earn at least $50,000 in royalties from sales of your invention there by others, or
- associated with a licensee or sales representative there who contracts to pay you royalties with a substantial advance or guarantee, or who will pay for your foreign filing in that country.

Note that even if an infringement occurs in a country where you didn't file, it still wouldn't have paid to file unless the infringement is substantial enough to justify the expense of filing, getting the patent, and the uncertainties of licensing and litigation.

The U.S., with its approximately 300 million people, provides a huge marketplace that should be a more-than-adequate market from which to make your fortune, especially if it's your first invention. In comparison, most foreign countries are relatively insignificant. For example, Switzerland is smaller in size than San Bernardino County in California and smaller in population than Los Angeles County; Canada has fewer people than California. In other words, filing in the U.S. usually gives you ten to 50 times more bang for your buck than filing abroad, which costs ten to 50 times as much anyway.

I.   The Patent Laws of Other Countries Are Different

Despite the Paris Convention and other treaties covering patent applications, and except for Canada, whose patent laws and practice are practically identical to ours, almost all countries have some differences from the U.S. in their substantive patent laws and practices. These differences have been reduced under the GATT treaty, but some that still exist are as follows:

- In the U.S., once an application is examined and allowed, the patent issues without any further proceedings. However, most foreign countries have an opposition proceeding under which the application is published and anyone who believes the invention isn't patentable can cite additional prior art to the patent office in order to block the patent.
- In the U.S. the patent must be applied for in the name of the actual inventor, but in most foreign countries any assignee (usually the inventor's employer-company) can apply in its own name.
- Many smaller countries (for example, Belgium and Portugal) don't conduct novelty examinations on applications that are filed there directly (not through the EPO), but instead simply issue a patent on every application filed and leave it up to the courts (in the

event of an infringement) to determine whether the invention was novel and unobvious.
- Some jurisdictions (the EPO, France, Germany, Italy, Australia, the Netherlands) require the payment of annual maintenance fees while the application is pending. But if you file in these countries (except Australia) through the EPO, no individual country fees are due until the European patent issues and is registered in each country; however, annual EPO fees are due until the Europatent issues.
- Most foreign countries don't have the one-year grace period the U.S. has. Thus you must get an effective filing date in most countries (either by actual filing there or by filing in the U.S. and then filing a corresponding Convention application there within one year) before publication of the invention. Most foreign countries consider any publication in any country as prior art, but some recognize only publications in their country as prior art.
- If two different applicants file respective patent applications on the same invention, most countries will award a patent to the first to file, a simple, economical, and easy-for-a-layperson system. However, the U.S. and the Philippines award the patent to the "first to invent," a system that requires an expensive, complicated, and lawyer-conducted trial proceeding called an interference (see Chapter 13).
- In Japan, the filing and translation fees are very high. Then, examination must be separately requested within seven years, requiring another stiff fee. After examination is requested, it takes about three years before the Japanese Patent Office, which is severely understaffed, gets around to it. Getting the application allowed is very difficult. However, it will be given more respect than in the U.S. That is, competitors will be far less likely to infringe or challenge it. Nevertheless, Japanese courts tend to interpret patents very narrowly.

J.   The Ways to File Abroad

Until several years ago, there was only one way to foreign file, namely, to file a separate application in each country in which you wished to file. As this was a cumbersome and expensive process, many of the countries got together to simplify things. Now there are four basic approaches to filing abroad in Convention countries. You may end up using different approaches for different countries, or the same approach for all. The chart below, Fig. 12B, summarizes these alternatives. In essence, they are:

Route A: This is the most common. File in U.S. Then file in non-Convention countries before publication or sale. (For more information about filing in non-Convention countries, see Section E, above.) Then, within one year, under the Paris Convention, file a PCT application to cover the PCT countries and jurisdictions (including the EPO). Select the PTO or EPO for the search. Then, within 19 months from your U.S. filing date, elect Chapter II of the PCT to get the application examined, either in the PTO or EPO. Finally, by 30 months from your U.S. filing date, file national applications (you'll have to hire agents and spend big bucks) in the EPO and non-EPO PCT countries.

Route B: This is the same as Route A, except that you don't elect Chapter II of the PCT, but instead file directly in the EPO and non-EPO countries within 20 months from your U.S. filing date.

Route C: This is the same as Route A, except that the PCT is eliminated entirely and you file Convention applications in the EPO and non-EPO countries within 12 months from your U.S. filing date.

Route D: This is the same as Route C, except that you file directly in the individual EPO countries (rather than the EPO).

Route E: In addition, if you've filed a Provisional Patent Application (PPA), and by the time almost one year elapses from your PPA's filing date you want to file in the U.S. and abroad, you can do so in three basic ways: (1) File a PCT application yourself, naming the U.S. and all other desired PCT countries. File in non-PCT Convention countries using agents. By 19 months from your PPA filing date, elect Chapter II of the PCT and select examination in the PTO or EPO. By 30 months from your PPA filing date, file, via agents, national applications in the EPO and non-EPO countries and file yourself in the U.S., claiming priority of your PCT application. (2) File separate applications in the U.S. and PCT yourself. Continue as in Route A for your PCT application. (3) File separate applications in the U.S. and either (a) use agents to file in non-EPO countries and the EPO (Route C), or (b) use agents to file national Convention applications in individual countries in Europe and elsewhere (Route D).

Let's discuss each of these alternatives in more detail.

1. Route A: Non-Convention/ Convention (PCT and Non-PCT/Chapter II/ National)

Route A is the most popular way to go. Not surprisingly, it's also the cheapest way to go in the short run, since you won't have to file national applications (with foreign patent agents and the huge expense they entail—indicated by boxes with double lines on the chart) until 30 months from

your U.S. filing date. Under Route A, you file in the U.S. first and then go abroad through the PCT, insofar as possible. Here's how it works for U.S. inventors:

- First file in the U.S. in the usual manner.
- Next file directly in any non-Convention countries you desire, before your application or invention is published, but after you get your foreign-filing license or six months has elapsed from your U.S. filing date.
- Then, before one year from your U.S. filing date, file a PCT request form and a separate "international application" with the U.S. PTO within 12 months from your filing date. The application designates the PCT member countries or jurisdictions (such as the EPO) in which you desire coverage.
- The request and application are forwarded to the "International Searching Authority" (a branch of the PTO) or the EPO (if you've elected to have your search made there) where an "international search report" is prepared. If you select the PTO, the examination will generally be done by the same examiner who handles your U.S. application.
- Copies of the search report and application are then forwarded to the countries designated in the application. Cite any new references to the PTO on your basic U.S. case through another Information Disclosure Statement.
- Elect to file under Chapter II within 19 months of your U.S. filing date. You'll get an examination report and prosecute the application similar to the way you do with a U.S. application and you'll ultimately get your claims allowed or rejected.
- Within 30 months from your U.S. filing date, you must hire agents and prosecute the application in the individual countries. You must also provide a translation (except in the EPO) and must pay any fees that are required. While separate prosecution is required in each country, it's commonly made easier by the fact that the PCT member countries generally rely on the international search and examination.

a. How to Prepare and File an International Application

To file an international application under the PCT, first prepare your original U.S. application and drawings in the A4 international format. The main differences between the PCT and U.S. national formats (both of which are acceptable for U.S. applications) are the drawing size and margins, location of page numbers, and spacing between typed lines. (These differences are detailed in Chapter 10.)

Also, obtain a "Request" (Form PCT/RO/101) and transmittal letter (Form PTO 1382) from Box PCT, Assis-

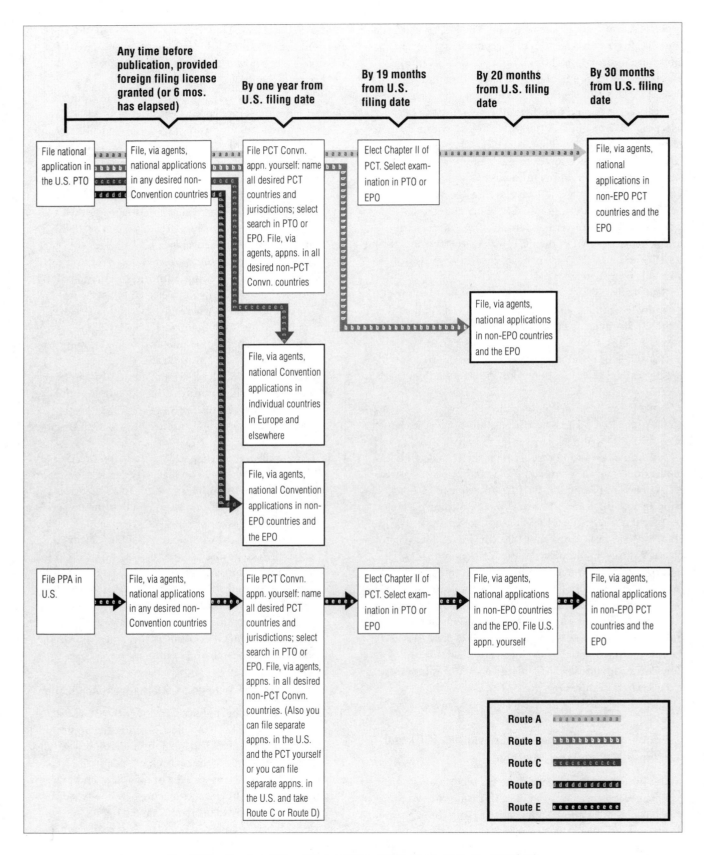

Fig. 12B—Foreign Filing Routes (After Filing Basic U.S. Application)

tant Commission for Patents, Washington, DC 20231, tel. 703-305-3257 (Fax 703-305-3230). Ask for the latest fees when you call. Complete the forms (full instructions will be attached), requesting the PTO to prepare a certified copy of your U.S. application for use with your PCT application, and attach a copy of your application in PCT (A4) format (with drawings) and a check payable to the Assistant Commissioner for Patents for the international application filing fees as computed on the Request form.

b. PCT Fees

The fee for a certified copy of your U.S. application is listed in Appendix 4, Fee Schedule. The PCT fees frequently vary due to exchange rate fluctuations. They're composed of several parts as follows:

- Transmittal Fee
- Search Fee: (a) if you haven't already filed in the U.S. (that is, you filed your first application in the PCT, rather than the U.S.—very rare—see Subpart 6, below); (b) if you've already filed in the U.S. (the usual case); and (c) if you want to use the EPO as your searching authority (recommended)
- International Fee
- Country Designation Fees (the EPO counts as one country).

A common course of action is to designate the EPO and Japan with an EPO search. You should designate the EPO as your searching authority if you intend to file there since they generally do a better search than the U.S. PTO and you'll save money and time in the EPO later. But be warned: Sometimes the EPO does such a good search that you might have to abandon both your U.S. and EPO applications.

c. How to File PCT and Non-PCT Convention Applications

To file the PCT application, mail the Transmittal Letter, Request, copy of your application and drawings (both on A4 size), and check to: Box PCT, Assistant Commissioner for Patents, Washington, DC 20231, which, as mentioned, is a designated receiving office for the International Bureau. Like Convention applications, the international (PCT) application should be filed within one year of your U.S. filing date, also known as the priority date.

I advise filing the PCT application at least a month before the anniversary of your U.S. filing date, so you'll have time to correct any serious deficiencies. But you can mail the PCT application as late as the last day of the one-year period from your U.S. filing date if you use Express Mail and complete the Express Mail Certification on page 1 of the Transmittal Letter. (Never use a plain Certificate of

Mailing (see Chapter 13, Section H) for any PCT correspondence.)

To file any non-PCT Convention applications, use a foreign patent agent in each country you select to prepare an appropriate application. The easiest way to do this is to send the agent a copy of your U.S. application and ask what else is needed. The requirements vary from country to country, but special drawings in each country's format will always be needed. You can have your foreign agent prepare these, or you can have these prepared yourself at lesser cost by the same companies that make drawings for U.S. divisional applications. (See discussion of "Divisional Applications" in Chapter 14, Section C.) Also, the agent will send you a power of attorney form that you'll have to sign and sometimes get notarized, certified by your county clerk, and legalized by the consulate of the country to which the form is being sent. Also you'll generally need a certified copy of your U.S. application; this can be obtained from the PTO. (See Appendix 4, Fee Schedule.) The cost for filing a foreign application in each individual country is about $1,000 to $5,000, depending on the country, the length of your application, and whether a translation is required.

If you wish to correspond directly with the foreign patent agents yourself, you'll first have to get the name of a patent agent in each country. See Section K, below.

d. What Happens to Your International Application?

You'll receive a filing receipt and separate serial number for your international application, and the application will eventually be transmitted for filing to the countries (including the EPO) you've designated on your request form. If you make any minor errors in your PCT application, the PCT Dept. of the U.S. PTO will give you a month to correct them.

e.   Search Report

When you receive your PCT search report (either from the PTO or EPO), you can comment on it and amend your claims if necessary, but no extended prosecution or negotiation is permitted.

f.   Chapter II

Within 19 months of your U.S. filing date, you elect Chapter II, selecting either the PTO or EPO for examination. Get the forms (PCT/IPEA/401) from the PCT Department of the PTO, and also get the latest fees for Chapter II. If you select the EPO to do the examination, you must file the papers with the EPO in Munich (address in Section C, above) and pay the fee in Deutschmarks. You'll get an examination report where claims will actually be allowed or rejected. You can amend your application once and even interview your examiner.

g.   National Stage

Within 30 months from your U.S. filing date, you must hire an agent in Europe (get one in London or Munich) and file an EPO application based on your PCT application. Also, you must have an agent in each non-EPO PCT country (such as Japan or Australia) in which you wish to file and get national applications on file in these countries. Expect to pay very stiff fees.

As mentioned, each of the separate countries and the EPO will rely to a great extent on the international examination they'll receive from the International Bureau (in most cases this will be the EPO search or an adoption of the U.S. search). Thus, one advantage of the PCT approach is that you'll save much of what used to be the agonizing, extremely expensive job of separately and fully prosecuting an application in each country in which you elected to file.

2.   Route B: Bypass Chapter II of PCT

Route B is the same as Route A, except that instead of electing Chapter II of the PCT, you file the national applications sooner in the EPO and non-EPO countries. You have, as indicated, 20 months from your U.S. filing date to do this. You file your EPO and non-EPO applications in the same way you did it under Route A—that is, you elect agents, send them copies of all of your papers, and tell them you

want to file national applications in their countries based upon your U.S. and PCT applications.

Route B will cost more than Route A in the short run, but will be cheaper in the long run, since you've skipped the expense of Chapter II of the PCT.

3.   Route C: Convention Applications in EPO and Non-EPO Countries

Under Route C, you bypass the PCT entirely and file, through agents, national convention applications in the EPO and non-EPO countries within 12 months of your U.S. filing date. This is the cheapest way to go in the long run if you wish to file in several European countries. An EPO filing, while expensive, is generally considered cheaper than separate filings if:

   a.   Two or more non-English-speaking countries are involved (for example, it's cheaper to file in the EPO than to file separate applications in France and Germany), or

   b.   The U.K. and more than one non-English country is involved. Conversely, it's cheaper to file separate applications in the U.K. and Germany, for instance, than to go through the EPO.

As mentioned, to file a Convention application in the EPO you'll have to go through a European patent agent, unless you have an address in one of the EPO countries, in which case you can do it yourself. Correspondence with the EPO must be in English if your application is based on your U.S. case.

Including the agent's fee, expect to spend a stiff fee to get your application on file and examined in about six countries. (See Appendix 4, Fee Schedule.) Additional large fees will be incurred for prosecution (getting your application approved once it's filed) and issuance. Then you'll have to arrange to get translations and individual agents for the respective countries you designate. For more information, write to the EPO for a copy of *How to Get a European Patent* (address in Section C, above).

4.   Route D: Convention Applications in Individual Countries

Here you bypass both the PCT and the EPO. It's not a wise idea to bypass the EPO unless you want to file in just two countries in Europe—in which case it's usually cheaper to make individual filings rather than go through the EPO. This is the simplest way to go, on the charts, although it can get very complex and involve a lot of parallel correspondence and paperwork, since you'll have to make simultaneous prosecutions in each country. Filing is effected by sending a certified copy of your U.S. application to a patent agent in each country and instructing the agent to file a Convention application based upon your U.S. application. The agent will tell you what else is needed.

5. Route E: PPA Filed

If you've filed a PPA, your choices and procedures are the same as Routes A to D, except that at each stage there's another national country in which you can file: the U.S.A. I recommend you file in the U.S., separately, by one year after you file your PPA, because it's simpler and somewhat cheaper. However, if you want to delay your U.S. filing, you can name the U.S. in your PCT application when you file your PCT application within one year after your PPA's filing date. You can file your U.S. national application by 20 months after your PPA date, or by 30 months if you elect Chapter II of the PCT by 19 months. Your U.S. application should be identical to a "regular" U.S. application, except that you should add the following sentence to the PAD (Form 10-2) to get the benefit of your PCT filing date: "I hereby claim foreign priority benefits under 35 USC 119 of the PCT patent application, Ser. No. _____, Filed 199___."

6. File the PCT Application First

Although not listed on the chart because it's not a very popular method, if you haven't filed a PPA you can file a PCT application first (before you file anything) and then file in the U.S. and PCT countries (including the EPO) through the PCT. File in the non-PCT Convention countries through the Convention.

If you haven't filed a PPA and you know for certain, before you file anywhere, that you'll want to file in the U.S. and at least one foreign PCT country, then you can save some fees and effort by filing the PCT application first, before you file in the U.S. In your PCT application you must designate the U.S. and any foreign PCT countries (including the EPO) you desire. Then, within one year of your PCT filing date, you should file Convention applications, based upon your PCT application, in any non-PCT countries, such as Mexico and China, you desire.

Within 20 months of your PCT filing date (30 months if you elected Chapter II), file separately under the PCT in each country or jurisdiction you've designated in your PCT application, including the U.S. and the EPO. Then order (from the PTO) a certified copy of your PCT application and file this within a few months after your U.S. filing date.

Whether you're filing in a PCT or non-PCT jurisdiction based upon a PCT filing, your foreign patent agents will tell you what you'll need to file PCT-based applications in their countries; allow at least two months before the 20- or 30-month deadline to give them (and you) time to prepare the applications and translations, if necessary.

K. Resources to Assist in Foreign Filing

There are a number of resources to assist you in foreign filing your patent application. Let's look at them separately.

1. Foreign Patent Agents

As I've mentioned, if you desire to file abroad you'll almost certainly need to find a foreign patent agent who's familiar with patent prosecution in the countries where you desire protection. (In most countries, patent professionals are called "agents" rather than attorneys. As in the U.S., foreign agents are licensed to represent clients before their patent office, but not their courts.) Your best bet is to find one through a U.S. patent attorney (see Chapter 6, Section F), as most are associated with one or more patent agents in other major countries.

If you don't know a U.S. patent attorney or someone who's familiar with foreign patent agents, there are several other ways to obtain the names. One is to look in the telephone directory of the city where the patent office of the foreign country is located. Most large libraries have foreign telephone directories. Another simple way is to inquire at the consulate of the country; most foreign countries have consulates in major U.S. cities and these should have a list of patent agents.

A third possibility is to hire a local patent attorney to do the work for you, although this involves an intermediary's costs. Because of the complicated nature of foreign filing, many patent attorneys even use their own intermediaries, namely, specialized patent-law firms in New York, Chicago, or Los Angeles, which handle foreign filing exclusively.

A fourth possibility is to hire a British firm of patent agents to do all your foreign filing. The reason for this is that they speak fairly good English and they're familiar with foreign filing. This would be especially appropriate if you're filing with the EPO, but most German agents in Munich, although not as fluent in English, have the compensating advantage of their physical proximity to the EPO. Finally, you can look in the *Martindale-Hubbell Law Directory* (in any law library) which lists some foreign patent agents in each country.

Whichever way you get your foreign patent agent, be careful, since some foreign patent agents, like some U.S. patent attorneys and agents, are not competent and/or are inclined to overcharge.

2. Written Materials

As you've gathered by now, filing abroad can become very complicated. If you want to learn more, and get the latest information (if the print date of this book is old), including the laws of each country, see *Patents Throughout the World*, by Greene (Clark Boardman). This book is revised annually, so be sure you have the most recent version. Also, you can call the consulate of any country to get information on their patent laws. For more information on how to utilize the PCT, a brochure, "The PCT Applicant's Guide," is available free from the PCT Department of the U.S. PTO, and a comprehensive book, *The PCT Applicant's Guide,* is available from World Intellectual Property Organization, Post Office Box 18, 1211 Geneva 20, Switzerland. (For more information on the EPO, see Section C, above.)

Bonne chance et au revoir! ■

INVENTOR'S COMMANDMENT #22

Never admit or state anything negative about your invention on the record (in writing), since anything negative you admit will be used against you later by an adversary.

INVENTOR'S COMMANDMENT #23

Whenever you have a patent application pending, you must be available to receive Office Actions (letters) from the PTO and you must respond to every OA within the time it allots, since your application will go abandoned if you don't file a timely response.

INVENTOR'S COMMANDMENT #24

You may never add any "new matter" (technical information not in the application as filed) to any patent application.

INVENTOR'S COMMANDMENT #25

In order to answer properly an Office Action from the PTO, you must respond to each and every point (objection or rejection) in the OA, either by suitable argument or by complying as required.

INVENTOR'S COMMANDMENT #26

When drafting an amendment in response to the first Office Action, do your very best job, including a complete response, all available arguments for patentability, and the narrowest and most comprehensive claims possible, since the next OA will almost certainly be made final, foreclosing any future changes.

There's an old saying in the law: "You can sue the bishop of Boston for bastardy." This means that you can file a lawsuit against anyone for anything. Whether you can prove your case and win is, of course, a very different matter.

Similarly, anyone can file a patent application on anything. But getting the Patent and Trademark Office (PTO) to issue you a patent is, of course, a very different matter.

This chapter tells you how to get the PTO to deliver, assuming your invention meets the standards of patentability (Chapter 5). This material is sure to seem confusing the first time you read it. A little familiarity with the process, however, should do a world of good when it comes to your understanding. Sections A to N of this chapter apply to utility patent application except as noted in Section P.

A. What Happens After Your Patent Application Is Filed?

It will be helpful to review exactly what will occur after your patent application is filed.

1. Receipt Postcard

After sending your patent application to the PTO, you'll receive your receipt postcard back in about two to four weeks. It will be stamped with a date and an eight-digit number—for example, "U.S. Patent & TM Office, 22 August 1991; 07/801,666." The date is the "deposit" date (date of receipt), and the number is the serial number (sometimes called "application number") of your application.

2. Official Filing Receipt

About a month later (if you followed my instructions in Chapter 10) you should receive an official filing receipt. This is a blue sheet containing the following:
- the name(s) of the inventor(s)
- the title of your patent application
- the examining group to which your application has been assigned
- the filing date and serial number of your application
- the number of claims (total and independent)
- the filing fee you paid
- your name and address
- the words "Small Entity" if you filed an SED (Form 10-3), and
- the words "Foreign Filing License Granted [date]" if the invention hasn't been militarily classified (most won't be).

Check all of this information carefully; it's what's entered into the PTO's data-processing system about your application. If the filing receipt has any errors, write a brief letter or send a fax to the Application Branch (see number in Appendix 5, Mail, Telephone and Computer Communications With the PTO). The caption should be as in Form 13-1, but substitute "Request for Corrected Filing Receipt" instead of "Amendment" and point out the errors and request a new filing receipt.

Once you receive the blue official filing receipt sheet, your patent application is officially pending and you may label your invention and any descriptive literature "Patent Pending," or "Patent Applied For." They have the same legal meaning.

If for any reason you didn't comply with an item on the checklist in Chapter 10, so that your application hasn't been filed properly (for example, you forgot the SED, your check bounced, or you forgot to sign the PAD (Form 10-2)), you won't get the blue filing receipt. Instead, the Application Branch of the PTO will send you a deficiency notice telling you what's needed and what surcharge (fine) you'll have to pay for the error of your ways. Once you comply with the deficiency notice (they usually give you a month), you'll get your blue filing receipt a few weeks later.

IF YOU RECEIVE A FOREIGN FILING LICENSE

The words "foreign filing license" mean that you can foreign file at any time, rather than waiting six months. However, you still should wait until approximately nine months have passed before considering filing abroad in Convention countries in order to allow time for you to receive a possible office action, so you'll have better information about patentability and to accumulate additional commercial information on your invention. You should file abroad in non-Convention countries before you sell or publish details of the invention.

3. Patent Pending Status

What does it mean to say "patent pending?" Many people believe that a person who copies an invention on which a patent is pending is liable for infringement. This isn't true. As explained in Chapter 1, you have no monopoly or rights until your patent actually issues. In other words, a manufactured article claimed in a pending patent application can be freely copied by anyone. However, even though "patent

pending" status can't be used to preclude others from copying the invention, this usually isn't necessary. This is because if a patent later issues, the infringer takes the chance that you'll use your patent to enforce your monopoly—that is, stop any further production and marketing. In this case, the money already spent on expensive tooling will have been mostly wasted. (If you're willing to license the infringer under your patent, the infringer's tooling outlay will be worthwhile, but few infringers will be willing to take this chance.)

After your application is filed, you may publish articles on your invention without loss of any legal rights in the U.S. or foreign Convention countries (see Chapter 12), but you'll lose rights in non-Convention Countries (Chapter 12). However, it's not desirable to reveal details of your invention to potential competitors at this early stage, especially since your application may not become a patent.

Note that it's a criminal offense to use the words "patent applied for" or "patent pending" (they mean the same thing) in any advertising when there's no active, applicable regular or Provisional Patent Application on file.

4. Send in Your Information Disclosure Statement (IDS)

If you haven't done so already, after receiving your official filing receipt send in your Information Disclosure Statement as discussed in Chapter 10, Section N, together with a PTO-1449 form and copies of the references you listed on the form. Remember that the PTO likes the IDS to be filed within three months of the application's filing date. Don't forget to print your serial number and filing date on the forms.

If you don't file the IDS within three months of your filing date, or before your first Office Action, or within three months after entry into the "national" stage for references cited in foreign applications, the PTO will still consider it provided you file it *before* a final action or a notice of allowance is sent, and (1) pay a "Late IDS Fee" (see Appendix 4, Fee Schedule), or (2) include a certificate as follows:

"Each item of information contained in this Information Disclosure Statement (IDS) was cited in a communication from a foreign patent office in a counterpart foreign patent application not more than three months prior to the filing of such IDS, or no item of information contained in this IDS was cited in a communication from a foreign patent office in a counterpart foreign patent application, or, to my knowledge after making reasonable inquiry, was known to any individual designated in 37 CFR § 1.56(c) [inventor, attorney, assignee, etc.] more than three months prior to the filing of such IDS."

If you file the IDS after a final action or notice of allowance is sent, but before you pay the issue fee, you *must* include the above certificate, a petition requesting consideration of the IDS, and a petition fee—see Fee Schedule. (Strangely this petition fee is less than the "before final action" Late IDS Fee.)

If you send in an IDS and later discover any additional references—for example, in the course of foreign prosecution—you must bring these to the attention of the PTO through a supplemental IDS.

5.   First Office Action

About six months to two years after the filing date you'll receive a communication from the PTO known as a "first office action" (OA), sometimes called an "official letter." It consists of forms and a letter from the examiner in charge of your application, describing what is wrong with your application and why it cannot yet be allowed. (Rarely will an application be allowed in the first OA.)

Specifically, the OA may:
- reject claims
- list defects in the specification and/or drawings
- cite and enclose copies of prior art that the examiner believes shows your invention is either:
  - (a) not novel, or
  - (b) obvious, and/or
- raise various other objections.

To find out approximately when you'll receive the first OA from the PTO, you can call the clerk of the examining group where your application has been assigned. The name of this group will be typed on your filing receipt. PTO phone numbers change frequently, but are published irregularly in the *Official Gazette* (OG), and in the first OG published each year. Each issue of the OG again gives OA date information for patent applications. Also, you can call the PTO's main number (see Appendix 5, Mail, Telephone and Computer Communications With the PTO) to find the telephone number of your group.

6.   Response to First Office Action

The OA itself will specify an interval, usually three months from the date the OA was mailed, within which you must file a response. Your response must take whatever action is necessary to overcome the objections and rejections listed in the OA. The response you file is technically called an "amendment" (assuming it contains any changes) and the entire process of correspondence (office actions and amendments) to and from the PTO is known as "patent application prosecution," although no one is "prosecuted" in the usual sense. I show you how to draft your response in Section F, below.

7.   Second/Final Office Action

About two to six months after you file your first amendment, you'll receive a second OA from the PTO; this will usually be designated a "final" OA by the PTO. A final OA is supposed to end the prosecution stage before the examiner. However, as we'll see later, this is far from true. In other words, a "final action" is rarely final. Again you have three months to reply.

8.   Notice of Allowance

Assuming you submit what is necessary to get your application in condition for allowance, you'll be sent a Notice of Allowance, indicating that all of your claims are allowed and that an issue fee is due within three months. (Usually you'll get a "Notice of Allowability" before or with the formal allowance; this merely states that your claims are all allowed, the Notice of Allowance will be sent, and whether formal drawings are due.) When you pay the issue fee, you can also order ten or more printed copies of your patent at the usual charge.

9.   Issue Fee and Issue Notification

Several months after you pay the issue fee (see Appendix 4, Fee Schedule) and file formal drawings (if you didn't do so before), you'll receive an Issue Notification from the PTO, indicating the issue date and number of your patent.

10.   Receipt of Official Patent Deed

Shortly after the date your patent issues, you'll receive your official "Letters Patent" deed from the PTO. Any printed copies of the patent that you've ordered will arrive in a separate envelope.

B.   General Considerations During Patent Prosecution

Patent application prosecution is generally more difficult than the preparation of the initial application. Assuming that you're going to handle the prosecution phase pretty much on your own, I recommend that you keep the following general considerations in mind.

1.   The PTO Can Write Claims for You

As I mentioned in Chapter 9 (claims drafting), you can ask the PTO to write a claim for you if you wish. Then you can either accept this claim or amend it if you think you can get it past the examiner.

2.   Consultation With a Patent Professional Might Be Wise

You might wish to consult with a patent expert at this point of the proceedings. Paying $200–$600 (if you use a "discount" patent attorney—see Chapter 6) to have an expert amend your claims and argument (which is usually what's required) may prove to be relatively cheap in the long run if you can afford the expense now. As you review the following, often dense, material, remember that expert outside help is available.

3.   Intervals Are Approximate

Except for official periods, such as the three-month period for response to an OA or to pay the issue fee, the dates and times I've given in this chapter are only approximate and are gleaned from recent experience. They can vary quite widely, depending on conditions in the PTO at the time you file your patent application. You have to be patient (patent prosecution is largely a waiting game), but if you don't receive any communication from the PTO for a long time, say over 1.5 years after you file your application, you should check the latest *Official Gazette* for the status of the cases in your group. Also, if it's over six months after you file an amendment, you should make a call, or send a letter, to the examiner or examining group to determine the status of your case.

4.   You'll Be Able to Correct Technical Errors

Don't worry too much about minor technical errors (except for dates—see next consideration) when dealing with the PTO. If you make one, you'll be given an opportunity to correct it. The PTO has so many rules and regulations that even patent attorneys who deal with them all the time can't remember them all. Also, the PTO is flexible in giving do-it-yourself applicants opportunities to correct errors that don't affect the substance of the application.

5.   Dates Are Crucial

Every OA that you receive from the PTO will specify an interval by which you must reply to the OA. If you fail to reply in the time the PTO allots you, the penalty is draconian: your application will go abandoned, although it can be revived at a price. (See Section Q, below.) Thus, you should write the due date for every OA promptly on the OA and on your calendar and heed it carefully. If you're not the type who can faithfully heed due dates, you must do something about this—for example, by hiring a methodical friend to bug you, or even by turning the whole job of prosecution over to a patent attorney.

6.   Situations Not Covered

If any situation occurs that isn't covered in this book, and you can't find the answer by looking in the *Rules of Practice* or *Manual of Patent Examining Procedure* (see Subsection 9, below, for how to obtain these), call the PTO, consult an attorney or agent, or use common sense and do what you would expect to be the logical thing to do in such a situation.

Newly Discovered Reference: For example, if after you've filed your patent application you find a prior-art reference that considerably narrows what you thought your invention to be, bring it to the attention of the PTO by way of another (supplemental) IDS and PTO-1449, and submit an amendment substituting narrower claims that avoid the reference. (You don't have to send in an IDS to cite any references cited by the examiner with an Office Action.) Remember that you have a continuing duty to disclose all material information about your invention to the PTO. (See Form 10-2.)

Embodiment Changes: If you discover that an embodiment of your invention doesn't work, delete it from your application. (See Section E, below, for how to do this.) If you discover a new embodiment of your invention that supersedes the present embodiments, file a continuation-in-part application. (See Chapter 14.)

Small Entity Changes: If you license or assign your application to a large entity (or cancel a license or your application is reassigned back to you), you should send a letter to the PTO asking that your small-entity status be canceled (or send in the appropriate SEDs to establish SE status).

Change of Address: If you change your address, you should send an appropriate letter (caption as in Form 13-1 but headed "Change of Applicant's Address") to the PTO.

PTO Mistakes: If the examiner cites a prior-art reference against your application that is later than the filing date, obviously the examiner made an error (this happens occasionally) and you should call or write to bring it to the examiner's attention so that a new office action can be issued. If the PTO fails to send you a copy of a reference that it has cited against you (this happens often), send an appropriate paper (captioned as in Form 13-1) headed "Request for Copy of Missing Reference" to the PTO. If a part of the OA doesn't make sense, or a part seems to have been omitted, send an immediate "Request for Clarification of Office Action."

Finally, as a wise person said, "Don't be afraid to ask dumb questions: they're easier to handle than dumb mistakes."

7. Standards of Patentability Vary Widely

While I've tried to give the proper standards of patentability in this book (see Chapter 5), what actually happens when your application is examined will vary, depending upon the personality, whims, and current emotions of the examiner assigned to handle it. Most examiners adhere to the basic standards of patentability outlined here and are competent, knowledgeable, and occasionally helpful when it comes to telling you what to do to put the case in condition for allowance. Unfortunately, some examiners are very new and inexperienced, new to the U.S. and unfamiliar with English, and/or incompetent or superficial, and even mean, which can sometimes lead them to make arbitrary, irrational rulings and deny patents that should be granted or vice versa. Services have deteriorated everywhere in recent years, but especially in the PTO.

The solution to the problem with an unreasonably tough or inexperienced examiner is to, first, be persistent. Go to the PTO (or hire a patent attorney to go) to interview your examiner. If necessary, appeal. Appealing is a powerful weapon against a tough examiner. Examiners don't like to write answers to appeal briefs since these take a lot of time. Also, they may have to have an appeal conference with another examiner, and it looks bad on their record if they have many appeals or get reversed often.

The problem with an easy examiner is that your allowed application might not stand up in court (should this ever become necessary). Accordingly, if you believe that your examiner is not rigorous enough (for instance, all your claims are allowed in the first office action), make especially sure yourself that at least some of your claims are clearly patentable, in the sense that they will withstand a court challenge. (See Chapter 15.)

It may help to know that examiners themselves have to contend with two opposing forces: on the one hand, they're expected to dispose of (allow or get the applicant to abandon) a certain number of cases, but on the other hand, they're subject to a quality review program to make sure they're not too lenient.

Note that even if you have a great invention that is quite patentable, but you haven't claimed it properly, many U.S. PTO examiners, unlike their counterparts in the European Patent Offices, won't volunteer help or constructive suggestions or try to assist you. They'll simply reject your claims or make a requirement and leave it to you to figure out how to do what's necessary to remedy the situation. Thus, it's up to you to claim and fight for what's rightfully yours. Never automatically accept any examiner's rejection.

UNLESS MRS. FLLOYD GETS SOME ONE TO PAY ATTENTION TO HER PROBLEM, I THINK SHE MAY GET VIOLENT.

8. Dealing With the PTO Can Be Frustrating and Unfair

Dealing with the PTO, as with any other government agency, can sometimes be a very difficult, time-consuming, and frustrating experience. I could spend a whole chapter listing the errors and mistakes I've encountered recently, but one example will suffice. I once filed an application for an inventor whose last name was "Loe." The filing receipt came back with the name "Lee." After several letters and calls with no response, a "corrected" filing receipt arrived with the name spelled "Leo." After a few more calls and much frustration, a correct filing receipt finally arrived. Put succinctly, dealing with the PTO is not like dealing with Federal Express. All I can tell you is to be philosophical, scrupulously check your correspondence with the PTO to make sure they get it right, and persist in correcting errors when they occur.

As far as the unfairness goes—there are many situations when you deal with the PTO (and the IRS) where you'll find an inherent unfairness due to non-reciprocity. For example, while you have to reply to an OA when the PTO tells you to, they can reply to you whenever they get around to it. While you have to make your claims and specification clear, grammatical, and free of spelling errors, you'll often find that the correspondence you receive from the PTO doesn't meet these standards. While you have to pay a stiff fine if you forget to sign your check or make some other inadvertent error, the PTO never is liable, no matter how negligent they are. In other words, you're playing on an unlevel field. There's nothing you can do about this unfairness except, again, to be philosophical and resign yourself to accept the rules of the game before you play.

One inventor was so frustrated that he sued his examiner and the PTO for negligence. The judge said, "This is the sad tale of an inventor frustrated by the bureaucratic mindset and Byzantine workings of the PTO." While he won in trial court, the appellate court reversed, holding that examiners are not legally responsible for their actions.

9. PTO Reference Books

During patent prosecution, you may need to refer to the MPEP, the PTO's *Rules of Practice* and/or the patent statutes. The latter two can be obtained from regional government bookstores in paperbound forms, and all three can be obtained from the GPO, the PTO's Bulletin Board System, the PTO's Internet sites, and the CASSIS CD-ROMs at any PTDL. The PTO's patent rules are given the prefix number "1." to distinguish them from trademark rules "2." and copyright rules "3." For example, Patent Rule 111, referred to later in this chapter, is officially identified as Title 37 of the Code of Federal Regulations, Section 1.111, or in legal citation form, 37 CFR 1.111. The *Manual of Patent Examining Procedure* (MPEP), which is often referred to as the "examiner's bible," covers almost any situation you can encounter in patent prosecution and contains the patent rules and statutes. It's an expensive, large, loose-leaf volume about 4 megabytes of text, so downloading will take a while if you get it from the PTO's BBS or via the Internet.

10. Never Make Negative Statements on the Record

When dealing with the PTO, you should never say or write anything that derogates your invention, and you should never admit that any prior-art reference shows (includes) any feature of your invention. Admittedly, this advice may be very difficult to follow in some situations, but it's extremely important that you comply with it. Why? Correspondence with the PTO will be put into your official file (called your "file wrapper"), and any negative admission by you that is included in the correspondence will be used against your patent if it ever becomes involved in litigation. Thus, if you always anticipate that your patent may later be involved in litigation, you'll do a much better job in the prosecution phase. This is so important that I've made it Inventor's Commandment #22, at the beginning of this chapter.

REMEMBER YOUR DUTY TO DISCLOSE

You do have a duty to disclose all information, such as relevant prior art, known to you that bears on the patentability of your invention (see Chapter 10, Section N), but you do not have to (and shouldn't) admit or state anything negative about your invention, even if what you disclose is very close to your invention. Of course, if you find a prior-art reference that you feel is so close that you believe your invention is not patentable, you should abandon your application.

11. Be Available to Answer Office Actions

As mentioned, you'll normally be required to respond to a PTO office action within three months. If an OA is sent while you're away or unavailable and you fail to reply to it, your application will, as stated in Subsection 5, above, be considered abandoned. Thus, I've provided Inventor's Commandment #23, at the beginning of this chapter, to give you ample warning. If you will be unavailable for an extended period while your application is pending, you should empower a patent attorney to handle it for you or arrange to have your mail forwarded by a reliable friend or relative. Unfortunately, the PTO won't allow you to appoint a layperson to represent you, unless you can show strong need exists; see PTO Rule 342 and write to the Chairman, Committee on Enrollment, at the PTO.

12. Consider Foreign Filing

About eight to ten months after you file your patent application, you should consider whether you want to file for coverage in other countries, as stated in Inventor's Commandment #21 (Chapter 12). Foreign filing is extremely expensive, time-consuming, and arduous, so do it only if you have a very important, innovative invention or a foreign licensee who will pay the freight.

There are international conventions or agreements among all countries that entitle you to the benefit of your U.S. filing date on any foreign applications you file within one year after you file your U.S. regular or provisional application. (Refer back to Chapter 12 to see how to file for a patent in other countries.)

13. You Can Call and Visit Your Examiner

If you have any questions about your application, or any reference that is cited against it, you are permitted to call, and/or make an appointment with and visit, the examiner in charge of your application. Your examiner's telephone number will be listed on official letters that you receive from the PTO. However, usually only one, or at most two, applicant-initiated interviews are permitted. So save this privilege for when you really need it. If you have an interview, you must summarize its substance (unless the examiner does so) in the next amendment. An interview is often a very valuable way to get a difficult case allowed, since communication is greatly enhanced when you and the examiner can discuss your differences and reach an understanding through the give and take and multiple feedback loops an interview permits. Also, it's harder to say "no" directly to a person face-to-face. Lastly, an interview provides an excellent opportunity to bring in and demonstrate a working prototype or sample of the invention to the examiner; this is usually an excellent persuader. However, I recommend that you try to avoid calling or interviewing any examiner on Fridays, since, like most of us, they're likely to be less attentive then. An excellent guide for negotiating with examiners is presented by Examining Group Director A.L. Smith at p. 168 of the 1990 February *Journal of the Patent and Trademark Office Society*. (This is available in most academic and business libraries as well as in Patent Depository libraries.)

14. No New Matter Can Be Added to Your Application

Virtually every inventor I've ever dealt with has asked me, at one time or another, about adding a new development or embodiment of their invention to their pending application. I must always answer in the negative. This is because once your application is filed, the PTO's Rule 118 prohibits you from adding any "new matter" to it. (New matter consists of any technical information, including dimensions, materials, etc., that was not present in your application as originally filed.) This prohibition makes sense since, if patent applicants were permitted to add continuing improvements and changes to their applications, the date of invention, and what was invented when, would be too difficult to determine.

Because of this widespread misconception, and because of the frequency with which PTO examiners must object when "pro se" (no attorney) applicants add new matter, I made this prohibition the subject of Inventor's Commandment #24, at the beginning of this chapter.

If you do want to add any new developments to your application, consider a special type of supplementary application (termed a "continuation-in-part application" or CIP and covered in Chapter 14) or, if your improvement is really significant, an independent, subsequent patent application.

New matter should be distinguished from prior art that may be discovered after an application has been filed. You are obligated to inform the PTO about any newly discovered, relevant prior art. (See Subsection 6, above.) Such prior art doesn't form part of your specification, nor does it affect the nature of your invention. Rather, it provides the PTO with more information by which to judge your invention for patentability. Also note that broadening claims is not new matter.

15. Official Dates Are When the PTO Receives Your Submission

Every paper that you send to or receive from the PTO has an official date. This is the date on which it was mailed from or received by the PTO. You should put your actual date of mailing on anything you send to the PTO, but the date of the PTO's "Received" stamp on your paper will be the "official" date of the paper. If you send in your application by Express Mail with an EM Certification (see Chapter 10), the PTO will stamp it as of the date you express mailed it, even though they receive it one to three days later. This is because, under PTO Rule 10, they consider your local post office their agent to receive your correspondence, provided you use EM.

16. Know Who Has the Ball

To use an analogy drawn from the game of basketball, during patent prosecution the "ball" (burden of action) will always be either on your side or the PTO's. If you just sent in your case, the ball will be with the PTO until they return your postcard, send you an official filing receipt, and send you a first office action. It doesn't go back to your side until

that first OA. Once they send the first OA, you have the ball and must usually take action within three months. Once you file an amendment, the PTO has the ball again, and so on. You should always know the status of your case—that is, whose side has the ball.

17. Reread Appropriate Chapters

When you respond to an OA, you should go back and reread the chapter that covers the issue you need to address. For example, if a claim is disallowed for prolixity, reread Chapter 9 (drafting claims). If the application is disallowed on prior-art grounds, reread Chapter 5. If your specification or drawings aren't in proper form, reread Chapters 8 and 10.

18. Respond to Each and Every Point in the Office Action

A typical OA will contain several criticisms (termed "objections" and/or "rejections"), such as drawing objections, specification objections, claim rejections for indefiniteness, and claim rejections based upon prior art. You must, as stated in Inventor's Commandment #25, at the beginning of this chapter, respond to each and every criticism in your next amendment or your amendment will be considered nonresponsive. (You'll usually be given two weeks to complete the amendment.) A suitable response can be an argument against the criticism or some action to eliminate the criticism—for example, by canceling claims, amending the specification, supplying new drawings or substituting different claims and arguing that the substituted claims are patentable over the prior art cited.

19. Form Paragraphs

Your actual office action, unlike the sample below, will usually include several form paragraphs that quote statutes or rules. Examiners love to use such form paragraphs. Therefore, don't assume, if you receive an office action with numerous form paragraphs that quote basic statutes and rules, that you've been singled out or that your application is substandard: all attorneys get OAs with these form paragraphs as well. Also, the form paragraphs that the examiner chose may sometimes be inapplicable or only partially applicable. If so, courteously point this out in your response.

20. Preliminary and Supplemental Amendments

In addition to the "regular" amendments discussed in this chapter (sent in response to an OA), you can also file a Preliminary Amendment before your first OA to correct any errors. Also, you may file a Supplemental Amendment (after you file a regular amendment, but before the next OA) to correct any errors or omissions in your Amendment. However, remember the rule against adding any new matter to your patent application.

21. Twenty-Year Term Considerations

In view of the new 20-year term, it behooves you to expedite the prosecution by filing a Petition to Make Special (Chapter 10), replying to Office Actions as soon as possible, and interviewing your examiner. Also file any divisional, continuation, or CIP applications (See Chapter 14) as soon as possible, since they'll expire 20 years from the filing date of your original, parent case.

C. A Sample Office Action

Now that you have an overview of the patent application prosecution process and the general principles that apply to it, it's time to get more concrete. Fig. 13A, below, shows a sample OA in an imaginary patent application. A study of this example will enable you to deal with your first OA far more effectively. It has been purposely written to include the most common objections and rejections; an actual OA is usually not this complicated and quotes applicable statutes. First let's look at Fig. 13A/1 (p. 1 of the OA).

At the top of the OA, the examiner's name and his examining section (Art Unit 254) are given. Art Unit 254 is part of Examining Group 250. Before that, in the large brackets, are the serial number, filing date, and inventor's name. To the right is the date the OA was mailed; this is its official date.

Below the address of the attorney, the first box that is checked indicates: "This application has been examined," denoting that this is the first OA in this application. If it had been a second and non-final OA, the second box, "Responsive to communication filed on [date]," would have been checked; had it been a final OA, the third box, "This action is made final," would have been checked.

The next paragraph indicates that the period for response will expire in three months and that failure to respond will cause the application to be abandoned. Since the OA was mailed 1995-11-21, the period for response expires 1996-2-21. If the last date of the period falls on a Saturday, Sunday or holiday, the period for response expires on the next business day.

Under "Part I," the check at box 1 indicates that two attachments, a "Notice of References Cited" and a "Notice re Patent Drawing," are part of the OA. A typical Notice of References Cited is shown in Fig. 13A/4, below, and the drawing notice is shown in Fig. 13A/5.

Under "Part II—Summary of Action," the examiner has checked various boxes to indicate what action he has taken with the application. He has rejected all seven claims pending. He has also acknowledged that informal drawings were filed and has indicated that these will be acceptable until allowable subject matter is indicated.

Now it's time to look at Figs. 13A/2 and 13A/3 (pp. 2 and 3 of the OA).

On p. 2 of the Office Action, the examiner gives his specific reasons for rejecting or objecting to the claims.

The first paragraph of p. 2 of the OA objects to the drawings because they fail to show certain features recited in the claims. Remember (Chapter 10) that the drawings must show every feature recited in the claims.

The second paragraph objects to the specification as inadequate. As stated in Chapter 8, the specification must teach, in full, clear and exact detail, how one skilled in the art would make and use the invention. This is a potentially serious and fatal flaw, since it is not permissible to add new matter (see Section B14, above) to supply the missing description.

In the third paragraph, the examiner rejects all of the claims under Section 112, since they are based on an inadequate specification for reasons stated in the second paragraph.

The fourth paragraph rejects Claims 1 to 6 on the Ohman reference (see Fig. 13A/4—p. 4 of the OA), under Section 102. This means that the examiner feels that these claims contain no novelty over Ohman. The requirement that the claims contain novel physical features was discussed in Chapters 5 and 9.

At the bottom of p. 2 of the OA, the examiner has rejected Claim 7 under Section 112 since a "said" clause in Claim 7 has no proper antecedent in parent, independent Claim 1 from which Claim 7 depends. Remember (Chapter 9) that every "said" clause must contain an identical antecedent earlier in the claim or in a parent claim. Many examiners, especially young ones, lean heavily on any Section 112 defects.

In the last paragraph of p. 2 of the OA (Fig. 13A/2-3), the examiner has rejected Claim 7, under our old and troublesome friend Section 103, as unpatentable over two references. Note that the examiner states what each reference shows and why it would be obvious to combine the teachings of these references. Also note that by using two references, or by relying on Section 103, the examiner has tacitly admitted that this claim has satisfied the novelty (Section 102) requirement. (See Chapter 5, Fig. 5A.)

The examiner next summarizes by stating that no claim is allowed.

UNITED STATES DEPARTMENT OF COMMERCE
Patent and Trademark Office
Address: COMMISSIONER OF PATENTS AND TRADEMARKS
Washington, D.C. 20231

SERIAL NUMBER	FILING DATE	FIRST NAMED APPLICANT	ATTORNEY DOCKET NO.
07/345,678	1995 Aug 9	LeRoy Inventor	

EXAMINER
HEYMAN, J

ART UNIT	PAPER NUMBER
254	3

Portia Barrister
1237 Chancery Lane
Puyallup, WA 98371-3841

DATE MAILED:

G5-11-21

This is a communication from the examiner in charge of your application.
COMMISSIONER OF PATENTS AND TRADEMARKS

☑ This application has been examined   ☐ Responsive to communication filed on _____   ☐ This action is made final.

A shortened statutory period for response to this action is set to expire __3__ month(s), __0__ days from the date of this letter.
Failure to respond within the period for response will cause the application to become abandoned.   35 U.S.C. 133

Part I   THE FOLLOWING ATTACHMENT(S) ARE PART OF THIS ACTION:

1. ☑ Notice of References Cited by Examiner, PTO-892.   2. ☑ Notice re Patent Drawing, PTO-948.
3. ☐ Notice of Art Cited by Applicant, PTO-1449.   4. ☐ Notice of Informal Patent Application, Form PTO-152
5. ☐ Information on How to Effect Drawing Changes, PTO-1474.   6. ☐ _____

Part II   SUMMARY OF ACTION

1. ☑ Claims ___1—7___ are pending in the application.

   Of the above, claims _____ are withdrawn from consideration.

2. ☐ Claims _____ have been cancelled.

3. ☐ Claims _____ are allowed.

4. ☑ Claims ___1—7___ are rejected.

5. ☐ Claims _____ are objected to.

6. ☐ Claims _____ are subject to restriction or election requirement.

7. ☑ This application has been filed with informal drawings which are acceptable for examination purposes until such time as allowable subject matter is indicated.

8. ☐ Allowable subject matter having been indicated, formal drawings are required in response to this Office action.

9. ☐ The corrected or substitute drawings have been received on _____. These drawings are ☐ acceptable;
   ☐ not acceptable (see explanation).

10. ☐ The ☐ proposed drawing correction and/or the ☐ proposed additional or substitute sheet(s) of drawings, filed on _____.
    has (have) been ☐ approved by the examiner. ☐ disapproved by the examiner (see explanation).

11. ☐ The proposed drawing correction, filed _____, has been ☐ approved. ☐ disapproved (see explanation). However,
    the Patent and Trademark Office no longer makes drawing changes. It is now applicant's responsibility to ensure that the drawings are
    corrected. Corrections **MUST** be effected in accordance with the instructions set forth on the attached letter "INFORMATION ON HOW TO
    EFFECT DRAWING CHANGES", PTO-1474.

12. ☐ Acknowledgment is made of the claim for priority under 35 U.S.C. 119. The certified copy has ☐ been received ☐ not been received

    ☐ been filed in parent application, serial no. _____; filed on _____.

13. ☐ Since this application appears to be in condition for allowance except for formal matters, prosecution as to the merits is closed in
    accordance with the practice under Ex parte Quayle, 1935 C.D. 11; 453 O.G. 213.

14. ☐ Other

PTOL-326 (Rev. 7-82)   **EXAMINER'S ACTION**

Fig. 13A/1—Sample Office Action

Serial No. 07/345,678   -2-

Art Unit 254

The drawing is objected to under Rule 1.83(a) in that all the features recited in the claims are not shown. See Claims 1 and 2 regarding the "electronic counter means" and "first and second solid state counters."

The specification is objected to under Rule 1.71(b) as inadequate. In particular, there is insufficient information regarding the "counter," "counter memory" and how the counter controls the illumination of the lights. Applicant is required to amplify the disclosure in this regard without the introduction of new matter, 608.04 MPEP.

Claims 1-7 are rejected under 35 U.S.C. § 112, 1st. paragraph, as based on an insufficient disclosure. See above.

Insofar as adequate, Claims 1-6 are rejected under 35 U.S.C. § 102(b) as fully anticipated by Ohman. Ohman shows an electronic cribbage board counter that fully meets these claims. See Fig. 1. The microprocessor 300 shown in Fig. 3 inherently includes the counter means of Claims 1 and 2.

Claim 7 is rejected under 35 U.S.C. § 112, ¶ 2. The term "said LCD readout" lacks proper antecedent basis in parent independent claim 1 as claim 1 recites only an "LCD monitor."

Claim 7 is rejected under 35 U.S.C. § 103 as unpatentable over Ohman in view of Morin. Ohman shows an electronic cribbage board counter, as stated. Morin shows an LCD tally monitor. It would be obvious to substitute Morin's LCD tally monitor for Ohman's mechanical readout, since the

Fig. 13A/2—Sample Office Action

substitution of LCD readouts for mechanical readouts is an expedient well known to those skilled in the art. See column 13, lines 34-41 of Morin, which indicate that in lieu of the LCD readout shown, other types of readouts may be used.

No claim is allowed.

The remaining art cited shows other electronic board games containing the claimed structure. Note Morin, which shows the details of a computer as containing first and second counter means.

Any inquiry concerning this communication should be directed to Examiner Heyman at telephone number 703-557-4777.

Heyman/EW

95/11/14

John S. Heyman

Examiner

Group Art Unit 254

Fig. 13A/3—Sample Office Action

FORM PTO-892	U.S. DEPARTMENT OF COMMERCE PATENT AND TRADEMARK OFFICE	SERIAL NO. 07/345,678	GROUP ART UNIT 254	ATTACHMENT TO PAPER NUMBER	3

NOTICE OF REFERENCES CITED

APPLICANT(S)
LeRoy Inventor

U.S. PATENT DOCUMENTS

*		DOCUMENT NO.	DATE	NAME	CLASS	SUBCLASS	FILING DATE IF APPROPRIATE
	A	4 3 6 8 5 1 6	1/1983	Morin	377	5	
	B						
	C						
	D						
	E						
	F						
	G						
	H						
	I						
	J						
	K						

FOREIGN PATENT DOCUMENTS

		DOCUMENT NO.	DATE	COUNTRY	NAME	CLASS	SUB-CLASS	PERTINENT SHTS. DWGS	PP. SPEC.
	L	8 1 0 1 7 6 6	6/1981	International P.U.B. (ACT)	Ohman	273	148R	5	21
	M	1 1 9 5 0 0 1	10/1985	Canada	Mah	273	148R	3	14
	N	2 1 7 3 4 0 6	10/1986	Gr. Britain	Armstrong	273	148R	3	6
	O								
	P								
	Q								

OTHER PRIOR ART (Including Author, Title, Date, Pertinent Pages, Etc.)

R	
S	
T	
U	

EXAMINER J.S. Heyman	DATE 4-1-9X	

* A Copy of this reference is not being furnished with this office action.
(See Manual of patent Examining Procedure, section 707.05(a).)

Fig. 13A/4—Notice of References Cited

Rcd 95028

Form PTO 948 (Rev. 10-93)   U.S. DEPARTMENT OF COMMERCE - Patent and Trademark Office   Application No. **07/883567**

NOTICE OF DRAFTSPERSON'S PATENT DRAWING REVIEW

PTO Draftpersons review all originally filed drawings regardless of whether they are designated as formal or informal. Additionally, patent Examiners will review the drawings for compliance with the regulations. Direct telephone inquiries concerning this review to the Drawing Review Branch, 703-305-8404.

The drawings filed (insert date) **9/27/95** , are
A. _____ not objected to by the Draftsperson under 37 CFR 1.84 or 1.152.
B. _✓_ objected to by the Draftsperson under 37 CFR 1.84 or 1.152 as indicated below. The Examiner will require submission of new, corrected drawings when necessary. Corrected drawings must be submitted according to the instructions on the back of this Notice.

1. DRAWINGS. 37 CFR 1.84(a): Acceptable categories of drawings:
Black ink. Color.
_____ Not black solid lines. Fig(s)_____
_____ Color drawings are not acceptable until petition is granted.

2. PHOTOGRAPHS. 37 CFR 1.84(b)
_____ Photographs are not acceptable until petition is granted.

3. GRAPHIC FORMS. 37 CFR 1.84 (d)
_____ Chemical or mathematical formula not labeled as separate figure. Fig(s)_____
_____ Group of waveforms not presented as a single figure, using common vertical axis with time extending along horizontal axis. Fig(s)_____
_____ Individuals waveform not identified with a separate letter designation adjacent to the vertical axis. Fig(s)_____

4. TYPE OF PAPER. 37 CFR 1.84(e)
_____ Paper not flexible, strong, white, smooth, nonshiny, and durable. Sheet(s)_____
_____ Erasures, alterations, overwritings, interlineations, cracks, creases, and folds not allowed. Sheet(s)_____

Transparent objectionable Figs 1, 3

5. SIZE OF PAPER. 37 CFR 1.84(f): Acceptable paper sizes:
_____ 21.6 cm. by 35.6 cm. (8 1/2 by 14 inches)
_____ 21.6 cm. by 33.1 cm. (8 1/2 by 13 inches)
_____ 21.6 cm. by 27.9 cm. (8 1/2 by 11 inches)
_____ 21.0 cm. by 29.7 cm. (DIN size A4)
_____ All drawing sheets not the same size. Sheet(s)_____
_____ Drawing sheet not an acceptable size. Sheet(s)_____

6. MARGINS. 37 CFR 1.84(g): Acceptable margins: _4 S128_

Paper size			
21.6 cm. X 35.6 cm.	21.6 cm. X 33.1 cm.	21 cm. X 27.9 cm.	21 cm. X 29.7 cm.
(8 1/2 X 14 inches)	(8 1/2 X 13 inches)	(8 1/2 X 11 inches)	(DIN Size A4)
T 5.1 cm. (2")	2.5 cm. (1")	2.5 cm. (1")	2.5cm.
L .64 cm. (1/4")	.64 cm. (1/4")	.64 cm. (1/4")	2.5 cm.
R .64 cm. (1/4")	.64 cm. (1/4")	.64 cm. (1/4")	1.5 cm.
B .64 cm. (1/4")	.64 cm. (1/4")	.64 cm. (1/4")	1.0 cm.

Margins do not conform to chart above.
Sheet(s)_____
_____Top (T) _____ Left (L) _____Right (R) _____ Bottom (B)

7. VIEWS. 37 CFR 1.84(h)
REMINDER: Specification may require revision to correspond to drawing changes.
_____ All views not grouped together. Fig(s)_____
_____ Views connected by projection lines. Fig(s)_____
_____ Views contain center lines. Fig(s)_____
Partial views. 37 CFR 1.84(h)(2)
_____ Separate sheets not linked edge to edge. Fig(s)_____
_____ View and enlarged view not labeled separately. Fig(s)_____
_____ Long view relationship between different parts not clear and unambiguous. 37 CFR 1.84(h)(2)(ii) Fig(s)_____
Sectional views. 37 CFR 1.84(h)(3)
_____ Hatching not indicated for sectional portions of an object. Fig(s)_____
_✓_ Hatching of regularly spaced oblique parallel lines not spaced sufficiently. Fig(s)_____
_____ Hatching not at substantial angle to surrounding axes or principal lines. Fig(s)__3____
_____ Cross section not drawn same as view with parts in cross section with regularly spaced parallel oblique strokes. Fig(s)_____
_____ Hatching of juxtaposed different elements not angled in a different way. Fig(s)_____
Alternate position. 37 CFR 1.84(h)(4)
_____ A separate view required for a moved position. Fig(s)_____

_____ Modified forms. 37 CFR 1.84(h)(5)
Modified forms of construction must be shown in separate views. Fig(s)_____

8. ARRANGEMENT OF VIEWS. 37 CFR 1.84(i)
_____ View placed upon another view or within outline of another. Fig(s)_____
_____ Words do not appear in a horizontal, left-to-right fashion when page is either upright or turned so that the top becomes the right side, except for graphs. Fig(s)_____

9. SCALE. 37 CFR 1.84(k)
_____ Scale not large enough to show mechanism without crowding when drawing is reduced in size to two-thirds in reproduction. Fig(s)_____
_____ Indication such as "actual size" or "scale 1/2" not permitted. Fig(s)_____
_____ Elements of same view not in proportion to each other. Fig(s)_____

10. CHARACTER OF LINES, NUMBERS, & LETTERS. 37 CFR 1.84(l)
_✓_ Lines, numbers & letters not uniformly thick and well defined, clean, durable, and black (except for color drawings). Fig(s)_____

11. SHADING. 37 CFR 1.84(m)
_____ Shading used for other than shape of spherical, cylindrical, and conical elements of an object, or for flat parts. Fig(s)_____
_____ Solid black shading areas not permitted. Fig(s)_____

12. NUMBERS, LETTERS, & REFERENCE CHARACTERS. 37 CFR 1.84(p)
_____ Numbers and reference characters not plain and legible. 37 CFR 1.84(p)(l) Fig(s)_____
_____ Numbers and reference characters used in conjuction with brackets, inverted commas, or enclosed within outlines. 37 CFR 1.84(p)(l) Fig(s)_____
_____ Numbers and reference characters not oriented in same direction as the view. 37 CFR 1.84(p)(l) Fig(s)_____
_____ English alphabet not used. 37 CFR 1.84(p)(2) Fig(s)_____
_____ Numbers, letters, and reference characters do not measure at least .32 cm. (1/8 inch) in height. 37 CFR(p)(3) Fig(s)_____

13. LEAD LINES. 37 CFR 1.84(q)
_____ Lead lines cross each other. Fig(s)_____
_____ Lead lines missing. Fig(s)_____
_____ Lead lines not as short as possible. Fig(s)_____

14. NUMBERING OF SHEETS OF DRAWINGS. 37 CFR 1.84(t)
_____ Number appears in top margin. Fig(s)_____
_____ Number not larger than reference characters. Fig(s)_____
_____ Sheets not numbered consecutively, and in Arabic numerals, beginning with number 1. Sheet(s)_____

15. NUMBER OF VIEWS. 37 CFR 1.84(u)
_____ Views not numbered consecutively, and in Arabic numerals, beginning with number 1. Fig(s)_____
_____ View numbers not preceded by the abbreviation Fig. Fig(s)_____
_____ Single view contains a view number and the abbreviation Fig. Fig(s)_____
_____ Numbers not larger than reference characters. Fig(s)_____

16. CORRECTIONS. 37 CFR 1.84(w)
_____ Corrections not durable and permanent. Fig(s)_____

17. DESIGN DRAWING. 37 CFR 1.152
_____ Surface shading shown not appropriate. Fig(s)_____
_____ Solid black shading not used for color contrast. Fig(s)_____

ATTACHMENT TO PAPER NO. **9**   REVIEWER **CBR**   DATE **10/25/95**

Applicant's Copy

Fig. 13A/5—Draftman's Drawing Objection Sheet
Although the PTO form still refers to four sizes of paper, new rules only allow two sizes—8 1/2" X 11" and A4.

Finally he refers to certain other prior art, which he cites but does not apply, to provide background and to put on the record in case he wants to use it later.

The examiner will sign the office action at the bottom and list his telephone number above his official name stamp.

Next, we turn to Fig. 13A/4 (the Notice of References Cited). It lists one U.S. and three foreign patents. All of these references will be attached to the OA, except any checked in the column marked with the asterisk(*), which were furnished in a prior office action, a prior related application, or were furnished by you in your Information Disclosure Statement. The "Document Number" column generally lists patent numbers.

The date column indicates the date the patent issued, or the document was published. If this date is later than your filing date, the reference is not a good reference against your application, unless it is a U.S. patent filed before your application. In the latter instance, the examiner is supposed to indicate the filing date of the patent reference in the last column.

Finally, note the Notice of Draftperson's Patent Drawing Review (Fig. 13A/5). This sheet comes from the PTO's Drafting Department and has been inserted since they found several self-explanatory defects in the drawings.

If you've sent in your IDS and PTO-1449 (Chapter 10, Section N), the OA will also include a copy of your PTO-1449, and a list of your references will be included under "References Cited" in the printed patent.

When the PTO cites patents as prior-art references, some inventors react in various illogical ways, as indicated by the following Common Misconceptions:

Common Misconception: *The PTO can't cite foreign or non-English patents or other publications against a U.S. patent application.*

Fact: *As indicated in Chapter 5, any publication, including a patent from anywhere in the world, in any language, is valid prior art against your patent application, provided it was published before your filing date, or before your earliest provable date of invention, up to one year before your filing date.*

Common Misconception: *An in-force foreign patent that shows or claims your invention will prevent you from making the invention in the U.S.*

Fact: *A patent of any country is enforceable only within the geographical area of that country and has no enforceability elsewhere. Thus, for example, a French patent is enforceable only in France and has no enforceability or effect in the U.S. It is a good prior-art reference in the U.S.*

Common Misconception: *If an examiner cites an in-force U.S. patent as a prior-art reference against your application, this means that your invention, if manufactured, sold, or used, would infringe this patent.*

Fact: *The only way you can tell if your invention would infringe any patent is to compare the patent's claims against your invention. Most cited in-force patents would not be infringed by your invention, since their claims are directed to a different invention. Again, examiners hardly ever read claims of patents they cite and the PTO is never concerned with infringements.*

Common Misconception: *If an examiner cites a very old prior-art reference against your application, it is not as good a reference as an in-force patent or a very recent reference.*

Fact: *The age of a reference is totally irrelevant, so long as its date is earlier than your filing date or your earliest provable date of invention. (See Chapter 5.)*

D. What to Do When You Receive an Office Action

When you receive an OA, don't panic or be intimidated. It's common for some examiners to reject all claims, even if the rejections are not valid. This type of rejection is termed a "shotgun" or "shoot-from-the-hip" rejection. Although they shouldn't do so, examiners sometimes do this because of the pressure of work, and sometimes to force you to state more clearly the essence of your invention and its true distinguishing features. You'll find that even if your examiner rejects all of your claims, if you approach your OA in a calm, rational, and methodical manner, as outlined below, you shouldn't have too much difficulty in ultimately getting your patent if your invention meets the legal tests for patentability.

IF THE PTO SUGGESTS YOU GET AN ATTORNEY

Some examiners insert a form paragraph in an OA, suggesting that you hire a patent attorney, regardless of how well the application is prepared, if there is no attorney of record. This has been done in several cases I prepared, but where I did not appear as the attorney of record. You can safely ignore this form paragraph, unless you feel uncomfortable without an attorney.

1.   Record Due Date on Your Calendar and OA, And Mount OA in Your File

After you get your office action, write the due date of your response right on it, and also on your calendar so you don't forget it. You should actually write the date thrice on your calendar: once on the date it's actually due, once one week before it's due, and once one month before it's due. If the due date falls on a weekend or holiday, your due date is the next business day. Also mount the OA in your file (see Inventor's Commandment #17 in Chapter 10) so you won't lose it.

2.   Check the References and Review Your Application

Check all your prior-art references carefully to make sure you've received all the correct references as listed in the Notice of References Cited. If there's any discrepancy, call or write the examiner at once. This call will not count as an interview (you are limited to two interviews).

If you sent in an IDS and PTO-1449, the examiner will send, with your first OA, a copy of your PTO-1449, with the blank adjacent each reference initialed to show that the examiner has considered it. If you don't get the PTO-1449 back, check with your examiner; otherwise, the references you cited on your PTO-1449 won't be listed on your patent when it's printed

Next, read the OA carefully and make a detailed written summary of it so that you'll have it impressed in your mind. After that, reread your application, noting all grammatical and other errors in the specification, claims, and drawings that you would like to correct or improve. Remember, however, that you can't add any "new matter" to your application. Also, if you really want to do a bang-up job, if any significant new reference(s) has been cited by the PTO, you can make a note to add a brief discussion of it to the prior art part of your specification; don't forget to "knock" it as usual.

3.   Read and Analyze Each Cited Reference, Except Patent Claims

Next, read every applied prior-art reference (except the claims of patent references) completely and carefully. (You don't have to read the non-applied (background) references that carefully, but you should review them to be sure none is more relevant than an applied reference.) Make sure that you take enough time to completely understand each reference and how it works. However, as I mentioned in Chapter 6 in connection with conducting a patentability search, don't read the claims of any patent cited as a reference.

Why not? Because the patent has not been cited for what it claims, but rather for what it shows about the prior art. The claims generally only repeat parts of the specification and are not directly relevant to the patent prosecution process, since they are only used to determine whether infringement exists. If you think of cited patents as magazine articles, you'll avoid this "claims trap" that most laypersons fall into.

Write a brief summary of each reference, preferably on the reference itself, even if it has an adequate abstract, in order to familiarize yourself with it in your own words.

"Swearing Behind" References: Under the PTO's Rule 131, you can "swear behind" and thus eliminate certain cited references as prior art to your application, provided you can prove that your *date of invention* is earlier than the *effective date* of the reference. (Remember from Chapter 5, Section E, that your *date of invention* is the earliest of (1) your *filing date (regular or PPA)*, (2) your *date of building and testing,* or (3) your *date of conception* followed by diligence. The *effective date* of any U.S. patent reference is its *filing date* and the *effective date* of any other reference is its *publication date.)*

If the PTO cites a reference against your application that has an *effective date* later than your *date of invention,* and you can prove your *date of invention* (you'll be able to if you've followed my recording instructions in Chapter 3!), you're in luck: you can swear behind this reference and thereby eliminate it from consideration. Typical references that you can swear behind are U.S. patents with *filing dates,* and other publications with *publication dates* earlier than your *filing date* but later than your *date of invention.*

To swear behind such a reference, you must submit a declaration containing facts with attached copies of documents showing that you *built and tested* the invention, or conceived the invention and were thereafter *diligent* in building and testing or filing it before the *effective date* of the reference. See MPEP § 715 for details.

If you've filed a PPA and need to rely on its filing date, merely refer to it by its Serial Number and Filing Date and point out to the examiner that a reference that the examiner cited is ineffective because you have an earlier effective filing date due to your PPA. Remember, however, that if your PPA didn't disclose your invention completely in accordance with Sec. 112, ¶ 1, you won't be entitled to rely on it.

One-Year-Rule and Interference Limitations: Two important limitations exist on your right to swear behind: (1) Because of the "one-year rule" (Chapter 5, Section E), you can't swear behind any reference (U.S. patent or otherwise) with a *publication date* over one year before your *filing date.* (There's no limitation as to how far you can swear back if the reference is a U.S. patent which issued less than one year before your *filing date.*) (2) You can't swear behind a

U.S. patent which claims the same invention as yours; the only way you can overcome such a patent is to get into interference with it and win "priority." (See Chapter 15.)

4.   Make a Comparison Chart

Next, you'll find it helpful to make a comparison chart showing every feature of your invention across the top of the chart and listing the references down the left-hand side of the chart, as in Fig. 13B.

Fig. 13B—Comparison Chart

Be sure to break up your invention so that all possible features of it, even those not already claimed, are covered and listed across the top of the chart. Remember that a feature can be the combination of two known separate features. Then indicate, by checking the appropriate boxes, those features of your invention that are not shown by each reference. This chart, if done correctly and completely, will be of tremendous aid in drafting your response to the first OA.

5.   Follow the Flowchart

Figure 13C provides a comprehensive, self-explanatory flowchart for dealing with all prior-art (Sections 102 and 103) rejections. Fig. 13D provides a list of all possible arguments I've found against obviousness rejections. Follow the charts and list carefully, together with the next four sections for each claim (or set of claims) rejected.

6.   Compare Your Broadest Claim With the Cited References for Novelty

If the examiner applies any prior-art references under Section 102, you'll need to deal with the novelty question. However, if the reference is said to apply under Section 103

(obviousness), the examiner is tacitly admitting that you've made it past Section 102—that is, your claimed structure is novel. Therefore, you won't have to go through the full analysis in this section. Instead, review the section briefly, and then concentrate on Section 7.

First, reread your broadest claim to see which features it recites. Remember, only positively recited physical structure or acts count. Then consider whether these physical features distinguish your invention from each reference cited against this claim. Don't pay any attention to the advantages of your invention, your statements of function, or your where-by clauses. Only focus on the physical features, including those that are in the form of a means clause followed by a function.

EXAMPLE: "A lever having a threaded end with a counter-balance thereon" is a proper physical recitation that can distinguish your invention from the prior art. The phrase "means for counterbalancing" is a means clause followed by a function and is equivalent to a physical recitation. But "said lever counterbalancing said arm" is a mere statement of result or function and can't be used to distinguish the prior art.

If only one reference has been cited against your broadest claim, consider whether your claim distinguishes over this reference under Section 102 (that is—whether your claimed structure is novel; see Chapter 5, Section E). In other words, are there any features recited in the claim that are not shown in the reference being cited against it? If not, the claim is "fully met" or anticipated by this reference and will have to be narrowed.

Remember that the examiner is entitled to interpret any claim in any reasonable way against you. That is, if a claim, or any word in a claim, has two reasonable interpretations, the examiner is entitled to take the one least favorable to you when determining if your claim has novel physical structure under Section 102. For example, suppose your invention uses a clamp that is halfway between two ends of a rod and a reference shows a clamp near one end of a rod. If your claim recites that the clamp is "intermediate" the ends of the rod, this won't distinguish over the reference since "intermediate" means "between" as well as "in the middle." The remedy? Recite that your claim is "substantially in the middle" of the rod in order to distinguish over the reference under Section 102 (but not necessarily under Section 103).

Suppose the physical features of your claim are all shown in a prior-art reference, but the prior-art reference's physical features are used for a different purpose than yours. For example, you claim "a depression in a wall plate for holding a clock" and the prior art shows a large oil drip pan under a milling machine; this pan literally constitutes

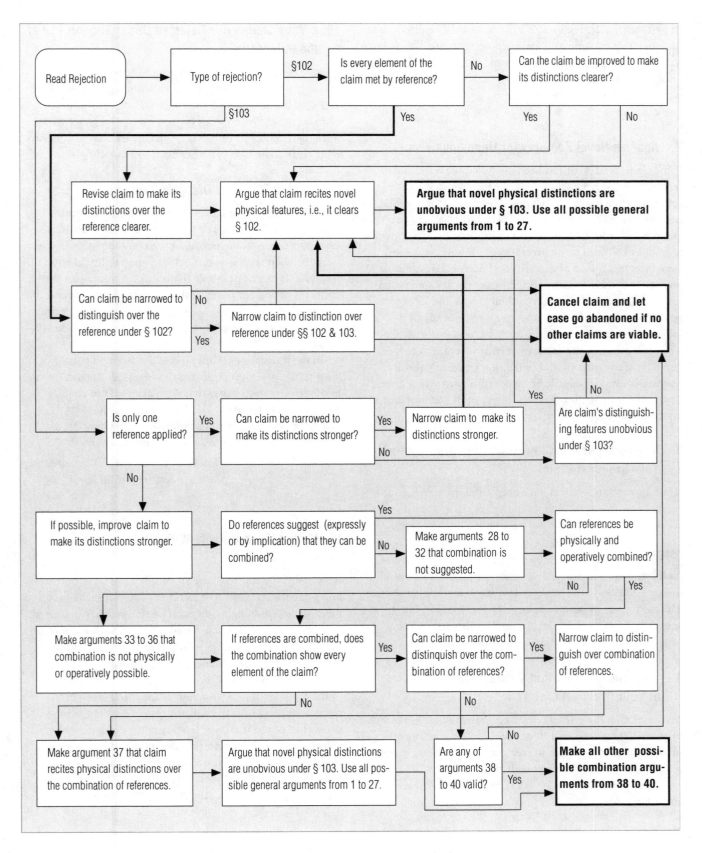

Fig. 13C—Flowchart for Handling Prior-Art Rejections

"a plate with a depression." Thus your claim literally "reads on" the prior art, but your claimed elements are directed to a different purpose than the elements of the prior-art reference. Unfortunately, the rejection is valid: you'll have to narrow the claim, or consider claiming your structure as a "new use" invention. (See Chapters 5 and 8.)

7.   Analyze Novel Features for Unobviousness

If the claim recites (or has been amended to recite) novel features, consider whether these are unobvious over the reference cited against it. All possible reasons for arguing unobviousness are listed in Fig. 13D (Part I). When you use any reasons from this chart, you should not merely copy the reason, as I've seen some inventors do. Rather, you must state facts in support of each reason you use. For example, if you select Reason 1 (Unexpected Results) after stating that your novel claimed structure produces new and unexpected results, state precisely what they are—such as that it does a job faster or more reliably.

If you consider the features of your invention obvious, you'll have to narrow the claim, either by adding more features from your specification or from narrower (dependent) claims (refer to Fig. 13C, above) or by reciting the existing features more narrowly.

8.   If References Are Cited in Combination Against Your Broadest Claim

If two or more references have been cited in combination against your broadest claim, refer to Fig. 13D (Part II) to see whether the examiner has a point.

You should especially consider reasons 28 to 32— that is, ask yourself whether it is proper to combine these references in the manner that the examiner has done. Also note that when you use any of the reasons of Fig. 13D, you should not merely state the applicable reason, but also supporting facts that pertain to your invention.

9.   Does the Combination Disclose Subject Matter of Your Broadest Claim?

Assuming that the references are combined (whether or not they can be), ask yourself if the combination discloses the subject matter of your claim (reason 37). If not, are the distinctions in your claim patentable under Section 103 (reasons 1–27 and 38–40)? Also ask yourself whether there are any other errors in the examiner's logic or reasoning.

10. If Your Claims Are Rejected Under Section 112 of the Patent Laws

If your claim has been rejected under Section 112, a very common occurrence even for patent attorneys, the examiner feels that the language of your claim is not clear or proper, and you should try to work out alternative language that will satisfy this objection. Also, you can ask the examiner to write clear claims for you. (See Section F2i, below.)

11. What to Do If You Disagree With the Examiner

If you believe your broadest claim is patentable over the prior art and that there is a serious flaw in the examiner's logic, it is theoretically permissible to "stand pat"—that is, leave the claim as it is and argue its patentability in your response. It can be desirable to do this, to emphasize the rightness of your position, if the examiner is very wrong. If you do file a reply to an OA without changing the specification or claims, your reply is technically not an "amendment," so call it a "response."

In most situations, I advise you not to stand pat, since it's difficult psychologically for the examiner to back down. In other words, it's easier to get the examiner to change directions slightly than to make an about turn. Thus, to save the examiner's ego, it's best to try to make some amendment to the claim, even if it's insignificant.

Treat all persons you deal with as if they had a sign around their neck reading, "Make Me Feel Important."

—Mary Kay Ash

12. Making Amendments Without Narrowing Scope of Claim

It's usually possible to make amendments to a claim that don't narrow its scope. For example, you can recite that a member, which of necessity must be elongated, *is* elongated. By doing this, you have amended the claim without narrowing your scope of coverage. Also, in the electronic field, you can state that a circuit is energized by a direct-current source. For almost any claim you can add a whereby clause to the claim stating the function of the mechanism of the claim, and you can add a longer preamble stating in more detail (but not in narrower language) the environment of your invention. The important thing is to add some words to the claim(s), even if you already believe they distinguish over the prior art under Sections 102 and 103, in order to show that you're meeting the examiner part way.

PART I—GENERAL ARGUMENTS

1. **Unexpected Results:** The results achieved by the invention are new, unexpected, superior, disproportionate, unsuggested, unusual, critical, and/or surprising.

2. **Assumed Unworkability:** Up to now those skilled in the art thought or were skeptical that the techniques used in the invention were unworkable or presented an insuperable barrier.

3. **Assumed Insolubility:** Up to now those skilled in the art thought or found the problem solved by the invention was insoluble—that is, the invention converts failure into success. The failures of prior-art workers indicate that a solution was not obvious.

4. **Commercial Success:** The invention has attained commercial success. (Prove this by a declaration with supporting documents.)

5. **Unrecognized Problem:** The problem solved by the invention was never before even recognized. The recognition of an unrecognized problem militates in favor of patentability.

6. **Crowded Art:** The invention is classified in a crowded art; therefore, a small step forward should be regarded as significant.

7. **Omission of Element:** An element of a prior-art device has been omitted or a prior-art version has been made simpler without loss of capability.

8. **Unsuggested Modification:** The prior art lacks any suggestion that the reference should be modified in a manner required to meet the claims.

9. **Unappreciated Advantage:** Up to now those skilled in the art never appreciated the advantage of the invention, although it is inherent.

10. **Inoperative References:** The prior-art references that were relied upon are inoperative.

11. **Poor References:** The prior-art references are vague, foreign, conflicting, or very old, and, therefore, are weak and should be construed narrowly.

12. **Ancient Suggestion:** Although the invention may possibly have been suggested by the prior art, the suggestion is many years old, was never implemented, and produced greatly inferior results.

13. **Lack of Implementation:** If the invention were in fact obvious, because of its advantages, those skilled in the art surely would have implemented it by now. That is—the fact that those skilled in the art have not implemented the invention, despite its great advantages, indicates that it is not obvious.

14. **Misunderstood Reference:** The reference does not teach what the examiner relies upon it as supposedly teaching.

15. **Solution of Long-Felt and Unsolved Need:** The invention solves a long-felt, long-existing, but unsolved need.

16. **Commercial Acquiescence:** The invention has been licensed, especially to a competitor.

17. **Professional Recognition:** The invention has been given an award or recognized in a professional publication.

18. **Purchase Offers:** Others, especially accused infringers, have tried to purchase or take a license under the invention.

19. **Copying by Others:** Others have chosen to copy and implement the invention, rather than using the techniques of the prior art.

20. **Competitive Recognition:** The invention has been copied by an infringer; moreover, the infringer has made laudatory statements about it, or has admitted it is unobvious.

21. **Contrarian Invention:** The invention is contrary to the teachings of the prior art—that is, the invention goes against the grain of what the prior art teaches.

22. **Strained Interpretation:** The examiner has made a strained interpretation of the reference that could be made only by hindsight.

23. **Paper Patent:** The reference is a "paper patent"— that is, it was never implemented or commercialized and therefore should be construed narrowly. (Don't use if reference completely anticipates your invention.)

24. **New Principle of Operation:** The invention utilizes a new principle of operation. Applicant has blazed a trail, rather than followed one.

25. **Inability of Competitors:** Competitors were unable to copy the invention until they were able to learn its details through a publication or reverse engineering a commercial model; this indicates unobviousness.

26. **Solved Different Problem:** Applicant's invention solves a different problem than the reference, and such different problem is recited in the claims. *In re Wright*, 6 USPQ 2d 1959 (1988).

27. **No Convincing Reasoning:** The examiner has not presented a convincing line of reasoning as to why the claimed subject matter as a whole, including its differences over the prior art, would have been obvious.

Fig. 13D—Arguments Against Obviousness Rejections (Part I)

28. **Unsuggested Combination:** The prior-art references do not contain any suggestion (express or implied) that they be combined, or that they be combined in the manner suggested.

29. **References Are Individually Complete:** Each reference is complete and functional in itself, so there would be no reason to use parts from or add or substitute parts to any reference.

30. **References Take Different Approaches:** The references take mutually exclusive paths and reach different solutions to a similar problem. Since they teach away from each other, it would not be logical to combine them.

31. **References Teach Away:** The references themselves teach away (expressly or by implication) from the suggested combination.

32. **Reference Is From Different Field:** One reference is from a very different technical field than that of the invention—that is, it's "nonanalogous art."

33. **Impossible to Combine:** Those skilled in the art would find it physically impossible to combine the references in the manner suggested.

34. **Inoperative Combination:** If combined, the references would produce an inoperative combination.

35. **Modifications Necessary:** It would be necessary to make modifications, not taught in the prior art, in order to combine the references in the manner suggested.

36. **Mutually Exclusive Paths:** The references can't be legally combined because they take mutually exclusive paths to reach different solutions to a problem, and, therefore, by implication each teaches away from combining itself with the other.

37. **Claimed Features Lacking:** Even if combined, the references would not meet the claims.

38. **Synergism:** The whole (that is—the result achieved by the invention) is greater than the sum of its parts (that is—the respective results of the individual references).

39. **Multiplicity of Steps Required:** The combination suggested requires a series of separate, awkward combinative steps that are too involved to be considered obvious.

40. **Multiplicity of References:** The fact that a large number of references (over three) must be combined to meet the invention is evidence of unobviousness.

Fig. 13D—Arguments Against Obviousness Rejections (Part II)

13. Amending Your Claim When You Agree With the Examiner

If you believe your broadest claim isn't patentable as written, and you agree with all or part of the examiner's rejection, you'll have to narrow the claim by adding physical or structural limitations, or by narrowing the limitations already present, in the manner outlined in Chapter 9.

Here are some suggestions on how to approach the amendment of your claims:

a. Look for the physical feature(s) in Fig. 13B that constitute the essence of why your invention can be distinguished from the prior art. Then try to put this essence into your claim. Note that you should amend the main claim so as to distinguish physically over the references under Section 102. The physical distinctions should also be significant enough to define structure that is unobvious under Section 103. Merely reciting a single descriptive word will usually not be enough. For example, "Manifold" may not distinguish over a single pipe (even though it should), but reciting "a pipe with a plurality of outlets" will be explicit enough to do the trick. Save your actual reasons as to why the physical distinctions are unobvious for your remarks or for a "whereby" clause at the end of the claim. (Whereby clauses can state the advantages of the invention in a relatively informal manner, without as much concern for antecedents, etc.)

b. Don't make your main claim narrower than necessary. Often the limitation you are looking for can be found in one or more dependent claims. (To see how to combine a dependent claim with an independent claim, see Chapter 9, Section J.)

c. Show your invention and the cited references to friends or associates; often they can readily spot the distinguishing essence of your invention. (Remember to use the Proprietary Materials Agreement (Form 3-1) if you are maintaining the invention as a trade secret in the patent prosecution phase.)

d. After you've narrowed your main independent claim so that it distinguishes over the prior art cited by the patent examiner, and you feel the distinguishing features are patentable under Section 103 (that is, they're unobvious), do the same for all your other independent claims.

e. If you've changed any independent claims, change your dependent claims so that they completely and correctly correspond in language and numbering with your main claim. If you incorporate a limitation from a dependent claim into your main claim, cancel the dependent claim. This is because the dependent claim will no longer be able to add anything to narrow the independent claim. You may also think of other, narrower dependent claims to replace those that you've canceled; refer to the comparison chart to be sure you've claimed every feature.

COMPUTER TIP

One way to be sure the language of your dependent claims corresponds with that of your independent claim is to use a computer with a word-processing program with a "windows" function, so that you can display both claims on your monitor simultaneously. In this way, you'll be able to compare both claims easily.

f. You should write the narrowest possible claims you're willing to accept, since it will be difficult to amend again if your amended claims are rejected this time around. See Section J on final office actions.

g. Be sure all of the less-important specific features of your invention are recited in your amended dependent claims.

h. Try to distinguish by adding quantitative or relative, rather than qualitative, recitations to your claims, since these carry far more weight. For example, say "a rod at least one meter long" or "a rod that is longer than said post" not "a rod of great length" (or "strength").

CHANGING CLAIM LANGUAGE OR INVENTION

If you do amend your claims to define over the prior art, you should, of course, try to keep them as broad as possible and worded appropriately to cover your invention in its latest and most likely commercial embodiment. If you change the design of your invention from that shown and described in your application, this will not prejudice you so long as your claims are still broad enough to cover the new design; judges recognize that designs frequently change as inventions mature. If your design changes by a great amount, consider filing a CIP or a new application. (See Chapter 14.)

---

14. Plan an Outline of Your Response

Indicate in pencil on a copy of your application, or on separate sheets, the amendments you intend to make to your specification, your claims, your drawing, and your remarks. The "remarks" section of your amendment (as shown in Fig. 13E, below) should consist of:

- a brief summary of all your amendments
- a review of the rejections made by the examiner
- a review of the references cited by the examiner
- a summary of how you changed the claim, quoting your changes
- a statement of your claimed distinctions under Sections 102 and 103 if one reference was cited, together with arguments from Part I of Fig. 13D
- a statement of why the references can't be combined, followed by comments regarding Sections 102 and 103 if more than one reference was cited, together with arguments from Part II of Fig. 13D
- a request for reconsideration of the examiner's position
- a discussion of dependent and other main claims you have
- a discussion of any technical (Section 112) rejections
- any request for aid you may wish to make under MPEP 707.07(j) requesting the examiner to write claims, and
- a conclusion.

See Section G, below, for specifics on drafting your remarks.

At this point, read Fig. 13E, a sample successful amendment from an actual case (now a patent) to see the format customarily used. Continue to refer to Fig. 13E throughout the next four sections of this chapter.

In The United States Patent And Trademark Office

Appn. Number:	07/910,721
Appn. Filed:	1992 Jul 27
Applicants:	Nira Schwartz, Arie Shahar, and Richard Woods
Title:	Inspection Method Using Templates And Unique Histogram Analysis
Examiner/GAU:	Yon J. Couso/3303

San Francisco, 1994 Dec 23, Thu

Amendment A

Assistant Commissioner for Patents
Washington, District of Columbia   20231

Sir:

In response to the Office Action mailed 1993 Sep 23, please amend the above application as follows:

Title: Change to —Inspection Method Using Multiple Template Images,
Unique Histogram Analysis, and Multiple Gray Levels
Correlated To Addresses Of Template Images—

Specification:

P. 1, l. 7, change "1991, May 25." to
—1991 May 25, now patent 5,204,911, granted 1993 Apr 20.—.

P. 3, ll. 12 to 13, change "application Ser. Nr. 07/706,800" to —patent—.

P. 13, l. 8, after "borders" insert —of—.

P. 21, l. 13, change "bussas" to —buss as—.

Fig. 13E/1—Sample "Regular" Amendment

Claims: Cancel all claims of record and substitute new claims 37 to 54 as follows.

37. A method for inspecting products that move on a production line for defects, marks, and dimensional accuracy with the use of a sensor and a processing unit having a memory, comprising:

(a) providing and saving in said memory a plurality of computer-generated artificial template images, each of said plurality of computer-generated artificial template images having a plurality of predetermined coordinates and addresses mapped within said memory, said plurality of computer-generated artificial template images together defining a full template image.

(b) assigning a plurality of predetermined gray levels to each of said plurality of computer-generated artificial template images,

(c) creating a respective plurality of histogram vectors of said plurality of computer-generated artificial template images, each of said histogram vectors having values which are correlated to said coordinates and addresses mapped within said memory.

(d) creating a product image by sensing one of said products with said sensor, said product image comprising a multiplicity of pixels with intensity levels expressed as a plurality of respective gray levels.

(e) modifying said product image to produce a modified product image by converting said plurality of gray levels of said product image to a plurality of modified gray levels,

(f) creating a plurality of additional gray levels by mathematically combining said plurality of modified gray levels with said plurality of predetermined gray levels so that said plurality of additional gray levels are different from said plurality of modified gray levels or said plurality of predetermined gray levels, and

(g) analyzing said plurality of computer-generated artificial template images, said modified product image, and said plurality of additional gray levels for product inspection.

38. The method of claim 37, further including creating said additional gray levels by superposing said modified product image onto said template images by summing gray levels assigned to memory locations of said product image and said full template image, so as to produce a summation which represents a superposed image, and saving said summation in said memory.

39. The method of claim 38, further including creating a histogram vector of said superposed image.

40. The method of claim 39 wherein said creating said histogram vector of said superposed image is done so that said histogram vector is compressed.

41. The method of claim 39 wherein said creating of histogram vector of said superposed image is done by including gray levels that are smaller than the highest gray levels of said computer-generated artificial template images so that said histogram vector is truncated.

42. The method of claim 39, further including comparing values of said histogram vectors of said superposed image with those of said histogram vectors of said computer-generated artificial template image.

43. The method of claim 39, further including analyzing said histogram vectors of said superposed image by its discontinuities to indicate dimensions in numbers of pixels.

Fig. 13E/2—Sample "Regular" Amendment

Appn. Number 07/910,721   (Schwartz et al.)   GAU 3303   Amnt. B, contd.   4

44. The method of claim 39, further including analyzing any new gray level values which appear in said histogram vectors of said superposed image and were absent in said histogram of said computer-generated artificial template image.

45. The method of claim 39, further including analyzing said histogram vectors of said superposed image by its discontinuities to detect, size, and map said defects in numbers of pixels.

46. The method of claim 39, further including counting the number of pixels equal to gray levels in said histogram vector and saving the count in memory.

47. The method of claim 39, further including analyzing said histogram vectors of said superposed image by its discontinuities to detect marks and express their size in numbers of pixels.

48. The method of claim 37 wherein said modifying said product image to produce a modified product image is performed by converting said gray levels of said product image to modified gray levels which are higher than said gray levels of said full template image minus the lowest gray level of said computer-generated artificial template images.

49. The method of claim 37, further including creating a superposed image by superposing said modified product image onto said template image by summing gray levels assigned to memory locations of said product image and said computer-generated artificial template images, and saving the results of the

Appn. Number 07/910,721   (Schwartz et al.)   GAU 3303   Amnt. B, contd.   5

summation in said memory.

50. The method of claim 37 further including creating a truncated histogram vector of said superposed image by including gray levels that are smaller than the highest gray levels of said computer-generated artificial template image.

51. The method of claim 37, further including creating a compressed histogram vector of said superposed image.

52. The method of claim 37 wherein said products are printed circuit boards.

53. The method of claim 37, further including modifying the number of said template images to one.

54. The method of claim 37 wherein said providing and saving in memory is done so that said full template image has a size equal to a line created by a plurality of said pixels.

REMARKS—General

By the above amendment, Applicants have amended the title to emphasize the novelty of the invention.

Also applicants have rewritten all claims to define the invention more particularly and distinctly so as to overcome the technical rejections and define the invention patentably over the prior art.

The Objection To The Specification And The Claims Rejection Under § 112
The specification was objected to under § 112 since it was said to fail to teach how processor 106 works and there was no description as to how the plurality of template images were related to an inspection machine.

Fig. 13E/3—Sample "Regular" Amendment

Appn. Number 07/910,721　(Schwartz et al.)　GAU 3303　Amnt. B, contd.　6

Applicants request reconsideration and withdrawal of this objection since it is not necessary to teach how prior-art processor 106 works, and since the specification teaches how the plurality of template images relate to an inspection machine.

First, note that processor 106 is a known prior-art item of commerce, made and sold by the company indicated on p. 9 of the specification. There is no requirement that a patent application teach how such a prior-art machine works—only how to make and use the invention claimed. The present clearly teaches how to make and use the invention with processor 106. The present specification system uses processor 106 in a new manner and the present specification clearly teaches in detail how to use it as part of and in the practice of the invention on pp. 13 to 23.

Note that cited prior patent 5,204,911 to Schwartz and Shahar shows the same processor 106 in Fig 12 and discusses how it works under the discussion of Fig 12—see cols. 13 and 14. Thus the structure and operation of processor 106 was prior art and was well known prior to applicants' filing date.

As to how the plurality of template images are related to an inspection machine, the present specification clearly shows this as follows:

P. 5 of the specification states that Fig 2 shows a plurality of template images related to an inspection machine and that Fig 3 is a histogram of a template image of Fig 2. This is done in the inspection machine.

P. 13 of the specification discusses the histogram vector of Fig 3 and how it is saved in compressed form. This is done in the inspection machine.

Pp. 13-16 discusses how an image of the product to be inspected is obtained and stored and how the gray levels of the product image are modified by the look-up tables. This is done in the inspection machine.

Appn. Number 07/910,721　(Schwartz et al.)　GAU 3303　Amnt. B, contd.　7

Pp. 16-18 discuss how the template images are superposed with the product image; this is also done in the inspection machine.

Pp. 18-21 discuss how the histogram of Fig 6 is built from the superposed image, again using the inspection machine.

Pp. 21 to 23 discuss how the machine of Fig 7 of the invention uses the histogram of Fig 6 to complete the inspection.

Thus the present specification clearly and completely teaches how to make and use the invention in general, and how the template images are related to an inspection machine in particular.

Accordingly applicants submit that the specification does comply with § 112 and therefore request withdrawal of this objection.

The Rejection Of Claim 19 On Hashim and Gaborski Is Overcome

The last O.A. rejected independent claim 19 on Hashim and Gaborski. Claim 19 has been rewritten as new claim 37 to define patentably over these references, and any combination thereof. Applicants request reconsideration of this rejection, as now applicable to claim 37, for the following reasons:

(1) There is no justification, in Hashim and Gaborski, or in any other prior art separate from applicants' disclosure, which suggests that these references be combined, much less be combined in the manner proposed.

(2) The proposed combination would not be physically possible or operative.

(3) Even if Hashim and Gaborski were to be combined in the manner proposed, the proposed combination would not show all of the novel physical features of claim 37.

(4) These novel physical features of claim 37 produce new and unexpected results and hence are unobvious and patentable over these references.

Fig. 13E/4—Sample "Regular" Amendment

The References And Differences Of The Present Invention Thereover

Prior to discussing the claims and the above four points, applicants will first discuss the references and the general novelty of the present invention and its unobviousness over the references.

Hashim creates an image of a product, but modifies the image of the product using a transformation function. Hashim, col. 2, ll. 60-65. Applicants modify the product image using a different transformation function. Hashim modifies the gray levels in his template to either value 0 or value B related to threshold T (col. 2, l. 57, to col. 3, l. 22). Thus Hashim's procedure modifies the gray levels according to a value and not according to coordinates. Therefore Hashim's procedure of gray level modification does not enable preselected coordinates and addresses to be mapped inside any template image. Further it does not assign preselected gray levels to any preselected coordinates and addresses. Hashim creates a histogram to be used as a tool for modifying gray levels of his template images (col. 2, l. 57 to col. 3 l. 22). However his histogram cannot be used for evaluation of product dimensions or as an indication of any coordinate values, as can applicants' histogram.

Gaborski's template is composed of vertical lines which are spread apart. There are no coordinates mapping the bars inside the template by assigning preselected gray levels to them, as in applicant's invention. Gaborski creates a histogram to be used as a tool for inspection of maximum correlation between template image and product image. His histogram vector does not contain information about the product's coordinates and dimensional measurements, as applicants' histogram vector will supply.

The last O.A. notes that Hashim's system does the following:

(1) creates template images,
(2) creates product images,
(3) creates additional gray levels,
(4) modifies the additional gray levels to prevent ambiguity.

However in general, to create a group of gray levels ('A') that are different than gray levels of another group ('B') and the gray levels of still another group ('C'), the procedure of creating the gray levels of group 'A' must take into account the values of the gray levels of groups 'B' and 'C' to prevent ambiguity. Hashim does not do this, but applicants do.

When Hashim creates (modifies) his gray levels [step (4) above] he considers only gray levels within the image that he modifies (Hashim, col. 2, l. 57 to col. 3, l. 18). He does not consider nor is he aware of the gray levels of step (1) above when he performs his modification step (4). Therefore, he cannot have any assurance that ambiguity is prevented. Whatever algorithm he uses to operate on the equalized histogram, this is then scanned to ascertain the positions of the edges (col. 3, ll. 10 to 18); it is NOT done to prevent ambiguity.

With regard to the compression of the histogram vectors, applicants perform this for the first time. Until now no one ever thought of compressing histogram vectors or suggested same, much less actually did it. Applicants' method identifies and maps coordinates using gray levels. Using this, one may create a very long histogram vector, or a large number of short histograms. By compressing the histogram vector, applicants save valuable processing time and storage space. As stated, this procedure that was not done before, so neither it nor its concomitant advantages were known or appreciated.

Hashim And Gaborski Do Not Contain Any Justification To Support Their Combination, Much Less In The Manner Proposed

With regard to the proposed combination of Hashim and Gaborski, it is well known that in order for any prior-art references themselves to be validly combined for use in a prior-art § 103 rejection , *the references themselves* (or some other prior art) must suggest that they be combined. E.g., as was stated in In re Sernaker, 217 U.S.P.Q. 1, 6 (C.A.F.C. 1983):

"[P]rior art references in combination do not make an invention obvious unless something in the prior art references would

Fig. 13E/5—Sample "Regular" Amendment

Appn. Number 07/910,721   (Schwartz et al)   GAU 3303   Amnt. B, contd.   10

suggest the advantage to be derived from combining their teachings."

That the suggestion to combine the references should not come from applicant was forcefully stated in Orthopedic Equipment Co. v. United States, 217 U.S.P.Q. 193, 199 (CAFC 1983):

"It is wrong to use the patent in suit [here the patent application] as a guide through the maze of prior art references, combining the right references in the right way to achieve the result of the claims in suit [here the claims pending]. Monday morning quarterbacking is quite improper when resolving the question of nonobviousness in a court of law [here the PTO]."

As was further stated in Uniroyal, Inc. v. Rudkin-Wiley Corp., 5 U.S.P.Q.2d 1434 (C.A.F.C. 1988), "[w]here prior-art references require selective combination by the court to render obvious a subsequent invention, there must be some reason for the combination other than the hindsight gleaned from the invention itself. . . . *Something in the prior art must suggest the desirability and thus the obviousness of making the combination.*" [Emphasis supplied.]

In line with these decisions, recently the Board stated in Ex parte Levengood, 28 U.S.P.Q.2d 1300 (P.T.O.B.A.&I. 1993):

"In order to establish a *prima facie* case of obviousness, it is necessary for the examiner to *present evidence,* preferably in the form of some teaching, suggestion, incentive or inference in the applied prior art, or in the form of generally available knowledge, that one having ordinary skill in the art *would have been led* to combine the relevant teachings of the. applied references in the proposed manner to arrive at the claimed invention. ... That which is within the capabilities of one skilled in the art is not synonymous with obviousness. ... That one can *reconstruct and/or explain the theoretical mechanism of an*

Appn. Number 07/910,721   (Schwartz et al)   GAU 3303   Amnt. B, contd.   11

invention by means of logic and sound scientific reasoning does not afford the basis for an obviousness conclusion unless that logic and reasoning also supplies sufficient impetus to have led one of ordinary skill in the art to combine the teachings of the references to make the claimed invention.... Our reviewing courts have often advised the Patent and Trademark Office that it can satisfy the burden of establishing a *prima facie* case of obviousness only by showing some objective teaching in either the prior art, or knowledge generally available to one of ordinary skill in the art, that 'would lead' that individual 'to combine the relevant teachings of the references.' ... Accordingly, an examiner cannot establish obviousness by locating references which describe various aspects of a patent applicant's invention without also providing evidence of the motivating force which would impel one skilled in the art to do what the patent applicant has done."

In the present case, there is no reason given in the last O.A. to support the proposed combination, other than the statement "both references teach a histogram template". However the fact that both references teach a histogram template is not sufficient to gratuitously and selectively substitute parts of one reference (Gaborski's template library) for a part of another reference in order to meet applicants' novel claimed combination.

The O.A. noted (p. 5) that the combination of Hashim and Gaborski produces an advantage (broadens system performance). Applicants submit that the fact that the combination produces advantages militates in favor of *applicants* because it proves that the combination produces new and unexpected results and hence is unobvious.

As stated in the above Levengood case,

"That one can *reconstruct and/or explain the theoretical mechanism of an invention by means of logic and sound scientific reasoning does not afford the basis for an obviousness*

Fig. 13E/6—Sample "Regular" Amendment

Appn. Number 07/910,721   (Schwartz et al.)   GAU 3303   Amnt. B, contd.   12

conclusion unless that logic and reasoning also supplies sufficient impetus to have led one of ordinary skill in the art to combine the teachings of the references to make the claimed invention.".

Applicant therefore submits that combining Hashim and Gaborski is not legally justified and is therefore improper. Thus they submit that the rejection on these references is also improper and should be withdrawn.

Applicants respectfully request, if the claims are again rejected upon any combination of references, that the Examiner include an explanation, in accordance with M.P.E.P. § 706.02, Ex parte Clapp, 27 U.S.P.Q. 972 (P.O.B.A. 1985), and Ex parte Levengood, supra, a "factual basis to support his conclusion that it would have been obvious" to make the combination.

Even If Hashim And Gaborski Were To Be Combined In The Manner Proposed, The Proposed Combination Would Not Show All Of The Novel Physical Features Of Claim 37

However even if the combination of Hashim and Gaborski were legally justified, claim 37 would still have novel (and unobvious) physical features over the proposed combination. In other words, applicant's invention, as defined by claim 37, comprises much more than merely substituting a plurality of templates for one template.

Specifically, clauses (a) and (b) of claim 37 clearly distinguish applicant's template histograms from Gaborski's and Hashim's, or any possible combination thereof, since these clauses recite:

"(a) providing and saving in said memory a plurality of computer-generated artificial template images, each of said plurality of computer-generated artificial template images having a plurality of predetermined coordinates and addresses mapped within said memory, said plurality of computer-generated artificial template images together defining a full template image,

Appn. Number 07/910,721   (Schwartz et al.)   GAU 3303   Amnt. B, contd.   13

(b) assigning a plurality of predetermined gray levels to each of said plurality of computer-generated artificial template images."

Neither Hashim nor Gaborski show this feature because neither of their systems assign specific gray levels to any predetermined coordinates and addresses, as applicants' system does.

By assigning specific gray levels to predetermined coordinates and addresses, applicants' system causes the histogram vectors of clause (c) to have values correlated to addresses, a feature that is missing in ordinary histogram vectors, such as those of Hashim and Gaborski. Thus Hashim and Gaborski also lack the feature of clause (c), i.e.,:

(c) creating a respective plurality of histogram vectors of said plurality of computer-generated artificial template images, each of said histogram vectors having values which are correlated to said coordinates and addresses mapped within said memory,

Clause (f) also clearly distinguishes over Gaborski and Hashim since it recites:

"(f) creating a plurality of additional gray levels by mathematically combining said plurality of modified gray levels with said plurality of preselected gray levels so that said plurality of additional gray levels are different from said plurality of modified gray levels or said plurality of preselected gray levels".

Neither Hashim nor Gaborski create any additional gray levels by mathematically combining the plurality of modified gray levels with the plurality of preselected gray levels so that the additional gray levels are different from the modified gray levels and the preselected gray levels.

As stated above. When Hashim creates his gray levels [step (4) above] he considers only gray levels within the image that he modifies (Hashim, col. 2, l. 57 to col. 3 l. 18). He does not consider nor is he aware of the gray levels of step (1) above while his modification step (4) above is performed.

Fig. 13E/7—Sample "Regular" Amendment

Therefore, he cannot have any assurance that ambiguity is prevented and he does not combine any previous gray levels to arrive at his additional gray levels.

Thus applicants submit that their invention is much more than merely substituting a plurality of templates for one template and that claim 37 clearly recites novel physical subject matter which distinguishes over any possible combination of Hashim and Gaborski.

The Novel Physical Features Of Claim 37 Produce New And Unexpected Results And Hence Are Unobvious And Patentable Over These References Under § 103

Also applicants submit that the novel physical features of claim 37 are also unobvious and hence patentable under § 103 since they produce new and unexpected results over Hashim and Gaborski, or any combination thereof.

These new and unexpected results are the ability of applicants' system to locate addresses and coordinates in memory by referring to the gray levels in the histogram vectors. This in turn results in higher speed image processing for detecting defects and making dimensional measurements. Applicants' system therefore is vastly superior to that of either Hashim And Gaborski, or any possible combination thereof. The novel features of applicants' system which effect these differences are, as stated, clearly recited in claim 37.

The Dependent Claims Are A Fortiori Patentable Over Hashim And Gaborski

New dependent claims 38 to 54 incorporate all the subject matter of claim 37 and add additional subject matter which makes them a fortiori and independently patentable over these references.

Claim 38 additionally recites

"creating said additional gray levels by superposing said modified product image onto said template images by summing gray levels assigned to memory locations of said product image and said full

template image, so as to produce a summation which represents a superposed image, and saving said summation in said memory."

This is entirely foreign to Hashim and Gaborski, or any combination thereof since, as stated, the systems of these references do not sum any gray levels of the product image and the full template image. Hashim modifies the product image using a transformation function, rather than by summing. Gaborski does not sum either.

Claim 39 further adds "creating a histogram vector of said superposed image". Again this is clearly foreign to Hashim and Gaborski.

Claims 40, 41, 50, and 51 further add that the histogram vector is compressed or truncated. As stated above, this feature is novel with applicant and produces new and unexpected results—the saving of processing time and storage space.

The last O.A. stated that it would be obvious to compress the histogram vector "in order to **increase** the processing time". [Emphasis added.] As stated, compressing the vector **saves or decreases**, rather than increases, processing time. This is an important and significant advantage. Applicants request reconsideration of the statement that compression would be obvious since they submit that the facts that it is (a) novel, and (b) produces valuable new, improved, and unexpected results proves that it is <u>unobvious</u>.

Claim 42 recites comparing values of the histogram vectors of the superposed image with those of the histogram vectors of said computer-generated artificial template image. Neither Hashim nor Gaborski do this: Hashim compares two product images and Gaborski looks for maximum correlation.

Claims 43, 45, and 47 recite analyzing the histogram vectors of the superposed image by its discontinuities to indicate dimensions in numbers of pixels. Neither Hashim nor Gaborski do this: Hashim analyzes discontinuities in the product image itself.

Fig. 13E/8—Sample "Regular" Amendment

Claim 44 recites analyzing any new gray level values which appear in the histogram vectors of the superposed image and were absent in the histogram of the computer-generated artificial template image. Neither Hashim nor Gaborski do this: Hashim analyzes new gray levels for threshold levels in order to modify the product image.

Claim 46 recites counting the number of pixels equal to gray levels in the histogram vector and saving the count in memory. Neither Hashim nor Gaborski count pixels in the product image.

Claim 48 recites converting the gray levels of the product image to modified gray levels which are higher than the gray levels of the full template image minus the lowest gray level of the computer-generated artificial template images. Neither Hashim nor Gaborski convert gray levels while preventing ambiguity of gray levels: Hashim converts gray levels "to ascertain the positions of edges". Hashim. Col. 3, l. 12.

Claim 49 recites creating a superposed image by superposing the modified product image onto the template image by summing gray levels assigned to memory locations of the product image and the computer-generated artificial template images, and saving the results of the summation in memory. Neither Hashim nor Gaborski do this: Gaborski creates multiplications of the product image and the template image. However his template image is different from applicants' template and his product image is modified differently from applicants' product image.

Claim 53 recites modifying the number of said template images to one. Neither Hashim nor Gaborski do this.

Claim 54 recites that the providing and saving in memory is done so that the full template image has a size equal to a line created by a plurality of the pixels. Neither Hashim nor Gaborski deal with an image size of one line.

Accordingly applicants submit that the dependent claims are a fortiori patentable and should also be allowed.

Conclusion

For all of the above reasons, applicants submit that the specification and claims are now in proper form, and that the claims all define patentably over the prior art. Therefore they submit that this application is now in condition for allowance, which action they respectfully solicit.

Conditional Request For Constructive Assistance

Applicants have amended the specification and claims of this application so that they are proper, definite, and define novel structure which is also unobvious. If, for any reason this application are not believed to be in full condition for allowance, applicant respectfully requests the constructive assistance and suggestions of the Examiner pursuant to M.P.E.P. § 706.03(d) and § 707.07(j) in order that the undersigned can place this application in allowable condition as soon as possible and without the need for further proceedings.

Very respectfully,

Nira Schwartz   Arie Shahar   Richard Woods
                          Applicants Pro Se

950 Parker Street
Berkeley, CA 94710
Tel. (510) 549-1976; Fax (510) 548-5902

Certificate Of Mailing: I certify that on the date below this document and referenced attachments, if any, will be deposited with the U.S. Postal Service as first class mail in an envelope addressed to: "BOX NON-FEE AMENDMENTS, ASSISTANT COMMISSIONER FOR PATENTS, WASHINGTON, DC 20231."

1994 Dec 23
                    Nira Schwartz, Applicant

Fig. 13E/9—Sample "Regular" Amendment

E. Format for Amending the Specification and Claims

Form 13-1 in Appendix 7 provides the initial part of your amendment.

Fill in the serial number, filing date, your name, title of your application, and the examiner's name and examining unit or group art unit. The date on which you actually mail the amendment goes after "date," and the date of the office letter goes at the space indicated in the first paragraph. Put an appropriate letter (A, B, etc.) after "Amendment" to indicate which amendment it is (your first, second, etc.) Then immediately after the "In response to..." sentence make all the desired changes to your specification and claims, in the manner indicated below, before starting your remarks. (You should not format your amendment in the form of a personal letter to the examiner, as I have seen some inventors do.)

1. Changes to Specification

If you're going to make any changes to the specification, provide the heading "SPECIFICATION:" below the sentence printed on Form 13-1. Then indicate the specific places in your application where you want to make amendments and the actual amendments you wish to make. Use quotes to indicate existing words and dashes to sandwich words you wish to add. (On typewriters, a dash traditionally consists of two hyphens (--), but many computers can now type an actual dash (—).) For example:

Page 1, line 3, change "member" (2d occur.) to —lever—.

Page 5, lines 12 to 14, change "member 14... pivot 23" to —lever 14 is connected by way of arm 22 to bearing 23—.

Page 12, line 21, after "screw 18" insert —in contact with arm 22—.

Page 14, lines 12 to 13, delete "member 14... pivot 23."

When your amendment is received, the clerk of the examining group will make each change in red ink in handwriting on the official copy of your application in the manner you direct. Thus, you should insure that there is no ambiguity in your amendments. See the example above for how to change the word "member" where it occurs twice on a line.

Be sure that your amendments to the specification don't contain any "new matter." (See Section B14, above.)

If you have to make a large number of amendments to the specification, it's better to submit an entirely retyped specification, called a "substitute specification"; see MPEP § 608.01(q) for instructions.

2. Amendments to Claims

If you want to amend your claims, provide the heading "CLAIMS:" and then indicate specifically the claim changes you desire. There are three ways to amend any claim of a patent application:

a. By word cancellation and/or insert

b. By claim cancellation and substitution, and

c. By rewriting the claim with brackets and underscoring.

Let's look at each of these in more detail.

a. The Word-Cancellation-and/or-Insert Method

The word-cancellation-and/or-insert method can be used only if you are canceling words and/or are adding *no more than five words* to your claim. Claim amendments made by this method are done in exactly the same manner as specification amendments. For example:

Claim 1, line 5, change "said elongated member" to "—a lever having—."

b. The Cancellation-and-Substitution Method

The cancellation-and-substitution method can be used under any circumstances, but especially if you are adding more than five words to the claim. To use this method, you cancel the claim in question and substitute an entirely different claim. The new claim should be given the next-highest unused claim number. Thus, if you originally submitted 12 claims and you want to cancel Claim 1 and substitute a new claim, the new claim should be numbered 13. For example:

Claim 1, cancel and substitute new Claim 13, as follows:

13. An improved bicycle mechanism comprising [etc.]...

(Make sure that you also amend all claims that were dependent on Claim 1 so that they're now dependent on Claim 13 and so that their terms conform with those in Claim 13.)

When the case is allowed, the clerk of your examining division will renumber all of your claims in order, starting with 1.

c. The Bracket-and-Underscore Method

The bracket-and-underscore method is used when you don't have too many amendments to make to your claim and you want to point out to the examiner exactly where you're making the amendments. Under this method you retype your entire claim with the notation "(amended)" after the number of the claim (use the same number), put brackets around words to be deleted, and underscore material to be added. Note how the following claim reads originally (with bracketed words and without underscored words) and as amended (without bracketed words and with underscored words):

Claim 1, rewrite as Claim 1 (amended) as follows:

1. *(amended) A method [for] of stimulating the growth rate of swine by feeding them [aspirin in an amount effective to increase their rate of growth] a daily dose of aspirin of 0.25 gram per kilogram of body weight.*

Some examiners don't like the bracket and underscore method of amending claims because it makes things look too confusing; I agree and therefore rarely use it. If your typewriter doesn't have brackets (you're not permitted to use parentheses), you must make your brackets by hand or with virgules (slashes) and underscore lines, thus: ⌐ ⌐

WORD PROCESSING TIP
With the availability of word processing, I now usually cancel all of the previous claims, even if I'm making one or two minor changes, and resubmit all of the claims as part of the amendment. This is easy to do by incorporating the claims from your disk file of the original application into your amendment and making the changes you desire. Examiners like this method since it presents all of the claims together in clean copy form. I strongly recommend it, since it reduces errors in numbering, terms, etc. For example, if your original claims were 1 (independent) and 2 to 10 (dependent) and you want to amend Claim 1 only, you would cancel Claims 1 to 10 and substitute new Claims 11 to 20. Claim 11 would be a rewritten version of Claim 1 and Claims 12 to 20 would be identical to Claims 2 to 10, respectively, except that they would be made dependent upon Claim 11, rather than on Claim 1.

F. Drafting the Remarks

Next, add the "remarks" portion of your amendment. Some general rules for drafting remarks that I'll state first may seem silly, but they're the customary practice and to deviate substantially may make the examiner feel uncomfortable and take a negative attitude toward your invention.

1. General Rules for Drafting Remarks

Rule 1: As stated before, when writing your remarks observe Inventor's Commandment #22 by never admitting that any prior art anticipates or renders any part of your invention obvious. Similarly, never derogate your invention or any part of it.

Rule 2: Never get personal with the examiner. If you must refer to the examiner, always use the third person. For example, never state "You rejected…"; instead, state "The Examiner [note the capitalization] has rejected…" Better yet, state "The office action rejects…" or "Claim 1 was rejected…" Never, never address the examiner by name (except in the caption), and never make your amendment a "Dear Mr. [Examiner's Name]" letter. See the sample amendment of Fig. 13E, above, for how it's done.

Rule 3: If there's an error in the OA, refer to the error in the OA, and don't state that the examiner made the error. Even if you find the examiner made a completely stupid error, just deal with it in a very formal way, keep emotions and personalities out of your response, and don't invalidate the examiner. Remember, you've probably made some stupid errors in your life also, and you wouldn't want your nose rubbed in them.

Rule 4: When referring to yourself, always refer to yourself in the third person as "Applicant" and never as "I."

Rule 5: Stick to the issues in your remarks. Be relevant and to the point and don't discuss personalities or irrelevant issues. Never antagonize the examiner, no matter how much you'd like to. It's improper, and, if you turn the examiner against you, it can considerably narrow the scope of claims that are ultimately allowed.

Rule 6: Use only the legally relevant, logical arguments which are listed in Fig. 13D. Don't use arguments which, although plausible, aren't legally relevant or logical. Among these are: (1) the invention of a prior patent that anticipates your invention wasn't ever implemented; (2) a cited patent shouldn't have been granted or has less novelty than yours (the PTO isn't bound to repeat its past mistakes); and (3) you spent a lot of time and/or effort to come up with the invention. Also, some inventors have actually telephoned the patentee-inventor of a cited patent. This is a futile exercise, since there's nothing a patentee can do to help you; a patent speaks for itself. As a further example, if the examiner says pages 11 and 12 of your specification don't provide a clear description of the invention, tell why these pages do the job; don't simply explain how it works without reference to these pages.

Rule 7: Whenever you write any new claims or make any additions to a present claim, you must tell how they distinguish over the prior art the examiner has cited under Sections 102 and 103. Follow Inventor's Commandment #7 from Chapter 5, repeated below, and Patent Rule 111(b) and (c):

(b) In order to be entitled to reexamination or reconsideration, the applicant must make request therefor in writing, and must distinctly and specifically point out the supposed errors in the examiner's action; the applicant must respond

to every ground of objection and rejection in the prior office action (except that request may be made that objections or requirements as to form not necessarily to further reconsideration of the claim be held in abeyance until allowable subject matter is indicated), and the applicant's action must appear throughout to be a bona fide attempt to advance the case to final action. A general allegation that the claims define a patentable invention without specifically pointing out how the language of the claims patentably distinguish them from the references does not comply with the requirements of this section.

(c) In amending an application in response to a rejection, the applicant must clearly point out the patentable novelty that the applicant thinks the claims present in view of the state of the art disclosed by the references cited or the objection made. The applicant must also show how the amendments avoid such references or objections.

INVENTOR'S COMMANDMENT #7

To evaluate or argue the patentability of any invention, use a two-step process: a) First determine what novelty the invention has over the closest prior-art reference(s). Novelty can be a new physical (hardware) feature, a new combination of two separate old features, or a new use of an old feature; and b) Then determine if the novelty produces any new and unexpected results or otherwise indicates unobviousness.

Rule 8: If you do disagree and think the OA was wrong, you must tell exactly why you disagree. If you agree that a claim is obvious over the prior art, don't admit this in your response (see Inventor's Commandment #22); simply cancel the claim and don't give any reason for it, or if you must comment, state merely that it has been canceled in view of the coverage afforded by the remaining claims.

Rule 9: Make a careful, complete, and convincing presentation, but you don't have to overly agonize about words or minutiae. The reality is that many examiners don't read your remarks or else skim through them very rapidly. This is because they're generally working under a quota system, which means they have to dispose of (finally reject or allow) a certain number of cases in each fiscal quarter. Thus, the examiners are under time pressure and it takes a lot of time to read remarks. It's important to cover all the substantive points in the office action and to deal with every objection

and rejection. If you do make an error, as stated, the PTO will almost always give you an opportunity to correct it, rather than forcing you to abandon your application.

Two good ways to make sure your examiner reads and (hopefully) understands your points and reasons are to liberally sprinkle your amendment with boldfaced "arguing" headings which themselves tell your whole story (as is done in the sample amendment of Fig. 13E), and to keep your paragraphs short and inviting. For example, some arguing headings might be, "Briskin Does Not Show Any Elongated Lever," "Claim 1 Clearly Defines Over Warner Under Section 102," "Ihara Could Not Be Operatively Combined With Harolde," and "Applicant's Rasterizer Produces New and Unexpected Results Over Hearsh."

Rule 10: If possible, thank or praise the examiner if you can find a reason to do so with sincerity. Examiners get criticized and told they're all wet so often that they'll welcome any genuine, deserved praise.

Rule 11: Don't emphasize your beliefs; they're considered irrelevant. For example, don't say "Applicant *believes* this invention is patentable." Rather say, "Since the claims define novel structure that produces new and unexpected results as described above, Applicant *submits* that such claims are clearly patentable."

Rule 12: Although it's okay to state *briefly* why your invention is superior to that of the reference(s), the main thrust of your argument should be a legal argument that tells (a) how your invention, as claimed, differs from the reference(s), and (b) why these differences are important. Again, see Inventor's Commandment #7 above.

You may wonder whether it makes sense to put much effort into your remarks even though the chances are great they won't be carefully read. My opinion is that it does, because you never know. Think of your effort as a kind of insurance against being the one in five (or whatever) whose remarks are in fact subjected to close scrutiny.

Although it's difficult, I recommend that you do the best job you possibly can in Amendment A, since it will probably be the last chance you get to amend your claims in this application. This is so important and is violated so often, that I've made it Inventor's Commandment #26, at the beginning of this chapter. After you draft your amendment, I suggest that you wait a few days and come back and review it again, pretending that you're the examiner. This will probably give you important insights and enable you to improve it further.

2. How to Draft Your Remarks

Your remarks should first provide a brief summary of what you've done to the specification and claims. For example, you can state: "The specification has been amended editorially and to correct those errors noted by the examiner. Claims 1 to 5 have been rewritten as new Claims 13 to 18 to more particularly define the invention in a patentable manner over the cited prior art." Then briefly summarize what each claim recites, as is done in Fig. 13E, above. If the drawing has been objected to, state that it will be corrected after allowance. If you want to make a voluntary amendment to the drawing, state that a request is attached (Form 13-2) and tell why you want to amend the drawing.

a. Restate First Rejection

Restate the first rejection of the OA. For example, state: "Claims 1 to 5 were rejected as unpatentable over Jones in view of Smith." The examiner, thus oriented, saves the time it would take to reread the OA.

b. Review Each Reference Relied On in the Rejection

One or two sentences for each is sufficient. For example: "Reference A (Clark patent 3,925,777) shows a clock having a sequential single-digit readout…[etc.]."

c. Specifically Describe Any Changes and Argue Section 102 and Then Section 103.

Discuss specifically how the claim in question has been amended and how it recites structure that physically distin-

guishes over the references under Section 102. The flow-chart of Fig. 13C gives the specifics as to how to do that. For example, *"Claim 1, now rewritten as new claim 5, recites …" This language distinguishes over Smith under Section 102 because Smith does not show [etc.]. These distinctions are submitted to be of patentable merit under Section 103 because* [discuss new results that flow from your novel structure, giving as many reasons as you can from Fig. 13D, Part 1, and your completed Form 4-2]." (I find it helpful to keep the claim I'm discussing displayed in one window of my computer monitor while I type my remarks in another window. Often I need to amend the claim to distinguish further over a reference under § 102 as I write the remarks.)

> ### USING A 102/103 APPROACH
>
> You must use a 102/103 approach even if your claim was rejected on Section 102 alone. This 102/103 approach is useful if you don't understand the examiner's reasoning. That is, rather than try to figure out what the examiner was trying to say, or questioning the examiner, simply put forth a detailed, cogent 102/103 argument. This will usually win the day, or at worst, reframe the issues in your favor.

I can't emphasize enough that you should discuss how your invention, *as claimed*, distinguishes over—that is, has novel physical features not shown in—the reference, not how the reference differs from your invention, and not, at this stage, why your invention is better than the reference. Remember that under Section 112, a means plus a function is considered a physical recitation.

The following jingle may help you remember this important rule:

Never argue what's not in your claim
You'll miss the mark and may lose the game.

Also be logical in your arguments. For example, if you're claiming B and a reference shows A and B, don't argue that A is no good. Also, don't argue that a reference should be taken lightly—that is, it's a "paper patent," because its invention was never put into commercial use—unless you're absolutely sure of your facts and the reference isn't a dead ringer for your invention.

d. Refute Any Improper Combination of References

If a combination of several references has been cited against your claim, first state why the combination cannot properly be made and then discuss your distinctions under Section 103. For example: *The combination of Smith's lever with*

Jones's pedal mechanism is submitted to be improper because neither Smith nor Jones suggests such a combination, and one skilled in the art would have no reason to make such a combination. Moreover, the combination could not be made physically because the lever of the Smith type would not fit in or work with Jones's pedal mechanism because…. However, even if the combination could be made, Claim 1 distinguishes because the combination does not show [here quote language], *and these distinctions are patentable under Section 103 because* [discuss new results and give as many reasons as you can from Fig. 13D and Form 4-2].

If the references themselves don't suggest that they should be combined (Reasons 28–32 in Fig. 13D), you can use the arguments and cases from pp. 7 and 8 of Fig. 13E; this is a very common defect in many current rejections and the cases cited give powerful arguments.

e.   Note Secondary Factors of Unobviousness

If your invention has achieved any commercial success or has won any praise, this is relevant, and you should mention it here. If possible, submit copies of advertisements for your invention, copies of industry or trade praise, sales figures, a commercially sold sample, etc. These things reify the invention (that is, make it a "fait accompli") and impress most examiners.

f.   Draft Any Needed Declaration Under Rule 132 to Refute Technical Points Raised by Examiner

If you want to challenge any technical points raised by the examiner, such as proving that your invention works in a superior manner to a reference, that two references can't be combined, or that a cited reference works in a far inferior way to yours, you or an expert in the field should do the necessary research and make the necessary tests (including building and testing a model of the cited reference) and then submit a "Declaration Under Rule 132." The Declaration should have a caption as in Form 13-1 and an appropriate heading, such as "Rule 132 Declaration Regarding Inferior Performance of Elias Patent." The body of the Declaration should start,

Jane Inventor declares as follows:

    1. I am the inventor [or I am a mechanical engineer (state education, experience, and awards)] in the above patent application.

Then, in numbered paragraphs, detail your technical facts and/or reasons, including tests you made, etc., but state facts, not conclusions or arguments. Whenever you make any legal declaration or affidavit (as opposed to a brief or remarks), heed the words of the immortal Joe

Friday, of television's "Dragnet" fame: "Just the facts, ma'am." You can attach and refer to "exhibits"—that is, documents in support of your arguments.

Then conclude with a "declaration paragraph," as in the last paragraph of Form 10-3, and sign and date the declaration.

Similarly, if you want to mention any additional factors relating to your invention, such as commercial success or copying by an infringer, which are relevant to patentability, you can submit a similar Rule 132 declaration. You can attach relevant "Exhibits," such as a prototype, a commercial sample, advertising, or sales reports. As stated, working models usually make believers out of negative examiners.

g.   Request Reconsideration

Request reconsideration of the rejection(s) and allowance of the claim: "Therefore applicant submits that Claim 5 is allowable over the cited references and solicits reconsideration and allowance."

If you have dependent claims that were rejected, treat these in the same manner. Since a dependent claim incorporates all the limitations of the parent claim, you can state that the dependent claim is patentable for the same reasons given with respect to the parent claim, and then state that it is even more patentable because it adds additional limitations, which you should discuss briefly.

Discuss each of the other rejections in a similar manner, that is, review the rejection, review the reference, review your new claims, discuss why they distinguish, and request reconsideration and allowance.

h.   Respond to Rejections Under Section 112 for Lack of Clarity or Conciseness

If a technical rejection has been made (under Section 112), discuss how you've amended your claim and why your new claim is clear and understandable.

i.   Request Claim Drafting Assistance From PTO

Once again, I emphasize that if you feel you have patentable subject matter in your application but have difficulty in writing new claims, you can request that the examiner write new claims for you pursuant to MPEP Section 707.07(j). Your remarks are the place to do this. For example, state, "Therefore it is submitted that patentable subject matter is clearly present. If the examiner agrees but does not feel that the present claims are technically adequate, applicant respectfully requests that the examiner write acceptable claims pursuant to MPEP 707.07(j)." If the examiner writes any claims for you, don't rest on them unless you're sure that the broadest one is as broad as the prior art permits, using the criteria above and in Chapter 5. Remember, if you are dissatisfied with the examiner's claims, you can once again submit your own claims, you can submit the examiner's claims with whatever amendments you choose, or you can interview the examiner to discuss the matter. You should request claim drafting assistance when you file, or after the first OA, not after a final OA.

j. Repeat the Above for Any Other Rejections in the Office Action

After you've covered and hopefully decimated the first rejection in the manner discussed in subsections a to i, above, then do the same for each additional rejection.

k. Discuss Non-Applied References

If a reference of interest has been cited but not applied against any claim, state that you've reviewed it but that it doesn't show your invention or render it obvious.

l. Conclusion

Last, provide a conclusion that should repeat and summarize—for example, *"For all the reasons given above, applicant respectfully submits that the errors in the specification are corrected, the claims comply with Section 112, the claims define over the prior art under Section 102 [briefly repeat why], and the claimed distinctions are of patentable merit under Section 103 because of the new results [repeat them briefly again] provided. Accordingly, applicant submits that this application is now in full condition for allowance, which action applicant respectfully solicits."* Then add the closing, "Very respectfully," followed by your signature, typewritten name, your address, and telephone number on the left-hand side. If you have a co-inventor(s), all of you must sign the amendment.

m. Do Your Very Best Job

It's important to do your very best job in your first amendment, since it's the only full opportunity you'll get to answer the examiner's position. I suggest that after writing the amendment, you have a friend read it or you come back to it after a few days and read it from the viewpoint of your examiner. As stated in Inventor's Commandment #26, make sure your amendment in response to the first OA is complete, carefully crafted, and includes all arguments and the narrowest claims possible, since the next OA will be final.

G. Drawing Amendments

If your office action includes any objections to the drawings (or drawing), you must correct these before the case can issue and usually as soon as allowable subject matter is indicated. In addition, if you want to make any voluntary amendments to the drawings, you must get the examiner's approval in advance.

To deal with drawing objections, merely state in the beginning of your Remarks (see Section F, above) that the drawing objections are noted and are corrected with new drawings submitted herewith or will be corrected after allowance. To make the corrections you must file new (corrected) drawings for substitution for your original drawings. This is easy to do. Merely correct your Bristol board or Mylar film originals, or make new CAD originals, and file new, good xerographic (or CAD output) copies. All lines must be crisp, black, and sharp, and all objections on the drawing objection sheet must be corrected. Use Form 13-3 to submit your corrected replacement drawings.

If you have to correct your drawings, and you're doing so after allowance (the usual case), you should do so promptly after you receive the Notice of Allowance. This will give the PTO's drawing checkers time to review your corrected drawings and let you know within the statutory three-month period to pay the issue fee, if they're still improper. If your corrected drawings aren't approved, the PTO will give you until the end of the three-month period, or an additional 15 days, to file proper drawings. Be sure to put your name, Serial Number and Examination Group on the back of the drawings.

If you want to make voluntary amendments or corrections to your drawings, use the Drawing Amendment Approval Request Form 13-2, filling in all necessary blanks; mention the request and the reasons in the beginning of your Remarks. Indicate your desired changes in red ink on a photocopy of your drawing and attach it to Form 13-2.

Then, if the examiner approves your drawing amendments in the next OA, you can make the changes after (or before) allowance, by filing new, corrected drawings. Remember that you can't add any new matter to the drawings. However, you can correct obvious errors, such as a reversed diode, a missing reference numeral, or a missing line.

H. Typing and Mailing the Amendment

The amendment should be typed with double- or 1.5 line-spacing on legal- or letter-size paper with 1.5-inch top and 1-inch left, right, and bottom margins. I number my paragraphs and, as stated, include plenty of boldface or underlined "arguing" headings—for example, "The Elias Patent Fails to Show Any Schmitt Trigger." Don't forget to keep an identical copy of your amendment mounted in your file; the PTO won't return any paper you send them, although they will make a copy of any paper or record for the per-sheet photocopy charge in the Fee Schedule. Again, I recommend using a word processor or typing the amendment on easily erasable paper on which you can readily make corrections, and then sending a photocopy of the original, since easily erasable paper is not accepted by the PTO. The signatures of all inventors must be on the copy you send to the PTO.

DOCUMENTS WITH COPIES OF SIGNATURES NOW OKAY

The PTO now accepts documents which contain a copy of any required signature, provided you retain a copy of the document with an original signature, in case it's ever needed. (Original signatures are required only on (a) documents involving the registration of an attorney or agent and (b) certified copies.)

After your signature, add a "Certificate of Mailing" or a "Certificate of Facsimile Transmission" (don't use Express Mail) as follows:

CERTIFICATE OF MAILING

I hereby certify that this correspondence, and attachments, if any, will be deposited with the United States Postal Service by First Class Mail, postage prepaid, in an envelope addressed to "Box Non-Fee Amendments, Assistant Commissioner for Patents, Washington, DC 20231" on the date below.

Date: _____

Inventor's Signature: _____

Only one inventor needs to sign this certification. If you mail with this certificate, you can mail your amendment even at 23:59 on the last day of your response period—it doesn't have to go out on the day it's mailed. Even if you're mailing the amendment two months ahead of time you should use the Certificate anyway, since if the amendment is lost in the mail, causing your application technically to go abandoned, you can get it revived easily by filing a declara-

tion stating the full facts and enclosing a photocopy of the amendment with the Certificate of Mailing—see PTO Rule 8(b). Don't forget to attach a postcard to your amendment reading as in Fig. 13F.

Amendment A (5 pp) in Application of John A. Novel, Ser. Nr. 999,999, filed 199X Jan. 9, received today:

Fig. 13F—Back of Receipt Postcard for Amendment

You may also fax your amendment—see fax numbers in Appendix 5, Mail, Telephone and Computer Communications With the PTO. And add a faxing certificate as follows:

CERTIFICATE OF FACSIMILE TRANSMISSION

I certify that on the date below I will fax this communication, and attachments if any, to Group _____ of the Patent and Trademark Office at the following number: (703) _____.

Date: _____

Inventor's Signature: _____

DRAFT AMENDMENTS MAY BE FAXED FOR DISCUSSION

Applicants may now send a proposed amendment for discussion to "sound out" and negotiate with the examiner. Mark the amendment "DRAFT" or "PROPOSED AMENDMENT," do not sign it, and fax it to the examiner. Then call the examiner in a few days to discuss the amendment by phone or visit the examiner personally. You still must file a regular, signed amendment by the due date to avoid abandonment.

Make sure your amendment won't cause the total number of claims of your application to exceed 20, or the number of independent claims to exceed three. Otherwise, you'll have to pay an additional claims fee (strongly not recommended, since three independent and 20 total claims should be more than adequate).

CHECKLIST FOR SENDING IN A REGULAR AMENDMENT

Before you mail your amendment, please check the following list carefully to be sure that the amendment's complete and properly done.

☐ A01. Each point in the OA has been responded to.

☐ A02. Any needed drawing objection has been responded to.

☐ A03. The specification has been re-proofed and any needed corrections have been made.

☐ A04. The prior-art portion of the specification has been amended to account for any significant new prior art (optional).

☐ A05. No new matter is included in any amendments to the specification.

☐ A06. All new claims have been checked against the checklist in Chapter 9.

☐ A07. All claims recite structure which is physically different from every cited reference (Section 102).

☐ A08. The physically different structure in every claim is sufficiently different to produce new and unexpected results or otherwise be considered unobvious (Section 103).

☐ A09. The case includes several very narrow dependent claims with a variety of phraseologies so that you won't have to present them for the first time if the next action is made final.

☐ A10. The wording in the remarks is clear, grammatically correct, and understandable.

☐ A11. The remarks are written in short paragraphs with ample "arguing" headings.

☐ A12. The patentability of all new claims is argued with respect to the references, using a two-part approach: (a) The claim has physical distinctions over the references under Section 102. (b) The claimed physical distinctions produce new and unexpected results or are otherwise unobvious under Section 103.

☐ A13. All possible arguments for unobviousness (Fig. 13D) have been presented.

☐ A14. A request for claim-drafting assistance under MPEP 707.07(j) has been made, if desirable.

☐ A15. The amendment is 1.5 or double-spaced with an ample top margin for punching mounting holes.

☐ A16. The last page of the amendment includes your name, address, and phone number.

☐ A17. If the amendment will cause the case to have over 20 total or over three independent claims, the proper additional fee is included (if not previously paid).

☐ A18. The amendment is signed and dated (no pencil) by all applicants.

☐ A19. An identical file copy of the amendment has been made.

☐ A20. The amendment is being mailed or faxed on time or includes a properly completed Petition to Extend with the proper fee included.

☐ A21. A Certificate of Mailing or Faxing is typed in the amendment.

☐ A22. All pages are complete and present.

☐ A23. A receipt postcard is attached to the amendment, if you are mailing it.

☐ A24. The envelope is properly stamped and addressed to "Box Non-Fee Amendments, Assistant Commissioner for Patents, Washington, DC 20231." If you are sending any money with your amendment, omit "Box Non-Fee Amendments." If you're faxing the amendment, make sure you have the correct fax number for your examiner's group and you feed your pages carefully.

I. If Your Application Is Allowable

Hopefully, your first amendment will do the trick and the examiner will decide to allow the case. If so, you'll be sent a Notice of Allowability and/or a formal Notice of Allowance (N/A), the latter accompanied by an Issue Fee transmittal form. You have a statutory period of three months to pay the issue fee; the three-month period is not extendable and forms are self-explanatory. Be sure to send in a receipt postcard with your issue fee transmittal. You can also place an advance order for printed copies of your patent (a space is provided on the issue fee transmittal form) at this time; and the minimum order is ten. However, the printed copies aren't necessary, as you can make photocopies from your patent deed. Also, be sure to fill in the Certificate of Mailing on the reverse side of the Issue Fee Transmittal.

When you receive your N/A, make any needed drawing corrections at once (see Section F, above) and review the application and drawings once again very carefully to make sure everything is correct, logical, grammatical, and so on. If you want to make any amendments at this time, you can still do so, provided they don't affect the substance of the application. Generally, only grammatical changes are permitted after the N/A. The format of the amendment should be similar to that of Form 13-E, except that the first sentence should read, "Pursuant to Rule 312, applicant respectfully requests that the above application be amended as follows:".

Then make any amendments to your specification and claims in the previously used format. Under "Remarks," discuss the amendments, stating that they are not matters of substance and noting that they will require very little consideration by the examiner.

If you've amended your claims in any substantial way during prosecution, after the Notice of Allowance is received you should also file a Supplemental Declaration (Form 13-4) to indicate that you've invented the subject matter of the claims as amended and that you know of no prior art that would anticipate these claims.

Prior to sending in the issue fee, you should go through the following checklist:

CHECKLIST FOR PAYING AN ISSUE FEE

☐ A01. All needed drawing corrections have been made and corrected drawings are enclosed.

☐ A02. Any needed specification or claim amendments have been made (PTO Rule 312).

☐ A03. Issue Fee Transmittal Form is properly filled out and signed.

☐ A04. A completed Supplemental Declaration is being filed if any significant claim changes have been made during prosecution.

☐ A05. Check is attached for correct issue fee amount and signed; adequate funds are on deposit.

☐ A06. Receipt postcard is attached, stamped, and addressed.

☐ A07. Certificate of mailing (on reverse side of Notice of Allowance) is completed, signed, and dated.

☐ A08. Papers are mailed by due date (no extensions allowed).

☐ A09. A file copy of all issue fee transmittal papers has been made.

If you filed corrected drawings and the PTO's draftspersons approve them, you won't receive any notification, but if they're not approved, you'll receive another drawing objection sheet.

Once your issue fee is received, your application goes to the Government Printing Office and no further changes are permitted.

Several months after the issue fee is paid, you'll receive an Issue Notification Form, which will indicate the number of your patent and the date it will issue, usually a week or so after you receive the receipt. A few days after your patent issues, you'll receive the deed, or letters patent, and, separately, any additional printed copies you've ordered. (See Chapter 15, Section H, for a discussion of maintenance fees.)

J. If Your First Amendment Doesn't Result in Allowance

If your first amendment doesn't place the application in condition for allowance, the examiner will usually make the next OA final. However, if the second OA cites any new references, it won't be made final unless the examiner had to dig out the new references to meet some new limitations in your amended claims. If your second OA isn't made final, you should respond to it in the same manner as you responded to the first OA. However, if the second OA is called final—and it usually will be—note the provisions of Rules 113 and 116, which govern what happens after a final action is sent:

Rule 113—Final Rejection or Action

(a) On the second or any subsequent examination or consideration, the rejection or other action may be made final, whereupon applicant's response is limited to appeal in the case of rejection of any claim (Rule 191), or to amendment as specified in Rule 116. Petition may be taken to the Commissioner in the case of objections or requirements not involved in the rejection of any claim (Rule 181). Response to a final rejection or action must include cancellation or appeal from the rejection of, each claim so rejected, and, if any claim stands allowed, compliance with any requirement or objection as to form.

(b) In making such final rejection, the examiner shall repeat or state all grounds of rejection then considered applicable to the claims in the case, clearly stating the reasons therefor.

Rule 116—Amendments After Final Action

(a) After final rejection or action (Rule 113) amendments may be made canceling claims or complying with any requirement of form that has been made, and amendments presenting rejected claims in better form for consideration on appeal may be admitted; but the admission of any such amendment or its refusal, and any proceedings relative thereto shall not operate to relieve the application from its condition as subject to appeal or to save it from abandonment under Rule 135.

(b) If amendments touching the merits of the application be presented after final rejection, or after appeal has been taken, or when such amendment might not otherwise be proper, they may be admitted upon a showing of good and sufficient reasons why they are necessary and were not earlier presented.

These rules mean, in effect, that "final" isn't final after all. It's just that the rules shift a bit. If you want to continue prosecuting your patent application after a final OA, you must take one of the following actions:

1. Narrow, cancel, or fix the claims *as specified by the examiner.*
2. Argue with and convince the examiner to change position.
3. Try a further amendment narrowing the claims.
4. Appeal to the Board of Appeals and Patent Interferences (BAPI).
5. File a continuation application (see Chapter 14).
6. Petition the PTO Commissioner.
7. Abandon the application.

Let's examine these options in more detail.

1. Comply With Examiner's Requirements

If the examiner indicates that the case will be allowed if you amend the claims in a certain way, for example, if you cancel certain claims or add certain limitations to the claim, and you agree with the examiner's position, you should submit a complying amendment similar to the previously discussed amendment. However, instead of stating, "Please amend the above application as follows:" (Form 13-1), state "Applicant requests that the above application be amended as follows:" This is because the clerk won't enter any amendments after a final OA unless the examiner gives permission.

Generally, no other amendments after a final OA are permitted unless you can show very good reasons why they weren't presented earlier. If your amendment changes the claims in the manner required by the examiner to get them allowed, this will clearly entitle it to entry. You should file your complying amendment as soon as possible, since you have to get the case in full condition for allowance within the three-month period, plus any extensions you've bought. If you file an after-final amendment near the end of the three-month period and the examiner agrees that it places the application in condition for allowance, but the period has expired, you'll have to buy an appropriate extension (Form 13-5): a case can't be allowed when it's technically abandoned. If you file an amendment or argument and it doesn't convince the examiner to allow your case, the examiner will send you an "advisory action," telling you why, and the three-month period will continue to run.

2. Convince the Examiner

You can try to convince the examiner to change position, either by written argument, by phone, or in person. Phone and personal interviews are especially effective because of the multiple feedback loops and give-and-take they provide

in a short period. Also, it's more difficult to say no when facing someone, as any salesperson will tell you. Try to come to some agreement to get the case allowed. This is often an excellent, effective choice, especially if you have a friendly examiner and you're willing to compromise. Do this as soon as possible so you'll have time to appeal or file a continuation application, if necessary. (See Chapter 14, Section B.)

3. Amendment After Final Rejection

You can try a further amendment, narrowing your claims or submitting other claims, provided you raise no new issues. If the examiner agrees that the amendment narrows or changes the claims sufficiently to place the case in condition for allowance, the examiner will authorize its entry and allow the case. Otherwise, the examiner will send you an "advisory action," reiterating the examiner's former position, and you'll still have the opportunity to exercise the other choices. Even if the examiner doesn't want to enter the amendment because it raises new issues, the advisory action will state whether the amendment will be entered for purposes of appeal. The examiner will enter it for appeal if it places the case in better condition for appeal and neither raises any new issues nor requires further search or consideration.

You should file any amendment as soon as possible. The PTO will try to reply to After-Final amendments within one month if you do the following with a *red marker*: (1) mark the upper right of p.1 of your amendment "RESPONSE UNDER 37 CFR 1.116—EXPEDITED PROCEDURE-

EXAMINING GROUP NUMBER [insert #]," (2) address the envelope and the amendment "Box AF, Commr. of Pats... [etc.]," and (3) write "BOX AF" in the lower left of envelope.

If you do send in an amendment after a final OA, you should head it "Amendment Under Rule 116," request (not direct) that the case be amended as follows to place it in condition for allowance. Also comply with the following checklist.

CHECKLIST FOR SENDING AN AFTER-FINAL AMENDMENT

☐ A01. All points on the checklist for "regular" amendments, except point A09, have been considered.

☐ A02. The amendment requests (rather than directs) entry of the amendment.

☐ A03. The claim changes or cancellations either comply with the examiner's requirements or otherwise narrow or revise the claims to obviate the outstanding rejections.

☐ A04. The remarks state why the claim changes, if any, were not presented before.

☐ A05. The claims don't contain any new limitations or radical changes that would raise new issues.

☐ A06. The amendment is being sent in as soon as possible after final action.

☐ A07. The first page of the amendment and the envelope are marked in red as indicated above.

4. Appeal

If you don't see any further way to improve the claims, and if you believe the examiner's position is wrong, you can appeal to the BAPI (Board of Appeals and Patent Interferences), a tribunal of judges in the PTO. To appeal, you must:

• file a notice stating that you appeal to the BAPI from the examiner's final action

• enclose an appeal fee. (See Appendix 4, Fee Schedule.)

• file an appeal brief in triplicate, describing your invention and claims in issue and arguing the patentability of your claims. This brief is due within two months after you file your notice of appeal

• enclose a brief fee

• if you desire it, request an oral hearing and enclose a further hearing fee (see Appendix 4, Fee Schedule). If you want an oral hearing, you'll have to travel to the PTO in Arlington, Virginia, or ask for a telephone hearing, and

• as always, include a Certificate of Mailing with all correspondence.

For information on how to comply with the appeal procedure, see PTO Rules of Practice 191 to 198.

After you file an appeal brief, the examiner must file a responsive brief (termed an "Examiner's Answer") to maintain the rejection. To do this, the examiner must take another good, hard look at your case. Often this review will result in changing the examiner's mind. More commonly, the examiner will maintain the rejection and file an Examiner's Answer. You may then file a reply brief limited to any new arguments raised in the Examiner's Answer.

If you do have a hearing, you will be allowed 20 minutes for oral argument. Sometimes the examiner attends; if so, 15 minutes will be allowed for the examiner's presentation.

If the Board disagrees with the examiner, it will issue a written decision, generally sending the case back with instructions to allow the case. If it agrees with the examiner, its decision will state why it believes your invention to be unpatentable. The Board upholds the examiner in about 65% of the appeals.

If the Board upholds the examiner and you still believe your invention is patentable, you can take a further appeal within 60 days of the date of the BAPI's decision to the Court of Appeals for the Federal Circuit (CAFC). The CAFC is located in Washington, but sits in local areas regularly. If the CAFC upholds the PTO, you can even request the United States Supreme Court to hear your case, although the Supreme Court rarely hears patent appeals. (See Chapter 15, Section L, for more on the CAFC.)

Under the new GATT law, as indicated, patents expire 20 years from the filing date of the patent application, but the PTO will extended this term up to five years if delay occurs due to an appeal to the BAPI, the CAFC, or because of an interference. (35 USC § 154.)

Appeal briefs aren't easy to write, so I suggest you consult professional help if you want to appeal.

If the examiner has issued a ruling on a matter other than the patentability of your claims—for example, has refused to enter an amendment or has required the case to be restricted to one of several inventions—you have another option. Although you can't appeal from this type of decision you can petition the Commissioner of Patents and Trademarks to overrule the examiner. (See Subsection 6, "Petitions to the Commissioner," below.)

If you want to obtain the maximum term possible for your patent, and three years have elapsed since the filing date of your application (or the filing date of any parent applications if it's a divisional or continuation—see Chapter 14), I recommend that you appeal after the second office action if the case is still under rejection, even if your second action is not a final action. Why? As stated, under the new laws, your patent will expire 20 years from your first filing date, regardless of when your patent issues. However, the PTO must extend this 20-year term (for up to five more years) from the date you file an appeal until the date of a final decision on appeal, except that if any portion of the appeal period occurs within three years of your filing date, this will not be counted in extending the expiration date (Rule 701).

Thus any time you take to negotiate with the examiner or file another amendment will shorten your patent's term. However, if three years have elapsed after your first filing date, you can avoid this shortening and actually extend your patent's term by filing an appeal and doing any negotiation or filing any amendments while your appeal is pending. If you can't get the examiner to allow the case, just follow through with the appeal by filing a brief and fee within two months after the date you file the notice of appeal. If you do get the examiner to allow the case while it's on appeal, just file a notice withdrawing the appeal; your patent's term will be extended for the time your appeal was active.

5. Continuation Application

If you want to have your claims reviewed further in another round with the examiner, you can file a "continuation application." Filing a continuation application is a relatively simple procedure involving writing new claims, paying a new filing fee, and sending in a special form requesting that a continuation application examination be prepared. (See Chapter 14 for how to do this.) You'll receive a new serial number and filing date for the purpose of your patent's duration, but you'll be entitled to the benefit of the filing date of your original application for the purpose of determining the relevancy of prior art. Your application will be examined all over again with the new claims. You must actually file the continuation application before the end of the three-month period or any extensions you buy. (See Section Q, below.) The Certificate of Mailing (CM) should not be used. According to the PTO's Rules (8 and 10), a CM isn't effective when an application is being filed; you must actually get it physically on file before the other case goes abandoned, unless you use the Express Mail certificate (Chapter 10, Section L, and Chapter 14, Section B).

6. Petitions to the Commissioner for Non-Substantive Matters

The Commissioner of Patents and Trademarks has power to overrule almost anyone in the PTO except the BAPI (Rules 181-183). Thus, if you think you've been treated unfairly or illegally, you can petition the Commissioner to overrule a subordinate. For example, if the PTO's application branch has made a ruling regarding your patent application, such as that it's not entitled to the filing date you think you're entitled to (but not a rejection of your claims), you can petition the Commissioner to overrule this ruling.

If you petition the Commissioner for any reason, you must do so promptly after the occurrence of the event forming the subject matter of the petition, and you must make your grounds as strong and as complete as possible. Generally, most petitions must be accompanied by a verified showing and fee. A verified showing is a statement signed by you and either notarized or containing a declaration such as that in the last paragraph of Form 10-3. (The petition fee is indicated in Appendix 4, Fee Schedule.)

7. Abandon Your Application

Any action you wish to take in response to a final OA must be made within the three-month period for response or any time extensions you buy (see Section Q, below); otherwise the application will go abandoned. That is, you must either appeal, file a continuation application, or get the examiner to allow your application within the period for response. However, if you're going to file an amendment or an argument, you should do it as soon as possible, preferably within one month, so the examiner's reply will reach you in time for you to take any further needed action within the three-month period.

If all claims of your application are rejected in the final OA, and you agree with the examiner and can't find anything else patentable in your application, you'll have to allow the application to become abandoned, but don't give up without a fight or without thoroughly considering all factors involved.

If you do decide to allow your application to go abandoned, it will go abandoned automatically if you don't file a timely reply to the final action, since the ball's in your court. You'll be sent a Notice of Abandonment advising you that the case has gone abandoned because you failed to reply to an outstanding office action.

If you do abandon the application, but your invention has a unique shape and it hasn't been made available to the public, offered for sale, or sold more than a year ago, consider filing a design patent application on it.

K. Interferences

An interference is a proceeding conducted by the PTO (a Patent Interference Examiner and the BAPI). An interference is instituted to determine priority of inventorship—that is, who will get the patent when two or more inventors are claiming the same invention.

The PTO generally institutes an interference when they discover two patent applications claiming the same invention. However, since the PTO is such a large, complex, and populous organization, and since its employees do not always do perfect work, they sometimes make mistakes. Thus they may allow an application that should have been involved in an interference with another application to issue as a patent without declaring an interference.

If this occurs and then an examiner or other patent applicant sees the patent and believes it claims the same invention as a pending application, an interference can be declared with the patent, provided the issued patent has not been in force for more than one year.

How is the interference instituted by you, the applicant, if you believe that you, rather than someone else, deserves the patent? Simple. You merely copy (present) the claims of the in-force patent in your application, informing the patent examiner about the patent from which you copied the claims, and showing the examiner how such claims are supported in your application. Remember, you must copy the claims of any patent within one year after it issues.

MONITORING PATENT APPLICATIONS

If you really want to do a bang-up job of patent prosecution, you should find the class and subclass of your patent application (you can find this by calling the clerk of the examining division to which your application is assigned) and then monitor all patents which issue in the class/sub while your application's pending. If you find a patent which claims the same invention as yours, you should get interference with it by copying its claims in your application (see above). If you find a patent which is relevant prior art to your invention, you should cite it via a supplemental IDS (see part B6 above).

On the other hand, if you've been granted a patent, be aware that there may be other patent applicants whose applications contain the same invention as yours. All such applicants have one year from your patent's date of issuance to copy your claims in their applications to get their application into interference with your patent.

Procedurally, an interference is a very complex proceeding, which would take another book of this size to cover. Unless you have an exceptional grasp of patent law and formal advocacy techniques, definitely seek help from a patent attorney who's experienced in trial work. Unlike some of the other situations where I've recommended professional help, representation in an interference proceeding is usually very costly, usually running $10,000 to $25,000 or more.

Despite the need for professional help should an interference occur, there's much you can do on your own to help your case. The Boy Scout motto will do nicely here: Be prepared. If your application is one of the 2% that becomes involved in interference, sufficient advance preparation will go a long way toward helping your case. As I stressed in Chapter 3:

- Record all steps in your invention development (conception, building, and so on) carefully. (Inventor's Commandment #1)
- Be diligent in building, testing, and recording your invention—unless you've filed a Provisional Patent Application (PPA) and are relying on that filing as your priority date. (Inventor's Commandment #2)
- File a patent application promptly.

Who wins an interference? As briefly stated in Chapter 5, the winner in an interference will not necessarily be the first to file a patent application on the invention. Rather, the first inventor to "reduce the invention to practice" (file a patent application or build and test the invention) will prevail, *unless* the other party conceives the invention first and has been diligent in effecting a reduction to practice. This means that the typical interference involves lots of testimony and introduction of documents by both sides, all for the purpose of proving priority. It's this aspect of the interference that virtually necessitates professional help.

Although there are certain advantages to the U.S.'s "first to invent" system, almost all other countries, including Canada, have a "first to file" system, which eliminates interferences and their attendant tremendous expense, complexity, and time delays. Some have called the interference laws a "patent attorney's relief act." If you agree, write your Congressperson or have your inventors' club launch an effort to simplify this area of the law.

L. Statutory Invention Registration (SIR)

If you intend to abandon your application, but want to prevent anyone else from ever getting a valid patent on your invention, you can have an abstract and one drawing figure of your application published in the OG—Patents (see Chapter 6 and Appendix 2, Books of Use and Interest) and your application printed like a patent. This is called "converting your application to a Statutory Invention Registration (SIR)." For the reasons stated in Chapter 14, Section F, I strongly recommend against ever using a SIR.

M. If Your Application Claims More Than One Invention

Often patent applications claim several embodiments of an invention, and the PTO will regard these embodiments as separate inventions. The PTO will thus require you to "restrict" the application to just one of the inventions. The theory is that your filing fee entitles you to have only one invention examined.

Also, if two of your claims are directed to the same invention, but the examiner feels that the two claims are directed to subject matter that is classified in two separate subclasses (see Chapter 6), the examiner can require you to restrict the application—that is, to elect one set of claims for prosecution.

Another situation in which restriction may be required occurs when your application contains both method and apparatus claims. Even when both sets of claims are directed to the same invention, examiners often consider them two separate inventions and require you to elect either the method or the apparatus claims.

Generally speaking, it's very difficult to fight a PTO-imposed restriction. Fortunately, it's possible to file a second application (called a divisional application—see Chapter 14) if you think pursuing the nonelected claims is worth the cost (new filing fee) and if present indications are that your divisional application will comprise allowable subject matter. You can file the divisional application any time until your first (parent) application issues, and your divisional application will be entitled to the filing date of your parent application. However, you should file any divisional application(s) as soon as possible since, under the new GATT law, any patent which issues on the divisional application will expire 20 years from the filing date of the *original* application in the chain.

Another, related situation occurs when you claim several embodiments or "species" of one invention. In the first OA, the examiner may require you to elect claims to one species

for purpose of examination; this is to facilitate the search. If you don't get any generic claim allowed—that is, a claim that covers all of your different species—you'll be allowed to claim only the elected species; you can file divisional applications on the nonelected species. (In this case, the PTO will consider each species to be a separate invention.) If you do get a generic claim allowed, you'll be allowed to claim a reasonable number of different species of the invention (Rule 146).

N. Protests Against Allowance of Your Patent Application

Most other countries have a practice under which they permit the public to see pending and allowed applications before they issue in order to give the public a chance to cite prior art or otherwise object to the allowance of the application. However, there's no authorization for this practice in the U.S. Still, the PTO has occasionally instituted voluntary protest programs (none currently exists as of this printing) under which you're given the option of having your application published for protest after it's allowed. This means, among other things, that the confidentiality of your invention is given up, since an abstract of your application will be published in the OG. Then copies of your application can be obtained by any member of the public who wants to order them; anyone can then protest against the allowance of your application by citing reasons to show why your invention isn't patentable.

If you do have an opportunity to have your allowed application published for protest, I advise you to elect the procedure—the PTO will give you full instructions—since a patent application which survives the protest procedure (most do) will become a stronger patent. The disadvantages include:

- delay
- the possibility of more examination, and
- members of the public may cite fatally damaging prior art against your application.

However, I believe the advantages outweigh these disadvantages. You won't lose any trade secret rights you wouldn't otherwise give up since your application was allowed and was going to issue (be published) anyway.

HOW TO PROTEST A PENDING APPLICATION OF ANOTHER

If you know of any prior adverse information against a pending patent application of another and you want to bring this to the attention of the examiner to prevent the application from issuing, you can file a protest against such application. Use the caption of Form 13-1, filling in as much information as possible, and head the paper "Protest." List, enclose and explain the relevance of the prior art and any other information. If you don't know the application's Serial Number or the name of the applicant, provide and discuss as much information as you can (for instance, advertisements, specification sheets, news articles) to aid the examiner in locating the application.

O. NASA Declarations

If your invention relates to aerospace, the PTO will send you a form letter (PTOL-224) with your filing receipt or after your application is allowed. The letter will state that because your invention relates to aerospace, you'll have to file a declaration stating the "full facts" regarding the making of your invention. This is to be sure NASA has no rights in it. If you don't file the declaration, you won't get a Notice of Allowance. Fortunately, the PTO now includes a declaration form for you to fill out. Check the appropriate blanks, indicating that you made the invention on your own time, and with your own facilities, and materials, and not in performance of any NASA contract, if this is the case.

P. Design Patent Application Prosecution

Design patent application prosecution is much simpler than regular patent application prosecution, and, armed with the instructions of this chapter, you'll find it to be duck soup. Design patent application prosecution will never require anything but the most elementary changes to the specification and claim; the examiner will tell you exactly what to do. (Make the amendments in the manner specified in Section E, parts 1, 2.a, and 2.b.)

To be patentable, the *appearance* of your design, as a whole, must be unobvious to a designer of ordinary skill over the references (usually earlier design patents) that the examiner cites. If your design has significant differences over the cited prior art, it should be patentable; if not, you'll have to abandon your application, as there's no way to narrow or change the substance of the claim or drawings of a design patent application. If the examiner rejects your design as obvious over one or more references, you should use the 102-then-103 attack as explained in Sections F and J and Inventor's Commandment #7 for utility patent applications—that is, point out the differences in your design and then argue their importance and significance, albeit from an aesthetic viewpoint. To reject a design claim on two or more references, one must look basically like the claimed design. (*In re Harvey*, 29 U.S.P.Q.2d 1206 (Fed.Cir. 1993).)

If your design case is allowed, you must pay an issue fee (see Appendix 4, Fee Schedule), which makes the design patent effective for a term of 14 years from its date of issue. There are no maintenance fees for a design patent. You can convert a design application to a utility application, or vice versa, by filing a continuing application under 35 U.S.C. 120. However a design patent application may not claim priority of a PPA.

Q. What to Do If You Miss or Want to Extend a PTO Deadline

If you miss any PTO deadline—for example, the three-month period to reply to an OA—your application technically becomes abandoned, but you can buy an automatic extension. If your application goes abandoned, or if you want more time to reply to an OA, it can be "revived" or extended in any of three following ways:

- buying an extension
- petition to Revive if delay was "unavoidable"
- petition to Revive if delay was avoidable but unintentional.

Let's look at these separately and in more detail.

1. Buy an Extension Before the Six-Month Period Ends (Rules 136(a) and 17(a)-(d))

Most OAs give you three months from their mailing date to reply. If you don't reply within your three-month period, you can send in your reply at any time up to the end of the sixth month by buying an extension of up to three months at the prices indicated in the Fee Schedule. To buy an extension in this manner, simply mail your reply (amendment) by the last day of the fourth, fifth or sixth month, together with a "Petition for Extension of Time" (Form 13-5), completed as necessary, and a check. It is not necessary to apply in advance. Make sure you include a Certificate of Mailing on your amendment. You should calculate your total number of months from the date of the OA; don't add your extension months to your original due date. For example, assume your OA was mailed 1995 Feb 20 so that your three-month period originally expired 1995 May 22 (May 20 fell on a Saturday). You want to buy a three-month extension. Your total period is then six months from *February 20*— that is, to 1995 Aug 21—*not* three months from May 22. Remember that you can't buy an extension to send in your issue fee; the three-month statutory period from the Notice of Allowance is not extendable. Also, by statute you can't extend any response period beyond six months.

2. Petition to Revive If Delay Was "Unavoidable" (Rules 137(a) or 316(b), and 17(c))

If you failed to send in your amendment or issue fee within the regular three-month period and your delay was "unavoidable"—for example, you never received the OA, you had a death in the family that precluded your drafting an amendment, you suffered a severe illness, or your home burned down—you can petition to revive the application. The fee is indicated in the Fee Schedule and you should file three papers: (a) your reply, (b) a petition to revive, and (c) a declaration. The petition (use the heading of Form 13-1) should petition to revive the above application, state that the delay was unavoidable because (give the reason), as explained in the attached declaration. The declaration (use heading of Form 13-1 and make the last paragraph the same as that of Form 10-3) should state in detail the specific facts which caused the delay. Use numbered paragraphs and start it as follows:

A.B. declares as follows:
1. I am the applicant in the above application.

Then, give your reasons in short, specific, numbered, factual paragraphs. Refer to and attach copies of any documents you feel are relevant. Your petition and paper must be promptly filed after you become aware of the abandonment. If the case has been abandoned over six months, you must also include a fourth paper disclaiming the terminal part of the term of any patent granted on the application for a period equal to the period of abandonment and include a terminal disclaimer fee (Rules 137(c), 321, and 20(d)). If your petition under this paragraph is denied, you can still petition under the next paragraph if you do so within three months.

If you don't file your petition to revive under this part or the next part within six months, you'll have to accompany it with a terminal disclaimer to shorten your patent monopoly period. Follow Rule 321. You must file the petition within one year after the date of abandonment.

3. Petition to Revive If Delay Was Avoidable but Unintentional (Rules 137(b) or 316(c), and 17(m))

If you failed to send in your amendment or issue fee within the three-month period and your delay was "avoidable but unintentional" —such as, you merely dropped the ball, or misinterpreted the time to reply to the OA—you can still petition to revive the application, albeit at a much higher cost. You should file three papers:
- your reply
- a petition to revive (same as the petition in preceding paragraph, except state the delay was "unintentional"), and
- a declaration similar to that of the preceding paragraph, except you need merely state that the abandonment was unintentional (no reason is needed—the stiff fee [see Fee Schedule] is ample). As with the unavoidable delay petition, this petition must be filed within one year of the date it went abandoned. If you file it after six months of abandonment, you will have to file a terminal disclaimer and fee. ■

Your Application Can Have Children

INVENTOR'S COMMANDMENT #27

Acquire at least some familiarity with all types of extension applications (continuations, divisions, continuations-in-part, reissues, and substitutes) if you have a patent application pending, and be aware of the double-patenting trap and shortening of your monopoly period before filing any such extension application.

A. Available Extension Cases

As we saw in Chapter 13 (application prosecution), the patent laws and PTO rules allow you to do much more than either getting a patent or abandoning the application. In this sense, perhaps, a patent application can best be understood by comparing it to a family tree, as shown in Fig. 14A. The basic application is like a parent, and just like a parent has children, the parent application can be used to produce off-shoots. Depending on the situation, the parent application is called by many names (for example, "parent," "prior," "basic," or "original" application), while the offshoot applications are referred to as "daughter," "continuation," "divisional," "reissue," "independent," or "substitute" applications. If there are several successive extensions, the basic application is called the "grandparent" or "great-grandparent" application and the latest-filed application can be called a "granddaughter," "great-granddaughter," "continuation-of-a-continuation," etc., application.

Fig. 14A shows all of the different extensions you may file.

Note that some extensions come from the bottom point of the Basic Application (BA) or the basic patent. These are "sequential" extensions since they replace the BA or its patent.

Other extensions come from the sides of the BA; these are "parallel" extensions since they can exist in addition to the BA or its patent.

The various extensions are as follows:

- **Division:** If your basic application was held to cover two or more inventions, and you've had to restrict it to one of these inventions, and you want to file a separate application on the other or "nonelected" invention, you should file a *divisional application* (left side of chart). As indicated, your divisional patent can be in addition to your original patent.
- **Continuation:** If you want another round with the examiner, or a chance to try a new and different set of

claims after a final Office Action (OA), you should file a *continuation application*.

- **SIRs:** If you can't get or for some reason don't want a patent once you've filed your application, but want to be sure no one else will ever get a patent on the invention, you can have the PTO publish your patent application by converting it to a *Statutory Invention Registration* (SIR), or you can have your invention published as an Independent Defensive publication.
- **Reissue:** If you've received an original patent (middle of Fig. 14A), but you want to revise the claims of the patent or correct significant errors in the specification for some valid reason, you should file a *reissue application*. As indicated, your reissue patent takes the place of your original patent.
- **CIP:** If you've improved your basic invention in some material way during the pendency of your application, and you want to obtain specific claims to the improvement, you should file a *continuation-in-part* (CIP) application (right side of chart). As indicated, your CIP patent can exist with your original patent.
- **Substitute:** If you abandon your application and later refile a new application on the same invention, the new application, which, as indicated by the broken line, has no copendency or continuity with the original application, is termed a *substitute application*. Of course, no patent on your original application is possible.
- **Independent:** If you've made a major improvement in your basic invention that uses new concepts and can really stand by itself, you should file an *independent* application.

Now that I've identified the major types of patent applications, its time to examine each one in more detail. Before we do, however, a word of advice. As suggested in Chapter 13, the types of problems that will occasion your using the information in this chapter may make it appropriate for you to at least consult with an expert prior to making a decision. In other words, before you decide to file a continuation, etc., you should seriously consider seeing a patent lawyer. Also note that, of necessity, the chart is abbreviated (it doesn't cover extensions of extensions), so rely primarily on the text, rather than the chart.

B. Continuation Applications

A continuing or continuation application is concisely defined in the *Manual of Patent Examining Procedure* (MPEP), Section 201.07, as "a second application for the same invention claimed in a prior application and filed before the [prior application] becomes abandoned." A continuation

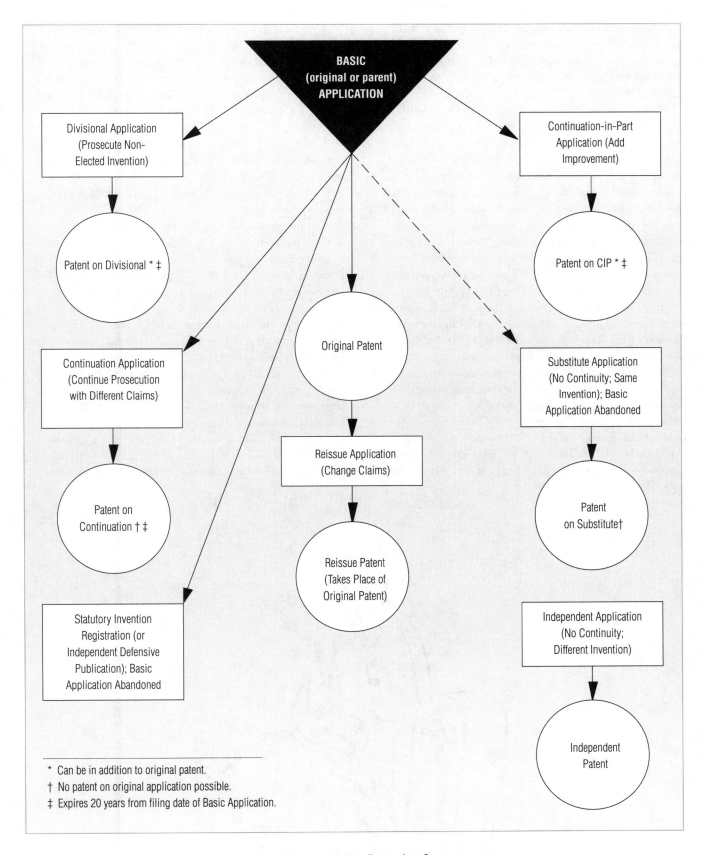

Fig. 14A—Available Extension Cases

application is almost always filed in response to a final rejection when you want to have another round with the examiner. If you don't file it within the response period (three months unless extended for a fee), you give up your right to file it at all.

If you think that it's inconsistent for the PTO to allow you to continue prosecuting claims to an invention after it has supposedly declared an office action "final," a word of explanation is in order. The word "final" is a word of art, meaning that it has a special, unusual meaning. A "final" action doesn't mean that the examiner has given the final word on your invention, but merely has decided to cut off your right to freely change your claims in your current application. In other words, you've gotten as many go-arounds as they're going to give you for your filing fee.

An historical explanation will make it even clearer. In the "old" days when I worked in the PTO (early '60s), patent prosecution proceeded at a leisurely pace. We examiners were allowed to send four or five OAs before we had to issue a final action. We issued a final OA only after an issue had been clearly defined and reached, or if it was a fourth or fifth OA. However, since the late 1960s, the PTO instituted a "compact prosecution" practice; under this practice the examiner is almost always supposed to make the second OA final. The purpose of this change was to obtain more income for the PTO (a continuation application gets the PTO an additional filing fee), to reduce the amount of work the PTO performed, and to shorten the backlog of pending applications.

However, two OAs are often not enough to define the invention adequately, reach an issue with the examiner, and complete the prosecution in a proper manner. Therefore, continuation applications are often filed nowadays, especially since the process has been made very simple by a new procedure, called the "File-Wrapper-Continuing" (FWC) procedure.

When you file an FWC continuation, the PTO uses your same file jacket and papers and merely assigns a new serial number and filing date. The procedure is covered by the PTO's Rule 62 and an FWC Request Form that I've provided as Form 14-1.

A continuation application must cover the same invention as the parent or basic application, and the parent or basic application must be abandoned when an FWC is filed. The continuation application is entitled to the benefit of the filing date of the parent application for purposes of overcoming prior art, although, as stated, the continuation receives its own filing date and serial number. The continuation's separate serial number and filing date are solely for PTO administrative purposes and have no legal effect.

You can also file a continuation of a continuation application. In fact, it's theoretically possible to file an unlimited sequence of continuation applications. But note that if an issue has been reached in the parent application, the examiner can, and usually will, make the first OA in a continuation application final. In other words, each continuation application will be quickly rejected unless you truly come up with a different slant on or definition of your invention not previously considered by the PTO.

When a patent issues on a continuation application, the heading of the patent will indicate that it's a continuation application. Also, the filing date and serial number of the parent (original, basic) application will be given in order to apprise the public of the patent's effective filing date.

To file an FWC continuation application, do the following:

- complete Form 14-1
- attach a new filing fee (large or small entity—see Appendix 4, Fee Schedule)
- attach a preliminary amendment containing the new claims you desire to prosecute or check the appropriate block on Form 14-1 if you want to have your Amendment under Rule 116 from the parent case entered, and
- as always, attach a receipt postcard. (See Chapter 10.)

To complete Form 14-1, check "continuation" in paragraph 1 and fill out all the other self-explanatory blanks in the form. For the Preliminary Amendment, use Form 13-1. You must either get your FWC Request in before the period for response to the final rejection expires (or any extensions you've bought—see Chapter 13), or you can mail your FWC Request on the last day of the period for response if you use the Express Mail Certification at the bottom of Form 14-1, as explained in Chapter 10. Send the papers to the usual PTO address, "Attention Box FWC."

Don't use the Certificate of Mailing in Chapter 13 to file any application; under PTO Rule 8, it won't be of any value in this situation. It's only useful for filing amendments and issue fees.

Complete Form 13-1 exactly as you would do with a regular amendment (see Chapter 13), with the following three exceptions:

1. Leave the serial number and filing date lines blank.
2. Below the caption, insert the serial number and filing date of the parent. For example, "(A continuation of Ser. Nr. 07/123,456, Filed 1995 Aug 9)."
3. Amend the specification by adding the following sentence before line 1 on page 1: "This is a continuation of application Ser. Nr. __/___,___, filed 199_ ___ _." (Insert the serial number and filing date of the parent case.)

Then proceed as usual: cancel the old claims and insert the new claims in the normal-amendment manner, numbered in sequence after the highest numbered claim of the prior application. Under "Remarks," you should state, "The above new claims are being submitted as part of the con-

tinuation application; these claims are submitted to be patentable over the art of record in the parent cases for the following reasons." Then give your reasons and arguments in the same manner as you would for a regular amendment, as stated in Chapter 13.

Be sure to include all the claims you desire in the preliminary amendment, since the first OA in the continuation may be made final if the examiner doesn't cite any new prior art.

Note that when you file a continuation application, the PTO will use the drawings of your parent application and abandon it as of the date of transfer.

As with a regular application, you'll receive your postcard back with the stamped serial number and filing date of your continuation application. Thereafter, you'll receive a blue filing receipt and first office action in due course.

If the claims that are finally allowed in a continuation application, or divisional application (see Section C, below) differ significantly from the claims originally presented in the parent application, file a Supplemental Declaration (Form 13-4) before or when you pay the issue fee.

CHANGING EXAMINERS

If you feel that the examiner in your parent case was unduly tough, it may be possible to get a different examiner in your continuation case by claiming your invention differently. The examining division to which a patent application is assigned is determined by the class and subclass to which the application is assigned, and this is in turn determined by the subject matter of the narrowest (longest or most specific) claim in the case.

EXAMPLE: Suppose you've invented a new gear for a bicycle and the narrowest claim of your parent case recites the fine details of the gear per se. Your case will be assigned to an examining division in the "gear" arts. If your "gear" examiner is a hardnose, you'll probably be able to get it into bicycles, a different examining division, by adding the bicycle to your narrowest claim. You can do this by providing a "bicycle" preamble for the claim (see Chapter 9) or by actually reciting other parts of the bike in the body of the claim. This may sometimes run you into an "old combination" rejection, but it's worth a try. If your narrowest claim is directed to a bike, your whole case will be classified in the bike division, and you'll have a different examiner.

Obviously, this maneuver can't be done in every instance, and you should do some research on the PTO's Examining Division art assignments (see the "Patent Examining Corps" page of any recent *Official Gazette*) to make sure your end run around a particular examiner will work.

Lastly, in an effort to get a new examiner, it also helps to change the title of your invention to one that is commensurate with your revised narrowest claim—for example, change "Gear with Anti-Backlash Pawl" to "—Bicycle Pedal Drive Gear—."

⚠ This is one of several situations where I believe a consultation with a patent attorney or agent may be called for, due to the artsy nature of claims drafting. (See Chapter 6, Section F.)

**OTHER WAYS TO FILE A
CONTINUATION, DIVISION OR CIP**

In addition to filing an FWC continuation application (Rule 62), continuation, divisional, and CIP applications can also be filed under Rule 53 (complete copy of specification and claims, drawings and signed new declarations (Patent Application Declaration and Small-Entity Declaration) must be filed while the parent is pending; most useful when both cases are to issue) and Rule 62 (same as Rule 53, but signed declarations can be omitted if certain steps are taken). I haven't provided forms or detailed instructions for Rule 53 and Rule 62 continuation cases since the FWC procedure is almost always used and since many traps exist under these other procedures. Consult a patent attorney if you believe the FWC procedure is inadequate for you.

⚠ **20-YEAR TERM**
Under the new GATT Law, signed 12/94 and effective 6/95, if you file a continuation application (or a continuation of a continuation) and get a patent on your continuation, the patent will expire 20 years after the filing date of your first, original, or parent application. So it behooves you to file any continuation as soon as possible and to prosecute it diligently if you don't want your monopoly to be shorter than the former 17-year term. Since any extension (continuation, division, or CIP) will expire 20 years from the filing date of its parent case, before filing any extension, consider whether you'll really need to rely upon the parent case's filing date. If you're certain that no adverse prior art has issued since the parent's filing date, you can have any new case expire 20 years from *its* filing date (rather than from the filing date of the original case) if your new case *doesn't* claim priority of your original case, i.e., if you file it as a regular patent application, rather than as an extension.

C. Divisional Applications

Now let's turn our attention to the divisional application.

A divisional application or "division" is "a later application for a distinct or independent invention, carved out of a pending application and disclosing and claiming only subject matter disclosed in the earlier or parent application" (MPEP 201.06). Divisional applications are filed when the PTO decides that two separate or distinct inventions have been claimed in the parent application (not permitted, since your filing fee entitles you to get only one invention examined), and you've agreed to restrict the parent application to the set of claims to one of the inventions. You have the option to file a separate, divisional application on the claims to the other invention. Divisional applications are so called because they cover subject matter that is "divided out" of the parent case.

A divisional application is entitled to the filing date of the parent case for purposes of overcoming prior art, although, like the continuation application, it receives its own serial number and filing date for PTO administrative purposes. A patent issuing on a divisional application will show the serial number and filing date of the parent application; this will be the divisional's effective filing date. The parent application of a divisional application can either issue as a patent or become abandoned if you feel it's not patentable over the prior art. But remember that the divisional application must be filed while the parent is pending. Also note that you can file a division of a continuation application, and a continuation of a divisional application. (Definitely consult an expert if you get into these murky waters.)

1. Use File-Wrapper-Continuing Procedure If the Parent Case Is to Be Abandoned

If the parent application is to be abandoned—that is, if you give up on the invention you elected and unsuccessfully prosecuted in the original case—you can file a sequential divisional application very easily by using the FWC procedure (Form 14-1). Merely check the "Division" block in paragraph 1 of the form, and check and fill in the appropriate "drawing" blocks at the end of paragraph 1. Most of the time you'll be using the same drawings of the parent case, but if you want to submit new drawings—for example, to delete extraneous figures to an abandoned embodiment—you can do so at this time. Check the other blocks as appropriate.

As with the continuation application, enclose a preliminary amendment to the daughter divisional case. Use Form 13-1. Amend the specification by inserting, at the beginning, the following sentence: "—This is a division of Ser. Nr. ___,___, Filed 199_ ___ ___, now abandoned—."

Amend the claims by canceling all of the claims to the elected invention of the parent case and submitting or leaving only claims to the divisional invention.

For example, suppose the parent case had Claims 1 to 20, of which Claims 1 to 10 were directed to the elected invention of the parent case (on which you couldn't get a patent) and Claims 11 to 20 were to the nonelected invention that you now want to prosecute in the divisional case. Your amendment would simply read: "CLAIMS: Cancel Claims 1 to 10." This will leave only Claims 11 to 20 pending. Alternatively, you can cancel all of the claims of the parent case and submit entirely new claims in your divisional application.

In the "Remarks" section, you can summarize what you've done and briefly point out why you think the divisional's claims are patentable. And don't forget the postcard and filing fee!

2. File a Complete Copy of the Divisional Application If Parent Case Won't Be Abandoned

If you're not abandoning the parent case—for example, if a patent is going to issue on the parent, and you want to get another, parallel patent on the invention that is the subject matter of the divisional application—things get a bit more complex, but they're still bearable. Instead of using the FWC procedure (Form 14-1) you'll have to proceed under Rule 53. File a complete copy of the divisional application, including a transmittal letter (Form 10-1), drawings (see below), filing fee, specification, claims, and abstract, PAD (Form 10-2), and SED (Form 10-3), postcard, and optionally, a Preliminary Amendment. Everything should be the same as if you were filing a completely new application (use the checklist of Chapter 10), with the following exceptions:

    a. Add the following sentence to the transmittal letter: "This is a division of Ser. Nr. __/___,___, Filed 199_ ___ __."

    b. Add the same sentence to paragraph 1 of the specification, either by typing it in the actual specification or by way of a Preliminary Amendment if you're using a copy of the specification from the parent case. Later on, after your patent on the parent case issues, add the following to the end of this sentence: "—, now patent 5,___,___, granted 199_ __ __.—."

    c. Delete any nonapplicable figures from the drawing— that is, any figures directed exclusively to the embodiment of the parent case.

    d. Amend the specification, either directly on the copy you file, or by a Preliminary Amendment, to remove any matter directed exclusively to the embodiment or invention of the parent case, and to make any editorial amendments you desire or which you've made in the parent case.

    e. Add the sentence of "a," above, to the Patent Application Declaration Disclosure Form (Form 10-2).

To supply drawings for the parallel divisional case, you have two choices:

    a. If you've made formal Mylar film or Bristol board originals of your drawings, you can file very good xerographic copies of these for your divisional's formal drawings.

    b. You can file rough xerographic copies as informal drawings and file formal drawings later, as explained in Chapter 10.

⚠ DOUBLE PATENT WARNING

You're not permitted to obtain two patents on the same invention; if you do, it's called "double patenting," a situation in which both patents may be held invalid. However, if in your parent case the examiner required you to restrict the application to one of several inventions, due to a special statute (35 USC 121), you can file your divisional(s) on the nonelected invention(s) with total immunity from double patenting. However, if the examiner didn't require you to restrict, and you're filing your divisional "voluntarily," you must be sure that it's to a clearly different invention than that claimed in the parent case; otherwise, both patents can be held invalid for "double patenting."

Once again, I recommend that you consult with a patent attorney in the event you (or the PTO) decide that a divisional application is indicated.

⚠ 20-YEAR TERM WARNING

The 20-year term warning for continuation applications in Section B also applies to divisional applications.

D. Continuation-in-Part and Independent Applications

As defined in MPEP 201.08, "a continuation-in-part" (CIP) is an application filed during the lifetime of an earlier application by the same applicant, repeating some substantial portion or all of the earlier application and adding matter not disclosed in the earlier application. CIP applications are not common; they're used whenever you wish to cover an improvement of your basic invention, for example, if you've discovered a new material or a better design. (Remember, you can't add these to a pending application because of the proscription on "new matter" discussed in Chapter 13.)

Generally, the parent application should be allowed to go abandoned when a CIP is filed, but if you do want the parent application to issue, you must be sure that the claims of the CIP application are patentably different—that is, they define subject matter which is unobvious over that of the parent application—or else the CIP and parent application patent can both be held invalid for double patenting, unless you file a terminal disclaimer. (See Section H, below.)

The advantage of a CIP application over a separate application is that the CIP is entitled to the filing date of the parent application for all subject matter common to both applications. However, if any claims of the CIP cover subject matter unique to the CIP, such claims are entitled to the filing date of the CIP only.

If your "improvement" of your basic application is different enough to be unobvious over the basic invention, an entirely separate, independent application, rather than a CIP, can be filed, but it's better to use a CIP application, since the common subject matter gets the filing date of the parent application.

CIP EXAMPLE 1: Suppose you've invented a bicycle gear with a new shape. You've claimed this shape in a patent application, which I'll call the parent application. After you file the parent application, your research shows you that the gear works much more quietly if it's made of a certain vanadium alloy (VA). The VA isn't patentable

over the invention of the parent case and your parent case's claims cover the gear no matter what material it's made of, but since the VA works much better, you'd like to add a few dependent claims specifically to cover a gear made of the VA. In this way, if there's an infringer who copies your gear made of the VA, you can show the judge that the infringer is infringing your specific as well as your broad claims and you may have specific claims to VA to fall back on if your broad claims are held invalid. You can't add the VA to the specification or the claims of the parent case since it would be verboten "new matter." The solution: file a CIP, describing the VA in the specification, and add a few dependent claims that recite that the gear is made of VA. To avoid any possibility of double patenting you should abandon the parent case or file a terminal disclaimer (see Section H), since the VA isn't patentable over the invention of the parent case. For purposes of clearing the prior art, your broad claims to the gear shape per se will get the benefit of the parent case's filing date, but the claims to the gear made of the VA will only be entitled to the later filing date of the CIP.

CIP EXAMPLE 2: On the other hand, suppose your gear shape works well, but you've come up with a related, but unobviously different shape that works better—that is, the new shape is patentable over the invention of the parent case. You would file a CIP with claims to the new shape and continue to prosecute the parent case to a patent. The CIP's claims generally will be entitled to only the CIP's filing date, but their CIP status will entitle you to refer back to the parent's filing date to show when you came up with the underlying concept common to the parent and CIP gears in case the CIP is ever involved in litigation or an interference.

CIP EXAMPLE 3: Lastly, suppose your gear shape works well, but you come up with an unrelated, and unobviously different shape that works better. You would file a new, independent application, not related to the "parent," with claims to the new gear shape. The two applications would be entirely separate.

You can file a CIP of a continuation or divisional application or vice versa in either case. It's also theoretically possible to file an unlimited number of successive CIP applications to cover successive improvements; there have been rare cases where inventors have filed chains of CIPs with as many as eight or more applications, each of which issued into a patent.

As with divisional applications, you can use the File-Wrapper-Continuing procedure for your CIP if you're abandoning the parent case, but if the parent will issue, you'll have to file a complete new set of papers for the CIP under Rules 53 or 62.

If you're allowing the parent case to go abandoned—that is, you're filing a sequential CIP—you should do the following:

- File the CIP using Form 14-1, in the same manner as you would file an FWC divisional, except check the "CIP" space in Form 14-1.
- Provide a Preliminary Amendment referring to the parent case, and with the new subject matter and claims you desire to add.
- Add any new drawings you desire.
- Attach a new declaration; use Form 13-4, which should refer to your Preliminary Amendment by its date.
- And don't forget the postcard and filing fee.

If your parent case will issue—that is, you're filing a parallel CIP—you can't use the FWC procedure or Form 14-1. Instead, use the same procedure as outlined above for filing a divisional when the parent case will issue, except substitute "continuation-in-part" for "divisional" in the transmittal letter and specification and add the following sentence to your PAD (Form 10-2): "I hereby claim the benefit under Title 35, United States Code, § 120 of the prior, copending United States application listed below and, insofar as the subject matter of each of the claims of this application is not disclosed in the manner provided by the first paragraph of Title 35, United States Code, § 112, I acknowledge the duty to disclose material information as defined in Title 37, Code of Federal Regulations, § 1.56(a), which occurred between the filing date of this application and the national or PCT international filing date of this application: Ser. Nr. _____, Filed 199_ ___." Don't forget the filing fee, postcard, and SED (Form 10-3). Also use the checklist of Chapter 10. The new subject matter of the CIP and any claims directed to it will be entitled to the CIP's filing date, not the filing date of the parent case.

If you're filing an independent application (rather than a CIP), do it in the usual manner (Chapters 7 to 10) except that you can add a heading and sentence to the specification as follows:

Cross-Reference to Related Application: This application is related to application Ser. Nr. ___, Filed ___, now patent Nr. ___, granted ___.

⚠ 20-YEAR TERM WARNING
The 20-year term warning for continuation applications in Section B also applies to CIP applications.

E. Reissue Applications

As stated in MPEP 201.05, "a reissue application is an application for a patent to take the place of an unexpired patent that's defective in some one or more particulars." Parts 1400 to 1401.12 of the MPEP discuss reissue applications extensively. If you've received a patent and believe that the claims are not broad enough, that they're too broad (you've discovered a new reference), or that there are some significant errors in the specification, you can file an application to get your original patent reissued at any time during its term. The reissue patent will take the place of your original patent and expire the same time as the original patent would have expired.

THE TWO-YEAR AND INTERVENING RIGHTS RULES

If you wish to broaden the claims of your patent through a reissue application, you must do so within two years from the date the original patent issued. Moreover, anyone who manufactures anything between the issue dates of the original patent and the reissue patent that infringes the broadened but not the original claims is entitled to "intervening rights." These preclude a valid suit against this person for infringement of the reissue patent's broadened claims. (35 USC 251, 252.)

EXAMPLE: Suppose you invent a new gear shape and get a patent, but unfortunately you included an unnecessary limitation in your independent claims, namely they all recite that the gear is made of carbon steel. If you discover your error within a two-year period after your patent's issue date, you can file an application to reissue the patent with broader claims—that is, claims that specify only the gear's shape and not its material. Your patent will be reissued with the broader claims. However, suppose that an infringer (Peg) made gears with your inventive shape, but out of aluminum, between the date of your original and reissue patents. Peg's aluminum gears would not infringe the claims of your original patent, but they would infringe the broader claims of the reissue. Nevertheless, Peg can continue to make her aluminum gears with impunity since she has "intervening rights" by virtue of her manufacture of the aluminum gears in the interim.

THE ANTI-RECAPTURE RULE

Note that a reissue can't be filed to "recapture" subject matter you deliberately gave up in the original case. In the example above, suppose that in your original case you put the "carbon steel" limitation in the claims to define over the prior art. Since this was a deliberate, conscious act, you aren't permitted to eliminate the "carbon steel" limitation (and thus "recapture" your broader claims) in a reissue.

To file a reissue application you must:
• Reproduce the entire specification of the original application (a copy of the printed patent pasted one column per page is acceptable), putting brackets around matter to be canceled and underlining matter to be added. When the reissue patent issues, it will include the brackets and underlining.
• Supply a request for a title report on the original patent (see Fee Schedule for amount) and offer to surrender the original patent deed.
• Provide a very detailed showing in your declaration as to why you believe the original patent to be wholly or partially inoperative or invalid; see Patent Rules 171-179.

Reissue patents are relatively rare and are identified by the letters "RE" followed by a five-digit number, for example, "Patent RE 26,420."

Due to the relatively complicated nature of reissue applications, I suggest that you consult a patent lawyer if you are interested in filing one.

F. Statutory Invention Registration

If you've filed a U.S. application and for some reason don't wish it to issue as a patent or can't obtain a patent on it, but want to be absolutely sure that no one else will ever be able to obtain a patent on it (for instance, you're manufacturing a product embodying the invention), you can elect to have an abstract of your application published in the *Official Gazette* and have your entire application published like a patent. Called a "Statutory Invention Registration" (SIR), this purely defensive procedure will cause your invention to become a prior-art reference, effective as of its filing date. The SIR will thus preclude anyone else from obtaining a patent on the invention, provided no application on the invention was filed earlier than yours. Your application will

then be printed and published like a patent, but you won't have any monopoly rights. (You will retain the right to revive your application and get into interference if a patent or application is discovered which claims your invention.)

I don't recommend use of the SIR procedure because of the generally higher fee required—it's cheaper to publish your own book about your invention or to list it with an invention register, such as ITD, Inc., P.O. Box 371-0371, Tinley Park, IL 60477; Technotec, 8100 34th Ave. South, Minneapolis, MN 55440 (about $160); or *Research Disclosure Magazine*, Industrial Opportunities, Ltd., Homewell, Havant, Hampshire, PO9 1EF, UK (about $100). If you have your invention published this way, the effective date of publication will be later than your filing date. However, the cost is generally much less and the later date won't make any difference unless someone has filed on the same invention before publication.

If you do choose to convert your application to an SIR, follow PTO Rules 293-297 and 17(n) or (o).

G. Substitute Applications

The term "substitute" is defined in MPEP 201.09 as "an application that is in essence a duplicate of an application by the same applicant that was abandoned before the filing date of the later case." A substitute can be filed for the same purpose as either a continuation, division, or CIP.

I hope you never have to file a substitute application, since it doesn't get the benefit of the filing date of the earlier case. This is because it wasn't filed while the earlier case was pending. Thus any prior art that issues after the filing date of the earlier case and before the filing date of the substitute case is good against the substitute case. If, however, you somehow abandon your application (not your invention) and you can't successfully petition the Commissioner of Patents to revive the application (see Chapter 13), you still may be able to cover your invention by filing a substitute application, assuming significant prior art hasn't been published in the meantime.

There are no special forms or procedures for filing a substitute application; just file it like you would a regular patent application, except that you can add a reference in the specification to the "parent" case. As stated, you won't get the benefit of your "parent" case's filing date, but the date of the parent case may be useful if you ever have to swear behind a reference (see Chapter 13) or prove earlier conception and/or reduction to practice—such as, in case of an interference. (See Chapter 13, Section K.) If your substitute application issues into a patent, the patent will expire 20 years from the filling date of the substitute.

H. Double Patenting and Terminal Disclaimers

Double patenting (DP) is a situation that exists when one person obtains two patents on the same invention, or on two inventions that are not patentably distinct. It's very important to avoid DP, since both patents can be held invalid by a court. Also, if the PTO sees that you have two applications pending that aren't patentably distinct, they will reject them on the grounds of potential DP. Thus, you must always be aware of the DP trap whenever you file a second case on an invention.

One way to avoid DP, even though you may be filing two cases on the same invention, occurs when the examiner has required restriction, as explained in Section C, above, under "Double Patent Warning." Another way is to file a Terminal Disclaimer (TD) in the later issuing case. Under a TD (Rules 130(b) and 321(b)), you agree to give up the terminal (end) period of your second patent so that both patents will expire together, thereby eliminating the harm to the public interest (extension of monopoly beyond normal term) of double patenting. I don't provide instructions on preparing and filing TDs, since the practice is tricky; I just want to make you aware of its existence so you'll know what options are available and when to consult an attorney. Also note that a TD can't be used to avoid DP if both cases claim the same invention; a TD can avoid DP only when the applications claim different inventions which aren't patentably distinct. ∎

CHAPTER

15

After Your Patent Issues:
Use, Maintenance and Infringement

INVENTOR'S COMMANDMENT #28

Once your patent issues, check it for printing errors, consider patent marking if you manufacture a product covered by the patent, be alert for infringements, and pay three maintenance fees (3.0 to 3.5, 7.0 to 7.5 and 11.0 to 11.5 years after issue) to keep it in force.

A. Always on Tuesdays

Several months after you pay the issue fee (Chapter 13), you'll receive an Issue Notification. This will indicate the number and issue date of your patent (approximately one or two weeks after you receive the notice). On the issue date, which will almost always be a Tuesday, the patent will be granted, published, and mailed to you so that several days later you'll receive your patent deed (also called "letters patent"). This consists of a copy of your patent on stiff paper, a fancy jacket, rivets, seal, and ribbon. You'll also receive (separately) the printed copies of your patent if you ordered them when you paid your issue fee. The highlights of your patent will also be listed in the *Official Gazette— Patents,* which is also almost always published on the Tuesday of grant.

B. Press Release

You may wish, when you learn the number and date of your patent, to prepare a press release about it. See any book on advertising to learn how to prepare a press release; it should cover the six facets of reporting:

> *I had six honest serving men*
> *They taught me all I knew;*
> *Their names were WHERE and WHAT and WHEN*
> *And WHY and HOW and WHO.*
> —Rudyard Kipling

Make your headline and text simple and short (250 words maximum), yet interesting and catchy—for example, "Midgeville Inventor Gets Patent on Jam-Free Bike Mechanism." Be conversational; don't use jargon or technical language. Type on only one side of the paper, double spaced, and include your name, address, phone number, and "For Immediate Release" at the top. If you have more than one page, number and type "more" at the bottom of each page (except the last) and staple the pages together. Type "30" or "###" at the end. If you have an interesting or important invention, send a letter or copy of your PR (as soon as you get the issue notice) to N.Y. Times Patent Columnist, 229 West 43d St., New York, NY 10036, and Julia Angwin, States News Service, Fax 202-737-1851; they may mention your patent in their regular column when your patent issues. Also send the PR to your local papers and trade magazines (each with a copy of your patent) on the day you get the patent.

C. Check Your Patent for Errors

First, proofread your patent carefully, preferably out loud with a friend or coworker. Carefully examine the information in the heading of the patent—serial number, filing date, title, your name, etc.—to make sure all is correct. Then read the patent word for word and compare it with the application in your file as amended during the prosecution phase.

If you find errors, you have several possible courses of action.

1. If the Errors Aren't Significant

If the errors aren't significant, that is, if the meaning you intended is obvious and clear, the PTO won't issue a Certificate of Correction, but you should make the error of record in the PTO's file of your patent. To do this, simply write a "make-of-record" letter to be put in the file of your patent, listing the errors you found. This letter should be captioned similarly to Form 15-1 (see below) with the patent number, issue date, and patentee(s) name(s) and should be headed, "Make-of-Record Letter for Errors in Printed Patent." It should then list all the errors in the patent.

2. Certificate of Correction

If any of the errors you discover are significant, that is, if the meaning is unclear because of a wrong reference numeral, missing or transposed words, failure to include a significant amendment, etc., you may obtain a Certificate of Correction. If the errors are the fault of the printer, the Certificate of Correction will be issued free. If the errors are your fault, that is, they appear in your file as well as in the printed patent, you still can get a Certificate of Correction, provided the error is of a clerical or minor nature and occurred in good faith. Examples are a wrong reference numeral or an omitted line or word. (The fee for a Certificate of Correction to fix your error is listed in Appendix 4, Fee Schedule.) To obtain one (in either case), do the following:

Step 1: Fill out Forms 15-1 and 15-2. In Form 15-1 (the request letter), insert the patent number, issue date, patentee(s), Ser. Nr., filing date, and the date you mailed the form. Check paragraph 2 if the error is the fault of the PTO; check paragraph 3 and insert the amount from the Fee Schedule if the error is your fault.

 In either case (whether you checked paragraph 2 or 3), in paragraph 4 list the places in the application file where the errors occurred and explain who was at fault; for example:

 "4. Specifically, on p. 4, line 12, of the specification, applicant erroneously typed '42' instead of '24' and neither applicant nor the examiner detected this error during prosecution."

 or

 "4. Specifically, on p. 4, line 12 of the specification, the reference numeral '24' has been erroneously printed by the GPO in the patent as '42' instead of '24.'"

Step 2: Complete the caption of Form 15-2 with the patent number, issue date, and inventor(s). (The PTO also furnishes carbon sets of the Certificate of Correction form gratis). In the body of Form 15-2, make the necessary corrections as if you were making an amendment (see Chapter 13) to the actual printed patent; for example:

 "Col. 3, line 54, change 'the diode' to —varistor 23—."

 Put your return address and the patent number on the bottom of Form 15-2.

Step 3: Send one copy of completed Form 15-1 and *two* copies of completed Form 15-2 to the PTO with a receipt postcard, and a check for the correct amount if the error was your fault. You'll get an approved copy of your Form 15-2 back in several months and the PTO will affix copies of it to the copies of your patent that it maintains in its storage facilities.

D. Patent Number Marking

If you already have sales blurbs promoting your invention, change them to indicate that your invention is "patented" rather than "patent pending." If you, or a licensee of yours, is manufacturing a product embodying the invention, you should consider marking your product with the patent number.

A section of the patent laws (35 USC 278) states that products embodying a patented invention may be marked with the legend "Pat." or "Patent," followed by the patent number. If you make or sell products embodying your invention that are properly marked, you can recover damages from any infringers you sue from the date you began marking, whether they see your notice or not. If you make or sell products but don't mark them with your patent number, or mark them "Patented" without the number, you can recover damages only from the date you notify the infringer of infringement, or from the date you file suit against the infringer, whichever is earlier.

The actual marking should be done on the product itself, on its package, or by means of a label affixed to the product. If you don't manufacture any product embodying the invention, or if the invention relates to a process that's not associated with a product and hence can't be marked, you can recover damages from an infringer for the entire period of infringement without marking.

The disadvantage of patent marking is that any sophisticated person who wants to copy your product can easily see the number of your patent, order the patent, read its claims, and attempt to design around the claims of your patent. If you don't mark your product, the potential infringer can still probably get this same information, but only through a lot more expense and effort. In other words, by not marking you may depend in part on human inertia to protect your invention from being copied. Many companies, therefore, favor *not* marking their patented products, or simply marking them "Patented" without including the number, relying on their own familiarity with the field to enable them to quickly spot and promptly notify any infringer of the existence of the patent.

E. Advertising Your Patent for Sale

If you still haven't licensed or sold your invention by the time your patent issues, you can advertise the availability of your patent for license or sale in one or more of several publications, such as:

 • *Patent Official Gazette,* Assistant Commissioner for Patents, Washington, DC 20231
 • *The International Invention Register*, P.O. Box 547, Fallbrook, CA 92028
 • *The Wall Street Journal, U.S.A. Today,* local newspapers in large cities, etc.

Contact the publications for listing information and fees.

F.   What Rights Does Your Patent Give You?

Now that you've actually obtained a patent, you'll undoubtedly want to know exactly what rights you receive under it. While I've indicated that a patent provides a monopoly on the manufacture, use, and sale of your invention that expires 20 years from the filing date of your application, I'll now specifically discuss what this means in the real world.

1.   Enforceable Monopoly on Manufacture, Use, and Sale

The grant of a patent gives you, or the person or corporation to whom you "assigned" (legally transferred) your patent or patent application, a monopoly on the invention *defined by the claims of the patent,* beginning with the patent's date of issuance and expiring 20 years from the date you filed your application (or the first application in the chain if your patent issued from a division, continuation, or continuation-in-part). (For applications issuing before 1995 Jun 8, the term is 17 years from issuance, and for applications filed before this date and issuing thereafter, the term is the greater of the 17- or 20-year term. Any term can be extended if you encountered a delay due to FDA processing of a new drug or medical device application, had to appeal or prosecute an interference, or had your application placed under a secrecy order. (35 USC 154-156.)) This monopoly gives you the right to bring a valid suit against anyone who makes, uses, sells, offers to sell, imports, files a new drug application on, actively induces infringement of your invention in the U.S., or imports a product made abroad by a process patented in the U.S.

You can use your ownership of the patent to make money in any of three ways:

1. Sell the patent outright.
2. License others to make, use, and/or sell the patented invention in return for royalties under a variety of conditions, subject to the antitrust laws mentioned in the note below. (See Chapter 16 for a more detailed discussion about the sale and licensing of patent rights.)
3. Use your patent to create a monopoly by preventing anyone else from making, using, or selling the invention. In this case you would manufacture the invention yourself (or have it manufactured for you) and charge more than you'd have to in a competitive situation, as Xerox did, and as Polaroid and Sony now do with their instant film, cameras, and the one-gun Trinitron CRT. In other words, a patent will give you the right (within limits) to fix the price of your product—a capitalist's dream!

> ### EXTENDING THE EFFECTIVENESS OF YOUR PATENT
>
> If you want to continue to make money from your creativity after your patent expires, you should plow back some of your royalties or proceeds from the sale of the patent for research so that you can invent further developments and improvements, and thereby get more and later patents so as effectively to extend your monopoly beyond its relatively short term.

ANTITRUST NOTE
Occasionally, companies or individuals who own a patent or manufacture a patented invention use their patent to extend their monopoly in ways that the antitrust laws prohibit (for example, compulsory package licensing, compulsory price fixing and other practices that impose undue restraints on free trade). This is very rarely a problem for the independent inventor but can occasionally raise problems for large corporations. For a discussion of antitrust law as it affects the use of patents, go to any law library and look for any books on patent-antitrust law, such as *Intellectual Property and Antitrust Law,* by William C. Holmes (Clark Boardman, 1985), or look under the heading "Patents," subhead, "antitrust," in any legal encyclopedia, such as *Corpus Juris Secundum.*

2.   Property Rights

The law considers a patent to be personal property that can be sold, given away, willed, or even seized by your creditors, just like your car, a share of stock, or any other item of personal property. Even though it's personal property, the actual patent deed you receive from the PTO has no inherent value; thus you need not put it in your safe-deposit box or take any steps to preserve it against loss. Your ownership of the patent is recorded in the PTO (just like the deed to your house is recorded by your county's Recorder of Deeds). If you lose the original deed, the PTO will sell you copies of the printed patent or certified copies of a title report showing that you're the owner.

3. Medical Procedure Exemption

Recently, one physician sued another for infringement of a patented ophthalmic surgery technique. In response, the medical establishment used its considerable clout to produce a federal statute exempting healthcare providers (for instance, doctors, nurses and hospitals) from liability for performing medical procedures covered by in-force patents. 35 U.S.C. §287(c). In view of this statute, it no longer makes sense to patent medical procedures, as such. However, the manufacture, use, sale, offer for sale and importation of patented medical devices and drugs can still infringe an applicable patent.

G. Be Wary of Offers to Provide Information About Your Patent

Soon after being awarded a patent, a client of mine received an offer by mail, advising that an "article" about her patent was published and offering to send her a copy of the article for $3.95. After anxiously sending in her money, she received the "article," a photocopy of a page from the PTO's *Official Gazette,* showing the usual main drawing figure and claim of her patent! Fortunately she was able to obtain a refund by threatening to call in the FTC and postal inspectors, but you may not be so lucky; new rackets originate all the time.

Another offer very frequently received by patentees, usually about a year or more after their patent issues, comes as a postcard, such as the following:

Important Notice

To: *Owners of U.S. Patent # 4688283*

Assignor

Our search of your U.S. patent shows the ⎣_[#]_⎦ most recent patents, issued after your patent, that the U.S. Patent Office has classified identically or cross-referenced in the same class and subclass as your patent.

    You may want to determine if your patent dominates the later patents, the activity of competitors, and the latest state of the art.

    For each of the later-issued patents we will send you the patent no., an abstract, a drawing, plus address-information on the inventor, and/or the owner or manufacturer for $1.00 each, plus a service charge of $60.00 if you **return THIS CARD** (or a copy) with your payment of $96.00. Make check or money order to ⎣_**(Name)**_⎦ payable on a **U.S. Bank.**

    Or send $60.00 for a list of later patent numbers.

CD 60

1-2-3-4-1   *Providing Patent Information Since 1976*   1-2-3-4-2

Fig. 15A—Postcard Offer of Dubious Value

I believe this offer has marginal utility to most inventors, and at a very high cost. I wouldn't accept the offer, since almost all patents in which earlier patents are cited as references are very different and extremely unlikely to be of any value to the owner of the earlier patent. You can obtain an enhanced version of the same service at a much lower cost by using a "forward search" service, such as Search Check, Inc., 2111 Jeff. Davis Hwy., P.O.B. 2327, Arlington, VA 22202, 703-979-7230, or through most of the computer search services in Chapter 6. These services can provide you with a list of *all* patents that have issued after yours, in which your patent was cited as a reference, for about $50.

A third offer is the "Patent Certificate." This offer is sent to many patentees in an official-looking letter from Washington, marked "U.S. Patent Certificate," "For Official Use Only" (next to the postage stamp), and "Important Patent Information." In reality, it's from a private company that wants to sell you a nicely framed version of your patent. Needless to say, this product is of no official value.

A fourth offer, definitely of questionable value, also comes on a postcard that states something similar to the following: "Our search of your patent has located X companies that manufacture, market, or sell products in a field allied to your invention." It offers to sell you the names of the X companies for a stiff fee, usually about $80. If you want to find the names of the companies that are in a similar field, I strongly advise that you save your money and instead take a trip to a store or library where you'll find plenty of suitable companies for free. (Use the techniques outlined in Chapter 11.)

A fifth offer is to include you in a compendium of inventors, such as a "Who's Who" of inventors, or an offer to sell you such a volume with your name included. Definitely not worth it, unless you like your ego stroked for a price.

Patentees receive other offers in the mail along the lines of the foregoing. Be sure to investigate and think about it carefully (or ask a trusted advisor) before you send anyone any money.

H. Maintenance Fees

In 1983, Congress allowed the PTO to institute a maintenance fee (MF) system. While MFs are new to the U.S., their use has been commonplace all over the world (except Canada) for decades. Under the U.S. MF system, your patent, when granted, will subsist in force for 20 years from the filing date of its application, provided three maintenance fees are paid.

If no MFs are paid, it will expire four years from grant. If a first MF is paid between years 3.0 and 3.5 from grant, the patent will be extended to expire eight years from grant. If a second (much higher) MF is paid between years 7.0 and 7.5, the patent will expire 12 years from grant. And if a third (much higher yet) MF is paid between years 11.0 and 11.5, the patent will expire at the end of the full 20 years from filing. This information is succinctly presented in Fig. 15B, an MF timing chart. The adjustable arrow indicates that the expiration date varies, depending upon the length of pendency of the application.

To help you remember when to pay your MFs, I've provided an MF Reminder Sheet as Form 15-3; a sample is completed in Fig. 15C. You should copy this sheet and fill it out in ink—except write the year of MF I (three years after issue) in pencil on the top line and leave the last three columns in the table blank. Put the sheet at the end of your current year's calendar and keep moving it ahead to the end of each new year's calendar at the end of each year, until the third year after issue when the fee is due. Write that the MF is due on the appropriate date on your calendar. Fill in the last three columns in the table. When you pay the first fee and receive your receipt statement, change the year at the top of the sheet to the seventh year after issue and repeat the process.

As indicated in Fig. 15B, if you forget to pay any fee during its normal six-month payment period, you can pay it in the six-month period (grace period) following its normal six-month payment period, provided you pay a penalty or surcharge. See Appendix 4, Fee Schedule.

If you forgot to pay a maintenance fee in the normal and grace periods, the patent will expire at the end of the grace period. However, an expired patent can be revived on petition if you show, by declaration, that the delay was "unavoidable" (Rule 378(b)), or "unintentional" (Rule 378(c)). An "unavoidable" petition must provide facts showing that you took reasonable care and steps to pay the fee in a timely manner, but were unable to do so—for example, because your house burned down. It must be accompanied by the MF, the MF transmittal letter, and the "unavoidable" fee (see Fee Schedule). An "unintentional" petition must merely state the nonpayment was unintentional, and it must be accompanied by the MF, the MF transmittal letter, and a very high "unintentional" fee (see Fee Schedule). It must be filed within two years after the end of the grace period. (See Chapter 13, Section Q, for how to prepare such a petition and declaration.) If any infringement occurred or was prepared for after the patent expired and before it was revived, the infringer has "intervening rights"—that is, infringement can be continued as if the patent was not revived. (35 USC § 41(c).)

Use Form 15-4 to pay the maintenance fees; the fees (large and small entity) are listed in the Fee Schedule. Be sure to complete every blank in the form, including the serial number of the application; otherwise the PTO won't accept your fee and the delay may carry you into the grace period, costing you a surcharge. (If you've assigned or

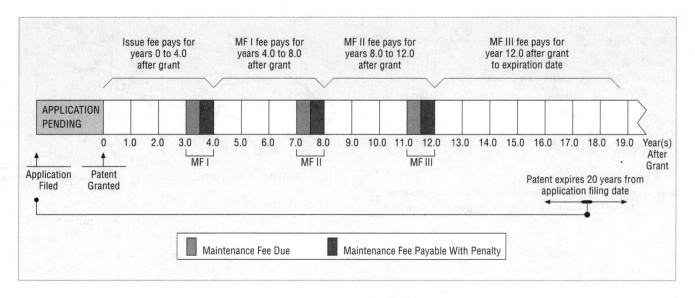

Fig. 15B—Maintenance Fee Timing Chart

Maintenance Fee Reminder

Next fee due: __98__ / __7__ / __16__
yr   mo   date
(Write year in pencil and change after each payment)

Patent Nr.: __5,032,015__   Issued: __1995/7/16__

Application Serial Nr.: __07/427,862__   Filed: __93/10/27__

Title: __"Shower Mirror with Valve"__

Patentee(s) (Inventor[s]/Applicant[s]): __T.R. Christianson__

Assignee(s) (if any): __ShowerTek, Inc.__

Expires __13/10/27__   (if all three maintenance fees are paid)[1].

☐ Small entity declaration was filed in application or patent.
(If not, large entity fees[2] must be paid.)

Maintenance Fee Number	Fee Due From:	To:	Sent Form & Check [4]	Amount	Received Receipt Statement
I. Due 3.0 - 3.5 YAI [3]	98 / 7 /16	99 / 1 / 16	/ /	$	/ /
II. Due 7.0 - 7.5 YAI	02 / 7 /16	03 / 1 / 16	/ /	$	/ /
III. Due 11.0 - 11.5 YAI	06 / 7 /16	07 / 1 / 16	/ /	$	/ /

Notes: _____
_____
_____
_____
_____
_____
_____
_____
_____
_____
_____
_____
_____
_____
_____

1. Expiration is 20 years from filing date of application for applications filed after 1995 Jun 7; 17 years from issue date for patents issuing before 1995 Jun 8; and the greater of 17– or 20– year term for patents issuing after 1995 Jun 7 and filed before 1995 Jun 8, provided you pay all three maintenance fees.

2. Please check all fee amounts before paying since PTO fees change often.

3. YAI = Years After Issue date.

4. Send payment at least a month before due date to allow time to take corrective action before entering grace (penalty) period in case PTO does not accept payment.

Fig. 15C—Maintenance Fee Reminder (Form 15-3 in Appendix 7)

licensed your patent to a large entity, check "large entity" on Form 15-4 and pay the large-entity fee.) If the PTO accepts your maintenance fee, they'll send you a Maintenance Fee Statement to this effect. Anyone can sign Form 15-4.

If you use the Certificate of Mailing at the end of the form, you can send in the fee on the last day of the period. If the last day of the period falls on a Saturday, Sunday, or holiday, it's extended to the next business day. And don't forget a postcard! Of course, if you feel, at any time a maintenance fee is due, that your invention's prospects have become nil, you shouldn't pay the fee. In this case, your patent will expire as indicated above.

The PTO won't accept a maintenance fee before its due period and may send you an MF reminder only after the due period expires, when you're in the six-month grace (penalty) period. They also may send you a Notice of Patent Expiration if you don't pay the fee in either the regular or grace periods. The PTO publishes the numbers of lapsed patents in the *Official Gazette*.

I. Legal Options If You Discover an Infringement of Your Patent

As stated in the Inventor's Commandment at the beginning of this chapter, once you get a patent you should monitor all products in its field and be alert for any infringement. If you find an infringer, you may wish that the earth would shake, the skies thunder, and a mighty lightning bolt would come down and vaporize the miscreant. In fact, nothing will happen and the infringement will continue unless you affirmatively do something about it. Although some think that the PTO plays a role in infringement situations, it doesn't. Rather, the patent owner must assume the full burden for stopping the infringer and obtaining damages. Here, viewed broadly, are the possible steps you can take:

- Ask the infringer to stop infringing and pay you compensation for the past infringement.
- Ask the infringer to pay you compensation for past infringement and royalties for future activity.
- Ask the infringer to buy your patent for a sum that will cover past infringement and the present value of future activity.
- If you're a manufacturer and the infringer has a patent of interest to you, exchange licenses with the infringer.
- Sue the infringer in federal court in the district where the infringer resides or has committed infringement (in the event your request is unsuccessful). If your suit is successful, you will be awarded damages and will

also get an injunction, precluding the infringer from using your invention in the future, during the remaining term of the patent.

The injunction is an order signed by a federal court, which, if violated, can subject the violator to contempt-of-court sanctions, including imprisonment and fines. Damages will be equivalent to a reasonable royalty you could have gotten had you licensed the patent or the profits the infringer made. In exceptional cases—if the infringer's conduct was flagrant or in bad faith—you may also be able to recover attorney fees and/or triple damages. Patent infringement damages and fees thus sometimes exceed the defendant-infringer's profits or even gross sales.

J. What to Do About Patent Infringement

Let's now take a closer look at what to do if your patent is infringed.

Step 1: Obtain Details of the Infringement

If you discover what you believe to be an infringement of your patent, obtain as many details and particulars about the infringing device or process and infringer as possible. To do this, procure service manuals, photographs, actual samples of the infringing device, advertisements, product-catalog sheets, etc., plus details of the individual or company that is committing the infringement.

Step 2: Compare Your Broadest Claim With Infringing Device

I have encountered many inventors, who, after being awarded a patent, somehow get the notion that it covers everything in the field, no matter what the claims recite. Of course, you'll know this isn't true if you understood the purpose of claims, discussed at the beginning of Chapter 9. A patent covers only what the claims recite, plus their equivalents and contributory components (see Steps 3 and 4, below). Thus you must compare your patent's claims with the physical nature of the infringing device or process.

To infringe your patent, the device in question must physically have or perform all of the elements contained in your patent's main or broadest claims. Even if the infringing device has additional elements, it will still infringe. For example, if your claim recites three elements, A, B, and C, and the infringing device has four elements, A, B, C, and D, it will infringe. But if the infringing device has only two of the three elements, A and B, it won't infringe. Similarly, if the supposed infringing device has three elements A, B, and

C′, it won't infringe, provided element C of your claim doesn't read on element C′ of the supposed infringing device. A patent claim is, in effect, a little statute that says, "If each and every one of the following elements is met, infringement occurs; if not all elements are met, there is no infringement; and if more than all elements claimed are present, infringement still occurs."

Each dependent claim incorporates all of the limitations of its superior claim(s) and is considered independently of its superior claim(s), even if its superior claim(s) are held invalid.

Moreover, even if your patent has 50 claims, you need prove that only one claim is infringed to prove infringement; your damages do not depend upon the number of claims which are infringed. And even if your claims don't literally read on the infringing device, there are still two ways you may be able to bag the infringer: the "doctrine of equivalents" and the "doctrine of contributory infringement."

Step 3: Apply the Doctrine of Equivalents

The law, recognizing that humans aren't perfect, provides an out if the essence of an invention is copied, but the claims aren't literally infringed. Under the doctrine of equivalents, even if each element of a patent's claim is not literally met by an element of the device, so long as the element of the device is the "equivalent" of the claimed element, the device can still infringe that element. A device element is equivalent if it performs the same function in the same way to achieve the same result as the claim element, or the role of the device element is substantially the same as that of the claim element. However, this doctrine does not apply if "file wrapper estoppel" exists, that is, the claim element was amended during prosecution to define over prior art.

EXAMPLE: Minerva Murgatroid of San Francisco has a patent on a mechanism for bunching broccoli. Its main claim recites the mechanism, including a recitation that the broccoli is banded with a wire-reinforced paper band. She didn't claim the band more broadly because she didn't read Chapter 9 and think to do so, this being the only type of band that would work at the time she got the patent.

A few years later, LeRoy Phillips of Philadelphia discovers a plastic broccoli band that will work just as well as Minerva's wire-reinforced band. He makes broccoli-banding machines and sells them, with his plastic bands, to Fred Farmer, who uses them to band broccoli on his farm in Fresno. Minerva can sue either LeRoy in Philadelphia or Fred in Fresno. Even though her main claim doesn't literally read on LeRoy's machine (that is, describe all of its physical elements), she can win the infringement suit since his plastic band is equivalent in structure, function, and result to the wire and paper band, the band material being a relatively minor change that won't get LeRoy or Fred off the hook.

THE NEGATIVE DOCTRINE OF EQUIVALENTS

There's a rarely used converse of the doctrine of equivalents, the so-called negative doctrine of equivalents. Under this, even if your claims literally read on the infringing device, but the infringing device has a different structure, function, or result than your invention, the device may be held not to infringe.

Step 4: Consider Whether a Contributory Infringement Has Occurred

If your claims don't read on the infringing device, but the infringing device is a specially made component that's only useful in a machine covered by your patent, the infringer may be liable under the doctrine of contributory infringement.

EXAMPLE: In the example above, LeRoy makes an entire broccoli-banding machine like Minerva's, except that he doesn't sell or supply any bands. Minerva's claims don't literally read on LeRoy's machine since her claims recite the band. Nevertheless, Minerva can bag Fred under the doctrine of contributory infringement, since his broccoli-banding machine is useful only in the machine of Minerva's patent claim and since it has no other non-infringing use.

Step 5: Find a Patent Attorney

When you first reasonably suspect that an infringement is occurring, you should promptly consult with a patent attorney. (See Chapter 6, Section F.) This is because you'll need to embark on a course of action that is very difficult for the non-lawyer to perform in its entirety. Unfortunately, the cost is high, and few patent attorneys will take this type of case on a contingent fee (you pay them only if you win). This means you'll have to pay the attorney up front (or at least partially up front). It depends on the complexity of your case, but an initial retainer of $10,000 would be typical. However, if you've got a very strong case and if the infringer is solvent (would be good for the damages if you win), it's possible that you may find an attorney who will take your case on a contingent-fee basis. If you do get an attorney to do this, you still may have to pay the out-of-pocket costs through trial; these can run as high as $50,000, so be sure you can afford them.

If, as will usually happen, you can't get a contingent-fee arrangement, you should be prepared for a shock: patent trial attorneys generally charge about $150 to $350 per hour, and a full-blown infringement suit can run to hundreds or even thousands of hours' work, most of it before trial! The American Intellectual Property Law Association, a trade group for patent attorneys, estimates the median cost of patent infringement actions for each side is $280,000 up to trial, and $518,000 through trial. You should be sure that your damages, if you win, will make this worthwhile. Also, be sure the defendant can pay any judgment you obtain. And don't depend on getting attorney fees or triple damages; these are awarded only in "exceptional cases"—that is, those where the defendant's conduct was flagrant.

Of course, what's sauce for the goose is sauce for the gander: since the infringer will usually have the same fee burden, he or she may be inclined to settle if your attorney writes a few letters and he or she thinks you're serious about suing. A substantial number of cases are in fact settled before suit is even brought and most are settled before trial.

Suits for patent infringement must be brought in federal court in the district where the infringer (who may be a corporation) resides, or is headquartered, or where the infringer has any place of business and has made, used, or sold the patented invention. Thus, if possible, you should select an attorney whose office is in one of these locations. If you do decide to do the substantial part of this yourself, especially where filing and prosecuting your case in court is involved, you'll need expert guidance that's beyond the scope of this book. I recommend *Patent Litigation: Procedure & Tactics*, by R. S. White, as a primary resource if you plan to conduct your own litigation.

The material in the following steps is not intended to help you do your own patent infringement litigation (it would take a big book just to get you started), but to give you an overview of what's involved so that you can play an active role in deciding on your course of action and, if a lawsuit is brought, helping your attorney bring its prosecution to a successful conclusion.

Step 6: Write a Letter

The first step to follow in the event an infringement has occurred is to write a letter. This letter can:

- Ask the infringer to stop infringing your patent and to pay you royalties for past activity, or
- Offer the infringer a license under your patent for future activity and again ask for a settlement for the past. Remember, any infringer is a potential licensee, so don't make war right away.

As is often the case, the letter may go unanswered, or your demands may not be acceded to. If so, you'll have to sue for patent infringement if you want to recover damages or an injunction. Also, if you actually charge anyone with infringement, rather than just offer a license, be prepared to follow through with a suit, since the infringer can sue you to have your patent declared invalid under what is known as a "declaratory judgment action."

Step 7: Act Promptly

The statute of limitations for patent infringement is six years, which means you cannot recover damages that occurred more than six years back from the date you filed suit. However, despite this rather lengthy limitations period, it's important that you not wait six years, but act rapidly once you become aware of an infringement. Otherwise, the infringer may reasonably argue that it continued to infringe because you appeared not to be concerned, and you may be prevented from collecting the bulk of the damages you would otherwise be entitled to. This would occur under the legal doctrines known as *estoppel* and *laches*, which generally mean that a court won't award you damages if your action (or lack of action in this case) in some way brought them about.

If you're selling a product embodying the invention and you failed to mark it with the patent number (see Section D, above), the six-year term of damages can be considerably shortened as a practical matter by application of the patent-marking statute (35 USC 287). On the other hand, you can bring suit even after your patent has expired and still go back six years during the time the patent was in force (again, provided that you had some valid reason for delaying your action).

Step 8: Who Should Be Sued?

Obviously, you can sue any manufacturer who makes, uses, sells, imports, or offers for sale any device or practices any process covered by the claims of your patent. You must bring suit against the manufacturer where (1) it has a place of business, and (2) has committed an act of infringement. (If you have a process patent which covers a process used abroad to make a device that is imported into the U.S., under a new statute, the device will be considered to infringe.)

You can also sue the retailer or ultimate purchaser of the invention (including a private individual) as well as the manufacturer. Suits against the retailer or customer are sometimes brought in order to find a court that's favorable, or at least geographically close, to the patent owner. If a suit is brought against the retailer or customer of a patented invention, under the Uniform Commercial Code the manufacturer of the patented invention must step in and defend or reimburse the customer's suit. If your infringer is an out-of-state manufacturer and you can sue its local retailer, it puts a tremendous burden on the manufacturer to defend at a distance.

IF THE INFRINGER HAS A GOVERNMENT CONTRACT

If the infringer of your patent is a company or individual who's making products embodying your invention under a government contract, you can sue only the government in the Court of Claims in Washington. You can't sue the company and you can't sue in your local jurisdiction. Moreover, you can't get an injunction prohibiting the company from manufacturing your invention, since the infringing device may be useful for national defense. In other words, we have compulsory licensing of any patent that covers an invention used by the government. You can, however, recover damages and interest.

Lastly, don't be afraid to take on a big company simply because they have more resources to defend a patent infringement suit than you have to prosecute it. You have the right to a jury trial. (See Section N, below) which more than equalizes the odds.

See the article, "The Truth About Patent Litigation for Patent Owners Contemplating Suit," by Vanderburg, at p. 331 of the *Journal of the Patent and Trademark Office Society* for 1991 April.

Step 9: Consider Stopping Importation of the Infringing Device

In addition, or as an alternative, to suing, if a device covered by your invention is being imported into the U.S. and the effect of such importation is to harm or prevent the establishment of a U.S. industry, or restrain or monopolize trade in the U.S., you can bring a proceeding before the International Trade Commission to have the device stopped at the port of entry. While such a proceeding is complex and expensive, it provides a remedy that is extremely powerful. The pertinent statute is 19 USC 1337(a), and two articles about ITC actions can be found in the *Journal of the Patent Office Society* for 1979 Mar., p. 115, and 1984 Dec., p. 660.

Step 10: Consider Ordering a Customs Survey

As an economical alternative to suing or filing an ITC action, you can order the U.S. Customs Service to make an import survey for two, four, or six months (cost: $1,000, $1,500, or $2,000, respectively) to determine the address of any importer whose goods appear to infringe. While such a survey will not stop any importation, it will provide you with valuable information and will delay the infringing goods, thereby burdening the importer. Write to Commissioner of Customs, Attn.: IPR Branch, Room 2104, U.S. Customs Service, 1301 Constitution Ave., Washington, DC 20229, for an import survey application.

DESIGN PATENT INFRINGEMENT

If you have a design patent, infringement is determined by the "eyeball" method: the drawings of the design patent are first compared with the prior art to determine the scope or novelty of the design invention. Then, with this in mind, they're compared with the accused infringing design to see if it incorporates the innovative essence or novelty of the design. As in most evidentiary trials, both sides will call in their "hired guns" (experts) to testify for their side; the trier of fact (jury or judge) will decide which side's experts are more convincing.

K. Product Clearance (Can I Legally Copy or Make That?)

This is the other side of the coin: Here I'll assume that, instead of having your own invention, you're interested in copying the invention or product of someone else or making a new product that you feel may be covered by someone else's patent. What can you legally do and how do you find out?

1. Common Misconceptions

Before giving you the applicable rules and information, first I want to dispel some widespread misconceptions so you'll start from neutral territory.

Common Misconception: If you make an identical copy of a device or circuit, you can be validly sued for infringement, even if the copied device is not patented.

Fact: You are free to copy any device or circuit, even to the minutest detail, so long as you do not infringe any applicable patent, trademark, or copyright, and so long as you don't copy any features that have a "secondary meaning." (See Chapter 1, Section R.)

Common Misconception: If a product is not marked "Patented" and it does not have a patent number, you are free to copy the product since the law requires patented products to be marked with the legend "Patented" and the patent number.

Fact: Patented products don't have to be marked as such: See "Patent Number Marking" (Section D).

Common Misconception: If a product that you intend to make is shown in the drawing of another's patent, you would be an infringer of that patent if you made the product.

Fact: Only the claims of a patent determine infringement. (See Chapters 9, 13, and Section J, above.)

Common Misconception: That which you do in your own home or for your own personal use will not infringe a patent that is otherwise applicable.

Fact: While "home infringement" may be difficult to detect, nevertheless it is a form of infringement that is legally actionable and can subject the infringer to paying damages and/or an injunction prohibiting further infringement.

Common Misconception: If you change a patented product a fixed percentage, say 20%, you won't be an infringer.

Fact: The amount you'll have to change a patented product to avoid infringement is not subject to quantitative analysis, but rather is determined by the breadth of the patent's claims. (See Section J, above.)

2. Find Out If There's an Applicable Patent and Whether You Will Infringe It

If you do want to manufacture a specific product or perform a specific process commercially, and you have some reason to believe it may be covered by an in-force patent or pending application, how can you find out whether you can proceed without infringing the patent in the process, or without infringing a patent that will issue in the future?

Unfortunately, there is no way to be 100% sure, because no search can cover pending patent applications. However I can give you some pretty specific instructions and guidelines.

If the process or product you wish to duplicate is already manufactured or used, look at the product, the literature accompanying it, and the packing material, to see if any patent number is given. If you can get the patent number, order the patent from the PTO. If the patent issued before 1995 Jun 8, it expired (or expires) 17 years from issue. Here's a rough guide that will help you make a rough determination as to when any patent issued: Patent #1 issued in 1836, #100,000 in 1870; #500,000 in 1893; #1,000,000 in 1911; #1,500,000 in 1924; #2,000,000 in 1935; #2,500,000 in 1950; #3,000,000 in 1961; #3,500,000 in 1970; #4,000,000 in 1977; #4,500,000 in 1985; #5,000,000 in 1991.

If the patent is in force, things usually aren't as bad as they seem. Often a patent that supposedly covers a product in reality may cover only a minor aspect of the product (such as the housing) that is easy to design around. Sometimes the patent doesn't cover the product at all: How can you be sure? The only way is to read its claims carefully, diagramming them if necessary, to know exactly what they cover. If what you want to manufacture is not covered by the claims, and if you feel there is no other patent on the item you wish to manufacture, you are free to do so.

If the product or process you wish to manufacture is simply marked "Patented" and carries no number, your task is more difficult. You can write to the company, asking for the number and date of their patent, or whether their patent is in force, but they're not bound to answer, and you'll have tipped your hand by communicating with them.

You can have a (relatively cheap) search made in the PTO of all of the patents issued to the company in question.

AFTER YOUR PATENT ISSUES: USE, MAINTENANCE AND INFRINGEMENT

Computer searches are good for this. (see Chapter 6, Section M). But there is no guarantee that this will uncover the manufacturer, since the patent may not be owned by the company in question; the manufacturer may simply be a licensee. The best way to determine whether an in-force patent is applicable is to make a search in the relevant classes and subclasses of the PTO (see Chapter 6), or have someone make the search for you. The search should seek to find any patent on the invention in question. This will involve a greater expenditure, but at least you will be fairly certain of your position. If, however, there is a patent pending on the product or process, there is no way to obtain any details, even if the manufacturer makes the product "patent pending"; thus, not all risks can be eliminated.

If the product or process you wish to manufacture has been known or used in the marketplace for over 17 years, you can be pretty sure that no in-force patent will be applicable, or that even if one is applicable, it is just about to expire anyway.

If you can't find any U.S. patents and the product or process is relatively new, you shouldn't feel free to copy it, because it may be the subject of a pending patent application. Although you can't search pending patent applications, since they're kept secret, you can often find some pending U.S. applications by searching for published corresponding foreign applications, which are published 18 months after filing. (To search published foreign applications, use one of the database searching services listed in Chapter 6, Section M.) Also, if the probable owner of a patent application you want to research has been selling the product under a trademark, such as "the Zorch widget," investigate the item in the PTO (trademark applications are not kept secret) to obtain the date of first use of the trademark in the United States. It's likely that the filing date of any patent application is just before the date of first trademark use.

If you find an applicable in-force patent or patent application, and you don't think you can break it, avoid it, or get a license at a reasonable royalty, consider designing around the patent or using older (non-patented) technology.

3. What to Do If an In-Force Patent Is Applicable

If there is an in-force patent applicable, and you still wish to manufacture the product, you have several alternatives:

- Although I don't advise it, some companies manufacture or use the product or process and hope that the patentee won't catch them. When they do this, they usually follow a good accounting practice, by keeping reasonable royalty reserves (see Chapter 16 for what is a reasonable royalty) in case they're ever caught. Also, they usually analyze the patent, or have a patent

attorney do so, to see if there are any good defenses to show that they were not a "willful" infringer, since willful infringers may be subject to triple damages or attorney fees in a lawsuit. They must always be aware that the patent owner may discover the infringement, and sue them, and get an injunction prohibiting further manufacturing. Although the idea of manufacturing without a license may seem deceitful, risky, and inadvisable, it is done frequently in U.S. (but not Japanese) industry; the infringer simply takes the full-speed-ahead-and-damn-the-torpedoes attitude and hopes to be able to negotiate a favorable settlement or break the patent if caught.

- You can ask the patent owner for a license to manufacture under the in-force patent. However, here you take the risk, if you aren't familiar with the patent owner's practices, of being refused a license. Moreover, you'll have shown your hand, so that if you do manufacture, the patent owner will be looking out for you and will certainly sue or accuse you of infringement in short order.

- You can make an extended validity search to try to "break" the patent. You should use a professional, experienced searcher to do this and should expect to spend a thousand or more dollars in order to make the widest and most complete search possible. Also, you should order a copy of the PTO's file of the patent (see Fee Schedule for cost) to see if there are any weaknesses or flaws in the patent that are not apparent from the printed patent itself. Again, the services of an experienced attorney should be employed here, because breaking patents requires a highly skilled practitioner.

- If you find highly relevant prior art, you can bring it to the attention of the patent owner and ask it to disclaim or dedicate the patent to the public. Or, you can send the art to the PTO to be put in the file of the patent (35 USC 301) or apply to have the patent re-examined (35 USC 302; see Section M, below). You can even sue the patent owner, if it has asserted the patent against you, for a judgment declaring the patent invalid. Be careful, however: Charlie Hall, the inventor of the waterbed, asserted his patent against Intex, a large waterbed manufacturer, offering them a fully paid license for only $25,000. Intex thought Hall's patent was invalid, however, so it sued him to have his patent declared invalid. Hall countersued for patent infringement. After many years of trials and appeals, Hall collected a jury award of $6,814,554.21.

- Your last alternative is to review the claims of the patent and then try to design around them. Often you will find that the claims of a patent, upon analysis, have one or more limitations that can be eliminated in your product or process so that you can make the patented invention even cheaper than the patentee. Alternatively, you can design around one of the elements of the patent, make an improved device, and get your own patent on it. Remember, if you don't infringe the independent claims, you won't have to worry about the dependent claims. (See Chapters 9 and 13, and Section J, above.)

4. If No In-Force Patent Is Applicable

Unless there is an in-force patent covering an item, anyone is free to make and manufacture identical copies of it, provided:

- One doesn't copy the trademark of the product
- The shape of the product itself is not considered a trademark (such as the shape of the *Fotomat* huts), and
- You don't copy "secondary meaning" features. (See Chapter 1.)

If you buy a product from another in the course of business, you don't have to worry about patent infringement. Under the Uniform Commercial Code, your vendor is obligated to indemnify you for any such infringement, although, technically, you can be validly sued for infringement.

I am reminded of the story of one manufacturer's effort to copy a small hardware item by having it manufactured cheaply in the Orient. He sent the item overseas with instructions to make several thousand identical copies of the item. Since he didn't give any further instructions, the Oriental manufacturer did as instructed, manufacturing and shipping back several thousand copies of the item, including a faithful copy of the embossed trademark of the manufacturer's competitor. The manufacturer then had to spend significant money obliterating the trademark, thereby losing his entire profit in the process.

L. The Court of Appeals for the Federal Circuit (CAFC)

Full-blown patent infringement suits are very expensive and can cost each side hundreds of thousands, and even millions, of dollars in attorney fees, travel and deposition expenses, witness fees, and telephone and secretarial expenses. Also, patent litigation can take one to ten years to complete. Thus, litigation favors wealthy or large corporations, which are far better equipped to defend and maintain

patent infringement suits than a single individual. In the past, if you discovered an infringement, it was usually to your advantage not to sue and to accept a settlement that was less than you thought you were owed. In short, "gold ruled the law."

The pendulum recently has swung back strongly in favor of the patent owner, however, primarily because of several important statutory and common-law changes. One of these is the Court of Appeals for the Federal Circuit (CAFC). All patent appeals, both from the PTO's refusal to grant a patent and from judgments in infringement suits brought in the U.S. District Courts around the country (federal trial courts are where patent infringement actions are first brought and decided), are now heard by the CAFC, which is headquartered in Washington, DC, but which travels around the U.S. to hear appeals in major cities. This means that one court decides all appeals and thus creates a body of legal interpretation that's uniform. Previously, appeals were decided by the various Circuit Courts of Appeal covering the area of the country where the U.S. District Court was located, with a resulting patchwork quilt of inconsistent decisions.

One happy result of the uniformity brought by CAFC has been the upholding of more patents and higher damage awards for infringement. While, as mentioned, patent infringement lawsuits and trials must still be brought and conducted in local U.S. District Courts, all of these courts are bound to follow the more pro-patentee decisions of the CAFC (under principles of common-law precedent).

Another pro-patentee change is the greater availability of a most powerful weapon—the preliminary injunction. Formerly, courts would grant a preliminary injunction (court order prohibiting the infringer from continuing the infringing activity) only if it appeared that, beyond question, the patentee would win. Now all the patentee need prove is a "reasonable likelihood of success."

M. Using the Re-Examination Process to Reduce the Expense of Patent Infringement Suits

Another valuable statutory change is the re-examination process (35 USC 302) in which the PTO can be asked to re-examine any in-force patent to determine whether prior art newly called to its attention knocks out one or more of the patent's claims. How does this help the patent holder? Suppose the patent holder decides to go after an infringer. Very soon after the first demand letter is sent, or suit is filed, the infringer will make a search and tell the patent holder of prior art that the infringer feels invalidates one or more claims in the patent. Formerly, if it still thought its patent was valid, the patent holder had to push ahead with an expensive patent infringement lawsuit and hope that the U.S. District Court judge (who is often unfamiliar with patent principles) would decide its way instead of for the infringer.

Now, instead of leaving the matter up to the judge, the patent holder can request a re-examination by the PTO—the request can be made before or during an infringement lawsuit. The PTO will re-examine the claims in light of the prior art and either issue a certificate of patentability, or unpatentability. In the case of the former, this opinion will weigh almost conclusively in favor of the patent holder in the ensuing litigation and quite often will lead to a favorable settlement beforehand. In the event the latter occurs (certificate of unpatentability), the unpatentable claims would be canceled automatically by the PTO. This would not result in victory for the patent holder, but would save time and money that otherwise would have been spent haggling in court.

The re-examination process can also be used to your advantage if you're accused of infringement. By obtaining a PTO certification that the patent holder's claims are unpatentable over the prior art, you may save yourself an expensive defense in court.

To institute a re-examination of any patent, anyone can file a request, together with the patent number, prior art, and the fee. (See Fee Schedule.) The fee appears huge, but is small compared with the expense of litigation. If the PTO feels that the prior art is relevant, it will conduct the re-examination; both sides can file a brief setting forth their arguments. If the PTO feels the newly cited art isn't relevant, it will terminate the proceeding and refund a large part of the fee.

N. Jury Trials

Juries love patent holders and have awarded very large damages in patent infringement actions, especially where an individual patent holder has sued a large corporation. Thus, if you sue on a patent, always demand a jury trial: most juries love injured individual inventors and usually award more than a judge will. Be aware, however, that the Supreme Court has recently removed much of juries' powers to decide the issue of infringement.

O. Arbitration

Instead of a lawsuit, if both parties agree, the entire infringement dispute can now be submitted to arbitration. In this case, an arbitrator, usually a patent attorney or retired judge, will hear from both sides in a relatively informal proceeding. The arbitrator will adjudicate the patent's validity, infringement, etc. The arbitrator's fee (about $5,000 to $20,000 and up) is far cheaper than the cost of a regular lawsuit complete with depositions, formal interrogatories, and other formal proceedings. In addition, it's much faster. Any arbitrator's award must be filed with the PTO. The American Arbitration Association is frequently used and has rules for arbitration of patent disputes, but the parties can use any arbitrator(s) they choose.

P. How Patent Rights Can Be Forfeited

Patents and their claims can be and often are retroactively declared invalid or unenforceable by the PTO or the courts for various reasons, such as:

- Relevant prior art that wasn't previously uncovered (Chapter 6)
- Public use or sale of the invention prior to the filing date of the patent application (Chapter 5, Section E)
- Misuse of the patent by its owner—for example, by committing antitrust violations, and

• Fraud on the PTO committed by the inventor—for example, by failing to reveal relevant facts about the invention and the prior art (Chapter 10, Section G).

In addition to losing your patent rights, you may discover that what you thought was a broad claim is so narrow as to be virtually useless. Generally, you'll discover this when your airtight infringement action goes down the drain when the PTO or the judge declares your patent non-infringed.

Most people are surprised to learn that patents, even though duly and legally issued, can be declared invalid, nonenforceable, or non-infringed. In other words, a patent isn't the invincible weapon many believe it to be. Rather, a patent can be defeated if it has weaknesses or if it isn't used in the proper manner. Still, 50% of patents that get to court are upheld. In addition, the percentage of patents that are treated as valid is higher than the court statistics indicate, since they don't count the many patents that don't get to court because the infringers saw the impossibility of invalidating them or didn't want to spend the $150,000 or more necessary to fight the patent.

An accused infringer of a patent can avoid liability (that is—defend against the infringement action) in three different ways:

• By showing that the claims of the patent aren't infringed
• By showing that the patent isn't enforceable, or
• By showing that the patent is invalid.

With regard to the first, non-infringement has already been covered above in Section J. Under the second, a patent can be declared nonenforceable if the owner of the patent has misused the patent in some way or has engaged in some illegal conduct that makes it inequitable for the owner to enforce the patent. Some examples of conduct that will preclude enforceability of a patent are:

• False marking (marking products with patent numbers that don't cover the product marked)
• Illegal licensing practices, such as false threats of infringement
• Various antitrust violations, such as package licensing
• Extended delay in bringing suit, which works to the prejudice of the accused infringer, and
• Fraud on the PTO, such as withholding a valuable reference from your Information Disclosure Statement, or failing to disclose the full and truthful information about your invention in your patent application. (See Inventor's Commandment #15 in Chapter 10.)

Third, the validity of the patent being sued on can be challenged by:

• Prior-art references that the PTO didn't discover or use properly
• Proof that the specific machine covered by the patent is inoperable
• A showing that disclosure of the patent is incomplete, that is, it doesn't teach one skilled in the art to make and use the patented invention
• A showing that the claims are too vague and indefinite under Section 112, or
• A showing that the patent was issued to the wrong inventor, etc.

As you can imagine, the subjects of patent non-enforceability and invalidity are also complex and difficult. In fact, it has been said that if enough money is spent, almost any patent can be "broken." However, patents are respected in many quarters and, as stated, billions of dollars change hands in the United States each year for the licensing and sale of patent rights.

Q. Your Patent Is Subject to Interference for One Year

For one year following the issuance of your patent, you are potentially subject to losing it if another inventor who has a pending application on the same invention can get the PTO to declare an interference. If the other inventor wins "priority" in the interference—that is, the PTO finds that the other inventor "reduced the invention to practice" (built and tested it or filed a patent application) before you, or conceived it first and was diligent in effecting a reduction to practice—you'll effectively lose your patent. While conflicts between patent applications and in-force patents are relatively uncommon, they do occur, due to the failure of the examiner to spot the interfering application before your patent issues. (See Chapter 13, Section K, for more on this.)

R. Taxes

I include this brief section because, unfortunately, most inventors give no thought whatever to taxes, either with regard to the money they spend to get their patents, or to the money they make when they sell or license their patents. I say "unfortunately" because the government will effectively subsidize your patent expenses by allowing you to deduct them. Because of space limitations, I can't provide a full guide to all of the patent-tax rules, but here are the basics. You should consult a tax professional or the IRS for the final word:

1. Your patent and invention expenses (search, drafting, models, testing, attorney fees, PTO filing fee, etc.) are deductible. Small disbursements (up to a few hundred dollars) will not generally be questioned if they are expensed (deducted 100% for the year incurred), but larger disbursements must be capitalized and depreciated over the life of the patent, or its estimated life (about 19 years), if it hasn't issued yet. Prosecution expenses can usually be expensed, however. Use Schedule C; the IRS considers that you're in the business of inventing. You can even deduct the cost of this book!

2. If you license your invention on a non-exclusive basis (see Chapter 16), you haven't given away all of your rights, so your royalties are considered ordinary income. Report on Schedule C or Schedule E.

3. If you sell all of your patent rights, or grant a full exclusive license, the IRS considers that you've sold it all; your receipts or royalties, even though received over a long number of years, are considered capital gains; report on Schedule D.

S. Patent Litigation Insurance

Because of the high cost of litigation, a cost assistance service is now available from several companies, including Lloyds of London, and Intellectual Property Insurance Services, Corp., 10503 Timberwood Circle, Louisville, KY 40223, 800-537-7863. These companies will, in return for an annual premium, reimburse the cost of patent enforcement litigation, up to the policy limit. You can even begin coverage while your patent application is pending. However, some companies may have a less-than-optimum rating and some may require you to jump through difficult hoops, such as getting an infringement and validity opinion from an independent attorney, before they will reimburse your expenses.

Also, if you're sued for patent infringement, your own general liability insurance may reimburse you for the cost of defending the suit; see the article about this at p. 527 of the 1991 July *Journal of the Patent and Trademark Office Society*.

CHAPTER

16

Ownership, Assignment, and Licensing of Inventions

INVENTOR'S COMMANDMENT # 29

File the patent application in the names of all actual inventors, but no one else. To transfer part or the entire ownership of an application or patent, the inventor-applicant(s) must sign an *assignment*, and to give permission to practice a claimed invention, they must use a *license agreement*.

INVENTOR'S COMMANDMENT # 30

If a patent has several owners, absent any agreement to the contrary the law permits any owner to practice the invention without accounting to any other owners. All joint owners should consider signing a Joint Owners' Agreement requiring cooperation and sharing of any profits from the patent.

In the simplest possible situation, a single inventor invents something, obtains a patent on it, manufactures it, and markets it directly to the public for the full period that the patent remains in force. In most instances, things are not that simple. Two or more people may be involved in the conception of the invention, and many more in its development and marketing. Established businesses may want to use the invention and be willing to pay large sums for the privilege. Employees and employers may disagree over who owns a particular invention that was developed at least partially on company time or with company materials or facilities. Thus, the entire question of invention ownership and utilization can at times become quite complex.

In this chapter, I outline some of the ways to deal with these various ownership questions and the common agreements that are used in the process. However, because the subject of invention ownership, licensing, and transfer is complicated, you'll probably want to retain a lawyer, if only to review your plans and paperwork.

A. The Property Nature of Patents

Before I begin explaining who owns an invention, it might be helpful to review exactly what patent ownership means. A patent should be thought of as a valuable property right.

This right, as I've stressed elsewhere in this book, gives you the right to exclude others from manufacturing, using, and selling your invention. This means that you have, in effect, an enforceable legal monopoly on the invention for the in-force period of the patent. If you do grant a company permission to use your invention, the law terms this permission a "license." As with most other intangible economic rights—such as the right to operate a business, the right to withdraw money from a bank account, and the right to vote stock in a corporation—patent rights, or a portion of them, can be sold to others, or licensed for a particular use over a particular period of time.

Unless it is patented, an invention has virtually no economic value to its inventor unless it is sold or licensed as a trade secret or with other intellectual property coverage (Chapter 1, Sections G to S). Because such sales are difficult for an inventor to make, patent ownership and invention ownership therefore often amount to the same thing.

B. Who Can Apply for a Patent?

As stated in Chapter 10, Section F, only the true inventor(s) can apply for a patent. As mentioned in Chapter 1, when it comes to eligibility to apply for a patent, the status of the applicant(s)-inventor(s) makes no difference, so long as each is a true inventor. That is, an applicant can be of any nationality, sex, age, or even incarcerated, insane, or deceased. (Insane and dead people can apply for patents through their personal representative.)

What happens to patent ownership if more than one person is involved in a particular invention? If other people are involved in the inventing stage, they're considered joint or co-inventors. Most often, the trick is to determine what type of activity constitutes invention. For instance, if one person came up with the concept of the invention, while the other merely built and tested it—that is, did not contribute any inventive concepts but merely did what any skilled artisan or model maker could do—the second person is not a co-inventor. Similarly, financiers, or others who provided financial, but not technical, input should not be listed as co-inventors.

On the other hand, if one person came up with the idea for an invention and the model maker then came up with valuable suggestions and contributions that went beyond the skill of an ordinary model maker or machinist and made the invention work far better, both people should be named as co-inventors on the patent application (see Chapter 10, Section F), provided the model maker's contribution is present in at least one claim.

The PTO and the courts don't recognize degrees of inventorship. Thus, the order in which the inventors are named on a patent application is legally irrelevant, although the first-named inventor's name will be more prominent in the printed patent.

If the joint inventors invented different parts of the claimed invention, they should keep good records as to what part each invented so that they can change the named inventors if one inventor's part is dropped later in the prosecution. Joint inventors need not have worked together either physically or at the same time, and each need not have made the same type or amount of contribution. To qualify as a co-inventor, as stated, an inventor need merely have contributed something to at least one claim of the application, even if it's a dependent claim.

When two or more persons work on an invention, disputes regarding inventorship sometimes arise later. For example, a model builder may later come back, after an application is filed, and claim to have been wrongfully excluded as a joint applicant. As I stated in Chapter 3, the best way to avoid such problems is for all inventors to keep a lab notebook—that is, a technical diary, which faithfully records all developments and is frequently signed by the inventor(s) and witnesses. In that way the complaining model builder can be answered by positive proof from the true inventor(s). Also using the Consultant's Agreement (Form 4-3) will eliminate many potential disputes. Absent such documentation, or agreement, expensive disputes can arise, with only vague memories to deal with.

It's important to include in your application all the inventors who are true inventors and to exclude those who aren't inventors. If it is discovered later that your inventorship is incorrect, and that the mistake resulted from bad faith, your patent can be held invalid, although this rarely happens. (If you do discover that the wrong inventor(s) is (are) named on a patent or patent application, this can be corrected under Patent Rules 48 or 324.)

Common Misconception: *If you want to make your financier a 50% owner of your invention, it is okay to do this by filing the patent application in both of your names.*

Fact: *A U.S. patent application must be filed in the name(s) of the true inventor(s) only. There are several legitimate ways to convey an interest in your invention to a non-inventor. (See Sections E and F, below.)*

Common Misconception: *If you came up with a bare idea for a valuable invention and your associate "took your ball and ran with it"—that is, built and tested the invention after hundreds of hours of work leading to final success, then your associate must be named as a co-inventor with you.*

Fact: *As stated above, only the true inventor(s)—that is, the one(s) who came up with the inventive concepts created in the claims—should be named as applicant(s). An associate who did only what any model maker would have done should not legally be named as co-inventor, no matter how much work was involved. On the other hand, if your associate contributed inventive concepts that made the invention workable, and that are recited in one or more claims, then the associate should be named as a joint inventor with you.*

C. Joint Owners' Agreement

Problems commonly arise in situations where there are two or more inventors or owners of a patent application or patent. These include questions as to who is entitled to commercially exploit the invention, financial shares, what type of accounting must be performed on partnership books, etc. Fortunately, most of these predictable problems can be ameliorated, if not completely prevented from arising, by the use of a Joint Owners' Agreement (JOA).

A JOA is also desirable because a federal statute (35 USC Section 262) provides that either of the joint owners of a patent may make, use, or sell the patented invention without the consent of and without accounting to (paying) the other joint owner(s). This statute seems unfair since it can work a severe hardship on one joint owner in either of two ways:

1. If one joint owner exploits and derives income from the patent while pushing the other aside, the passive joint owner will not be rewarded for any inventive

contribution (if an inventor) or any capital contribution (if an investor—that is, someone who has bought part of the patent).

2. If one joint owner works hard to engineer and develop a market for the patented product, the other joint owner can step in as a competitor without compensating the engineer or marketing pathmaker for the efforts accomplished.

The JOA that I provide as Form 16-1 prevents these results from occurring and also accomplishes the following:

- Prohibits any joint owner from exploiting the patent without everyone's consent, except that if there is a dissenter, a majority can act if consultation is unsuccessful

- Provides that in case of an equally divided vote, the parties will select an arbiter, whose decision shall control

- Provides that disputes are to be resolved by mediation or binding arbitration if mediation fails

- Provides that the parties shall share profits proportionately, according to their interests in expenditures and income, except that if one party does not agree to an expenditure, the other(s) can advance the amount in question, subject to double reimbursement from any income

- Provides that if an owner desires to manufacture or sell the patented invention, that owner must pay a reasonable royalty to all other owners, including the manufacturing owner.

You should not regard this agreement as cast in stone, but merely as one solution to an unfair statute. You may ignore, modify, add to, or replace this agreement with any understanding you wish, so long as you're aware of the problems of Section 262, as paraphrased above.

The manner of completing the JOA of Form 16-1 is straightforward. Fill it in after or concurrently with an assignment (Section E, below) or a joint patent application (Chapter 10). Fill in the names and respective percentages owned by each at the top of the form, identify the patent application (or patent) next, and have each joint owner sign and date the end of the form. As with all agreements, each joint owner should get and preserve an original signed copy. The JOA should not be filed in the PTO.

Time and space do not allow me to freely explain the possible ramifications of each paragraph in the JOA, or the many possible variations that might be more appropriate to your situation. If you want to be sure that your joint owner's agreement accurately reflects your needs, consult a patent attorney.

D. Special Issues Faced by the Employed Inventor

Many inventors are employed in industries that are at least somewhat related to the inventing they do on their own time. Such inventors naturally have a strong desire to learn what rights, if any, they have on inventions that they make during their employment, both on their own time and when they are on the job. This complex subject is covered in detail in *Who Owns Innovation? The Rights and Obligations of Employers and Employees*, by Spanner (Dow Jones Irwin 1984). I'll just cover the high points here.

Generally, the rights and obligations of employed inventors are covered by the Employment Agreement (EA) they sign with their employer—that is, the EA prevails—unless it conflicts with state law. (See below.) Below is an example (Fig. 16A) of a typical EA.

If you have no EA, you'll own all your inventions, subject to the employer's extensive "shop rights" (that is, a right to use the invention solely for the employer's business, without paying the employee) on inventions made using company time, facilities, or materials.

If you have an EA, it will almost certainly require that you assign (legally transfer) to your employer all inventions, which are:

1. Made during the term of employment. (Note that Form 16A asks you to list all inventions you owned prior to employment; those are excluded from the agreement.)

2. Related to the employer's existing or contemplated business

3. Made by using the employer's time (that is, the time for which the employee is paid), facilities, or materials, or

4. Made as a result of activity within the scope of the employee's duties.

Note that under items 1, 2, and 4, even if an employee makes an invention at home, on the employee's own time, the employer still can be entitled to ownership.

Also, you'll usually be bound to disclose *all* inventions to the employer (so the employer can determine if they're assignable). Lastly, most EAs will require you to keep your employer's trade secrets confidential during and after your employment. Some states, such as California, have enacted statutes (Calif. Labor Code, Sections 2780 et seq. and 2860) prohibiting the employer from requiring the employee to sign any EA that is broader than the foregoing—that is, the employee can't be made to turn over all inventions, no matter where and when made, to the employer, and also stating that everything an employee acquires from the employer (except salary) belongs to the employer.

Agreement

varian

IN CONSIDERATION of my employment or the continuance of my employment by VARIAN ASSOCIATES. I agree as follows:

1. For the purpose of this Agreement the term "the Company" shall include VARIAN ASSOCIATES. its subsidiaries and. or its affiliates in which VARIAN ASSOCIATES now or hereafter during the term of this Agreement owns more than twenty percent of the stock eligible to vote for directors and the assignees and licensees of VARIAN ASSOCIATES, its subsidiaries and affiliates.

2. I agree that all information and know-how. whether or not in writing, of a private, secret or confidential nature concerning the Company's business affairs, including its inventions, products, processes, projects, developments, and plans are and shall be the property of the Company, and I will not disclose the same to unauthorized persons or use the same for any unauthorized purposes without written approval by an officer of the Company, either during or after the term of my employment, until such. time as such information has become public knowledge. I also agree to treat all U. S. Government classified information and material in the manner specified by applicable Government regulations.

3. I agree that all files, letters, memos, reports, sketches, drawings, laboratory notebooks or other written material containing matter of the type set forth in paragraph 2 above which shall come into my custody or possession shall be and are the exclusive property of the Company to be used by me only in the performance of Company duties and that all such records or copies thereof in my custody or possession shall be delivered to the Company upon termination of my employment.

4. I agree that my obligation not to disclose or to use proprietory or confidential information of the types set forth in paragraphs 2 and 3 above also extends to such types of information of customers of the Company or suppliers to the Company who may have disclosed or entrusted such information to the Company or me in the course of business.

5. I hereby assign and agree to assign to the Company or its designee all my right. title and interest in and to all inventions, improvements, discoveries or technical developments, whether or not patentable. which I, solely or jointly with others, may conceive or reduce to practice during the term of my employment and which are conceived or first actually reduced to practice (a) in the utilization by the Company of my services in a technical or professional capacity in the areas of research, development, marketing, management, engineering or manufacturing. or (b) pursuant to any project of which I am a participant or member and that is either financed or directed by the Company, or (c) at the Company's expense, in whole or in part.   All other inventions, improvements, discoveries or technical developments shall remain my property.

6. I agree to promptly disclose to and to cooperate with the Company or its designee, both during and after employment, with respect to the procurement of patents for the establishment and maintenance of the Company's or its designee's rights and interests in said inventions, improvements, discoveries or developments, and to sign all papers which the Company may deem necessary or desirable for the purpose of vesting the Company or its designee with such rights, the expense thereof to be borne by the Company.

7. Since I am to assign to the Company certain inventions which I may conceive or first actually reduce to practice after I enter the employ of the Company, I have listed below all those inventions which I own at this time and which I believe should be brought to the attention of the Company to avoid future misunderstandings as to ownership.

8. I agree that I will make no claim for pecuniary award or compensation under the provisions of the Atomic Energy Act of 1954, as amended, with respect to any invention or discovery made or conceived by me, solely or jointly with others, in the course of or under any contracts that the Company now has or may have pertaining to work for the Atomic Energy Commission during the term of my employment.

DATE _____   EMPLOYEE _____

DATE _____   WITNESS _____

PRIOR INVENTIONS OWNED BY EMPLOYEE
(PLEASE USE REVERSE SIDE IF MORE SPACE IS REQUIRED)

_____

_____

_____

_____

111-1-3 R 1/69

Fig. 16A—Typical Employment Agreement

Suppose an employee makes an invention outside of the scope of her job (for example, an employee of Silicon Valley Chips (SVC) invents a new toilet valve), and her EA requires her to disclose to SVC all inventions made during the term of her employment at SVC. She should disclose the valve to her employer (regardless of whose time it was invented on) and then go ahead and do whatever she wants with it, since she owns it totally.

If the invention is clearly within the scope of the EA, or is in a gray area, I recommend first disclosing it to the employer. If the employer isn't interested in the invention after reviewing it, the employee can apply for a release, a document under which the employer reassigns or returns the invention to the employee (the employer may retain a "shop right" under the release—that is, a nontransferable right to use the invention for its own purposes and business only).

If the invention is in the gray area and the employer wants to exploit the invention, the employee can then try to negotiate some rights, such as a small royalty, or offer to have the matter decided by arbitration. Failing this, a lawsuit may be necessary, but I favor employees disclosing "gray-area" inventions so that their invention will not be engulfed in a cloud of ownership uncertainty.

Most EAs also require the invention-assigning employee to keep good records of inventions made and to cooperate in signing patent applications, giving testimony when needed, even after termination of employment. Most companies give the employee a small cash bonus, usually from one to several hundred dollars, when the employee signs a company patent application. This bonus is not in payment for the signing (the employee's wages are supposed to cover that) but to encourage employees to invent and turn in invention disclosures on their inventions. Some employers, such as Lockheed, give their inventor-employees a generous cut of the royalties from their invention, and some will even set up a subsidiary entity (partly owned by the employee-inventor) to exploit the invention. Most, however, prefer to reward highly creative employees via the salary route.

There is currently legislation as well as voluntary proposals within various engineering organizations to expand the rights of the employed inventor. One of these is to change the U.S. to the German system, where employees own their inventions but usually assign them to their employers in return for a generous cut, such as 20% of the profits or royalties.

E. Assignment of Invention and Patent Rights

Suppose you're an employed inventor and you make an invention on your employer's time and your employer wants to file a patent application on it in your name. This raises a problem. If it's filed in your name, how will the employer get ownership? Since inventions, patent applications, and patents aren't tangible things like a car, money, or goods, you can't transfer ownership by mere delivery, or even by mere delivery with a bill of sale or receipt. To make a transfer of ownership in the arcane patent world, you must sign an "assignment"—a legal document that the law will recognize as effective to make the transfer of ownership.

An assignment for transferring ownership of an invention and its patent application is provided as Form 16-2A (Appendix 7). A cover sheet and fee must be submitted to the PTO with any assignment to be recorded; the cover sheet is provided as Form 16-2B, and the fee is listed in Appendix 4, Fee Schedule. A completed assignment is shown in Fig. 16B.

As indicated, full assignments (transfer of 100% of the invention and its patent application) are usually made by employed inventors ("the assignors") who have agreed, in their EA, to assign all inventions they make within the scope of their employment to their employer (the "assignee"); in these cases the assignee is usually a corporation.

A partial assignment (transfer of less than 100%) is usually made where the assignee (the person getting the transferred interest) has financed all or part of the patent application.

The assignment document presented here, like the Joint Owners' Agreement, is but one of many possible alternatives. If you use it, you may want to change a number of provisions to fit your situation. Also, keep in mind my cautionary note regarding the joint owner's agreement, that is, a consultation with a patent attorney is advisable if you wish to fully understand how this agreement will affect your rights. For example, where there will be many owners of the patent application, the percentage interest of each should be specifically listed in the last sentence of paragraph 1.

To complete the assignment do the following:

Lines 1-3: Insert the names of the assignors (the inventor-patent applicants) on lines 1 and 2 of the first paragraph after "received," and insert their cities and states of residence after "of" on line 3.

Lines 4-6: Do the same for the assignee on line 4.

Line 7: Put the percentage of the patent rights being assigned (normally 100%).

Lines 8-9: Put the title of the invention on line 7.

Assignment of Invention and Patent Application

For value received, _____ Minerva Murgatroid _____ ,

of _Merion Station, PA_ _____

(hereinafter ASSIGNOR), hereby sells, assigns, transfers, and sets over unto _LeRoy Phillips_ ____

of _Philadelphia, PA_ _____

and her or his successors or assigns (hereinafter ASSIGNEE) _100_ % of the following: (A) ASSIGNOR'S

right, title and interest in and to the invention entitled " _____ Fusion System Using_ ____

Psychic Field _____ "

invented by ASSIGNOR; (B) the application for United States patent therefor, signed by ASSIGNOR on

199X Dec. 16 ,U.S. Patent and Trademark Office Serial Number ___ 06/777,432 ___ ,

filed ___ 199X Dec. 21 _____; (C) any patent or reissues of any patent that may be

granted thereon; and (D) any applications which are continuations, continuations-in-part, substitutes, or

divisions of said application. ASSIGNOR authorizes ASSIGNEE To enter the date of signature and/or Serial

Number and Filing Date in the spaces above. ASSIGNOR also authorizes and requests the Assistant Commis-

sioner for Patents to issue any resulting patent(s) as follows: ___ O ___ % to ASSIGNOR and __ 100 ___

% to ASSIGNEE. (The singular shall include the plural and vice versa herein.)

ASSIGNOR hereby further sells, assigns, transfers, and sets over unto ASSIGNEE, the above percentage of
ASSIGNOR'S entire right, title and interest in and to said invention in each and every country foreign to the
United States; and ASSIGNOR further conveys to ASSIGNEE the above percentage of all priority rights resulting
from the above-identified application for United States patent. ASSIGNOR agrees to execute all papers, give any
required testimony and perform other lawful acts, at ASSIGNEE'S expense, as ASSIGNEE may require to enable
ASSIGNEE to perfect ASSIGNEE'S interest in any resulting patent of the United States and countries foreign
thereto, and to acquire, hold, enforce, convey, and uphold the validity of said patent and reissues and extensions
thereof, and ASSIGNEE'S interest therein.

In testimony whereof ASSIGNOR has hereunto set its hand and seal on the date below.

Minerva Murgatroid _____

_____

State: _Pennsylvania_ _____

County: _Montgomery_ _____ } ss

Subscribed and sworn to before me _____ _Dec. 28_ _____ ,199 _X_ .

Henrietta Bossomy _____
Notary Public

SEAL

Fig. 16B—Completed Assignment Form (Form 16-2A in Appendix 7)

Lines 10-12: Put the date the patent application was signed (sometimes termed "executed" in the law) on line 11. If the application has already been filed, also put the serial number of the patent application on line 11 and put the filing date on line 12. Put the percentages owned by the assignor and assignee in the penultimate line of this paragraph.

Then, take the assignment to a notary, sign it before the notary, and have the notary write in the city, county, date, sign the assignment, and affix a notarial seal. While the PTO doesn't require the assignment to be notarized for it to be recorded (see below), it is wise to do so, as assignments that have been notarized are more readily admissible in court, and can be used in some foreign countries, should this ever be necessary.

F.   Record Your Assignment With the PTO

To be fully effective, the assignment must be recorded in the PTO, just as the deed to your house must be recorded with your county clerk. If the assignment is not recorded, and the assignors make a subsequent (fraudulent) assignment to a different assignee who is unaware of the first assignment, the second assignee's rights will prevail over those of the first assignee if the second assignee records the assignment first. This means any assignee should record its assignment as soon as possible after it's signed. To do this, merely send the assignment and cover sheet to the PTO with a recording fee (see Appendix 4, Fee Schedule). The PTO will stamp the assignment with "recording indicia" (a record of the date and place it has been recorded, such as, "Recorded 1995 Mar 14, Reel 2012, Frame 547"), make a copy of the assignment and cover sheet, and return the recorded assignment and cover sheet to the person requesting recording, just as your county's recorder did with the deed to the building in which you're living or working.

If the assignment has been made before the patent application is filed, it is permissible to send the assignment in with the application and have it recorded at that time (see Chapter 10, Section O), provided you fill in the date the application was signed (executed) on the assignment and cover sheet. (You won't be able to insert the serial (application) number or filing date since you don't know those yet.) However, even if the assignment is signed before filing, I prefer to wait until I can add the filing date and application (serial) number to it before sending it in for recording, since this will connect it to the application in an unequivocal way. If you send in the assignment after you file the application, mail the assignments, the cover sheet, a check for the fee, and a receipt postcard to "Box Assignment, Assistant Commissioner for Patents, Washington, DC 20231."

G.   Licensing of Inventions—An Overview

Usually, the owner of a patent application or patent needs to allow others to make and sell the patented invention. Inventors, after all, are rarely also manufacturers. When an inventor gives another permission to manufacture and market an invention in exchange for compensation (such as a royalty or flat payment), it is, as stated, done with a document termed a "license." It is essential that a license agreement be written and signed by the inventor or owner of the patent or patent application (the licensor) and the manufacturer (the licensee). Here are just a few major considerations and terms that can be written into a license agreement:

1. The proposed licensee can buy an option from you (the licensor) under which you give it the exclusive (or nonexclusive) right to obtain a license under your patent application or patent within a fixed time, say two years. The payment for this option can be merely the company's agreement to research and develop your invention (this is a typical arrangement), or it can involve a cash payment. The general rule is that the more you receive up front, the more seriously the licensee will view and promote your invention.

2. As noted, if you grant the company a license, the license can be *exclusive,* under which you agree to license only the company and no one else, or it can be *nonexclusive,* under which you license them but also have the right to license others. Exclusive licenses are more common, since manufacturers want to have a monopoly. Nonexclusive licenses are usually used where a very valuable invention exists and several manufacturers want licenses to get into the business. For example, Pilkington Brothers, the great British glass company, granted many nonexclusive licenses under its float glass patents.

3. The license, if granted, can be for the life of the patent, or just for a limited term, say five years, with an option to renew for succeeding five-year terms.

4. The license can require the payment of an advance that may be recoverable against royalties, or may it be in addition to royalties. You, of course, want to get as much money at the beginning as possible under the old "bird-in-the-hand" theory.

5. The license can require the payment of minimum annual royalty payments during each year of its existence. This is usually done when an exclusive license is granted.

6. The license rights can be transferred ("assigned") by your licensee to another manufacturer, or any such assignment can be prohibited. From your point of view, it's a good idea to try to get a provision included in the agreement prohibiting assignment without your approval.

There are hundreds of other, less important, considerations in licensing, which I won't discuss here. Licensing, as you may have gathered by now, is a difficult, complex subject, and one that requires knowledge as well as negotiation skill. Unfortunately, most invention licensing agreements tend to be tailor-made by large corporations to protect their interests. To date, no good self-help law book deals with the ins and outs of doing this. However, I refer to several standard patent law treatises in Appendix 2, Books of Use and Interest.

It's important to realize that even though you can make a great invention, prepare a patent application on it, and sell it to a manufacturer, you may not be able to represent yourself adequately in negotiating a license agreement unless you're familiar with licensing and adept at business. It's therefore often wise to hire a patent lawyer to review any contract that is offered to you. You'll find this will probably cost several hundred dollars or more, but the money will be

well spent, especially if you have a potentially good deal in the offing.

In fact, most reputable companies would prefer that you be represented by an attorney when you negotiate a license agreement and often give you money to pay an attorney. The reason for this is that an agreement between an unrepresented inventor and a much larger company is likely to be interpreted against the company by the courts. If the inventor is represented by an experienced lawyer, the courts will tend to treat the parties equally if a dispute later arises.

H. Universal License Agreement

If you do feel confident enough to represent yourself, and you're the type of person who can go through a long license agreement with nit-picking skill and then competently negotiate with corporate pros, more power to you. Start your quest by referring to the Universal License Agreement in Appendix 7 (Form 16-3). This agreement can be used to exclusively or nonexclusively license your invention as well as to license know-how. It can also be used to grant a potential licensee an option to evaluate your invention for a given period in return for a payment. As I've said, most companies will either prefer their own license agreement or to make one up from scratch, but you can use the Universal License Agreement for purposes of comparison.

Do you find the agreement long and complex? So do I. To deal with it easily, it's best to consider each of its parts separately. The sample shown (Fig. 16C) is for the first page of an exclusive license with an option grant and a know-how license.

Part 1: The licensor is the party, usually the inventor, who does the licensing, while the licensee is the party who is licensed—that is, given permission to use the invention, patent, know-how, etc.

The Patent Royalty rate is the percentage rate the licensee pays for use of the patent. I made this rate low (2%) purposely, since a know-how license has been granted at a rate of 3% for an overall (total) royalty of 5%. It's usually to an inventor's advantage to license know-how, as well as patent rights, and to make the know-how rate as high a proportion of the total rate as possible. This is because patents can be held invalid and can only be licensed for a limited term (the duration of the patent application plus the approximately 18-year term of the patent), usually a total of about 19 years; whereas a know-how license can extend indefinitely.

A licensing fee (advance) is customarily paid to the licensor upon signing the agreement as a reward for past work. In the agreement, the licensing fee is computed as an estimate of the first year's sales by multiplying (a) the Patent Royalty Rate by (b) the Estimated First Year's Sales in Units by (c) the Estimated Unit Price in dollars. Again, it's usually in the inventor's interest to get as large a signing bonus as possible, and not to have this money be set off against later royalty payments.

The "Exclusive" box is checked, indicating that only the licensee will be entitled to make, use or sell the invention. If the "Nonexclusive" box is checked, the licensor will be able to license others, and the licensee and the licensor will be able to make, use and sell the invention. The title, serial number, and filing date of the patent application are identified next.

The "Minimum Number of Units to Be Sold to Compute Minimum Annual Royalty" (whether or not they are actually sold) is provided to insure that the licensor receives an adequate income from the licensee inasmuch as he can't, under an exclusive license, license others to derive more income. This minimum annual royalty has been computed on the basis of a minimum annual number of units to be sold (rather than a fixed dollar amount) to give the licensor the benefit of inflation in unit price. While the manufacturer can cut the price of the licensed product and thereby reduce its royalty payments to you, it's generally not in its interest to do this, since it will be reducing its profits as well. However, if you want protection against this possibility, you can substitute a fixed dollar amount for the minimum annual royalty.

For the privilege of obtaining an option to exclusively evaluate the invention for the Option Term, an Option Premium (a one-time cash payment) has been paid to the licensor.

The Know-How Royalty Rate is stated and is added to the Patent Royalty Rate to get the total, or Running Royalty Rate.

Part 2: The effective date of the agreement is the date when the last signature is made.

Part 3: Here the Recitals provide the reasons or premises for the agreement. The recitals simply state that the licensor has an invention, a patent application, and possibly know-how, and the licensee desires to evaluate licensor's invention (if an option has been granted) and to make, use, and sell the licensed invention.

Part 4: This covers the parties' rights if an option has been granted. In this case, the regular license grant doesn't take effect yet, but the licensee has the exclusive right to investigate the invention for the option term indicated in Part 1. If the invention is favorable, the licensee will exercise its option and the patent license grant of Part 5 will take effect. If not, the option will not be exercised and all rights will revert to the licensor and the licensor will get the results of the licensee's investigation of the invention.

Part 5: This contains the actual license grant. This comes into play immediately if the invention is licensed or if an option is granted or if the option is granted and exercised. Remember, if an option is granted, the actual license isn't granted until the option is exercised. The license granted (exclusive or nonexclusive) gives the licensee the right to make, use and sell the Licensed Product in the U.S., and it includes any derivative applications and patents (see Chapter 14). If the "know-how" box of Part 1 has been checked, then know-how is also licensed.

Part 6: Know-how is covered in this part. If know-how is licensed, then the licensor is obligated to communicate all of its know-how to the licensee within one month, plus provide up to 80 hours of consultation to the licensee, with travel and other expenses paid by licensee. The licensor disclaims any guarantee that the know-how is workable. The know-how royalty is to be paid for three years and thereafter for so long as the licensee enjoys a U.S. competitive market share of at least 15%. This means that the licensor can enjoy know-how royalty payments indefinitely, provided its know-how was valuable enough to give the licensee a market share of over 15% after three years have passed.

Part 7: This concerns royalties and is the heart of the agreement.

Subpart A: If a Licensing Fee is paid; it's an advance against future royalties. If the estimated Licensing Fee has been computed inaccurately (Part 1) then an adjustment is made when royalties are paid. (Note: It is permissible to draft an agreement whereby the licensing fee is a one-time payment and not an advance against royalties.)

Subpart B: The running royalty is covered and is paid quarterly, within one month after the end of each quarter, together with a report of the sales made in the quarter.

Subpart C: The minimum annual royalty is to be paid if an exclusive license has been granted. The MAR payment is computed using the royalty rate times the minimum number of units of Part 1. Minimum annual royalties start as also stated in Part 1. If the minimum number of units is not sold in any year, the licensee must pay the appropriate makeup difference to the licensor with its payment for the fourth quarter.

Subpart D: If the minimum is not paid by licensee, either due to lack of sufficient sales or licensee's choice, then the license grant will be converted to a nonexclusive one, and the licensor can immediately license others.

Universal License Agreement

1. Parties and Summary of Terms:

Parties: This agreement is between:

Licensor: _Henry Beresofsky_ ,

of _Chernegov, Ukraine_ .

Licensee: _Chernobyl Reactor Works, Inc._ ,

of _Russian Hill, CA_ .

Summary: Type of License: ☒ Exclusive ☐ Nonexclusive

Invention Title: _Perpetual Energy Machine_ .

Patent Application Ser. Nr.: _07/123,456_ , Filing Date: _199X Aug 9_

If Exclusive License, minimum number of units to be sold to compute Minimum Annual Royalty (MAR): _____

MARs start first quarter of _199X_ .

☒ Option Granted: Premium $ _5,000_ For term of: _18_ (months)

Patent Royalty Rate _2.00_ % ☒ Know-How Licensed: Know-How Royalty Rate: _3.00_ %

Total Royalty Rate (Patent Royalty Rate plus Know-How Royalty, if applicable): _5.00_ %.

Estimated 1st year's sales (units): _200_ x Estimated Unit Price $ _1,000.00_

x Total Royalty Rate _5.00_ % = Licensing Fee $ _10,000.00_

2. Effective Date: This agreement shall be effective as of the latter of the signature dates below written and shall be referred to as the Agreement of such date.

3. Recitals:

    A. LICENSOR has developed an invention having the above title and warrants that LICENSOR has filed a patent application on such invention in the U.S. Patent and Trademark Office, which patent application is identified by the above title, Serial Number, and Filing Date. LICENSOR warrants that LICENSOR has full and exclusive right to grant this license on this invention and LICENSOR'S patent application. If the "Know-How Licensed" box above is checked, LICENSOR has also developed know-how in connection with said invention and warrants that LICENSOR owns and has the right to license said know-how.

    B. LICENSEE desires, if the "Option Granted" box above is checked, to exclusively investigate LICENSOR'S above invention for the term indicated. If said "Option Granted" box is not checked, or if said box is checked and LICENSEE investigates LICENSOR'S invention for the term indicated and such investigation is favorable, LICENSEE desires to make, use and sell the products embodying such invention and covered by the claims of LICENSOR'S patent application and any patent(s) issuing thereon (hereinafter "Licensed Product").

4. If Option Granted: If the "Option Granted" box above is checked, then (A) the patent license grant of Part 5 below shall not take effect except as defined in this part, and (B) LICENSOR hereby grants LICENSEE, for the option premium stated above, an exclusive option to investigate LICENSOR'S invention for the term indicated above, such term to commence from the date of this Agreement. LICENSOR will furnish LICENSEE with all information and know-how (if any) concerning LICENSOR'S invention in LICENSOR'S possession. LICENSEE will investigate LICENSOR'S invention for operability, costing, marketing, etc. LICENSEE shall report the results of its investigation to LICENSOR at any time before the end of the option term. If LICENSEE'S determination is favorable, it may thereupon exercise this option and the patent license grant of Part 5 below shall become effective. If LICENSEE'S determination is unfavorable, then said option shall not be exercised and no patent license grant shall take effect and all rights hereunder shall revert to LICENSOR and LICENSEE shall deliver to LICENSOR all results of its investigations for LICENSOR'S benefit.

5. Patent License If Option Exercised or If Option Not Granted: If the "Option Granted" box above is checked and LICENSEE has investigated LICENSOR'S invention and such investigation is favorable and

Fig. 16C—Completed First Page of Universal License Agreement (Form 16-3 in Appendix 7)

Subpart E: If the license is or becomes nonexclusive, then the licensor may not grant more favorable terms to any other licensee.

Subpart F: Patent royalties are not due after the patent expires, or if it is declared invalid, or if no patent is granted.

Subpart G: Late payments earn interest at 10%.

Subpart H: The "Net Factory Sales Price," on which royalties are based, is the factory selling price, less shipping, insurance, taxes, etc., if billed separately. If the units are imported, then the importer's gross selling price is the basis for royalties. The royalty paid on returns is deductible against future royalties.

Part 8: This requires the licensee to keep full records for at least two years after each payment, so that the licensor can verify the royalty payments.

Part 9: Here the licensee's sublicensees are bound by all of the terms of the agreement and the licensee must notify the licensor if it grants sublicenses. A licensee will usually grant a sublicense when it has the licensed product made for it by a contracting company.

Part 10: This simply states the parties' responsibilities for patent prosecution.

Subpart A: Requires the licensor to pay for prosecution of the U.S. patent application, together with the patent maintenance fees that are payable after the patent issues. If the licensor intends to abandon the patent application, it must notify the licensee at least two months in advance to give it the opportunity to take over.

Subpart B: The licensor may file for patent coverage abroad, but if it doesn't do so, then the licensee may do so. If licensor wants to license any foreign licensees, it has to give the licensee the opportunity of first refusal.

Subpart C: If the licensee takes over the U.S. patent prosecution, and is successful, then it can reduce its royalties by 25%, and can deduct its patent prosecution expenses. If the licensee elects to file abroad, then the royalty rate on foreign sales is 50% of the U.S. rate, less foreign prosecution expenses.

Part 11: This requires the licensee to mark products sold with the legend "patent pending" while the patent application is pending and with the patent number (see Chapter 15) after the patent issues.

Part 12: This states that if the patent is infringed, the licensor can sue to enforce its patent rights. If it doesn't choose to do so, the licensee may do so. If the licensee sues, it can keep 75% of this recovery, less costs of the suit.

Part 13-A: This clause states that licensor doesn't guarantee that its patent is valid or that it has any particular scope (breadth).

Part 13-B: This clause states, in effect, that if someone is injured by the patented product, the licensor is not liable.

Part 14: This clause states that the term or maximum duration of the agreement shall be until the last patent of licensor expires, unless know-how is licensed, in which case Part 6 governs the term.

Part 15: This clause covers the situations when the parties may terminate the agreement before the term expires. Under Subparts A and B, the licensor may terminate the agreement if the licensee defaults in making royalty payments, or if it ever declares bankruptcy. Subpart C, the antishelving clause, is very important. This protects the licensor in case the licensee stops production for 1.5 years, or doesn't start production within 1.5 years from the date the license agreement is signed. In these cases, the licensor can terminate the agreement.

Clauses like this one (and others) are designed to put teeth into the agreement to deter the licensee from defaulting: it is not enough to make a fair agreement; all agreements should also be structured to ensure the other party's performance by giving an incentive for performance, or a penalty for nonperformance.

Part 16: This clause states how and where notices under the agreement are to be sent.

Part 17: This clause provides that if the parties have any dispute, they shall submit the matter to mediation. If mediation can't resolve the dispute, the parties must submit the dispute to binding and final arbitration. In no case will the dispute go to a court for resolution, since litigation is extremely expensive and thus works to the detriment of the independent inventor.

Part 18: This clause allows the licensor to assign (legally transfer) its rights to anyone without permission, but the licensee needs advance permission of licensor to assign the licensee's rights unless it makes an assignment to its successor in business.

Part 19: This clause specifies that the laws of licensor's state shall govern interpretation of the agreement. Normally, state law on the interpretation of contracts doesn't vary much, but since a licensor is usually at an economic disadvantage, I've given it the benefit here. Also, it specifies that any lawsuit on the agreement shall be brought in licensor's county.

Part 20: This states that neither party shall take any action that hampers the rights of the other and that both parties shall engage in good faith and fair dealing. This clause is supposed to be read into any agreement, but I've expressly stated it in order to increase cooperation and reduce disputes.

Part 21: This states that in case of any mistake in the agreement, it shall be rectified to conform to the parties' intentions. The clause is designed to save a misdrafted agreement that otherwise might be thrown out.

Part 22: This makes it clear the agreement supersedes prior or concurrent oral, or prior written, understandings.

Part 23: This one states that the parties have carefully read the agreement and have consulted, or have been given an opportunity to consult, counsel and that each has received a signed original. This makes a challenge to the agreement more difficult.

All that remains is to sign and date the agreement. Each party should get an original, ink-signed copy.

Again, let me remind you that while the Universal Agreement incorporates most of the customary terms and covers many common licensing situations, it probably won't be appropriate for your situation without some modification. Obviously, if your arrangement won't fit within the terms of this agreement, or if you don't like any of the "fixed" terms, such as the 80 hours of consultation (Clause 6), the 15% market share (Clause 6), compulsory arbitration (Clause 17), etc., you should propose changes, or hire an expert to help you.

I. How Much Should You Get for Your Invention?

Many inventors seem to believe that patents are almost always licensed at a royalty rate of 5%. The 5% royalty generally means that you get 5% of the money received by

the factory for its sales of the item embodying your invention. This is sometimes termed 5% of the "ex-factory" price. This assumption is simply not true. While 5% is often used as a starting point in many license negotiations, very few licenses are granted at this rate. I've seen them run from 0.1% to 15% of the factory price of the licensed item (as high as 30% of the retail price for software).

As you've guessed, many factors affect the royalty rate. Obviously, the more desirable your invention is to the licensee, the better royalty you'll get, subject to industry norms. Here's a list of some factors that militate in favor of increasing the royalty rate; you should use as many of these as possible in your negotiations: Sales volume, selling price, low competition, profit margin, ingeniousness of product, amount of development work inventor has done, degree to which invention pervades product, size of licensed territory, amount of services or material/parts you furnish, absence of competition between licensee and licensor, degree of respect in field for patents, difficulty of licensee's avoiding patent, difficulty of making agreement, cost savings to licensee, and low start-up costs to implement invention. Of course, your bargaining skill will transcend all of these considerations. As business negotiating seminar leader C.L. Karrass says: "In business, you don't get what you deserve—you get what you negotiate." Also the custom of the industry will dominate—for example, toys usually get a royalty rate of 2.5 to 4%; medical products 6 to 7%. An exclusive license will entitle you to about 50% more than a nonexclusive license.

If your licensee doesn't want to pay the rate you ask, a good technique is to accept the lower rate they're willing to pay, with a proviso that the rate will be increased to the rate you want if "x" number of units are sold.

Instead of a negotiated percentage, some experts advocate getting a royalty equivalent to "one-third of the manufacturer's profit." This means that the company will take its selling price for your invention, say $10, subtract its cost of manufacture, including overhead, say $7, and give you one-third of the difference—that is, $1 = $^1/_3$ of its $3.00 profit. This type of royalty is often enticing to a manufacturer since the company only contemplates parting with a portion of its profit, not paying a fixed sum per item, whether the particular product turns out to be profitable or not. If your licensee is willing to accept this type of royalty, you can substitute this language in the Universal Agreement. But, if you do so, be sure you include an auditing right (such as Clause 8) to insure that you can verify its cost of manufacture.

LUMP SUM PAYMENT

If you're offered a single lump-sum payment for all your rights (this is rare), should you take it, and if so, how much should you get? To answer the first question, only you can decide if a relatively large bird in the hand is worth more than a potential (but by no means assured) stream of smaller, but aggregatively heavier, smaller birds in the bush over the years. To grapple with the second question, estimate the potential sales of your invention for the life of your patent application (one to three years), plus the term of the patent (approximately 18 years), then apply your royalty to this figure, and be willing to take half of this as a single payment lump sum for a fully paid-up license.

For example, suppose you expect your widget to be sold for the next 20 years (two years during patent pendency, and 18 years during life of patent), for an average factory price of 50 cents and an average yearly quantity of 150,000 units, and that application 5% royalty is fair. Applying the formula, the substitute lump-sum payment for your royalty would be 0.5 x 19 x 150,000 x $0.05, or $35,625. If you are offered much less than this, it could very well be unwise to sell.

Don't make Mary Jacobs' mistake. She invented the bra (out of two hankies and a ribbon) and was able to sell her patent for $15,000 in 1914. Although this was a princely sum then, she practically gave it away since (as you know) her invention soon took hold and her patent eventually was worth $15 *million*!

The disadvantage with the alternative lump-sum calculation is that it's very hard to estimate anything about what will happen in the next 20 years. Will sales go up or down? Will the product become obsolete or even more popular? Will competition affect its price, etc.? These are just some of the imponderables and unknowables, so, as stated, be extremely careful before selling your rights for a single lump-sum payment.

If you do have an opportunity to sell your invention, you should use the assignment form (Form 16-2A), changing "For value received" at the beginning of the form to "In exchange for $_____." For obvious reasons, make sure you actually receive the money by certified check or money order before you sign. Do not, under any circumstances, assign your patent in return for a series of payments: if your assignee defaults in the payments, you'll be left without your patent or your money, but with a big legal headache—getting your patent back. If someone wants to buy your patent for a series of payments, see a lawyer or legal forms book and make a suitable license with an agreement to assign only after all payments have been made.

APPENDIX

1

Abbreviations Used in *Patent It Yourself*

Throughout *Patent It Yourself* (PIY) I've used many abbreviations to save space and to spare you the tedium of repeatedly reading long phrases like "Manual of Patent Examining Procedure." I've tried to define each abbreviation the first time I've used it and again if I've used it at a location remote from the first usage. However, in case I've failed to define any abbreviation adequately, here's a list of (hopefully) all the abbreviations I've used in PIY:

A&ARTP	Attorneys and Agents Registered to Practice	GATT	General Agreement on Tariffs and Trade
AF	After Final	GPO	Government Printing Office
AIPO	African Intellectual Property Organization	IC	Inventors' Commandment
BA	Basic Application	IDS	Information Disclosure Statement
BAPI	Board of Appeals & Interferences	ITC	Intentional Trade Commission
BBS	Bulletin Board System	JOA	Joint Owners' Agreement
BNA	Bureau of National Affairs	JPTOS	Journal of the Patent and Trademark Office Society
BRS	Bibliographic Research Services	KISS	Keep It Simple, Stupid
CAD	Computer-Aided Drafting	MAR	Minimum Annual Royalty
CAFC	Court of Appeals for the Federal Circuit	MF	Maintenance Fee
CASSIS	Classification and Search Support Information System	MPEP	Manual of Patent Examining Procedure
CFR	Code of Federal Regulations	N/A	Notice of Allowance
CIP	Continuation-in-Part	N&UR	New and Unexpected Results
CM	Common Misconception; Certificate of Mailing	NCC	Non-Convention Country
CTRP	Constructive Reduction to Practice	NIH	Not Invented Here
D	Design Patent	N(N)C	Normally (Non-) Conductive
DDP	Disclosure Document Program	OA	Office Action
DOE	Department of Energy	OG	*Official Gazette*
DP	Double Patenting	P	Problem
EA	Employment Agreement	PA	Prior Art
EEC	European Economic Community	PAD	Patent Application Declaration
EM	Express Mail	PCT	Patent Cooperation Treaty
EPC	European Treaty Convention	PDL	Patent Depository Library
EPO	European Patent Office	PGL	Paranoia, Greed, Laziness
FDA	Food and Drug Administration	PPA	Provisional Patent Application
FWC	File-Wrapper-Continuing	Pre-Ex	Preliminary to Examination

PTDL	Patent and Trademark Depository Libraries	SPO	Shadow Patent Office
PTMS	Petition To Make Special	SSM	Statutory Subject Matter
PTO	Patent and Trademark Office (U.S.)	TD	Terminal Disclaimer
RPA	Regular Patent Application	TM	Trademark
RTP	Reduced to Practice	TN	Trade Name
S	Solution	TS	Trade Secret
SBA	Small Business Administration	UC	Unfair Competition
SD	Supporting Declaration	UCC	Uniform Commercial Code
SE	Small Entity	USC	United States Code
SED	Small-Entity Declaration	VA	Vanadium Alloy
SIR	Statutory Invention Registration		

■

Books of Use and Interest

It has been said that knowing where to look is half the battle of knowing the law. With this in mind, this section is provided to help you avoid having to hire a patent lawyer in case you encounter any situations or problems which this book does not cover. I've also provided a number of resources and publications I feel will be of interest to inventors and other creative people. I provide comment generally where the title of the book or source isn't self-explanatory. Most books which can't be found in a general or business library may be found in a law library. Most county courthouses and law schools have law libraries. Prices aren't indicated since they change frequently. This list isn't exclusive by any means: if you browse in your bookstore or a patent depository or law library, you'll find many other valuable books of interest.

Government Publications

Annual Index of Patents. Issued yearly in two volumes: *Patentees* and *Titles of Inventions.* U.S. Government Printing Office (GPO), Washington, DC 20402. Comes out long after the end of year to which it pertains—for instance, in September. Available in search and public libraries.

Attorneys and Agents Registered to Practice Before the U.S. Patent and Trademark Office. Annual. GPO. Contains alphabetical and geographical listings of all attorneys and agents.

Classification Definitions. GPO. Many loose-leaf volumes. Contains definitions for each of 66,000 subclasses. Available in search libraries.

Guide for the Preparation of Patent Drawings. GPO.

Index to Classification. Loose-leaf. Contains about 70,000 subclasses and cross-references arranged alphabetically. Search libraries.

Manual of Classification. GPO. Loose-leaf. Contains 300 search classes for patents arranged numerically, together with subclasses in each class. Search libraries.

Manual of Patent Examining Procedure. Revisions issued several times per year. GPO. Called "the patent examiner's bible," the MPEP provides answers to most questions about patent prosecution.

Official Gazette—Patents and O.G.—Trademarks. GPO. Weekly. Lists all patents and TMs issued and registered; also contains latest PCT fees and notices of interest. Available in search and public libraries.

Questions and Answers about Plant Patents. PTO. Free.

Questions and Answers about Trademarks. PTO. Free.

Rules of Practice in Patent Cases. (Title 37, Code of Federal Regulations.) GPO. Revised annually. The PTO's Rules of Practice. A must for all who prosecute their own patent applications. Almost always incomplete due to frequent rule changes. Look in *Official Gazette* (especially the first volume each year) for later rules.

The Story of the U.S. PTO. GPO. 1985.

In addition to being available in paper-bound publications, most of the above publications are now available on CD-ROMs, which are updated quarterly and which may be read on the computer in any Patent and Trademark Depository Library. (See list of libraries in Chapter 6.) They are also available on the Internet. (See Appendix 5, Mail, Telephone, and Computer Communications With the PTO.)

Law Books Relating to Patents

Copyright Your Software, by Fishman, S. Nolo Press, 1994.

Corpus Juris Secundum, vol. 69, Patents. A legal encyclopedia which will answer almost any question on patent law. West Pub. Co., St. Paul, 1958 (supplemented annually). Any law library.

Desk Encyclopedia of Intellectual Property, by McCarthy, J.T. BNA, 1991.

Drafting Patent License Agreements, by Mayers & Brunsvold, 3rd. ed., BNA, 1991.

The Inventor's Notebook, by Grissom, F., & Pressman, D., 2nd ed., Nolo Press, 1996.

Journal of the Patent and TM Office Society. Monthly. Box 2600, Arlington, VA 22202. Contains articles on patent law and advertisements by patent services: for instance, draftspersons, drawing reproducers, searchers.

Landis on The Mechanics of Patent Claim Drafting, by Faber, R., 1990, Practicing Law Institute, 810 Seventh Avenue, New York, NY 10019.

Patent and Trademark Laws. BNA. Revised annually.

The Patent Drawing Book, by Lo, J. and Pressman, D., 1st ed., Nolo Press, 1997.

Patent License Agreements, by Nordhaus, R.C. Jural, Chicago, IL 60626, 1976.

Patent Licensing Transactions—Forms, by Einhorn. Matthew Bender, New York, 1990. Contains many license agreement forms.

Patent Litigation Procedure & Tactics, by White, R.S. Matthew Bender, New York, 1974.

Patents Throughout the World, by Greene, A.M. Clark Boardman, 1980. Revised annually.

Small Business Administration. The SBA's list of free publications has three sections: "Management Aids," "Small Marketer's Aids" and "Small Business Bibliographies." Listed are dozens of excellent, concise business pamphlets, such as No. 82, *Reducing the Risks in Product Development*, and 6.004, *Selecting the Legal Structure for Your Firm.* Order from your local SBA office or SBA, Washington, DC 20416.

Software Development: A Legal Guide, by Fishman, S. Nolo Press, 1994.

Trade Secrets, by Milgrim, R.M. Matthew Bender, New York, 1967.

Walker on Patents (2nd ed. by Deller; 3rd ed. by Lipscomb). Bancroft-Whitney. A comprehensive legal treatise. Law libraries.

General Interest Books and Magazines Relating to Patents, Inventions and Trademarks

The Catalyst, by Harness, Charles R., Esq. Pocket Books, New York, 1980. Science fiction story involving a patent attorney, an invention, and an interference.

Complete Guide to Making Money With Your Ideas and Inventions, by Paige, R.E. Barnes & Noble, New York, 1976. Excellent guide to invention marketing.

Compu-Mark Directory of U.S. Trademarks. Thomson & Thomson, Quincy, MA. Available in search libraries.

Dream Merchant (a magazine for inventors with ads for products wanted and from model makers). 2309 Torrance Blvd., Suite 201, Torrance, CA 90501. Tel. 310-328-1925; Fax 310-328-1844. $16 for six issues/year.

Edison, The Man Who Made the Future, by Clark, R.W. Putnam, New York, 1977.

The Existential Pleasures of Engineering, by Florman, S.C. St. Martins, 1976. A brilliant, eloquent panegyric of technology; a crushing blow to Reich, Mumford, Rozak, et al.

Inventing: How the Masters Did It. Moore Pub., Durham, NC, 1974.

Man of High Fidelity: Edwin Howard Armstrong, by Lessing, L. Lippincott, Philadelphia, 1956. Biography of the inventor of frequency modulation; he committed suicide because of the delays and difficulties of patent litigation against the large radio companies, but his widow eventually collected millions in settlements.

The National Inventors Hall of Fame. *Biographies of Inductees.* NIHF Foundation, Room 1D01, Crystal Plaza 3, 2001 Jefferson Davis Hwy., Arlington, VA 22202. Free.

One Day at Kitty Hawk, by Walsh, J.E. Crowell, New York, 1975. The story of the development and sale of rights to the airplane.

Perpetual Motion: The History of An Obsession, by Ord-Hume, A. St. Martins, 1981. A must if you're filing on a perpetual-motion machine.

Trademark: How to Name a Business & Product, by McGrath, K., & Elias, S., with Sarah Shena. Nolo Press, 1996. The best self-help book on the topic.

Trademark Register of the United States. Annual. Trademark Register, Washington Bldg., Washington, DC 20005. Lists all registered trademarks by subject matter classes.

Publications Relating to Business

Apollo Handbook of Practical Public Relations, by Adams, A.B. Apollo Editions, New York, 1970. How to get publicity.

Applied Sciences and Technology Index. H.W. Wilson Co., Bronx, NY 10452. Lists engineering, scientific, and industrial periodical articles by subject.

Bacon's Publicity Checker—Magazines; Bacon's Publicity Checker—Newspapers. Annual. Bacon Pub. Co., Chicago. Classifies all sources of publicity.

Business Plans That Win $$$: Lessons From the MIT Enterprises Forum, by Rich, S.R., & Gumpert, D. Harper & Row, 1985.

California Manufacturers Register. Annual. 1115 S. Boyle Ave., Los Angeles, CA 90023.

Conover Mast Purchasing Directory. Conover Mast, Denver, CO 80206. Annual. Three volumes. Manufacturers listed alphabetically and by products. Also lists trademarks.

Dun & Bradstreet Reference Book. Six issues per year. Lists three million businesses in the United States and Canada. D&B also publishes specialized reference books and directories, such as *Apparel Trades Book* and *Metalworking Marketing Directory*.

The Entrepreneur's Manual. Brown, D. Ballantine, 1981.

Gale Directory of Publications and Broadcast Media. Annual. Ayer Press, Philadelphia, PA 19106. Lists United States newspapers and magazines geographically.

Getting to Yes; Negotiating Agreements Without Giving In, by Fisher, R., & Ury, W. Penguin, 1991.

Guide to American Directories. 9th ed. B. Klein Pubs., New York, 1975. Lists directories by industry, profession, and function.

How to Market a Product for Under $500! by Dobkin, J. Danielle Adams Pub., Box 100, Merion Station, PA 19066, 1996.

How to Write a Business Plan, by McKeever, M. 4th ed., Nolo Press, 1994.

Innovation and Entrepreneurship, by Drucker, P. Harper & Row, 1985. How any organization can become entrepreneurial.

International Yellow Pages. R.H. Donnelley Corp., New York, NY 10017. Similar to local Yellow Pages, but provides foreign business listings.

MacRae's Blue Book. MacRae's Blue Book Co., Hinsdale, IL 60521. Sources of industrial equipment, products, and materials. Also lists trademarks.

Marketing Without Advertising, by Phillips, M., & Rasberry, S., 2nd ed., Nolo Press, 1997.

The Partnership Book, by Clifford, D., & Warner, R., 5th ed., Nolo Press, 1997.

Pratt's Guide to Venture Capital Sources, Venture Economics, Inc., 1991.

R & D Partnerships, by Petillon, L.R., & Hull, R.J. Clark Boardman, 1985.

Thomas Register of American Manufacturers. Thomas Pub. Co., New York, NY 10001. Eleven volumes. Similar to *Conover Mast Directory* above.

Ulrich's International Periodicals Directory. R.R. Bowker Co., New York, NY 10036. Lists periodicals by subject.

Up Your Own Organization, by Dible, D.M. Entrepreneur Press, c/o Hawthorn Books, New York. How to start and finance a business.

What's What; A Visual Glossary of Everyday Objects, by Bragonier, R., Jr., and Fisher, J. Ballantine, 1981.

Books Relating to Self-Improvement

I believe that the real key to success and happiness, in inventing as well as life, lies principally within each individual's own mind. A positive, optimistic attitude, hard work and perseverance, the willingness to take full responsibility for one's own destiny, and living and thinking mainly in the present time—rather than luck, inherited abilities, and circumstances—are principally responsible for success and happiness. I have therefore provided a list of books whose main purpose is to prime you with the attitude to secure such success and happiness so that you'll be able to use *Patent It Yourself* as effectively as possible.

Explorations in Awareness, by Bois, S. Harper & Row, 1957. Break through mental blocks and preconceptions.

Higher Creativity—Liberating the Unconscious for Breakthrough Insights, by Harman, W., & Rheingold, H., J.P. Tarcher, 1984.

Language in Thought and Action, by Hayakawa, S.I., and A.R. 5th ed. Harcourt Brace Jovanovich, 1991.

Levels of Knowing & Existence, by Weinberg. H. Harper & Row, 1961. A new approach that answers many questions.

A New Guide to Rational Living, by Ellis, A., and Harper, R.A. Wilshire Book Co., Los Angeles, 1975.

People In Quandries, by Johnson, W. Harper & Row, 1946. Classic book on emotional problem solving.

The Psychology of Self-Esteem, by Branden, N. Nash, Los Angeles, 1971.

303 of the World's Worst Predictions, by Coffey, W. Tribeca Communications, Inc.

Your Erroneous Zones, by Dyer, W.W. Funk & Wagnalls, New York, 1976.

■

Glossary

This Glossary[1] provides a list of useful words to describe the hardware, parts, and functions of your invention in the specification and claims. The most esoteric of these words are briefly defined. While some definitions are similar, this is due to space limitations; all words have nuances in meanings.

If you're looking for a word to describe a certain part, look through the list for a likely prospect and then check a dictionary for its precise meaning. If you can't find the right word here, look in your search patents, in *What's What* or another visual dictionary, or in a thesaurus. If you can't find an appropriate word, you'll probably be able to get away with "member" or "means-plus-a-function" language. Also, for new fields, you may invent words, preferably using Latin or Greek roots, as Farnsworth did with "television," or by extending the meaning of words from analogous devices (e.g., "base" for a part of a transistor.) Very technical or specialized fields have their own vocabulary (e.g., "catamenial" in medicine, "syzygy" in astronomy); look in

appropriate tutorial texts for these. The words are grouped loosely by the following functions:

1. Structure
2. Mounting and Fastening
3. Springs
4. Numbers
5. Placement
6. Voids
7. Shape
8. Materials and Properties
9. Optics
10. Fluid Flow
11. Electronics
12. Movement
13. Rotation

[1] Expanded and used with kind permission and thanks from a list originally prepared by Louis B. Applebaum, Esq., of Newport, RI.

1. STRUCTURE

annulus (ring)

apron

arbor (shaft)

arm

bail (arch wire)

band

barrel

bascale (seesaw)

base

beam
 —cantilever
 —simple

belt

bib

blade

blower

board

body

boom

boss (projection)

bougie (body-insertion
 member)

boule (pear-shaped)

branch

breech (back part)

canard (front wing)

carriage

case

chord

cincture (encircling band)

clew (sail part)

column

configuration

container

conveyor

cornice (horiz. top of
 structure)

cover

cylinder

dasher (plunger, churn)

detent

device

die

disparate (dissimilar)

diversion

doctor blade (scraper)

dog (holder)

drum

echelon (staggered line)

element

enclosure

fence (stop on tool)

fillet (narrow strip)

fin

finger

finial

flange

fluke (triangular part)

flute (groove on shaft)

frame

frit (vitreous substance)

frustrum (cut-off area)

furcate (branch)

futtock (curved ship
 timber)

gauge

generatrix (path traced)

gnomon (sundial upright)

grommet

gudgeon (pivot)

gusset (triangular insert)

handle

head

header (base, support)

homologous

housing

hub

jacket

jaw

jib (crane arm)

lagging (support)

leg

lip

list (margin strip)

lobe

magazine

mandrel (tapered axle)

manifold

marginate (w/margin)

medium

member

mullion (dividing strip)

nacelle (pod)

neck

object

panel

particle

partition

piece

piston

placket (slit in garment)

platform

plug

pontoon

portion

post

projection

purlin (horiz. rafter
 support)

pylon (support)

rib

ring

rod

sash (frame)

screed (guide strip)

scroll

sear (catch)

shell

shoe

shoulder

skeleton

sleeve

snorkel

spar (pole support)

spline (projection on shaft)

spoke

sprag (spoke stop)

spur

stanchion

station

stay

stem

stent (stretcher)

step

stepped

stile (dividing strip)

stop

strake (ship plank)

strip

strut

tang (shank, tool)

tine

tip

tongue

trace (pivoted rod)

tracery (scrolling)

track

trave (crossbar)

truss

tuft

turret

tuyere (air pipe)

upright

volar (palm, sole)

wall

warp

woof (weft)

2. MOUNTING & FASTENING

attach

billet (tip of belt)

bolt

busing

cable

clamp

cleat (reinforcer)

clevis (U-shaped pin)

connection

couple

coupling

demountably

docking

dowel

engage

fay (join)

ferrule (barrel)

ferruminate (attach, solder)

fix

gland (sliding holder)

guy wire

harp (lamp shade support)

hold

holder

hook

imbricate (regular overlap)

joint

 —universal

keeper

key

latch

lock

lug

matrix

mount

nail

nut

pin

ribband (holds ribs)

rivet

scarf (notched joint)

screw

seam

seat

secure

set

sliding

solder

springably

support

thrust

weld

3. SPRINGS

air

bias

 —element

coil

compressed

elastic

expanded

helical

 —compression

 —tension

leaf

press

relaxed

resilient

springably

torsional

urge

4. NUMBERS

argument

compound

difference

dividend

divisor

equation

formula

index

lemma

minuend

modulo

multiplicand

multiplicity

multiplier

plurality

power

product

quotient

remainder

subtrahend

variable

5. PLACEMENT (RELATION)

adjacent

aft

aligned

angle

aposition (facing)

array

attached

axial

bottom

close

complementary

concentric

contiguous

contracted

course

crest

disposed

distal

divided

edge

engaged

evert (inside out)

extended

external

face

fiducial (reference)

film

fore

horizontal

integral

intermediate

internal

interposed

juxtaposed

layer

located

lower

mating

meshing

mesial (between)

normal

oblique

obtuse

offset

open

opposed

overlapping

parallel

perpendicular

positioned

projecting

prolapsed (out of place)

proximal

proximate

reference

removable

resting

rim

row

sandwich

section

slant

spacer

staggered

superimposed

supported

surface

surrounding

symmetrical

tilt

top

vernier (9:10 gauge)

vertical

6. Voids

aperture

bore

cavity

chamber

concavity

cutout

dimple

duct

embrasure (slant opening)

engraved

filister (groove)

foramen (opening)

fossa (depression)

gain (notch)

gap

groove

hole

hollow

intaglinated (engraved)

lumen (bore of tube)

mortise (cutout)

nock (notch on arrow)

notch

opening

orifice

passage

placket (garment slit)

rabbet (groove)

raceway

recess

separation

slit

slot

sulcus (groove)

ullage (lost liquid)

via (path)

void

7. Shape

acclivity (slope)

acicular (needle shaped)

agonic (no angle)

annular

anticline (peak)

arch

arcuate

barrel

bevel

bifurcated (2 branches)

bight (bend)

bucket

buckled

chamfer (beveled)

channel

circular

coin

concave

conical

convex

convoluted (curled in)

corner (inside, outside)

corrugated

crest

crimp

crispate (curled)

cup

cusp (projection)

cylinder

depression

dihedral (two-faced)

direction

disc

dome

drawing (pulling out)

elliptical

fairing (streamlined)

fin

flange

fold

fork

fossa (groove)

fundus (base)

furcate (branched)

helical

hook

incurvate (curved in)

line

lozenge (diamond shaped)

mammilated (nipple-shaped)

notch

oblate (flattened)

oblong

ogive (pointed arch)

orb (globe)

oval

parabolic

parallelogram

plane

prolate (cigar-shaped)

rectangular

reticulated (gridlike)

rhomboid (non-parallel sides)

rhombus (not lozenge)

round

salient (standing out)

serrated

setaceous (bristlelike)

sheet

shelf

sinusoidal

slab

spherical

spica (overlapping reverse spirals)

square

stamped

striated (grooved or ridged)

swaged (flattened)

swale (depression)

syncline (V-shaped)

taper terminus (end)

tesselated (tiled)

thill (horse joinder stake)

topology (unchangeable geometry)

tram (on wheels)

trefoil (three-leaved)

triangular

trihedral (3-sided)

trough

tubular

tumescence (detumescence)

turbinate (top/spiral shaped)

twist

upset (distorted)

vermiculate (worm-eaten)

volute (spiral)

wafer

web

wedge

xyresic (razor sharp)

8. MATERIALS & PROPERTIES

adhesive

concrete

cork

dappled (spotted)

denier (gauge)

dense

elastic

enlarged

fabric

fiber

flexible

foraminous

haptic (sense of touch)

humectant (moistener)

insulation

liquid

material

metal

nappy

opaque

pied (splotched)

plastic

porous

prill

refractory

resilient

rigid

rubber

sand

screen

shirred (gathered)

smectic (cleaning)

stratified (layered)

strong

sturdy

translucent

transparent

wood

xerotic (dry)

9. OPTICS

astigmatic

bezel

bulb

—fluorescent

—incandescent

fresnel

lamp

light

—beam

—ray

opaque

pellicle

pellucid (clear)

reflection

refraction

schlieren (streaks)

translucent

transmission

transparent

window

10. FLUID FLOW

accumulator

afferent (to center)

aspirator

bellows

bibb (valve)

bung (hole or stopper)

cock (valve)

conduit

connector

convection

cylinder

—piston

—rod

dashpot

diaphragm

discharge

dispenser

efferent (away from center)

filter

fitting

flue

gasket

hose

hydraulic

medium

navicular (like boat)

nozzle

obturator (blocker)

outlet

pipe

plunger

port

—inlet

—outlet

pump

—centrifugal

—gear

—piston

—reservoir

—seal

—siphon

—tank

—vane

sparge (spray)

sprue (vent tube)

tube

valve

—ball

—check

—control

—gate

—shutoff

wattle (intertwined wall)

weir (dam)

wicket (gate or door)

11. ELECTRONICS

adder

amplifier

astable

capacitance

clipping

conductor

contact

control element

demodulator

diode

electrode

electromagnet

filament

flip flop

gate (AND, OR, etc.)

impedance

inductance

insulator

integrated circuit

laser

lead

light emitting diode

line cord

liquid crystal

maser

memory

motor

multiplier

multivibrator

oscillator

pixel (CRT spot)

power supply

raster
read-and-write memory
read-only memory
resistance
sampling
Schmitt trigger
shift register
Shottky diode
socket
solenoid
switch
terminal
thermistor
transformer
transistor
triode
valve
varistor
wire
Zener diode

12. MOVEMENT

alternate
articulate (jointed)
avulsion (tear away)
cam
compression
cyclic
detent (click)
downward
draft (pull)
drag
drift pin
drill

eccentric
emergent
epicyclic (on circle)
extensible
extrude
grinding
impact
inclined plane
inertia
interval
lag
lead
lever
linkage
 —parallel
longitudinal
machine
meeting
nutate (to and fro)
pressing
propelling
pulverize
sagging
sequacious (regular)
severing
skive (peel)
slidable
snub (stop)
straight line
 —motion
terminating
toggle
torque
traction
transverse

traversing
triturate (grind to powder)
trochoid (roll on circle)
urging
vibrating
wedge

13. ROTATION

antifriction
—ball
—needle
—roller
—tapered
arbor (shaft)
bell crank
brake
—band
—disk
—shoe
bushing
cam
chain
clevis (circular holder)
clutch
—centrifugal
—one-way
—sprag (stop)
—toothed
cog (tooth)
connecting rod
crank arm
drive
—belt
—pulley
—sheave
—toothed

flexible coupling
friction
fulcrum
gear
—bevel
—crown
—internal
—non-circular
—pinion
—right angle
—spur
—wheel
—worm
guide
intermittent
—escapement
—geneva
—pawl
—pendulum
—ratchet
jack
journal
orbit
pivot
pulley
radial
radius bar
screw
seal
sheave (pulley)
sprocket
tappet (valve cam)
variable speed
ward (ridge or notch)
winch
yoke

4

Fee Schedule

These fees are good as of 1997 October 1, but you should check with the PTO, 703-308-HELP, its PCT Office, 703-308-3257, its Website (http://www.uspto.gov), a later printing, the *Nolo News* (published quarterly by Nolo Press), if it's much later, on the following Website: www.PatentItYourself.com/update.html. If you underpay any fee, PTO imposes a stiff surcharge. (If you overpay any fee, the PTO will send you a refund.) Two fees separated by a slash refer to large entity/small entity; single fees apply to both entities. PTO fees are listed in order for the patenting process.

Service or Item	Fee ($)	Form/Chapter
PTO Fees (Rule)		
Disclosure Document, filing (21(c))	10	3-3
Provisional Patent Appn., Filing	150/75	3
Printed Copy of Patent or Patent Order Coupon Utility/Design; Also for Copy of SIR (19(a))	3	Ch. 6
Copy of Patent With Color Drawings (19(a))	24	
Application Filing Fees:		
Utility Patent (incl. reissue) (16(a))	790/395	10-1, 14-1
Design Patent (16(f))	330/165	10-8
Plant Patent (16(g))	540/270	Ch. 10
Fee for Each Independent Claim Over Three (16(b))	82/41	10-1, 14-1
Fee for Each Claim Over Twenty (Independent or Dependent) (16(c))	22/11	Ch. 10
Surcharge—Multiple Dependent Claims in Any Application (16(d))	270/135	Ch. 10
Surcharge if Filing Fee or Declaration Late (16(e))	130/65	Ch. 10
Recording Assignment per Application or Patent Involved (21(h))	40	10-1
Surcharge if Any Check Bounces (21(m))	50	Ch. 10
Petitions to Commissioner:		
To Accept Color Drawings or Photos or B&W Photos for Drawings (17(k))	130	Ch. 10
Regarding Inventorship, Misc.,		
Maint. Fees, Interferences, Foreign		
Filing Licenses, Access to		Ch. 13
Records, Foreign Priority Papers,		
Amendments After Issue Fee, Defer/Withdraw a Case From Issue (17(k,l))	130	10-7
To Make Application Special (17(l))	130	Ch. 10

Service or Item	Fee ($)	Form/Chapter
Extensions to Reply to Office Action:		
1st Month (17(a))	110/55	13-5
2nd Month (17(b))	400/200	13-5
3rd Month (17(c))	950/475	13-55
4th Month (if available) (17(d))	1,510/755	13-5
Petition to Revive Abandoned Appn.:		
Unavoidable Delay (17(l))	110/55	Ch. 13
Unintentional Delay (17(m))	1,320/660	Ch. 13
Certified Copy Patent Application as Filed (19(b))	15	Ch. 12
Late IDS Fee (before final action)(17(p))	240	Ch. 13
Late IDS Fee (after final action or notice of allowance)	130	Ch. 13
Appeal to Board of Appeals & Pat. Intrfs.:		
Filing Notice of Appeal (17(e))	310/155	Ch. 13
Filing Brief (17(f))	310/155	Ch. 13
Oral Hearing (17(g))	270/135	Ch. 13
Application Issue Fees:		
Utility Patent (18(a))	1,320/660	Ch. 13
Design Patent (18(b))	450/225	Ch. 13
Plant Patent (18(c))	670/335	Ch. 13
Certificate to Correct Patent (Applicant's Mistake) (20(a))	100	15-1
Re-examination Fee (20(c))	2,520	Ch. 15
Utility Patent Maintenance Fees:		
I (3.5 years—pays for yrs 4 thru 8) (20(e))	1,050/525	15-3
II (7.5 years—pays for yrs 9 thru 12) (20(f))	2,100/1,050	15-3
III (11.5 years—pays for yrs 13 thru 17) (20(g))	3,160/1,580	15-3
Late Charge (in 6-month grace period) (20(h))	130/65	15-3
Petition to Revive (after patent expires)—unintentional delay (20(i))	1,640	15
Petition to Revive (after patent expires)—unavoidable delay (20(i))	700	15
Certified Copy of File & Contents—Issued Patent (19(b)(2))	150	Ch. 15
Certified Copy of Patent Assignment Record (19(b)(3))	25	Ch. 14
Disclaimer of Claims or Terminal Part of Term of Patent (20(d))	110/55	
Dedication of Entire Term or Terminal Part of Term of Patent	NC	

Service or Item	Fee ($)	Form/Chapter
Other Fees		
Trademark Application Filing (in PTO)	245	Ch. 1
Trademark Application Filing (in California)	120	Ch. 1
Copyright Application Filing (in Copyright Office)	20	Ch. 1
Filing a European or Japanese Pat. Appn., incl. agent's fee, approx.	4,000-5,000	Ch. 12
PCT Fees (Always check just before filing; these fees change frequently)		
Transmittal Fee	220	Ch. 12
Search Fees:		
In U.S. PTO		
—no corres. prior U.S. appn. filed	680	Ch. 12
—corres. prior U.S. appn. filed	430	Ch. 12
In European Patent Office	1,425	Ch. 12
International Fees:		
Basic (First 30 Sheets)	530	Ch. 12
Each Additional Sheet Over 30	10	Ch. 12
Designation Fee, each country or office up to 10	128	Ch. 12
11th and additional countries or offices	NC	Ch. 12
Chapter II Fees:		
Handling Fee	162	Ch. 12
Examination Fee		
In U.S. PTO	480	Ch. 12
In EPO	730	Ch. 12

Mail, Telephone and Computer Communications With the PTO

Patent and Trademark Office Mail Addresses

SPECIAL BOXES FOR PATENT MAIL

If you are sending mail in any of the "Type of Mail" categories below to the PTO, add the appropriate box below as the first line of your address as indicated. If your mail does not fall into one of these categories, e.g., an amendment with a fee for extra claims, simply address it using just the last two lines of the address below.

Box _____

Assistant Commissioner for Patents

Washington, DC 20231

Type of Mail	Box
Amendments and other responses after final action	AF
Petitions for Office of Petitions (to revive and accept late fees)	DAC
Design patent application and associated papers and fees	Design
Disclosure Documents and related correspondence	DD
File Wrapper Continuation Applications	FWC
Papers after Not. of Allowance & prior to issuance (no Assignments)	Issue Fee
Maintenance fees and correspondence	M Fee
Non-fee amendments to patent applications	Non-Fee Amendment
New patent application and associated papers and fees	Patent Application
Patent Cooperation Treaty mail	PCT
Diskettes for biotechnical applications	Sequence
Coupon orders for U.S. patent and trademark copies	9
Orders for certified copies of PTO documents	10
All assignments except those filed with new applications	Assignment

FEDERAL GOVERNMENT HOLIDAYS: The PTO is closed on weekends and the following holidays: New Year's Day, M. L. King Day, Presidents' Day, Memorial Day, Independence Day, Labor Day, Columbus Day, Veterans' Day, Thanksgiving, and Christmas. If any action falls due on a holiday or weekend, it is due on the next open-for-business day.

Patent and Trademark Office Telephone and Faxes

All numbers are in area code 703. These numbers were current as of spring 1995 but change often, so if it's much later, check the first *Official Gazette* of the year or a later one which has a new list.

Service or Department	Dial or Contact
Automated Information	557-INFO (557-4636)
Help Line	308-HELP (308-4357)
Abstracts of Title	308-9726; Fax 308-9759
Advance Orders, Non-Receipt (Patent Copies)	305-8237
Amino Acid Sequence Information Submissions	308-1123 (Seq. Rules); 308-4212 (CRF); 308-6856 (PatentIn)
Assignment Recordation	308-9723
Assignment Searches	308-2768
Attorneys' Roster	308-5278
Board of Patent Appeals and Interferences	603-3361
Bulletin Board System (BBS) Information	308-0322
CASSIS/CD-ROM (Classification & Search Info.)	308-0322 (System/CD-ROM 308-0322 (CD-ROM Products))
CD-ROM Products	308-0322
Certificates of Correction	305-8309
Certified Copies of Patent Applications	308-9726; Fax 308-9759
Certified Copies of Patent Assignment Documents	308-9726; Fax 308-9759
Chemical Examining Group 1100	308-0661; Fax 305-3599
Chemical Examining Group 1200	308-1235; Fax 308-4556
Chemical Examining Group 1300	308-0651; Fax 305-3601
Chemical Examining Group 1500	308-2351; Fax 305-3596 or 305-3612
Chemical Examining Group 1800	308-0196; Fax 308-4227
Complaints	Assistant Commr. for Patents, 305-8800. Fax: 305-8825
Copies of Applications as Filed	308-9726
Copies of File Wrapper and Contents	308-9726
Coupon Orders	308-0904
Deaf (TDD)	305-8059
Deceased, Filing Applications for	305-9282
Disclaimers	305-8408
Disclosure Document Program	308-0995
Drawing Corrections	305-8404
Electrical Examining Group 2100	308-1782; Fax 305-3432
Electrical Examining Group 2200	308-0511; Fax 305-3603
Electrical Examining Group 2300	305-9600; Fax 305-9564
Electrical Examining Group 2400	308-0771; Fax 305-3588
Electrical Examining Group 2500	308-0956; Fax 305-3594
Electrical Examining Group 2600	305-4700; Fax 305-9508
Electrical Examining Group 2900	305-3291; Fax 305-3599
Fee Rates	308-HELP
Fee Receipts	308-0904; Fax 308-3491

Fee Refunds .... 305-4229; Fax 305-8007; TDD 308-6695

File Histories 308-9726

File Wrapper Continuation Applications 308-1202

Forms .... 308-HELP; Fax 305-7786

GATT/TRIPs Information 800-PT0-2224

Issue Fee 305-8495

Maintenance Fees .... 308-5068, 308-5069; Fax 308-5077

Mechanical Examining Group 3100 ., ... 308-1113; Fax 305-7687

Mechanical Examining Group 3200 .... 308-1148; Fax 305-3762

Mechanical Examining Group 3300 .... 308-0858; Fax 305-3590

Mechanical Examining Group 3400 .... 308-0861; Fax 305-3463

Mechanical Examining Group 3500 .... 308-2168; Fax 305-3597

Modem for PTO BBS 308-8950

MPEP on CD-ROM or Diskette 308-0322

Nucleic Acid Information Submissions .... 308-1123 (Sequence); 308-4212 (CRF); 308-6856 (PatentIn)

Patent & Trademark Depository Library Program 308-3924

Patent Cooperation Treaty (PCT) 305-3257

Patent Copy Sales 305-8716

Patent Search Room 308-1057

Petitions, Abandonment, Withdrawal of .... Appropriate Examining Group Director

Petitions, Access to Application Files .... Office of Special Program Exam. 305-9282

Petitions, Amendment After Payment of Issue Fee .... Appropriate Examining Group Director

Petitions re Application Acceptance .... Office of Special Program Exam. 305-9282

Petitions re Assignments & Issuance of Patent .... Office of Petitions 305-9282

Petitions re Certificates of Correction, Refusal to Issue .... Office of Petitions 305-9282

Petitions re Disclaimers .... Office of Petitions 305-9282

Petitions re Divisional Reissues .... Office of Special Program Examination 305-9282

Petitions re Examiner's Requirements or Holdings .... Appropriate Examining Group Director

Petitions re Extensions of Time in Group .... Appropriate Examining Group Director

Petitions re Premature Final Rejection .... Appropriate Examining Group Director

Petitions re License to File in Foreign Countries .... Director, Group 2200 308-1721

Petitions re Representation by Non-Attorney .... Committee on Enrollment 308-9618

Petitions, Make Special re Mfgr. or Infringement .... Office of Special Program Exam. 305-9282

Petitions, Office of .... 305-9282; Fax 308-6916

Petitions re Patent Cooperation Treaty .... PCT Legal Division 308-6515

Petitions re Age, Health, Environment, Special
     Procedure, Energy, DNA, Supercond., AIDS/Cancer .... Appropriate Examining Group Director

Petitions re Refusal to Enter an Amendment .... Appropriate Examining Group Director

Petitions to Reinstate, Appeal Dismissed by Group .... Appropriate Examining Group Director

Petitions re Rejection, Premature Final .... Appropriate Examining Group Director

Petitions, Reopen Prosecution After Decision by BPAI .... Appropriate Examining Group Director

Petitions re Restriction Requirement .... Appropriate Examining Group Director

Petitions to Revive an Abandoned Application .... Office of Petitions 305-9282

Petitions re Statutory Invention Registrations (SIRs) .... Group 2200 308-0766

Petitions to Invoke Supervisory Authority of Commr. .... Office of Petitions 305-9282

Petitions re Suspension of Action .... Appropriate Examining Group Director

Petitions re Suspension of Rules .... Office of Petitions 305-9282

Petitions re Withdraw from Issue .... Office of Petitions 305-9282

Protest Against Pending Patent Applications 305-9282

Publications, General Info 557-INFO

Scientific and Technical Information Center .... 308-0810 (electrical, mechanical); 308-4506 (chemical)

Status, Patent .... 308-1844 or examining group

Statutory Invention Registrations (SIRs) .... 308-0766 (Group 2200)

Subscription MPEP (Paper Version) .... Government Printing Office 202-512-1800

Technical Questions .... Exam. Grp. or Special Prgrms Office; 305-9282; Fax 308-6916

Terminal Disclaimers (Double Patenting Rejection) .... Appropriate Examining Group

Terminal Disclaimers, General 305-8408

PTO Fax Numbers

Application Processing Division 305-9863

Assignment Svcs (Refund/Status Requests) 308-7124

Board of Patent Appeals & Interferences 603-3541

Certification Services 308-9759

Office of Petitions 308-6916

Office of Special Program Examination 308-6916

Patent Cooperation Treaty 305-3230

Patent and Trademark Copy Sales 305-8759

Patent Examining Group 1100 305-3599

Patent Examining Group 1200 308-4556

Patent Examining Group 1300 305-3601

Patent Examining Group 1500 .... 305-3596/3612

Patent Examining Group 1800 305-4227

Patent Examining Group 2100 305-3432

Patent Examining Group 2200 305-3603

Patent Examining Group 2300 305-9564

Patent Examining Group 2400 305-3588

Patent Examining Group 2500 305-3594

Patent Examining Group 2600 305-9508

Patent Examining Group 2900 305-3599

Patent Examining Group 3100 305-7687

Patent Examining Group 3200 305-3762

Patent Examining Group 3300 305-3590

Patent Examining Group 3400 305-3463

Patent Examining Group 3500 305-3597

Patent Maintenance Fee Information 308-5077

Refunds 305-8007

Patent and Trademark Internet Addresses

PTO Home Page .... http://www.uspto.gov/

File Transfer Protocol .... ftp.uspto.gov

The Patent and Trademark Office Bulletin Board System

The Patent and Trademark Office has an electronic Bulletin Board System (PTOBBS) which is open to the public. To access the PTOBBS, you need a computer with a modem and software. You can access the PTOBBS either directly or through FedWorld. FedWorld itself may be accessed directly or via the Internet.

    The PTOBBS enables you, for the cost of a long-distance call, or through the Internet, to view and download the following files:

1. News and Bulletins

Contains news items, press releases from the PTO and the Department of Commerce; bulletins specific to the PTOBBS and its users; reports such as Top Patenting Companies (the ten companies that issued the most patents for a particular year); the PTO's Strategic Plan; and PTO employment announcements.

2. Services and Products

Describes what's available from the PTO's Patent Copy Sales and in the PTO's Public Search Room. Contains brochures detailing CD-ROM, tape, and other media products available from the PTO's Office of Information Products Development, including the Technology Assessment and Forecast Program. Contains a description of PKWareR PKUnzip software used to decompress files from the PTOBBS.

3. Patent Information

Contains the current week's *Official Gazette* notices for patents; list of weekly and cumulative expired patents; the most recent PTO fee schedule for patents, trademarks, and general services; and the bibliographic data of the 12 current weekly issues of patents.

4. Files to Download

Contains the OG notices and a list of patents issued for the last 52 weeks, and miscellaneous compressed files, such as the Attorney Roster, master file of expired patents, the Manual of Patent Examining Procedure, the Trademark Manual of Examining Procedure, Goods & Services Manual, and Design Code manuals. Software (PKWareR) for decompressing these files is also available for downloading.

5. Utilities

Provides access to user-changeable parameters, including passwords and registration information.

6. Directory Information

Contains telephone listings for the PTO, Patent and Trademark Depository Libraries (PTDLs), including those which give the public access to the PTO's Automated Patent System (APS), as well as the PTOBBS table of contents.

7. Trademark Information

Contains *Official Gazette* notices for trademarks, the most recent PTO fee schedule for patents, trademarks, and general services.

8. Join Conference

Leave messages, helpful hints, problems and solutions, and comments in three different conferences accessible to PTOBBS users.

9. Message to Sysop

PTOBBS users may leave a message for the Sysop for comments, questions, or problems.

10. Electronic Mail: Communicate with the Sysop or other PTOBBS users

To access the PTOBBS directly, dial 703-305-8950. From Internet, connect via FedWorld by telnet connect to fedworld.gov or use the address 192.239.93.307. Once in FedWorld, select UDD116 from menu. The PTOBBS allows terminal emulation to be set for ASCII, ANSI, or RIP. (If problems are encountered with access through FedWorld, call the NTIS FedWorld Help Desk at 703-487-4608.) ■

Quick Reference Timing Chart

The following is a summary of some of the more important timing intervals that apply in intangible property law. This list is not intended to be comprehensive, and certain exceptions may be applicable, so check the pertinent parts of this book, or with a patent attorney if you have a special situation or need more precise advice.

From the date of first publication, offer of sale, sale, or public or commercial use
(excluding experimental use) of anything embodying an invention, one must file a
U.S. utility, design, or plant patent application within .... 1 year.

From the date of filing a PPA, one must file a utility patent application within .... 1 year.

To preserve foreign-filing rights in Convention Countries, one must not sell or
publicly disclose details of an invention until .... after U.S. filing date.

To preserve foreign-filing rights in Non-Convention Countries (NCCs), one must
not publicly disclose or sell invention until .... after foreign-filing date in NCC.

From the PTO's mailing date, one must file a response to most office actions within .... 3 months.

The maximum statutory time to reply to an Office Action, provided extensions are bought, is .... 6 months.

The full term of a utility or plant patent is .... 20 years.

The full term of a design patent is .... 14 years.

From the date of issue (grant) the issue fee will keep a utility patent in force for the first .... 4 years.

Timely payment of Maintenance Fee I (between year 3.0 and 3.5, or 3.5 and 4.0 with late charge)
will keep a utility patent in force for another .... 4 years.

Timely payment of Maintenance Fee II (between year 7.0 and 7.5, or 7.5 and 8.0 with late charge)
will keep a utility patent in force for another .... 4 years.

Timely payment of Maintenance Fee III (between year 11.0 and 11.5, or 11.5 and 12.0 with late charge)
will keep a utility patent in force until expiration which occurs .... 20 years after filing.

For works not made for hire, the copyright term is .... author's life + 50 years.

For works made for hire, the copyright term is the shorter of .... 75 years from publication or
100 years from creation.

To get statutory damages and attorney fees, one must apply to register a copyright
before infringement begins or within .... 3 months of publication.

A California state trademark registration lasts for .... 10 years.

A U.S. (federal) trademark registration lasts for .... 10 years.

State and U.S. trademark registrations can be renewed .... in perpetuity.

If kept secret, and provided it's not discovered independently, a trade secret
will be enforceable against those who discover it illegally .... in perpetuity.

Unless a foreign filing license has been granted, after filing a U.S. patent application,
before foreign filing a patent application, you must wait .... 6 months.

From the U.S. filing date, to obtain priority, one must file a foreign
Convention application (PCT, EPO or industrial countries) within .... 1 year.

One must file a foreign Non-Convention application (most non-industrial countries) .... before invention becomes publicly known.

From the U.S. filing date, after filing a PCT application, if examination
in the foreign jurisdiction is desired, one must file abroad within .... 20 months.

From the U.S. filing date, after filing a PCT application, if examination in the U.S. PTO
or the European Patent Office is desired (Chapter II), one must file a request within .... 19 months.

From the U.S. filing date, after filing a PCT application and electing Chapter II, one must file abroad within .... 30 months.

■

Form numbers indicate the chapters in which the forms are discussed; for example, Form 10-7 is discussed in Chapter 10.

Form numbers indicate the chapters in which the forms are discussed; for example, Form 10-7 is discussed in Chapter 10.

Proprietary Materials Agreement
(Keep Confidential/Non-Disclosure Agreement)

PROPRIETARY MATERIALS (items, documents, or models loaned—describe or identify fully, including number of sheets): _____

_____

_____

_____

PROPRIETARY MATERIALS loaned by (name and address): _____

_____

_____ ("LENDER")

PROPRIETARY MATERIALS loaned to (name and address): _____

_____

_____ ("BORROWER")

BORROWER acknowledges and agrees as follows:

(1) Borrower:

    (a) has received the above Proprietary Materials from Lender (_____)

    (b) understands that LENDER will immediately send the above PROPRIETARY MATERIALS to BORROWER upon LENDER'S receipt, from BORROWER, of a signed copy of this Agreement (____)

    [BORROWER cross out (a) and initial (b), or vice versa, as appropriate]

(2) These PROPRIETARY MATERIALS contain valuable proprietary information of LENDER. This proprietary information constitutes a trade secret of LENDER and loss or outside disclosure of these materials or the information contained within these materials will harm lender economically.

(3) BORROWER acknowledges that these PROPRIETARY MATERIALS are furnished to BORROWER under the following conditions:

    (a) These PROPRIETARY MATERIALS and the information they contain shall be used by BORROWER solely to review or evaluate a proposal or information from, supply a quotation to, or provide a component or item for LENDER.

    (b) BORROWER agrees not to disclose these PROPRIETARY MATERIALS or the information they contain except to any persons within BORROWER'S organization having a good faith "need to know" same for the purpose of fulfilling the terms of this Agreement. If necessary, BORROWER may make additional copies of this Agreement and have each such person sign a copy of this Agreement and furnish such copy(ies) to LENDER.

    (c) BORROWER and all persons within BORROWER'S organization shall exercise a high degree of care to safeguard these PROPRIETARY MATERIALS and the information they contain from access or disclosure to all unauthorized persons.

    (d) BORROWER shall not make any copies of these PROPRIETARY MATERIALS except upon written permission of LENDER and BORROWER and shall return all PROPRIETARY MATERIALS (including any copies made) to LENDER at any time upon request by LENDER.

(4) These terms shall not apply to any information which BORROWER can document becomes part of the general public knowledge without fault of BORROWER or comes into BORROWER'S possession in good faith without restriction.

BORROWER: _____
(Name of Organization or Individual)

By: _____

_____
(Name and Title)

Date: _____ / _____ / _____

Other persons within BORROWER'S organization obtaining access to PROPRIETARY MATERIALS:

_____   ____ / ____ / ____

Print Name: _____

_____   ____ / ____ / ____

Print Name: _____

Proprietary Materials Agreement
(Keep Confidential/Non-Disclosure Agreement)

PROPRIETARY MATERIALS (items, documents, or models loaned—describe or identify fully, including number of sheets): _____

_____

_____

_____

PROPRIETARY MATERIALS loaned by (name and address): _____

_____

_____ ("LENDER")

PROPRIETARY MATERIALS loaned to (name and address): _____

_____

_____ ("BORROWER")

BORROWER acknowledges and agrees as follows:

(1) Borrower:

   (a) has received the above Proprietary Materials from Lender (_____)

   (b) understands that LENDER will immediately send the above PROPRIETARY MATERIALS to BORROWER upon LENDER'S receipt, from BORROWER, of a signed copy of this Agreement (____)

   [BORROWER cross out (a) and initial (b), or vice versa, as appropriate]

(2) These PROPRIETARY MATERIALS contain valuable proprietary information of LENDER. This proprietary information constitutes a trade secret of LENDER and loss or outside disclosure of these materials or the information contained within these materials will harm lender economically.

(3) BORROWER acknowledges that these PROPRIETARY MATERIALS are furnished to BORROWER under the following conditions:

   (a) These PROPRIETARY MATERIALS and the information they contain shall be used by BORROWER solely to review or evaluate a proposal or information from, supply a quotation to, or provide a component or item for LENDER.

   (b) BORROWER agrees not to disclose these PROPRIETARY MATERIALS or the information they contain except to any persons within BORROWER'S organization having a good faith "need to know" same for the purpose of fulfilling the terms of this Agreement. If necessary, BORROWER may make additional copies of this Agreement and have each such person sign a copy of this Agreement and furnish such copy(ies) to LENDER.

   (c) BORROWER and all persons within BORROWER'S organization shall exercise a high degree of care to safeguard these PROPRIETARY MATERIALS and the information they contain from access or disclosure to all unauthorized persons.

   (d) BORROWER shall not make any copies of these PROPRIETARY MATERIALS except upon written permission of LENDER and BORROWER and shall return all PROPRIETARY MATERIALS (including any copies made) to LENDER at any time upon request by LENDER.

(4) These terms shall not apply to any information which BORROWER can document becomes part of the general public knowledge without fault of BORROWER or comes into BORROWER'S possession in good faith without restriction.

BORROWER: _____
(Name of Organization or Individual)

By: _____

_____
(Name and Title)

Date: ____ / ____ / ____

Other persons within BORROWER'S organization obtaining access to PROPRIETARY MATERIALS:

_____ ____ / ____ / ____

Print Name: _____

_____ ____ / ____ / ____

Print Name: _____

Invention Disclosure

Sheet _____ of _____

Inventor(s): _____

Address(es): _____

Title of Invention: _____

To record **Conception**, describe: 1. Circumstances of conception, 2. Purposes and advantages of invention, 3. Description, 4. Sketches, 5. Ramifications, 6. Possible novel features, and 7. Closest known prior art. To record **Building and Testing**, describe: 1. Any previous disclosure of conception, 2. Construction, 3. Ramifications, 4. Tests, and 5. Test results. Include sketches and photos, where possible. Continue on additional identical copies of this sheet if necessary; inventors and witnesses should sign all sheets.

Inventor(s): _____   Date:____ / ____ / ____

_____   Date:____ / ____ / ____

The above confidential information is Witnessed and Understood:

_____   Date:____ / ____ / ____

_____   Date:____ / ____ / ____

Date: _____

Box DD
Assistant Commissioner for Patents
Washington, District of Columbia 20231
Request for Participation in Disclosure Document Program:

Disclosure of _____
                                          Your Name(s)

Entitled: _____
                        Title of Disclosure

Sir:

Attached is a copy of a disclosure of my above-entitled invention (consisting of _____ sheets of written description and _____ separate drawings or photos), a $_____ check and a stamped receipt postcard.

The undersigned respectfully requests that this disclosure be accepted and retained for two years (or longer if it is later referred to in a paper filed in a patent application) under the Disclosure Document Program and that the enclosed postcard be date stamped, numbered and returned.

The undersigned understands that (1) this disclosure document is neither a patent application nor a substitute for one, (2) its receipt date will not become the effective filing date of a later-filed patent application, (3) it will be retained for two years and then destroyed unless it is referred to in a patent application, (4) this two-year retention period is not a "grace period" during which a patent application can be filed without loss of benefits, (5) in addition to this document, proof of diligence in building and testing the invention, and/or filing a patent application on the invention, may be vital in case of an interference, and in other situations, (6) if such building and testing is done, signed, and dated, records of such should additionally be made and these should be witnessed and dated by disinterested individuals (not the PTO), and (7) if any public use or sale of the invention is made in the U.S., or any publication is made anywhere, no valid patent can be granted on the invention unless a patent application is filed on it within one year of any such public use, sale or publication, regardless of the filing date of this Disclosure Document.

Very respectfully,

_____   _____
Signature of Inventor   Signature of Joint Inventor

_____   _____
c/o (Print Name)   Print Name

_____   _____
Address   Address

_____   _____

Enclosures:
As stated above

In the United States Patent and Trademark Office

Serial Number: _____

Appn. Filed: _____

Applicant(s): _____

Appn. Title: _____

Examiner/GAU: _____

Disclosure Document Reference Letter

Date: _____

Assistant Commissioner for Patents

Washington, District of Columbia 20231

Sir:

A disclosure document as identified below was previously filed in the Patent and Trademark Office. As this disclosure relates to the above patent application, applicant(s) request that this Disclosure Document be retained and referenced to the above application.

Disclosure Document Title: _____

Disclosure Document Number: _____

Disclosure Document Filing Date: _____

Very Respectfully,

_____   _____
Signed Name   Signed Name

_____   _____
Printed Name, First Applicant   Printed Name, Joint Applicant

_____   _____
Address of First Applicant   Address of Joint Applicant

_____   _____

In the United States Patent and Trademark Office

Box Provisional Patent Application   Mailed 199 _____

Assistant Commissioner for Patents

Washington, District of Columbia 20231

Sir:

Please file the enclosed Provisional Patent Application (PPA) papers listed below under 37 C.F.R. § 1.53(b)(2).

Each of the undersigned understands:

A. This PPA is not a substitute for a Regular Patent Application (RPA), cannot be converted to an RPA, cannot get into interference with an RPA of another person, cannot be amended, will not be published, cannot claim any foreign priority, and will not mature into a patent;

B. If an RPA referring to this PPA is not filed within one year of the filing date of this PPA, this PPA will be worthless and will be destroyed;

C. Any desired foreign Convention applications (including PCT applications) based upon this PPA *must* be filed within one year of the filing date of this PPA;

D. This PPA *must* contain a written description of the invention, and of the manner and process of making and using it, in such full, clear, concise, and exact terms as to enable any person skilled in the art to which it pertains, or with which it is most nearly connected, to make and use the same, and shall set forth the best mode contemplated by the inventor of carrying out his invention. 35 U.S.C. § 112, ¶ 1. Otherwise this PPA will be worthless.

E. Any RPA will be entitled to claim the benefit of this PPA only if such RPA names at least one inventor of this PPA and this PPA discloses such inventor's invention, as claimed in at least one claim of the RPA, in the matter provided in Item D above.

Tentative Applicant # 1, Name: _____

Tentative Applicant # 2, Name: _____

Title: _____

(x) Specification, sheets: _____   ( ) Drawing(s), sheets : _____

( ) Small Entity Declaration(s), number: _____ .

(x) Check for $ _____   for   ( ) small entity   ( ) large entity filing fee

(x) Return Receipt Postcard Addressed to Applicant # 1.

Very respectfully,

_____   _____
Applicant # 1 Signature   Applicant # 2 Signature

_____   _____
Address (Send Correspondence Here)   Address

_____   _____

Express Mail Label # (_____)   **; Date of Deposit 199** _____

I hereby certify that this paper or fee is being deposited with the United States Postal Service using "Express Mail Post Office to Addressee" service under 37 CFR 1.10 on the date indicated above and is addressed to "Box Provisional Patent Application, Assistant Commissioner for Patents, Washington, DC 20231."

Signed: _____
                                                                Inventor

Form 3-5: Provisional Patent Application Cover Letter

Positive and Negative Factors Evaluation

Inventor(s): _____   Invention: _____

_____   _____

Factor	Weight (−100 to +100)	Factor	Weight (−100 to +100)
1. Cost	_____	28. Markup	_____
2. Weight	_____	29. Inferior Performance	_____
3. Size	_____	30. "Sexy" Packaging	_____
4. Safety/Health	_____	31. Miscellaneous	_____
5. Speed	_____	32. Long Life Cycle	_____
6. Ease of Use	_____	33. Related Product Addability	_____
7. Ease of Production	_____	34. Satisfies Existing Need	_____
8. Durability	_____	35. Legality	_____
9. Repairability	_____	36. Operability	_____
10. Novelty	_____	37. Development	_____
11. Convenience/Social Benefit/ Mechanization	_____	38. Profitability	_____
12. Reliability	_____	39. Obsolescence	_____
13. Ecology	_____	40. Incompatibility	_____
14. Salability	_____	41. Product Liability Risk	_____
15. Appearance	_____	42. Market Dependence	_____
16. Viewability	_____	43. Difficulty of Distribution	_____
17. Precision	_____	44. Service Requirements	_____
18. Noise	_____	45. New Tooling Required	_____
19. Odor	_____	46. Inertia Must Be Overcome	_____
20. Taste	_____	47. Too Advanced Technically	_____
21. Market Size	_____	48. Substantial Learning Required	_____
22. Trend of Demand	_____	49. Difficult to Promote	_____
23. Seasonal Demand	_____	50. Lack of Market	_____
24. Difficulty of Market Penetration	_____	51. Crowded Field	_____
25. Potential Competition	_____	52. Commodities	_____
26. Quality	_____	53. Combination Products	_____
27. Excitement	_____	54. Entrenched Competition	_____
		55. Instant Anachronism	_____

TOTAL _____

Signed: _____   Date: _____
_____Inventor(s)

Positive and Negative Factors Summary

Inventor(s): _____   Invention: _____

_____   _____

List Factors With Positive Values	Weight	List Factors With Negative Values	Weight
_____	_____	_____	_____
_____	_____	_____	_____
_____	_____	_____	_____
_____	_____	_____	_____
_____	_____	_____	_____
_____	_____	_____	_____
_____	_____	_____	_____
_____	_____	_____	_____
_____	_____	_____	_____
_____	_____	_____	_____
_____	_____	_____	_____
_____	_____	_____	_____
_____	_____	_____	_____
_____	_____	_____	_____
_____	_____	_____	_____
_____	_____	_____	_____
_____	_____	_____	_____
_____	_____	_____	_____
_____	_____	_____	_____
_____	_____	_____	_____
_____	_____	_____	_____
_____	_____	_____	_____
_____	_____	_____	_____

Positive Total _____   Negative Total _____

NET (Positive Total less Negative Total): _____

Signed: _____   Date: _____
        Inventor(s)

Form 4-2

Consultant's Work Agreement

1. **Parties**: This Work Agreement is made between the following parties:

   Name(s) _____

   Address(es): _____

   _____

   (hereinafter Contractor), and

   Name(s): _____

   Address(es): _____

   _____

   (hereinafter Consultant).

2. **Name of Project:** _____

   _____

   _____

3. **Work to Be Performed by Consultant:** _____

   _____

   _____

4. **Work/Payment Schedule:** _____

   _____

   _____

5. **Date:** This Agreement shall be effective as of the latter date below written.

6. **Recitals:** Contractor has one or more ideas relating to the above project and desires to have such project developed more completely, as specified in the above statement of Work. Consultant has certain skills desired by Contractor relating to performance of the above Work.

7. **Performance:** Consultant will perform the above work for Contractor, in accordance with the above-scheduled Work/Payment Schedule and Contractor will make the above scheduled payments to Consultant. Any changes to the Work to Be Performed or the Work/Payment Schedule shall be described in a writing referring to this Agreement and signed and dated by both parties. Time is of the essence of this Agreement, and if Consultant fails to perform according to the above work schedule, contractor may (a) void this agreement and pay consultant 50% of what would otherwise be due, or (b) require that Consultant pay contractor a penalty of $_____ per day.

8. **Intellectual Property:** All intellectual property, including trademarks, writings, information, trade secrets, inventions, discoveries, or improvements, whether or not registrable or patentable, which are conceived, constructed, or written by Consultant and arise out of or are related to work and services performed under this agreement, are, or shall become and remain the sole and exclusive property of Contractor, whether or not such intellectual property is conceived during the time such work and services are performed or billed.

9A. **Protection of Intellectual Property:** Contractor and Consultant recognize that under U.S. patent laws, all patent applications must be filed in the name of the true and actual inventor(s) of the subject matter sought to be patented. Thus if Consultant makes any patentable inventions relating to the above project, Consultant agrees to be named as an applicant in any U.S. patent application(s) filed on such invention(s). Actual ownership of such patent applications shall be governed by clause 8.

9B. Consultant shall promptly disclose to Contractor in writing all information pertaining to any intellectual property generated or conceived by Consultant under this Agreement. Consultant hereby assigns and agrees to assign all of Consultant's rights to such intellectual property, including patent rights and foreign priority rights. Consultant hereby expressly agrees, without further charge for time, to do all things and sign all documents deemed by Contractor to be necessary or appropriate to invest in intellectual property, including obtaining for and vesting in Contractor all U.S. and foreign patents and patent applications which Contractor desires to obtain to cover such intellectual property, provided that Contractor shall bear all expenses relating thereto. All reasonable local travel time and expenses shall be borne by Consultant.

10. **Trade Secrets:** Consultant recognizes that all information relating to the above Project disclosed to Consultant by Contractor, and all information generated by Consultant in the performance of the above Work, is a valuable trade secret of Contractor and Consultant shall treat all such information as strictly confidential, during and after the performance of Work under this Agreement. Specifically Consultant shall not reveal, publish, or communicate any such information to anyone other than Contractor, and shall safeguard all such information from access to anyone other than Contractor, except upon the express written authorization of Contractor. This clause shall not apply to any information which Consultant can document in writing is presently in or enters the public domain from a bona fide source other than Consultant.

11. **Return of Property:** Consultant agrees to return all written materials and objects received from Contractor, to deliver to Contractor all objects and a copy (and all copies and originals if requested by Contractor) of all written materials resulting from or relating to work performed under this Agreement, and not to deliver to any person, organization, or publisher, or cause to be published, any such written material without prior written authorization.

12. **Conflicts of Interest:** Consultant recognizes a fiduciary obligation to Contractor arising out of the work and services performed under this agreement and accordingly will not offer Consultant's service to or perform services for any competitor, potential or actual, of Contractor for the above Project, or perform any other acts which may result in any conflict of interest by Consultant, during and after the term of this Agreement.

13. **Mediation and Arbitration:** If any dispute arises under this Agreement, the parties shall negotiate in good faith to settle such dispute. If the parties cannot resolve such dispute themselves, then either party may submit the dispute to mediation by a mediator approved by both parties. If the parties cannot agree to any mediator, or if either party does not wish to abide by any decision of the mediator, they shall submit the dispute to arbitration by any mutually acceptable arbitrator, or the American Arbitration Association (AAA). If the AAA is selected, the arbitration shall take place under the auspices of the nearest branch of such to both parties. The costs of the arbitration proceeding shall be borne according to the decision of the arbitrator, who may apportion costs equally, or in accordance with any finding or fault or lack of good faith of either party. The arbitrator's award shall be non-appealable and enforceable in any court of competent jurisdiction.

14. **Governing Law:** This Agreement shall be governed by and interpreted under and according to the laws of the State of _____ .

15. **Signatures:** The parties have indicated their agreement to all of the above terms by signing this Agreement on the respective dates below indicated. Each party has received an original signed copy hereof.

Contractor:_____ Date: _____

Consultant:_____ Date: _____

Consultant's Work Agreement

1. **Parties**: This Work Agreement is made between the following parties:

   Name(s) _____

   Address(es): _____

   _____

   (hereinafter Contractor), and

   Name(s): _____

   Address(es): _____

   _____

   (hereinafter Consultant).

2. **Name of Project:** _____

   _____

   _____

3. **Work to Be Performed by Consultant:** _____

   _____

   _____

4. **Work/Payment Schedule:** _____

   _____

   _____

5. **Date:** This Agreement shall be effective as of the latter date below written.

6. **Recitals:** Contractor has one or more ideas relating to the above project and desires to have such project developed more completely, as specified in the above statement of Work. Consultant has certain skills desired by Contractor relating to performance of the above Work.

7. **Performance:** Consultant will perform the above work for Contractor, in accordance with the above-scheduled Work/Payment Schedule and Contractor will make the above scheduled payments to Consultant. Any changes to the Work to Be Performed or the Work/Payment Schedule shall be described in a writing referring to this Agreement and signed and dated by both parties. Time is of the essence of this Agreement, and if Consultant fails to perform according to the above work schedule, contractor may (a) void this agreement and pay consultant 50% of what would otherwise be due, or (b) require that Consultant pay contractor a penalty of $_____ per day.

8. **Intellectual Property:** All intellectual property, including trademarks, writings, information, trade secrets, inventions, discoveries, or improvements, whether or not registrable or patentable, which are conceived, constructed, or written by Consultant and arise out of or are related to work and services performed under this agreement, are, or shall become and remain the sole and exclusive property of Contractor, whether or not such intellectual property is conceived during the time such work and services are performed or billed.

9A. **Protection of Intellectual Property:** Contractor and Consultant recognize that under U.S. patent laws, all patent applications must be filed in the name of the true and actual inventor(s) of the subject matter sought to be patented. Thus if Consultant makes any patentable inventions relating to the above project, Consultant agrees to be named as an applicant in any U.S. patent application(s) filed on such invention(s). Actual ownership of such patent applications shall be governed by clause 8.

9B. Consultant shall promptly disclose to Contractor in writing all information pertaining to any intellectual property generated or conceived by Consultant under this Agreement. Consultant hereby assigns and agrees to assign all of Consultant's rights to such intellectual property, including patent rights and foreign priority rights. Consultant hereby expressly agrees, without further charge for time, to do all things and sign all documents deemed by Contractor to be necessary or appropriate to invest in intellectual property, including obtaining for and vesting in Contractor all U.S. and foreign patents and patent applications which Contractor desires to obtain to cover such intellectual property, provided that Contractor shall bear all expenses relating thereto. All reasonable local travel time and expenses shall be borne by Consultant.

10. **Trade Secrets:** Consultant recognizes that all information relating to the above Project disclosed to Consultant by Contractor, and all information generated by Consultant in the performance of the above Work, is a valuable trade secret of Contractor and Consultant shall treat all such information as strictly confidential, during and after the performance of Work under this Agreement. Specifically Consultant shall not reveal, publish, or communicate any such information to anyone other than Contractor, and shall safeguard all such information from access to anyone other than Contractor, except upon the express written authorization of Contractor. This clause shall not apply to any information which Consultant can document in writing is presently in or enters the public domain from a bona fide source other than Consultant.

11. **Return of Property:** Consultant agrees to return all written materials and objects received from Contractor, to deliver to Contractor all objects and a copy (and all copies and originals if requested by Contractor) of all written materials resulting from or relating to work performed under this Agreement, and not to deliver to any person, organization, or publisher, or cause to be published, any such written material without prior written authorization.

12. **Conflicts of Interest:** Consultant recognizes a fiduciary obligation to Contractor arising out of the work and services performed under this agreement and accordingly will not offer Consultant's service to or perform services for any competitor, potential or actual, of Contractor for the above Project, or perform any other acts which may result in any conflict of interest by Consultant, during and after the term of this Agreement.

13. **Mediation and Arbitration:** If any dispute arises under this Agreement, the parties shall negotiate in good faith to settle such dispute. If the parties cannot resolve such dispute themselves, then either party may submit the dispute to mediation by a mediator approved by both parties. If the parties cannot agree to any mediator, or if either party does not wish to abide by any decision of the mediator, they shall submit the dispute to arbitration by any mutually acceptable arbitrator, or the American Arbitration Association (AAA). If the AAA is selected, the arbitration shall take place under the auspices of the nearest branch of such to both parties. The costs of the arbitration proceeding shall be borne according to the decision of the arbitrator, who may apportion costs equally, or in accordance with any finding or fault or lack of good faith of either party. The arbitrator's award shall be non-appealable and enforceable in any court of competent jurisdiction.

14. **Governing Law:** This Agreement shall be governed by and interpreted under and according to the laws of the State of _____ .

15. **Signatures:** The parties have indicated their agreement to all of the above terms by signing this Agreement on the respective dates below indicated. Each party has received an original signed copy hereof.

Contractor:_____ Date: _____

Consultant:_____ Date: _____

Searcher's Worksheet

Sheet _____ of _____

Inventor(s): _____

Invention Description (use key words and variations): _____

_____

_____

Selected Search Classifications

Class/Sub   Description   Checked   Comments
_____

_____   _____   _____   _____

_____   _____   _____   _____

_____   _____   _____   _____

_____   _____   _____   _____

_____   _____   _____   _____

_____   _____   _____   _____

_____   _____   _____   _____

Patents (and Other References) Thought Relevant

Patent #   Name or Country   Date   Class/Sub   Comment
_____

(blank entry lines)

Searcher: _____   Date: _____

Form 6-1

Drawing Reference Numerals Worksheet

PART NAME

10 _____
12 _____
14 _____
16 _____
18 _____
20 _____
22 _____
24 _____
26 _____
28 _____
30 _____
32 _____
34 _____
36 _____
38 _____
40 _____
42 _____
44 _____
46 _____
48 _____
50 _____
52 _____
54 _____
56 _____
58 _____
60 _____
62 _____
64 _____
66 _____
68 _____
70 _____
72 _____
74 _____
76 _____
78 _____
80 _____
82 _____

PART NAME

84 _____
86 _____
88 _____
90 _____
92 _____
94 _____
96 _____
98 _____
100 _____
102 _____
104 _____
106 _____
108 _____
110 _____
112 _____
114 _____
116 _____
118 _____
120 _____
122 _____
124 _____
126 _____
128 _____
130 _____
132 _____
134 _____
136 _____
138 _____
140 _____
142 _____
144 _____
146 _____
148 _____
150 _____
152 _____
154 _____
156 _____

In the United States Patent and Trademark Office

Mailed 199_____

Box Patent Application

Assistant Commissioner for Patents

Washington, District of Columbia 20231

Sir:

Please file the following enclosed patent application papers:

Applicant #1, Name: _____

Applicant #2, Name: _____

Title: _____

☐ Specification, Claims, and Abstract: Nr. of Sheets _____

☐ Declaration: Date Signed: _____

☐ Drawing(s): Nr. of Sheets Enc.: Formal: _____ Informal: _____

☐ Small Entity Declaration of Inventor(s)   ☐ SED of Non-Inventor / Assignee / Licensee

☐ Assignment enclosed with cover sheet and recordal fee; please record and return.

☐ Check for $ _____ for:

    ☐ $ _____ for filing fee (not more than three independent claims and twenty total claims are presented).

    ☐ $ _____ additional if Assignment is enclosed for recordal.

☐ Disclosure Document Program reference letter.

☐ Pursuant to 35 U.S.C. §119(e)(i), applicant(s) claim priority of Provisional Patent Application Ser. Nr. _____ ,

    filed _____ .

☐ Return Receipt Postcard Addressed to Applicant #1.

☐ **Request Under MPEP § 707.07(j):** The undersigned, a pro se applicant, respectfully requests that if the Examiner finds patentable subject matter disclosed in this application, but feels that Applicant's present claims are not entirely suitable, the Examiner draft one or more allowable claims for applicant.

Very respectfully,

_____   _____
Applicant #1 Signature   Applicant #2 Signature

_____   _____
Address (Send Correspondence Here)   Address

_____   _____

Express Mail Label # (_____)   **; Date of Deposit 199** _____

I hereby certify that this paper or fee is being deposited with the United States Postal Service using "Express Mail Post Office to Addressee" service under 37 CFR 1.10 on the date indicated above and is addressed to "Box Patent Application, Assistant Commissioner for Patents, Washington, DC 20231."

Signed: _____
                                                       Inventor

Form 10-1: Patent Application Transmittal Letter

In the United States Patent and Trademark Office

Mailed 199_____

Box Patent Application
Assistant Commissioner for Patents
Washington, District of Columbia 20231

Fee Transmittal

First-Named Applicant _____

Title of Invention: " _____ "

Total Payment Enclosed (From Calculation Below): $ _____ ☐ Check   ☐ Money Order

Sir:

Enclosed is the following small entity filing fee for the above patent application:

Fee Code	Fee Description	Fee ($)
214	Provisional Pat. Appn. Filing Fee	_____
201	Basic Utility Appn. Filing Fee	_____
206	Basic Design Appn. Filing Fee	_____
	Subtotal (1)	==============

203	Total Claims: _____ − 20 = _____ ; X _____ (fee for each claim over 20) = _____
202	Tot. Indep. Claims _____ − 3 = _____ ; X _____ (fee for each indep. claim over 3) = _____
	Subtotal (2) ==============

Total Payment Enclosed [Sum of Subtotals (1) and (2)]   ============

Very respectfully,

_____
Signature of First-Named Applicant

_____
Print Name of First-Named Applicant

_____
Address

_____

_____

Declaration for Utility or Design Patent Application

As a below-named inventor, I hereby declare that my residence, post office address, and citizenship are as stated below next to my name and that I believe that I am the original, first, and sole inventor [if only one name is listed below] or an original, first, and joint inventor [if plural names are listed below] of the subject matter which is claimed and for which a patent is sought on the invention, the specification of which is attached hereto and which has the following title:

" _____ "

I have reviewed and understand the contents of the above-identified specification, including the claims, as amended by any amendment specifically referred to in the oath or declaration. I acknowledge a duty to disclose information which is material to the examination of this application in accordance with Title 37, Code of Federal Regulations, Section 1.56(a).

I hereby declare that all statements made herein of my own knowledge are true and that all statements made on information and belief are believed to be true; and further that these statements were made with the knowledge that willful false statements and the like so made are punishable by fine or imprisonment, or both, under Title 18, United States Code, Section 1001, and that such willful false statements may jeopardize the validity of the application or any patent issued thereon.

Please send correspondence and make telephone calls to the First Inventor below.

Signature: Sole/First Inventor: _____

Print Name: _____ Date: _____

Legal Residence:* _____ Citizen of: _____

Post Office Address: _____

_____

Telephone: _____

Signature: Joint/Second Inventor: _____

Print Name: _____ Date: _____

Legal Residence:* _____ Citizen of: _____

Post Office Address: _____

_____

Telephone: _____

* City and state, county and state or city, state and country, if foreign.

In the United States Patent and Trademark Office

First/Sole Applicant: _____

Joint/Second Applicant: _____

Title: "_____"

Small Entity Declaration—Independent Inventor(s)

As a below-named inventor, I hereby declare that I qualify as an independent inventor as defined in 37 CFR 1.9(c) for purposes of paying reduced fees under Section 41(a) and (b) of Title 35 United States Code, to the Patent and Trademark Office with regard to my above-identified invention described in the specification filed herewith. I have not assigned, granted, conveyed, or licensed—and am under no obligation under any contract or law to assign, grant, convey, or license—any rights in the invention to either (a) any person who could not be classified as an independent inventor under 37 CFR 1.9(c) if that person had made the invention, or (b) any concern which would not qualify as either (i) a small business concern under 37 CFR 1.9(d) or (ii) a nonprofit organization under 37 CFR 1.9(e).

Each person, concern, or organization to which I have assigned, granted, conveyed, or licensed—or am under an obligation under contract or law to assign, grant, convey, or license—any rights in the invention is listed below:

☐ There is no such person, concern, or organization.

☐ Any applicable person, concern, or organization is listed below:[*]

Full Name: _____

Address: _____

_____

I acknowledge a duty to file, in the above application for patent, notification of any change in status resulting in loss of entitlement to small entity status prior to paying, or at the time of paying, the earliest of the issue fee or any maintenance fee due after the date on which status as a small entity is no longer appropriate (37 CFR 1.28(b)).

I hereby declare that all statements made herein of my own knowledge are true and that all statements made on information and belief are believed to be true; and further that these statements were made with the knowledge that willful false statements and the like so made are punishable by fine or imprisonment or both, under Section 1001 of Title 18 of the United States Code, and that such willful false statements may jeopardize the validity of the application, any patent issuing thereon, or any patent to which this verified statement is directed.

_____   _____
Signature of Sole/First Inventor   Signature of Joint/Second Inventor

_____   _____
Print Name of Sole/First Inventor   Print Name of Joint/Second Inventor

_____   _____
Date of Signature   Date of Signature

*Note: A separate Small Entity Statement is required from any listed entity.

In the United States Patent and Trademark Office

First/Sole Applicant: _____

Joint/Second Applicant: _____

Title: " _____ "

Small Entity Declaration—Non-Inventor Individual

I hereby declare that I am making this verified statement to support a claim by _____

_____

for small entity status for purposes of paying reduced fees under 35 USC 41(a) & (b) with regard to the above-entitled invention of the above applicants and described in the specification filed herewith.

I hereby declare that I would qualify as an independent inventor as defined in 37 CFR 1.9(c) for the purpose of paying reduced fees under 35 USC 41(a) & (b) if I had made the above-identified invention.

I have not assigned, granted, conveyed, or licensed—and am under no obligation under any contract or law to assign, grant, convey, or license—any rights in the invention to either (a) any person who could not be classified as an independent inventor under 37 CFR 1.9(c) if that person had made the invention, or (b) any concern which would not qualify as either (i) a small business concern under 37 CFR 1.9(d) or (ii) a nonprofit organization under 37 CFR 1.9(e).

I have not assigned, granted, conveyed, or licensed—and am not under any obligation under contract or law to assign, grant, convey, or license—any rights in the invention to any person, concern, or organization.

I acknowledge a duty to file, in the above application for patent, notification of any change in status resulting in loss of entitlement to small entity status prior to paying, or at the time of paying, the earliest of the issue fee or any maintenance fee due after the date on which status as a small entity is no longer appropriate (37 CFR 1.28(b)).

I hereby declare that all statements made herein of my own knowledge are true and that all statements made on information and belief are believed to be true; and further that these statements were made with the knowledge that willful false statements and the like so made are punishable by fine or imprisonment, or both, under Section 1001 of Title 18 of the United States Code, and that such willful false statements may jeopardize the validity of the application, any patent issuing thereon, or any patent to which this verified statement is directed.

_____   _____
Signature of Non-Inventor   Date of Signature

_____
Print Name and Address of Non-Inventor

_____

_____

In the United States Patent and Trademark Office

First/Sole Applicant: _____

Joint/Second Applicant: _____

Title: "_____"

Small Entity Declaration—Small Business Concern

I hereby declare that I am

☐ the owner of the small business concern identified below:

☐ an officer of the small business concern empowered to act on behalf of the concern identified below:

    Name of Concern: _____

    Address of Concern: _____

    _____

I hereby declare that the above identified small business concern qualifies as a small business concern as defined in 13 CFR 121.3-18, and reproduced in 37 CFR 1.9(d), for purposes of paying reduced fees under section 41(a) and (b) of Title 35, United States Code, in that the number of employees of the concern, including those of its affiliates, does not exceed 500 persons. For purposes of this statement, (1) the number of employees of the business concern is the average over the previous fiscal year of the concern of the persons employed on a full-time, part-time or temporary basis during each of the pay periods of the fiscal year, and (2) concerns are affiliates of each other when either, directly or indirectly, one concern controls or has the power to control the other, or a third party or parties controls or has the power to control both.

I hereby declare that rights under contract or law have been conveyed to and remain with the small business concern identified above with regard to the above entitled invention of the above applicants and the specification filed herewith.

I acknowledge a duty to file, in the above application for patent, notification of any change in status resulting in loss of entitlement to small entity status prior to paying, or at the time of paying, the earliest of the issue fee or any maintenance fee due after the date on which status as a small entity is no longer appropriate (37 CFR 1.28(b)).

I hereby declare that all statements made herein of my own knowledge are true and that all statements made on information and belief are believed to be true; and further that these statements were made with the knowledge that willful false statements and the like so made are punishable by fine or imprisonment or both, under Section 1001 of Title 18 of the United States Code, and that such willful false statements may jeopardize the validity of the application, any patent issuing thereon, or any patent to which this verified statement is directed.

_____   _____
Signature of Officer of Small Business Concern   Date

_____
Name and Title of Officer

_____
Address of Officer

In the United States Patent and Trademark Office

First/Sole Applicant: _____

Joint/Second Applicant: _____

Title: " _____ "

Small Entity Declaration—Nonprofit Organization

I hereby declare that I am an official empowered to act on behalf of the nonprofit organization identified below:

Name of Organization _____

Address of Organization _____

_____

Type of Organization:

☐ University or Other Institution of Higher Education

☐ Tax Exempt Under Internal Revenue Service Code (26 USC 501(a) and 501(c) (3))

☐ Nonprofit Scientific or Educational Under Statute of State of the United States of America

(Name of State _____)

(Citation of Statute _____)

☐ Would Qualify as Tax Exempt Under Internal Revenue Service Code (26 USC 501(a) and 501(c) (3)) if located in the United States of America

☐ Would Qualify as Nonprofit Scientific or Educational Under Statute of State of the United States of America if located in the United States of America

(Name of State _____)

(Citation of Statute _____)

I hereby declare the nonprofit organization identified above qualifies as a nonprofit organization as defined in 37 CFR 1.9(e) for purposes of paying reduced fees under section 41(a) and (b) of Title 35 , United States Code, with regard to the above-entitled invention of the above applicant(s) and the specification filed herewith.

I hereby declare that rights under contract or law have been conveyed to and remain with the nonprofit organization with regard to the above identified invention.

I acknowledge a duty to file, in the above application for patent, notification of any change in status resulting in loss of entitlement to small entity status prior to paying, or at the time of paying, the earliest of the issue fee or any maintenance fee due after the date on which status as a small entity is no longer appropriate (37 CFR 1.28(b)).

I hereby declare that all statements made herein of my own knowledge are true and that all statements made on information and belief are believed to be true; and further that these statements were made with the knowledge that willful false statements and the like so made are punishable by fine or imprisonment or both, under Section 1001 of Title 18 of the United States Code, and that such willful false statements may jeopardize the validity of the application, any patent issuing thereon, or any patent to which this verified statement is directed.

_____   _____

Signature or Officer of Non-Profit Organization   Date

_____

Name and Title of Officer

_____

Address of Officer

_____

In the United States Patent and Trademark Office

Serial Number: _____

Appn. Filed: _____

Applicant(s): _____

Appn. Title: _____

Examiner/GAU: _____

Mailed: _____

At: _____

Information Disclosure Statement

Assistant Commissioner for Patents

Washington, District of Columbia 20231

Sir:

Attached is a completed Form PTO-1449 and copies of the pertinent parts of the references cited thereon. Following are comments on any non-English-language references pursuant to Rule 98:

Very respectfully,

Applicant(s): _____

_____

Enc.: PTO-1449 & References

c/o: _____

_____

_____

Telephone: _____

FORM PTO-1449 (Substitute)

LIST OF PRIOR ART CITED BY APPLICANT

(Use several sheets if necessary)

ATTY. DOCKET NO.	SERIAL NO.
APPLICANT	
FILING DATE	GROUP

U.S. PATENT DOCUMENTS

*EXAMINER INITIAL		DOCUMENT NUMBER	DATE	NAME	CLASS	SUBCLASS	FILING DATE IF APPROPRIATE
	AA						
	AB						
	AC						
	AD						
	AE						
	AF						
	AG						
	AH						
	AI						
	AJ						
	AK						

FOREIGN PATENT DOCUMENTS

	AL						
	AM						
	AN						
	AO						
	AP						

OTHER PRIOR ART *(Including Author, Title, Date, Pertinent Pages, Etc.)*

	AR						
	AS						
	AT						

EXAMINER	DATE CONSIDERED

*EXAMINER: *Initial if reference considered, whether or not citation is in conformance with MPEP 609; Draw line through citation if not in conformance and not considered. Include copy of this form with next communication to applicant.*

In the United States Patent and Trademark Office

Serial Number: _____

Appn. Filed: _____

Applicant(s): _____

Appn. Title: _____

Examiner/GAU: _____

Mailed: _____

At: _____

Petition to Make Special

Assistant Commissioner for Patents

Washington, District of Columbia 20231

Sir:

Applicant hereby respectfully petitions that the above application be made special under MPEP Sec. 708.02 for the following reason; attached is a declaration in support thereof:

I.   ☐ Manufacturer Available;*

II. ☐ Infringement Exists;*

III. ☐ Applicant's Health Is Poor;

IV. ☐ Applicant's Age Is 65 or Greater;

V.   ☐ Environmental Quality Will Be Enhanced;

VI.   ☐ Energy Savings Will Result;

VII. ☐ Recombinant DNA Is Involved;*

VIII. ☐ Special Procedure: Search Was Made;*

IX . ☐ Superconductivity Is Advanced;

X .   ☐ Relates to HIV/AIDS or Cancer.*

* ☐   Also attached, since reason I, II, VII, VIII, or X has been checked, is the $ _____ Petition Fee pursuant to Rules 102 and 17(i).

Very respectfully,

Applicant(s): _____

_____

Attachment(s): Fee if indicated and supporting Declaration

c/o: _____

_____

_____

Telephone: _____

Design Patent Application—Preamble, Specification, and Claim

Box Design

Assistant Commissioner for Patents

Washington, District of Columbia 20231

Sir:

Preamble:

The petitioner(s) whose signature(s) appear on the declaration attached respectfully request that Letters Patent be granted to such petitioner(s) for the new and original design set forth in the following specification. The filing fee of $_____, _____ sheets of drawings (3 copies ea.), a patent application declaration, a small entity declaration, and a return receipt postcard are attached.

Specification:

The undersigned has (have) invented a new, original, and ornamental design entitled

" _____ "

of which the following is a specification. Reference is made to the accompanying drawings which form a part hereof, the figures of which are described as follows:

Fig. 1 is a _____ view.

Fig. 2 is a _____ view.

Claim: I (We) Claim:

The ornamental design for a _____

_____ , as shown.

Express Mail Label # (_____) **; Date of Deposit 199** _____

I hereby certify that this paper or fee is being deposited with the United States Postal Service using "Express Mail Post Office to Addressee" service under 37 CFR 1.10 on the date indicated above and is addressed to "Assistant Commissioner for Patents, Washington, DC 20231."

Signed: _____

Inventor

In the United States Patent and Trademark Office

Serial Number: _____

Appn. Filed: _____

Applicant(s): _____

Appn. Title: _____

Examiner/GAU: _____

Mailed: _____

At: _____

Amendment _____

Assistant Commissioner for Patents

Washington, District of Columbia 20231

Sir:

In response to the Office Letter mailed _____, 19_____ , please amend the above application as follows:

In the United States Patent and Trademark Office

Serial Number: _____

Appn. Filed: _____

Applicant(s): _____

Appn. Title: _____

Examiner/GAU: _____

Mailed: _____

At: _____

Request for Approval of Proposed Drawing Amendment

Assistant Commissioner for Patents

Washington, District of Columbia 20231

Sir:

Applicant(s) respectfully request(s) permission to amend the drawing(s) of the above application after allowance. The proposed changes are indicated in red on the photocopy(ies) of Fig.(s) _____

or sheets _____ thereof attached below.

Very respectfully,

Applicant(s): _____

_____

c/o: _____

_____

_____

Tel.: _____

Certificate of Mailing

I certify that this correspondence will be deposited with the United States Postal Service as first class mail with proper postage affixed in an envelope addressed to: "Assistant Commissioner for Patents, Washington, DC 20231" on the date below.

Date: 199 _____ _____ , Applicant

In the United States Patent and Trademark Office

Serial Number: _____

Appn. Filed: _____

Applicant(s): _____

Appn. Title: _____

Examiner/GAU: _____

Mailed: _____

At: _____

Submission of Corrected Drawings

Assistant Commissioner for Patents

Washington, District of Columbia 20231

Attn: Chief Draftsperson

Sir:

New drawing sheet(s) (_____) for the above application is/are enclosed, corrected as necessary. Please substitute this/these for the corresponding sheet(s) on file.

Very respectfully,

Applicant(s): _____

_____

c/o: _____

_____

_____

Tel.: _____

Certificate of Mailing

I certify that this correspondence will be deposited with the United States Postal Service as first class mail with proper postage affixed in an envelope addressed to: "Assistant Commissioner for Patents, Washington, DC 20231" on the date below.

Date: 199 _____   _____, Applicant

In the United States Patent and Trademark Office

Serial Number: _____

Appn. Filed: _____

Applicant(s): _____

Appn. Title: _____

Examiner/GAU: _____

Mailed: _____

At: _____

Supplemental Declaration
(for Use After Close of Prosecution or With Continuation-in-Part Application)

As an applicant in the above-identified application, I declare as follows:

1. If only one inventor is named below, I am a sole inventor, and if more than one inventor is named below, I am a joint inventor with the inventor(s) named below of the subject matter of the above-identified application.

2. I have reviewed and understand the contents of the specification and claims, as originally filed, and as amended by the amendment(s) dated _____ .

3. I believe that I, and the other inventor(s) named below if more than one inventor is named below, am the original and first inventor or inventors of the subject matter which is claimed and for which a patent is sought.

4. I acknowledge the duty to disclose information which is material to the examination of the application in accordance with 37 C.F.R. Section 1.56(a), and if this oath accompanies or refers to a continuation-in-part application, I acknowledge the duty to disclose material information as defined in 37 C.F.R. Section 1.56(a) which occurred between the filing date of the prior application and the national or PCT international filing date of the continuation-in-part application.

5. I hereby declare that all statements made herein of my own knowledge are true and that all statements made on information and belief are believed to be true, and further that these statements were made with the knowledge that willful false statements and the like so made are punishable by fine or imprisonment, or both, under Section 1001 of Title 18 of the United States Code, and that such willful false statements may jeopardize the validity of the application, any patent issuing thereon, or any patent to which this verified statement is directed.

_____   _____
Signature of Inventor   Signature of Joint Inventor

_____   _____
Printed Name of Inventor   Printed Name of Joint Inventor

_____   _____
Date   Date

In the United States Patent and Trademark Office

Serial Number: _____

Appn. Filed: _____

Applicant(s): _____

Appn. Title: _____

Examiner/GAU: _____

Mailed: _____

At: _____

Petition for Extension of Time
(Rules 136 and 17(a)-(d))

Outstanding Office Action Mailed 199 _____

Original Period for Response Expired 199 _____

Request for Extension of _____ Month(s) to 199 _____

Sml. Ent. Petn. Fee Enc.: ☐ $ _____ (1 mo.); ☐ $ _____ (2 mo.); ☐ $ _____ (3 mo.); ☐ $ _____ (4 mo.)

Assistant Commissioner for Patents

Washington, District of Columbia 20231

Sir:

In the above application, applicant(s) respectfully petition that the period for response to the outstanding Office Action indicated above be extended for the additional month(s), also indicated above. A response to such Office Action and the above Petition Fee (Small Entity) are enclosed herewith. (This extension will not extend the time over the statutory period of six months from the date of the Office Action.)

Very respectfully,

Applicant(s): _____

_____

c/o: _____

_____

_____

Tel.: _____

Certificate of Mailing

I certify that this correspondence will be deposited with the United States Postal Service as first class mail with proper postage affixed in an envelope addressed to: "Assistant Commissioner for Patents, Washington, DC 20231" on the date below.

Date: 199 _____   _____ , Applicant

In the United States Patent and Trademark Office

Serial Number: _____

Appn. Filed: _____

Applicant(s): _____

Appn. Title: _____

Examiner/GAU: _____

Mailed: _____

At: _____

Request for File-Wrapper-Continuing Application

Box FWC

Assistant Commissioner for Patents

Washington, District of Columbia 20231

Sir:

Pursuant to Rule 62, please file a file-wrapper-continuing application of the above pending complete application. This Rule 62 continuing application is being actually filed in the PTO or express mailed during the pendency of the above application. It should be a ☐ Continuation-in-Part ☐ Division ☐ Continuation of the above application. Please use the specification (including the claims and abstract) of the above application and also use the Declaration therefrom if this is a Continuation or Division.

    ☐ Enclosed is a Preliminary Amendment for this Rule 62 Application.

    ☐ Please enter the Amendment Under Rule 116 in the parent application.

    ☐ Enclosed is a new Declaration if this is a CIP application.

    Please use ☐ the drawings of the above application ☐ the new drawing(s) enclosed (_____ sheets).

    After entry of this Preliminary Amendment (or any Amendments under Rule 116 in the above application) there will be not more than 3 independent claims and 20 total claims. A small entity declaration ☐ was enclosed for the above application ☐ is enclosed. Thus the filing fee for the Rule 62 Application will be $_____; a check for this amount is enclosed.

Very respectfully,

Applicant(s): _____

_____

Enc(s): Filing Fee; Also New Declaration and/or Amendment, if indicated

c/o: _____

_____

_____

Tel.: _____

Express Mail Label # ⟨_____⟩ **; Date of Deposit 199** _____

I hereby certify that this paper or fee is being deposited with the United States Postal Service using "Express Mail Post Office to Addressee" service under 37 CFR 1.10 on the date indicated above and is addressed to "Box FWC, Assistant Commissioner for Patents, Washington, DC 20231."

Signed: _____

Inventor

In the United States Patent and Trademark Office

Patent No.: _____

Issued: _____

Patentee(s): _____

Ser. Nr.: _____

Filed: _____

Request for Certificate of Correction

Date: _____

Assistant Commissioner for Patents

Washington, District of Columbia 20231

Sir:

1. The above patent contains significant error, as indicated on the attached Certificate of Correction form (submitted in duplicate). These errors arose at the respective places in the application file indicated below.

☐ 2. Since such error arose through the fault of the Patent and Trademark Office, it is requested that the Certificate be issued at no cost to applicant.

☐ 3. Such error arose through the fault of applicant(s). A check for $ _____ for the fee is enclosed. Such error is of a clerical or minor nature and occurred in good faith and therefore issuance of the Certificate of Correction is respectfully requested.

4. Specifically,

Very respectfully,

_____   _____
Patentee   Co-Patentee

Encs.

_____   _____
Address

_____   _____

(_____) _____ – _____
Phone

United States Patent and Trademark Office
Certificate of Correction

Patent No.:

Dated:

Inventor(s):

It is certified that error appears in the above-identified patent and that said Letters Patent are hereby corrected as shown below:

Mailing Address of Sender: Patent No.:

_____   _____

_____

_____

Maintenance Fee Reminder

Next fee due: _____ / _____ / _____
yr   mo   date

(Write year in pencil and change after each payment)

Patent Nr.: _____   Issued: _____

Application Serial Nr.: _____   Filed: _____

Title: _____

Patentee(s) (Inventor[s]/Applicant[s]): _____

Assignee(s) (if any): _____

Expires _____ (if all three maintenance fees are paid).[1]

☐ Small entity declaration was filed in application or patent.

(If not, large entity fees[2] must be paid.)

Maintenance Fee Number	Fee Due From:	To:	Sent Form & Check [4]	Amount	Received Receipt Statement
I. Due 3.0 - 3.5 YAI [3]	/ /	/ /	/ /	$	/ /
II. Due 7.0 - 7.5 YAI	/ /	/ /	/ /	$	/ /
III. Due 11.0 - 11.5 YAI	/ /	/ /	/ /	$	/ /

Notes: _____

_____

_____

_____

_____

_____

_____

_____

_____

_____

_____

_____

_____

1. Expiration is 20 years from filing date of application for applications filed after 1995 Jun 7; 17 years from issue date for patents issuing before 1995 Jun 8; and the greater of a 17– or 20–year term for patents issuing after 1995 Jun 7 and filed before 1995 Jun 8, provided you pay all three maintenance fees.

2. Please check all fee amounts before paying since PTO fees change often.

3. YAI = Years After Issue date.

4. Send payment at least a month before due date to allow time to take corrective action before entering grace (penalty) period in case PTO does not accept payment.

In the United States Patent and Trademark Office

Patent No.: _____

Issued: _____

Patentee(s): _____

Ser. Nr.: _____

Filed: _____

Submission of Maintenance Fee

Box M Fee

Assistant Commissioner for Patents

Washington, District of Columbia 20231

Sir:

Enclosed is the following maintenance fee for the above patent: this fee is for a ☐ large entity ☐ small entity, since a small-entity declaration was filed in connection with the above application and small entity status is still proper.

☐ 3.5 yr fee; $ _____; due 3.0 to 3.5 yrs after issue; covers yrs 4.0 thru 8.0.

☐ 7.5 yr fee; $ _____; due 7.0 to 7.5 yrs after issue; covers yrs 8.0 thru 12.0.

☐ 11.5 yr fee; $ _____; due 11.0 to 11.5 yrs after issue; covers yrs 12.0 thru expiration.

☐ Also enclosed is a surcharge of $ _____ (total enclosed $ _____) since this fee is being filed in the six-month grace period after the above due period.

Very respectfully,

_____
Either Patentee/ Assignee

_____
Address

_____

(_____) _____ – _____
Phone

Certificate of Mailing

I certify that this correspondence will be deposited with the United States Postal Service as first class mail with proper postage affixed in an envelope addressed to: "Box M Fee, Assistant Commissioner for Patents, Washington, DC 20231" on the date below.

Date: 199 _____   _____ , Applicant

Joint Owners' Agreement

This agreement is made by and between the following parties who, by separate assignment or as joint applicants, own the following respective shares of the invention, patent application or patent identified below:

_____ of _____ , _____ %,

_____ of _____ , _____ %,

_____ of _____ , _____ %,

Invention Title: _____

Patent Application Ser. Nr.: _____ , Filed: _____

Patent Nr.: _____ , Issued: _____

Applicants: _____

_____

The above patent application data is to be filled in as soon as it becomes available if the application has not yet been filed.

The parties desire to stipulate the terms under which they will exploit this invention and patent application and therefore agree as follows:

1. **No Action Without Everyone's Consent:** None of the parties to this agreement shall license, use, make, or sell the invention or application, or take any other action, other than normal prosecution, without the written consent and cooperation of the other party or parties (hereinafter "parties") to this agreement, except as provided below. Any action so taken shall be committed to a writing signed by all of the parties, or as many parties as consent, with copies to all other parties.

2. **Decisions:** In case any decision must be made in connection with the invention or the patent application, including foreign filing, appealing from an adverse decision in the Patent and Trademark Office, or any opportunity to license, sell, make, or use the invention or application, the parties shall consult on such opportunity and a majority decision shall control. In the event the parties are equally divided, the matter shall be decided in accordance with Paragraph 5 below. After a decision is so made, all parties shall abide by the decision and shall cooperate fully by whatever means are necessary to implement and give full force to such decision. However, if an offer is involved and there is time for any parties to obtain a better or different offer, they shall be entitled to do so and the decision shall be postponed for up to one month to allow such other parties to act.

3. **Proportionate Sharing:** The parties to this agreement shall share, in the percentages indicated above, in all income from, liabilities, and expenditures agreed to be made by any decision under Part 2 above in connection with the invention or patent application. In case a decision is made to make any expenditure, as for foreign patent application filing, exploitation, etc., and a minority or other parties opposes such expenditure or is unable to contribute his or her proportionate share, then the others shall advance the minority or other parties' share of the expenditure. Such others shall be reimbursed by the minority or other parties by double the amount so advanced from the minority or other parties' proportionate share of any income received, provided such income has some reasonable connection with the expenditure. No party

shall be entitled to reimbursement or credit for any labor unless agreed to in advance by all of the parties hereto.

4. **If Any Parties Desire to Manufacture, Etc.:** If any parties who do not constitute all of the parties to this agreement desire to manufacture, distribute, or sell any product or service embodying the above invention, they may do so with the written consent of the other parties under Part 1 above. The cost of the product or service shall include, in addition to normal profit, labor, commission, and/or overhead, etc., provision for a reasonable royalty which shall be paid for the term of the above patent application and any patent which may issue thereon. Such royalty shall be determined before any action is taken under this part and as if a valid patent on the invention had been licensed to an unrelated exclusive licensee (or a nonexclusive licensee if the patent is licensed to others) in an arm's length transaction. Such royalty shall be distributed to all of the parties hereto according to their proportionate shares and on a quarterly basis, accompanied by a written royalty report and sent within one month after the close of each calendar quarter.

5. **In Case of Dispute:** In case any dispute, disagreement, or need for any decision arises out of this agreement or in connection with the invention or patent application, and the parties cannot settle the matter or come to a decision in accordance with Paragraph 2, above, the parties shall first confer as much as necessary to settle the disagreement; all parties shall act and compromise to at least the degree a reasonable person would act. If the parties cannot settle their differences or come to a decision on their own, they shall submit the dispute or matter to mediation and decision by an impartial third party or professional mediator agreed to by all of the parties. If the parties cannot agree on a mediator, or cannot come to an agreement after mediation, then they shall submit the matter to binding arbitration with a mutually acceptable arbitrator or the American Arbitration Association. The arbitrator shall settle the dispute in whatever manner he or she feels will do substantial justice, recognizing the rights of all parties and commercial realities of the marketplace. The parties shall abide by the terms of the arbitrator's decision and shall cooperate fully and do any acts necessary to implement such decision. The costs of the arbitrator shall be advanced by all of the parties or in accordance with Part 3 above and the arbitrator may make any allocation of arbitration costs he or she feels is reasonable.

6. **Non-Frustration:** No party to this Agreement shall commit any act or take any action which frustrates or hampers the rights of another party under this Agreement. Each party shall act in good faith and engage in fair dealing when taking any action under or related to this Agreement.

_____

Date: _____

_____

Date: _____

_____

Date: _____

Assignment of Invention and Patent Application

For value received, _____ ,

_____

of _____

_____

(hereinafter ASSIGNOR), hereby sells, assigns, transfers, and sets over unto _____

_____

of _____

and her or his successors or assigns (hereinafter ASSIGNEE) _____% of the following: (A) ASSIGNOR'S

right, title and interest in and to the invention entitled " _____

_____ "

invented by ASSIGNOR; (B) the application for United States patent therefor, signed by ASSIGNOR on

_____ ,U.S. Patent and Trademark Office Serial Number _____ ,

filed _____; (C) any patent or reissues of any patent that may be

granted thereon; and (D) any applications which are continuations, continuations-in-part, substitutes, or

divisions of said application. ASSIGNOR authorizes ASSIGNEE to enter the date of signature and/or Serial

Number and Filing Date in the spaces above. ASSIGNOR also authorizes and requests the Assistant Commis-

sioner for Patents to issue any resulting patent(s) as follows: _____ % to ASSIGNOR and _____

% to ASSIGNEE. (The singular shall include the plural and vice versa herein.)

ASSIGNOR hereby further sells, assigns, transfers, and sets over unto ASSIGNEE, the above percentage of
ASSIGNOR'S entire right, title and interest in and to said invention in each and every country foreign to the
United States; and ASSIGNOR further conveys to ASSIGNEE the above percentage of all priority rights resulting
from the above-identified application for United States patent. ASSIGNOR agrees to execute all papers, give any
required testimony and perform other lawful acts, at ASSIGNEE'S expense, as ASSIGNEE may require to enable
ASSIGNEE to perfect ASSIGNEE'S interest in any resulting patent of the United States and countries foreign
thereto, and to acquire, hold, enforce, convey, and uphold the validity of said patent and reissues and extensions
thereof, and ASSIGNEE'S interest therein.

In testimony whereof ASSIGNOR has hereunto set its hand and seal on the date below.

_____

_____

State: _____

County: _____ } ss

Subscribed and sworn to before me _____ ,199 _____ .

_____
Notary Public

SEAL

RECORDATION FORM COVER SHEET

PATENTS ONLY

Tab settings ⇨ ⇨ ⇨ ▼   ▼   ▼   ▼   ▼   ▼   ▼

To the Honorable Commissioner of Patents and Trademarks: Please record the attached original documents or copy thereof.

1. Name of conveying party(ies): Additional name(s) of conveying party(ies) attached? ❑ Yes ❑ No	2. Name and address of receiving party(ies): Name: _____ Internal Address: _____ _____ _____ Street Address: _____ _____ City: _____ State: ___ ZIP: _____ Additional name(s) & address(es) attached? ❑ Yes ❑ No

3. Nature of conveyance:

❑ Assignment   ❑ Merger

❑ Security Agreement   ❑ Change of Name

❑ Other _____

Execution Date: _____

4. Application number(s) or patent number(s):

If this document is being filed together with a new application, the execution date of the application is: _____

A. Patent Application No.(s)   B. Patent No.(s)

Additional numbers attached? ❑ Yes ❑ No

5. Name and address of party to whom correspondence concerning document should be mailed: Name: _____ Internal Address: _____ _____ _____ Street Address: _____ _____ City: _____ State: _____ ZIP: _____	6. Total number of applications and patents involved: [ ] 7. Total fee (37 CFR 3.41)..............$_____ ❑ Enclosed ❑ Authorized to be charged to deposit account 8. Deposit account number: (Attach duplicate copy of this page if paying by deposit account)

DO NOT USE THIS SPACE

9. Statement and signature
To the best of my knowledge and belief, the foregoing information is true and correct and any attached copy is a true copy of the original document.

_____   _____   Date [ ]

Name of Person Signing   Signature

Total number of pages comprising cover sheet: [ ]

Universal License Agreement

1. Parties and Summary of Terms:

Parties: This agreement is between:

Licensor: _____ ,

of _____ .

Licensee: _____ ,

of _____ .

Summary: Type of License: ☐ Exclusive   ☐ Nonexclusive

Invention Title: _____ .

Patent Application Ser. Nr.: _____ , Filing Date: _____

If Exclusive License, minimum number of units to be sold to compute Minimum Annual Royalty (MAR): _____

  MARs start first quarter of _____ .

☐ Option Granted: Premium $ _____ For term of: _____ (months)

Patent Royalty Rate _____ %   ☐ Know-How Licensed: Know-How Royalty Rate: _____ %

Total Royalty Rate (Patent Royalty Rate plus Know-How Royalty, if applicable): _____ %.

Estimated 1st year's sales (units): _____ x Estimated Unit Price $ _____

  x Total Royalty Rate _____ % = Licensing Fee $ _____

2. Effective Date: This agreement shall be effective as of the latter of the signature dates below written and shall be referred to as the Agreement of such date.

3. Recitals:

    A. LICENSOR has developed an invention having the above title and warrants that LICENSOR has filed a patent application on such invention in the U.S. Patent and Trademark Office, which patent application is identified by the above title, Serial Number, and Filing Date. LICENSOR warrants that LICENSOR has full and exclusive right to grant this license on this invention and LICENSOR'S patent application. If the "Know-How Licensed" box above is checked, LICENSOR has also developed know-how in connection with said invention and warrants that LICENSOR owns and has the right to license said know-how.

    B. LICENSEE desires, if the "Option Granted" box above is checked, to exclusively investigate LICENSOR'S above invention for the term indicated. If said "Option Granted" box is not checked, or if said box is checked and LICENSEE investigates LICENSOR'S invention for the term indicated and such investigation is favorable, LICENSEE desires to make, use and sell the products embodying such invention and covered by the claims of LICENSOR'S patent application and any patent(s) issuing thereon (hereinafter "Licensed Product").

4. If Option Granted: If the "Option Granted" box above is checked, then (A) the patent license grant of Part 5 below shall not take effect except as defined in this part, and (B) LICENSOR hereby grants LICENSEE, for the option premium stated above, an exclusive option to investigate LICENSOR'S invention for the term indicated above, such term to commence from the date of this Agreement. LICENSOR will furnish LICENSEE with all information and know-how (if any) concerning LICENSOR'S invention in LICENSOR'S possession. LICENSEE will investigate LICENSOR'S invention for operability, costing, marketing, etc. LICENSEE shall report the results of its investigation to LICENSOR at any time before the end of the option term. If LICENSEE'S determination is favorable, it may thereupon exercise this option and the patent license grant of Part 5 below shall become effective. If LICENSEE'S determination is unfavorable, then said option shall not be exercised and no patent license grant shall take effect and all rights hereunder shall revert to LICENSOR and LICENSEE shall deliver to LICENSOR all results of its investigations for LICENSOR'S benefit.

5. Patent License If Option Exercised or If Option Not Granted: If the "Option Granted" box above is checked and LICENSEE has investigated LICENSOR'S invention and such investigation is favorable and

LICENSEE has exercised its option, or if said box is not checked, then LICENSOR hereby grants to LICENSEE, subject to the terms and conditions herein, a patent license of the type (Exclusive or Nonexclusive) checked above. Such patent license shall include the right to grant sublicenses, to make, have made, use, and sell the Licensed Product throughout the United States, its territories, and possessions. Such patent license shall be under LICENSOR'S patent application, any continuations, divisions, continuations-in-part, substitutes, reissues of any patent from any of such applications (hereinafter and hereinbefore LICENSOR'S patent application), any patent(s) issuing thereon, and if the "Know-How Licensed" box is checked above, any know-how transferred to LICENSEE.

6. **If Know-How Licensed:** If the "Know-How" box above is checked, LICENSOR shall communicate to LICENSEE all of LICENSOR'S know-how in respect of LICENSOR'S invention within one month after the date of this Agreement and shall be available to consult with LICENSEE, for up to 80 hours, with respect to the licensed invention and know-how. All travel and other expenses of LICENSOR for such consultation shall be reimbursed by LICENSEE within one month after LICENSOR submits its voucher therefor. LICENSOR makes no warranty regarding the value, suitability, or workability of such know-how. The royalty applicable for such know-how shall be paid, at the rate indicated above, for a minimum of three years from the date of this Agreement if no option is granted, or for three years from the date of exercise if an option is granted and exercised by LICENSOR, and thereafter for so long as LICENSEE makes, uses, or sells Licensed Products and has a share in the United States for of at least 15% of the competitive market for Licensed Products.

7. **Royalties:**

   A. **Licensing Fee:** Unless the "Option Granted" box above is checked, LICENSEE shall pay to LICENSOR, upon execution of this Agreement, a nonrefundable Licensing Fee. This Licensing Fee shall also serve as an advance against future royalties. Such Licensing Fee shall be computed as follows: (A) Take the Total Royalty Rate in percent, as stated above. (B) Multiply by LICENSEE'S Estimate of Its First Year's Sales, in units of Licensed Product, as stated above. (C) Multiply by LICENSEE'S Estimated Unit Price of Licensed Product, in dollars, as stated above. (D) The combined product shall be the Licensing Fee, in dollars, as stated above. When LICENSEE begins actual sales of the Licensed Product, it shall certify its Actual Net Factory Sales Price of Licensed Product to LICENSOR in writing and shall either (1) simultaneously pay LICENSOR any difference due if the Actual Net Factory Sales Price of Licensed Product is more than the Estimated Unit Price, stated above, or (2) advise LICENSOR of any credit to which LICENSEE is entitled if the Actual Net Factory Sales Price of Licensed Product is less than the above Estimated Unit Price. In the latter case, LICENSEE may deduct such credit from its first royalty remittance to LICENSOR, under subpart B below. If an option is granted and exercised under Part 4 above, then LICENSEE shall pay this Licensing Fee to LICENSOR if and when LICENSEE exercises its option.

   B. **Royalty:** If the "Option Granted" box above is not checked, or if said box is checked and LICENSEE has exercised its option under Part 4, LICENSEE shall also pay to LICENSOR a Total Royalty, at the rate stated above. Such royalty shall be at the Patent Royalty Rate stated in Part 1 above, plus, if the "Know-How Licensed" box above is checked, a Know-How Royalty at the Know-How Royalty Rate stated above. Said Total Royalty shall be computed on LICENSEE'S Net Factory Sales Price of Licensed Product. Such Total Royalty shall accrue when the Licensed Products are first sold or disposed of by LICENSEE, or by any sublicensee of LICENSEE. LICENSEE shall pay the Total Royalty due to LICENSOR within one month after the end of each calendar quarter, together with a written report to LICENSOR of the number of units, respective sales prices, and total sales made in such quarter, together with a full itemization of any adjustments made pursuant to subpart F below. LICENSEE'S first report and payment shall be made within one month after the end of the first calendar quarter following the execution of this Agreement. No royalties shall be paid by LICENSEE to LICENSOR until after the Licensing Fee under subpart A above has been earned, but LICENSEE shall make a quarterly report hereunder for every calendar quarter after the execution hereof, whether or not any royalty payment is due for such quarter, except that if an option is granted, LICENSEE shall not make any royalty reports until and if LICENSEE exercises its option.

C. **Minimum Annual Royalties:** If the "Exclusive" box above is checked, so that this is an exclusive license, then this subpart C and subpart D shall be applicable. But if the "Nonexclusive" box is checked above, then these subparts C and D shall be inapplicable. There shall be no minimum annual royalties due under this Agreement until the "Year Commencing," as identified in Part 1 above. For the exclusivity privilege of the patent license grant under Part 5 above, a Minimum Annual Royalty shall be due beginning with such royalty year and for each royalty year ending on the anniversary of such royalty year thereafter. Such Minimum Annual Royalty shall be equal to the Patent Royalty which would have been due if the "Minimum Number of Units [of Licensed Product] to Be Sold to Compute Minimum Annual Royalty" identified in Part 1 above were sold during such royalty year. If less than such number of units of Licensed Product are sold in any royalty year, then the Patent Royalty payable for the fourth quarter of such year shall be increased so as to cause the Patent Royalties paid for such year to equal said Minimum Annual Royalty. If an option is granted under Parts 1 and 4, then no Minimum Annual Royalties shall be due in any case until and if LICENSEE exercises its option.

D. **If Minimum Not Paid:** If this part is applicable and if sales of Licensed Product in any royalty year do not equal or exceed the minimum number of units identified in Part 1 above, LICENSEE may choose not to pay the Minimum Annual Royalty under subpart C above. In this case, LICENSEE shall so notify LICENSOR by the date on which the last royalty for such year is due, i.e., within one month after any anniversary of the date identified in Part 1 above. Thereupon the license grant under Part 4 above shall be converted to a nonexclusive grant, and LICENSOR may immediately license others under the above patent.

E. **Most Favored Licensee:** If this license is nonexclusive, or if it becomes nonexclusive under subpart D above, then (a) LICENSOR shall not grant any other license under the above patent to any other party under any terms which are more favorable than those which LICENSEE pays or enjoys under this Agreement, and (b) LICENSOR shall promptly advise LICENSEE of any such other grant and the terms thereof.

F. **When No Royalties Due:** No Patent Royalties shall be due under this Agreement after the above patent expires or if it is declared invalid by a court of competent jurisdiction from which no appeal can be taken. Also, if LICENSOR'S patent application becomes finally abandoned without any patent issuing, then the Patent Royalty under this Agreement shall be terminated as of the date of abandonment. Any Know-How Royalties under Part 6 above shall continue after any Patent Royalties terminate, provided such Know-How Royalties are otherwise due under such Part 6.

G. **Late Payments:** If any payment due under this Agreement is not timely paid, then the unpaid balance shall bear interest until paid at an annual rate of 10% until the delinquent balance is paid. Such interest shall be compounded monthly.

H. **Net Factory Sales Price:** "Net Factory Sales Price" is defined as the gross factory selling price of Licensed Product, or the U.S. importer's gross selling price if Licensed Product is made abroad, less usual trade discounts actually allowed, but not including advertising allowances or fees or commissions paid to employees or agents of LICENSEE. The Net Factory Sales Price shall not include (1) packing costs, if itemized separately, (2) import and export taxes, excise and other sales taxes, and customs duties, and (3) costs of insurance and transportation, if separately billed, from the place of manufacture if in the U.S., or from the place of importation if manufactured abroad, to the customer's premises or next point of distribution or sale. Bona fide returns may be deducted from units shipped in computing the royalty payable after such returns are made.

8. **Records:** LICENSEE and any of its sublicensees shall keep full, clear, and accurate records with respect to sales subject to royalty under this Agreement. The records shall be made in a manner such that the royalty reports made

pursuant to Part 7B can be verified. LICENSOR, or its authorized agent, shall have the right to examine and audit such records upon reasonable notice during normal business hours, but not more than twice per year. In case of any dispute as to the sufficiency or accuracy of such records, LICENSOR may have any independent auditor examine and certify such records. LICENSEE shall make prompt adjustment to compensate for any errors or omissions disclosed by any such examination and certification of LICENSEE'S records. If LICENSOR does not examine LICENSEE'S records or question any royalty report within two years from the date thereof, then such report shall be considered final and LICENSOR shall have no further right to contest such report.

9. **Sublicensees:** If LICENSEE grants any sublicenses hereunder, it shall notify LICENSOR within one month from any such grant and shall provide LICENSOR with a true copy of any sublicense agreement. Any sublicensee of LICENSEE under this Agreement shall be bound by all of the terms applying to LICENSEE hereunder and LICENSEE shall be responsible for the obligations and duties of any of its sublicensees.

10. **Patent Prosecution:**

   A. Domestic: LICENSOR shall, at LICENSOR'S own expense, prosecute its above U.S. patent application, and any continuations, divisions, continuations-in-part, substitutes, and reissues of such patent application or any patent thereon, at its own expense, until all applicable patents issue or any patent application becomes finally abandoned. LICENSOR shall also pay any maintenance fees which are due on any patent(s) which issue on said patent application. If for any reason LICENSOR intends to abandon any patent application hereunder, it shall notify LICENSEE at least two months in advance of any such abandonment so as to give LICENSEE the opportunity to take over prosecution of any such application and maintenance of any patent. If LICENSEE takes over prosecution, LICENSOR shall cooperate with LICENSEE in any manner LICENSEE requires, at LICENSEE'S expense.

   B. Foreign: LICENSOR shall have the opportunity, but not the obligation, to file corresponding foreign patent applications to any patent application under subpart A above. If LICENSOR files any such foreign patent applications, LICENSOR may license, sell, or otherwise exploit the invention, Licensed Product, or any such foreign application in any countries foreign to the United States as it chooses, provided that LICENSOR must give LICENSEE a right of first refusal and at least one month to exercise this right before undertaking any such foreign exploitation. If LICENSOR chooses not to file any corresponding foreign applications under this part, it shall notify LICENSEE at least one month prior to the first anniversary of the above patent application so as to give LICENSEE the opportunity to file corresponding foreign patent applications if it so chooses.

   C. If Licensee Acts: If LICENSEE takes over prosecution of any U.S. patent application under subpart A above, and LICENSEE is successful so that a patent issues, then LICENSEE shall pay LICENSOR royalties thereafter at a rate of 75% of the royalty rate and any applicable minimum under Part 7C above and LICENSEE shall be entitled to deduct prosecution and maintenance expenses from its royalty payments. If LICENSEE elects to prosecute any foreign patent applications under subpart B above, then LICENSEE shall pay LICENSOR royalties of 50% of the royalty rate under Part 7 above for any applicable foreign sales, less all foreign prosecution and maintenance expenses incurred by LICENSEE.

11. **Marking:** LICENSEE shall mark all units of Licensed Product, or its container if direct marking is not feasible, with the legend "Patent Pending" until any patent(s) issue from the above patent application. When any patent(s) issue, LICENSOR shall promptly notify LICENSEE and thereafter LICENSEE shall mark all units of Licensed Product which it sells with proper notice of patent marking under 35 U.S.C. Section 287.

12. **If Infringement Occurs:** If either party discovers that the above patent is infringed, it shall communicate the details to the other party. LICENSOR shall thereupon have the right, but not the obligation, to take whatever action it deems necessary, including the filing of lawsuits, to protect the rights of the parties to this Agreement and to terminate such infringement. LICENSEE shall cooperate with LICENSOR if LICENSOR takes any such action, but all expenses of LICENSOR shall be borne by LICENSOR. If LICENSOR recovers any damages or compensation for

any action it takes hereunder, LICENSOR shall retain 100% of such damages. If LICENSOR does not wish to take any action hereunder, LICENSEE shall also have the right, but not the obligation, to take any such action, in which case LICENSOR shall cooperate with LICENSEE, but all of LICENSEE'S expenses shall be borne by LICENSEE. LICENSEE shall receive 75% of any damages or compensation it recovers for any such infringement and shall pay 25% of such damages or compensation to LICENSOR, after deducting its costs, including attorney fees.

13. Disclaimer and Hold Harmless:

    A. Disclaimer of Warranty: Nothing herein shall be construed as a warranty or representation by LICENSOR as to the scope or validity of the above patent application or any patent issuing thereon.

    B. Product Liability: LICENSEE shall hold LICENSOR harmless from any product liability actions involving Licensed Product.

14. Term: The term of this Agreement shall end with the expiration of the last of any patent(s) which issues on LICENSOR'S patent application, unless terminated sooner for any reason provided herein, or unless know-how is licensed, in which case the terms of Part 6 shall cover the term of this Agreement.

15. Termination: This Agreement may be terminated under and according to any of the following contingencies:

    A. Default: If LICENSEE fails to make any payment on the date such payment is due under this Agreement, or if LICENSEE makes any other default under or breach of this Agreement, LICENSOR shall have the right to terminate this Agreement upon giving three months' written Notice of Intent to Terminate, specifying such failure, breach, or default to LICENSEE. If LICENSEE fails to make any payment in arrears, or otherwise fails to cure the breach or default within such three-month period, then LICENSOR may then send a written Notice of Termination to LICENSEE, whereupon this Agreement shall terminate in one month from the date of such Notice of Termination. If this Agreement is terminated hereunder, LICENSEE shall not be relieved of any of its obligations to the date of termination and LICENSOR may act to enforce LICENSEE'S obligations after any such termination.

    B. Bankruptcy, Etc.: If LICENSEE shall go into receivership, bankruptcy, or insolvency, or make an assignment for the benefit of creditors, or go out of business, this Agreement shall be immediately terminable by LICENSOR by written notice, but without prejudice to any rights of LICENSOR hereunder.

    C. Antishelving: If LICENSEE discontinues its sales or manufacture of Licensed Product without intent to resume, it shall so notify LICENSOR within one month of such discontinuance, whereupon LICENSOR shall have the right to terminate this Agreement upon one month's written notice, even if this Agreement has been converted to a nonexclusive grant under Part 7D above. If LICENSEE does not begin manufacture or sales of Licensed Product within one and one-half years from the date of this Agreement or the date of its option exercise if an option is granted, or, after commencing manufacture and sales of Licensed Product, discontinues its manufacture and sales of Licensed Product for one and one-half years, LICENSOR shall have the right to terminate this Agreement upon one months' written notice, unless LICENSEE can show that it in good faith intends and is actually working to resume or begin manufacture or sales, and has a reasonable basis to justify its delay. In such case LICENSEE shall advise LICENSOR in writing, before the end of such one-and-one-half-year period, of the circumstances involved and LICENSEE shall thereupon have up to an additional year to resume or begin manufacture or sales. It is the intent of the parties hereto that LICENSOR shall not be deprived of the opportunity, for an unreasonable length of time, to exclusively license its patent if LICENSEE has discontinued or has not commenced manufacture or sales of Licensed Product. In no case shall LICENSOR have the right to terminate this Agreement if and so long as LICENSEE is paying LICENSOR minimum annual royalties under Part 7C above.

16. Notices: All notices, payments, or statements under this Agreement shall be in writing and shall be sent by first-class certified mail, return receipt requested, postage prepaid, to the party concerned at the above address, or to any substituted address given by notice hereunder. Any such notice, payment, or statement shall be considered sent or made on the day deposited in the mails. Payments and statements may be sent by ordinary mail.

17. **Mediation and Arbitration:** If any dispute arises under this Agreement, the parties shall negotiate in good faith to settle such dispute. If the parties cannot resolve such dispute themselves, then either party may submit the dispute to mediation by a mediator approved by both parties. The parties shall both cooperate with the mediator. If the parties cannot agree to any mediator, or if either party does not wish to abide by any decision of the mediator, then they shall submit the dispute to arbitration by any mutually acceptable arbitrator. If no arbitrator is mutually acceptable, then they shall submit the matter to arbitration under the rules of the American Arbitration Association (AAA). Under any arbitration, both parties shall cooperate with and agree to abide finally by any decision of the arbitration proceeding. If the AAA is selected, the arbitration shall take place under the auspices of the nearest branch of the AAA to the other party. The costs of the arbitration proceeding shall be borne according to the decision of the arbitrator, who may apportion costs equally, or in accordance with any finding of fault or lack of good faith of either party. The arbitrator's award shall be non-appealable and enforceable in any court of competent jurisdiction.

18. **Assignment:** The rights of LICENSOR under this Agreement shall be assignable or otherwise transferrable, in whole or in part, by LICENSOR and shall vest LICENSOR'S assigns or transferees with the same rights and obligations as were held by LICENSOR. This Agreement shall be assignable by LICENSEE to any entity that succeeds to the business of LICENSEE to which Licensed Products relate or to any other entity if LICENSOR'S permission is first obtained in writing.

19. **Jurisdiction and Venue:** This Agreement shall be interpreted under the laws of LICENSOR'S state, as given in Part 1 above. Any action related to this Agreement shall be brought in the county of LICENSOR'S above address; LICENSEE hereby consents to such venue.

20. **Non-Frustration:** Neither party to this Agreement shall commit any act or take any action which frustrates or hampers the rights of the other party under this Agreement. Each party shall act in good faith and engage in fair dealing when taking any action under or related to this Agreement.

21. **Rectification:** In case of any mistake in this Agreement, including any error, ambiguity, illegality, contradiction, or omission, this Agreement shall be interpreted as if such mistake were rectified in a manner which implements the intent of the parties as nearly as possible and effects substantial fairness, considering all pertinent circumstances.

22. **Entire Agreement:** This Agreement sets forth the entire understanding between the parties and supersedes any prior or contemporaneous oral understandings and any prior written agreements.

23. **Signatures:** The parties, having carefully read this Agreement and having consulted or have been given an opportunity to consult counsel, have indicated their agreement to all of the above terms by signing this Agreement on the respective dates below indicated. LICENSEE and LICENSOR have each received a copy of this Agreement with both LICENSEE'S and LICENSOR'S original ink signatures thereon.

Licensor: _____   Date: _____

Print Licensor's Name _____

Licensee: _____   Date: _____

Print Licensee's Name:_____

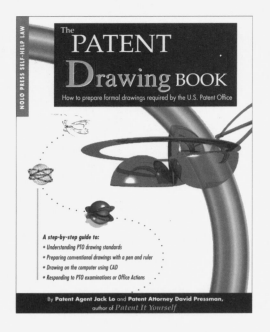

The Patent Drawing Book

How to Prepare Formal Drawings
Required by the U.S. Patent Office

By Patent Agent Jack Lo and Patent Attorney David Pressman

1st Edition • $29.95

Got it in mind but not on paper? Professional patent drafters charge hundreds of dollars to prepare patent drawings, but you can use this book to do it yourself. This invaluable guide and companion to David Pressman's bestselling *Patent It Yourself* will tell you exactly what you need to do to draw your invention and meet every one of the Patent and Trademark Office guidelines. Whether you're preparing conventional drawings with pen and ruler or using computer automated drawing programs or photographic techniques, this book will guide you step by step through the entire process, from understanding PTO drawing standards to responding to PTO examinations and Office Actions.

NOLO PRESS • 950 Parker Street, Berkeley, CA 94710

NOLO PRESS

Index

CATALOG

...more from Nolo Press

CALL 800-992-6656 OR USE THE ORDER FORM IN THE BACK OF THE BOOK

		EDITION	PRICE	CODE

HOMEOWNERS, LANDLORDS & TENANTS

Dog Law	3rd	$14.95	DOG
▣ Every Landlord's Legal Guide (National Edition)	1st	$34.95	ELLI
How to Buy a House in California	4th	$24.95	BHCA
Leases & Rental Agreements (Quick & Legal Series)	1st	$18.95	LEAR
Neighbor Law: Fences, Trees, Boundaries & Noise	2nd	$16.95	NEI
Safe Homes, Safe Neighborhoods: Stopping Crime Where You Live	1st	$14.95	SAFE

HUMOR

29 Reasons Not to Go to Law School	4th	$9.95	29R
Poetic Justice	1st	$9.95	PJ

IMMIGRATION

How to Become a United States Citizen	5th	$14.95	CIT
How to Get a Green Card: Legal Ways to Stay in the U.S.A.	2nd	$24.95	GRN
U.S. Immigration Made Easy	5th	$39.95	IMEZ

MONEY MATTERS

Chapter 13 Bankruptcy: Repay Your Debts	2nd	$29.95	CH13
Credit Repair (Quick & Legal Series)	1st	$15.95	CREP
How to File for Bankruptcy	6th	$26.95	HFB
Money Troubles: Legal Strategies to Cope With Your Debts	4th	$19.95	MT
Nolo's Law Form Kit: Personal Bankruptcy	1st	$14.95	KBNK
Stand Up to the IRS	3rd	$24.95	SIRS

PATENTS AND COPYRIGHTS

The Copyright Handbook: How to Protect and Use Written Works	4th	$29.95	COHA
Copyright Your Software	1st	$39.95	CYS
The Patent Drawing Book	1st	$29.95	DRAW
Patent, Copyright & Trademark: A Desk Reference to Intellectual Property Law	1st	$24.95	PCTM
Patent It Yourself	6th	$44.95	PAT
▣ Software Development: A Legal Guide (Book with disk—PC)	1st	$44.95	SFT

RESEARCH & REFERENCE

● Law on the Net, (Book w/CD-ROM—Windows/Macintosh)	2nd	$39.95	LAWN
Legal Research: How to Find & Understand the Law	4th	$19.95	LRES

SENIORS

Beat the Nursing Home Trap	2nd	$18.95	ELD
Social Security, Medicare & Pensions	6th	$19.95	SOA

SOFTWARE
Call for special direct discounts on Software

Living Trust Maker 2.0—Macintosh	2.0	$79.95	LTM2
Living Trust Maker 2.0—Windows	2.0	$79.95	LTWI2
Small Business Legal Pro Deluxe CD—Windows/Macintosh CD-ROM	2.0	$79.95	SBCD
Nolo's Partnership Maker 1.0—DOS	1.0	$79.95	PAGI1
Personal RecordKeeper 4.0—Macintosh	4.0	$49.95	RKM4
Personal RecordKeeper 4.0—Windows	4.0	$49.95	RKP4
Patent It Yourself 1.0—Windows	1.0	$229.95	PYP12
WillMaker 6.0—Macintosh	6.0	$49.95	WM6B
WillMaker 6.0—Windows	6.0	$49.95	WIW6B

Special Upgrade Offer
Get 25% off the latest edition off your Nolo book

It's important to have the most current legal information. Because laws and legal procedures change often, we update our books regularly. To help keep you up-to-date we are extending this special upgrade offer. Cut out and mail the title portion of the cover of your old Nolo book and we'll give you 25% off the retail price of the NEW EDITION of that book when you purchase directly from us. For more information call us at 1-800-992-6656. This offer is to individuals only.

▣ Book with disk

● Book with CD-ROM

ORDER FORM

Code	Quantity	Title	Unit price	Total
		Subtotal		
		California residents add Sales Tax		
		Basic Shipping ($6.00 for 1 item; $7.00 for 2 or more)		
		UPS RUSH delivery $7.50–any size order*		
		TOTAL		

Name

Address

(UPS to street address, Priority Mail to P.O. boxes)

* Delivered in 3 business days from receipt of order.
S.F. Bay Area use regular shipping.

FOR FASTER SERVICE, USE YOUR CREDIT CARD AND OUR TOLL-FREE NUMBERS

Order 24 hours a day	1-800-992-6656
Fax your order	1-800-645-0895
e-mail	cs@nolo.com
General Information	1-510-549-1976
Customer Service	1-800-728-3555, Mon.-Fri. 9am-5pm, PST

METHOD OF PAYMENT

☐ Check enclosed
☐ VISA   ☐ MasterCard   ☐ Discover Card   ☐ American Express

Account #   Expiration Date

Authorizing Signature

Daytime Phone

PRICES SUBJECT TO CHANGE.

VISIT OUR OUTLET STORES!

You'll find our complete line of books and software, all at a discount.

BERKELEY
950 Parker Street
Berkeley, CA 94710
1-510-704-2248

SAN JOSE
111 N. Market Street, #115
San Jose, CA 95113
1-408-271-7240

VISIT US ONLINE!

on the Internet
www.nolo.com

N O L O   P R E S S   9 5 0   P A R K E R   S T . ,   B E R K E L E Y ,   C A   9 4 7 1 0

Patent, Copyright and Trademark

A Desk Reference to Intellectual Property Law

by Attorney Stephen Elias

$24.95 • PCTM

This invaluable bestseller provides a plain-English, easy-to-understand overview of patent, copyright, trademark and trade secret law. Clear concise definitions, contextual examples, and sample forms and agreements demystify one of the most complex and confusing areas of the law.

Software Development

A Legal Guide

by Attorney Stephen Fishman

$44.95 • SFT

This book is an invaluable guide to the tangle of complex legal rules regulating software development and protection. It includes step-by-step instructions and all the forms needed to register a software copyright with the U.S. Copyright Office, along with practical, thorough and comprehensive advice about copyright law. All contracts, agreements and legal forms are provided on disk.

Small Business Legal Pro Deluxe CD

$79.95 • Windows/Macintosh • SBCD2

This comprehensive CD-ROM contains all the legal information a small business needs to thrive. It features over 100 forms, business letters and documents, and its fully searchable index makes finding information a breeze. It also contains the complete text of six of Nolo's bestselling business titles: *The Legal Guide for Starting and Running a Small Business, Volumes 1 & 2, Tax Savvy for Small Business, The Employer's Legal Handbook, Marketing Without Advertising,* and *Everybody's Guide to Small Claims Court.*

The Inventor's Notebook

by Fred Grissom and Attorney David Pressman

$19.95 • INOT

The best way to protect your patent is to keep good records. *The Inventor's Notebook* helps you document the major steps that all successful inventors must take. A companion to *Patent It Yourself,* it also includes worksheets, forms, instructions, references to relevant areas of patent law and a bibliography of legal and non-legal aids, as well as valuable information on internet research, intellectual property law, marketing and financing.

Trademark

How to Name Your Business and Product

by Attorneys Kate McGrath & Stephen Elias with Trademark Attorney Sarah Shena

$29.95 • TRD

Essential for all small business owners, this book shows them how to choose, use and protect the names and symbols that identify their services or products. The newly revised third edition contains all the official forms and instructions necessary to register a federal trademark or servicemark with the U.S. Patent and Trademark Office.

Wage Slave No More

The Independent Contractor's Legal Guide

by Attorney Stephen Fishman

$29.95 • WAGE

This invaluable book tells you everything you need to know to work successfully and legally as an independent contractor. It includes 15 independent contractor agreements tailored for specific occupations, and a general agreement you can customize to fit any occupation. All agreements are included as tear-outs and on disk.

Take 1 minute & Get a 1-year *Nolo News* subscription free!*

CALL
1-800-992-6656

FAX
1-800-645-0895

E-MAIL
NOLOSUB@NOLOPRESS.com

OR MAIL US THIS POSTAGE-PAID REGISTRATION CARD

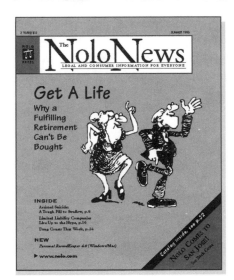

With our quarterly magazine, the *Nolo News*, you'll

- **Learn** about important legal changes that affect you
- **Find out first** about new Nolo products
- **Keep current** with practical articles on everyday law
- **Get answers** to your legal questions in *Ask Auntie Nolo's* advice column
- **Save money** with special Subscriber Only discounts
- **Tickle your funny bone** with our famous *Lawyer Joke* column.

It only takes 1 minute to reserve your free 1-year subscription or to extend your **NOLO** *News* subscription.

REGISTRATION CARD

NAME _____ DATE _____

ADDRESS _____

PHONE NUMBER _____

CITY _____ STATE _____ ZIP _____

WHERE DID YOU HEAR ABOUT THIS BOOK? _____

WHERE DID YOU PURCHASE THIS PRODUCT? _____

DID YOU CONSULT A LAWYER? (PLEASE CIRCLE ONE)   YES   NO   NOT APPLICABLE

DID YOU FIND THIS BOOK HELPFUL?   (VERY)   5   4   3   2   1   (NOT AT ALL)

SUGGESTIONS FOR IMPROVING THIS PRODUCT _____

WAS IT EASY TO USE?   (VERY EASY)   5   4   3   2   1   (VERY DIFFICULT)

DO YOU OWN A COMPUTER? IF SO, WHICH FORMAT? (PLEASE CIRCLE ONE)   WINDOWS   DOS   MAC

PAT 6.2

The CD-ROM in the back of this book contains Try & Buy Versions of our self-help legal software, including Patent It Yourself 1.2 for Windows, a full stand-alone program that helps you prepare and file your U.S. patent application. This invaluable program:

- guides you step-by-step through the entire patent process
- produces all the forms you'll need to prosecute your patent
- gives you extensive program and legal help, including an online version of the *Patent It Yourself* book, and much more

This CD also contains TRY & BUY VERSIONS of these best-selling Nolo programs:

WillMaker 6.0 • Personal RecordKeeper 4.0
Living Trust Maker 2.0 • Small Business Legal Pro Deluxe 2.0

FREE BONUS! Just for fun, we've also included a free copy of *Nolo's Ultimate Lawyer Joke Collection* on the CD.

See the face of the disk for instructions on how view installation instructions.

If you have a Macintosh, or if you don't have a CD-ROM drive but would like to take part in the Try & Buy experience, don't worry. Just visit our website at www.nolo.com and click on the Software icon.